ALMANACS OF AMERICAN WARS

Vietnam War
Almanac

James H. Willbanks

Facts On File
An imprint of Infobase Publishing

Vietnam War Almanac

Copyright © 2009 by James H. Willbanks

Facts On File, Inc.
An imprint of Infobase Publishing
132 West 31st Street
New York NY 10001

Library of Congress Cataloging-in-Publication Data

Willbanks, James H., 1947–
    Vietnam War almanac / James H. Willbanks.—1st ed.
        p. cm. — (Almanacs of American wars)
    Includes bibliographical references and index.
    ISBN 978-0-8160-7102-9 (hc : alk. paper) 1. Vietnam War, 1961–1975—Almanacs.
    2. Vietnam War, 1961–1975—Chronology. I. Title.
    DS557.7.W552 2008
    959.704′3—dc22   2008006881

Text design by Erika K. Arroyo
Cover design by Pehrsson Design/Salvatore Luongo
Maps by Patricia Meschino

Printed in the United States of America

VB Hermitage 10 9 8 7 6 5 4 3 2 1

*This book is dedicated to our son, Russell,
currently serving in Iraq, and our beloved daughter,
Jennifer Willbanks Schaad, whom we lost this year;
she will live in our hearts forever.*

CONTENTS

PREFACE

The Vietnam War was the most divisive conflict in American history since the Civil War. The ramifications of the war and its outcome can still be felt today. The United States became involved in Vietnam within the larger context of the cold war and its containment policy. Vietnam itself was of no intrinsic value to U.S. national interests, but according to the domino theory, its control by the Communists threatened all of Southeast Asia. Having witnessed the appeasement of totalitarian governments that led to World War II, successive U.S. presidents believed that the struggle in Vietnam fitted the pattern of communism's worldwide expansion and so responded with aid, first to the French and then to the Republic of Vietnam. Later, as the United States poured more resources into Vietnam, the conflict came to be seen as a test of American resolve, and it became harder to disengage; the credibility of the United States was at risk. When the National Liberation Front and the leadership in Hanoi responded to the increased U.S. effort in Vietnam, the conflict rapidly escalated, evolving into a bloody war of attrition. The Tet Offensive of 1968, although a serious defeat at the tactical level for the Communists, became a great psychological victory when it convinced many Americans that the war could not be won. This led to President Lyndon Johnson deciding not to run for reelection and paved the way for Richard Nixon's victory in the 1968 election.

Under Nixon's direction, the U.S. objective changed from winning the war to finding a face-saving way out of the conflict. This proved difficult to do, while still honoring the American commitment to its South Vietnamese ally. Nevertheless, Nixon launched a dual program of U.S. troop withdrawals and "Vietnamization," a comprehensive effort to bolster the combat capabilities of the South Vietnamese forces so they could assume responsibility for the war. At the same time, he launched an illegal, secret bombing campaign against Cambodia. He would also send U.S. and South Vietnamese ground troops into Cambodia and South Vietnamese forces into Laos. Although the South Vietnamese sustained a serious setback in Laos, they withstood a massive North Vietnamese invasion in 1972, bolstered by U.S. advisers and American air support. Nixon declared Vietnamization a success. With the invasion blunted, Henry Kissinger, Nixon's national security advisor, who had conducted secret negotiations with the Communists in Paris since 1969, worked out a draft agreement to end the war with his counterpart, Le Duc Tho. President Nguyen Van Thieu, alarmed that the agreement did not call for the withdrawal of North Vietnamese forces, balked and demanded significant revisions to the draft. The North Vietnamese refused to accept these demands, and Nixon responded with what became known as the Christmas bombing. The North Vietnamese returned to the negotiating table in late December, and Kissinger and Le Duc Tho worked out an agreement, the Agreement on Ending the War and Restoring the Peace in Vietnam, which was signed on January 27, 1973. Thieu's protestations about the North Vietnamese troops left in the south were ignored, and the agreement was essentially the same one that had been agreed to by the United States and North Vietnam before the Christmas bombing.

Although the Paris peace accords ended the war for the United States, which withdrew all American troops by March 1973, the cease-fire provided only the briefest respite before the fighting by North and South Vietnamese troops for control of the countryside began again in earnest. During the bitter fighting that ensued, the South Vietnamese held their own throughout 1973, but in 1974 the tide began to turn against them. At the same time, the U.S. Congress began to reduce the aid to the South Vietnamese. The South Vietnamese sustained another body blow when Richard Nixon resigned in disgrace in August 1974.

In late December 1974, the North Vietnamese launched a major corps-level attack against Phuoc Long Province, north of Saigon along the Cambodian border, as a "test case" to determine how the Vietnamese would handle a large-scale attack and what would be the response of the United States. The ARVN defenses were quickly overrun and Gerald Ford, Nixon's unelected successor, now prohibited from direct intervention by law, could only redouble efforts to secure additional aid for the South Vietnamese. Encouraged by the rapid collapse of the South Vietnamese forces and stunned by the lack of a meaningful response from Washington, Hanoi directed a new campaign designed to set the conditions for a final victory to be achieved by follow-on operations in 1976. Campaign 275 was launched in March 1975 with Ban Me Thuot in the Central Highlands as the primary objective. The North Vietnamese forces quickly overran Darlac Province as the South Vietnamese forces fell back in disarray. When the North Vietnamese pressed the attack in the northern half of South Vietnam, the South Vietnamese forces disintegrated in panic. The North Vietnamese pushed rapidly down the coast and on April 30, 1975, North Vietnamese tanks crashed through the gates of the presidential palace in Saigon and the South Vietnamese surrendered unconditionally. The Republic of Vietnam, whose forces had been soundly defeated in 55 days, ceased to be a sovereign nation and the two Vietnams were reunited under Communist control.

It had been a bloody war for all the belligerents. The Communists admit to 1.1 million deaths from 1954 to 1975. They claim 2 million civilian casualties, but this has not been confirmed and U.S. figures estimate 30,000 killed by U.S. bombing of the North. The South Vietnamese lost more than 110,000 military personnel killed, with nearly a half-million wounded. Civilian casualties in the South are estimated at over 400,000.

The Republic of Vietnam fell two years after the departure of the United States from Vietnam. Although U.S. forces had not been defeated in the field, the nation had essentially lost the first war in its history. In the process, more than 58,000

Americans died, and more than 300,000 U.S. servicemen were wounded, many maimed for life. The total cost of the war exceeded $130 billion. The war almost rent American society and forever destroyed the concept of cold war consensus in foreign policy. It scarred the American psyche, caused many Americans to question America's place in the world, and resulted in a national malaise that lasted for many years.

The Vietnam War has been a source of intense study for scholars and policy makers. Among the most crucial questions that have been addressed is why the United States committed itself to such a large military effort in Vietnam and why it failed to achieved its goals and objectives. The postwar debate continues, and much about the war is still misunderstood. The purpose of this book is to examine the early history of Vietnam, the First Indochina War, how America became involved in Southeast Asia, how the United States fought the war, and the events that led to the fall of South Vietnam.

ACKNOWLEDGMENTS

I wish to acknowledge the major sources used for this work. All of them are referenced in the Selected Bibliography of the *Almanac*, but several require special mention. These include David L. Anderson, *The Columbia Guide to the Vietnam War* (Columbia University Press, 2002); John S. Bowman, editor, *The Vietnam War: Day by Day* (Brompton Books, 1989); Leo Daugherty, *The Vietnam War Day by Day* (Lewis International, 2002); Hal Drake, editor, *Vietnam Front Pages* (Macmillan Publishing, 1986); William J. Duiker, *Historical Dictionary of Vietnam* (Scarecrow Press, 1989); Stanley I. Kutler, editor, *Encyclopedia of the Vietnam War* (Macmillan Library Reference USA, 1996); Marc Leepson, editor, *Webster's New World Dictionary of the Vietnam War* (Simon and Schuster Macmillan, 1999); Edwin E. Moïse, *Historical Dictionary of the Vietnam War* (Scarecrow Press, 2001); James S. Olson, *Dictionary of the Vietnam War* (Greenwood Press, 1988); *Pentagon Papers* (Gravel edition, Beacon Press, 1971); David Burns Sigler, *Vietnam Battle Chronology: U.S. Army and Marine Corps Combat Operations, 1965–1973* (McFarland, 1992); Shelby L. Stanton, *Vietnam Order of Battle* (Galahad Books, 1981); Harry G. Summers, Jr., *Historical Atlas of the Vietnam War* (Houghton Mifflin, 1995) and *Vietnam War Almanac* (Facts On File, 1985); Spencer C. Tucker, editor, *Encyclopedia of the Vietnam War: A Political, Social, and Military History* (ABC-CLIO, 1998).

There were also several official multi-volume service histories that proved invaluable. These include the *U.S. Marines in Vietnam*, U.S. Marine Corps History and Museums Division, the *U.S. Army in Vietnam* by the U.S. Army Center of Military History, *The United States Air Force in Southeast Asia*, the Air Force History Office, and *The United States Navy and the Vietnam Conflict*, Naval History Division. Additionally, the Indochina Monograph series written by former South Vietnamese senior officers and published by the U.S. Army Center of Military History were very useful.

Among the primary sources consulted were those found at the Military History Institute, Carlisle, Pennsylvania; the Gerald R. Ford Presidential Library, Ann Arbor, Michigan; the Lyndon Baines Johnson Presidential Library, Austin, Texas; and the National Archives, College Park, Maryland. For many of the photos used in this book and numerous other materials and sources, I am grateful to Steve Maxner and the staff of the Vietnam Center and Archive at Texas Tech University in Lubbock. A special note of thanks goes to the staff and administration of the Combined Arms Research Library, Fort Leavenworth, Kansas.

As in all my endeavors, I am indebted to Diana, my wife and best friend of more than 40 years, for her unstinting support and encouragement.

INTRODUCTION

U.S. involvement in the Vietnam War can be traced through five distinct phases: the combined French-U.S. advisory phase (1950–55); the U.S. advisory phase (1955–64); force buildup and combat phase (1965–67); large-unit offensive combat operations (1967–69); and Vietnamization (1969–73). Even though the last U.S. forces departed Saigon in 1973, the war did not end for the Vietnamese. The fighting extended into 1974, when the North Vietnamese began the offensive that would culminate in the fall of Saigon in April 1975.

The genesis of U.S. involvement in Vietnam can be found in the confrontation that developed between East and West following the end of World War II. With the emergence of the cold war, the United States turned to a policy of containment to counter the perceived spread of communism. This policy led President Harry Truman to provide aid to France in its war against the Viet Minh in Vietnam; between 1950 and 1954, the United States provided France more than $2.6 billion in military aid. From the beginning, U.S. policy supported the development of an independent Vietnamese army and a U.S. role in its organization and training. Ultimately, however, the French were defeated at the Battle of Dien Bien Phu in 1954.

The subsequent Geneva Accords temporarily partitioned Vietnam at the 17th parallel, pending elections, but essentially established two Vietnams, leaving Ho Chi Minh and the Communists in charge in the north and a noncommunist state in the south under Emperor Bao Dai. This resulted in the next phase of the war in which, for the better part of 10 years, the United States would support the government of Ngo Dinh Diem, Bao Dai's prime minister who succeeded him in 1955 after a questionable national election. President Dwight Eisenhower and his successor, John F. Kennedy, threw their support behind Diem in the hopes that he and a non-Communist Republic of Vietnam would act as a counterweight to the Communist-controlled North. This period was marked by a significant American effort to build South Vietnamese forces capable of defending against the growing insurgency. Diem refused to institute meaningful reforms that might have won him the support of the people. Instead, he attempted to suppress any opposition, which led to a major confrontation with Buddhists. Ultimately, the United States lost faith in Diem and gave tacit approval for a coup that was carried out by several South Vietnamese generals in early November 1963 and resulted in the deaths of Diem and his brother.

Less than a month later, President Kennedy was assassinated and Lyndon Baines Johnson inherited the conflict in Vietnam. This issued in the third phase of the war, which initially saw the use of American airpower against North Vietnam in retaliation for an escalation of the war in the South. When this proved insufficient, Johnson ordered the deployment of U.S. ground troops to South Vietnam. By the end of 1966, there were over 190,000 American combat troops in Vietnam.

The fourth phase of the war began when General William Westmoreland, the commander of American forces in Vietnam, launched a series of large-scale search and destroy operations to find and kill the enemy. Meanwhile, the Communist forces, directed by Hanoi, had settled in for a protracted war designed to exhaust the Americans. The result was a bloody war of attrition that caused heavy casualties on both sides.

The turning point in the war was the Communist Tet Offensive of 1968. Although the offensive was a significant defeat for the Communists at the tactical level, it proved to be a great psychological victory that changed the nature of the U.S. commitment in Vietnam and issued in the next phase of the war. Under Richard Nixon, who was elected in the wake of the Tet Offensive, American objectives shifted from winning the war to a prolonged disengagement, during which U.S. forces were gradually withdrawn as the responsibility for the war was shifted to the South Vietnamese.

The signing of the Paris peace accords in January 1973 signaled the end of the war for the United States, while issuing in a new phase of the war for the Vietnamese. Bitter fighting lasted for two years until the South Vietnamese fell apart in the face of a new North Vietnamese offensive in the spring of 1975. Although U.S. forces had been gone for two years when South Vietnam fell, the North Vietnamese triumph was perceived as the first loss of a war by the United States. To understand how this happened, it is useful to look at the country in some detail and consider a brief review of its early history.

THE COUNTRY

Vietnam stretches for over 1,650 kilometers (1,000 miles) along the eastern coast of the Indochinese Peninsula, making it slightly larger than Italy and a bit smaller than Japan. It is bounded on the north by China and on the west by Laos and Cambodia. Vietnam is on the South China Sea and has over 2,500 kilometers (1,500 miles) of coastline. However, three-quarters of the country consists of mountains and hills. The highest summit is the 3,160-meter-high Phan Si Pan, in the Hoang Lien Son mountain range in the province of Lao Cai, near the Chinese border in the northwest. The Truong Son Mountains (Annamite Cordillera), which form the Central Highlands, run almost the full length of Vietnam along its borders with Laos and Cambodia.

The country is S-shaped, broad in the north and south and very narrow in the center, where at one point it is only 50 kilometers wide. Some geographers have likened the country, with its three regions—Bac Bo (north), Trung Bo (center), and Nam Bo (south)—to a bamboo pole supporting a basket of rice at each end. These baskets represent the country's two main cultivated areas, the rich deltas of the Red River in the north and the Mekong River in the south. The Mekong River is one of the longest in Asia, flowing from its source in the mountains of Tibet, across China, through Burma (Myanmar) into Laos and northern Thailand, and then across Cambodia before flowing through southern Vietnam into the South China Sea.

In 1960, the two largest cities in Vietnam were Hanoi (population about 600,000) in the north and Saigon (population about 1.6 million) in the south. The cities are almost exactly 700 miles apart and are, respectively, located in the alluvial plains of the Red River and the Mekong. The next largest cities were Danang, with a population of 240,000, and Hue, with a population of 140,000 in 1960. At that time, of the approximately 30.5 million people living in Vietnam (16.5 million north of the 17th parallel and 14 million south of it), close to 29 million lived on only about 20 percent of the land. The remaining 1.5 million people, mostly indigenous tribes, lived in the mountains and plateaus of the Chaîne Annamitique, a north-south mountain range originating in China and Tibet, and extending south to about 50 miles north of the city formerly known as Saigon.

The people of Vietnam developed as a distinct ethnic group between 200 B.C. and A.D. 200 through a fusion of people of Indonesian stock with Viet and Thai immigrants from the north and Chinese who arrived around 200 B.C. and ruled until A.D. 938. Vietnamese civilization was also profoundly influenced by both China and India. When European missionaries arrived, the Vietnamese people were predominantly Mahayana Buddhist, but they were also strongly influenced by Confucianism, Daoism, and animism. Although the preponderance of Vietnam's population when the Europeans arrived were *Kinh*, the term used to describe the Viet race, Vietnam was also home to ethnic minorities living in the mountainous regions in central and southern Vietnam; these were called "montagnards" by the French.

Early History

Nearly 5,000 years ago, according to legend, Hung Vuong was crowned the king of Van Lang, a kingdom that encompassed most of present-day northern and central Vietnam. Van Lang was governed by 18 successive Hung kings but fell to Thuc Phan, king of neighboring Au Viet, in 258 B.C. Thuc Phan took the name of An Duong Vuong and established the kingdom of Au Lac, building his capital at Phuc An (north of present-day Hanoi).

Fifty years later, Au Lac fell to Trieu Da, a warlord from the south of China who established the independent kingdom of Nam Viet. The new kingdom also included much of present-day southern China. Trieu Da established the Trieu dynasty in 208 B.C. Less than a century later, the Han emperor Wu Di sent his army to conquer Nam Viet. Despite Nam Viet's fierce resistance, the Chinese prevailed and Nam Viet became a Chinese protectorate under the name of Giao Chi. The Chinese ruled Vietnam almost continually for the next one thousand years.

Periodically, there were revolts by the Viet people, like the one by the Trung Sisters in A.D. 39, but the success of these uprisings was short-lived and the Chinese maintained control of the territory until A.D. 938. During this period, the Chinese made concerted efforts to establish their culture and civilization in Nam Viet, which they renamed An Nam.

The decline of the Tang dynasty in China gave the Viets an opportunity to throw off the Chinese yoke. They conducted a protracted war that culminated with the defeat of the Chinese in A.D. 938 at the naval battle of Bach Dang, east of Haiphong. The victor, Ngo Quyen, renamed the country Dai Viet, but the defeat of the Chinese only resulted in a period of chaos as the Vietnamese warlords fought among themselves.

The situation stabilized somewhat in A.D. 968 when the most powerful of the feudal lords, Dinh Bo Linh, reunited the fragmented country under the name of Dai Co Viet, taking the imperial title of Dinh Tien Hoang De. A succession of emperors from a series of dynasties pacified the countryside and began the process of "nam tien," the movement south, launching a military campaign against the Chams, a Hindu kingdom that had appeared around present-day Danang in the late second century. This period was marked by a succession of revolts and instability. The monk Khuong Viet managed to establish Buddhism in the ensuing period, which served as a long-overdue stabilizing factor in the kingdom.

The Ly dynasty, which reigned over the country for more than two centuries (1009–1225), was the first of the enduring national dynasties. During this period, the independence of the Vietnamese kingdom was consolidated, but it was marked by constant conflict with the Chinese, Khmers, and Chams. The continuous confrontation with the Chams resulted in the annexation of new territory to the south, which the Vietnamese aggressively colonized. During the Ly dynasty, Buddhism became the national religion.

After a period of civil strife, the Tran dynasty overthrew the Ly dynasty in 1225. During the Ly dynasty, Vietnam was beset by Kublai Khan and the Mongols, but the Mongol fleet was defeated at the Battle of Bach Dang River in 1288.

The Tran dynasty was overthrown in 1400 by Ho Qui Ly. The Tran loyalists and the Chams encouraged the Chinese to intervene, which they did in 1407. During the brief period in which they once again controlled Vietnam, the Chinese imposed a harsh rule that attempted to destroy the Vietnamese national identity. This resulted in a resistance movement, known as the Lam Son Uprising, which was organized and led by Le Loi, a man renowned for his courage and generosity. He led a guerrilla war against the Chinese rulers, which proved ultimately successful in 1428.

Le Loi took the name Le Thai To and founded the Le dynasty. Le Loi and his successors instituted a vast program of agrarian reform and land redistribution. The legal system was reorganized and the penal system revised. In 1471, the army of Le Thanh Tong won a victory over the southern Champa army. The national territory was gradually expanded to the southward, until finally the Champa kingdom was completely absorbed and assimilated.

By the late 16th century, the decline of the Le dynasty resulted in a period of internal strife that eventually led to the division of Vietnam between the Trinh lords, who ruled in the north, and the Nguyen lords, who controlled the south.

This division of Vietnam would indirectly pave the way for the French to gain a foothold in Indochina. According to Chinese records, the first recorded Vietnamese contact with Europeans occurred in A.D. 166 when Roman travelers arrived in the Red River Delta. The first Portuguese sailors landed near Danang in 1516, to be followed by Dominican missionaries 11 years later. For the next few decades, the Portuguese traded with the Vietnamese, setting up a commercial colony at Faifo (present-day Hoi An).

Franciscan missionaries from the Philippines settled in central Vietnam in 1580, followed in 1615 by the Jesuits. One of the most influential of the early Jesuits was French priest Alexandre de Rhodes, who transliterated the Viet language into *quoc nhu*, a Latin-based written alphabet that came to be used in Vietnamese writing in place of the previously used Chinese characters.

By the late 17th century, most of the European traders had departed because trade with Vietnam had not proved sufficiently profitable. However, the missionaries remained. The Vietnamese, particularly in the north, proved receptive to Catholicism, but Vietnamese officials restricted the activities of the missionaries and persecuted their followers. Determined to convert the Vietnamese to Catholicism, the missionaries campaigned for a greater French political and military role in Vietnam.

In 1765, a rebellion broke out in the town of Tay Son, near Qui Nhon. By 1773, the Tay Son rebels controlled the whole of central Vietnam and in 1783 they captured Saigon and the rest of the south. Prince Nguyen Ahn, the only survivor of the defeated Nguyen clan, fled to Thailand where he requested military assistance from the Thais. There he also met with the French Jesuit missionary Pigneau de Behaine, bishop of Adran, who saw an opportunity to expand the Catholic Church's influence in Vietnam. De Behaine agreed to act as Nguyen Ahn's intermediary in seeking military assistance from the French. After de Behaine arrived in Paris, Louis XVI agreed to send a military expedition to Vietnam, but then, beset by his own internal concerns, reversed his decision. Undaunted, de Behaine returned to Vietnam, on the way stopping in India, where he convinced French merchants to finance a mercenary force. He and his hired army set sail for Vietnam in June 1789.

With the aid of the French mercenaries, Nguyen Ahn subdued the Tay Son rebels, proclaiming himself Emperor Gia Long in 1802. For the first time in two centuries, Vietnam was united, with Hue as its new national capital. Although Nguyen Ahn had achieved victory largely through French assistance, as emperor, he remained suspicious of France's designs on the country. His successors would become increasingly anti-French and anti-Catholic, setting up a confrontation that would have disastrous consequences for Vietnam.

When seven French missionaries and a number of their Catholic converts were executed in the 1830s, French Catholics demanded that their government intervene. France's military activity in Indochina began in 1847, when the French navy attacked Danang harbor in response to Emperor Thieu Tri's oppression of French missionaries; however, it was not until 1858 that the French military effort began in earnest. That year, a joint military force of 14 ships from France and the Spanish colony of the Philippines stormed Danang after the killing of several missionaries; this time, the French did not withdraw but landed forces to occupy the city.

The occupation of Danang was followed by successive French advances over the next 40 years. In 1861, they took Saigon. Six year later, the entire southern part of the country, rechristened by the French as Cochin China, was annexed as a French colony. The French extended control to the north in 1883. The central part of Vietnam, renamed by the French as Annam, and the north, or Tonkin, became French protectorates. In 1887, the French announced the creation of the Indochinese Union, made up of Cochin China, Annam, Tonkin, and Cambodia; in 1893, they also added Laos to the Union. This effectively ended the existence of an independent Vietnam state.

From the beginning, French colonial rule was, for the most part, politically repressive and economically exploitative. Not surprisingly, this resulted in the organization of various Vietnamese nationalist resistance movements, which became increasingly active. There were periodic uprisings, but the French responded quickly and brutally, maintaining their stranglehold on the colonies. However, they were unsuccessful in stamping out nationalist sentiment, and a number of anti-colonialist movements, including the Communists, continued their resistance efforts against the French.

The outbreak of World War II proved an unexpected opportunity for the anti-colonialists. The pro-Nazi Vichy government of France accepted the Japanese occupation of Indochina; in exchange, it was allowed to continue administering Vietnam. In 1941, Ho Chi Minh, one of the founders of the Indochinese Communist Party, formed the Viet Nam Doc Lap Dong Minh (League for the Independence of Vietnam). The Viet Minh, as it became more popularly known, portrayed itself as a broad nationalist organization, but was dominated by the Communists. During the war, the Viet Minh resisted the Japanese occupation and aided the Allies.

In 1945, realizing that Allied victory was inevitable, Japan overthrew the French in Vietnam, imprisoned their civil servants, and declared Vietnam "independent" under Japanese "protection," with Emperor Bao Dai as head of state. When Japan surrendered later in the year, this provided the opportunity that Ho had been waiting for, and he called for a general uprising, which later became known as the August Revolution. The Viet Minh quickly seized power and Bao Dai abdicated in favor of the new government. On September 2, Ho declared the independence of the Democratic Republic of Vietnam. This set up a confrontation between Ho and the French, who wished to re-establish control in Vietnam.

Ho attempted to negotiate Vietnam's status with the French, but relations quickly deteriorated. Hostilities continued to mount, reaching a peak in November 1946 when the French shelled Haiphong after an obscure customs dispute, killing hundreds of Vietnamese civilians. In December, Ho ordered a general offensive against the French in Hanoi and at French garrisons in northern and central Vietnam. This proved to be the beginning of the First Indochina War between France and the Viet Minh. Later, Vietnam would become a cold war battlefield when Ho turned to the Chinese and the Soviets for assistance and support, leading the United States to support France, and ultimately to the direct U.S. involvement that would result in America's longest war.

How to Use This Almanac

The purpose of this almanac is to provide a day-to-day account of the Vietnam War beginning with some of the most important events of early Vietnamese history as background, a review of the major events of the First Indochina War that led to U.S. involvement in Southeast Asia, a detailed account of America's war in Vietnam, and the aftermath of the conflict for Vietnam and the United States.

Once the United States becomes fully committed in Vietnam in 1964, the sequence of events becomes very complicated, with a number of different actions happening on each day. In the interest of clarity, the entries from that point on in the chronology will be classified by category using the following subheadings:

USA – Government: All matters related to U.S. government decisions and actions including those of the executive and legislative branches.

USA – Military: All matters related to high-level U.S. military decisions, actions, plans, and orders of the Department of Defense, Joint Chiefs of Staff, or Headquarters, Military Assistance Command, Vietnam (MACV).

USA – Domestic: Politics, media, public opinion, and other matters having to do with the home front.

Diplomacy: Diplomatic discourse between sovereign states and international governmental organizations.

Ground War: Operations, engagements, and battles on the ground in Vietnam. This category will also include air operations in support of U.S. and South Vietnamese ground troops.

Air War: Air operations in the Southeast Asia theater of operations.

Sea War: Surface warfare at sea.

River War: Warfare in the inland waterways of South Vietnam.

Covert War: Undercover operations conducted by special forces units.

Terrorism: Operations meant to terrorize primarily noncombatants in order to make a political point.

POWs: Actions and events having to do with captured combatants.

War Crimes: Violations of the laws of war.

South Vietnam: Politics, government, administration, and wartime direction of the Republic of Vietnam.

North Vietnam: Politics, government, administration, and wartime direction of the Democratic Republic of Vietnam.

NLF (National Liberation Front): The organization in South Vietnam that included a broad array of nationalist elements but was dominated and directed by the Lao Dong Party of the Democratic Republic of Vietnam.

Cambodia: Activities of and within the sovereign state of Cambodia, including warfare within its boundaries.

Laos: Activities of and within the sovereign state of Laos, including warfare within its boundaries.

International: Actions of nations and international figures. Given the nature of their involvement in the war in Vietnam, separate subheadings will be used for separate nations, to include:

   USSR

   China

   Thailand

Korea

Australia

New Zealand

The Philippines

Negotiations: The actions and interplay among the belligerents in their attempts to bring an end to the war.

Refugees: The experiences of those made homeless (and "nationless") by the war and its outcome.

The two military forces that opposed the United States and the Republic of Vietnam are properly known as the People's Liberation Armed Forces (PLAF) and the People's Army of Vietnam (PAVN). However, for the purpose of simplicity, the chronology will generally use the more popular terms: Viet Cong (VC) and North Vietnamese Army (NVA).

Discussion of each ground operation will normally be a one-time entry indicating start date, completion date, location (province and corps tactical region), and casualties (when reported in source documents).

It should be noted that preparing a chronology of this type is problematic. Not every event can be reported, but an effort was made to include as much as possible—and certainly the most important events and those that provide a feel for the rhythm of the conflict over time. Also, assigning exact dates to some events depends on how one defines the start and completion of that event. An additional problem is that the United States and Vietnam are in different time zones and are separated by the International Date Line; therefore, the convention used will be one that is commonly used in this series, that is, as much as possible, the dates presented are listed at the time the event is taking place in the place where it is happening. In most cases, unless otherwise stated, the 24-hour military clock will be used to denote specific times.

The author is solely responsible for any errors of either commission or omission.

 CHRONOLOGY

2879 B.C.

Legendary Hung Vuong founds the kingdom of Van Lang, establishing the Hung dynasty.

1800–1400 B.C.

Phung Nguyen culture, the Early Bronze Age.

258 B.C.

Thuc Phan, king of Au Viet, conquers Van Lang, establishing the new kingdom of Au Lac, taking the name An Duong Vuong, and locating his capital at Phuc An.

208 B.C.

Chinese general Chao T'o (Trieu Da) conquers Au Lac and establishes the independent kingdom of Nam Viet ("Southern Viet") under his rule.

111 B.C.

Chinese Han dynasty conquers Nam Viet, marking the beginning of a thousand years of direct Chinese rule. During this time, the Viet people will develop a fierce resistance against outside rule.

A.D. 39–43

Trung sisters lead unsuccessful revolt against Chinese rule, but eventually become legendary martyrs after the Chinese regain control.

542–544

Ly Bi leads uprising against China's Liang dynasty to create independent kingdom of Van Xuan.

938

Vietnamese under Ngo Quyen defeat Chinese at the Battle of Bach Dang River.

939

Ngo Quyen becomes king of new, independent Nam Viet and begins 900-year March to the South (Nam Tien) that will eventually extend Vietnamese control through Champa (south-central coastal area of present day Vietnam) and ultimately into the Mekong River Delta.

968

Dinh Bo Linh declares himself emperor, naming his empire Dai Co Viet.

970–975

Dinh Bo Linh gains Chinese recognition of Nam Viet's independence by negotiating a nonaggression treaty with China's Song (Sung) dynasty in exchange for tribute to be paid to the Chinese every three years.

1009

Ly Thai To becomes emperor, establishing Ly dynasty.

1010

Hanoi established.

1054

Emperor Ly Thanh Ton renames the country Dai Viet ("Greater Viet"), the name by which it will commonly be known until the 19th century.

1225

Tran dynasty replaces Ly dynasty.

1288

April
Vietnamese under Tran Hung Dao defeat invading Mongols at Second Battle of Bach Dang River.

1407

Chinese Ming dynasty reoccupies Dai Viet after toppling the Ho dynasty.

1418

Le Loi organizes the Lam Son Uprising in opposition against Chinese rule.

1428

Le Loi defeats Chinese, reestablishing independent Dai Viet and becoming king under the name of Le Thai To. Under the Le dynasty, Vietnamese expansion to the south continues.

1471

Le Thanh Tong defeats the southern army of the kingdom of Champa and establishes a protectorate over the kingdom, greatly expanding Vietnamese territory and dominion.

1527

Vietnam fragments politically; Nguyen family in the south and Trinh family in the north divide control of Vietnam at approximately the 17th parallel, issuing in a period of internal strife and bloody fighting that will not be resolved until the 19th century.

1535

Portuguese sailors under the command of Captain Antonio da Faria land at Danang Bay. This first wave of Europeans to reach Vietnam fails to achieve a foothold in the area. They are followed by the Dutch, English, and French, who are no more successful at this time.

1543

Descendants of the Le dynasty occupy the country's southern capital after a series of fierce battles. The southern court is founded near Thanh Hoa.

1592

The death of Mac dynasty's last king, Mac Mau Hop, ends the succession wars.

1627

French missionary Alexandre de Rhodes codifies *quoc ngu,* an adoption of the Roman alphabet to the Vietnamese language.

1672

Lord Trinh consents to partition the country at the Linh River.

1771

Tay Son Rebellion begins under Nguyen Hue, who leads a peasant uprising against the Nguyen dynasty in the south. The uprising will last for seven years and result in deposing both the Nguyen family and the Trinh family in the north.

1778

December
Nguyen Hue declares himself emperor.

1779

January
Nguyen Hue attacks and defeats invading Chinese forces at Thang Long (Hanoi) during Tet holiday.

1802

June
Nguyen Anh, one of the last surviving Nguyen Lords, overthrows the Tay Son forces with the aid of French missionary Pigneau de Behaine and French mercenaries. He takes control of a reunified Vietnam that extends from Hanoi to Saigon and declares himself Emperor Gia Long, founding the Nguyen dynasty. He renames the country Vietnam and establishes his capital at Hue. Gia Long allows French missionaries to remain in Vietnam, but regards Christianity as potentially subversive.

1857

September
Unable to gain a foothold in Vietnam peacefully, the French send a fleet under Admiral Rigault de Genouilly to attack Tourane (Danang). The fleet bombards the city and then lands troops, capturing Danang and gaining control of the area by 1858. Although decimated by disease, the French forces push south.

1861

French forces capture Saigon and later defeat the Vietnamese army, gaining control of Gia Dinh and surrounding provinces.

1862

June
Emperor Tu Duc cedes the three eastern provinces of Cochin China to France under the Treaty of Saigon.

1863

August
France imposes protectorate on Cambodia.

1867

France occupies the three western provinces of Cochin China.

1883

August 25
Vietnam signs Treaty of Hue with France, creating French protectorates in Annam and Tonkin, effectively establishing French control of Vietnam.

1885

A general uprising by the Vietnamese against French rule fails. In Tonkin, the French begin a 12-year "pacification" program.

1887

The French form the Indochinese Union, which consists of Tonkin, Annam, Cochin China, and Cambodia. These colonies are to be administered by a governor-general under the Ministry of Colonies in Paris.

1893

Emperor Ham Nghi and Phan Dinh Phung organize a royalist movement and stage an unsuccessful uprising at Ha Tinh. France imposes protectorate on Laos, which becomes part of the Indochinese Union.

1904

Phan Boi Chau forms anticolonialist Modernization Society.

1905

Japanese victory over Russia convinces Vietnamese nationalists that Western power is no longer invincible.

1907

Eastward Movement is established by Phan Boi Chau and Cuong De, but is discovered and crushed by the French.

1912

Phan Boi Chau founds Vietnamese Restoration Society.

1919

During the Versailles Peace Conference, a number of Vietnamese residing in Paris draw up an eight-point petition requesting independence for Vietnam. One of them, Nguyen Ai Quoc ("Nguyen the Patriot," later known as Ho Chi Minh), unsuccessfully tries to meet with President Woodrow Wilson to plead the Vietnamese case. The Vietnamese petition for independence is never given serious consideration by the conferees at Versailles.

1920

Nguyen Ai Quoc (Ho Chi Minh) participates in the founding of the French Communist Party.

1923

Nguyen Ai Quoc goes to Moscow to be trained as an agent of the Communist International.

1925

Twelve-year-old emperor Bao Dai ascends the throne. In Canton, China, Nguyen Ai Quoc founds the Revolutionary Youth League of Vietnam, the first truly Marxist organization in Indochina. At the same time, the Vietnam Quoc Dan Dang (VNQDD), or Vietnam Nationalist Party, is founded in opposition to the Revolutionary Youth League.

1930

An uprising in Yen Bay, northwest of Hanoi, is put down by French authorities and the Vietnam Nationalist Party (VNQDD) is all but destroyed. In Kowloon, Nguyen Ai Quoc forms the Communist Party of Vietnam; in Hong Kong, the Indochinese Communist Party is formed, also under the leadership of Nguyen Ai Quoc.

1932

French authorities prevent young emperor Bao Dai, just returned from studying in France, from carrying out his plan to shape a political role for the royal court. Nationalist groups of various political persuasions continue to organize and resist French rule from within and outside the country.

1940

September 22

Japan occupies French Indochina. Heavy fighting results at Lang Son and Dong Dang, but Japanese reach agreement with Vichy government officials whereby French resistance ceases and the French colonial administration is left intact to "rule." Ultimately, the Japanese occupy and control Vietnam for the course of the war.

1941

May 10

Indochinese Communist Party creates Viet Minh or Vietnam Independence League (Viet Nam Doc Lap Dong Minh) as a united front of organizations opposed to Japanese and French rule. Under the direction of Vo Nguyen Giap, the Viet Minh organize guerrilla and intelligence networks to operate against the Japanese and the French.

1942–1943

Nguyen Ai Quoc goes to China in 1942 to solicit aid from Chiang Kai-shek in the fight against the Japanese, but he is arrested by the Nationalist Chinese and held prisoner for 13 months. Promising to work to further Chinese interests, which include designs on Vietnam, he returns to Vietnam in the spring of 1943. Taking the name of Ho Chi Minh ("Ho, the Enlightened One"), he and the Viet Minh assist the OSS (U.S. Office of Strategic Services) in rescuing downed American and other Allied pilots, sabotaging Japanese efforts and generally keeping them off balance in Vietnam.

1944

December 22

With Ho Chi Minh's support, Vo Nguyen Giap sets up an armed propaganda brigade of 34 Vietnamese and begins to attack French outposts in northern Vietnam.

1945

March 9

Japanese occupation troops remove French officials in Indochina and recognize an "independent" Vietnam with Emperor Bao Dai as nominal ruler under Japanese protection.

August 13–14

Japan formally accepts unconditional surrender. Japanese forces in Indochina remain in control for the interim.

August 15

Charles de Gaulle appoints Admiral Georges Thierry d'Argenlieu as high commissioner for Indochina, with instructions to restore French sovereignty over France's colonies in Southeast Asia.

August 16–29

In Hanoi, Ho Chi Minh and his People's Congress create a National Liberation Committee of Vietnam to form a provisional government. On the 18th, the Japanese transfer power in Indochina to the Viet Minh. On the 23rd, Bao Dai, thinking that the Viet Minh are still working with the OSS and can guarantee independence for Vietnam, abdicates his throne and becomes First Citizen Vinh Thuy. On the 29th, Ho and the Liberation Committee establish a provisional government and include Bao Dai as "supreme advisor." This becomes known as the August Revolution. Meanwhile, Ho writes at least eight letters to President Harry S. Truman and the U.S. State Department asking for recognition of the new government and American aid in gaining Vietnam's independence from France. The U.S. government is not excited about supporting French colonialism, but also does not want to turn Vietnam over to Communist control; there is no evidence that Ho's letters were ever answered.

September 2
Ho Chi Minh, with American OSS officers at his side, declares the independence of the Democratic Republic of Vietnam (DRV) with its capital in Hanoi.

September 12
British troops arrive in Saigon to accept surrender of the Japanese. In accordance with the Potsdam Agreements, 5,000 troops of the 20th Indian Division, commanded by General Douglas Gracey, arrive in southern Indochina. Gracey, who detests the Viet Minh, begins to turn over control to French authorities.

September 14
Nationalist Chinese troops enter North Vietnam to disarm Japanese troops north of the 16th parallel.

September 16
The new government under Ho Chi Minh organizes Tuan Le Vang (Gold Week), appealing to the people to turn in gold and other valuables so that the government might purchase arms from the Chinese. Much of the money goes to bribe Chinese commander Lu Han to secure his support and end aid to the nationalist parties.

September 21–24
The Viet Minh under Ho try to enforce their control, but are opposed by various Vietnamese nationalist groups, French colonials trying to regain power, and representatives of the French colonial government determined to reassert sovereignty. Thousands of Nationalist Chinese troops move into the north, while General Gracey attempts to assert control in the south. He declares martial law and subsequently rearms some 1,400 French soldiers imprisoned by the Japanese. He will even use Japanese troops to assist his British, Indian and Gurkha troops to help maintain order. On September 22, the French troops, mostly battle-hardened foreign legionnaires, remove the Viet Minh's executive committee from Saigon city hall and go on a rampage, attacking Viet Minh and killing innocent civilians. The Viet Minh respond by organizing a general strike in Saigon on the 24th, shutting down all commerce along with electricity and water supplies. In a suburb of Saigon, members of Binh Xuyen, a Vietnamese criminal organization, massacre 10 French and Eurasion civilians. The resulting bloody clash between the Viet Minh and French troops is considered by many Vietnamese to be the beginning of the First Indochina War. The 24th also marks the arrival in Saigon of General Jacques-Philippe Leclerc, the newly appointed French military commander in Vietnam, who declares, "We have come to reclaim our inheritance."

September 26
Lieutenant Colonel Peter Dewey (USA), head of the OSS mission in Vietnam, is shot by Viet Minh troops (who evidently mistake him for a Frenchman) on the road to the airport in Saigon. Dewey becomes the first American to die in Vietnam. Before his death, Dewey files a report on the deepening crisis in Vietnam, stating his opinion that the United States "ought to clear out of Southeast Asia."

October 25

With 35,000 newly arrived French troops, General Leclerc begins the reconquest of Indochina for France, predicting that it will take about a month for "mopping-up operations." The Viet Minh immediately begin a guerrilla campaign to harass the French troops.

November

The Viet Minh ostensibly dissolve the Indochinese Communist Party, hopefully to win support from the Chinese Nationalists for their resistance against the French. However, in February the Chinese will sign a treaty with the French, agreeing to withdraw Chinese troops from Vietnam and allow the French to return in exchange for French concessions in Shanghai and other Chinese ports. This agreement effectively negates any possibility of Chinese support for the Vietnamese.

1946

January

Viet Minh elect a national assembly, which includes VNQDD and and other nationalist members, and form a coalition government headed by Ho Chi Minh.

March 6

Ho signs an agreement with the French that allows French forces back into northern Vietnam to replace Nationalist Chinese forces, in exchange for French recognition of his Democratic Republic of Vietnam as a "free" Vietnam within the French Union. However, the status of the new state is not clearly defined and specifics are deferred to future negotiations.

May

Ho Chi Minh travels to France for negotiations.

June 1

A conference begins at Fontainebleau with Ho Chi Minh and a delegation of Vietnamese in attendance. They are hoping to clarify the status of the "new state" and negotiate full independence and unity for Vietnam. However, progress is stymied when High Commissioner Georges Thierry d'Argenlieu declares the Republic of Cochin China a separate autonomous state, violating the March agreement.

August 27

French president Charles de Gaulle declares, "France is a great power. Without the overseas territories, she would be in danger of no longer being one." French policy is now clear.

September

Ho Chi Minh signs a modus vivendi with French authorities, which he later describes as "better than nothing." The agreement covers a cessation of hostilities and facilitates French resumption of economic and cultural activities in return for a more liberal regime.

November 20–28

Armed clashes between Vietnamese and French forces break out at Lang Son and Haiphong. Wanting to teach the Vietnamese a "lesson," the French commander in Haiphong gives the Vietnamese an ultimatum, telling them they have two hours in which to withdraw from the French section of the city, the Chinese quarter, and the port. When the Vietnamese do not comply, the French launch an air, sea, and land bombardment, with the preponderance of the fire coming from the French navy cruiser *Suffren*. An undetermined number of Vietnamese are killed (estimates range from 200 to 6,000). Fighting in Haiphong will be over by November 28, but Vietnamese-French relations are at an all time low.

December 19

The French demand the disarming of the Vietnamese militia, which has been steadily sniping at French troops. In Hanoi, the Viet Minh launches its first large-scale attack against the French, beginning what comes to be known as the Indochina War, which will last for eight years.

December 20

The Voice of Vietnam radio proclaims Ho's call for a "National Resistance War."

1947

January

The French begin punitive raids on villages supporting the Viet Minh.

February 4

French public opinion poll reveals that 36 percent of French people favor use of force in Vietnam, while 42 percent favor negotiations and 8 percent believe that France should leave Indochina altogether.

April

Having lost almost all towns in Tonkin and northern Annam, the Viet Minh forces under General Vo Nguyen Giap withdraw into the Viet Bac, the mountainous region north of Hanoi, to organize and train for the coming conflict. Giap adopts a policy of avoiding all-out confrontation and prepares to fight a protracted war.

August 15

High Commissioner Emile Bollaert devises a plan to offer independence for Vietnam within the French Union, accompanied by a unilateral cease-fire and an offer to negotiate with all Vietnamese parties and groups. The plan is never implemented, because the French do not go far enough in granting real independence to Vietnam.

October

General Etienne Valluy, leading the largest French military operation to date, fails to wipe out the Viet Minh in one stroke. The Viet Minh bide their time and conduct guerrilla warfare designed to wear down French forces until they are able to meet the French in large-scale open warfare.

October 7–December 22
French forces launch Operation Lea, a series of attacks on Viet Minh positions near the Chinese border. Directed by General Raoul Salan, the operation involves 12,000 men during a three-week period over some 80,000 square miles of nearly impenetrable terrain northeast of the Viet Bac region. The operation results in more than 9,000 Viet Minh casualties, but most of the 40,000 guerrillas slip away through gaps in the French lines.

1948

April
The French induce Emperor Bao Dai to return to Vietnam.

June 5
High Commissioner Bollaert and General Nguyen Van Xuan sign the Baie d'Along Agreement, which names Bao Dai chief of state and recognizes the independence of Vietnam within the French Union. Vietnamese from all sides condemn the Bao Dai government as a French puppet.

1949

March 8
The Elysée Agreement outlining general principles affecting French-Vietnamese relations is signed by French president Vincent Auriol and Bao Dai. France recognizes an "independent" state of Vietnam with Bao Dai as its leader and promises to help build a national anti-Communist army.

July
The French establish the Vietnamese National Army.

October
Mao Zedong's Communist forces defeat Chiang Kai-shek's Nationalist army, ending the decades-long Chinese Civil War.

1950

January 14
The newly established People's Republic of China formally recognizes the Democratic Republic of Vietnam led by Ho Chi Minh and agrees to furnish military assistance to the Viet Minh. Shortly thereafter, China begins sending military advisers and modern weapons and equipment to the Viet Minh. With supplies coming in, General Giap declares that the guerrilla phase is now over and that the counteroffensive can begin. He will subsequently transform the guerrillas into a conventional army that will include five light divisions and one heavy division.

January 30
The Soviet Union extends diplomatic recognition to the Democratic Republic of Vietnam.

February 7

The United States and Great Britain extend de jure recognition of the state of Vietnam and the Bao Dai regime. Later in the month, France will request U.S. military aid.

February 27

The National Security Council signs NSC 64, a memorandum recommending "that all practicable measures be taken" to block further Communist expansion in Southeast Asia.

May 8

United States announces that an agreement has been reached with France for the United States to provide military and economic assistance to aid the pro-French regimes of Vietnam, Laos, and Cambodia.

May 25–27

French and Viet Minh forces fight a pitched battle at Dong Khe. The French defenders are overwhelmed by Viet Minh artillery and human wave attacks, but the Viet Minh are forced to withdraw when the French surprise them by dropping a battalion of paratroopers on the town.

June 25

Korean War begins when North Korean People's Army attacks south across the thirty-eighth parallel.

June 27

President Truman announces that he is increasing the military aid program for Vietnam that he initiated earlier in the year. This includes a military mission and military advisers. Aid is to be funneled through the French.

July 26

United States commits $15 million in military aid to the French for the war effort in Indochina. American military advisers will accompany the flow of U.S. tanks, planes, artillery, and other equipment and supplies to Vietnam. Over the next four years, the United States will spend $3 billion on the French war and by 1954 will provide 80 percent of all war supplies used by the French.

August 3

A U.S. Military Assistance Advisory Group Indochina (MAAG-I) is formed in Saigon. The mission of the 35-man group is to screen French requests for American military aid, assist in the training of South Vietnamese troops, and advise on strategy.

September 16

As part of General Giap's first major counteroffensive against the French, the Viet Minh launch second attack on Dong Khe. The Viet Minh overrun the position, cutting French communications with Cao Bang and French garrisons to the northwest.

October 7–17

French garrison at Cao Bang is wiped out by Viet Minh and the French garrison at Lang Son is evacuated, leaving northern Tonkin from the sea to the Red River in Viet Minh hands. In the battles in September and October, the French sustain 6,000 casualties and lose large stores of military equipment to the Viet Minh.

December

General Jean de Lattre de Tassigny, one of France's most illustrious generals, is appointed commander in Vietnam and also named high commissioner, giving him civilian as well as military authority. Upon his arrival in Vietnam, he will invigorate the morale of the French forces and adopt a more offensive approach to defeating the Viet Minh.

December 22

Napalm is used for the first time in Vietnam, against Viet Minh forces at Tien Yen.

December 23

United States signs a Mutual Defense Assistance Agreement with France and the French Associated States of Indochina (Vietnam, Cambodia, and Laos).

1951

January 13–15

A Viet Minh force of 20,000 soldiers begins a series of attacks on fortified French positions in the Red River Delta. French troops strike back with devastating results. In the first attack at Vinh Yen near Hanoi, French air support plays a major role. The Viet Minh forces withdraw, suffering heavy losses.

February

The Lao Dong Party (Worker's Party of Vietnam) is created in Hanoi as the successor to the Indochinese Communist Party.

March 23–28

Viet Minh forces attack French outpost at Mao Khe near Haiphong, but are forced to withdraw with heavy casualties after being pounded by French naval gunfire and airstrikes.

May 29–June 18

As part of ongoing counteroffensive, Viet Minh forces attack French positions in the Day River area southeast of Hanoi, but French reinforcements combined with air strikes and gunboat support result in resounding defeat for the Viet Minh. Giap's leadership is questioned by the Viet Minh leadership, but he retains his post as head of the army. He will subsequently begin a general withdrawal of his forces from the Red River Delta. Among the French casualties in this round of fighting is Bernard de Lattre, the only son of the French commander and high commissioner.

September

General de Lattre travels to Washington seeking more aid from the United States.

September 7

The United States signs an agreement with Saigon for direct aid to South Vietnam. American presence in Saigon is increased as civilian government employees join the U.S. military personnel already there.

October

General Giap orders his 312th Division against the French position at Nghia Lo. The French reinforce the threatened position with paratroopers and Giap's forces withdraw.

November

De Lattre initiates a "meat grinder" battle at Hoa Binh, a city on the Black River 80 kilometers southwest of Hanoi. He wants to lure Giap into a major battle of attrition designed to inflict the maximum punishment on the Viet Minh. However, de Lattre overextends his forces by setting up too many outposts. During the battle, which lasts until February 1952, Giap takes advantage and inflicts heavy casualties on the French, but his forces are hit hard as well. He withdraws, allowing the French to retake their positions.

November 20

Stricken by cancer, De Lattre is replaced by Raoul Salan. De Lattre returns home and dies in Paris two months later, just after being promoted to the rank of marshal.

December 9

Giap's forces attack French outpost at Tu Vu on the Black River. Giap now avoids conventional warfare and instead wages hit and run attacks followed by a retreat into the dense jungles. The objective of this campaign is to cut French supply lines.

December 31

French casualties in Vietnam surpass 90,000.

1952

January

General Salan orders the withdrawal of French forces from posts along the Black River between Hoa Binh and Viet Tri and finally Viet Binh.

February

French forces withdraw from Hoa Binh. General Giap's forces continually ambush French forces during the retreat and destroy many elements of the French rear guard. Casualties for each side surpass 5,000 during the Black River fighting.

Summer

During this period both sides focus on preparing for future operations. The Viet Minh bring their divisions up to full strength and concentrate on training with new weapons supplied by China. The French prepare for an all-out offensive and receive more American supplies, small arms, tanks, and aircraft.

July

President Truman promotes the American Legation in Saigon to Embassy status.

October

In preparation for a new offensive, General Giap orders his troops into the delta area between the Black and Red Rivers.

October 17

General Giap's forces attack Nghia Lo and overrun the French position, followed by nearby outposts. The Viet Minh then advance westward.

October 29–November 30

General Salan launches Operation Lorraine, which involves 30,000 troops in the largest French military operation of the war. Salan hopes that by striking Giap's base areas around Nghia Lo in the Viet Bac region, he can compel the Communists to abandon the effort to conquer the Thai Highlands, but the operation will be largely unsuccessful because Giap ignores the French maneuvers and keeps his forces in position along the Black River.

November 4

Dwight D. Eisenhower is elected president. During his administration, the Indochina War will cease to be regarded as a colonial war, and the fighting in Vietnam will become a war between communism and the "free world." The new president will greatly increase U.S. military aid to the French in Vietnam. However, for many of Eisenhower's closest advisers, in particular Secretary of State John Foster Dulles and Vice President Richard Nixon, the possibility of direct Chinese intervention in Vietnam becomes a matter of urgent preoccupation.

1953

March 3

Soviet leader Joseph Stalin dies and is succeeded by Georgi Malenkov and Nikita Khrushchev.

April

U.S. vice president Richard Nixon visits Vietnam and tells the French, "It is impossible to lay down arms until victory is won."

April 14

Communist forces mass to invade Laos. After initially deploying his divisions, General Giap, realizing that he cannot sustain his primitive supply lines, withdraws his forces. However, the Viet Minh now have freedom of movement through a large part of northern Laos and can dominate the territory west of the Black River while other forces keep the French tied down.

May 20

General Henri Navarre assumes command of French Union forces in Vietnam; using a phrase that will haunt Americans in later years, he proclaims, "Now we can see, [success in Vietnam] clearly, like light at the end of a tunnel." He focuses his attention on the grave deterioration of the French military position, particularly in the North, devising a plan for a major buildup of French forces preparatory to a massive attack against the Viet Minh.

July 27

With the signing of the Korean armistice at Panmunjom, Chinese aid to Vietnam, such as trucks, artillery and antiaircraft guns, increases.

September 30

Eisenhower approves $385,000,000 over the $400,000,000 already budgeted for military aid for Vietnam. By April 1954 aid to Indochina will reach $1,133,000,000 out of a total U.S. foreign aid budget of $3,497,000,000.

November

The French begin Operation Castor, which includes the occupation of a series of entrenched outposts protecting a small base to be established in the isolated jungle valley at Dien Bien Phu in northwest Vietnam. General Navarre will place 15,000 French troops there 200 miles behind enemy lines as part of an effort to defend Laos and hopefully lure the Viet Minh into a pitched battle where the French can achieve a decisive victory. During the opening days of this operation, 800 French paratroopers parachute into Dien Bien Phu and begin preparations for a fortified camp, building two airstrips to link the base with Hanoi.

November 20

General Giap's forces take the last French stronghold in northwest Tonkin, and soon the entire Chinese border is open. He immediately begins massing his troops and artillery in the Dien Bien Phu area, sensing the potential for a decisive blow against the French. Giap's troops manually drag 200 heavy howitzers up rugged mountainsides to target the French positions in the Dien Bien Phu valley.

1954

January

The French begin Operation Alante, which is designed to clear the coastal areas of Viet Minh, but the operation will end in March without achieving its objective.

January 25–February 18

Foreign ministers of the Big Four—the United States, Britain, France, and the Soviet Union—meet in Britain. In February they agree to hold a conference on Korea and Indochina in Geneva in April.

March

The Dien Bien Phu garrison now includes a dozen battalions, two groups of 75 mm guns, 28 105 mm howitzers, four 155 mm howitzers, mortars, and 10 light tanks. Six Grumman fighters armed with napalm are on alert on the airfield. Three main bastions form the defense of the larger airstrip, while the main stronghold includes the village itself. Four smaller outposts form the outer defenses.

March 13

A force of 40,000 to 50,000 Viet Minh armed with heavy artillery attacks the French garrison at Dien Bien Phu. Using artillery they have hauled up the sides of the surrounding mountains, the Viet Minh pound the French positions and shut down the airstrips; after five days it is clear that the French are in serious trouble, for they are forced to rely on parachute drops for resupply. Giap's troops begin construction of a maze of tunnels and trenches, slowly inching their way toward the main French positions.

March 20

The French urgently appeal to Washington for help. John Foster Dulles, a firm believer in General Navarre's plan, is shocked. Admiral Arthur Radford and the Joint Chiefs of Staff consider possible military options: sending American combat troops to the rescue; a massive but conventional air strike by B-29 bombers, the mining of Haiphong Harbor; and even the employment of several tactical nuclear bombs.

March 25

The National Security Council tentatively approves the Radford plan, which calls for massive B-29 airstrikes from the Philippines and carrier strikes from the Gulf of Tonkin involving up to 350 aircraft. President Eisenhower wants to consult with the British before making a decision to launch the airstrikes.

April 7

At a news conference discussing the importance of defending Dien Bien Phu, President Eisenhower espouses what will become known as the "domino theory," saying, "You have a row of dominoes set up, and you knock over the first one and what will happen to the last one is the certainty that it will go over quickly. So you have the beginning of a disintegration that will have the most profound circumstances."

April 16

Vice President Richard Nixon tells a convention of newspaper editors that the United States may be "putting our own boys in [Indochina] . . . regardless of allied support."

April 24

Admiral Radford and Secretary of State John Foster Dulles meet Anthony Eden in Paris to convey a message from the president that he is prepared to ask Congress for a joint resolution approving American air strikes in support of the French at Dien Bien Phu. Eden is opposed, but promises to convey the message to the British government.

April 25

Prime Minister Winston Churchill rejects the U.S. proposal because he thinks the situation is too far gone and that the air strikes "might well bring the world to the verge of a major war."

April 26

The Far Eastern Conference opens in Geneva while the Viet Minh continue to lay siege to the French garrison at Dien Bien Phu. Delegations from the United States, Britain, China, Soviet Union, France, Vietnam (Viet Minh and representatives of Bao Dai), Cambodia, and Laos begin negotiations to end the war in Vietnam as part of a larger settlement of Indochina problems. The Viet Minh, now certain of victory at Dien Bien Phu, are in no mood to compromise. The U.S. delegation, under orders from Dulles not to negotiate with or recognize the Chinese delegation, does not participate in the discussions and acts only as observers.

April 29

At a press conference, President Eisenhower denies that there is a U.S. plan for massive air strikes in support of the French at Dien Bien Phu. Unwilling to go it alone without Great Britain's support, President Eisenhower rejects the French request for U.S. military intervention and dismisses the conventional air raid option.

May 7

At 5:30 P.M., the remnants of the French garrison at Dien Bien Phu surrender to the Viet Minh after suffering 1,600 killed, 4,800 wounded, and 1,600 missing. The Viet Minh immediately send their 8,000 prisoners on a 500-mile march to prison camps. During the battle, two U.S. civilian fliers, James "Earthquake McGoon" McGovern, Jr., and Wallace Buford, are shot down and killed.

May 8

The Geneva peace talks continue. The French are publicly opposed to any solution that involves a partition of Vietnam, but behind the scenes they are considering this as a compromise. The Chinese indicate a willingness to support partition, for they have no desire to continue a war that might spill over into China and, additionally, do not want the Vietnamese to become too strong. Negotiations will drag on for six weeks as the French reject the demands made by the Viet Minh's chief delegate, Pham Van Dong.

June 1

Colonel Edward G. Lansdale (USAF) arrives in Vietnam to assume the duties of chief of the Saigon Military Mission. Lansdale, actually a member of the CIA, has been sent to Vietnam to run covert, political-psychological operations aimed at disrupting the government of North Vietnam.

June 16

At Geneva, China's Chou En-lai suggests that the Viet Minh withdraw their troops from Laos and Cambodia. He is supported by Vyacheslav Molotov of the Soviet Union. China and the Soviets bring pressure to bear on the Viet Minh not to disrupt the conference. The Viet Minh delegation will later complain that their Communist brethren sold them out, but they cannot afford to offend the Chinese because they cannot be certain of expelling the French without Chinese support.

June 17

France's newly elected prime minister, Pierre Mendès-France, declares that he will resign as head of the French government if he is unable to obtain a cease-fire in Indochina by July 20.

June 18

At his chateau in Cannes, France, Bao Dai appoints Ngo Dinh Diem prime minister of the state of Vietnam.

June 26

Ngo Dinh Diem, newly chosen premier of South Vietnam, flies into Saigon, where only a few of his Catholic supporters meet him.

July 7

Diem, having completed the organization of his cabinet, formally assumes office as premier.

July 20–21

At Geneva, French and Viet Minh representatives sign an agreement providing for an armistice in the French-Viet Minh War. Another document, entitled the "Final Declaration of the Geneva Conference," calls for temporarily partitioning Vietnam at the 17th parallel, creating North and South Vietnam, and recognizes the independence and neutrality of Laos and Cambodia. The agreement provides for a national election to be held in two years to address the issue of reunification. The agreement also calls for a period of 300 days in which all persons may pass freely from one zone to the other and for the establishment of an International Control Commission made up of representatives from India, Canada, and Poland to oversee the implementation of these agreements.

August

Hundreds of thousands of refugees, mostly Catholics, begin moving from North Vietnam to South Vietnam under terms of the Geneva Accords. Colonel Edward Lansdale and his CIA team play a key role in encouraging Catholics and others opposed to the Viet Minh to leave the north. The United States and France provide aircraft and ships to move the refugees south. Once resettled in the south, the Catholics will provide a firm base of support for Ngo Dinh Diem, himself a Catholic.

August 8–12

In Washington, the National Security Council concludes that the Geneva settlement was a "disaster" that "completed a major forward stride of Communism which may lead to the loss of Southeast Asia."

August 11

U.S. Military Assistance Advisory Group in Saigon reaches 342 men.

August 20

President Eisenhower approves a National Security Council paper titled "Review of U.S. Policy in the Far East," which supports Secretary of State Dulles's view that the United States should support Diem, while encouraging Diem to broaden his government and establish more democratic institutions.

September 8

An agreement is signed at Manila establishing a military alliance that becomes the Southeast Asia Treaty Organization (SEATO), aimed at checking Communist expansion. Signatories are France, United States, Great Britain, Australia, New Zealand, the Philippines, Pakistan, and Thailand, who pledge themselves to "act to meet the common danger" in the event of aggression against any signatory state. A separate protocol to SEATO designates Laos, Cambodia, and "the free territory under the jurisdiction of the State of Vietnam [South Vietnam]" as areas subject to the provisions of the treaty. This agreement provides a justification for U.S. support of anti-Communist regimes in Southeast Asia.

September 11

Prime Minister Diem suspends the chief of staff, General Nguyen Van Hinh, and orders him to leave for France. This is an attempt to consolidate Diem's control of the military following the earlier arrest of two other officers charged with plotting against the government. Hinh refuses to relinquish his command or obey Diem's order to leave the country.

September 19

Diem accuses General Hinh of rebellion after Hinh released a statement demanding that the country be given a "strong and popular" new government. A few days later Hinh stations tanks around the presidential palace, which is guarded by police controlled by Diem's enemies, the Binh Xuyen. Diem stalls for time until loyal militia units can be brought up from Annam. Hoa Hao and Cao Dai sect leaders, who have formed a united front with the Binh Xuyen in opposing Diem, send the Binh Xuyen's Le Van Vien to Paris to seek permission from Emperor Bao Dai, nominally head of state, for a coup against Diem.

September 20

Nine of Diem's 15 cabinet members resign, apparently convinced that his government will be overthrown. In response, Diem turns to his family and friends, whom he will install as members of his cabinet.

September 24

Forty-eight hours before the projected joint action of the sects against Diem, he announces the formation of a coalition government including four Hoa Hao and two Cao Dai leaders, effectively ending the first great test of his regime. General Hinh left Vietnam for France on November 20.

October

The Vietnamese Marine Corps (VNMC) is formally organized with U.S. marine colonel Victor J. Croizat as its senior American adviser. At two-battalion strength by the end of the year, the VNMC will become a well-disciplined unit that will form the nucleus of a force that will eventually expand and become part of South Vietnam's strategic reserve forces.

October 5

The last French troops depart Hanoi.

October 11

Following the French departure from Hanoi, Ho Chi Minh and the Viet Minh return after eight years in the jungle and formally take over Hanoi and North Vietnam. The long war with the French has devastated the North, which is plagued by severe economic problems. In addition, on Diem's instructions, departing anti-Communist Vietnamese heading south dismantle public facilities and loot factories, crippling some essential services in Hanoi.

October 24

President Eisenhower advises Ngo Dinh Diem that the United States will provide support and assistance directly to South Vietnam, instead of channeling it through French authorities, but only if democratic reforms continue uninterrupted.

November 3

President Eisenhower sends General Lawton J. Collins, the U.S. representative on the military committee of NATO, to Vietnam to convey assurances of direct U.S. aid and "coordinate the operation of all U.S. agencies in that country."

November 17

General Collins arrives in Saigon. Affirming $100 million in U.S. aid, he announces that the aid is for "Diem and his Government only." Collins warns that the South Vietnamese army will receive U.S. military aid only if it supports Diem; he announces that U.S. military personnel will be assigned to help train that army.

November 20

Premier Mendès-France visits Washington. On his return to Paris, he discloses the agreements made during his visit: (1) France will relinquish control of the economy, commerce and finances of Vietnam; (2) command of the National Army will be transferred to the Vietnamese government; (3) responsibility for training the Vietnamese army will be transferred to the United States; (4) U.S. aid will go directly to Saigon; and (5) the French Expeditionary Corps will withdraw from Vietnam.

December

The People's Republic of China and Hanoi conclude an aid agreement, by which the PRC agrees to provide technical assistance and equipment for improving North Vietnam's roads, railroads, postal and telegraph systems, and waterworks. Under this agreement, Chinese technicians will supervise the repair of the Hanoi-Lang Son railroad.

1955

January 1

In Hanoi, at a five-and-one-half-hour parade attended by over 200,000, Ho Chi Minh makes his first public appearance in over eight years.

In Saigon, Lieutenant General John W. O'Daniel assumes duties as chief of the U.S. Military Assistance Advisory Group–Indochina; the focus of his efforts will be to assist the South Vietnamese government in organizing and training the South Vietnamese army.

In Washington, the U.S. government pledges additional military aid for South Vietnam, citing the aid agreement of December 23, 1950, signed by the United States, France, and the Associated States of Indochina.

February 1

The Franco-American Training Relations and Instruction Mission (TRIM) is established to conduct the training of South Vietnamese forces by U.S. and French military advisory personnel.

February 3

President Diem introduces the first of a series of agrarian reform measures urged by his U.S. advisers with a decree governing levels of rent for farm land. Instead of redistributing land to the poor, Diem's land reform program ends up by taking back what the peasants were given by the Viet Minh and returning it to the landlords, forcing peasants to pay for the land they considered theirs on terms they cannot meet. By 1960, 75 percent of the land will be owned by 15 percent of the people. The Communists will capitalize on unresolved peasant unrest throughout Diem's regime.

February 12
U.S. Military Assistance Advisory Group takes over sole responsibility from the French for training and organizing the South Vietnamese army.

March 7
The United States and Vietnam sign a new agreement supplementing the earlier economic cooperation agreements of September 1951.

March 28
Diem launches a campaign against the Binh Xuyen, a private armed group of 40,000 that controls the Saigon-Cholon police and the national security police. Diem sends troops to take over the Saigon police headquarters. The Binh Xuyen withdraw but fighting breaks out. The Hoa Hao sect forces under Generals Ba Cut and Tran Van Soai join the Binh Xuyen in a blockade of Saigon.

April 26
Fighting renews in Saigon when Diem dismisses Lai Van Sang, director-general of the national security police, and orders the Binh Xuyen to cease operations in Saigon; the Binh Xuyen refuse and Saigon turns into a battlefield. As the situation worsens, Bao Dai summons Diem to Cannes, but Diem refuses.

April 27
Based on recommendations from General Collins, Secretary of State Dulles agrees to withdraw support from Diem, who has refused to institute any meaningful reform programs and is beset by the Binh Xuyen. Dulles cables the embassy in Saigon to find a replacement. However, Colonel Edward Lansdale of the CIA, a staunch supporter of Diem, presses the embassy to support Diem.

April 28
Encouraged by Colonel Lansdale to persevere, Diem orders a counterattack against the Binh Xuyen, which succeeds in expelling them from their Saigon strongholds. The U.S. embassy is instructed to destroy the earlier communication from Washington.

May 7–13
Three-power talks on the South Vietnamese question are held in Paris between French premier Edgar Faure, Foreign Minister Pinay, British foreign secretary Harold Macmillan, and U.S. secretary of state John Foster Dulles. After the meeting, Faure announces that neither France nor the United States intend to interfere in South Vietnam's internal affairs, but both countries will support Diem's government and urge that it become more representative. The next day Diem declares that as a sovereign country South Vietnam will not be bound by decisions taken at conferences in which it was not a participant.

May 10
South Vietnam formally requests U.S. instructors for its armed forces.

May 16
The United States agrees to furnish direct military aid to Cambodia.

May 20

The French command withdraws its troops from the Saigon-Cholon area, thereby depriving remaining Cao Dai and Hoa Hao sect forces of French support.

June 5

Diem initiates a new offensive against the remaining Hoa Hao forces; within two weeks, sect forces will have been routed and most sect leaders flee into Cambodia. Hoa Hao resistance is reduced to sporadic guerrilla operations.

June 6

North Vietnamese foreign minister Pham Van Dong announces that his government is prepared to open consultations with South Vietnam in preparation for holding the nationwide elections in 1956 as called for in the Geneva Accords.

July 6

Diem declares in a broadcast that since the state of Vietnam did not sign the Geneva Accords, South Vietnam is not bound by them and the elections called for by the accords will not be held. Washington will support Diem in this declaration.

July 7

Following a trip to Beijing by Ho Chi Minh and his ministers of finance, industry, agriculture, education, and health, Chinese officials announce that the PRC will provide 800 million yuan (about $200 million) in economic aid to North Vietnam.

July 18

Following a visit from Ho Chi Minh and his ministers, the Soviet Union announces that it will grant Hanoi 400 million rubles ($100 million) in economic aid. This grant will finance an ambitious industrialization program in North Vietnam.

July 20

Diem rejects North Vietnam's invitation to discuss nationwide elections on the grounds that the people will not be able to express their will freely.

August 10

Declaring that the State of Vietnam is "the only legal state" and charging that free elections are impossible in the Communist North, Diem reaffirms the announcement he made in his broadcast of July 6 in which he stated that South Vietnam was not bound by the Geneva Accords, which it did not sign.

August 16

The last French high commissioner in Vietnam departs.

August 31

Secretary of State John Foster Dulles announces that the United States supports the position of the government of Vietnam regarding its refusal to hold national elections to reunify the two Vietnam states.

October 6

Diem's Ministry of the Interior announces that a referendum is scheduled for October 23 to decide whether Bao Dai or Diem will be the rightful head of state.

October 18

Bao Dai announces in a communiqué from his office in Paris that he has dismissed Diem from the premiership and annulled his authority and power. In a message to the Vietnamese people, which Diem's censors suppress, Bao Dai declares, "police methods and personal dictatorship must be brought to an end, and I can no longer continue to lend my name and my authority to a man who will drag you into ruin, famine and war."

October 23

The national referendum results in a 98 percent vote against Bao Dai and for Diem, who becomes chief of state. The election is by all accounts rigged, with the CIA's Colonel Lansdale once again playing an important role. In Saigon, Diem receives one-third more votes than there are registered voters.

October 24

Lieutenant General Samuel T. Williams replaces General John W. O'Daniel as senior U.S. Army officer in Vietnam and as commander of MAAG-Indochina; he eliminates "Indochina" from the mission title, renaming it the U.S. Military Assistance Advisory Goup-Vietnam (MAAG-V). Under his command, the MAAG will concentrate on preparing the South Vietnamese armed forces for a conventional attack from North Vietnam.

October 26

Diem proclaims the Republic of Vietnam with himself as its first president. He is also prime minister, defense minister, and supreme commander of the armed forces (now officially called the Republic of Vietnam Armed Forces, or RVNAF). The new regime is recognized immediately by France, the United States, Great Britain, Australia, New Zealand, Italy, Japan, Thailand, and South Korea.

December

All of about 150 French companies still operating in North Vietnam are nationalized.

December 12

The United States consulate in Hanoi is closed, effectively severing diplomatic relations with North Vietnam.

December 13

Hanoi officially announces that, by this date, more than 100,000 people have taken part in the People's Agricultural Reform Tribunals, which began in 1953 but were temporarily halted until after the French were defeated. During these tribunals, "landlords" in villages near Hanoi were tried for their "transgressions"; many of those charged as landlords own only two to four acres. Thousands are executed or sent to forced labor camps during this period of ideological cleansing ordered by Ho Chi Minh.

December 19

The Southeast Asia Collective Defense Treaty (SEATO), having been ratified by the Senate and President Eisenhower, officially goes into effect.

1956

January 11

South Vietnamese president Ngo Dinh Diem issues Ordinance No. 6, allowing the internment of those "considered as dangerous to national defense and common security." This marks the beginning of Diem's campaign to eliminate the Viet Minh cadres who had remained in the South to prepare for the planned national elections.

February 18

While visiting Beijing, Cambodia's Prince Norodom Sihanouk renounces SEATO protection for his nation.

March 31

Prince Souvanna Phouma becomes prime minister in Laos.

April 13

Hoa Hao guerrilla commander Ba Cut is captured by General Duong Van Minh. He is publicly executed on July 13, signifying the end of Hoa Hao resistance. With the Cao Dai already subdued, Diem has successfully neutralized two groups that had long defied his regime.

April 28

The last French soldiers depart and the French Military High Command disbands; the U.S. MAAG assumes full responsibility for the training of South Vietnamese forces.

May

The United States sends 350 additional military men designated as Temporary Equipment Recovery Team (TERM) to Saigon to help recover and redistribute equipment abandoned by the French. They will stay on as a permanent part of the MAAG.

May 25

Diem again reiterates his refusal to recognize the Geneva Accords, stating that "the absence of all liberties in North Vietnam makes impractical at this moment any approach to the problem of electoral and pre-electoral discussions."

July 7

A new constitution, written at Diem's direction, is officially announced on the second anniversary of Diem's accession to power. The new constitution gives the president, with a term of office of six years, veto power over the unicameral legislative assembly, whose members are elected for four years. The president may rule by decree when the assembly is not in session. Both the president and assembly are chosen by direct vote. Freedom of speech and assembly are guaranteed, but may be suspended during the next four years if the president declares a state of emergency.

July 20

Deadline set by Geneva Accords for nationwide elections passes. From this point on, an initially disorganized and uncoordinated insurgency begins in the South.

August 5
Souvanna Phouma and the Communist Prince Souphanouvong agree to a coalition government in Laos.

August 24
Ho Chi Minh apologizes to the North Vietnamese people for the excesses of the land reform campaign, dismisses Truong Chinh as party secretary, and initiates a "Campaign for the Rectification of Errors."

November 8
North Vietnam's People's Agricultural Reform Tribunals are officially abolished; between 10,000 and 15,000 persons are estimated to have been killed, with another 50,000 to 100,000 imprisoned. Most are eventually released.

November 10–20
Hanoi sends the 325th Division to suppress an open rebellion that has broken out over the repressive land reform campaign in Ho Chi Minh's native Nghe An Province; about a thousand peasants are killed or wounded and several thousand are arrested and deported. The Viet Minh blame the Chinese for pushing them to institute the disastrous land reform campaign.

December
By the end of the year, President Diem has eliminated 90 percent of the former Viet Minh cells in the Mekong Delta, but his ruthless drive against all dissidents does little to enhance his popularity, and he loses many potential allies in the process.

1957

January 3
The International Control Commission declares that neither North Vietnam nor South Vietnam has carried out the Geneva Accords.

January 24
The Soviet Union proposes a permanent division of Vietnam into North and South, with the two nations admitted separately to the United Nations. The United States rejects the proposal, unwilling to recognize Communist North Vietnam.

May 8
During Diem's visit to the United States (May 5–19), President Eisenhower calls him the "miracle man" of Asia and reaffirms support for his regime, declaring "The cost of defending freedom, of defending America, must be paid in many forms and in many places . . . military as well as economic help is currently needed in Vietnam."

May 11
Presidents Diem and Eisenhower issue a joint communiqué that reaffirms the United States' continuing support of South Vietnam in its stand against communism.

President Ngo Dinh Diem is welcomed in ceremonies at Washington National Airport, May 1957. *(National Archives)*

May 29
Communist Pathet Lao forces attempt to seize power in Laos.

June 24
The U.S. Army's 1st Special Forces Group is activated on Okinawa. This unit will send advisers to Vietnam to help organize and train the initial contingent of South Vietnamese Special Forces at the commando training center in Nha Trang.

October
Communist insurgent activity in South Vietnam begins in earnest when a decision is made in Hanoi to organize 37 armed companies in the Mekong Delta. Prior to this point, the remaining Viet Minh cadres in the South have been conducting a somewhat uncoordinated program of assassination and sabotage directed against the Diem regime. With the reorganization, the insurgency will intensify.

October 21
Captain Harry Cramer, Jr., dies in a munitions handling accident, becoming the first American killed in the Second Indochina War.

October 22
Thirteen U.S. military personnel are wounded in three terrorist bombings of MAAG and U.S. Information Service installations in Saigon. The rising tide of guerrilla

activity in South Vietnam reaches an estimated 30 terrorist incidents, and at least 75 local officials are assassinated or kidnapped in the last quarter of 1957.

December

By the end of 1957, Diem's government announces that at least 300,000 refugees from the North have been settled in 300 new villages in the South. Meanwhile, the fledgling insurgency continues with an ongoing program of harassment, sabotage, and assassination (over 400 minor officials by this time) meant to disrupt social, political, and economic progress in South Vietnam.

1958

January

Communist guerrillas attack a plantation north of Saigon.

March 7

North Vietnam's Pham Van Dong proposes in a letter to Diem that representatives of North and South Vietnam meet to discuss a reduction in the number of troops on both sides and the establishment of trade relations with a view toward eventual reunification. The letter strongly criticizes the United States for meddling in the internal affairs of Asian countries, particularly Vietnam.

April 26

Diem's government responds to Pham Van Dong's letter by flatly rejecting his offer of a meeting, characterizing it as "phoney" and a "propaganda trick." Stating that the South Vietnamese government also desires normalization of relations aimed at reunification, the South Vietnamese statement provides a list of conditions necessary for opening North-South discussions.

June

The Communists form a coordinated command structure in the eastern Mekong Delta. Most of the 37 companies organized in October 1957 are located in the western Mekong Delta.

June 25

Cambodia charges that South Vietnamese troops have violated Cambodian territory since 1957, but the allegation is denied by South Vietnam's foreign minister.

December

The CIA comes into possession of a document from the Lao Dong Party Central Committee in Hanoi. Resolution 15 states that the decision has been made to "open a new stage of the struggle" and increase the level of the armed insurgency in the South.

1959

January

The CIA receives a copy of an order from the Central Committee in Hanoi directing the establishment of two guerrilla operation bases, one in the western Central

Highlands and one in Tay Ninh Province, near the Cambodian border and not too far from Saigon.

April

The Lao Dong Party establishes the 559th Transportation Group and charges it with controlling the infiltration of insurgents into the South. This military unit will be responsible for providing men and supplies to support the armed struggle in South Vietnam; this operation marks the beginning of the effort that will result in the building of the Ho Chi Minh Trail through Laos and Cambodia. The trail will eventually expand into a 1,500-mile-long network of jungle and mountain passes extending from North Vietnam along Vietnam's western border through Laos and parts of Cambodia, funneling a constant stream of soldiers and supplies into South Vietnam.

April 4

In an address at Gettysburg College in Pennsylvania, President Eisenhower makes a commitment to maintain South Vietnam as a free and independent state. He asserts the "inescapable conclusion that our own national interests demand" U.S. support of South Vietnam.

May

At the 15th Plenum of the Lao Dong Party Central Committee in Hanoi, North Vietnam's leaders formally decide to take control of the growing insurgency in the South.

In South Vietnam, the CIA begins to pick up indications of large-scale infiltration from the North, which had begun in 1955. These indications are viewed by intelligence analysts in Washington as the beginning of North Vietnamese intervention in the South.

U.S. Commander in Chief, Pacific, authorizes U.S. military advisers down to the regimental level of South Vietnam's armed forces.

June–July

Communist Pathet Lao forces attempt to gain control over northern Laos, receiving some Vietnamese Communist assistance.

July

The Lao Dong Party in Hanoi organizes Group 759 to oversee shipment of men and supplies from North Vietnam to the South down what will become known as the Ho Chi Minh Trail. The activities of Groups 559 and 759 are kept secret since they are in clear violation of the Geneva Accords.

July 8

Major Dale R. Buis and Master Sergeant Chester M. Ovnand are killed when guerrillas strike the MAAG compound in Bien Hoa, 20 miles northeast of Saigon; they are the first two Americans to die from hostile fire.

August

Diem passes a law authorizing severe repression of Communists and other dissidents. The insurgent campaign of assassination of local officials accelerates dramatically; between 1959 and 1961, the number killed rises from 1,200 to 4,000 per year. Diem reacts by appointing more military men to administrative posts.

August 10
An insurgent force of 400 raiders attacks the large Michelin rubber plantation north of Saigon, easily defeating South Vietnamese security forces and capturing more than 100 weapons and 5 million piasters (approximately $143,000).

August 30
General elections are held in South Vietnam and result in an overwhelming victory for the Diem government. Two opposition members, Dr. Phan Quang Dan and Nguyen Tran, are elected as independents when their party, the Democratic Bloc, is refused registration. However, they are refused seats when the assembly meets and later are found guilty and fined on trumped up charges of electoral law infractions.

September 12
In Hanoi, Pham Van Dong tells the French consul, "You must remember that we will be in Saigon tomorrow." In November he will tell the Canadian commissioner, "We will drive the Americans into the sea." These comments are passed on to the U.S. embassy in Saigon, which forwards the remarks to Washington as evidence of the intentions of North Vietnam in the worsening situation in the South.

September 26
The 2nd Liberation Battalion ambushes two South Vietnamese companies from the 23rd Division, killing 12 men and capturing most of their weapons.

October 26
New South Vietnamese constitution, heavily weighted toward control by the executive branch, goes into effect. The Republic of Vietnam is divided into 41 provinces, then subdivided into districts and villages.

December 31
General Phoumi Nosavan seizes control in Laos.

There are approximately 760 U.S. military personnel now in Vietnam; the South Vietnamese armed forces now total 243,000 personnel.

1960

January 1
In Hanoi, the First National Assembly, with Ho Chi Minh's approval, passes the first socialist constitution.

January 17
An uprising begins in Ben Tre Province, some 100 miles from Saigon in the Mekong Delta. Villagers armed with mattocks, machetes, spears, swords, and sharpened bamboo sticks have joined slightly better armed dissidents to storm civil guard posts and overthrow village administrations. Largely in reaction to oppressive measures

employed by the Diem regime in the construction and maintenance of "agrovilles," the peasants, for the first time under the direction of former Viet Minh cadres, organize a defense and survive a counterattack. For the first time, a popular armed insurrection achieves victory on a provincial scale.

February 5

Saigon government requests that Washington double U.S. Military Assistance and Advisory Group strength from 342 to 685.

April

North Vietnam imposes universal military conscription and begins infiltration of cadres into South Vietnam.

In South Vietnam, 18 distinguished nationalists send a petition to President Diem urging him to reform his family-run and increasingly corrupt government. Diem ignores their advice and instead closes several opposition newspapers and arrests journalists and intellectuals.

April 17

Despite the approval of the International Control Commission (ICC) for an increase in U.S. advisers in South Vietnam, Hanoi lodges a protest with the chairmen of the 1954 Geneva Conference (Britain and the Soviet Union) against the "formidable" increase in the U.S. advisory group, charging that the United States is attempting to turn South Vietnam into "a U.S. military base for the preparation of a new war."

August

A U.S. national intelligence estimate notes that areas under Communist control in South Vietnam will continue to expand unless the South Vietnamese government can protect the peasants and win their cooperation and support.

August 9

In Laos, Captain Kong Le occupies Vientiane and urges restoration of a neutral state under Prince Souvanna Phouma; this is effectively the beginning of the Laotian civil war.

September 5

At the third congress of the Lao Dong Party in Hanoi, the leadership calls for intensified struggle in the south and formation of a "broad national united front."

In Saigon, Lieutenant General Lionel McGarr replaces Lt. Gen. Samuel T. Williams as commander, Military Assistance Advisory Group–Vietnam; Williams had served since October 1955.

September 16

In a cable to Secretary of State Christian A. Herter, the U.S. ambassador in Saigon, Elbridge Durbrow, analyzes two separate but related threats to the Diem regime: danger from demonstration or coup, predominantly "non-Communist" in origin; and the danger of a gradual Viet Cong extension of control over the countryside. He suggests methods Diem might use to mitigate both threats—including sending his brother Nhu abroad and improving relations with the peasantry—and ends by declaring, "If Diem's position in country continues to deteriorate as a result of failure to adopt political, psychological, economic and security measures, it may become necessary for U.S. government to begin considerable alternative courses of action and leaders in order to achieve our objective."

November 8
John F. Kennedy defeats Richard M. Nixon in election for president of the United States.

November 11–12
In an aborted coup attempt, paratroop battalions and a marine unit under the direction of Colonel Nguyen Van Thi and Lieutenant Colonel Vuong Van Dong surround Diem in the presidential palace. Colonel Thi declares that Diem has "shown himself incapable of saving the country from Communism and protecting national unity." Diem stalls until loyal troops arrive and the coup fails. He subsequently cracks down on all perceived "enemies of the state." From this time on, many in the military, including Diem's former allies, plot against him.

December 4
Despite American diplomatic pressure, Diem continues to resist instituting economic and political reforms. Ambassador Durbrow cables Washington, "We may well be forced, in the not too distant future, to undertake the difficult task of identifying and supporting alternative leadership."

December 16
In Laos, the forces of Phoumi Nosavan capture Vientiane.

December 20
Hanoi announces the formation of the National Front for the Liberation of the South, more commonly known as the National Liberation Front, or NLF, at a conference held "somewhere in the South." Designed to replicate the Viet Minh as an umbrella nationalist organization, it reaches out to all those who oppose the Diem regime. One hundred delegates representing more than a dozen political parties and religious groups, including remnants of the Cao Dai, Hoa Hao, and Binh Xuyen, are in attendance. From the beginning, the NLF is completely dominated by the Lao Dong Party's central committee and serves as the North's shadow government in South Vietnam. The Saigon regime dubs the NLF and its armed forces the "Viet Cong," a pejorative contraction of *Viet Nam Cong San* (Vietnamese Communists). This label, created by Diem's publicists, is designed to brand the rebels as Communists, and will come to be applied generally to the supporters and participants of the insurgency.

December 31
Approximately 900 U.S. military personnel are now in Vietnam; strength of South Vietnamese armed forces remains at 243,000.

1961

January 1
President-elect John F. Kennedy appoints Dean Rusk as secretary of state, Robert McNamara as secretary of defense, and McGeorge Bundy as National Security Advisor.

January 4
Prince Boun Oum organizes a pro-Western government in Laos; North Vietnam and the USSR send aid to the Communist Pathet Lao insurgents.

January 6
Soviet premier Nikita Khrushchev declares that the Soviet Union will back all "wars of national liberation" around the world. This pronouncement will greatly influence the incoming Kennedy administration in support of a strategy of "counterinsurgency" in Vietnam.

January 19
Outgoing president Dwight D. Eisenhower warns incoming President John F. Kennedy that Laos is "the key to the entire area of Southeast Asia" and might require the direct intervention of U.S. combat troops.

January 20
John F. Kennedy is inaugurated as 35th president of the United States.

January 25
In the first news conference of his administration, President Kennedy announces support for a "neutral Laos."

January 28
President Kennedy approves a Vietnam counterinsurgency plan that calls for government reform and military restructuring as the basis for expanded U.S. assistance.

March
Republic of Vietnam Campaign Medal with "1960 Device" is authorized by the government of the Republic of Vietnam for members of the U.S. armed forces who serve in Vietnam for a minimum of six months.

March 23
In a television news conference, President Kennedy warns of Communist expansion in Laos and says that a cease-fire must precede the start of negotiations to establish a neutral and independent nation there.

An American SC-47 intelligence-gathering plane en route from Vientiane in Laos to Saigon is shot down over the Plain of Jars while checking radio frequencies used by Russian planes delivering arms to the Pathet Lao. Subsequently, at President Kennedy's suggestion, RT-33 aircraft borrowed from the Philippine Air Force and painted with Laotian markings are used for reconnaissance over Laos.

March 28
A national intelligence estimate prepared for President Kennedy reports that the situation in Vietnam has deteriorated in the previous six months and predicts that "An extremely critical period for President Ngo Dinh Diem and the Republic of Vietnam lies immediately ahead." The report claims that more than one-half of the rural region south and southwest of Saigon is under Communist control and states that the discontent that gave rise to the barely failed coup against Diem the preceding November

has not been dealt with. The report concludes by questioning Diem's ability to rally the people against the Communists.

April

U.S.-supported Bay of Pigs invasion of Cuba fails.

Frederick Nolting replaces Elbridge Durbrow as U.S. ambassador to South Vietnam.

April 1

Four hundred Viet Cong attack a village in Kien Hoa Province but are beaten back by South Vietnamese troops.

April 3

More than a hundred Viet Cong guerrillas are killed in an attack on Ben Cat, north of Saigon.

April 12

Walt W. Rostow, senior White House specialist on Southeast Asia and a principle architect of U.S. counterinsurgency doctrine, delivers a memorandum to President Kennedy recommending that there be a "gearing up [of] the whole Viet-Nam operation." His nine proposals, almost all of which eventually become policy, include sending the vice president to Vietnam for a personal assessment, increasing the number of American Special Forces, increasing funds for Diem, and "persuading Diem to move more rapidly to broaden the base of his Government, as well as to decrease its centralization and improve its efficiency."

April 19

U.S. Military Assistance Advisory Group–Laos is created and eventually directs Green Beret "White Star" mobile training teams in support of Royal Lao forces.

April 26–29

President Kennedy meets with the National Security Council to decide whether to send troops into Laos. During the course of the discussion, the threat to South Vietnam is addressed when Deputy Secretary of Defense Roswell L. Gilpatric proposes discussions with President Diem on "possibility of a defensive security alliance." Additionally, he recommends quick expansion of South Vietnam's forces by 40,000 and the deployment of 2,000 U.S. trainers and Special Forces troops to prevent an invasion of South Vietnam from Laos. In addition to what would be the first major input of U.S. troops, on April 29 the Joint Chiefs of Staff cables Admiral Harry Felt to be prepared to send one brigade with air elements to northeastern Thailand and another to Danang, as a threat to intervene in Laos. Kennedy ultimately decides against these deployments, but will increase the number of U.S. advisers in South Vietnam.

May 4

At a press conference Secretary of State Dean Rusk reports that Viet Cong forces have grown to 12,000 men and have killed or kidnapped more than 3,000 persons in 1960. While declaring that the United States will supply South Vietnam with every possible assistance, he refuses to say whether the United States will intervene militarily. At a press conference the next day, President Kennedy says that consideration is being given to the use of U.S. forces.

May 9
President Kennedy dispatches Vice President Lyndon Johnson to Vietnam to make a firsthand assessment of the situation.

May 11
President Kennedy approves sending 400 Special Forces troops and 100 other U.S. military advisers to South Vietnam to train South Vietnamese soldiers in methods of "counter-insurgency" to fight the Viet Cong. On this day, Kennedy orders the start of clandestine operations against North Vietnam, to be conducted by South Vietnamese agents directed and trained by the CIA and U.S. Special Forces troops. These orders also call for infiltration of South Vietnamese forces into Laos to locate and disrupt Communist bases and supply lines there.

May 12
Vice President Lyndon Johnson meets with President Diem in Saigon, hailing him as the "Winston Churchill of Asia." He finds Diem uninterested in the deployment of U.S. combat troops except in the event of open invasion by the North Vietnamese.

May 16
A 14-nation conference on Laos is convened in Geneva.

May 23
Upon his return from Asia, Vice President Johnson reports to President Kennedy, recommending a "strong program of action" in Vietnam. Echoing domino theorists, Johnson says that the loss of Vietnam would compel the United States to fight "on the beaches of Waikiki" and eventually on "our own shores." Focusing on Thailand and Vietnam, he asserts that the United States must either aid these countries or "pull back our defenses to San Francisco and a 'Fortress America' concept." He says that Asian leaders do not want American troops involved in Southeast Asia, but Johnson feels that open attack would bring calls for U.S. combat troops.

June 4
President Kennedy meets with Premier Khrushchev of the Soviet Union in Vienna to discuss the situation in Berlin. During their discussions, they agree to support a neutral and independent Laos. While satisfied with this solution for Laos, Kennedy rejects neutrality for Vietnam even though Hanoi appears prepared to agree, believing that South Vietnam is the place to make a stand against the further spread of communism.

June 9
President Diem requests U.S. troops for training his armed forces and asks for U.S. assistance in increasing the South Vietnamese army by 100,000 men, to 270,000, accompanied by "considerable" U.S. build-up with "selected elements of the American armed forces." In August, Washington agrees to finance a 30,000-man increase but postpones a decision on the buildup of U.S. advisers.

June 16

Following a meeting between President Kennedy and South Vietnam's Nguyen Dinh Thuan, the Vietnamese acting defense minister, an agreement is reached for direct training and combat supervision of Vietnamese troops by U.S. instructors.

July 2

Hanoi captures at least three members of Lansdale's U.S.-trained First Observation Group when their U.S. C-47 aircraft is shot down (or experiences engine trouble). The First Observation Group is the clandestine warfare unit ordered by President Kennedy in May 1961. Initially, the detachment had only 340 men but eventually expands to 805. The group's activities were at first focused on the Viet Cong but soon shifted entirely to operations against North Vietnam.

July 16

In what is described as Vietnam's bloodiest battle since the 1954 armistice with the French, Army of the Republic of Vietnam (ARVN) forces kill 169 Viet Cong in fighting in the Plain of Jars marsh area 80 miles west of Saigon.

September 1–4

Viet Cong forces carry out a series of attacks in Kontum Province.

September 18

A VC battalion of over 1,500 besieges the provincial capital of Phuoc Vinh, 60 kilometers north of Saigon. During August there are 41 engagements between government troops and Viet Cong units in South Vietnam.

September 21

The U.S. Army's 5th Special Forces Group is activated at Fort Bragg, North Carolina. Eventually the group will deploy to South Vietnam and assume control of all Special Forces operations in-country. Based on his belief in the potential of the Special Forces in counterinsurgency, President Kennedy visits the Special Warfare Center to review the program, and authorizes the Special Forces to wear the distinctive green beret that becomes their symbol.

September 29

In Saigon, President Diem meets with Ambassador Frederick Nolting and Admiral Harry Felt, commander in chief of U.S. Pacific forces. Diem expresses his desire for a mutual defense treaty with the United States and an accelerated American "build-up" to include tactical air squadrons to help break up the larger VC units that have recently been massing for attacks.

October 1

Southeast Asia Treaty Organization (SEATO) representatives meet in Bangkok to discuss guerrilla warfare in South Vietnam.

October 2

Addressing the Vietnamese National Assembly, President Diem declares that the VC guerrilla campaign has grown into a "real war" in which the enemy attacks "with regular units fully and completely equipped" and "seeks a strategic position in Southeast Asia in conformity with the orders of the Communist International."

October 5

U.S. military intelligence estimates that 80 percent to 90 percent of the 17,000 Viet Cong guerrillas in South Vietnam have been locally recruited and do not depend on external supplies.

October 8

In Laos, the warring factions agree to form a neutral coalition headed by Prince Souvanna Phouma.

October 11

At a meeting of the National Security Council, a proposal is put before President Kennedy urging that the United States accept "as our real and ultimate objective the defeat of the Viet-cong." In a supplemental note, the Joint Chiefs of Staff estimate, that 40,000 U.S. troops could clean up "the Vietcong threat" and another 120,000 could cope with possible North Vietnamese or Chinese Communist intervention. President Kennedy decides to send General Maxwell Taylor to Vietnam to study the situation and consider possible strategies.

Operation Farm Gate begins when President Kennedy orders the U.S. Air Force to send a combat detachment to South Vietnam to assist the Republic of Vietnam Air Force (VNAF). In response, the Air Force forms the 4400th Combat Crew Training Squadron and dispatches 155 officers and airmen to Bien Hoa Airfield. The unit immediately begins training VNAF pilots and crews.

October 13

The Diem government sends an urgent request through Ambassador Frederick Nolting for U.S. combat units to be introduced into South Vietnam as "combat trainer units," as well as for additional aircraft and a symbolic U.S. presence in the Central Highlands to prevent attacks there.

October 18

Diem declares a state of national emergency because of increased Viet Cong activity and the severe floods that have beset South Vietnam.

October 18–24

President Kennedy's chief military adviser, General Maxwell Taylor, and Special Assistant for National Security Affairs Walt Rostow conduct a second fact-finding trip to South Vietnam. Despite the declaration of national emergency, Diem does not repeat the earlier request for American combat troops, but does ask for tactical aviation, helicopter companies, coastal patrol forces, and ground transport. He reiterates his desire for a bilateral defense treaty with the United States.

November

U.S. Special Forces medical specialists are deployed to Vietnam to provide assistance to the Montagnard tribes around Pleiku; from this beginning, the Civilian Irregular Defense Group (CIDG) program will evolve, whereby the CIA and Special Forces will organize and train paramilitary forces among the ethnic and religious minorities of South Vietnam to combat Communist forces in the border areas with Laos and Cambodia.

November 1

Writing President Kennedy from Vietnam, General Taylor reports that prompt U.S. military, economic, and political action can lead to victory without a U.S. takeover of the war. He advocates a "massive joint effort" with South Vietnam to cope with the flood and the VC. He tells Kennedy that the disastrous flooding in the Mekong Delta could provide a potential cover for the introduction of 6,000 to 8,000 U.S. combat troops that would serve to "reverse the present downward trend of events." The issue for the president becomes somewhat clouded when Secretary of State Dean Rusk, cabling from Japan, acknowledges the great importance of Southeast Asia, but warns about the risks of making a military commitment without reciprocal political reforms by President Diem.

November 3

President Kennedy receives the formal Taylor-Rostow report, which recommends a change in the U.S. role from advisory only to "limited partnership" with the South Vietnamese. The report urges increased U.S. economic aid and military advisory support to include intensive training of local self-defense forces and large increases in airplanes, helicopters, and support personnel. A secret appendix recommends deployment of 8,000 American combat troops that could be used to support ARVN in military operations. The report concludes that, if all else fails, the United States "could probably save its position in Vietnam by bombing the North."

November 8

Secretary of Defense Robert McNamara and Secretary of State Dean Rusk send a joint memorandum to President Kennedy essentially agreeing with the findings of the Taylor-Rostow Report and recommending that the United States "now take the decision to commit ourselves to the objective of preventing the fall of South Vietnam to the Communists."

November 12

It is reported that four U.S. F-101 jets are engaged in photo reconnaissance missions in South Vietnam focused on locating guerrilla units in remote areas vulnerable to air attack.

November 15

U.S. Air Force 2nd Advanced Echelon (later designated "Division") is activated at Bien Hoa Air Base.

November 16

In accordance with President Kennedy's earlier decision to increase military aid to South Vietnam without committing U.S. combat troops, U.S. Air Force cargo planes begin shuttling in more U.S. instructors and advisers.

November 21

White House issues National Security Action Memorandum 111, spelling out President Kennedy's response to the Taylor-Rostow Report and the recommendations of Secretaries McNamara and Rusk. Although the president declines to send American ground combat troops, the United States will underwrite an increase in the RVNAF and provide advisers throughout the military structure down to battalion level and in each provincial capital. In return, the Diem government will be urged to begin reform measures to win more support from the Vietnamese people.

December 4

Armed Forces Expeditionary Medal is authorized by Presidential Executive Order 10977 for award to U.S. military personnel participating in "operations of assistance for a friendly foreign nation." The order applies to U.S. personnel serving in Vietnam after July 1, 1958, and in Laos after April 19, 1961.

December 8

Washington issues a report accusing North Vietnam of aggression against the South and warning of a "clear and present danger" of Communist victory.

December 11

The ferry carrier USNS *Core* arrives in Saigon with the 8th and 57th Transportation Companies, the first U.S. helicopter units sent to Vietnam as part of the expanded military aid ordered by President Kennedy. On board are 33 Vertol H-21C Shawnee helicopters and 400 air and ground crewmen to operate and maintain them. Their assignment will be airlifting ARVN troops into combat.

December 14

The American decision on the U.S. troop build-up in South Vietnam is formally announced in a public exchange of letters between Presidents Kennedy and Diem. Kennedy writes, "We shall promptly increase our assistance to your defense effort."

December 15

President Kennedy renews the U.S. commitment to preserve the independence of Vietnam and pledges American assistance to Vietnam's defense effort.

December 16

Joint Chiefs of Staff authorizes U.S. Air Force pilots serving as advisers engaged in Operation Farm Gate to undertake combat missions, providing at least one Vietnamese trainee is carried on board the strike aircraft for training purposes.

December 20

According to the *New York Times*, about 2,000 uniformed U.S. troops and specialists are "operating in battle areas with South Vietnamese forces" and are authorized to return fire if fired upon.

December 22

Specialist Fourth Class James T. Davis, a cryptologist from the U.S. Army's 3rd Radio Research Unit working with a South Vietnamese signals intelligence unit, is killed in action during a firefight with the VC, making him the first American to die in direct combat action.

December 26
Specialist Fourth Class George Fryett is the first American captured by the VC. He will be released in June 1962.

December 31
The total number of U.S. military personnel in Vietnam reaches 3,200. South Vietnamese military strength remains at 243,000. Total insurgent forces are estimated at 26,700. Fourteen Americans have been killed or wounded in combat. Two army helicopter units are flying combat missions in support of the ARVN; U.S. Air Force personnel are instructing VNAF and flying combat missions; U.S. Navy Mine Division 73 (a tender and five sweepers) is patrolling from Danang south along the coastline; U.S. aircraft from Thailand and Seventh Fleet carriers are flying surveillance and reconnaissance missions over Vietnam; and six C-123 aircraft equipped for support of defoliant operations have received "diplomatic clearance" to enter South Vietnam. In 1961, $65 million of U.S. military equipment and $136 million in economic aid have been delivered to South Vietnam.

1962

January
The United States installs a tactical air control system in South Vietnam and provides additional aircraft for combat and airlift support.

January 4
The United States and South Vietnam announce in a joint communiqué that they will cooperate in starting "a broad economic and social program aimed at providing every Vietnamese with the means for improving his standard of living . . . Measures to strengthen South Vietnam's defense in the military field are being taken simultaneously."

U.S. Air Force C-123s conduct defoliation mission as part of Operation Ranch Hand. *(Texas Tech University Vietnam Archive)*

January 8
An American civilian contractor is killed in a VC ambush near Saigon.

January 10
Accusing Diem of creating "a military dictatorship based on ruthless terror," the Soviet Union also denounces the United States for "gross interference" in South Vietnam's internal affairs and for "open violations" of the international agreements on Indochina that are responsible "for the present worsening of the situation in South Vietnam."

January 12
In South Vietnam, the U.S. Air Force launches Operation Ranch Hand, a "modern technological

area-denial technique" designed to defoliate the roads and trails used by the Viet Cong. Flying C-123 Providers, U.S. personnel will dump an estimated 19 million gallons of defoliating herbicides (Agent Orange, named for the color of its metal containers, is the most frequently used) over 10 percent to 20 percent of Vietnam and parts of Laos in the years between 1962 and 1971. The operation succeeds in killing vegetation but not in stopping the Viet Cong. The herbicide has a small proportion of dioxin, a chemical that, at least in larger doses, is considered a carcinogen and/or otherwise dangerous to human beings. Long after the war is over, thousands of veterans of Vietnam and Vietnamese citizens will attribute many medical, genetic (in their offspring), and psychological problems to exposure to Agent Orange.

January 13
As part of the ongoing Operation Farm Gate, U.S. Air Force pilots fly T-28 fighter-bombers on their first combat missions in support of a South Vietnamese outpost under Viet Cong attack. By the end of the month, 229 missions will have been flown.

January 15
Asked at a news conference if U.S. troops are fighting in Vietnam, President Kennedy answers "No." This is technically correct, but U.S. soldiers are serving as combat advisers with the South Vietnamese army, and U.S. pilots are flying missions with the South Vietnamese air force.

In South Vietnam, the People's Revolutionary Party is founded. Ostensibly independent of the Communist Lao Dong Party in the North, this organization consolidates Communist control of the NLF.

January 27
Secretary of Defense McNamara forwards a memorandum from the Joint Chiefs of Staff to President Kennedy that urges the deployment of "suitable" U.S. forces to Vietnam, saying that it is clear that the South Vietnamese cannot handle the insurgency alone. The Joint Chiefs of Staff asserts that failure to deploy forces at this time "will merely extend the date when such action must be taken and will make our ultimate task proportionately more difficult."

February
The 39th Signal Battalion, a communication unit, is the first unit of regular U.S. ground forces to arrive in Vietnam.

February 2
The first U.S. Air Force plane is lost in South Vietnam. The C-123 aircraft crashes while spraying defoliant on a Viet Cong ambush site as part of Operation Ranch Hand.

February 3
The "Strategic Hamlet" program begins in South Vietnam. This program, which is essentially a resumption of Diem's "agroville" program, is designed to provide security and a better life for the rural populace by settling them in protected hamlets where government cadres can carry out economic and political programs, while at

the same time depriving the Viet Cong of their peasant support base. Conceived in 1961, this program is derived from British counterinsurgency expert Sir Robert Thompson's experiences in quashing the 1950s Malayan emergency. However, the situation in Vietnam is more complex than in Malaya and the Strategic Hamlet program in South Vietnam proves to be ill-conceived, expensive, and ineffective.

February 4
First U.S. helicopter is shot down in Vietnam. It was one of 15 helicopters ferrying ARVN troops into battle near the village of Hong My.

February 7
Two additional U.S. Army aviation units arrive, bringing American military strength in South Vietnam to 4,000.

February 8
U.S. Military Assistance Command, Vietnam (USMACV), under the command of General Paul D. Harkins, is established with headquarters in Saigon as part of the substantial increase in the U.S. commitment in Vietnam. The new headquarters will assume overall responsibility for the U.S. advisory effort and other U.S. military assistance to South Vietnam. A Defense Department spokesman said the move stresses that "we intend to win" the struggle in Southeast Asia.

February 11
The first Operation Farm Gate casualties occur when an SC-47 crashes about 70 miles north of Saigon, killing nine U.S. and South Vietnamese crewmen.

February 14
At a news conference, President Kennedy says that "the training missions we have [in South Vietnam] have been instructed that if they are fired upon, they are of course to fire back, but we have not sent combat troops in [the] generally understood sense of the word." The next day former vice president Nixon expresses hope that President Kennedy will "step up the build-up and under no circumstances curtail it because of possible criticism."

February 17
High administration officials in Washington tell the press that the war in Vietnam is being fought under a "counter-guerrilla strategy" in which U.S. combat troops should play no part.

February 27
South Vietnamese president Diem survives another coup attempt when two VNAF pilots try to kill him and his brother Ngo Dinh Nhu by bombing and strafing the presidential palace. Neither Diem nor any of his staff are injured. The attack confirms Diem's conviction that his main adversaries are domestic; as a result he retreats deeper into himself, delegating more authority to his brother Nhu, who sets about to eliminate all dissidents.

March 15
U.S. Army Advisory Campaign officially begins.

March 18

Secretary of Defense McNamara acknowledges in a press conference that American "training" of the South Vietnamese "occasionally takes place under combat conditions."

March 22

Operation Sunrise, South Vietnam's first long-range counteroffensive against the Viet Cong, is launched in Binh Duong Province, 35 miles north of Saigon, as part of the Strategic Hamlet program. The plan calls for ARVN troops to establish 14 fortified hamlets in War Zone D, north of Saigon. By the end of the year, only four of the planned hamlets have been constructed and occupied. The operation, which ends in 1963, will ultimately be a failure and the Viet Cong will once again control the area.

March 23

The first U.S. Army regular unit, the 39th Signal Battalion, arrives in Vietnam.

April 9

Two U.S. soldiers are killed in a Viet Cong ambush while on a combat operation with South Vietnamese troops. Questioned about the deaths in a news conference two days later, President Kennedy remarks, "We are attempting to help Vietnam maintain its independence and not fall under the domination of the Communists . . . We cannot desist in Vietnam."

During ceremonies in Saigon, the Vietnamese air force pledges support for President Ngo Dinh Diem after a political uprising and an attempt on the president's life, March 1962. *(National Archives)*

April 15

Arriving aboard the aircraft carrier *Princeton,* the first U.S. Marine Corps air unit lands in South Vietnam. The 362nd Marine Medium Helicopter Squadron (HMM-362) with 450 marines and 15 Sikorsky UH-34D Sea Horse helicopters will be based near Soc Trang, 100 miles southwest of Saigon. The unit, dubbed "Task Force Shoofly," reinforces the three U.S. Army helicopter companies already in Vietnam. The unit's mission will be to carry supplies and troops in support of the South Vietnamese army. They fly their first combat mission on April 22.

May

Some 5,000 U.S. troops are serving in South Vietnam, plus a total of 124 U.S. aircraft including two U.S. Air Force C-123 squadrons and four helicopter companies in-country. Intelligence reports indicate that the Viet Cong are forming battalion-sized units in several parts of Central Vietnam.

May 6–27

In Laos, Phoumi Nosavan's forces are routed, paving the way for a settlement in the ongoing civil war.

May 11

Secretary of Defense McNamara makes the first of many trips to Vietnam and meets with President Diem. After 48 hours in the country he concludes that "every quantitative . . . measurement shows that we are winning the war."

May 17

President Kennedy sends 3,000 marines and 50 jet fighters to Thailand in response to Communist expansion in Laos. To thwart the Soviet-supported Pathet Lao, who have been massing near the Thai border, the marines are flown to Udorn, which is 35 miles from the Laotian capital of Vientiane. This show of force had been requested by the Thai government. The marines will be withdrawn by the beginning of August.

In Saigon, President Diem, continuing his campaign against dissidents, passes several presidential decrees forbidding the holding of any meeting for any purpose without prior government approval.

May 25

A report of the International Control Commission (ICC) for Vietnam charges North Vietnam with subversion and aggression in South Vietnam. It also charges that the United States is violating the Geneva Accords with its military buildup in South Vietnam, and accuses South Vietnam of violating the 1954 Geneva Accords by accepting U.S. military aid and establishing "a factual military alliance" with the United States. The Polish delegation, following the Soviet line, does not support the report's findings.

June

Students for a Democratic Society (SDS) issues its Port Huron Statement, calling for "true democracy" in the United States and an end to the arms race. The SDS will become increasingly radicalized and will organize teach-ins and demonstrations to protest the war after U.S. ground forces are committed.

June 12

Three Laotian factions sign an agreement for the establishment of a neutralist regime under Souvanna Phouma.

July

A team of 30 Australian military advisers arrives in Vietnam to join with American advisory teams training South Vietnamese military forces.

July 18

The largest helicopter lift in Vietnam thus far takes South Vietnamese troops north of Saigon in 18 marine helicopters, 12 U.S. Army helicopters, and 11 helicopters belonging to the Vietnamese air force.

July 23

Geneva Accords on Laos signed at second Geneva Conference. The declaration and protocol on the neutrality of Laos is signed at the 14-nation conference in Geneva.

At a Honolulu conference on Vietnam strategy, Secretary of Defense McNamara orders plans to be made for U.S. withdrawal from Vietnam and the reduction of aid to Saigon. His orders reflect what is perceived as "tremendous progress" during early 1962, as well as reservations concerning domestic support for long-term U.S. involvement in Southeast Asia.

August 1

Marine helicopter squadron HMM-362 is replaced by HMM-163 after flying 50 combat assaults with South Vietnamese troops and suffering no casualties.

President Kennedy signs the Foreign Assistance Act of 1962, which provides ". . . military assistance to countries which are on the rim of the Communist world and under direct attack."

August 22

Kennedy administration officials quoted in the *New York Times* estimate that there are 20,000 guerrilla troops in South Vietnam. Despite hundreds of engagements during the preceding two months and encouraging victories for South Vietnamese forces during the first six months of the year, the Viet Cong have grown in numbers, and some U.S. officials feel that the war has become stalemated.

October 1

General Earle Wheeler replaces General George Decker as Army chief of staff. General Maxwell Taylor replaces General Lyman Lemnitzer as chairman of the Joint Chiefs of Staff.

October 14

An air force reconnaissance flight photographs nuclear-armed Soviet missiles in Cuba, causing a major showdown between President Kennedy and Soviet premier Khrushchev that results in what will become known as the Cuban Missile Crisis.

October 15

Despite State Department denials, several sources report that U.S. helicopter crewmen have begun to fire first on Viet Cong troops encountered during missions in support of South Vietnamese troops.

October 19

Operation Morning Star, a major South Vietnamese effort to clear Tay Ninh Province, north of Saigon, ends in failure. Five thousand South Vietnamese troops ferried by U.S. helicopters kill only 40 Viet Cong in eight days and capture two others. One UH-1 is lost. U.S. officials call the operation a waste and disclaim any responsibility for it.

October 28

Khrushchev orders withdrawal of missiles from Cuba, ending the crisis.

December 2

Following a trip to Vietnam at President Kennedy's request, Senate Majority Leader Mike Mansfield (D-Mont.) informs Congress that after eight years and $2 billion, U.S. efforts to set up an independent Vietnam are "not even at the beginning of the beginning." Originally a supporter of President Ngo Dinh Diem, Mansfield places blame for the deteriorating situation in Vietnam squarely on the Diem regime for its failure to share power, suggesting that the Americans have simply taken the unenviable place formerly occupied by the French. His reversal surprises and irritates President Kennedy.

December 3

Roger Hilsman, director of the State Department Bureau of Intelligence and Research, sends a memorandum entitled "The Situation and Short-Term Prospects in South Vietnam" to Secretary of State Rusk. Acknowledging that government control of the countryside has improved slightly, he asserts that the VC are prepared for a long struggle and have expanded considerably in size and influence. According to Hilsman, successful counterinsurgency in Vietnam will take several years of greater effort by both the United States and the South Vietnamese government and that real success hinges upon Diem gaining the support of the peasants through social and military measures he has so far failed to implement. Hilsman warns that a non-Communist coup against Diem "could occur at any time" and would "probably halt and possibly reverse the momentum of the government's counterinsurgency effort."

December 29

Saigon announces that 4,077 strategic hamlets have been completed out of a projected total of 11,182, and now house 39 percent of the South Vietnamese population. These figures are considered questionable by U.S. officials.

December 31

President Kennedy authorizes the expansion of Operation Farm Gate.

Approximately 11,300 U.S. advisory and support personnel are now in Vietnam. One hundred and nine Americans have been killed or wounded during the previous year, almost eight times as many as in 1961. U.S. Army and Marine Corps aviation units have flown over 50,000 sorties, about one-half of which were combat support missions. China claims to have armed the Viet Cong with more than 90,000 rifles and machine guns this year, and trained guerrilla forces in South Vietnam are estimated at 25,000, with active Viet Cong sympathizers numbered at 150,000. The Viet Cong are now killing and kidnapping 1,000 local officials per month. South Vietnamese government regular troops number 243,000 plus 65,000 Self Defense Corps members trained to defend their villages.

1963

January 2

At Ap Bac, a village in the Mekong Delta 50 miles southwest of Saigon, 2,500 troops of the ARVN 7th Infantry Division equipped with armored personnel carriers and supported by fighter-bombers and U.S. helicopters suffer a humiliating defeat at the hands of 320 VC guerrillas from the 261st Main Force Battalion. Uncharacteristically, the Viet Cong stand and fight against a bungled ARVN attack during which three U.S. advisers are killed, eight are wounded, and five American helicopters shot down. The ARVN suffers 80 killed and 100 wounded, and the VC escape with only light losses. The engagement, symbolic of the ARVN's many problems, clearly demonstrates that government troops can neither cope with the strategy nor match the fighting spirit of the Viet Cong. Despite candid assessments of the poor ARVN performance by Lieutenant Colonel John Paul Vann and other U.S. advisers, Headquarters MACV declares the battle a victory for South Vietnamese forces because the VC quit the area after the fighting. The poor performance of the South Vietnamese troops is an indicator that the United States will eventually be compelled to escalate the war by committing American ground troops to fight the Communists.

In Hanoi, the Lao Dong Party declares the battle at Ap Bac a great victory and says that it "signified the coming of the new revolutionary armed forces in the South."

February 11

Senior White House aide Michael V. Forrestal advises President Kennedy to expect a long and costly war. "No one really knows how many of the 20,000 'Viet Cong' killed last year were only innocent, or at least persuadable, villagers, whether the strategic hamlet program is providing enough government services to counteract the sacrifices it requires, or how the mute class of villagers react to the charges against Diem of dictatorship and nepotism." He warns that, in his opinion, Viet Cong recruitment in South Vietnam is effective enough to continue the war even without infiltration from the North.

Vietnamese paratroopers jump from U.S. Air Force C-123 transports in the initial assault wave of Operation Phi Hoa II in Tay Ninh Province, March 1963. *(National Archives)*

February 24
A U.S. Senate panel reports that annual American aid to South Vietnam totals $400 million and that 12,000 Americans are stationed there "on dangerous assignment."

February 26
U.S. helicopter crews escorting ARVN troops are cleared to shoot first when encountering enemy soldiers. Two days before, one U.S. soldier was killed when Viet Cong ground-fire downed two of three U.S. Army H-21 helicopters airlifting government soldiers about 100 miles north of Saigon.

April 11
One hundred U.S. troops of the Hawaiian-based 25th Infantry Division are sent to South Vietnam to reinforce U.S. Army aviation units by serving as door gunners aboard Army H-21 helicopters.

April 17
Diem initiates Operation "Open Arms" (Chieu Hoi) designed to subvert the Communist military effort and convince their troops to desert or rally to the South Vietnamese cause. The campaign promises clemency and material benefits to Viet Cong guerrillas if they abandon the war against his government.

May 5
The Americans for Democratic Action (ADA) group issues a resolution demanding that the United States government withdraw its troops from Vietnam.

May 8
Buddhists riot in the streets of Hue after they are denied the right to display the multicolored Buddhist flag during the celebration of Buddha's birthday. Government troops fire on the crowd, which numbers 20,000. Nine persons are killed, including seven children and one woman, and about 20 are wounded. Diem blames the incident on the Viet Cong and refuses Buddhist demands that the officials responsible be punished. Countrywide Buddhist demonstrations continue into August as the resentment against Diem's regime intensifies. U.S. ambassador Nolting urges Diem to be conciliatory, but Diem refuses.

June 7
Diem's sister-in-law Madame Nhu, self-styled First Lady of Vietnam, alleges that the Buddhists are being manipulated by the Americans. Pressure from Deputy Ambassador William Trueheart forces Diem to create a committee to investigate the Hue incident, but it is only for show and has no real authority.

June 10
MACV commander General Paul Harkins is reported to have warned U.S. military personnel to avoid duty with Vietnamese military units involved in the suppression of Buddhists.

June 11
Buddhist monk Thich Quang Duc publicly immolates himself in Saigon to protest repression by the Diem regime. Diem remains stubborn, despite repeated U.S. appeals, and his special committee of inquiry confirms his contention that the Viet

Cong were responsible for the Hue incident. By November, six Buddhist monks have followed Thich Quang Duc's example. Ngo Dinh Nhu's wife, Madame Nhu, exacerbates the crisis by referring to the self-immolations as Buddhist "barbecues" and offers to supply matches.

June 27

President Kennedy appoints Henry Cabot Lodge, his former Republican political opponent, to succeed Nolting as ambassador to Vietnam beginning August 1. The president wants bipartisanship in his Vietnam foreign policy.

July 4

General Tran Van Don informs Lucien Conein of the CIA that certain South Vietnamese officers are planning a coup against Diem. The CIA has already reported that such plans are under way. Kennedy is initially opposed to the coup, preferring that Diem purge his entourage and institute more liberal reforms. However, it will soon be apparent that Diem refuses to do either.

July 30

Ninety Viet Cong are killed in a four-hour battle in the Ca Mau Peninsula at the southernmost tip of South Vietnam. Three government soldiers are killed in the action.

August 20

President Diem declares martial law at the urging of General Tran Van Don ostensibly to prosecute the war more effectively. Don's real purpose is to set conditions for the coup being contemplated by himself and a number of his fellow officers. Diem hopes to implicate the army in the campaign against the Buddhists conceived by his brother, Ngo Dinh Nhu.

August 21

South Vietnamese special forces loyal to President Diem's brother, Nhu, attack Buddhist pagodas in Saigon, Hue, and several other cities, destroying property and beating and arresting 1,400 Buddhists and students. In response, several large-scale demonstrations break out in a number of cities. Diem proclaims a three-week curfew. In Washington, President Kennedy and his administration see these actions as the last straw.

August 22

Diem's foreign minister, Vu Van Mau, and his ambassador to the United States, Tran Van Chuong, resign in protest over Diem's treatment of the Buddhists. Henry Cabot Lodge arrives in Saigon to replace Frederick Nolting as U.S. ambassador to South Vietnam. He reports back to Washington that Diem's brother, Nhu, is behind the attacks against the Buddhists. Lodge also says that a group of South Vietnamese generals are seeking U.S. support for a coup against Diem.

August 24

Ambassador Lodge receives a State Department cable stating that the United States can no longer tolerate Nhu's influence in Diem's regime. This message also directs Lodge to tell the South Vietnamese generals that Washington is prepared to discontinue economic and military aid to Diem if he does not remove Nhu and institute the necessary reforms.

August 26

Lodge meets with Diem for the first time. Diem refuses to drop Nhu and will not discuss the reforms that President Kennedy wants. Following the meeting, Lodge will try to convince the Kennedy administration to support the dissident generals.

August 27

Cambodia severs diplomatic relations with South Vietnam in protest over border violations and persecution of the Buddhists.

August 28

The CIA chief of station in Saigon reports to Washington that the situation has reached a "point of no return" and that if the coup does not take place or fails, "VN [Vietnam] runs serious risk of being lost . . ."

August 29

Ambassador Lodge sends a message to Washington stating ". . . there is no possibility, in my view, that the war can be won under the Diem administration." In reply, Secretary of State Dean Rusk cables Lodge that he is "authorized to announce suspension of aid through Diem government at a time and under conditions of your choice."

August 30

Two U.S. pilots are killed and three other Americans wounded when enemy gunfire brings down their helicopter in Tay Ninh Province, 55 miles north of Saigon.

August 31

Ambassador Lodge reports to Washington that the conspiracy and coup have collapsed. He also reports hearing that Nhu was secretly dealing with the Viet Cong. Subsequently, the members of the National Security Council meet, without the president present, to discuss "where we go from here." The discussion reveals the differences of opinion within the Kennedy administration. Paul Kattenberg, just returned from Saigon, proposes disengagement from Vietnam because, in his opinion, the war effort is irretrievable, with or without Diem. In response, Secretary of State Rusk declares that it is "unrealistic" to insist that Nhu "must go," and in any event "we will not pull out of Vietnam until the war is won." Secretary of Defense McNamara agrees with Rusk, asserting that the United States is winning. Vice President Johnson suggests that "we should stop playing cops and robbers . . . and once again go about winning the war."

September

The U.S. Army establishes the 145th Aviation Battalion in Vietnam.

September 2

In a CBS-TV interview with Walter Cronkite, President Kennedy rebuffs French president Charles de Gaulle's proposal for a neutral, united Vietnam, rejecting any policy that would lead to the withdrawal of U.S. troops from Vietnam before the Viet Cong menace has been eliminated. While reasserting the U.S. commitment to stay in Vietnam, Kennedy describes Diem as "out of touch with the people" and calls South Vietnam's repressive actions against the Buddhists "very unwise." He also states that the war in Vietnam cannot be won "unless the people support the effort," and that the Diem government might regain that support "with changes in policy and perhaps in personnel."

The *Times* of Saigon charges that the CIA had planned a coup against Diem for 28 August. After intrigues by Diem's brother Nhu, who intimates that he might deal with the Communists, Roger Hilsman advises Secretary of State Rusk that the United States should encourage the South Vietnamese generals who have been discussing a coup against Diem, and he suggests attacking North Vietnam if Hanoi interferes with the coup.

September 10
General Victor Krulak (USMC) and Joseph Mendenhall of the State Department report to President Kennedy on their recent fact-finding mission to Vietnam. Krulak concludes that the war is going well, but Mendenhall concludes from talks with bureaucrats and politicians that Diem is near collapse. Presented with such diametrically opposed assessments, Kennedy is moved to ask, "You two did visit the same country, didn't you?"

September 11
At least 90 soldiers and civilians are killed in fighting during a government counterattack to retake the Ca Mau Peninsula towns of Cai Nouc and Dam Doi.

September 14
Washington decides to suspend economic subsidies to South Vietnamese commercial imports and freeze loans for developmental projects; both are parts of the effort to pressure Diem into making reforms. However, they also serve as a clear sign to those planning a coup against Diem.

September 17
White House sends a message to Ambassador Lodge saying that the administration sees "no good opportunity for action to remove present government in immediate future" and for the present wants to focus on forcing Diem to affect needed reform by applying "such pressures as are available to secure whatever modest improvements on the scene may be possible."

September 24
McNamara and General Taylor arrive in Vietnam after being dispatched by President Kennedy, who is dissatisfied with the report of Krulak and Mendenhall. They were charged to determine whether the country's military situation had deteriorated as a result of the clash between the government and the Buddhists.

October 2
Upon their return, President Kennedy receives the report of the McNamara-Taylor mission. The report is generally optimistic, citing "real progress" in the war but noting that the anti-Buddhist campaign has hurt the war effort. They recommend sanctions against the Diem regime but, unaware that the generals' plotting

continues, report that there is "no solid evidence of the possibility of a successful coup" and recommend that the administration continue to work with Diem.

October 5
Lodge reports to Kennedy that the coup against Diem appears to be on again. General Duong Van Minh, meeting with CIA operative Lucien Conein, asks for assurances that the United States will not thwart a coup, and that economic and military aid will continue. Kennedy cables Lodge instructing him that "no initiative should now be taken to give any active covert encouragement to a coup," but that contacts should be made with "alternative leadership."

October 7
Madame Nhu arrives in the United States for a short visit despite being rebuffed by the Kennedy administration, which refuses officially to acknowledge her presence or to extend diplomatic courtesies to her.

October 18
General Harkins informs President Diem that the United States will deny funds to the Vietnamese Special Forces, who had played a leading role in attacks against the Buddhists, if the funds are used for purposes other than fighting the Viet Cong. Washington will also not renew the annual agreement supplying the government with surplus food, which is sold to pay South Vietnamese troops. These actions serve to convince the dissident generals that they have Washington's approval for the coup.

October 22
General Harkins informs General Don at a British Embassy reception that he knows of the coup and considers it a mistake that will detract from the war against the Communists. The following day Don tells Lucien Conein of the CIA that he has postponed the coup set for October 26.

October 25
Prompted by concerns over a public relations fallout if the coup fails, White House aide McGeorge Bundy sends a cablegram to Lodge seeking assurances that the coup will succeed.

October 27
Lodge meets with Diem, but reports to Washington that the meeting was a "fruitless, frustrating" exchange.

October 29
A U.S. military spokesman reports that government troops have killed 44 guerrillas in a battle at three strategic hamlets in Quang Ngai Province during the past two days.

   At a National Security Council meeting, Kennedy's confidence in the coup is shaken when Diem's performance is supported by General Taylor, citing messages from General Harkins. Kennedy's main concern is now whether the coup can succeed. He cables Lodge to ask the generals to postpone "until chances are better."

Lodge never delivers this message. In the end, Kennedy's message leaves the final judgment to Lodge to decide on the prospects for the coup's success, asserting that once the coup is under way, "it is in the interest of the U.S. Government that it should succeed."

November 1

Lodge has a routine mid-morning meeting with Diem at the presidential palace. At 1:30 P.M., the coup begins when the forces of Major Generals Duong Van Minh, Ton That Dinh, and Tran Van Don begin the takeover of the government, seizing the police headquarters, radio stations, the airport, and other installations and launching attacks on the presidential palace and the Special Forces barracks. Diem and his brother Nhu are trapped inside the palace and reject all calls to surrender. At 4:30 P.M., Diem telephones Ambassador Lodge to ask where the United States stands. Lodge offers to provide Diem and his brother sanctuary and safe conduct out of the country if he resigns. Diem refuses, saying that he will restore order. In the end, Diem is unable to summon any support, so he and Nhu escape through a secret tunnel and go into hiding at St. Francis Xavier Church in Cholon, the Chinese section of the capital.

ARVN troops in front of the presidential offices following the coup against Ngo Dinh Diem, November 1963 *(Texas Tech University Vietnam Archive)*

November 2

At about 6:00 A.M., Diem begins negotiating with the generals, who have assured Lodge that Diem's life will be spared. Diem finally agrees to surrender, and a U.S.-built M113 armored personnel carrier is sent to pick up him and his brother in Cholon. Major Duong Huu Nghia and General Minh's bodyguard, Captain Nguyen Van Nhung, murder Diem and Nhu on their way to the Joint General Staff headquarters, at Minh's orders. At the White House, a meeting is interrupted with the news of Diem's death. According to witnesses, President Kennedy's face turns a ghostly white and he immediately leaves the room. Later, the president records in his private diary, "I feel that we must bear a good deal of responsibility for it."

November 4

Ambassador Lodge cables Kennedy predicting that the change of regime will shorten the war against the Viet Cong. The United States recognizes the new provisional government of South Vietnam. Former vice president Nguyen Ngoc Tho, a Buddhist, becomes premier but the real power is held by the Revolutionary Military Committee headed by General Duong Van Minh. The new government pledges not to become a dictatorship and announces, "the best weapon to fight communism is democracy and liberty."

November 9
The United States announces resumption of its commodity-import aid program to South Vietnam, previously suspended in August.

November 15
Major General Charles Timmes announces in Saigon that 1,000 of 15,000 American advisers in South Vietnam will be withdrawn beginning December 3.

November 19
In Cambodia, Prince Sihanouk, charging that the CIA is trying to oust him from power, declares an end to all U.S. military and economic aid.

November 22
President Kennedy is assassinated in Dallas, Texas; Vice President Lyndon Johnson assumes the presidency.

November 24
President Johnson decides that there will be no break from the Kennedy policies, reaffirming the U.S. intention to continue military and economic support to South Vietnam. He instructs Lodge, in Washington for consultations following Diem's death, to communicate his intention to the South Vietnamese generals.

November 25
South Vietnamese officials announce that 150 guerrillas have been killed in two days of fighting in the Mekong Delta.

November 26
Johnson administration issues National Security Action Memorandum 273, which officially reaffirms the U.S. commitment to the Republic of Vietnam and pledges "to assist the people and Government of that country to win their contest against the externally directed and supported Communist conspiracy." Johnson also gave his personal sanction for a stepped-up program of "clandestine operations by the GVN (Government of Vietnam) against the North."

December
Watching the events unfold in Saigon and Washington, Ho Chi Minh and senior staff make plans for the future. They are happy with Viet Cong progress during recent months, but they realize that there will be no rapid victory. It is clear that Lyndon Johnson plans to continue the U.S. involvement, perhaps deploying as many as 100,000 U.S. combat troops in Vietnam. Viet Minh veteran Colonel Bui Tin, who had been conducting covert inspections of the Viet Cong for the Hanoi leadership for five months, reports that they are poorly organized, lacking in leadership, and unprepared for a long campaign. Partly due to his report, Hanoi decides to start sending regular army troops into the South and to authorize direct attacks against U.S. personnel in the South.

December 2
The South Vietnamese junta orders a temporary halt to the strategic hamlet program. Senior U.S. representative in Long An Province Barl Young reports that three-

quarters of the strategic hamlets in his province have been destroyed, either by the Viet Cong, the peasants, or a combination of both. In a report that is typical of the rising tide of pessimistic news from Vietnam, Young asserts that Minh and his government are ineffective at best, saying, "The only progress in Long An has been by the Viet Cong."

December 14
A U.S. military spokesman in Saigon reports that Viet Cong attacks on hamlets, outposts, and patrols in November have resulted in 2,800 government casualties and 2,900 Viet Cong losses. According to intelligence estimates, the VC have captured enough weapons to arm five 300-man battalions.

December 19
Secretary of Defense McNamara arrives in Saigon to evaluate the new government's war effort against the Viet Cong.

December 21
In his formal report to President Johnson, McNamara, who remains publicly optimistic, says that the new regime in Saigon is "indecisive and drifting." The situation in South Vietnam is "very disturbing" and that "current trends, unless reversed in the next two or three months, would lead to neutralization at best or more likely to a Communist-controlled state." He concludes that, "We should watch the situation very carefully, running scared, hoping for the best, but preparing for more forceful moves if the situation does not show early signs of improvement." His assessment lays the groundwork for decisions that will lead to an intensification of the covert war against North Vietnam, and increased American aid to the South.

December 24
In response to growing pressure from the military to widen and "Americanize" the war, President Johnson tells the Joint Chiefs of Staff, "Just let me get elected, and then you can have your war."

December 31
Some 16,300 U.S. military personnel are now in Vietnam; South Vietnamese forces remain at 243,000. A total of 489 Americans have been killed or wounded in Vietnam this year, well over four times the previous year's total. South Vietnam has received $500 million in U.S. aid in 1963.

1964

January 2
USA – GOVERNMENT: President Johnson receives a report prepared by Major General Victor H. Krulak (USMC), special assistant for counterinsurgency and special activities for the Joint Chiefs of Staff. The report outlines an elaborate series of clandestine operations against North Vietnam "to result in substantial destruction, economic loss and harassment." Collectively, these operations, which will be carried out in three phases, will be instituted as "Oplan 34A."

January 4

SOUTH VIETNAM: The 11 main Buddhist sects in South Vietnam, concluding a four-day convention in Saigon, announce that they are forming an institute for secular affairs to coordinate Buddhist political and social activities. This is seen as a move to present a united front against a government the Buddhists regard as insensitive to their goals.

USA – MILITARY: A U.S. military spokesman in Saigon reports that there has been a considerable increase in arms shipments from Communist nations to the VC and that they are "better equipped and better organized than 12 months ago." U.S. military sources also claim that the bulk of the arms and equipment come from Chinese and North Vietnamese ports via Cambodia and the Mekong River in South Vietnam.

GROUND WAR: An offensive that began on December 31 when 10 ARVN battalions set out to destroy a VC force of two battalions in the Ben Suc area some 40 miles west of Saigon, ends when the Communist forces escape. Only two VC are killed while the South Vietnamese lose 15. U.S. military advisers with the ARVN openly describe the operation as a failure.

January 5

GROUND WAR: In Long An Province, 25 miles southwest of Saigon, a 500-man VC battalion escapes from an ARVN encirclement. Ground fire hits 15 U.S. planes supporting the action, and five American advisers are wounded. Nine ARVN are killed and VC casualties are estimated at 60 to 70.

January 6

SOUTH VIETNAM: Major General Duong Van Minh, chairman of the Military Revolutionary Council, issues decrees that centralize government and military power in himself and two other officers, Major General Tran Van Don and Major General Le Van Kim. The new regime will prove both unresponsive to the people of South Vietnam and politically unstable.

January 13

GROUND WAR: VC take over two strategic hamlets in Pleiku Province, burning 135 houses and kidnapping seven government officials.

January 14

USA – MILITARY: Lieutenant General William C. Westmoreland is appointed deputy to General Paul Harkins, chief of U.S. Military Assistance Command Vietnam (MACV). It is generally accepted that Westmoreland will soon replace Harkins, whose insistently optimistic views on the progress of the war have come under increasing criticism in Washington.

SOUTH VIETNAM: A joint U.S.-South Vietnamese report concludes that the government's war against the VC in the Mekong Delta "cannot be won" unless there are major reforms in the administration of the villages and strategic hamlets. The report recommends an end to both the forcible removal of peasants into strategic hamlets and the corruption and mismanagement that prevails in such villages.

GROUND WAR: Viet Cong guerrillas down a U.S. B-26 bomber, killing two American flyers.

January 16
USA – GOVERNMENT: President Johnson officially approves Operations Plan 34A, clandestine operations to be conducted by South Vietnamese forces supported by the United States to gather intelligence and conduct sabotage to destabilize the North Vietnamese regime.

January 17
GROUND WAR: Five U.S. helicopter crewmen are killed and three are wounded while supporting a major ARVN attack on Communist bases in the Mekong Delta.

January 18
SOUTH VIETNAM: The USS *Providence,* flagship of the Seventh Fleet, arrives in Saigon on what Washington describes as a "goodwill mission." In addition to underlining U.S. support for South Vietnam, the action is also designed to show to all powers in the Far East, the U.S. commitment.

January 22
USA – MILITARY: The Joint Chiefs of Staff informs Defense Secretary McNamara that its members "are wholly in favor of executing the covert actions against North Vietnam," but they do not believe "these efforts will have a decisive effect on the Communist determination to support the insurgency, and it is our view that we must therefore be prepared fully to undertake a much higher level of activity . . ." They recommend "aerial bombing of key North Vietnam targets" and "commit[ment of] additional U.S. forces, as necessary, in support of the combat action within South Vietnam."

January 23
GROUND WAR: A battalion-size Viet Cong force carries out the first significant action on the Ca Mau Peninsula in two months when it makes a pre-dawn attack on Nam Can, an isolated district capital.

January 27
USA – GOVERNMENT: Defense Secretary McNamara appears before the House Armed Services Committee in closed session (his testimony is made public on February 18) and insists that the "bulk of the U.S. armed forces in Vietnam can be expected to leave by the end of 1965," but that "the survival of an independent Government in South Vietnam is so important to the security of Southeast Asia and to the free world that I can conceive of no alternative other than to take all necessary measures within our capability to prevent a Communist victory."

January 29
USA – DOMESTIC: At a news conference, Governor Nelson Rockefeller of New York, a candidate for the Republican nomination for president, attacks the "double talk" of the Johnson administration and calls for a "full accounting" of the situation in Vietnam.

January 30
SOUTH VIETNAM: A junta headed by General Nguyen Khanh, 37-year-old commander of the ARVN I Corps, deposes General Minh in a bloodless coup and seizes control of the government in Saigon. General Minh is placed under house arrest and the figurehead premier, Nguyen Ngoc Tho, is arrested and incarcerated. U.S. Ambassador Lodge had known of Khanh's plans, but dismissed them as just another rumor.

January 31
SOUTH VIETNAM: General Khanh assumes the chairmanship of the Military Revolutionary Council and moves quickly to gain U.S. support for his regime. However, he shows no more aptitude for governing than had Minh. Many ARVN officers turn against Khanh when he attempts to try rival Generals Tran Van Don and Le Van Kim on trumped-up charges.

February 1
COVERT WAR: Covert operations under Oplan 34A begin against North Vietnam.
TERRORISM: One U.S. soldier is killed and five are injured by a bomb blast in Saigon.
USA – GOVERNMENT: At a press conference, President Johnson says he has General Khanh's pledge to increase the war effort against the Viet Cong and that he, in turn, has pledged full U.S. support for the new regime. Johnson also says he is prepared to consider any plan that truly ensures the neutralization of both North and South Vietnam.

February 3
GROUND WAR: A Viet Cong force raids the U.S. military compound at Kontum and one U.S. officer is killed.

February 4
GROUND WAR: VC troops overrun an ARVN battalion headquarters at Hau My, killing 12 and wounding 20 ARVN troops; elsewhere, VC forces ambush an ARVN battalion in Thua Thien Province, killing eight.

February 5–6
SOUTH VIETNAM: About 1,000 students demonstrate in Saigon for the return to power of General Minh, whom General Khanh had released from house arrest and persuaded to stay on as a figurehead.

February 6
NORTH VIETNAM: Soviet premier Aleksey Kosygin arrives in Hanoi; he pledges support for North Vietnam in its effort toward the unification of Vietnam and condemns American policy.
GROUND WAR: Some 500 VC cross the border from a base camp in Cambodia and seize three strategic hamlets at Ben Cau; they are forced to withdraw after a 14-hour battle and reportedly lose 100 men, while ARVN losses number 114.

February 7
TERRORISM: A bomb explodes in a Saigon bar, killing five Vietnamese and wounding six U.S. servicemen and 20 civilians. President Johnson orders the withdrawal of American dependents from South Vietnam.

February 8

SOUTH VIETNAM: General Khanh announces the formation of a new Vietnamese government with himself as premier; General Minh is named chief of state, a position without real authority.

February 9

TERRORISM: A bomb explodes at the Saigon stadium, killing two Americans and injuring 20. U.S. authorities in Saigon denounce the indiscriminate bombings of the previous two days and take steps to tighten security measures at all U.S. installations in Saigon.

February 13

SOUTH VIETNAM: General Khanh visits ARVN troops in the field as part of the Vietnamese New Year observances and announces a 20 percent pay increase for all servicemen up to and including the rank of corporal.

USA – GOVERNMENT: Walt Rostow writes a memo to Secretary of State Rusk in which he argues that the United States should seriously consider bombing Hanoi. Saying that Ho Chi Minh "has an industrial complex to protect: he is no longer a guerrilla fighter with nothing to lose," Rostow suggests that bombing might be enough to convince Ho to order the Viet Cong to hold their activities in the South. Rostow also recommends that President Johnson obtain a congressional resolution to give him authority to wage war—evidently the first time this thought has been put into writing by an administration official.

DIPLOMACY: British prime minister Alec Douglas-Home, visiting President Johnson in Washington, reaffirms his nation's support for the U.S. defense of South Vietnam and attacks statements by Britons who have been urging that the United States withdraw from Vietnam.

February 16

TERRORISM: The recent round of Communist terrorist operations continues with a bomb explosion in a movie theater for U.S. personnel in Saigon, killing three Americans and wounding 50. U.S. officials announce that the VC are evidently conducting a terrorist campaign to force a face-losing evacuation of army and diplomatic dependents.

NORTH VIETNAM: In Hanoi, an article in an official newspaper hails the Soviet Union's pledge of support for the struggle against "U.S. imperialists."

February 19

USA – GOVERNMENT: The CIA sends a memo to the secretaries of defense, state, and other top officials, concluding that, based on information from its Saigon office, South Vietnam is making little progress in its war against the Communists.

GROUND WAR: The VC shoot down two VNAF planes and one U.S. pilot is killed.

CAMBODIA: Prince Sihanouk proposes that the United States, Thailand, South Vietnam and Cambodia sign an agreement to "recognize" Cambodia's neutrality and territorial integrity.

February 20
USA – GOVERNMENT: After a strategy meeting, President Johnson orders that "contingency planning for pressures against North Vietnam should be speeded up" to "produce the maximum credible deterrent effect on Hanoi."

February 21
USA – GOVERNMENT: In a speech in Los Angeles, President Johnson says that the war in Vietnam is primarily an internal contest but warns that "those engaged in external direction and supply" are playing a "dangerous game."

February 24
GROUND WAR: Viet Cong guerrillas ambush an ARVN convoy in the Saigon area, killing six soldiers and wounding nine.

February 25
GROUND WAR: ARVN troops launch attacks on various Viet Cong positions near the border of Cambodia and South Vietnam.

TERRORISM: VC forces blow up a train on the Saigon-Danang run, killing 11.

USSR: A statement issued by the Soviet news agency TASS demands the withdrawal of U.S. military aid and a halt to "interference" in South Vietnam's affairs; it also states that the Soviet Union will not stand idly by if the United States extends the war to North Vietnam.

February 26
GROUND WAR: Despite a five to one advantage in manpower an ARVN force fails to defeat a VC battalion near Long Dinh. Although encircled by some 3,000 ARVN troops, 600 soldiers of the VC 514th Battalion fight their way out during an eight-hour battle; the VC sustain 40 killed while only 16 ARVN are killed, after the South Vietnamese troops call in air and artillery strikes rather than engage the enemy directly. General Khanh is so angry that he dismisses three of his four corps commanders and five of his nine division commanders.

February 27
USA – GOVERNMENT: At a press conference, Secretary of State Rusk says that recent U.S. warnings to North Vietnam are reminders that aggression is "serious business." Rusk makes it clear that the United States rejects any political settlement that involves American withdrawal, which he maintains would leave South Vietnam exposed to a Communist takeover.

March
COVERT WAR: After a temporary delay because of bad weather, the destroyer USS *Craig* begins operations in the Gulf of Tonkin that are called for by Oplan 34A. The purpose of these missions, which are code-named DeSoto, is to gather intelligence about North Vietnamese coastal defense installations.

March 1
USA – GOVERNMENT: William Bundy, deputy secretary of defense for international security affairs, sends President Johnson a series of recommendations for extending

the war against North Vietnam, which include the blockading of Haiphong harbor and the bombing of North Vietnamese railways. Bundy points out that such actions will require some form of legislative endorsement short of a declaration of war, and he recommends that the president obtain a congressional resolution.

March 2

SOUTH VIETNAM: General Khanh charges that the French are plotting to assassinate him and impose a neutralist settlement.

USA – MILITARY: The Joint Chiefs of Staff submits a memo entitled "Removal of Restrictions for Air and Ground Cross Border Operations," requesting the authority to conduct operations in Laos to eliminate it as a Communist sanctuary.

TERRORISM: Two Vietnamese are killed and 10 injured by a grenade tossed into a crowded marketplace in Duc Ton.

March 3

DIPLOMACY: Secretary General U Thant says that he sees no effective role for the United Nations in the Vietnam conflict.

March 4

SOUTH VIETNAM: Americans in Vietnam report growing sentiment in the country for neutrality, but the U.S. government advises President Khanh not to sever relations with France, which is reportedly behind the neutralist movement. In a move apparently made to encourage the French, the VC release four French citizens they have held prisoner.

March 5

USA – MILITARY: The Joint Chiefs of Staff orders a U.S. Air Force air commando training advisory team to Thailand to train Lao pilots in counterinsurgency tactics; this had been proposed in December 1963 and the plan approved by Thailand's government in February 1964.

March 7

SOUTH VIETNAM: In a 15-page policy paper, General Khanh sets forth a comprehensive reform program to rebuild South Vietnam's political and administrative structures and raise the standard of living.

USA – GOVERNMENT: In a press conference, President Johnson says that the United States will move armed forces to and from South Vietnam depending on the need; he also says no decision has been made on removing U.S. dependents from Vietnam.

GROUND WAR: In scattered clashes, the ARVN report killing 52 VC and capturing 33.

March 8

SOUTH VIETNAM: Defense Secretary McNamara and General Maxwell Taylor, chairman of the JCS, arrive in Vietnam on a fact-finding mission; they are briefed by General Nguyen Khanh and Ambassador Henry Cabot Lodge. In a press conference, McNamara states that General Khanh "has our admiration, our respect and our complete support." He announces that "We shall stay for as long as it takes. We shall provide whatever help is required to win the battle against the Communist insurgents."

March 9

SOUTH VIETNAM: General Nguyen Khanh takes McNamara and Taylor on a tour of the countryside to demonstrate U.S. commitment to his regime. At one stop, McNamara describes Khanh, in memorized Vietnamese, as the country's "best possible leader." One U.S. helicopter accompanying the group crashes, killing two U.S. airmen.

DIPLOMACY: The South Vietnamese government agrees to the four-power talks proposed by Cambodia to guarantee the latter's neutrality.

GROUND WAR: VC attack Can Tho and destroy fuel tanks there.

March 14

GROUND WAR: ARVN troops claim to have trapped over 500 VC suspects in a raid in Kien Phong Province and to have captured about 300 VC suspects in Cai Cai. In separate actions, a U.S. helicopter and a spotter plane are downed and six Americans are killed.

LAOS: General Phoumi Nosavan, the Laotian rightist leader, and General Nguyen Khanh of South Vietnam agree to allow South Vietnamese troops to enter Laos in "hot pursuit" of Communist forces.

March 16

USA – GOVERNMENT: McNamara sends memorandum to President Johnson outlining the findings of his recent trip to South Vietnam. He reports that "the situation has unquestionably been growing worse" and calls for "new and significant pressures upon North Vietnam." The first, to be launched on 72 hours' notice, is described as "Border Control and Retaliatory Actions" and includes ARVN ground operations against infiltration routes along the Ho Chi Minh Trail in southeastern Laos, "hot pursuit" of the Viet Cong into Cambodia, retaliatory air strikes into North Vietnam by VNAF "on a tit-for-tat basis" in response to guerrilla attacks, and "aerial mining . . . of the major ports in North Vietnam." The second program, called "Graduated Overt Military Pressure," which is to be readied for initiation on 30 days' notice, includes a long-range "program of graduated military pressure," characterized by air attacks against military and possibly industrial targets in North Vietnam. To accomplish these missions, the South Vietnamese air force and the ongoing Operation Farm Gate will be reinforced by three squadrons of U.S. Air Force B-57 jet bombers flown in from Japan.

March 17

USA – GOVERNMENT: President Johnson presides over a crucial session of the National Security Council at which Secretary of Defense McNamara and General Maxwell Taylor present a full review of the situation in Vietnam as they observed it. McNamara, who had publicly pronounced improvement in the situation in South Vietnam, tells the president that conditions have deteriorated since his last visit there and that 40 percent of the countryside is now under Viet Cong control or influence. He reiterates the recommendations he had made in the previous day's memorandum. President Johnson approves the recommendations, directing that contingency planning "proceed energetically." The statement issued to the public afterward says that the United States will increase military and economic aid to support General Khanh's new plan for fighting the VC.

March 18
USA – DOMESTIC: Senator Barry Goldwater (R-Ariz.), candidate for the Republican nomination for president, attacks President Johnson's handling of the war and calls for more deliberate steps to achieve "victory."

March 20
USA – GOVERNMENT: President Johnson sends a cable to Ambassador Lodge in which he says he is intent on "knocking down the idea of neutralization wherever it rears its ugly head." He explains that administration "planning for action against the North is on a contingency basis at present, and immediate problem in this area is to develop the strongest possible military and political base for possible later action."
CAMBODIA: South Vietnamese ground and air forces attack the Cambodian village of Chantrea. U.S. military advisers participate, and a U.S. observer plane is downed. The U.S. and South Vietnamese governments will apologize to Cambodia for the raids, but Sihanouk demands reparations.

March 23
CAMBODIA: The talks between Cambodia and South Vietnam collapse over border violations, and the South Vietnamese delegation departs. Sihanouk calls for a Geneva conference on Cambodia.

March 24
GROUND WAR: The ARVN claims two major victories in Kien Phong and Hau Nghia Provinces, with high casualties for the VC, but a U.S. pilot is killed while supporting the action.

March 25–31
CAMBODIA: Sihanouk continues to force his demands for reparations and apologies from the United States for the raid on Chantrea while demanding a full-scale conference in Geneva. France intervenes and persuades Sihanouk to soften his demands, but Sihanouk continues to deny that Cambodia provides sanctuaries for Viet Cong.

March 28
GROUND WAR: U.S. Army and Vietnamese air force helicopters are called in to rescue South Vietnamese soldiers from Ap Giao Hiep, an outpost surrounded by the Viet Cong.

March 29
USA – GOVERNMENT: Defense Secretary McNamara announces that the United States will provide South Vietnam with $50,000,000 annually to finance the expansion of its armed forces (in addition to the current annual aid of $500,000).

March 30
SOUTH VIETNAM: General Khanh initiates a "clear and hold" policy so that "the Viet Cong won't come right back." Part of this effort will be a program of training for ARVN officers on how to run local governments properly.

March 31

GROUND WAR: An unidentified U.S. official in Saigon announces that the "momentum" of the Viet Cong has been checked.

USA – DOMESTIC: Governor Nelson Rockefeller of New York demands that Ambassador Lodge resign and fully explain U.S. policy in Vietnam.

April

NORTH VIETNAM: Following up on a decision made in late 1963, the leadership in Hanoi begins to send regular army troops into South Vietnam. A large number of engineer construction battalions from the People's Army of Vietnam (PAVN), more commonly known as the North Vietnamese Army (NVA), are deployed to improve the Ho Chi Minh Trail network in preparation for the movement south of main force PAVN units to join the fight with the Viet Cong. While the road network is being improved, combat units undergo special training and political indoctrination in preparation for their departure for the south.

April 1–3

USA – DOMESTIC: Former vice president Richard Nixon visits Vietnam and issues a series of statements sharply criticizing Johnson administration policies for "compromise and improvisations," calling for continued aid, and promising to make the situation an issue in the forthcoming U.S. presidential campaign.

April 4

GROUND WAR: In fighting at the Phuoc Tan outpost, six U.S. advisers are wounded and 12 ARVN are killed.

April 5

SOUTH VIETNAM: A new draft law authorizes conscription into the Civil Guard and the Self Defense Corps, the two paramilitary forces that bear the brunt of the fight at the hamlet and village level against the Viet Cong; both forces have suffered a lack of volunteers and a rise in desertions.

April 8

GROUND WAR: South Vietnamese troops kill some 75 Viet Cong in capturing a key guerrilla base in Kontum Province, 300 miles north of Saigon, which is considered an important distribution point for arms and personnel coming down the Ho Chi Minh Trail.

April 9–12

GROUND WAR: During four days of major fighting in the Mekong Delta, 50 ARVN soldiers and four American advisers are killed.

April 11–15

GROUND WAR: In a five-day battle, the longest and heaviest to date, at Kien Long, 135 miles south of Saigon, South Vietnamese forces retake the ground they had earlier lost to the VC, but 70 South Vietnamese militiamen are killed and 55 ARVN are lost. Viet Cong casualties are estimated at 175 killed.

April 13–15

DIPLOMACY: The Ministerial Council of the Southeast Asia Treaty Organization (SEATO) holds its 10th annual meeting in Manila. French foreign minister Maurice Couve de Murville argues on behalf of De Gaulle's plan for "neutralization" of Vietnam, but the other delegates reject this and agree on a final communiqué that states "that defeat of the Communist campaign is essential not only to the security of Vietnam but that of Southeast Asia."

April 14

USA – MILITARY: It is announced that the U.S. Military Assistance Advisory Group (MAAG) in Vietnam will be combined with the Military Assistance Command Vietnam (MACV) to reduce duplication of effort and make more efficient use of U.S. service personnel.

April 15–18

USA – DOMESTIC: Former vice president Nixon, returning from his 24-day trip through Asia, gives a number of speeches in New York City and Washington in which he criticizes the Johnson administration's handling of the situation in Vietnam and calls for extending the war into North Vietnam and Laos.

April 17

USA – MILITARY: The Joint Chiefs of Staff approves Operation Plan 37-64, prepared in the Honolulu headquarters of CINCPAC, which details how many planes and what bomb tonnages would be required for each phase of air raids against specific targets in North Vietnam. This contingency plan is drawn up in response to President Johnson's decisions and orders at the March 17 National Security Council meeting.

TERRORISM: In Saigon, terrorists toss a bomb into a U.S. bus and injure two U.S. soldiers.

April 17–20

USA – GOVERNMENT: Secretary of State Dean Rusk, William Bundy, and General Earle Wheeler, army chief of staff, visit Saigon where they review the latest U.S. plans for covert actions against North Vietnam with Ambassador Lodge. Rusk visits a fortified hamlet with General Khanh and tells the villagers that "we are comrades in your struggle." Later, back in Washington, Rusk reports that the military situation is critical, but says that Khanh is "on the right track."

April 17–23

LAOS: Souvanna Phouma goes to the Plain of Jars in the north of Laos to confer with leaders of opposing factions in an effort to demilitarize and neutralize Laos. The talks fail, however, and Phouma returns to Vientiane and announces his intention to resign. On the 19th several generals attempt a coup, but with the support of the U.S. ambassador, Phouma regains control of a coalition government. The Johnson administration views Phouma as the only hope for some kind of moderate and stable government, but the Communist Pathet Lao reject his coalition and go on the offensive.

April 19

GROUND WAR: Viet Cong guerrillas strike in four provinces, in one place within 14 miles of Saigon, but South Vietnam forces halt their advance.

April 20

GROUND WAR: After the Viet Cong seize the outpost at Huong Hoa Ha, ARVN forces counterattack and inflict heavy losses on the VC. U.S. officials publicly praise this as one of the most successful operations of the war, but in private many U.S. military officials still believe that the ARVN are combat ineffective and will not be victorious in the long run against the Communists.

April 21

USA – DOMESTIC: Republican leaders of the Senate, Everett Dirksen (Ill.), and the House, Charles Halleck (In.), hold a joint news conference in Washington and charge that the Johnson administration is concealing the extent of U.S. involvement in the war. To support their charge, they read from the letters of an air force captain killed in Vietnam: "They tell you people we're just in a training situation. . . . But we're at war, we are doing the flying and fighting . . . the only reason [the Vietnamese 'students'] are on board is, in case we crash, there is one American 'adviser' and one Vietnamese 'student.'" The air force officer was part of Operation Farm Gate, which had begun in February 1962.

April 22

USA – GOVERNMENT: President Johnson, trying to quiet the rising protests against the growing U.S. commitment in South Vietnam, summons congressional leaders to the White House for briefings by Defense Secretary McNamara and CIA director John McCone to convince them that progress is being made in the war against the Viet Cong.

GROUND WAR: Twenty-nine U.S. helicopters airlift about 600 Vietnamese troops to the Mekong Delta in Kien Phong Province, about 80 miles south of Saigon, to double the number of troops used in a mopping up operation there.

April 23

GROUND WAR: In a clash with the Viet Cong in Trung Lap, one American is killed and three are wounded.

DIPLOMACY: In France, Premier Georges Pompidou reemphasizes his country's desire to see Vietnam neutralized and says that this will require that the United States deal with Communist China.

April 24

USA – GOVERNMENT: In a news conference, Defense Secretary McNamara says that he does not mind Senator Wayne Morse's description of the conflict in Vietnam as "McNamara's War." The Oregon senator has been using this verbiage in public comments about the war.

April 25

USA – MILITARY: President Johnson announces that General William Westmoreland will replace General Paul Harkins as head of U.S. Military Assistance Command, Vietnam (as of June 20). Westmoreland, influenced by his World War II and Korean experiences, will eventually become fixated on attrition warfare based on the assumption that the Communists can not sustain large-unit fighting because they lack sufficient logistical capabilities.

GROUND WAR: South Vietnamese forces rout a Viet Cong battalion at Binh Chanh.

April 30

DIPLOMACY: Secretary of State Rusk flies to Ottawa, Canada, to make secret arrangements with J. Blair Seaborn, Canada's new representative on the International Control Commission; Seaborn will be visiting Hanoi in June and Rusk wants him to convey the offer of U.S. economic aid to Premier Pham Van Dong if the North Vietnamese will call off their forces and cease their support of the Viet Cong.

GROUND WAR: Viet Cong guerrillas penetrate Long An, a provincial capital, and capture 74 Viet Cong defectors; other VC forces attack Tan An and kill six women and five children.

May 2

TERRORISM: The USNS *Card*, an escort carrier being used as an aircraft and helicopter ferry, sinks at its dock in Saigon, presumably from an explosive charge assumed to have been placed by Viet Cong terrorists. No one is injured and eventually the ship will be raised and repaired.

May 3

TERRORISM: A terrorist throws a bomb into the crowd viewing the USNS *Card*, sunk at its dock, and eight U.S. servicemen are wounded.

GROUND WAR: One hundred ARVN Rangers are wiped out by a Viet Cong attack, 25 miles northwest of Saigon.

May 4

SOUTH VIETNAM: General Khanh, sensing a decline in his fortunes and a lack of support for his efforts, tells Ambassador Lodge that he wants to declare full-scale war on North Vietnam. He says he wants the United States to start bombing the North and send 10,000 U.S. Special Forces troops "to cover the whole Cambodian-Laotian border." Lodge does not inform him that the United States had already developed its own plan to bomb the North.

USA – GOVERNMENT: In secret testimony before the House Armed Services Committee (released June 19) William Bundy, now assistant secretary of state for East Asian and Pacific affairs, says that the United States must drive the Communists out of South Vietnam even if it means "attacking countries to the north."

May 5

USA – GOVERNMENT: The United States announces it is freezing all assets of North Vietnam and barring any further financial and commercial transactions between the two countries.

AIR WAR: Ten U.S. servicemen are among 16 killed when a USAF transport plane crashes at Tan Hiep.

May 7

SOUTH VIETNAM: General Khanh says that his country would appreciate aid from other countries in addition to the United States.

May 8–14

CAMBODIA: Cambodian forces destroy an ARVN armored personnel carrier that strays into Cambodia in pursuit of VC troops. Khanh immediately apologizes, but asserts that the real problem is that Cambodia allowed the Viet Cong to take refuge there in the first place. On May 9, a clash between Cambodians and ARVN troops leaves seven Cambodians dead. Cambodian students in Phnom Penh demonstrate, demanding the withdrawal of all U.S. military personnel in their country. It is then alleged (but later denied) that Cambodian aircraft strafed ARVN troops searching for Viet Cong. The Cambodian government asks that the United Nations send a mission to Cambodia to disprove charges it shelters Viet Cong.

May 9

TERRORISM: A terrorist is captured trying to place an explosive charge under a Saigon bridge over which Defense Secretary McNamara's car is to pass on May 12.

May 12–13

SOUTH VIETNAM: Defense Secretary McNamara and General Maxwell Taylor visit Vietnam for their fifth fact-finding mission. While McNamara reiterates U.S. support for South Vietnam, he also tells Khanh privately that, although the United States does not "rule out" bombing the North, "such actions must be supplementary to and not a substitute for successful counter-insurgency in the South" and that "we do not intend to provide military support nor undertake the military objective of 'rolling back' Communist control in North Vietnam."

May 12–14

USA – MILITARY: Amid charges that U.S. pilots in Vietnam are endangered (and even losing their lives) due to obsolescent South Vietnamese planes, it is announced that 60 U.S. Navy dive bombers are being sent to Vietnam and that 40 refurbished, propeller-driven B-26 bombers are being readied for Vietnam.

May 14

USA – GOVERNMENT: Defense Secretary McNamara, having returned to Washington, presents a plan to President Johnson calling for increased military aid to South Vietnam.
GROUND WAR: A Viet Cong battalion wipes out an ARVN relief force, 20 miles north of Saigon; 54 ARVN are killed and 50 wounded. The next day, a U.S. military adviser criticizes ARVN combat performance.

May 15

SOUTH VIETNAM: President Khanh signs a decree that abolishes restrictions imposed by the Diem regime on Buddhists and grants them the same rights as Catholics.
USA – GOVERNMENT: Defense Secretary McNamara reports to the National Security Council on the situation in Vietnam; President Johnson informs congressional leaders attending the session that he will probably seek more aid for South Vietnam.

May 16
USA – DOMESTIC: Governor Rockefeller accepts President Johnson's offer to brief all Republican candidates for the presidency; afterward, he will agree with a questioner that Americans are not getting the full story of the situation. Senator Goldwater openly charges that U.S. pilots are dying because of obsolescent planes.

May 16–17
LAOS: The Communist Pathet Lao launch an offensive on the Plain of Jars that threatens to collapse the pro-American government of Premier Souvanna Phouma. When word of this situation reaches Washington, President Johnson alerts troops in Okinawa and orders the Seventh Fleet in the South China Sea to prepare for possible military action. Officials begin drawing up a resolution that Johnson might present to Congress to get it to declare that the independence and integrity of Laos are vital to U.S. interests.

May 17–19
USA – GOVERNMENT: Secretary of State Rusk visits Saigon primarily to get Ambassador Lodge's support for the "retaliatory" actions being contemplated by the Johnson administration. Lodge counsels more reliance on the South Vietnamese forces and increased efforts to apply the "carrot" of inducements to North Vietnam before applying the "stick" of heavy bombing.

May 18
USA – GOVERNMENT: President Johnson, in a special message to Congress, asks for an additional $125,000,000 for economic and military aid to Vietnam.

May 19–21
LAOS: The United States initiates low-altitude reconnaissance flights over southern Laos (on the 19th) and northern Laos (on the 21st) by U.S. Navy and U.S. Air Force jets; these flights are code-named Yankee Team. At the same time, the United States releases bomb fuses and more T-28s to the Laotian Air Force. Souvanna Phouma has been consulted about the flights and has given his approval.

May 20
DIPLOMACY: France proposes reconvening a 14-nation conference on Laos in Geneva; the proposal is rejected by the United States and Great Britain, but accepted by the Soviet Union, Poland, Cambodia, India, and Communist China.

May 21
DIPLOMACY: UN Security Council meets to consider Cambodia's charge that the United States directs South Vietnam's raids into Cambodia. U.S. ambassador Adlai Stevenson calls for a clear marking of the border and the stationing of some force to police the border.

May 22
USA – GOVERNMENT: In a major speech before the American Law Institute in Washington, Secretary of State Rusk explicitly accuses North Vietnam of initiating and directing the aggression in South Vietnam. U.S. withdrawal, said Rusk, "would mean

not only grievous losses to the free world in Southeast and Southern Asia but a drastic loss of confidence in the will and capacity of the free world."

GROUND WAR: ARVN forces conclude a month-long campaign in the Do Xa region by overrunning the headquarters of General Don, a top Viet Cong leader. Although Don escapes capture, Saigon claims this operation will set back the Viet Cong's efforts for many months.

May 22–31

THAILAND: Thailand mobilizes its border provinces against incursions by the Pathet Lao and agrees to the use of its bases by the U.S. Air Force for reconnaissance, search and rescue, and even attacks against the Pathet Lao. By the end of the year, some 75 U.S. aircraft will be based in Thailand to assist in operations against the Pathet Lao.

May 23

USA – GOVERNMENT: Assistant Secretary of State William Bundy draws up a 30-day program that culminates in full-scale bombing of North Vietnam. He submits the plan as a formal draft presidential memorandum for consideration by an executive committee of the National Security Council. Parts of this scenario will be executed when the situation in Vietnam continues to deteriorate.

May 24–28

USA – DOMESTIC: Senator Barry Goldwater, vying for the Republican nomination for the presidency, gives an interview in which he proposes the use of low-yield atomic bombs to defoliate forests and the bombing of bridges, roads, and railroad lines that bring supplies from Communist China. During the storm of controversy that follows, Goldwater tries to back away from these drastic actions—claiming that he did not mean to advocate the use of atomic bombs, only that he was "repeating a suggestion made by competent military people." However, Goldwater is never able to shake the image of an extremist, which will work heavily against him when he runs against Lyndon Johnson.

May 25

USA – GOVERNMENT: William Bundy drafts a joint congressional resolution that would give the president authority to take whatever steps he deems necessary in Vietnam.

DIPLOMACY: During a discussion of the Cambodia-South Vietnam issue in the UN Security Council, France splits from the United States and Great Britain's position and urges the council to pass a resolution "deploring" South Vietnam's violations of the border.

May 26

CAMBODIA: Sihanouk says he welcomes UN inquiry teams or UN troops to police the disputed border with South Vietnam.

May 27

SOUTH VIETNAM: President Khanh announces that South Vietnam forces will "liberate" North Vietnam after defeating the Communists in the south.

DIPLOMACY: Poland proposes a new Laos conference that would not include discussions of Vietnam.

May 28
DIPLOMACY: Canada's Prime Minister Lester Pearson meets President Johnson in New York and they discuss the forthcoming trip to Hanoi by James Seaborn, Canada's delegate to the International Control Commission, who is to convey a message from the United States that it does not want to destroy the North Vietnamese regime but is determined to protect South Vietnam—a thinly veiled threat to bomb North Vietnam.
GROUND WAR: VC troops overrun Nho Dung and kidnap the hamlet chief; at Quang Ngai, VC snipers kill two ARVN soldiers.

June 1–2
USA – GOVERNMENT: Top U.S. officials gather for a two-day strategy session on Vietnam at Admiral Harry Felt's Pacific Command Headquarters in Honolulu. Lodge and Westmoreland fly to Hawaii with Secretary of State Rusk, who stopped off in Saigon on his way back from attending the funeral of Indian prime minister Jawaharlal Nehru. They are joined by McNamara, William Bundy, John McCone of the CIA, and others. Much of the discussion focuses on the projected air campaign against North Vietnam, including the development of a list of 94 targets. Lodge argues for beginning the bombing soon, reflecting his nervousness over the shakiness of the Saigon regime. However, the major outcome of the conference will be a recommendation that major actions "be delayed for some time yet."

June 2
USA – GOVERNMENT: In a news conference, President Lyndon Johnson reasserts U.S. commitment to defend Vietnam, but says he knows of no plans to extend the war into North Vietnam.
DIPLOMACY: The United States and Cambodia agree on a proposal to form a three-party commission to visit the Cambodian border within 45 days to resolve the ongoing crisis between Cambodia and South Vietnam.

June 3
USA – GOVERNMENT: Rusk, McNamara, and the other officials return to Washington and report to President Johnson on the Honolulu conference. William Bundy prepares the briefing paper for Secretary Rusk and advises more time to "refine our plans and estimates," as well as an "urgent" public relations campaign at home to "get at the basic doubts" about U.S. interests in Vietnam and "the importance of our stake there."
GROUND WAR: Viet Cong guerrillas enter the strategic hamlet of Khanh Hoi-Dong Hung and kidnap 47 men.

June 4
USA – GOVERNMENT: As a result of the report to President Johnson, Defense Secretary McNamara orders the U.S. Army to take "immediate action . . . to improve the effectiveness and readiness status of its matériel prestocked for possible use in

Southeast Asia." Specifically, he orders the army to augment stocks at Korat, Thailand, near the Laotian border, to support potential combat operations by a U.S. Army infantry brigade and to give "first priority" at the Okinawa Forward Depot to stocking equipment that would be required for another army brigade flown to the island staging base on sudden notice.

DIPLOMACY: The UN Security Council approves the compromise plan for a commission to investigate the situation on the Cambodian-Vietnamese border, and on June 6 will name Brazil, the Ivory Coast, and Morocco to form the commission.

June 6–9

AIR WAR: Two U.S. Navy jets flying low-altitude target reconnaissance missions over Laos—part of Operation Yankee Team—are shot down by Pathet Lao ground fire. Washington immediately orders armed jet fighters to escort the reconnaissance flights, and by June 9 escort jets are attacking Pathet Lao gun positions. The downing of the two planes is made public, but the subsequent strikes by the escort jets are not.

June 7

SOUTH VIETNAM: Some 35,000 Roman Catholic Vietnamese demonstrate in Saigon against what they allege is government favoritism toward Buddhists.

GROUND WAR: U.S. officials report that the Viet Cong are blockading a 600-square-mile area south of Ca Mau in the Mekong Delta to starve the residents and deprive the South Vietnamese of charcoal supplies that come from that area.

June 8

AUSTRALIA: Australian training teams with ARVN forces exchange fire with Viet Cong guerrillas on the same day that the Australian government sends six transport planes and more army instructors as combat advisers. The government in Canberra also calls for all SEATO members to increase their support for South Vietnam.

June 9

USA – GOVERNMENT: The CIA submits a memo in response to a formal question from President Johnson, who asks, "Would the rest of Southeast Asia necessarily fall if Laos and South Vietnam came under North Vietnamese control?" In its answer, the CIA concludes that Cambodia was probably the only nation in the area that would immediately fall. Although the CIA analysts do not deny that the loss of South Vietnam and Laos "would be profoundly damaging to the U.S. position in the Far East," the memo concludes that the United States, with its Pacific bases and its allies such as the Philippines and Japan, would have enough power to deter China and North Vietnam from any further aggression or expansion. Having solicited this analysis, it appears that the president and senior advisers are not inclined to adjust policy based on a report that challenges the "domino theory."

June 10–11

LAOS: Embarrassed by the disclosure of U.S. participation in air operations in Laos, Souvanna Phouma threatens to resign if the flights do not stop. U.S. ambassador to Laos Leonard Unger persuades Souvanna to change his mind, and after a temporary suspension, the U.S. State Department announces on the 11th that the reconnaissance flights will continue "as necessary" but that "operational aspects would not be discussed." This will result in the describing of all U.S. air operations in Laos during the coming years as "reconnaissance flights." On the 11th, Thai pilots in planes with Laotian air force markings bomb the Pathet Lao headquarters at Khang Khay, destroying the Chinese mission and killing one civilian.

June 12
GROUND WAR: ARVN troops attack a Communist convoy from Laos and kill 27 guerrillas.
DIPLOMACY: In Paris, de Gaulle calls for an end to all foreign intervention in South Vietnam. In Berlin, West German chancellor Ludwig Erhard pledges more aid to South Vietnam.

June 13
GROUND WAR: Seven ARVN and one U.S. soldier are killed in an ambush. Viet Cong mines derail three trains, blow up two trucks, and kill six Vietnamese.

June 14
USA – MILITARY: General Westmoreland travels to Malaysia to study the methods used by the British to defeat Communist guerrillas there.
USA – GOVERNMENT: In a speech at Williams College, Secretary of State Rusk emphasizes the U.S. determination to support its Southeast Asian allies.
RIVER WAR: A South Vietnamese river patrol is ambushed by Viet Cong but manages to kill 23 guerrillas in the confrontation.
AIR WAR: The U.S. military allows its own pilots operating out of Thailand to hit "targets of opportunity" in Laos.
AUSTRALIA: The opposition Labour Party attacks the government for failing to provide the Australian public with more information about the situation in Vietnam and the activities of the Australian personnel there in support of the South Vietnamese and Americans.

June 15
USA – GOVERNMENT: At a meeting of the National Security Council, McGeorge Bundy, the president's national security advisor, informs Rusk, McNamara, and the others present that President Johnson has decided to postpone a decision on the resolution that William Bundy had been preparing for submission to Congress asking for authority to wage war. Johnson and his aides will later deny that this decision was based on politics.
AIR WAR: VNAF A-1 Skyraiders turn back Viet Cong attackers at Lap Vo.

June 17
USA – GOVERNMENT: Amid speculation that Ambassador Lodge will have to be replaced in Vietnam because of his possible role as a Republican presidential candidate, there is also rumor that Attorney General Robert Kennedy might be named to succeed Lodge.
USA – MILITARY: An unnamed top U.S. military adviser departing Vietnam after three years reports that the Viet Cong have greatly improved as a military force. He

also claims that over 90 percent of the VC's weapons have been captured from South Vietnamese forces armed by U.S. military aid.

GROUND WAR: ARVN forces beat back a Viet Cong attack on Duc Hoa, killing 19 but taking 51 casualties of their own.

June 18

DIPLOMACY: In the first of two meetings with North Vietnam's premier Pham Van Dong, J. Blair Seaborn, the chief Canadian delegate to the ICC, is asked by the U.S. government to appraise the situation in Hanoi—specifically, to see whether the North Vietnamese leaders are ready to pull back from the war and to convey to the premier that the United States is fully aware of the degree to which Hanoi controls the Viet Cong and "in the event of escalation, the greatest devastation would of course result for the D.R.V. itself." When Seaborn returns to Saigon, he sends two long reports to the U.S. State Department.

June 19

USA – GOVERNMENT: Secretary of State Rusk, in a news conference, states that the U.S. commitment to the security of Southeast Asia, is "unlimited" and comparable to the American commitment to West Berlin, and that the United States demands full compliance with the Geneva Accords both in South Vietnam and Laos.

TERRORISM: In South Vietnam, terrorists blow up four cars of a passenger train and kill 20 South Vietnamese.

June 20

USA – MILITARY: General Paul Harkins is succeeded as head of USMACV by his deputy, Lieutenant General William C. Westmoreland, who is subsequently promoted to general.

June 23

USA – GOVERNMENT: At a news conference, President Johnson announces that Henry Cabot Lodge has resigned as ambassador to South Vietnam and that his replacement will be General Maxwell Taylor. Johnson makes a point of insisting that this change will in no way affect the U.S. commitment to South Vietnam.

USA – MILITARY: It is announced that General Westmoreland is to become the "executive agent" to supervise the pacification programs in three provinces around Saigon, the first stage of a plan to coordinate the entire U.S. military and civilian program in South Vietnam under the military command.

June 24

USA – DOMESTIC: A dispute among Republicans develops, with some supporting Lodge's claims that Vietnam should not become an issue in the campaign while others try to link his resignation as ambassador to a disagreement with the Johnson administration's policies.

GROUND WAR: Seventeen Viet Cong are killed and 11 captured during a search for two missing U.S. soldiers (who are later reported dead).

June 25

NORTH VIETNAM: Foreign Minister Xuan Thuy writes to Communist China and other signers of the Geneva Accords and urges them "to demand that the U.S.

government give up its design of . . . provocation and sabotage against North Vietnam."

GROUND WAR: Viet Cong capture a civil guard platoon without firing a shot in Quang Tri Province.

June 26

GROUND WAR: In Quang Ngai Province, South Vietnamese troops attack a Viet Cong training center and kill 50 guerrilla recruits. Elsewhere, ARVN troops in armored personnel carriers engage a Viet Cong force in Bau Cot, killing some 100 guerrillas.

TERRORISM: A bomb explodes in an airport hangar near where General Westmoreland is addressing U.S. servicemen returning to the United States; two Americans are injured but Westmoreland is unharmed.

June 27

GROUND WAR: ARVN Rangers trap a Viet Cong battalion near Long Hoi and inflict heavy casualties.

AIR WAR: Two American pilots are killed when their fighter-bomber is shot down.

June 29

GROUND WAR: Two outposts are overwhelmed by Viet Cong in the Saigon area.

GROUND WAR: Four Americans are killed when their helicopter crashes during a mission in the Mekong Delta.

NEW ZEALAND: Twenty-four New Zealand army engineers arrive in Saigon as a token of that country's support for South Vietnam.

July 1

GROUND WAR: A U.S. Army helicopter is downed and its pilot and gunner are killed; elsewhere, a Viet Cong sniper kills a U.S. helicopter pilot and injures three other Americans who have landed to pick up a wounded serviceman. At a news conference in Saigon, a U.S. military spokesman reports that U.S. helicopters are now flying 1,300–1,400 hours a week, explaining the rising losses of U.S. aircraft and personnel.

July 2

USA – DOMESTIC: At a joint news conference, Senate Republican leader Everett Dirksen (Ill.) and House Republican leader Charles Halleck (In.) say that the war will be a campaign issue because "Johnson's indecision has made it one."

GROUND WAR: The VC ambush a 36-truck ARVN ammo convoy in the Pleiku-Qui Nhon area, but the convoy is saved when two U.S. helicopters arrive and drive off the attackers; however, 29 South Vietnamese troops are killed and 24 wounded.

TERRORISM: In Saigon, terrorists throw a bomb at a U.S. officers' billet and two Americans are killed.

July 3

USA – MILITARY: General Harold K. Johnson replaces General Earle Wheeler as chief of staff, U.S. Army. Wheeler becomes the chairman of the Joint Chiefs of Staff, replacing General Maxwell Taylor, who will become the U.S. ambassador to South Vietnam.

GROUND WAR: Viet Cong overrun a South Vietnamese camp at Kontum and kill 44 ARVN soldiers, wounding 22, including three U.S. advisers. In central Vietnam, Viet Cong wipe out the defenders of three strategic hamlets.

July 4
GROUND WAR: VC forces attack a U.S. Special Forces training camp at Polei Krong, seize the camp's arms and ammunition, and leave 41 South Vietnamese dead and two Americans wounded.

July 6
GROUND WAR: At Nam Dong in the northern highlands, an estimated 500-man Viet Cong force attacks an American Special Forces camp but is forced to withdraw after a bitter five-hour battle that kills 57 Vietnamese defenders, two Americans, and one Australian military adviser. An estimated 40 Viet Cong are killed during the battle. Captain Roger C. Donlon will later be awarded the Medal of Honor for valor during this battle, the first such award for the war in Vietnam.

July 7
SOUTH VIETNAM: General Maxwell Taylor, the new U.S. ambassador, arrives in Saigon. As a military man with considerable experience in Vietnam, he is looked upon by everyone—the South Vietnamese government, the U.S. military establishment, and the Johnson administration—as the ideal individual to coordinate and invigorate the war effort.

TERRORISM: A bomb is thrown at the U.S. embassy and two grenades explode elsewhere in Saigon; no one is injured and only slight damage is caused.

July 8
DIPLOMACY: UN secretary-general U Thant proposes that the Geneva conference that ended in 1954 be reconvened to negotiate peace in Vietnam.

USA – GOVERNMENT: President Johnson decrees that a Vietnam service medal be awarded to Americans serving in the conflict, even though there has been no official declaration of war.

July 9
CHINA: Communist China pledges to help defend North Vietnam if U.S. forces attack on the ground.

July 11–12
GROUND WAR: In what is regarded as the largest battle of the war to date, at least 1,000 Viet Cong troops twice attack the South Vietnamese outpost at Chong Thien and then ambush the relief force. The VC seize 100 weapons and 200 ARVN soldiers are killed or wounded in the battle.

July 13
SOUTH VIETNAM: The Vietnamese air force commander, Nguyen Cao Ky, claims he has 30 Vietnamese pilots trained and ready to fly jet fighter-bombers against North Vietnam.

GROUND WAR: Viet Cong forces ambush an ARVN convoy, 40 miles south of Saigon, killing 16 ARVN soldiers and three U.S. soldiers.

July 14

GROUND WAR: U.S. military intelligence publicly charges that North Vietnamese regular army officers command and fight in so-called Viet Cong forces in the northern provinces, where Viet Cong strength has doubled in the past six months. Only the day before, General Khanh had referred to the "invasion" of South Vietnam by North Vietnamese Army forces.

July 15–16

USA – DOMESTIC: Senator Barry Goldwater is chosen as the Republican nominee for president at the Republican National Convention in San Francisco. During his acceptance speech Goldwater declares, "Extremism in the defense of liberty is no vice." Although he will go to great trouble during his subsequent campaign to explain that he never meant to advocate using atomic weapons in tactical or strategic situations, he has definitely called for a more aggressive approach by the United States, and the Democrats portray him as a trigger-happy warmonger.

July 16

GROUND WAR: South Vietnamese forces claim that they have killed 100 Viet Cong in a clash in Vinh Binh Province; the ARVN suffered 17 dead and 45 wounded. Within the past two days, there have been 15 other clashes between South Vietnamese and Communist forces throughout South Vietnam, indicative of the stepped-up activity by the Viet Cong, evidently bolstered by North Vietnamese forces.

July 19

SOUTH VIETNAM: General Khanh starts a "March North" campaign of military slogans and oratory at a "unification rally" in Saigon, calling for an expansion of the war to North Vietnam. This breaks a promise he had made to Ambassador Lodge and Secretary Rusk in a May meeting, to consult with Washington before publicly announcing any attention of declaring war on the North.

July 19–30

DIPLOMACY: The UN team that has been inspecting the Cambodian-South Vietnamese border returns and on the 28th urges prompt action by the Security Council to avoid further conflict. Meanwhile, Cambodia continues to accuse South Vietnam of new acts of aggression, and on the 29th, Cambodia charges that the United States and South Vietnam used chemical weapons, killing 76 Cambodians in six villages. The United States promptly denies any use of chemical weapons, and South Vietnam claims that it is Viet Cong troops masquerading as ARVN forces that have been attacking Cambodian border villages.

July 20

GROUND WAR: Viet Cong forces overrun Cai Be, the capital of Dinh Tuong Province, killing 11 South Vietnamese militiamen, 10 women, and 30 children.

July 21

GROUND WAR: Viet Cong ambush a convoy in Chuong Thien Province and kill 26 ARVN and wound about 100.

July 22

SOUTH VIETNAM: Air Vice-Marshal Nguyen Cao Ky, at a news conference, reveals that "combat teams" have been sent on sabotage missions into North Vietnam and that South Vietnamese pilots are being trained for possible large-scale attacks. He further states that he personally flew a plane over North Vietnam on one such mission. U.S. officials refuse to confirm Ky's statements but concede that some flights had been made in previous years.

July 23

FRANCE: At a news conference in Paris, President Charles de Gaulle proposes that the United States, France, the Soviet Union, and Communist China negotiate an end to the hostilities in Vietnam and Laos by agreeing to leave the Indo-Chinese peninsula, guaranteeing its neutrality and independence, and providing economic and technical aid.

July 23–24

SOUTH VIETNAM: Ambassador Taylor meets with General Khanh to register U.S. disapproval of the recent calls by Khanh and Ky to extend the war into North Vietnam. Both meetings are reported to have been "heated" but it is also reported that Khanh stood firmly against Taylor's reprimands, arguing that the war had entered a new phase because of the presence of North Vietnamese forces in the South. Khanh offers to resign at the second meeting, but Taylor dissuades him. In a news conference in Washington on the 24th, President Johnson insists that U.S.-South Vietnamese relations are good.

July 25

USA – GOVERNMENT: Ambassador Taylor cables Washington a warning about Khanh and the "March North" campaign, recommending that the United States "engage in contingency planning [with the South Vietnamese] for various forms of extended action . . ." Such planning, he says, will placate Khanh and his generals, while gaining time needed to stabilize the Saigon government.

USA – MILITARY: Following a meeting of the National Security Council to discuss the recent events in Saigon, the Joint Chiefs of Staff draws up a memo proposing air strikes—in unmarked planes flown by non-American crews—against targets in North Vietnam, including the coastal bases for Hanoi's flotilla of torpedo boats. The memo is forwarded to Secretary Rusk on July 30.

July 26

SOUTH VIETNAM: General Khanh and the top South Vietnamese military leaders hold secret talks at Dalat; it is reliably reported that some of those present call for expanding the war into North Vietnam and Laos.

July 27

USA – GOVERNMENT: It is announced that the United States will send an additional 5,000 U.S. troops to Vietnam to complement about 16,000 already there. Military spokesmen and Washington officials insist that this does not represent any change in policy, that new troops will only intensify present U.S. advisory efforts.

July 29

GROUND WAR: The U.S. military raises its estimates of Communist forces in South Vietnam to 28,000–34,000 regular Viet Cong troops and another 60,000–80,000 guerrillas, and claims that about 30 percent of units formed in the past eight months are made up of troops who have infiltrated from North Vietnam.

July 30–31

SEA WAR: South Vietnamese navy conducts commando raids along North Vietnamese coast. About midnight, six special "Swift" PT boats used by the South Vietnamese for their covert raids, attack two islands in the Tonkin Gulf, Hon Me and Hon Ngu. Although unable to land any commandos, the boats fire on island installations. Radar and radio transmissions are monitored by the USS *Maddox,* a destroyer on a DeSoto intelligence gathering mission about 120 miles away. The *Maddox* will report sighting patrol boats in the Gulf but will be told that these were the Swifts returning from their undercover raid.

July 31

USA – GOVERNMENT: Secretary of State Dean Rusk, in a news conference, admits there are differences between the United States and South Vietnam on the issue of extending the war into North Vietnam, yet he insists there is agreement on the general conduct of the war and that U.S. warnings to Communist China and North Vietnam indicate total U.S. commitment.

SOUTH VIETNAM: Saigon charges that the attack in Dinh Tuong Province on July 20 was conducted by PAVN regulars led by Chinese Communist advisers.

SOUTH KOREA: The national assembly approves aid to South Vietnam.

August 1

TERRORISM: A bomb explodes in a Saigon bar, wounding five U.S. servicemen and 18 South Vietnamese.

NORTH VIETNAM: Hanoi accuses the United States and South Vietnam of having authorized and conducted the raids on the two North Vietnamese islands on July 30–31.

August 1–2

LAOS: Thai pilots, flying U.S. T-28s on covert missions from their base in Laos, bomb and strafe North Vietnamese villages along the Laotian border.

August 2

SEA WAR: North Vietnamese torpedo boats attack the destroyer *Maddox.* The American ship has been cruising around the Tonkin Gulf about 28 miles off the North Vietnamese coastline, monitoring North Vietnamese radio and radar signals following the attack by South Vietnamese PT boats on two North Vietnamese islands as part of Oplan 34A. U.S. crews interpret one North Vietnamese message as indicating that they are preparing for "military operations," which the *Maddox's* captain John Herrick assumes means some sort of retaliatory attack. His superiors order him to remain in the area. Early that afternoon, three North Vietnamese patrol boats begin to chase the *Maddox.* About 1500 hours, Captain Herrick orders his crew to commence firing as the North Vietnamese boats come within 10,000 yards and he radios the U.S. aircraft carrier *Ticonderoga* for air support. The North Vietnamese boats each fire one torpedo at the *Maddox*, but two miss and the third fails to explode. U.S. gunfire hits one of the North Vietnamese boats, and then three U.S. Crusader jets proceed to strafe them. Within 20 minutes, one of the boats is sunk and two are crippled; only one bullet hits the *Maddox* and there are no U.S. casualties. The *Maddox* is ordered to withdraw and await further instruction.

USA – GOVERNMENT: Because of the time difference, President Johnson is informed of the incident on the morning of the 2nd. With a presidential campaign underway, he wants to appear firm yet restrained. He rejects any reprisals against North Vietnam and in his first use of the "hot line" to Russia, tells Khrushchev that he has no desire to extend the conflict. In the first U.S. diplomatic note ever sent to Hanoi, Johnson warns that "grave consequences would inevitably result from any further unprovoked offensive military action" against U.S. ships "on the high seas."

USA – MILITARY: Despite Johnson's measured response, the U.S. military command takes several critical actions. U.S. combat troops are placed on alert and additional fighter-bombers are sent to South Vietnam and Thailand. The carrier *Constellation* is ordered to the South China Sea to join the *Ticonderoga*. Admiral Sharp, U.S. commander in chief Pacific, orders a second destroyer, the *C. Turner Joy*, to join the *Maddox* to "assert the right of freedom of the seas," but the ships are instructed not to approach closer than 11 nautical miles to the North Vietnamese coast.

August 3–4

COVERT WAR: South Vietnamese patrol boats conduct two more clandestine attacks under Oplan 34A against North Vietnamese radar installations at Cape Vinh Son and an installation at the Cua Ron estuary. The commanders of the *Maddox* and *C. Turner Joy* are aware of the situation and try to avoid becoming associated with the South Vietnamese operations, but Admiral Sharp orders them to stay close by "to assert our legitimate rights."

August 4

SEA WAR: At 8:00 in the evening, the destroyers *Maddox* and *C. Turner Joy* intercept radio messages from the North Vietnamese that give Captain Herrick of the *Maddox* "the impression" that their patrol boats are planning an attack. Herrick calls for air support from the *Ticonderoga* and eight Crusader jets soon appear overhead. In the darkness, neither the pilots nor the ship crews see any enemy craft, but at about 10 o'clock the sonar operators report torpedoes in the water. The U.S. destroyers maneuver to avoid the torpedoes and begin to fire at the North Vietnamese patrol boats. When the action ends about two hours later, U.S. officers report sinking two and possibly three of the PT boats. After the incident, no American is sure of ever having seen any enemy boats nor any enemy gunfire. Captain Herrick immediately communicates his doubts to his superiors and urges a "thorough reconnaissance in daylight." Shortly thereafter, he informs Admiral Sharp that the blips on the radar scope were apparently "freak weather effects" while the torpedo sonar signatures were probably due to an "over-eager" radar operator.

USA – GOVERNMENT: Because of the time difference, it is only 0920 hours in Washington when the Pentagon receives the report of a potential attack on the U.S.

destroyers. When a more detailed report is received at 1100 hours, President Johnson is immediately informed and McNamara convenes a meeting with the Joint Chiefs of Staff to discuss possibilities for retaliation. Shortly thereafter, at a National Security Council meeting in the White House, McNamara, Dean Rusk, and McGeorge Bundy recommend to the president that reprisal air strikes be ordered. Johnson is cautious at first, but at a follow-on meeting in the afternoon, he gives the order to execute the reprisal raids. He also decides to seek the congressional resolution he had tabled earlier and discusses with his advisers the deployment of additional air strike forces for the opening stages of Operation Plan 37–64, an extended bombing campaign against North Vietnam.

Meanwhile, Admiral Sharp in Honolulu is still trying to get confirmation from the *Maddox* and *C. Turner Joy* that an attack has taken place. By 1723 hours, Admiral Sharp calls the Pentagon to say that he is satisfied that the attack has occurred. By 1845 hours, President Johnson has met with 16 congressional leaders to inform them of the second unprovoked attack and that he has ordered reprisal attacks. He also tells them he plans to ask for a congressional resolution to support his actions. By 2330 hours, McNamara is informed by Sharp that the initial wave of strike aircraft from the *Ticonderoga* had launched at 2243 and is on its way to the targets. At 2336 hours, President Johnson appears on national television and announces that reprisal raids are underway in response to unprovoked attacks on U.S. warships, characterizing them as a "limited and fitting" response and assuring the viewing audience that, "We still seek no wider war."

August 5

AIR WAR: In the early morning hours, the retaliatory raids, code-named Pierce Arrow, commence when carrier aircraft from the American Seventh Fleet attack the bases used by the torpedo boats and other military targets in North Vietnam. F-8 Crusaders, A-1 Skyraiders, and A-4 Skyhawks, flying from the carriers *Ticonderoga* and *Constellation* in the South China Sea, fly 64 sorties against North Vietnamese coastal targets. They destroy or damage 25 North Vietnamese PT boats (claimed by U.S. officials to be about one-half of the North Vietnamese navy) at bases at Hon Gai, Loc Ghao, Phuc Loi, and Quang Khe; destroy seven antiaircraft installations at Vinh; and severely damage an oil storage depot at Phuc Loi. Two U.S. planes are shot down. One pilot, Lieutenant (j.g.) Everett Alvarez, parachutes to safety, but breaks his back in the process and is taken prisoner by the North Vietnamese. He is the first of some 600 U.S. airmen who will be captured during the war and will not be released until the cease-fire agreement is signed in 1973.

USA – GOVERNMENT: At a news conference, McNamara announces the results of the air strikes and describes the moves that are under way to reinforce U.S. forces in the Pacific area. These include the transfer of an attack carrier group to the western Pacific, the deployment of interceptor and fighter-bomber aircraft to Vietnam and Thailand, the relocation of combat aircraft to advance bases in the Pacific, the deployment of an antisubmarine task force group into the South China Sea, and the alert of selected army and marine forces who will be readied for movement. McNamara admits that these actions are being taken in case there is some form of military reaction from North Vietnam and its allies, but he does not reveal that these actions are part of the Operation Plan 37-64 that the Johnson administration has been planning for months.

USA – DOMESTIC: Opinion polls indicate 85 percent of Americans support President Johnson's bombing decision. Numerous newspaper editorials also come out in support of the president.

INTERNATIONAL: North Vietnam and its Communist bloc allies condemn the U.S. retaliatory strikes. China warns that it will "not sit idly by" while the United States commits "deliberate aggression" against North Vietnam. America's allies generally support the U.S. actions, but some qualify that support. British prime minister Douglas-Home defends the American action as "in accordance with the inherent right of self-defense." France renews its call for an international conference to address the situation in Southeast Asia.

DIPLOMACY: In the UN Security Council, the United States charges that the North Vietnamese attacked the U.S. vessels and Adlai Stevenson defends the air strikes as a "defensive measure." The Soviet delegation condemns the United States for its "acts of aggression" against North Vietnam. A resolution is passed asking both North and South Vietnam to participate in the Security Council debate.

August 6

USA – GOVERNMENT: President Johnson rules out any further raids against North Vietnam. Defense Secretary McNamara and Secretary of State Rusk testify on behalf of proposed resolution in secret sessions of the Senate and House foreign relations committees. Saying that there is "no connection" between the activities of the U.S. destroyers and any action by South Vietnam, McNamara and Rusk present the Johnson administration's arguments for a resolution authorizing the president "to take all necessary measures." The resolution has been drafted by the White House and is sponsored by Senator J. W. Fulbright (D-Ark.) and Representative Thomas E. Morgan (D-Pa.). When debate begins on the resolution, only Senators Wayne Morse (D-Oreg.) and Ernest Gruening (D-Alaska) oppose the measure.

USA – DOMESTIC: The New York stock market, reacting to the news of the crisis in Vietnam, experiences its sharpest decline since the death of President Kennedy. Various rallies and peace vigils are held across the United States protesting the bombing raids. Republican presidential candidate Barry Goldwater says that he supports President Johnson's ordering of the retaliatory raids, but that he intends to make the whole question of Vietnam a campaign issue.

AIR WAR: One U.S. bomber crashes and three are damaged during the U.S. military buildup in Thailand and South Vietnam.

August 6–13

DIPLOMACY: The U.S. State Department cables J. Blair Seaborn, the Canadian who made contacts with the North Vietnamese in June, to tell Hanoi that the United States does not understand why the North Vietnamese PT boats attacked the U.S. ships, but that the U.S. response "for the moment will be limited and fitting." However, he is instructed to point out that additional air power is being deployed to South Vietnam and Thailand. When he sees Pham Van Dong on the 13th, the North Vietnamese premier is furious and indicates that his country is prepared to fight if necessary, but also states that he wants to keep open communication channels with the United States. Seaborn reports to the State Department after his visit that he believes that Hanoi sees "no need to compromise."

August 7

USA – GOVERNMENT: The U.S. Congress passes Public Law 88-408, which becomes known as the Gulf of Tonkin Resolution, giving President Johnson the power to take whatever actions he deems necessary to defend Southeast Asia, including "the use of armed force." The resolution passes 82–2 in the Senate (Senators Morse and Gruening are the only dissenting votes) and 416–0 in the House of Representatives. President Johnson signs it into law on August 10. Despite the initial support for the resolution, it will become increasingly controversial as Johnson uses it to enlarge U.S. commitment to the war in Vietnam. It will remain in effect until repealed in May 1970.

SOUTH VIETNAM: General Khanh declares a "state of emergency." Attempting to take advantage of the heightened tensions, he reimposes censorship and announces other controls. He justifies these acts by declaring that South Vietnam is threatened by a large-scale Communist attack.

NORTH VIETNAM: Hanoi charges that U.S. planes "again intrude repeatedly" into North Vietnamese airspace, but the Pentagon categorically denies this.

INTERNATIONAL: Foreign Minister Gromyko of the Soviet Union again condemns the U.S. action and pledges his nation's full support to North Vietnam. In Beijing, thousands of demonstrators march in support of Hanoi. In London, Lord Russell condemns the American raids. In Calcutta, a thousand leftist students demonstrate against the United States. Not all are against the Americans, and Britain announces that its Far East Fleet is ready for any emergency action to support the United States.

August 8

USA – GOVERNMENT: President Johnson says at a news conference that the U.S. air strikes and the congressional resolution demonstrate the United States' "determination to resist and repel aggression" in Southeast Asia.

SOUTH VIETNAM: A U.S. intelligence report concludes that the Communists are winning the hearts and minds of the South Vietnamese populace and the VC are increasing in strength even though they are sustaining heavy casualties on the battlefield.

USA – MILITARY: The DeSoto intelligence missions are suspended.

August 9

NORTH VIETNAM: Hanoi rejects the call from the United Nations to participate in a Security Council debate on the Tonkin Gulf crisis, maintaining that only the Geneva agreement signatories have jurisdiction in the matter.

August 10

USA – GOVERNMENT: Ambassador Taylor in Saigon cables the president a situation report on South Vietnam. He says that the Khanh regime has only "a 50-50 chance of lasting out the year." Accordingly, he recommends that the United States "be prepared to implement contingency plans against North Vietnam with optimum readiness by Jan. 1, 1965."

August 11

NORTH VIETNAM: Lieutenant Everett Alvarez, the U.S. Navy pilot shot down and captured during the Pierce Arrow raids, is paraded through the streets of Hon Gay.

USA – GOVERNMENT: William Bundy draws up a memorandum outlining graduated phases of escalation during the period August through December, but ramping up toward a full-scale air war against North Vietnam with "a contingency date, as suggested by Ambassador Taylor, of 1 January 1965." The later phase will include systematic bombing raids of North Vietnam and the mining of Haiphong Harbor. Bundy, however, concludes that there should be a "holding phase" until the end of August in order not to "take the onus off the Communist side for escalation."

USA – MILITARY: The Pentagon announces that Communist China has moved MiG fighters into bases in North Vietnam; it also insists that the USS *Maddox*, despite claims to the contrary, never approached closer than 12 miles to the North Vietnamese shoreline.

August 12

GROUND WAR: The Viet Cong distribute leaflets claiming that they will fire only on South Vietnamese units accompanied by U.S. advisers, but this promise is almost immediately broken. Near Ap Cao Cang, 90 U.S. and 12 South Vietnamese helicopters airlift about 1,000 ARVN troops into a Viet Cong base. Other ARVN troops converge on the area from the ground, but the 2,000-man guerrilla force slips away. Only four Viet Cong are killed, while one U.S. helicopter is downed, killing the pilot.

USA – DOMESTIC: Presidential candidate Barry Goldwater charges that President Johnson's "impulsive action" in the Vietnam crisis proves that Johnson is prepared "to use any weapon necessary." Goldwater asserts that this includes nuclear weapons, trying to demonstrate that Johnson is saying the same thing that Goldwater did in the controversial remarks he made earlier in the campaign. Rusk and McNamara immediately deny that Johnson has authorized the use of such weapons and call Goldwater's charge "both unjustified and irresponsible."

August 14

NORTH VIETNAM: Hanoi is reported to be holding air-raid drills for fear of more U.S. attacks. The government urges all civilians with nonessential posts to leave the city.

GROUND WAR: ARVN troops ambush a Viet Cong unit south of Saigon. Meanwhile, Viet Cong guerrillas attack three hamlets in Vinh Binh Province. A U.S. helicopter crashes 50 miles northwest of Saigon, killing three U.S. airmen.

USA – GOVERNMENT: A summary of William Bundy's memorandum of August 11 is cabled to Ambassador Taylor, Ambassador Leonard Unger in Laos, and to Admiral Sharp in Honolulu for comment that will "permit further review and refinement" of the document.

August 16

SOUTH VIETNAM: General Nguyen Khanh is elected president by the Military Revolutionary Council, ousts Duong Van Minh as chief of state, and installs a new constitution, claimed to be modeled on that of the United States. Khanh says that he is not becoming a military dictator, but it is clear that he is now the chief power in the Saigon government.

August 16–September 1

DIPLOMACY: Henry Cabot Lodge, former ambassador to South Vietnam, goes to Western Europe as a personal emissary of President Johnson to explain U.S. policy in Vietnam and to obtain more support for South Vietnam from allies. Lodge returns with pledges from West Germany, Holland, Belgium, Great Britain, and Spain to provide nonmilitary technical aid to Saigon, but none agree to provide military support.

August 17

USA – MILITARY: Admiral Sharp cables Washington commenting on William Bundy's August 11 memorandum, saying, "Pressures against the other side once instituted should not be relaxed by any actions or lack of them which could destroy the benefits of the rewarding steps previously taken." He concludes that the U.S. actions in Tonkin Gulf "have created a momentum which can lead to the attainment of our objectives in S.E. Asia."

August 17–19

GROUND WAR: In the Mekong Delta, ARVN troops battle the Viet Cong in three days of fighting, after which the South Vietnamese claim 280 guerrillas killed. However, U.S. military advisers report finding only 10 VC bodies and no sign of the other 270.

August 18

USA – GOVERNMENT: Ambassador Taylor cables Washington from Saigon saying that he does not think that the Viet Cong can be defeated and the Saigon government preserved by "a counterguerrilla war confined to South Vietnam." Accordingly, he calls for "a carefully orchestrated bombing attack on North Vietnam" to prevent "a complete collapse of national morale" in Saigon. He also advocates sending U.S. Army Hawk antiaircraft missiles to Danang and Saigon to protect the airfields there from retaliatory Communist air attacks and American marines to Danang to protect the airbase against possible ground attacks.

August 19

AIR WAR: VNAF fighter-bombers, some piloted by U.S. pilots, attack a major VC headquarters south of Saigon.

August 20

GROUND WAR: Viet Cong forces overrun the outpost of Phu Tuc, killing seven, wounding 15, and capturing the remaining defenders. When an ARVN unit responds, it is ambushed and four U.S. military advisers are killed.

NORTH VIETNAM: In a message to the UN Security Council, Hanoi rejects the U.S. charge that North Vietnam has committed "deliberate aggression" against U.S. ships and declares the reports of a second attack "an imaginary story."

August 21–25
SOUTH VIETNAM: Chaos reigns as opposition to General Khanh's new government grows. Buddhists charge the government with "anti-Buddhist" policies held over from the Diem years. Student demonstrations turn into street riots with the students marching on Khanh's office, storming the national radio station, and stoning U.S. Army billets. Khanh meets with the student leaders, promising to civilianize the government, but he cannot placate the demonstrators and anti-government violence spreads to other cities. The Revolutionary Council issues a proclamation that withdraws the constitution announced on August 16 and promises to elect a new head of state who will convene a national assembly to reform the government "consistent with the aspirations of the people."

August 22
GROUND WAR: Over 1,000 ARVN casualties are reported in heavy fighting in the Viet Cong stronghold of Tay Ninh Province.

August 26
USA – DOMESTIC: Lyndon B. Johnson is nominated to run for re-election at the Democratic National Convention in Atlantic City, New Jersey. His running mate will be Hubert H. Humphrey. During the campaign, Johnson will declare, "We are about to send American boys nine or ten thousand miles away from home to do what Asian boys ought to be doing for themselves."

USA – MILITARY: The Joint Chiefs of Staff sends a memorandum to the secretary of defense concurring with Ambassador Taylor's August 18 cable. It asserts that an air war against the North is now "essential to prevent a collapse of the U.S. position in Southeast Asia."

August 26–29
SOUTH VIETNAM: Demonstrations and violence continue in protests against the government. In Danang, at least nine people are killed in clashes between Buddhists and Catholics. The Buddhists also attack a U.S.–run hospital and kill four patients. In the Catholic town of Thanh Bo, the Buddhists burn down 450 of 500 houses and the two Catholic churches. The Revolutionary Council disbands and proposes a provisional triumvirate made up of Duong Van Minh, Tran Thien Khiem, and Nguyen Khanh, with Khanh to retain the title of prime minister. This body would rule for two months, by which time a national convention will elect a provisional leader. This does not placate the demonstrators, and paratroopers are required to restore order after Catholic activists attempt to storm the council meeting place. General Khanh leaves for Dalat; after his departure, it is announced that he has suffered a physical and mental "breakdown" and has gone to Dalat to recuperate. Nguyen Xuen Oanh, a Harvard-educated economist and former professor of Trinity College in Connecticut, is chosen to lead the caretaker government for the next two months.

August 29
USA – GOVERNMENT: The Defense Department issues the official casualty list revealing that 274 Americans have been killed in Vietnam between December 1961 and August 17, 1964. President Johnson assures the American people that he has "tried very carefully to restrain ourselves and not to enlarge the war." He says that the United States will continue to aid the South Vietnamese, but will not fight the war for them.

August 30
SOUTH VIETNAM: In Saigon, 50,000 Catholics participate in the funeral procession for six victims killed in the rioting. The South Vietnamese government charges that the Communists instigated the recent trouble.
CHINA: The Communist China press agency charges that the Soviet Union is supporting the United States in a move to intervene in Vietnam through the agency of the United Nations.

August 31
SOUTH VIETNAM: Ambassador Taylor confers at Dalat with Khanh and reports that he appears "rested and recovered" and ready to return to Saigon to assume the premier duties. In Hue, Buddhist leaders announce the formation of the People's Revolutionary Council, which, although anti-Communist, will challenge U.S. policies.
USA – MILITARY: Admiral Thomas Moorer, chief of naval operations, announces that U.S. warships will remain on alert in the South China Sea off North Vietnam in case there is any counterattack by North Vietnamese forces.
JAPAN: In Tokyo for a meeting of the Joint Security Consultative Committee, Admiral Sharp briefs the Japanese on the situation in Vietnam and acknowledges that the Japanese have just allotted $500,000 in aid for South Vietnam.

September
USA – MILITARY: The JCS organizes Sigma II, a war game that is to estimate the possible results of a U.S. air offensive against North Vietnam. One team represents the United States and the other North Vietnam. The conclusion is that the Communists are not going to stop fighting, no matter how much North Vietnam is bombed.
DIPLOMACY: UN secretary-general U Thant tries to set up direct talks between the United States and North Vietnam in Rangoon, Burma. Secretary of State Rusk claims that meeting with North Vietnam would mean "the acceptance or the confirmation of aggression." Nothing comes of U Thant's effort.
USSR: Premier Khrushchev is also secretly trying to get Hanoi to negotiate with Washington, offering the prospect of increased aid.

September 2–3
SOUTH VIETNAM: General Khanh returns to Saigon on September 2 and holds talks with Generals Minh and Khiem, the two other members of the "triumvirate." Khanh resumes his position as premier, dissolves the triumvirate, and reappoints Duong Van Minh as chief of state, though the latter is still very much in charge. Khanh appeals to Buddhists and students to support the government.

CAMBODIA: Phnom Penh charges that South Vietnam aircraft spread poisonous chemicals on Cambodian territory in August. In response, Saigon charges that VC forces are operating from five bases in Cambodian sanctuaries.

September 3
USA – GOVERNMENT: John T. McNaughton, assistant secretary of defense for international security affairs, in a memorandum for Secretary McNamara outlines a plan of provocation designed "to provide good grounds for us to escalate if we wished . . ." The plan includes South Vietnamese air strikes on Laos infiltration routes, coastal raids on North Vietnam, and resumption of U.S. destroyer patrols in the Gulf of Tonkin.

September 4
GROUND WAR: A U.S. helicopter crewman is killed by VC gunfire, five other U.S. servicemen are injured in other operations, and the ARVN claims it has killed 70 guerrillas in a major clash in Quang Ngai Province.

September 5
NORTH VIETNAM: Hanoi renews appeal to Geneva Conference cochairmen to reconvene the conference.

September 7
USA – GOVERNMENT: Ambassador Taylor arrives in Washington to brief the administration on the situation in South Vietnam. He and Johnson are joined by Rusk, McNamara, the Bundy brothers, John McCone, and General Earle Wheeler, chairman of the Joint Chiefs. The consensus is that air strikes on North Vietnam will be necessary sooner or later, but for the present they decide against adopting the provocation strategy advocated by McNaughton in his September 3 memorandum "while the GVN is struggling to its feet."

SOUTH VIETNAM: Saigon charges that Cambodian forces have been shelling South Vietnamese territory in support of the VC and that Cambodian planes have been violating South Vietnamese airspace.

September 8
SOUTH VIETNAM: General Duong Van Minh is named chairman of the military tribunal; Minh will have the duties of chief of state, but Khanh remains the real power in the government.

CAMBODIA: U.S. Air Force jets come to the aid of South Vietnamese planes that report being chased by Cambodian jets, but no fire is exchanged.

September 9
SOUTH VIETNAM: General Khanh lifts press censorship and appoints two civilians to government posts to replace military men, but announces that he will retain his post as defense minister.

USA – GOVERNMENT: Ambassador Taylor reports to Congress and then holds a news conference, in which he states that General Khanh is "very definitely head of the interim government" and that the situation in Vietnam is "essentially normal."

USSR: Soviets warn Japan that it must expect some military retaliation if it allows U.S. bases there to be used for military action against North Vietnam.

September 10

USA – GOVERNMENT: In National Security Action Memorandum 314, President Johnson authorizes a series of measures "to assist morale in South Vietnam and show the Communists we still mean business," but at the same time "seeking to keep the risks low and under our control at each stage." These measures include covert action, such as resumption of the De Soto patrols and the South Vietnamese coastal raids, while a crucial item calls for asking Premier Souvanna Phouma of Laos to permit "limited GVN air and ground operations" into southeastern Laos along with air strikes by Laotian planes and possible use of U.S. armed aerial reconnaissance in Laos.

Henry Cabot Lodge, President Johnson's special personal emissary, reports to the president on his trip throughout Europe. They issue a statement that claims that all Western European governments except France view the Vietnam struggle as a "free world" issue, not just a regional problem.

September 11

LAOS: The U.S. ambassadors to Thailand and Laos meet with Ambassador Taylor in Saigon and decide that the South Vietnamese air force will not participate in the stepped-up air action in Laos authorized by President Johnson's memorandum of September 10. However, T-28s based in Laos and U.S. Navy and Air Force planes that are part of Yankee Team will continue their covert operations in Laos. It is also agreed that South Vietnamese troops will be able to make incursions into Laos up to 12 miles, but that Souvanna Phouma will not be informed so he can honestly deny such operations and not weaken his government.

September 12

SOUTH VIETNAM: Saigon sends a letter to the ICC saying that South Vietnam is prepared to disarm and end all U.S. support as soon as North Vietnam ceases the activities of the Viet Cong.

USA – DOMESTIC: Vice presidential candidate Hubert Humphrey says that the United States must remain in Vietnam but makes it clear that the primary responsibility for winning the war and achieving peace rests with the South Vietnamese.

SEA WAR: The U.S. Navy destroyers *Edwards* and *Morton* resume the DeSoto patrols in the Gulf of Tonkin.

September 13–14

SOUTH VIETNAM: Dissident army officers led by General Lam Van Phat, a Roman Catholic who was dismissed as interior minister on September 3, and General Duong Van Duc, commander of IV Corps, attempt to overthrow Khanh's government, calling their movement the People's Council for the Salvation of the Nation. Ambassador Taylor is en route back to Saigon, but his deputy, Alexis Johnson, meets with the cabinet and encourages them to remain loyal to Khanh. Meanwhile, government troops loyal to Khanh move against the coup's main base near Tan Son Nhut. The final blow to the coup comes when Air Vice Marshal Nguyen Cao Ky orders VNAF planes over the insurgent generals' headquarters and threatens to bomb them if they do not surrender. By the 14th, Ky is holding a news conference with the dissident leaders and claiming "there was no coup."

September 15
GROUND WAR: The NLF calls for a general military offensive to take advantage of the disarray among the South Vietnamese leadership, particularly after the abortive coup of September 13–14.

September 16
SOUTH VIETNAM: The two chief leaders of the coup attempt, Generals Phat and Duc, are arrested, as are three other rebel generals.

September 18–19
SEA WAR: The two U.S. destroyers on De Soto patrols in the Gulf of Tonkin, *Edwards* and *Morton,* are pursued at night by four unidentified vessels, presumed to be North Vietnamese PT boats. The destroyers fire hundreds of shells, but never see any ships and do not detect any torpedoes. President Johnson does not authorize any retaliation and subsequently suspends the De Soto patrols.

September 18
GROUND WAR: South Vietnam claims that two PAVN companies invaded South Vietnam, in Quang Tri Province, but that they were defeated with heavy casualties. U.S. military advisers question whether these were actually North Vietnamese troops; in fact, NVA units are beginning to infiltrate to the South.
RIVER WAR: VC artillery sink two South Vietnamese landing craft conducting operations on the Mekong River.

September 19
SOUTH VIETNAM: General Khanh's government makes several major changes in the military command, in part a response to demands of officers who emerged as loyal in the recent coup attempt.
CAMBODIA: Khanh threatens to close the Mekong River to international commercial traffic unless Cambodia ceases all hostile actions.

September 21–28
SOUTH VIETNAM: Rhadé (or Edé) hill tribesmen in the central plateau, who have no sympathy for Saigon or the Viet Cong, rebel against the South Vietnamese government and demand autonomy. In the process, they kill 50 ARVN troops at a U.S. Special Forces camp at Ban Me Thuot in Darlac Province. Eventually, the uprising is put down, partly through the influence of the tribesmen's Special Forces advisers. Khanh blames the uprising on "Communists and foreigners."

September 22
USA – DOMESTIC: Republican presidential candidate Goldwater charges that President Johnson lied to the American people and that he is "recklessly" committing the United States to war. Having previously described it as "McNamara's War," he now calls it "Johnson's War."

September 25–27
SOUTH VIETNAM: Rumors of another coup cause government troops to take up key positions around Saigon, but nothing materializes. Anti-government riots in Qui Nhon, one of the centers of Buddhist protests during August, are also put down by government forces.

September 26
SOUTH VIETNAM: Khanh forms a 17-member "High National Council" that he charges with setting up a provisional government and drafting a new constitution.
GROUND WAR: Heavy fighting breaks out between South Vietnamese forces and the VC in the Mekong Delta; one U.S.-piloted aircraft is shot down and one U.S. soldier is killed.

September 28
GROUND WAR: ARVN forces claim a victory in a battle with the Viet Cong in Go Cong Province, but are defeated in a clash in Kien Giang Province, where one U.S. soldier is killed.

September 30
USA – DOMESTIC: First large-scale anti-war demonstration in the United States is staged at University of California–Berkeley by students and faculty opposed to the war, but national polls indicate that a majority of Americans support the president's policy on the war.
USA – MILITARY: General Westmoreland initiates Hop Tac, a pacification operation focused on six provinces around Saigon and based on tactics used by the British in fighting the Communists in Malaya.

October
USA – GOVERNMENT: Undersecretary of State George Ball dictates a private 67-page memo that he sees as "a challenge to the assumptions of our current Vietnam policy." He argues that an intensified U.S. air war against North Vietnam will lead to a still greater escalation on both sides, "leading at the end of the road, to the direct intervention of China and nuclear war." He writes that, "Once on the tiger's back we cannot be sure of picking the place to dismount." As for the assumption behind the domino theory—that a loss in Vietnam will inevitably lead to the loss of America's credibility and so to the loss of a series of nations—Ball concludes, "What we might gain by establishing the steadfastness of our commitments, we could lose by an erosion of confidence in our judgments." Ball sends copies of the memo to Rusk, McNamara, and McGeorge Bundy, but no one bothers to send a copy to President Johnson until February 1965.
USA – MILITARY: U.S. Fifth Special Forces Group deploys to Vietnam from Fort Bragg, North Carolina, to oversee Special Forces operations in-country.
GROUND WAR: Tactical units of the PAVN are beginning a steady influx into the South over the Ho Chi Minh Trail.

October 2
SOUTH VIETNAM: General Khanh announces that his government and U.S. authorities are revising the program that has been arming the Montagnards. In reference

to the recent troubles with the tribesmen, he threatens to use force to put down further disorder.

October 4

USA – GOVERNMENT: President Johnson issues an order to reactivate coastal raids by South Vietnamese boats as part of Oplan 34A.

GROUND WAR: ARVN troops suffer heavy casualties from a Viet Cong ambush some 15 miles north of Saigon.

October 5

USA – GOVERNMENT: Senator Gaylord Nelson (D-Wis.), disturbed by growing reports that the Johnson administration is preparing to extend U.S. operations in Vietnam, states that Congress did not intend the Gulf of Tonkin Resolution (August 7) as an endorsement of any escalation of the war.

USA – DOMESTIC: Republican presidential candidate Barry Goldwater announces that if he is elected he will ask ex-president Eisenhower to visit Vietnam and report on the situation there; Eisenhower's aides quickly announce that he has not committed himself.

October 7

SOUTH VIETNAM: General Tran Thien Khiem, a member of the government triumvirate, leaves on a "goodwill mission" to various Asian nations; in fact, he is being forced into exile.

USA – DOMESTIC: Former vice president Richard Nixon claims that Vietnam will be lost within a year and all of Southeast Asia within three years if the United States does not quickly change its policy.

GROUND WAR: VC ground fire brings down a U.S. helicopter, killing five U.S. servicemen.

October 8

USA – GOVERNMENT: Secretary of State Rusk, in a news conference, insists that the administration's decisions about the conflict in Vietnam have "nothing to do" with the election and denies that information is being withheld because of the ongoing campaign.

Former Viet Cong member makes radio appeal to former comrades to rally to the ARVN during the Chieu Hoi (Open Arms) program. *(Texas Tech University Vietnam Archive)*

October 9

SOUTH VIETNAM: General Khanh says that South Vietnam now has the capability of bombing North Vietnam or China without U.S. aid, but he says no such action is imminent.

October 10

SOUTH VIETNAM: Saigon claims that 16,101 Communist soldiers or agents have deserted during the last 20 months under the ongoing *Chieu Hoi* ("Open Arms") program. Some of these defectors will fight with U.S. and ARVN forces and will become known as Kit Carson Scouts.

DIPLOMACY: In Cairo, participants at a meeting of nonaligned nations urge that a conference be called in Geneva to negotiate an end to the conflict in Vietnam.

October 11
GROUND WAR: The VC burn 200 structures in attacks on eight fortified hamlets in the Pleiku area. Elsewhere, two U.S. soldiers are killed by a landmine explosion.

October 13
USA – MILITARY: The United States announces it is setting up a third helicopter company in the Mekong Delta area controlled by the Viet Cong.

October 14
LAOS: U.S. aircraft are permitted to fly cover for Laotian planes on operations against Communist movements on the Ho Chi Minh Trail.

October 14–15
USSR: After 10 years in power, Nikita Khrushchev is ousted as both premier and chief of the Communist Party, replaced by Leonid Brezhnev as first secretary of the party and Aleksey Kosygin as premier. The new Russian leadership will increase military aid to North Vietnam and will not try to persuade them to attempt a negotiated end to hostilities.

October 19
GROUND WAR: Thirteen U.S. servicemen and four U.S. civilians believed to be held as prisoners by the VC for over two years have not been allowed to contact their families, and the Red Cross has been unable to make contact with them.

October 20
SOUTH VIETNAM: The High National Council (established on September 26) issues a new draft constitution providing for a chief of state, a premier, a cabinet, and a legislative assembly; its preamble explicitly states that "the armed forces have rightfully asserted that they would return to their purely military duties and gradually hand over the powers to a civilian government."
GROUND WAR: MACV reports that a helicopter operation, 80 miles southwest of Saigon, killed 34 Viet Cong guerrillas.

October 20–28
CAMBODIA: Relations between Cambodia, South Vietnam, and the United States reach a new low when South Vietnamese planes strafe a Cambodian village. When Cambodia protests, Saigon charges Cambodia once again with providing refuge for Communist forces. On the 22nd, the United States charges that Cambodian troops crossed over into South Vietnam and seized a U.S. officer advising ARVN forces; on the 25th, the officer's body is recovered just inside South Vietnam and Cambodia is accused of placing the body there to allow the rescue force to be fired on. Then on the 24th, Cambodians shoot down a USAF C-123, loaded with ammunition; eight U.S. servicemen are lost. By the 28th, the United States admits that the plane did stray over Cambodian territory by mistake, but argues that such incidents arise because of the poorly defined border and the activities of the VC in the area. Despite

the charges and threats from Sihanouk, and despite the U.S. losses in personnel and planes, neither side pursues the matter, avoiding further armed confrontation.

October 22

NORTH VIETNAM: It is reported that Hanoi's government radio is increasing its propaganda broadcasts into South Vietnam, noting the criticisms of the Johnson administration's handling of the war being made by various U.S. senators.

October 23

SOUTH VIETNAM: The 20 military officers and civilians on trial, charged with an attempted coup September 13–14, are acquitted. As part of this attempt by Nguyen Khanh to placate a growing dissident element in the armed forces, he also appoints to high posts the five generals arrested when he seized power in January.

October 24–29

SOUTH VIETNAM: The High National Council chooses Phan Khac Suu, a 63-year-old engineer, as chief of state. Nguyen Khanh resigns as premier on the 26th, and on the 29th, Tran Van Huong, former mayor of Saigon, is named premier.

October 28

AIR WAR: U.S. T-28s, piloted by Thais, bomb and strafe North Vietnamese villages in the Mugia Pass area.

GROUND WAR: One U.S. soldier is wounded when the VC down a U.S. Army helicopter, and elsewhere another U.S. soldier is killed and two wounded in a VC ambush.

November 1

SOUTH VIETNAM: One year after the overthrow and assassination of Ngo Dinh Diem, a survey of South Vietnam reveals that it has deteriorated in both the military and political spheres.

GROUND WAR: Viet Cong attack Bien Hoa Air Base, 12 miles north of Saigon, killing five U.S. servicemen and two Vietnamese, wounding about 76, destroying two B-57 bombers, and damaging another 20 U.S. and Vietnamese aircraft. Word of the attack reaches Washington early in the morning, and the JCS calls the attack "a deliberate act of escalation" and recommends "a prompt and strong response." Ambassador Taylor urges bombing "selected" targets in North Vietnam. President Johnson, well aware that the presidential election will be underway within 48 hours, essentially decides to do nothing except order the immediate replacement of destroyed and damaged planes. However, he appoints an interagency working group to draw up various political and military options for direct action against North Vietnam.

CAMBODIA: The U.S. embassy in Phnom Penh evacuates dependents from Cambodia because of the recent increase in anti-U.S. demonstrations following charges of U.S. involvement in border incidents. Wreckage of the C-123 shot down on October 4 is now displayed in Phnom Penh.

November 2

USA – DOMESTIC: On the last day before the election, presidential candidate Barry Goldwater and former vice president Richard Nixon attack the president's handling of the war in Vietnam. The Republican candidate challenges Johnson to admit to the American people that the United States is involved in an undeclared war in Vietnam.

USSR: The Soviet Union delivers a major shipment of arms to Cambodia, to replace U.S. equipment no longer available. Within two days, the Soviet Union will also be calling for a new international conference to guarantee Cambodia's neutrality.

November 3

USA – DOMESTIC: With 61 percent of the popular vote, Lyndon Johnson is elected in a landslide victory, the biggest to date in U.S. history, defeating Goldwater by over 16 million votes. Goldwater is defeated because many Americans believe Johnson is less likely to escalate U.S. involvement in Southeast Asia. The Democrats also achieve big majorities in both the U.S. House and Senate.

USA – GOVERNMENT: An interagency working group appointed by the president and headed by William Bundy holds its first meeting. This group is charged by Johnson to reexamine the entire American policy toward Vietnam and to recommend to the National Security Council a broad range of options.

November 5

GROUND WAR: Heavily armed VC, attempting to kidnap a Vietnamese official, get within rifle-range of the U.S. embassy in Saigon.

November 5–6

SOUTH VIETNAM: Buddhists charge that Premier Huong has deliberately denied them any role in the government, students are angry that they will lose their draft exemptions, some charge he has ignored political leaders, while others charge he has appointed ministers who served under Ngo Dinh Diem and Emperor Bao Dai. Huong warns he will not hesitate to use force to suppress violent demonstrations, but on the 6th he speaks in a more conciliatory way, admitting his government's weakness and appealing to all dissident groups to cooperate.

November 6

GROUND WAR: U.S. military advisers openly express their disgust when ARVN officers refuse to order their boats and troops along a canal they regard as militarily insecure, delaying a major operation planned to break the VC's hold on the Mekong Delta town of Nam Can.

November 7

SOUTH VIETNAM: The South Vietnam government bans the sale of the current issue of *Newsweek* because it carries a photograph showing a VC prisoner being tortured by ARVN personnel.

GROUND WAR: The latest U.S. intelligence analysis claims that the VC now number about 30,000 full-time professional soldiers, many of whom are North Vietnamese.

November 7–10

GROUND WAR: After VNAF aircraft bomb a Communist stronghold near Bien Hoa, 1,200 ARVN troops push through the jungles in the area, all part of the attempt to find the guerrillas that attacked the U.S. air base.

November 10
USA – GOVERNMENT: Secretary of Defense McNamara says, at a news conference, that the United States has no plans to send combat troops into Vietnam; when asked whether the United States intends to increase its activities in Vietnam, he replies, "wait and see."

AUSTRALIA: Prime Minister Robert Menzies announces that his country will strengthen its defenses to meet the growing Communist threat in Southeast Asia.

November 10–14
SOUTH VIETNAM: Major floods in the region north of Saigon disrupt military operations, while Viet Cong forces attack rescue operations and relief convoys.

November 11
SOUTH VIETNAM: Saigon police announce they have uncovered a ring involving officials from the Khanh government that sold exemptions to Vietnamese youths called up for military service.

USA – DOMESTIC: NBC-TV shows a film provided by a Japanese agency that gives the North Vietnamese version of the conflict between the United States and North Vietnam; the film shows the first U.S. POW, Lt. Everett Alvarez, who was shot down and captured during the initial retaliatory strikes following the Gulf of Tonkin incident.

November 12
GROUND WAR: In two separate attacks in Binh Tuy Province, VC kill 34 ARVN soldiers and wound 40.

November 15–18
CAMBODIA: Prince Sihanouk says that if the United States wants to improve its relations with Cambodia, it must order the South Vietnamese to stop their attacks on border areas and stop charging that the VC are allowed to use Cambodia as a sanctuary and supply route. Claiming that the South Vietnamese have killed 100 Cambodians, Sihanouk demands that the United States and Saigon pay one bulldozer or one million riels for each Cambodian killed.

November 17
GROUND WAR: In a skirmish in Bien Hoa Province, one U.S. military adviser and four ARVN soldiers are killed, while another American adviser and six ARVN soldiers are wounded.

November 18
GROUND WAR: In the largest airmobile operation of the war to date, 116 U.S. and South Vietnamese helicopters fly some 1,100 ARVN troops into Bingh Duong and Tay Ninh Provinces to attack what is claimed to be a major Communist stronghold. General Khanh personally directs the operation, but it makes only light contact with the VC.

November 19
GROUND WAR: ARVN troops kill 17 VC and capture 21 in an airmobile operation in Quang Nam Province. Elsewhere, over 7,000 ARVN troops converge on enemy

positions in a forested area near Thu Dau Mot, but they find that the VC have slipped away.

TERRORISM: A VC mine planted on the Saigon-Hue railroad derails a train, killing four railroad workers and injuring 17 South Vietnamese and one U.S. military adviser.

November 20

NORTH VIETNAM: It is reported that delegations from 10 Communist-bloc countries are meeting in Hanoi to express "solidarity with North Vietnam against US imperialism."

November 22–28

SOUTH VIETNAM: In Saigon, a clash breaks out between thousands of Buddhist marchers and police near the palace of chief of state Phan Khac Suu, ending the moratorium on violent demonstrations that the Buddhists have voluntarily observed since November 6. The confrontation continues for the next few days. On the 26th, the government declares martial law, banning demonstrations and putting troops in the streets; on the 28th, Buddhist leaders announce that they will resort to a nonviolent campaign of noncooperation.

November 24

USA – GOVERNMENT: A select committee of the National Security Council made up of Rusk, McNamara, General Wheeler, John McCone of the CIA, and Undersecretary of State George Ball meets to discuss the options prepared by the "Bundy working group." Ball "indicated doubt" that bombing the North would improve the situation in South Vietnam and "argued against" a judgment that a VC victory in South Vietnam would have a falling-domino effect on the rest of Asia. However, the rest of the attendees favor bombing North Vietnam; only the timing is debated.

November 25

LAOS: William Sullivan arrives in Vientiane as the new U.S. ambassador.

November 27

USA – GOVERNMENT: Ambassador Maxwell Taylor arrives in Washington to join the discussions ongoing in the select committee of the National Security Council. Saying that victory in South Vietnam "is very much in doubt," he calls for an escalation of U.S. bombing of North Vietnam, but only after Saigon leaders demonstrate a willingness to achieve political stability, replace incompetent officials, and get with the war effort. Then, the United States should pursue a two-phased program culminating in the bombing of infiltration facilities south of the 19th parallel in North Vietnam.

November 28

USA – GOVERNMENT: Secretaries Rusk and McNamara, Ambassador Taylor, and other members of the select committee of the National Security Council agree to recommend to the president that he adopt Taylor's plan for a two-stage escalation of bombing of North Vietnam. This day, in response to a reporter's question at a news conference at his ranch in Texas, the president says he "anticipates no dramatic announcement" to come out of the select committee's sessions.

December

SEA WAR: U.S. Navy Task Group 77 (TF77)—including the attack carriers *Hancock*, *Coral Sea*, and *Ranger*—is assigned to rendezvous about 75 miles out in the Gulf of Tonkin. This area will be called Yankee Station (as opposed to the U.S. ships assigned to the waters off South Vietnam, which are on Dixie Station).

GROUND WAR: MACV releases a study that shows November to have been one of the most successful months in the war to date, with some 1,370 guerrillas reported killed and 370 captured, and with the ratio of guerrillas killed to South Vietnamese dead (the "kill ratio") at its most favorable level since 1961.

December 1 and 3

USA – GOVERNMENT: In two crucial meetings at the White House, President Johnson and his top-ranking advisers agree to a two-phase bombing plan. Phase I will involve air strikes by U.S. Air Force and Navy jets against infiltration routes and facilities in the Laotian panhandle. Phase II will extend the air strikes to a widening selection of targets in North Vietnam. Johnson makes it clear that Phase II is tied to a "serious attempt" by the Saigon leadership to achieve some political stability and get on with the war. In a news conference on the 3rd, Taylor indicates that he has been authorized to improve South Vietnam's war efforts and "that he was going to hold 'across-the-board' discussions with GVN [Government of Vietnam]." However, he says nothing about the bombing operations planned.

December 2

USA – DOMESTIC: Richard Nixon calls on the United States to bomb Viet Cong supply routes, even if it requires extending the war.

GROUND WAR: Viet Cong overrun the district headquarters at Thien Gao, an area supposedly controlled by the South Vietnamese government; the Viet Cong kill the district chief and capture a number of weapons.

December 3

USA – MILITARY: It is announced that the first U.S. women to serve as military advisers will be assigned to a South Vietnamese Women's Army Corps training camp at Saigon.

December 4

USA – GOVERNMENT: William Bundy leaves for Australia and New Zealand to brief their government leaders on the two-phase bombing plan. Other governments supporting the U.S. efforts will also be briefed, although most governments will not be told of the plans for Phase II, the extension of the bombing into the North.

SOUTH VIETNAM: General Khanh, still commander in chief of the military forces of South Vietnam, meets with other high-ranking military leaders at Dalat, and they issue an appeal to all dissident groups to support the government.

GROUND WAR: The Viet Cong move into Phuoc Tuy Province, southeast of Saigon, and commence a series of attacks that culminate in a major defeat of ARVN forces at Binh Gia, 40 miles from Saigon, from December 28, 1964, to January 4, 1965. For several weeks about 1,000 Viet Cong had been making their way in small groups from Tay Ninh Province, northwest of Saigon, and then joined forces to conduct the surprise attacks.

December 5
USA – MILITARY: The first Congressional Medal of Honor awarded to a U.S. serviceman for action in Vietnam is presented to Captain Roger Donlon for his heroic action during a battle at Nam Dong Special Forces camp on July 6, 1964.

GROUND WAR: A major attack by the Viet Cong at Tan Phu in the Mekong Delta leaves seven U.S. advisers wounded and 23 ARVN soldiers killed and 50 wounded. Fifty Viet Cong are reported killed in the action.

December 7–9
GROUND WAR: The Viet Cong attack and capture the district headquarters at An Lao and much of the surrounding valley. ARVN troops regain control only after reinforcements are airlifted into the area by U.S. helicopters; during the battle, one U.S. Army officer and one U.S. soldier are killed. There are over 300 South Vietnamese casualties and as many as 7,000 villagers are temporarily forced to abandon their homes.

DIPLOMACY: Prime Minister Harold Wilson of Britain is briefed on the forthcoming bombing plan for Vietnam during a state visit to Washington.

December 7–11
SOUTH VIETNAM: Ambassador Taylor, having returned from Washington, holds a series of meetings with Premier Huong, General Khanh, and other South Vietnamese leaders to exact the desired assurances in exchange for the planned bombing campaign. The South Vietnamese leaders issue a communiqué on the 11th, drafted by U.S. officials, describing the additional aid that the United States will supply to strengthen South Vietnam's military forces (which South Vietnam agrees to increase by 100,000 men) and to "further economic assistance for a variety of reforms of industrial, urban, and rural development." Nothing is said of the plans to start the new bombing raids.

December 10
LAOS: Ambassador Sullivan in Laos gets Souvanna Phouma to allow U.S. planes to bomb the Communist supply routes in Laos.

December 11
SOUTH VIETNAM: As soon as the communiqué announcing increased U.S. support for the government is released, Buddhist leaders announce a campaign to oust Premier Huong, particularly because they claim he is being kept in power by the Americans.

December 12
USA – GOVERNMENT: At a meeting of the National Security Council, the final details for Operation Barrel Roll, the name given to the first phase of the bombing plan approved by President Johnson on December 1, are reviewed and approved. It is "agreed that there would be no public operations statements about armed reconnaissance unless

a plane were lost." In such a case, the government will insist that the U.S. plane was simply on escort duty as requested by the Laotians.

USA – MILITARY: A C-123 transport aircraft crashes during take-off at the Danang airport and two U.S. servicemen are killed. Because the Defense Department does not provide any explanation for the plane's mission, the incident leads to public speculation that the U.S. Air Force is engaging in some kind of secret operations.

TERRORISM: A bomb planted in a Saigon bar explodes and injures two Americans and four Vietnamese.

December 13–17

CAMBODIA: U.S. and Cambodian representatives meet in New Delhi, India, in an effort to work out such issues as the border raids and alleged support for the Viet Cong, but the talks quickly break down.

December 14

USA – DOMESTIC: A survey of Americans reveals that one-quarter do not know there is any fighting going on in Vietnam.

GROUND WAR: Four U.S. Army officers are killed when the Viet Cong attack an ARVN division headquarters in Thu Dau Mot.

LAOS: Operation Barrel Roll begins with U.S. planes attacking "targets of opportunity" in northern Laos.

December 15

GROUND WAR: Reports reach Saigon of recent battles in Soc Trang and Chuong Thien Provinces and in the An Loa Valley that have left 580 ARVN troops missing and 40 known dead. These losses are part of the highest South Vietnamese casualty figures for a seven-day period in the war to date.

DIPLOMACY: Secretary of State Dean Rusk, addressing the Ministers' Council of the North Atlantic Treaty Organization, says that the entire non-Communist world has a stake in the war in Vietnam and he asks that NATO countries provide more tangible aid. Some will eventually respond with economic aid for Saigon, but none will provide troops.

December 17

GROUND WAR: ARVN forces blow up a network of Viet Cong tunnels some 15 miles northeast of Saigon, capturing 16 VC soldiers who survive the blasts.

December 18

USA – GOVERNMENT: Secretary McNamara sets the level of Barrel Roll attacks for the first 30 days of Phase I at two missions of four aircraft apiece each week.

December 19

GROUND WAR: Viet Cong disguised as ARVN paratroopers ambush a South Vietnamese convoy returning to Saigon after escorting General Khanh to Cap St. Jacques (Vung Tau) on the coast. It is believed that the VC expected Khanh to be in the convoy.

December 19–20

SOUTH VIETNAM: General Khanh, in a temporary alliance with the so-called Young Turks, a group of younger generals led by Air Vice-Marshal Nguyen Cao Ky and

General Nguyen Van Thieu, stages another bloodless coup. Khanh dissolves the High National Council, arrests individuals who oppose his rule, and conducts a purge of military leadership. Ambassador Taylor summons the Young Turks to the embassy and "read them the riot act." Taylor says that Americans are "tired of coups" and warns them that the United States will not "carry you forever." Telling them "that all the military plans which I know you would like to carry out are dependent on government stability," he tries to get them to agree to restore the High National Council, but they refuse.

December 21–23

SOUTH VIETNAM: General Khanh tells a reporter from the *New York Herald Tribune* that the High National Council "will not be reactivated" just to satisfy the United States. On the 22nd, Khanh issues an order from the Armed Forces Council saying that the military will retain control of the government.

December 24

TERRORISM: Viet Cong saboteurs, disguised as ARVN soldiers, detonate a car bomb outside the Brinks Hotel, a U.S. officers billet in Saigon. Two Americans are killed and 65 Americans and Vietnamese injured. President Johnson declines to authorize reprisal air strikes against the North, despite vigorous recommendations by Taylor, Westmoreland, the Joint Chiefs of Staff, and other senior U.S. officials.

December 25

SOUTH VIETNAM: Premier Huong broadcasts a Christmas message to U.S. personnel in Vietnam. General Khanh will issue his own Christmas message with thanks to the U.S. troops two days later.

USA – MILITARY: The Pentagon releases figures showing that most of the approximately 23,000 U.S. military personnel now serving in Vietnam are not volunteers but have been assigned there.

POWs: The Red Cross announces that it has tried to send packages to the 17 or more Americans believed being held in North Vietnam, but it has no assurances that the packages were delivered.

December 26

SOUTH VIETNAM: The Armed Forces Council orders paratroopers into Saigon and extends martial law, primarily to signal Buddhists and any other potential resisters that the military government will not allow opposition to its control.

December 27–28

GROUND WAR: Although outnumbered, ARVN troops capture a Viet Cong head-quarters, seize a record cache of enemy arms, and claim 85 guerrillas killed in a two-day battle. ARVN casualties include 19 dead and 49 wounded; eight American advisers are also wounded.

December 28–January 2

GROUND WAR: The Viet Cong capture the village of Binh Gia, 40 miles southeast of Saigon and hold it for eight hours. ARVN forces recapture the village but only after three battalions are brought in on helicopters. On January 2, two companies of Rangers, accompanied by tanks, are ambushed by Viet Cong on a nearby rubber plantation. Throughout the protracted fighting, the South Vietnamese forces continually demonstrate inept leadership and poor motivation.

December 31

USA – GOVERNMENT: Ambassador Taylor, Deputy Ambassador Johnson, and General Westmoreland, despairing of trading a bombing campaign against the North for a stable Saigon government that will prosecute the war in the South, send a joint message to Washington, saying that the United States should go ahead with the air campaign against the North "under any conceivable alliance condition short of complete abandonment of South Vietnam."

YEAR-END SUMMARY: Despite the Johnson administration's claim to the contrary, a full-scale war is now raging in South Vietnam. There are about 23,300 U.S. military personnel in-country, an increase of more than 6,000 since President Johnson took office. U.S. casualty figures include 140 killed, 1,138 wounded, and 11 missing in action. Free world military forces include some 2,000 Korean military advisers, small units and advisers from Australia and New Zealand, with Thailand and the Philippines preparing units for deployment to South Vietnam. During the year, South Vietnamese armed forces increased to 514,000 (265,000 regular forces and some 290,000 militia and paramilitary forces). South Vietnamese casualties for the year are estimated at 7,000 military personnel killed, 16,700 wounded, and 500 missing or captured. It is estimated that the Communist forces in South Vietnam number some 34,000 main-force soldiers, but a steady stream of North Vietnamese soldiers are moving down the Ho Chi Minh Trail to join the fight. Additionally, the Communists control as much as 50 percent of South Vietnam. U.S. intelligence estimates that 17,000 Communists were killed during the year and 4,200 captured.

1965

January 2

GROUND WAR: The six-day Battle of Binh Gia comes to an end; five Americans are killed and three are wounded—the highest U.S. casualties sustained in a single battle to date. Total losses for the operation around Binh Gia include some 200 South Vietnamese killed, plus 300 more wounded or missing. VC losses are estimated at about 120 dead.

January 3

SOUTH VIETNAM: Thousands of anti-government demonstrators in Saigon clash with government marines and police. There are also demonstrations in Hue, where students organize strikes against the local government. The main resistance to the Saigon regime comes from Buddhists, who are strongly opposed to Tran Van Huong, who became premier on November 4, 1964.

January 4

USA – GOVERNMENT: In his State of the Union message, President Johnson reaffirms the U.S. commitment to support South Vietnam in combating Communist aggression, saying that, "Our own security is tied to the peace of Asia."

GROUND WAR: The VC make another attack on ARVN positions in Binh Gia, accounting for additional casualties among the South Vietnamese troops and their American advisers.

January 6
USA – GOVERNMENT: An Associated Press survey of 83 U.S. senators shows considerable disagreement on the Johnson administration's handling of the situation in Vietnam. William Bundy submits a memo to Secretary of State Dean Rusk, predicting that the "situation in Vietnam is now likely to come apart more rapidly than we had anticipated." He urges "stronger action."

January 8
GROUND WAR: Viet Cong forces ambush an ARVN company near Tan Bu and one U.S. adviser is killed. Elsewhere, ARVN claims to have killed 53 Viet Cong near Quang Nam and routed attackers in the Hue area.

January 9
SOUTH VIETNAM: Under pressure from U.S. officials, General Khanh and the Armed Forces Council agree to support the civilian government of Premier Tran Van Huong. They pledge to confine their activities to the military realm and to convene a national convention to "assume legislative powers" and draw up a permanent constitution.

January 11
USA – GOVERNMENT: In a cable to Saigon, Secretary of State Rusk instructs Ambassador Taylor "to avoid actions that would further commit the United States to any particular form of political solution" to the turmoil in Saigon.

January 11–27
SOUTH VIETNAM: The major cities, including Saigon and Hue, and much of central Vietnam are disrupted by demonstrations and strikes led by the Buddhists, who demand the ouster of the Huong government. Because the demonstrators perceive that the Americans are supporting the regime in Saigon, they turn their ire on U.S. facilities. In Hue, a mob of 3,000 Buddhists storms the U.S. Information Service office and burns more than 5,000 books. U.S. vice consul in Hue, Anthony Lake, is stoned by the mob when he tries to enter the building to put out the fire, but he is not hurt. Although Huong tries to appease the Buddhists by rearranging his government, they are not placated and continue their demonstrations and strikes.

January 12
JAPAN: Prime Minister Sato, addressing the National Press Club in Washington, says that the problem in Vietnam cannot be solved by the "rational approach" of the West but should be left to the Asians themselves.

January 13
LAOS: The U.S. press reports that two U.S. Air Force jet fighters have been shot down over Laos while escorting bombers in attacks on the Ho Chi Minh Trail, which passes from North Vietnam through Laos into South Vietnam. In actuality,

the downed aircraft are part of the secret air war in Laos called Operation Barrel Roll, which began in December 1964, but these reports "blew the lid" on U.S. air operations over Laos.

January 17
SOUTH VIETNAM: It is reported that about 30 percent of South Vietnamese draftees desert within their first six weeks in service.

January 19
USA – GOVERNMENT: Senator Wayne Morse (D-Oreg.) condemns the U.S. air operations in Laos, saying that they violate the 1962 Geneva Accords and warning that "there is no hope of avoiding a massive war in Asia, if U.S. policy towards Southeast Asia were to continue without change."

January 20
SOUTH VIETNAM: A revised cabinet assumes office, as Premier Tran Van Huong tries to placate the Buddhists.

January 21
GROUND WAR: Some 1,500 ARVN troops are transported by helicopter to confront a large VC unit in the Mekong Delta province of Kien Hoa; the ARVN report killing 46 and capturing 61.

January 24
SOUTH VIETNAM: The Armed Forces Council, headed by Nguyen Khanh, resolves to get rid of Premier Tran Van Huong, who is the focus of Buddhist ire.

January 26
USA – DOMESTIC: Former vice president Richard Nixon, in a speech in New York City, charges that the United States is "losing the war in Vietnam" and calls for U.S. bombing of Communist supply routes. He says that to negotiate with the VC or "neutralize" South Vietnam is "surrendering on the installment plan."

SOUTH VIETNAM: A Buddhist girl in Nha Trang immolates herself as part of the continuing Buddhist protest against the regime in Saigon.

January 27–28
SOUTH VIETNAM: The Armed Forces Council ousts Premier Huong and his civilian government in a bloodless coup; General Nguyen Khanh is empowered to establish a new government. The council announces that it will observe the constitution of October 1964 and that the promised elections for a national congress will proceed. The Buddhist leaders immediately order their followers to stop the antigovernment demonstrations and hunger strikes, but they do not hide their dislike of Khanh and the U.S. influence.

February
SOUTH VIETNAM: There are reliable reports that the VC control much of the South Vietnamese countryside through a highly organized "shadow government."

SEA WAR: The aircraft carriers *Hancock* and *Coral Sea* are ordered to depart the waters off Vietnam and rejoin the Seventh Fleet, as part of an apparent reaction to the reduction in the number of aggressive actions.

February 1
CUBA: A Cuban publication reports that Cubans are helping to train the Viet Cong.

February 3
USA – DOMESTIC: A poll of some 600 prominent Americans, conducted by the Council on Foreign Relations, reveals that most approve of U.S. aims in Vietnam but feel the Johnson administration policy is failing; many advocate immediate withdrawal but some call for widening the war.

February 4
SOUTH VIETNAM: McGeorge Bundy, special assistant for national security, arrives in Saigon for talks with the U.S. ambassador, General Maxwell Taylor, about how to deal with the political situation in Saigon.

February 6
NORTH VIETNAM: Soviet premier Aleksey Kosygin arrives in Hanoi. There is worldwide speculation that this visit and Bundy's visit to Saigon are linked and that the United States and the Soviet Union have agreed to pressure their "clients" into negotiations. Both Bundy and Kosygin deny that this is the case.

February 7
GROUND WAR: Viet Cong attack the U.S. Army helicopter base at Camp Holloway and simultaneously blow up the nearby U.S. advisers' barracks at Pleiku in the Central Highlands, killing nine and wounding 76 U.S. servicemen, mostly from the 52nd Combat Aviation Battalion. Losses in materiel include 10 aircraft destroyed and 15 damaged. At the same time, the VC also destroy part of the fuel dump in Phu Yan Province. When word of these attacks arrives, McGeorge Bundy joins Westmoreland and Taylor at MACV headquarters and they telephone President Johnson to urge immediate retaliatory air raids against North Vietnam. Bundy follows this with a memorandum to the president advocating "a policy of sustained reprisal" against North Vietnam.

USA – GOVERNMENT: President Johnson convenes his top advisers to discuss "appropriate and fitting" retaliatory raids in response to the VC attacks on U.S. installations in South Vietnam; all present except Senator Mike Mansfield (D-Mont.) and Vice President Hubert Humphrey concur. As a result, Humphrey is kept out of Johnson's Vietnam planning for about a year, until he satisfies Johnson that he will support presidential policies.

AIR WAR: As part of the already-planned Operation Flaming Dart, 49 U.S. Navy jets from the carriers *Coral Sea* and *Hancock* drop bombs on barracks and staging areas at Dong Hoi, a guerrilla training camp 40 miles north of the 17th parallel in North Vietnam in retaliation for VC attacks on Pleiku.

February 8
SOUTH VIETNAM. A prearranged plan for evacuating U.S. dependents goes into effect and wives and children are airlifted out of Saigon in case North Vietnam, or another Communist power, decides to retaliate for the Flaming Dart raids on North Vietnam.

AIR WAR: In a follow-up to Flaming Dart, South Vietnamese air vice-marshal Nguyen Cao Ky leads a raid, escorted by U.S. jets, to bomb a North Vietnamese military communications center at Vinh Linh.

USA – GOVERNMENT: McGeorge Bundy, just returned from Vietnam, defends the air raids as "right and necessary." Senate Majority Leader Mansfield (D-Mont.) and GOP leader Everett Dirksen (R-Ill.) support the president's decision, but Senators Wayne Morse (D-Oreg.) and Ernest Gruening (D-Alas.) oppose the action.

February 9

USA – MILITARY: U.S. Marine Corps Hawk air defense missile battalion is deployed to Danang.

INTERNATIONAL: There is considerable reaction around the world to what is perceived as a new escalation by the United States in Vietnam. Predictably, both Communist China and the Soviet Union threaten to intervene if the United States continues to apply its military might on behalf of the South Vietnamese government. In Moscow, some 2,000 demonstrators, led by Vietnamese and Chinese students and clearly supported by the authorities, attack the U.S. embassy. Britain and Australia support the U.S. action, but France calls for negotiations.

February 10

TERRORISM: Viet Cong terrorists blow up the U.S. barracks at Qui Nhon, 75 miles east of Pleiku on the central coast by planting a 100-pound explosive charge under the building; 23 American soldiers from the 140th Maintenance Detachment are killed and 22 are wounded.

February 11

AIR WAR: In retaliation for the Qui Nhon attack, President Johnson orders a second and heavier reprisal raid, Flaming Dart II. Some 160 U.S. and South Vietnamese planes, both land and carrier-based, bomb the barracks and staging points at Chan Hoa and Chap Le, 160 miles and 40 miles respectively, north of the 17th parallel. Three U.S. Navy planes are downed, but only one pilot is rescued.

February 12–16

INTERNATIONAL: The world continues to react to American air raids on North Vietnam. The Communist Chinese threaten to send "volunteers" to aid the Viet Cong. There are anti-U.S. demonstrations in various cities, including a break-in at the U.S. embassy in Budapest, Hungary, by some 200 Asian and African students. U Thant, secretary-general of the United Nations, calls for peace talks inside and outside the United Nations.

February 13

USA – GOVERNMENT: President Johnson decides to undertake the sustained bombing of North Vietnam that he and his advisers have discussed for a year. The objective of the campaign is to employ air power in ever-intensifying degrees "to send a message" in an effort to persuade North Vietnam to abandon its support of the Viet Cong and enter negotiations to end the war on terms favorable to South Vietnam and the United States. It is also meant to boost the morale of South Vietnamese and demonstrate U.S. resolve. Called Operation Rolling Thunder, the bombing campaign will go on for over three years, with occasional suspensions, until President Johnson calls a halt to it on October 31, 1968.

February 16

SOUTH VIETNAM: The Armed Forces Council, which seized power on January 27, appoints Dr. Phan Huy Quat as premier and reappoints Phan Khac Suu as chief of state. Quat, a physician with considerable experience in government, appoints a cabinet that includes representatives from many of Vietnam's political, religious, and military factions.

USA – GOVERNMENT: Former president Harry Truman issues a statement that gives his full support to President Johnson's policies in Vietnam and attacks the "irresponsible critics . . . who have neither all the facts—nor the answers."

February 17

SOUTH VIETNAM: The Armed Forces Council announces the formation of a 20-member national legislative council.

USA – GOVERNMENT: President Johnson meets with former president Dwight D. Eisenhower to demonstrate the caliber of his supporters.

February 18

USA – GOVERNMENT: The State Department sends secret cables to the U.S. ambassadors in London and eight embassies in the Far East advising of the forthcoming

Secretary of Defense Robert S. McNamara conducts a press conference at the Pentagon, February 1965. *(National Archives)*

bombing operations over North Vietnam and instructing the American ambassadors to inform the governments concerned "in strictest confidence" and to report reactions. They are to stress that "all actions will be adequate and measured and fitting to [North Vietnam's] aggression."

AIR WAR: American pilots fly B-57 Canberra bombers and North American F-100 jet fighters against the VC near An Khe in support of ARVN troops in the first mission in which no South Vietnamese airmen participate, indicating an escalation in U.S. involvement in the air war.

February 19

USA – GOVERNMENT: The first Rolling Thunder raid originally scheduled for February 20 is postponed because of the upheaval in the South Vietnamese government. The State Department sends a message to the nine U.S. embassies previously contacted, rescinding until further notice the instructions to notify heads of government of the planned air war.

February 19–25

SOUTH VIETNAM: Dissident ARVN officers move several battalions into Saigon with the intention of ousting General Khanh from leadership, but he escapes to Dalat. Ky meets with the dissident officers and agrees to their demand for the dismissal of Khanh. Shortly before dawn on February 21, Khanh submits his resignation, claiming that a "foreign hand" was behind the coup. On February 25, as a face-saving device and to get him out of the country, General Khanh is appointed "roving ambassador" by the "Young Turks" who had ousted him and departs South Vietnam never to return.

February 22–26

USA – MILITARY: General Westmoreland cables Washington to request two battalions of U.S. Marines to protect the U.S. airbase at Danang. Ambassador Taylor, aware of Westmoreland's plan, disagrees and cables President Johnson that he has "grave reservations" and warns that such a step could encourage South Vietnam to "shuck off greater responsibilities" and that "it will be very difficult to hold the line" once the deployment begins, thus leading to a growing American commitment. The Joint Chiefs of Staff, however, supports Westmoreland's request and on February 26, Washington cables Taylor and Westmoreland that the troops will be sent, and that Taylor should "secure GVN [Government of South Vietnam] approval."

February 24

AIR WAR: U.S. Air Force aircraft from Bien Hoa and Danang airbases attack VC concentrations in Binh Dinh Province in support of a CIDG company and their Special Forces advisers.

February 25

SOUTH KOREA: The first contingent of South Korean troops from "Peace Dove" Engineer Task Force arrives at Bien Hoa. The 600-man task force begins construction of a major circumferential highway around Saigon.

February 27

USA – GOVERNMENT: U.S. State Department issues 14,000-word "White Paper" detailing North Vietnam's "aggression" and its "campaign to conquer South Vietnam." Citing "massive evidence," including testimony of North Vietnamese troops who had defected or been captured in South Vietnam, this report claims that nearly 20,000 Viet Cong military and technical personnel have entered South Vietnam through the "infiltration pipeline" along the Ho Chi Minh Trail from the North and they remain under military command from Hanoi.

March 1–4

SOUTH VIETNAM: As directed by President Johnson, Ambassador Taylor calls on Premier Phan Huy Quat to inform him that the United States is prepared to send 3,500 U.S. Marines to Vietnam. Three days later, a formal request is submitted by the U.S. embassy asking the South Vietnamese government to "invite" the United States to send the marines. Premier Quat, a figurehead, has to obtain approval from the real power, General Nguyen Van Thieu, chief of the Armed Forces Council. Thieu approves, but asks that the marines be "brought ashore in the most inconspicuous way feasible."

This is also the day that a South Vietnamese government official first states conditions for ending the war that "the Communists have provoked." According to the official, the Communists must stop all infiltration, subversions, and sabotage, and offer "concrete, efficient, and appropriate means" to guarantee South Vietnam's security.

March 2

AIR WAR: Operation Rolling Thunder, the sustained aerial bombardment of North Vietnam, is initiated. In the largest raid to date, over 100 U.S. Air Force jet bombers strike an ammunition depot at Xom Bang, 10 miles inside North Vietnam, while 60 South Vietnamese Air Force Skyraiders bomb the Quang Khe naval base, 65 miles north of the 17th parallel. Six U.S. planes are downed, but only one U.S. pilot is not recovered. Captain Hayden J. Lockhart, flying an F-100, is shot down and becomes the first air force pilot to be taken prisoner by the North Vietnamese.

USA – GOVERNMENT: In Washington, President Johnson has not yet approved any extended series of bombing raids. For the next two weeks, he will consider the conflicting proposals of various military and civilian leaders. The official position is that this air raid does not represent a change in U.S. policy, but it does imply the possibility of additional raids until North Vietnam ends its support of the Viet Cong.

March 3

AIR WAR: Over 30 USAF jets strike targets along the Ho Chi Minh Trail. The U.S. State Department announces that these raids are authorized by the powers granted to President Johnson in the August 1964 Tonkin Gulf Resolution.

March 3–5

INTERNATIONAL: The concern about the escalation of the conflict in Vietnam grows in the international community. Communists condemn the new bombing campaign; Cuba announces that it will aid North Vietnam. In Moscow, 2,000 students attack the U.S. embassy. In Canada, Prime Minister Lester Pearson expresses concern about the risk of additional escalation, but says he understands the U.S. position. In Britain, however, there is mounting pressure against the government's support for U.S. policies.

March 5

USA – MILITARY: Military reports are surfacing of complaints by U.S. servicemen in Vietnam about shortages of ammunition and equipment, while some of these items are being sold on the black market in Saigon. At the Danang air base, the United States is clearing a 500-yard peripheral zone and moving thousands of South Vietnamese from the area; an eight-mile-deep special military sector is being established around the air base. All of this lends credence to rumors that U.S. Marines will be sent to Vietnam.

March 6

USA – GOVERNMENT: The White House confirms that the United States is sending two battalions of U.S. Marines (3,500 men) at the request of South Vietnam to be deployed in security work at the Danang air base, freeing South Vietnamese troops for combat.

March 7

USA – MILITARY: U.S. Advisory Campaign officially ends. During this phase of the war, U.S. troops peak at 23,310.

March 8

USA – MILITARY: The USS *Henrico, Union,* and *Vancouver,* carrying the 9th Marine Expeditionary Brigade, take up station some 4,000 yards off Red Beach Two, north of Danang, and begin to land the marines, who arrive on the beach at 0815 hours, where they are met by sightseers, South Vietnamese officers, Vietnamese girls with leis, and four American soldiers with a large sign that reads: "Welcome Gallant Marines." General Westmoreland, who had expected the marines to maintain a low profile, is reportedly "appalled." Within two hours, Battalion Landing Team 1/3 (1st Battalion 3rd Marines) begins landing at Danang air base. At the same time, 1st Marine Aircraft Wing deploys from Japan and Okinawa to Vietnam to support U.S. Marine operations in I Corps.

March 9

USA – GOVERNMENT: President Johnson authorizes the use of napalm by U.S. planes bombing targets in North Vietnam.

GROUND WAR: The marines continue to land. Among today's arrivals is the first U.S. armor—an M48A3 tank of the 3rd Marine Tank Battalion. It will be followed in a few days by more tanks, including those with flame-throwing capability. There is scattered firing from VC hidden ashore, but no marines are hit. The mission of the marines, now numbering 5,000, is restricted to the defense of the airbase, both from the immediate perimeter and from the high ground along a ridge to the west.

DIPLOMACY: The U.S. State Department formally rejects U Thant's proposal of February 24 that the United States join with other major powers in negotiating a solution to the war, on the grounds that the government cannot support any such plan until North Vietnam ceases its "aggression."

March 10

USA – MILITARY: A Pentagon press release declares that the marines at Danang are there at the "request" of the South Vietnamese government; but in reality the regime has been neither consulted nor informed in advance. South Vietnamese premier Phan Huy Quat later says that there had been a general understanding that U.S. troops would be committed, but that he "only learned the details at the last minute."

USA – DOMESTIC: Expressing support for the Johnson administration's policies in Vietnam, the Republican Party Coordinating Committee attacks Democratic Party members who raise "disruptive voices of appeasement."

March 11

SEA WAR: U.S. Navy's Seventh Fleet begins Operation Market Time, the blockade of South Vietnam coastal waters to detect and interdict waterborne infiltration and resupply by seizing or destroying enemy craft. The navy assigns two destroyers and six destroyer escorts to this mission. The Coastal Surveillance Force will eventually assume this mission.

March 12

GROUND WAR: The last of the initial marine ground contingent arrives. This brings the total number of U.S. military personnel in South Vietnam to 27,000.

March 13

USA – MILITARY: General Westmoreland begins work on a report titled "Commander's Estimate of the Situation in South Vietnam," which he will complete on March 26. The completed report predicts that the bombing campaign against the North will not show tangible results until June at the earliest and that, in the meantime, the South Vietnamese army will need American reinforcements. Therefore, the final report will recommend an increase of 40,000 U.S. troops. This will bring the total U.S. troop commitment to 70,000 and provide 17 maneuver battalions. The report also indicates that even more troops might be needed if the bombing fails to achieve results.

March 14–15

AIR WAR: In some of the heaviest raids of the air war so far, 24 South Vietnamese planes, led by Air Vice-Marshal Ky and supported by U.S. jets strike barracks and depots on Con Co ("Tiger") Island, 20 miles off the coast of North Vietnam. The next day, 100 American aircraft strike the ammunition depot at Phu Qui, 100 miles south of Hanoi. This is the second set of raids in Operation Rolling Thunder and the first in which U.S. planes use napalm.

March 15

USA – MILITARY: General Harold K. Johnson, army chief of staff, reports to President Johnson and Secretary McNamara upon his return from a fact-finding trip to Vietnam. He admits that the recent air raids have not affected the course of the war and recommends a division of American troops be dispatched to South Vietnam to hold coastal enclaves and defend the Central Highlands in order to free Saigon government forces for offensive action against the VC. General Johnson also advocates creating a four-division force of U.S. and SEATO troops to patrol the DMZ along the border separating North and South Vietnam and the Laotian border region. The president does not accept these recommendations.

March 16

USA – GOVERNMENT: Undersecretary of State George Ball openly criticizes France for repudiating the "common burden" of the anti-Communist world by failing to support U.S. efforts in South Vietnam.

March 16–19

INTERNATIONAL: In London, Soviet foreign minister Andrei Gromyko begins conferring with British government leaders for five days, but, after five days, the British are unable to persuade the Russians to join in convening peace talks on the situation in Vietnam.

March 17

AIR WAR: The South Vietnamese air force bombs the village of Man Guang in the Danang area, killing some 45 civilians, including 37 children; the government claims that the VC flag had been flying over the village.

March 18

USA – GOVERNMENT: A rift begins to develop in South Vietnam between the U.S. military and the press corps, who charge that curbs on coverage are so strict as to constitute censorship. U.S. military and government spokesmen claim that South Vietnam has imposed some of the restrictions.

March 19

AIR WAR: In the fourth Rolling Thunder raid, 110 U.S. planes bomb military targets at Phu Van and Vinh Son in North Vietnam.

March 20

USA – MILITARY: The Joint Chiefs of Staff proposes sending two American divisions and one South Korean division to South Vietnam, about 100,000 troops, for offensive operations against the Viet Cong.

March 21

AIR WAR: U.S. and South Vietnamese planes attack the North Vietnamese base at Vu Can, 15 miles north of the DMZ.

March 22–24

USA – GOVERNMENT: The State Department confirms a report out of Saigon that the United States has supplied the South Vietnamese armed forces with a "non-lethal gas which disables temporarily" for use "in tactical situations in which the Viet Cong intermingle with or take refuge among non-combatants, rather than use artillery or aerial bombardment." The gas has already been used three times—with little effect. This triggers a storm of criticism around the world; the North Vietnamese and the Soviets loudly protest this introduction of "poison gas" into the war. Secretary of State Rusk insists at a news conference on March 24 that the United States is "not embarking upon gas warfare," but is merely employing "a gas which has been commonly adopted by the police forces of the world as riot-control agents."

March 23

AIR WAR: U.S. and South Vietnamese planes bomb a radar station at Ba Binh, 10 miles north of the 17th parallel, and attack a North Vietnamese convoy on Route 1.

USSR: Leonid Brezhnev hints that the Soviet Union may join the North Vietnamese in the war and claims that many Russians have already volunteered to serve. U.S. authorities and most Western diplomats continue to doubt that the Soviet Union will allow Russian personnel to become involved in the war.

March 24
USA – GOVERNMENT: Testifying before a Senate committee, Secretary of Defense McNamara claims that if the Communists are allowed to win in Vietnam, the United States will have to renew the struggle elsewhere. On this same day, John McNaughton, assistant secretary of defense for international security affairs, and one of McNamara's most trusted associates, drafts a crucial memo titled "Plan for Action for South Vietnam," to be used in the National Security Council sessions on April 1–2. His conclusion is that the situation cannot be saved without "extreme measures."

USA – DOMESTIC: The first "teach-in" is conducted at the University of Michigan at Ann Arbor where some 200 faculty participate by holding special seminars. On March 26, there will be a similar teach-in at Columbia University in New York City; this form of protest eventually will spread to many colleges and universities.

AIR WAR: U.S. and South Vietnamese planes attack North Vietnam radar and military radio stations and sink four ships at Quang Khe harbor.

CHINA: The official Communist newspaper says that China is ready to aid the Viet Cong with men and materiel if requested, but it is clear from the statement that the Chinese are releasing it to preempt the Soviet Union in order to appear as a closer ally of the Vietnamese.

March 25
USA – GOVERNMENT: During a statement about aiding Southeast Asian nations, President Lyndon Johnson makes an indirect offer of "economic and social cooperation" to North Vietnam if peace can be restored. Nothing comes of the offer.

March 26
AIR WAR: Forty U.S. planes bomb four radar sites in North Vietnam as Operation Rolling Thunder continues.

USSR: The Communist Party's Central Committee in Moscow ratifies a defense accord with North Vietnam.

March 27
USA – MILITARY: The Joint Chiefs of Staff presents a proposal for an intense bombing campaign that will start on road and rail lines south of the 20th parallel and then "march north" week by week to isolate North Vietnam from China by cutting road and rail lines north of Hanoi. The later phases of the campaign would target port facilities and industries outside populated areas. However, the president and Secretary McNamara decline to approve a multi-week program, preferring to retain continual control over timing and individual target selection.

It is revealed today that U.S. and South Vietnamese planes are using herbicides to defoliate jungles and destroy crops.

SOUTH VIETNAM: Lightning strikes U.S. camp defenses at Plei Do Lin and triggers land mine explosions that result in 88 casualties.

March 29

USA – GOVERNMENT: The JCS proposal to send three divisions to South Vietnam is discussed at a meeting among the Joint Chiefs, Secretary McNamara, and Ambassador Taylor, who is in Washington for the April 1–2 National Security Council meeting. Taylor opposes the plan because he feels that the South Vietnamese might resent the presence of so many foreign troops and that there was still no military necessity for them. The proposal will be one of the topics of discussion at the NSC deliberations.

GROUND WAR: ARVN troops discover a Viet Cong camp some 60 miles northwest of Saigon, in Tay Ninh Province, and confiscate supplies, rations, and ammunition.

AIR WAR: Forty-two U.S. planes drop 45 tons of bombs on the Bach Long radar station in North Vietnam.

March 30

TERRORISM: A terrorist bomb, detonated outside the American embassy in Saigon, virtually destroys the building and kills 19 Vietnamese, two Americans, and a Filipino while wounding 183 others, among them Deputy Ambassador U. Alexis Johnson. Although some U.S. military leaders urge special retaliatory raids on North Vietnam, President Johnson refuses permission. Congress quickly appropriates $1 million to reconstruct the embassy.

March 31

USA – GOVERNMENT: President Johnson, responding to questions from reporters about administration plans and policy in South Vietnam, says, "I know of no far-reaching strategy that is being suggested or promulgated." In fact, he is contemplating giving the order to authorize U.S. troops to go from defensive to offensive tactics in Vietnam.

AIR WAR: Over 70 USAF planes make the largest incendiary attack to date on a Viet Cong concentration in the Boi Loi Forest, 25 miles northwest of Saigon. To establish that this is not a retaliatory raid for the previous day's bombing of the embassy, U.S. spokesmen state that the raid has been planned for months, and that preparations included spraying to defoliate trees and using leaflets and loudspeakers to warn the civilian population to leave the area.

April

USA – MILITARY: U.S. 1st Logistics Command is formed at Long Binh near Saigon to control logistics buildup in Vietnam.

AIR WAR: U.S. Air Force begins Operation Steel Tiger to strike targets in the Laotian panhandle to interdict troops and supply movement down the Ho Chi Minh Trail.

April 1

DIPLOMACY: The heads of state of 17 nonaligned nations appeal to the United Nations, the United States, Britain, the Soviet Union, and North and South Vietnam to redress the situation in Vietnam by "peaceful solution through negotiations." President Johnson will formally respond on April 8, saying that the United States agrees with the goals but can not negotiate until North Vietnam ceases its aggression against South Vietnam.

GROUND WAR: In one of the largest battles since early February, ARVN troops clash with Viet Cong forces 25 miles south of Danang.

April 1–2

USA – GOVERNMENT: During two days of National Security Council meetings, President Johnson considers deploying more ground troops to Vietnam. Ultimately, Johnson accedes to Westmoreland's request for additional marines and will authorize the deployment of two more battalions and an increase of 18,000–20,000 support troops. Ambassador Taylor, called to Washington for the meeting, insists that the troops continue to be restricted to defending U.S. bases and other installations along the coast. Westmoreland argues that "a good offense is the best defense." Johnson backs his general and authorizes the U.S. forces to go on the offensive. In statements to the public at this time, the president conceals his change in the mission for the forces in South Vietnam, telling reporters that "no far-reaching strategy . . . is being suggested or promulgated."

April 3–5

AIR WAR: In the farthest north raids of the Rolling Thunder operation and the first explicitly aimed at nonmilitary targets, U.S. and South Vietnamese planes bomb a series of bridges and roads in North Vietnam, to include the major rail links to Hanoi. Four Russian-built MiG fighters attack the U.S. planes in the first reported combat by the North Vietnamese air force. Six U.S. aircraft are shot down on these raids.

April 4

AUSTRALIA: Prime Minister Robert Menzies says that the U.S. intervention in Vietnam is an act of moral courage, in that Americans have accepted the challenge presented by communism to "human freedom."

April 5–7

GROUND WAR: A fierce three-day battle in the Mekong Delta leaves six Americans dead and a reported 276 Viet Cong fatal casualties. In an air and amphibious assault at Vinh Loc on the Ca Mau Peninsula, 16 ARVN troops are killed.

April 6

USA – GOVERNMENT: McGeorge Bundy drafts and signs National Security Action Memorandum 328 on behalf of the president; this "pivotal document" constitutes the "marching orders" developed in NSC meetings on April 1–2 that authorize U.S. personnel to take the offensive to secure "enclaves" and support ARVN operations. The memorandum says that the means approved by the president "should be taken as rapidly as practicable," but in such a way as to "minimize any appearance of sudden changes in policy."

April 7

USA – GOVERNMENT: In a major policy speech broadcast from Johns Hopkins University (and seen or heard by an estimated 60,000,000 people), President Johnson says that the United States is ready to engage in "unconditional discussions" to settle the war. However, in the course of his speech, he sets forth several conditions before any negotiations will take place. Additionally, he calls for a vast economic plan for Southeast Asia, for which he will ask Congress to approve $1 billion. Western nations and U Thant of the United Nations support Johnson's call for negotiations.

April 8

NORTH VIETNAM: Premier Pham Van Dong, at a meeting of the National Assembly in Hanoi, sets four conditions for negotiations and peace: independence for all Vietnamese, nonintervention by foreign powers, political settlement of all issues, and reunification of the country. These four points will remain fixed as the Communists' nonnegotiable conditions.

AIR WAR: U.S. jets fly 63 sorties against Viet Cong concentrations in Kontum Province.

April 9

AIR WAR: In the course of U.S. raids over North Vietnam, four carrier-based F-4 Phantom jets clash with Chinese MiGs off Hainan Island, the large Chinese island southeast of Haiphong. On April 12, the United States will admit that one Phantom and its two pilots were lost during the engagement.

April 9–12

DIPLOMACY: North Vietnam, China, and the Soviet Union reject the proposal for negotiations made by President Johnson on April 7, calling it a "trick."

April 10–14

USA – MILITARY: The 5,000 U.S. Marines already stationed in the area of Danang are reinforced with the arrival of the 2nd Battalion, 3rd Marines and the 3rd Battalion, 4th Marines, which are deployed at Hue-Phu Bai and Danang. The marines immediately push their patrol perimeters out past the immediate defenses of the U.S. installations, establishing active rather than passive defense measures. Meanwhile, the F-4B Phantom II jets of VMFA-531 arrive at Danang, becoming the first marine fixed-wing tactical aircraft to utilize the base.

April 11

USA – MILITARY: General Westmoreland cables Admiral Sharp, U.S. commander in chief, Pacific, reiterating an earlier request for the U.S. Army's 173rd Airborne Brigade in Okinawa.

GROUND WAR: ARVN troops battle Viet Cong forces north of Bong Son, along Highway 1 in the Central Highlands.

April 13

AIR WAR: U.S. and South Vietnamese aircraft strike the Thanh Yuen bridge and two radar positions previously hit in North Vietnam.

April 14

USA – MILITARY: In response to General Westmoreland's April 11 request, the Joint Chiefs of Staff orders the deployment of the 173rd Airborne Brigade from Okinawa to the Bien Hoa–Vung Tau area "to secure vital U.S. installations." Ambassador Taylor cables the State Department saying that the order "comes as a complete surprise." He still resists the increase of U.S. combat personnel on the ground in Vietnam and asks that deployment of the brigade be held up, but he is overruled.

GROUND WAR: It is reported that South Vietnamese forces have discovered some 4 million pounds of rice and 21 stolen trucks in a Viet Cong stronghold 30 miles north of Saigon.

AIR WAR: Thirty U.S. Air Force planes bomb the radar installations on Hon Mat Island.

April 15–16

AIR WAR: U.S. planes conduct armed reconnaissance along Highways 7 and 8 in North Vietnam and bomb the boat landing at Muong Sen. Other U.S. planes fly the first night operation in North Vietnam. It is being reported, meanwhile, that sites near Hanoi are being prepared for SAM II missiles to be provided by the Soviet Union. South Vietnamese bombers, led by Air Vice-Marshal Ky, sink four ships in another night raid. In the largest air strike of the war to date, U.S. and South Vietnamese planes drop 1,000 tons of bombs on a major Viet Cong stronghold in Tay Ninh Province, preparatory to an airlift of ARVN troops into the area the next day.

April 17

USA – GOVERNMENT: President Johnson, in a statement from his ranch at Johnson City, Texas, says that the United States will continue its air strikes against North Vietnam but also reaffirms his willingness to participate in "unconditional discussion." Ambassador Taylor cables McGeorge Bundy protesting the "hasty and ill-conceived" proposal for the deployment of more ground forces to South Vietnam.

USSR: After secret talks in Moscow, Leonid Brezhnev and North Vietnamese foreign secretary Le Duan issue a joint communiqué reiterating that the Soviet Union will send volunteers if North Vietnam requests them.

April 18

USA – DOMESTIC: Newspaper publishers claim there is widespread support for Johnson's policies. Two Queens College students report that they have collected 2,000 signatures on a petition backing the president's policies.

INTERNATIONAL: In his annual Easter message, Pope Paul VI calls for "constructive collaboration" to obtain peace but does not mention Vietnam by name.

AIR WAR: U.S. war planes hit several targets throughout North Vietnam, including troop barracks at Dong Thanh, a ferryboat in Song Trac River, and highways in the region north of the DMZ.

April 19–20

USA – GOVERNMENT: U.S. military and civilian leaders, including Secretary of Defense McNamara and JCS chairman Earle Wheeler, meet in Honolulu with General Westmoreland and Ambassador Taylor. The conferees agree to double U.S.

military forces from the present approved level of 40,200 to 82,000 and to seek additional forces of up to some 7,250 men from Australia and South Korea, providing a total of 17 maneuver battalions. They discuss but do not recommend a possible later deployment of 11 U.S. and six South Korean battalions, which would bring the total U.S.-"third country" combat capability to 34 battalions.

April 21

USA – GOVERNMENT: Secretary McNamara forwards the Honolulu recommendations to the president, together with a notation on possible later deployment of the army's 1st Cavalry Division (Airmobile) and the Third Marine Expeditionary Force.

SOUTH VIETNAM: To protest the conduct of the war by his government, a 16-year-old novice Buddhist monk immolates himself. Another monk will set himself aflame three days later.

GROUND WAR: The CIA and the Defense Intelligence Agency report that a regiment of the 325th PAVN Division has been identified in South Vietnam, a "most ominous" development that proves that main force North Vietnamese battalions have entered the war. This is clear proof that the conflict is no longer solely an externally supported insurgency; it now includes effectively an invasion from North Vietnam.

April 22

GROUND WAR: A patrol of the 3rd Marine Reconnaissance Battalion engages the Viet Cong for the first time at Binh Thai, nine miles southwest of Danang, with no U.S. casualties. Elsewhere, VC guerrillas infiltrate within three miles of Danang and fire on a South Vietnamese radio station.

AIR WAR: The virtual round-the-clock bombing raids by U.S. and South Vietnamese air forces in recent weeks have destroyed so many bridges and highways that North Vietnamese supply routes and transportation are said to be seriously impaired.

April 23

USA – GOVERNMENT: In a speech before the American Society of International Law, Secretary of State Rusk attacks the "gullibility of educated men and the stubborn disregard of plain facts by men who are supposed to be helping our young to learn"; this is in reference to the growing number of academics who are criticizing the bombing raids but not the violence perpetrated by the Communists.

April 24

USA – GOVERNMENT: President Johnson issues an executive order designating Vietnam a "combat area" and authorizes "hostile fire" pay, retroactive to January 1, 1964.

AIR WAR: Over 200 U.S. and South Vietnamese planes bomb bridges and ferries in North Vietnam in a concentrated effort to destroy supply routes to the South.

April 26

USA – GOVERNMENT: In a televised news conference, Secretary of Defense McNamara reports that the infiltration of both arms and personnel into South Vietnam "has grown progressively more flagrant and more unconstrained." McNamara, however, refuses to answer questions from the press as to whether the United States planned to send more troops. The war, he said, is now costing the nation about $1.5 billion per year.

USA – DOMESTIC: A Louis Harris poll indicates that some 57 percent of Americans support Johnson's handling of the war.

CAMBODIA: Some 20,000 people, mostly students, attack the U.S. embassy in Phnom Penh and rip down the U.S. flag in protest.

April 27

USA – GOVERNMENT: President Johnson renews his offer of "unconditional discussions . . . with any government concerned," and defends the U.S. bombing raids, saying, "Our restraint was viewed as weakness. We could no longer stand by while attacks mounted."

USA – DOMESTIC: Former presidential candidate Barry Goldwater says Johnson's policies are the same that he advocated in 1964.

April 28

USA – GOVERNMENT: CIA director John A. McCone sends a personal memo to President Johnson stating his view that unless the United States is willing to intensify the bombing of North Vietnam, there is no utility in committing more U.S. ground troops.

April 30

USA – MILITARY: The JCS presents a detailed program for deploying 48,000 U.S. and 5,250 third-country troops in Vietnam—an increase over the numbers agreed to in the Honolulu conference, but one that includes "a healthy support package." The JCS says that these additional forces are "to bolster GVN forces during their continued build-up, secure bases and installations, conduct counterinsurgency combat operations with the RVNAF" and prepare for the arrival of additional U.S. ground forces.

May

USA – MILITARY: U.S. III Marine Amphibious Force headquarters is established in Danang to control marine combat operations in I Corps; III MAF will be the senior marine headquarters in-country, replacing 9th Marine Expeditionary Brigade.

May 2

CHINA: A Beijing radio broadcast charges that the Soviet Union, which is reportedly backing some kind of peace conference before the total withdrawal of U.S. forces, has joined the "U.S. aggressors" in a "peace negotiation swindle."

GROUND WAR: The first patrols by U.S. Marines in tanks are met only by scattered sniper fire.

May 3

USA – MILITARY: About 3,500 men of the U.S. Army's 173rd Airborne Brigade begin landing in South Vietnam; the unit deploys from Okinawa and will conduct combat operations in the III Corps tactical zone initially. The brigade is the first U.S. Army combat unit assigned to Vietnam. Part of the brigade goes to Bien Hoa air base, 20 miles northwest of Saigon, others to the base at Vung Tau. The 173rd Airborne Brigade includes the 3rd Battalion, 319th Artillery, the first U.S. artillery unit assigned to Vietnam.

May 4

USA – DOMESTIC: A three-man "truth team," sent out by the State Department to explain the administration's policies in Vietnam, makes its first stop at the University of Iowa. There (and later) it meets considerable opposition, but its members will claim that such opposition represents a minority view.

AIR WAR: U.S. planes sink three boats said to be carrying Viet Cong guerrillas near Danang.

May 4–7

USA – GOVERNMENT: President Johnson asks Congress for a $700 million supplemental appropriation "to meet mounting military requirements in Vietnam." The House will pass the bill, 408–7, on May 5; the Senate will approve it 88–3 and Johnson will sign it on May 7.

May 6

SOUTH VIETNAM: The Armed Forces Council dissolves; its leader, General Nguyen Van Thieu, says this shows that the civilian regime of Premier Quat can govern and that the military leaders have no political ambitions.

May 7

USA – MILITARY: A 6,000-man brigade of the 4th Marines deploys to Chu Lai, on the coast some 55 miles south of Danang, to build a second jet air base, including a new type of field, a Short Airfield for Tactical Support (SATS)—a 4,000-foot airstrip of aluminum matting, with arrestor wires as on an aircraft carrier. (A catapult will be installed two years later; until then, the planes will make rocket-assisted takeoffs.) By June 1, the field will be operational.

May 9–10

GROUND WAR: A two-day battle in the Binh Duong area, 25 miles northwest of Saigon, begins when the VC start shelling ARVN positions near Thu Dau Mot. Afterward it will be revealed that ARVN troops fled from the engagement when they became frightened by their own planes flying overhead.

May 10

AIR WAR: U.S. and South Vietnamese planes strike at 12 bridges in North Vietnam and claim to have knocked out four.

May 10–15

GROUND WAR: More than a thousand Viet Cong troops overrun Song Be, the capital of Phuoc Long Province, and occupy it for seven hours before ARVN forces recover it supported by a heavy air attack. Five U.S. military advisers and 48 South Vietnamese are killed, and 85 Viet Cong are reported killed. U.S. and ARVN forces will pursue the Viet Cong for several days but fail to engage them. The Americans later charge that the Viet Cong attacked their compound after overrunning the adjacent ARVN camp, which failed to offer any resistance.

May 11

USA – MILITARY: General Westmoreland and Deputy Premier Nguyen Van Thieu make a parachute jump together. Also this day, the 1st Marine Aircraft Wing flies in to establish its advance headquarters at Danang.

May 12

DIPLOMACY: The U.S. ambassador in Moscow, Foy Kohler, tries to deliver a message from Washington to the North Vietnamese embassy, which says that the United States will suspend bombing of North Vietnam for several delays in hope of eliciting reciprocal "constructive" gestures from the North Vietnamese. This effort will be known as Operation Mayflower (all subsequent diplomatic moves will be code-named for flowers). The North Vietnamese refuse even to receive Kohler and return the message unopened.

GROUND WAR: Soldiers of the 173rd Airborne Brigade conduct combat operations near Bien Hoa Air Base but encounter no enemy contact.

May 13

USA – GOVERNMENT: President Johnson, in a nationally televised address, accuses Communist China of opposing a political solution that could be in the best interests even of North Vietnam, because China's goal is to dominate "all of Asia."

NORTH VIETNAM: Hanoi claims the Viet Cong held their first "congress" in a "liberated area" of South Vietnam in early May. According to the announcement, the meeting is attended by the National Liberation Front's president, Nguyen Huu Tho, and 150 "outstanding cadres and fighters" from the Viet Cong.

GROUND WAR: Disguised as South Vietnamese troops, Viet Cong guerrillas attack a textile mill only five miles north of Saigon, killing eight and wounding 11.

May 13–18

AIR WAR: President Johnson orders a pause in Operation Rolling Thunder in the hope that it may elicit a favorable response from Hanoi. By this action, the president intends to "clear a path either toward restoration of peace or toward increased military action, depending on the reaction of the Communists." North Vietnam's only response is to charge on May 18 that the halt was only "an effort to camouflage American intensification of the war and deceive world opinion."

May 14

USA – DOMESTIC: George Meany, president of the AFL-CIO, criticizes "academic" opponents of President Johnson's conduct of the war. Organized labor largely supports the administration's Vietnam policies.

May 15

AIR WAR: Despite a plea by South Vietnamese Buddhists for a pause in observance of Buddha's birthday, U.S. and South Vietnamese aircraft fly 150 missions against VC targets in South Vietnam.

May 15–16

USA – DOMESTIC: A major "teach-in" is held in a lecture hall in Washington, D.C., and broadcast by a radio-telephone network to over 100 colleges. It lasts 15½ hours and features prominent academic and governmental figures who defend or attack the administration's policies in Vietnam. McGeorge Bundy had agreed to participate, but he leaves for the Dominican Republic to monitor the assignment of U.S. troops there. President Johnson has sent the troops to put down what he regards as an attempted Communist takeover.

May 16

AIR WAR: What is described as "an accidental explosion of a bomb on one aircraft which spread to others" at the Bien Hoa air base leaves 27 U.S. servicemen and four South Vietnamese dead and some 95 Americans injured; over 40 U.S. and South Vietnamese planes, including 10 B-57s, are destroyed.

USA – DOMESTIC: A Gallup poll shows a slight decline (from 55 percent to 52 percent) in the number of Americans who support the administration's policies in Vietnam.

May 18

USA – GOVERNMENT: President Johnson releases a memo from Secretary of Defense McNamara showing how the recently appropriated $700 million will be spent on the military.

May 19

USA – DOMESTIC: Henry Cabot Lodge, back from a trip through Asia, insists that the nations he visited did not want the United States to negotiate an end to the war but were concerned about U.S. willingness to stay in Vietnam.

AIR WAR: The United States resumes bombing raids over North Vietnam, striking at oil storage tanks. There is disappointment that North Vietnam did not respond to the bombing pause.

USSR: The Soviet Union warns Thailand against allowing the United States to use Thai bases to raid over North Vietnam.

May 20

SOUTH VIETNAM: The government alleges that there has been a plot to assassinate Premier Quat; most of those arrested are Roman Catholics and military personnel, whose main complaint seems to be that Quat is not taking a hard enough line against pro-Communist and neutralist elements.

May 22

NORTH VIETNAM: It is now officially confirmed by U.S. intelligence that the Soviet Union is building antiaircraft missile sites in and around Hanoi.

USA – DOMESTIC: The mother of a Haverford College student who has been involved in showing Viet Cong propaganda films on college campuses asks that his scholarship be revoked.

AIR WAR: U.S. planes bomb a military complex at Quan Soui, an ammunition depot at Phu Qui, and five other targets in North Vietnam.

May 24

INTERNATIONAL: Cyrus Eaton, an industrialist who has dedicated himself to working for world peace, reports that, at a recent meeting in Moscow, Premier Aleksey Kosygin warned him that the Soviet Union and China would combine their resources and turn against the United States unless it changed its policies in Vietnam. Eaton also reports that President Anastas Mikoyan suggested that the world was threatened by nuclear war. Secretary of State Rusk will respond to Eaton's observations two days later, claiming that the United States does not give "undue importance" to Kosygin's comments, but warning the Soviet Union and China to avoid further military involvement.

GROUND WAR: Over 2,200 ARVN troops launch an offensive in Kontum, a strategic area in the Central Highlands, in an attempt to disrupt a Viet Cong buildup reportedly aimed at taking control there when the monsoon season begins.

May 25
SOUTH VIETNAM: President Phan Khac Suu refuses to sign a decree of Premier Quat's calling for some cabinet changes, creating another government crisis in Saigon; the National Legislative Council will uphold all of Quat's demands on June 4.

May 26
AUSTRALIA/NEW ZEALAND: Eight hundred Australian troops depart for Vietnam, and New Zealand announces that it will send an artillery battalion.

May 27
SEA WAR: U.S. warships begin to provide naval gunfire against Viet Cong targets in the central coastal area of South Vietnam. At first this gunfire is limited to destroyers armed with five-inch guns, but cruisers will soon be called in and eventually a battleship mounting 16-inch guns will provide support.

May 28–June 1
GROUND WAR: Near Ba Gia in Quang Ngai Province in the northern part of South Vietnam, an ARVN battalion is ambushed and overrun by the VC. ARVN reinforcements are also ambushed. Only three U.S. advisers and about 60 of the South Vietnamese troops manage to escape. Although the Viet Cong suffer a reported loss of several hundred soldiers, the two ARVN battalions are decimated, suffering 392 killed and losing 446 weapons during the fighting. This battle demonstrates to the U.S. military the continuing difficulties that the South Vietnamese military faces in confronting their Communist foe.

May 31
AIR WAR: U.S. planes bomb an ammunition depot at Hoi Jan, west of Hanoi, and try again to drop the Thanh Hoa Bridge. Navy Seabees complete the runway at Chu Lai.

June
USA – MILITARY: U.S. forces in Vietnam pursue the "enclave" strategy first suggested by Ambassador Taylor. Under this concept, U.S. forces will control the densely populated coastal areas, freeing up the ARVN to recover and take control of the countryside while the government builds credibility and legitimacy. The marines are now at Danang, Phu Bai, and Chu Lai, while the army will defend the area around Vung Tau in the III Corps tactical zone.

June 1

CHINA: Beijing warns again that the increasing U.S. role in the war justifies China's own increased support to North Vietnam.

June 1–14

AIR WAR: U.S. planes continue bombing raids on military installations throughout North Vietnam. Visitors to Hanoi report that almost one-third of the city's population has been evacuated and that the city is now ringed by antiaircraft sites.

June 2

USA – DOMESTIC: The prominent American poet Robert Lowell rejects an invitation to attend an arts festival at the White House because he opposes the administration's policies in Vietnam.

GROUND WAR: As U.S. Marines and ARVN troops mount a joint operation against Viet Cong forces in the area of the Chu Lai air base, they are supported by naval gunfire from the USS *Canberra* offshore.

AUSTRALIA: Australia deploys the 1st Battalion of the Royal Australian Regiment to Vietnam for combat operations in III Corps. The first contingent of Australians arrives by plane in Saigon; they will join the U.S. 173rd Airborne Brigade at the Bien Hoa air base. Four hundred Australian combat troops will arrive by ship on June 8; they will join 80 of their countrymen already serving as military advisers with the ARVN.

June 3

DIPLOMACY: Britain's foreign secretary Michael Stewart proposes a conference to end the fighting and remove all foreign troops from South Vietnam, with a ceasefire to begin either before or during the talks. Stewart also reveals that the Soviet Union has rejected the British plan for reconvening the Geneva conference.

GROUND WAR: In two ambushes in the area of Pleiku, at Binh Chanh and Phu Bon, the Viet Cong destroy another battalion of ARVN troops.

June 4

USA – MILITARY: Major General Lewis Walt takes command of the III Marine Amphibious Force and the 3rd Division from Major General William Collins. U.S. officials confirm that at least six Russian Ilyushin-28 light jet bombers are now in North Vietnam.

June 5

USA – MILITARY: The State Department confirms that U.S. troops assigned to guard U.S. installations in Vietnam are in fact engaging in some combat against Communist forces.

June 7

USA – MILITARY: General Westmoreland sends a long message to the Pacific commander for relay to the Joint Chiefs, describing the deteriorating battlefield situation. Citing the ARVN's continuing "difficulty in coping with this increased VC activity," he requests a total of 34 battalions of U.S. combat troops, plus another 10 to be provided, at American expense, by South Korea. This request leads to the "44-battalion" debate within the Johnson administration because it is clear that such a commitment will drastically change the U.S. role in Vietnam. When questioned as to how he will deploy so many troops, Westmoreland will reply (on June 13) that he must be free to move U.S. forces around Vietnam.

June 8–9

USA – GOVERNMENT: State Department press officer Robert McCloskey reports that President Johnson has decided that "American forces would be available for combat support together with Vietnamese forces when and if necessary." This apparently innocuous statement, which seems to describe a mission change for U.S. troops, produces an immediate response in the press. In an attempt to quell the outcry, the White House issues a statement that claims "There has been no change in the missions of United States ground combat units in Vietnam," but it goes on to state that Westmoreland does have the authority to employ troops "in support of Vietnamese forces faced with aggressive attack." This statement, because of its ambiguity, serves only to exacerbate the situation and contributes to what is being described as "the credibility gap."

June 10

USA – GOVERNMENT: Amid rising criticism of the new combat role of U.S. forces in Vietnam, Attorney General Nicholas Katzenbach writes to assure the president that he has the power to commit large-scale forces, without going back to Congress.

June 10–13

GROUND WAR: Some 1,500 Viet Cong start a mortar attack on the district capital of Dong Xoai, about 60 miles northeast of Saigon, and then quickly overrun the town's military headquarters and an adjoining militia compound. Other Viet Cong also raid a U.S. Special Forces camp about a mile away. U.S. helicopters fly in ARVN reinforcements, and at first the Viet Cong seem to be in retreat, but they renew their attack and soon isolate and cut down the ARVN troops. Heavy U.S. air strikes eventually help to drive off the Viet Cong, but not before the ARVN have lost some 800 to 900 men and the United States loses seven killed, 12 missing and presumed dead, and 15 wounded. The Viet Cong are estimated to have lost 350 in the ground combat and perhaps several hundred more in air attacks. On the last day, a battalion of U.S. paratroopers is flown into an airstrip near Dong Xoai, but Westmoreland never sends them into battle. During the fighting, Second Lieutenant Charles Q. Williams of 5th Special Forces Group single-handedly knocks out a Viet Cong machine gun and guides helicopters into the area to evacuate the wounded. Himself wounded four times in the engagement, Williams will later receive the Congressional Medal of Honor for his actions in the battle.

June 11

USA – GOVERNMENT: Ambassador Taylor, in Washington for consultations, reports to President Johnson and Congress, and speaks at several public forums, in each case providing a pessimistic outlook on the situation in Vietnam.

June 12–13

SOUTH VIETNAM: Mounting Roman Catholic opposition to Premier Quat's government leads him to resign, and the next day a faction of officers, known as the "Young Turks," led by Air Vice-Marshal Ky, and Generals Nguyen Van Thieu and Nguyen Hun Co, announce formation of a National Leadership Committee. General Thieu is subsequently designated chief of state. This was the ninth government in less than two years.

June 15

USA – GOVERNMENT: Senator J. William Fulbright (D-Ark.), in a speech in the Senate, calls for a "negotiated settlement involving major concessions by both sides," yet he is opposed to "unconditional withdrawal of American support from South Vietnam." Fulbright will become one of the most vocal critics of the war and the Johnson administration's handling of it.

TERRORISM: Communist terrorists explode a bomb in the Saigon airport that wounds at least 22 persons, including 20 U.S. servicemen.

June 15–30

AIR WAR: U.S. planes bomb targets in North Vietnam every day, but are still prohibited from bombing Hanoi and the Soviet missile sites. On June 17, two U.S. Navy jets down two Communist MiGs, and one more three days later. U.S. planes also drop almost 3 million leaflets urging the North Vietnamese to get their leaders to end the war.

June 16

USA – GOVERNMENT: Secretary of Defense McNamara announces that 21,000 more U.S. troops are to be sent to Vietnam. He also claims that it is now known that North Vietnamese regular troops had infiltrated South Vietnam before the U.S. bombing began.

June 17

USA – GOVERNMENT: Ambassador Taylor sends a report to Washington confirming "the seriousness of the military situation as reported by General Westmoreland" and also points up the very tenuous hold the new government has on the country.

USA – DOMESTIC: Former president Dwight D. Eisenhower, while admitting the complexities of the situation, urges Americans to support President Johnson's policies.

DIPLOMACY: Representatives of Ceylon and three nations of the British Commonwealth—Ghana, Nigeria, and Trinidad and Tobago—say they will visit the principal nations involved and try to find a way to end the war. North Vietnam, the Soviet Union, and Communist China immediately reject their plan; the proposed visits are never made.

AIR WAR: For the first time, 27 B-52 Stratofortress jet bombers fly from Guam to strike a Viet Cong concentration in a heavily forested area of Binh Duong Province. Such flights, under the aegis of the Strategic Air Command, become known as Operation Arc Light. One B-52 is lost in a collision, and the raid is revealed to have cost $20 million. Some military leaders question the worth of such raids, but the raids will be conducted for the rest of the war as the Arc Light missions are extended throughout Southeast Asia.

June 19
SOUTH VIETNAM: Air Vice-Marshal Nguyen Cao Ky assumes the premiership of the ninth government within the last 20 months. He promises to rule with an iron hand and will start by demanding full mobilization.

June 22
USA – GOVERNMENT: General Wheeler cables Westmoreland asking if the 44 battalions will be enough to convince enemy forces that they cannot win. Westmoreland replies that "there was no evidence that the VC/DRV would alter their plans regardless of what the U.S. did in the next six months." He says, however, that the 44 battalions will establish a favorable balance of power by the end of the year, but to seize the initiative, further forces would be required in 1966.
AIR WAR: U.S. planes bomb targets only 80 miles from the Chinese border, the deepest raids into North Vietnam so far.

June 24
SOUTH VIETNAM: Premier Ky announces austerity measures, which include extending martial law and curfew, imposing price controls, and cutting salaries of top government officials.
POWs: Hanoi Radio announces that the Viet Cong have shot Sergeant Harold G. Bennett (USA), who had been captured in December 1964 while serving as an adviser with the Vietnamese Rangers, in retaliation for South Vietnam's execution of a convicted Viet Cong terrorist on June 22.

June 25
USA – GOVERNMENT: President Johnson appeals to the United Nations to persuade North Vietnam to negotiate a peace.
TERRORISM: Thirty-one people, including nine Americans, are killed in a bomb explosion in a riverboat restaurant in Saigon.

June 26
NORTH VIETNAM: Hanoi Radio reports that the Viet Cong now have "death lists," headed by the names of Ambassador Taylor, his deputy, U. Alexis Johnson, Premier Ky, and General Thieu.
USA – MILITARY: General Westmoreland is given formal authority to commit U.S. forces to battle when he decides they are necessary "to strengthen the relative position of the GVN [Government of Vietnam] forces."
GROUND WAR: Using what is described as "human wave" tactics, about 1,000 Viet Cong attack an ARVN position near Duc Hoa, 20 miles northwest of Saigon; they are finally dispersed by aerial bombing.

June 28–30
GROUND WAR: In the first major ground offensive ordered for U.S. forces, 3,000 troops of the 173rd Airborne Brigade in conjunction with an Australian battalion

and a Vietnamese airborne unit launch a sweep of a jungle area known as War Zone D, 20 miles northeast of Saigon. The operation is called off after three days when it fails to make any major contract with the enemy, but one American is killed and nine Americans and four Australians are wounded. The State Department assures the American public that the operation was in accord with Johnson administration policy on the role of U.S. troops.

June 30
SOUTH VIETNAM: Premier Ky suspends all Vietnamese-language newspapers.

July
USA – MILITARY: U.S. Army Vietnam is formed at Long Binh near Saigon to support army operations in Vietnam. The 2nd Brigade, 1st Infantry Division, deploys to Vietnam from Fort Riley, Kansas, for combat operations in III Corps. The 1st Brigade, 101st Airborne Division, deploys to Vietnam from Fort Campbell, Kentucky, for combat operations in II Corps. The number of American soldiers, airmen, marines, and sailors in South Vietnam now exceeds 50,000.

July 1
USA – GOVERNMENT: Undersecretary of State George Ball, convinced that the United States is "pouring its resources down the drain in the wrong place," submits a memo to President Johnson advising against the enlargement of the U.S. commitment in Vietnam. Saying that "there was absolutely no assurance that the U.S. could with the provision of more ground forces achieve its political objectives in Vietnam," he warns that to do so risks involving ourselves in "a costly and indeterminate struggle." Ball concludes that "humiliation would be more likely than the achievement of our objectives" and advises that the United States "cut its losses" by not committing more troops, restricting the combat role of those in place, and seeking to negotiate a way out of the war. Ball's recommendations will have little impact on the president.

GROUND WAR: The U.S. air base at Danang comes under attack by the Viet Cong for the first time when an 85-man enemy sapper team infiltrates the airfield, blowing up three planes and heavily damaging three others; one USAF man is killed and three U.S. Marines are wounded.

July 2
USA – GOVERNMENT: The State Department reports that 20 percent fewer ships from non-Communist nations are calling at North Vietnamese ports. This suggests that whether by political or military pressure, the United States is beginning to isolate North Vietnam.

USA – DOMESTIC: The Reverend Martin Luther King, Jr., leader of the civil rights struggle by African Americans, says that he is so convinced the war must be ended that he may join the peace rallies and teach-ins.

July 3
USA – GOVERNMENT: The Vietnam Service Medal is authorized by Presidential Order 11231.

July 4

USA – GOVERNMENT: Secretary of State Dean Rusk makes an Independence Day broadcast over the Voice of America, stating that the United States is still waiting to hear what North Vietnam will do in return for a cessation of U.S. bombing.

July 4–7

GROUND WAR: ARVN troops retake an outpost near Ba Gia from the Viet Cong, who will attack on several occasions during the next few days but be repulsed by the South Vietnamese troops.

July 6

GROUND WAR: The headquarters unit of the 9th Marines begins to land at Danang.

July 6–9

GROUND WAR: B-52s based at Anderson Airbase on Guam bomb War Zone D again. Then a 2,500-man task force of South Vietnamese, U.S. units from the 173rd Airborne Brigade, and Australian troops moves in to search the area. An Australian platoon is ambushed, and at the end of the operation, it is reported that 10 Americans and one Australian were killed. Some 150 Viet Cong are reported dead (it is also reported that they removed many of their wounded through tunnels).

July 7

USA – GOVERNMENT: Representative Gerald Ford (R-Mich.) urges President Johnson to bomb antiaircraft sites that are ready to receive Soviet missiles.

July 8

USA – GOVERNMENT: Ambassador Maxwell Taylor resigns from his post in Vietnam; he will be replaced by former ambassador Henry Cabot Lodge. Taylor, having lost the debate about increasing the U.S. ground commitment at the Honolulu conference in April, returns to Washington haunted by a sense of failure.

USA – MILITARY: At a court-martial in Okinawa, a U.S. Army captain pleads not guilty to charges of feigning mental illness to get out of Vietnam.

July 8–13

DIPLOMACY: Prime Minister Harold Wilson of Great Britain sends an envoy to Hanoi to persuade the North Vietnamese to consider negotiations, but the envoy is rebuffed.

July 9

USA – GOVERNMENT: At a news conference, President Johnson confirms that the government is considering limited mobilization, to include a call-up of reservists, larger draft quotas, and increased defense expenditures, to cope with the situation in Vietnam.

July 9–13

GROUND WAR: Viet Cong attack An Hoa island, and five Americans are killed in the first day's fighting; in the ensuing days, many civilians will be killed in the crossfire. On July 13, the VC overrun the last outpost and kill all 26 ARVN defenders.

July 10

POWs: In a gesture evidently to gain favor with the South Vietnamese people, the Viet Cong release 60 ARVN soldiers captured on June 8 at Dong Xoai.

AIR WAR: U.S. planes continue their heavy raids in South Vietnam, claiming to have killed 580 guerrillas. In the air over North Vietnam, U.S. Phantom jets, escorting fighter-bombers in a raid on the Yen Sen ammunition depot northwest of Hanoi, shoot down two MiG-17s with Sidewinder air-to-air missiles, the first air force air-to-air victories of the Vietnam War.

July 11

NORTH VIETNAM: The government announces that the first contingent of "volunteers" has left to serve in South Vietnam.

USA – GOVERNMENT: Secretary Rusk states that the "idea of sanctuary is dead," meaning that the United States will attack any part of North Vietnam it chooses to.

AIR WAR: U.S. planes inflict heavy damage on a river shipping area northwest of Hue.

July 12

USA – GOVERNMENT: Vice President Hubert Humphrey defends the administration's conduct of the war and warns its critics not to mistake appeasement for peace.

GROUND WAR: A marine patrol from the 3rd Reconnaissance Battalion is ambushed by the VC near Danang. Wounded, the platoon leader, First Lieutenant Frank Reasoner of Kellogg, Idaho, kills two Viet Cong and organizes his men into a hasty defense, then races through machine-gun fire to rescue his injured radio operator. Reasoner succumbs to his wounds, but later is named the first marine to earn the Medal of Honor in the Vietnam War.

July 14

AIR WAR: U.S. planes hit targets only 40 miles from the border of China, the closest raids to the border to date.

July 15

SOUTH VIETNAM: In an English newspaper interview, Premier Ky is quoted as saying that Adolf Hitler is one of his "heroes." Confronted with outraged protest, Ky first denies making this statement, then admits that he meant only that he admired the way Hitler rallied the German people.

USA – MILITARY: With the arrival of 3,000 U.S. troops, the total U.S. force in Vietnam is now 71,000. The Department of Defense announces that it is imposing "voluntary" curbs on the press in reporting such specifics as casualties, troop movements, and participating units.

AUSTRALIA/NEW ZEALAND: New Zealand deploys a field artillery battery to Vietnam for combat operations in support of the Australian forces in III Corps.

July 16–21

USA – GOVERNMENT: Secretary of Defense Robert McNamara conducts a fact-finding mission in South Vietnam, and Henry Cabot Lodge arrives in Saigon to assume

Secretary of Defense Robert S. McNamara and Gen. Westmoreland talk with Gen. Thi, I Corps Commander, July 1965. *(National Archives)*

his post as ambassador. McNamara is informed by secret cable from Deputy Secretary of Defense Cyrus Vance that Johnson has decided to give General Westmoreland the additional troops he had requested. On leaving Saigon, McNamara is asked at a press conference about the situation in-country; he admits that "There has been deterioration since I was last here, 15 months ago."

July 17

GROUND WAR: A large ARVN force clears and reopens Route 19, the strategic route through the Central Highlands. For the first time in six weeks, an armed convoy from Qui Nhon gets through to Pleiku without being attacked by the Viet Cong. However, it is reported that six of the 10 main roads leading out of Saigon are completely controlled by the Viet Cong.

July 18

USA – MILITARY: Secretary of Defense McNamara, visiting the carrier USS *Independence* off Vietnam, assists in launching a bombing raid.

AIR WAR: In a raid over North Vietnam, Commander Jeremiah Denton (USN) is shot down and captured. He will remain one of the most prominent U.S. POWs until the end of the war; he will later be elected to Congress.

LAOS: Souvanna Phouma holds elections, but the polls are open only to a limited elite who must vote for carefully screened candidates. The Communist Pathet Lao boycott these elections.

July 20

USA – GOVERNMENT: Secretary of Defense McNamara, upon his return from his weeklong trip to Vietnam, revises an earlier memorandum for the president prepared on July 1. In the revised memo, McNamara recommends an increase in U.S.–Third Country presence and a change in the mission of those forces from one of providing support and reinforcement for the ARVN to a more active role "to gain and hold the initiative . . . pressing the fight against VC-DRV main force units in South Vietnam to run them to ground and destroy them . . ." He concludes that the troop increase and Westmoreland's proposed course of action "stands a good chance of achieving an acceptable outcome within a reasonable time."

NORTH VIETNAM: On the 20th anniversary of the signing of the Geneva Accords, Ho Chi Minh says that his people will fight 20 more years or as long as it takes to achieve victory. Premier Ky, also speaking on this occasion in Saigon, reaffirms his determination to fight for the "liberation" of North Vietnam.

LAOS: Government planes bomb trucks carrying supplies for the Viet Cong on the Ho Chi Minh Trail.

July 21

USA – GOVERNMENT: President Johnson begins a weeklong series of conferences with his civilian and military advisers on Vietnam and also with private citizens he trusts. He appears to be considering all options, but it is clear to most observers that he has made up his mind to provide more combat troops, as requested by Westmoreland and recommended by McNamara.

AIR WAR: Thirty Guam-based B-52s bomb the Viet Cong in War Zone D again; fighter-bombers then move in for precision strikes on the same area.

July 23

SOUTH VIETNAM: Chief of State Thieu decrees that the death penalty may be imposed for those supporting "neutralism."

USA – GOVERNMENT: Some of President Johnson's advisers tell him that he should give the American public all the facts, ask for an increase in taxes, mobilize the reserves, and declare a state of national emergency. However, the president rejects this approach, informing his staff that he wants any decisions implemented in a "low-key manner" in order to avoid an abrupt challenge to the Communists, and to avoid undue concern and excitement in the Congress and any negative impact on domestic public opinion.

July 24

USA – MILITARY: The Pentagon reports that since 1961, U.S. wounded in Vietnam outnumber those killed by 5 to 1, the highest such ratio in any American conflict.

AIR WAR: Four U.S. F-4C Phantom jets escorting a formation of U.S. bombers on a raid over munitions manufacturing facilities at Kang Chi, 55 miles northwest of

Hanoi, are fired at for the first time by antiaircraft missiles; one plane is shot down and the other three damaged.

SEA WAR: U.S. destroyers shell a fleet of suspected Viet Cong junks and sink 23.

July 25

USA – GOVERNMENT: President Johnson informs a small group of Democratic and Republican congressional leaders of his decision to increase the number of ground troops in Vietnam.

July 27

USA – GOVERNMENT: The U.S. government confirms that Secretary of State Rusk has talked with members of the International Red Cross about improving the treatment of POWs on both sides.

AIR WAR: Forty-six U.S. Air Force F-105 fighter-bombers attack the missile installation that fired at U.S. planes on July 24 and another missile installation 40 miles northwest of Hanoi. One missile launcher is destroyed, another damaged, but five U.S. planes are shot down.

July 28

USA – GOVERNMENT: President Johnson announces that he has ordered an increase in U.S. military forces in Vietnam, from the present 75,000 to 125,000, and that he will order additional increases if the situation calls for it. He says, "I have asked the commanding general, General Westmoreland, what more he needs to meet this mounting aggression. He has told me. And we will meet his needs. We cannot be defeated by force of arms. We will stand in Vietnam." To fill the increase in military manpower needs, he announces that the monthly draft calls will be doubled from 17,000 to 35,000. There is an immediate reaction to Johnson's announcement. Most members of Congress are reported to favor Johnson's decision; U.S. state governors, now convened for their annual conference, also support a resolution backing Johnson. Hanoi immediately attacks Johnson, condemning the U.S. troop increase.

AIR WAR: U.S. and South Vietnamese bombers hit a Buddhist monastery by mistake, killing two monks and wounding ten.

July 29

USA – DOMESTIC: One survey shows general support for Johnson's decision to send more troops, but another, more specialized, shows a shift from complete support to uncertainty.

USA – MILITARY: The first 4,000 paratroopers of the 101st Airborne Division arrive in Vietnam, landing at Cam Ranh Bay. They make a demonstration jump immediately after arriving, observed by General Westmoreland and outgoing ambassador Taylor, both former commanders of the division also known as "the Screaming Eagles."

July 30

INTERNATIONAL: It is reported that 29 nations now give some kind of aid to South Vietnam; this aid runs the gamut from materiel and funds to personnel, but only Korea, Thailand, Philippines, Australia, and New Zealand send troops.

DIPLOMACY: The United States formally requests that the United Nations Security Council help settle the war in Vietnam.

August 1

USA – GOVERNMENT: President Johnson charges that Congressman Gerald Ford (R-Mich.) has misrepresented events by claiming that prominent Democrats dissuaded Johnson from calling up the reserves. Ford denies that he ever said this, but the disagreement is only a reflection of one of the most controversial aspects of the war—Johnson's failure to call up the reserves.

GROUND WAR: The VC strike 20 South Vietnamese outposts.

AIR WAR: U.S. aircraft bomb 11 bridges, destroying two, and hit three radar installations in North Vietnam.

SEA WAR: Operation Market Time, the monitoring of sea traffic along the Vietnam coast to cut off supplies to the Viet Cong, is removed from the U.S. Seventh Fleet and assigned to a newly created coastal surveillance force, but it will continue to be controlled by the U.S. Navy.

August 2

GROUND WAR: U.S. troops end a six-day operation in Phuoc Tuy Province, during which they fail to make contact with the Viet Cong.

August 2–3

USA – MILITARY: In Honolulu, General Wheeler, chairman of the Joint Chiefs of Staff, meets with Admiral Sharp, CINCPAC, to discuss plans for stepping up U.S. forces in Vietnam. A U.S. Army spokesman in Washington confirms that the United States has begun transferring troops from U.S. Army Europe on a "volunteer" basis.

August 2–11

GROUND WAR: A Viet Cong force of about 3,000 soldiers strikes at a South Vietnamese special forces camp at Duc Co near the Cambodian border. Two ARVN airborne battalions are flown in as reinforcements, but the VC will not be repulsed until U.S. troops from the 1st Infantry Division and 173rd Airborne Brigade are inserted into the battle.

August 3

SOUTH VIETNAM: Peasants in Hau Nghia Province are reported to be demonstrating against both the VC and the South Vietnamese government.

USA – DOMESTIC: CBS TV shows pictures of men from the 1st Battalion, 9th Marines, setting fire to huts in the village of Cam Ne, six miles southwest of Danang despite a report that the Viet Cong had already fled the area. The broadcast sparks a rash of indignation, both at home and overseas.

USA – MILITARY: The Department of Defense announces that it is increasing the monthly draft quota from 17,000 in August to 27,400 in September and 36,000 in October. It also announces that the navy will require 4,600 draftees, the first such action since 1956.

August 5

GROUND WAR: Viet Cong sappers penetrate U.S. defenses and blow up the Esso oil storage tanks on the Hai Vai Peninsula, across the bay from Danang. Two million gallons of fuel are destroyed—almost 40 percent of the U.S. supply in South Vietnam—but U.S. military officials claim that the loss does not affect combat operations.

August 6

SOUTH VIETNAM: A U.S. B-57 with a full load of bombs crashes into a residential section of Nha Trang. Although the crew survives, 12 Vietnamese on the ground are killed.

August 7

AIR WAR: U.S. aircraft bomb the explosives plant at Lang Chi in North Vietnam.
CHINA: The Chinese government warns that it may send forces to Vietnam to fight for the Communist cause if necessary.

August 8

AIR WAR: U.S. aircraft fly over 250 missions in South Vietnam, striking numerous suspected Viet Cong concentrations.

August 12

USA – GOVERNMENT: At the swearing in ceremony for the new ambassador to Vietnam, Henry Cabot Lodge, President Johnson proclaims that the United States will not continue to fight in Vietnam "if its help were not wanted and requested."
USA – DOMESTIC: Reverend Martin Luther King, Jr., criticizes President Johnson for his failure to enter negotiations with the Viet Cong to end the war and threatens to appeal personally to the Communists, even if it means violating federal law.
AIR WAR: A navy A-4 Skyhawk becomes the second U.S. aircraft shot down by a surface-to-air missile over North Vietnam.

August 13

GROUND WAR: ARVN troops score a major victory when they kill over 250 Viet Cong in a battle in the Mekong Delta, suffering only light casualties in the process.
AIR WAR: Five U.S. Navy warplanes are downed over Hanoi by antiaircraft fire.

August 14

NORTH VIETNAM: In a message purportedly from an American defector from the Korean War living in Beijing, Hanoi Radio broadcasts an appeal to American troops, particularly African Americans, to "get out."
USA – MILITARY: Advance units of the 7th Marines land at Chu Lai, bringing U.S. Marine strength in South Vietnam to four regiments and four air groups. The marines are given responsibility for the conduct of combat operations in southern I Corps and northern II Corps.
AIR WAR: U.S. and VNAF aircraft continue the intensified air campaign in South Vietnam.
SOUTH KOREA: The National Assembly approves sending troops to fight in South Vietnam; in exchange for sending one combat division to Vietnam, the United States agrees to equip five South Korean divisions.

August 16

TERRORISM: Two car bombs explode at the National Police Headquarters in Saigon, killing eight policemen and wounding 17. The Viet Cong claim credit for the attack, but there is some speculation that it is the work of a dissident group of South Vietnamese who have attempted a coup.

GROUND WAR: VC guerrillas attack a U.S. Marine tank unit near Danang but suffer six killed in the process.

August 18–24

GROUND WAR: U.S. Marines conduct Operation Starlite on the Van Tuong Peninsula 16 miles south of Chu Lai, Quang Ngai Province, I Corps. In this, the first major operation of the Vietnam War conducted only by U.S. troops, 5,500 marines from the 3rd, 4th, and 7th Marines destroy a Viet Cong stronghold, scoring a resounding victory. Ground forces, artillery from Chu Lai, naval gunfire, and air support combine to kill nearly 700 Vietcong soldiers. U.S. forces sustain nine marines dead and 34 wounded.

August 21

AIR WAR: It is revealed that U.S. pilots have received approval to destroy any Soviet-made missiles they see while raiding North Vietnam, a major change from previous orders that restricted them to bombing only previously approved targets.

August 22–October 2

GROUND WAR: U.S. Task Force Collins from the 101st Airborne Division conducts Operation Highland, a clearing operation to secure An Khe base for the incoming

U.S. Marines wade through mud during the conduct of a patrol 12 miles south-southwest of Danang, date unknown. *(National Archives)*

1st Cavalry Division in Binh Dinh Province, II Corps. Casualties are U.S.: 21 KIA; NVA/VC: 692.

August 23
GROUND WAR: The Viet Cong shell the air base at Bien Hoa, damaging 49 planes.

August 26
GROUND WAR: The Viet Cong overrun an ARVN outpost just 10 miles from Saigon.
AIR WAR: USAF B-52 bombers strike suspected Viet Cong concentrations in War Zone D, while fighter-bombers attack a radar site in North Vietnam.

August 27
GROUND WAR: ARVN forces clear Route 21 between Ninh Hoa and Ban Me Thuot in the Central Highlands, II Corps, to permit supply convoys to pass.
AIR WAR: U.S. and South Vietnamese warplanes fly over 300 missions in South Vietnam.

August 28
GROUND WAR: After an all-night battle in the Can Tho area of the Mekong Delta, a Viet Cong battalion is forced to withdraw, leaving behind over 50 dead.

August 31
SOUTH VIETNAM: Premier Nguyen Cao Ky announces that South Vietnam will not negotiate with the Communists without guarantees that North Vietnamese troops will be withdrawn from the South. He also promises that his government will institute major reforms to correct economic and social injustices.
USA – GOVERNMENT: In the United States, President Johnson signs into law a bill making it illegal to destroy or mutilate a U.S. draft card, with penalties of up to five years and a $10,000 fine.
USA – MILITARY: In order to curb black marketeering in South Vietnam, it is decided that foreign troops, including U.S. forces, will be paid in scrip.
AIR WAR: U.S. aircraft continue to bomb targets in North Vietnam, while in the South, B-52s strike Viet Cong troop concentrations in War Zone D and in Quang Tin Province.

September
USA – MILITARY: The U.S. I Field Force Vietnam headquarters is formed at Nha Trang to coordinate army combat operations in the Central Highlands. The 1st Cavalry Division (Airmobile) deploys to Vietnam from Fort Benning, Georgia, for combat operations in II Corps.

September 2
USA – MILITARY: The United States announces that over 100 U.S. servicemen are volunteering every day for duty in South Vietnam—a sharp increase since the marines landed in March.

September 3
AIR WAR: U.S. and South Vietnamese planes fly 532 air missions over Vietnam, the highest number of missions in one day so far in the war.

September 5
USA – DOMESTIC: Former vice president Richard Nixon affirms his support of U.S. policy on a visit to Saigon: "There is only one basis for negotiation . . . a communist withdrawal."

September 7–10
GROUND WAR: U.S. Marines and South Vietnamese forces follow up Operation Starlite with Operation Piranha on the Batangan Peninsula, 23 miles south of their base at Chu Lai, Quang Ngai Province, I Corps. Purpose of the operation is to find and destroy remnants of the 1st Viet Cong Regiment. Casualties are: U.S.: 2 KIA, 14 WIA; ARVN: 5 KIA, 33 WIA; NVA/VC: 183 KIA, 360 POW.

September 9
AIR WAR: U.S. warplanes hit a bridge just 17 miles from the North Vietnamese border with China.

September 10
USA – MILITARY: U.S. aircraft drop 10,000 tons of toys and supplies over five towns in South Vietnam.

September 11
USA – MILITARY: Advance elements of the 1st Cavalry Division (Airmobile) begin to arrive in South Vietnam at Qui Nhon. The arrival of the entire division will bring U.S. troop strength in South Vietnam to 125,000. The division will initially be based at the newly established Camp Radcliff in An Khe.

USA – GOVERNMENT: Representative Gerald R. Ford (R-Mich.) charges that the Johnson administration is deceiving Americans about the actual cost of the war.

September 14–15
GROUND WAR: ARVN paratroopers and their U.S. advisers jump into the Ben Cat area, 20 miles north of Saigon. This is the first major parachute assault of the war by the South Vietnamese. Although they fail to make contact with the enemy, they achieve their goal of clearing Route 13, at least for the time being.

September 15
SOUTH VIETNAM: To affirm their loyalty to the government of South Vietnam, 500 Montagnards turn over their weapons at a ceremony in Ban Me Thuot attended by Premier Ky.

DIPLOMACY: In Tokyo, U.S. deputy ambassador Alexis Johnson warns Japan and other noncommunist nations that they cannot continue to remain apart from the struggle in Vietnam, because fundamental issues are at stake.

September 16
AIR WAR: In their first strike over the Mekong Delta, B-52 bombers hit targets in Vinh Binh Province.

September 17
GROUND WAR: ARVN troops claim that the Viet Cong used gas grenades when attacking an outpost near Quang Ngai, but the claim will never be substantiated.

September 17–19
AIR WAR: In three incidents, U.S. planes strike so close to the DMZ that at least 60 South Vietnamese civilians are reported killed or wounded. General Westmoreland orders that special precautions be taken to avoid causing harm to civilians, but simultaneously calls for redrawing the borders of the free strike zone.

September 18–21
GROUND WAR: U.S. troops from the 1st Brigade, 101st Airborne Division, conduct Operation Gibraltar, a search and destroy sweep northeast of An Khe in Binh Dinh Province to secure the 1st Cavalry Division's base camp. During this operation, the American troops defeat a Viet Cong regiment, the first defeat of an enemy main force unit by the U.S. Army. Casualties are U.S.: 13 KIA, 44 WIA; NVA/VC: 226 KIA, 9 POW.

September 20
AIR WAR: Seven U.S. aircraft are lost in raids over North and South Vietnam. The Chinese claim to have shot down a U.S. F-104 jet over Hainan island and captured its pilot; a U.S. spokesman claims that the plane developed a mechanical problem over the Gulf of Tonkin.

September 23
GROUND WAR: During an engagement near Ben Cat, U.S. troops kill 12 VC and report finding a large arms cache.

September 23–26
SOUTH VIETNAM: The South Vietnamese government executes three accused VC agents held at Danang. Three days later, a clandestine VC radio station announces the execution of two U.S. soldiers held captive since 1963 as "war criminals," in retaliation for the execution of their agents by the South Vietnamese.

September 29
NORTH VIETNAM: Hanoi publishes the text of a letter it has written to the Red Cross claiming that, as there is no formal state of war, U.S. pilots shot down over the North will not receive the rights of prisoners of war and will be treated as "war criminals." The U.S. State Department protests.

September 30
AIR WAR: Two U.S. Air Force jets are shot down, one by a surface-to-air missile, while bombing the Minh Binh bridge in North Vietnam.

October
USA – MILITARY: The 1st Infantry Division deploys to Vietnam from Fort Riley, Kansas; it will initially be stationed in Bien Hoa Province, III Corps. U.S. Navy establishes support base at Danang.

GROUND WAR: U.S. Special Forces launches a clandestine operation called Shining Brass in which specially trained teams are inserted into Laos to watch and disrupt traffic along the Ho Chi Minh Trail; these high-risk missions, controlled and executed by MACV Special Operations Group, are launched from Kham Duc Special Forces Camp in Quang Tin Province, I Corps.

SOUTH KOREA: South Korea deploys its Capital Division and a marine brigade to South Vietnam; the Korean troops will conduct combat operations in II Corps.

October 5

USA – MILITARY: After a long debate, the administration in Washington authorizes use of tear gas by U.S. troops in Vietnam.

CHINA: Beijing claims that Chinese gunners downed a U.S. plane intruding into China's Kwang Si Province; the U.S. Department of Defense will not confirm the incident, but acknowledges that one plane did not return from a bombing mission 50 miles northeast of Hanoi.

October 6

AIR WAR: U.S. B-52s hit suspected VC bases in Tay Ninh Province near the Cambodian border.

October 6–November 19

GROUND WAR: In the first large-scale operation since arriving the previous month, the 1st Air Cavalry Division (Airmobile) joins with South Vietnamese marines to conduct Operation Happy Valley, a search and clear operation conducted in Binh Dinh Province, II Corps. Although they fail to trap the North Vietnamese 325th Infantry Division, they do reopen the Pleiku-An Khe highway and destroy a 50-bed enemy hospital equipped with U.S. medical supplies.

October 10

GROUND WAR: A company from the 173rd Airborne Brigade is ambushed in the "Iron Triangle" area in III Corps; eight Americans are killed and 25 wounded.

October 12

USA – GOVERNMENT: Senator John Stennis (D-Miss.) states that it may be necessary to keep U.S. forces in Vietnam for another 15 years. The Defense Department orders a draft call for 45,224 men for December, the largest quota of men drafted since the Korean War in 1950.

October 15–16

USA – DOMESTIC: The student-run National Coordinating Committee to end the War in Vietnam sponsors nationwide demonstrations in some 40 U.S. cities. During one of these demonstrations, David Miller, a relief program volunteer, becomes the first U.S. war protester to burn his draft card. He is later arrested by agents from the Federal Bureau of Investigation.

October 16

INTERNATIONAL: Protests against U.S. policy in Vietnam are held in London, Rome, Brussels, Copenhagen, and Stockholm to coincide with the demonstrations being conducted in the United States.

JAPAN: Premier Sato of Japan announces that Japan will send no troops to Vietnam, even if it is requested to do so by the United States.

October 19–27

GROUND WAR: North Vietnamese troops launch a major assault on a U.S. Special Forces camp at Plei Me in the Central Highlands, 25 miles northwest of Pleiku. During a week of savage fighting, defenders of the besieged outpost, which is manned by 400 Montagnards, 12 Green Berets, and a handful of South Vietnamese guerrilla specialists, repel repeated VC attacks with the aid of numerous allied air strikes and several hundred ARVN reinforcements. With the camp secured, General Westmoreland decides to seize the initiative and sends in the 1st Cavalry Division (Airmobile) to "find, fix, and defeat the enemy forces that threatened Plei Me."

October 20–November 5
GROUND WAR: The U.S. 1st Cavalry Division (Airmobile) conducts Operation Good Friend in Binh Dinh Province, II Corps, to provide security for the arrival and establishment of the Republic of Korea's Capital Division Cavalry Regiment at Binh Khe.

October 21
TERRORISM: A terrorist mine explodes in the marketplace at Tra On, a town in the Mekong Delta 75 miles southeast of Saigon, killing 11 persons and wounding 54.
USA – DOMESTIC: The United Auto Workers' executive board issues a statement declaring its support of administration policy in Vietnam.

October 22
USA – MILITARY: In a Honolulu interview, Admiral U.S. Grant Sharp, Pacific area commander, claims that Allied forces have "stopped losing" the war. He further states that he does not believe China will enter the conflict.

October 23
USA – DOMESTIC: The Americans for Democratic Freedom denounces a probe into suspected communist influence on the war protest and anti-draft movement as a blatant attempt to "stifle criticism" of government policy.

October 23–November 9
GROUND WAR: The U.S. 1st Cavalry Division (Airmobile) and South Vietnamese troops conduct Operation All the Way in Pleiku Province, II Corps, a follow-on operation to the clash at the Plei Me Special Forces camp. The purpose of the operation is to seek out and destroy Communist forces operating in the area. Casualties are U.S.: 57 KIA, 192 WIA; NAV/VC: 216 KIA, 138 POW.

October 27
GROUND WAR: The Korean Capital (Tiger) Division arrives in South Vietnam and assumes the mission of providing security in the Qui Nhon area.

October 27–28
GROUND WAR: VC forces damage and destroy a number of Allied aircraft in two separate raids on marine air bases. The first raid occurs at the Marble Mountain base, in which VC commandos, under cover of mortar fire, force their way onto the runway and toss grenades into open helicopter cockpits. During the fighting, the marines kill 17 of the 30-man assault force. The second attack

Soldiers from C Battery, 2nd Battalion, 19th Artillery, prepare to support 1st Cavalry operations southwest of Pleiku Special Forces Camp, November 1965. *(Texas Tech University Vietnam Archive)*

occurs at Chu Lai, where a VC mortar attack destroys two jet fighters and damages five other aircraft.

October 30

USA – DOMESTIC: In New York City, military veterans lead a parade in support of government policy in Vietnam. Led by five recipients of the Congressional Medal of Honor, 25,000 people march in support of America's action in Vietnam.

GROUND WAR: Ten miles from Danang, U.S. Marines repel a VC human wave attack, killing 56 guerrillas. A search of the dead uncovers a sketch of marine positions on the body of a 13-year-old boy who had been selling drinks to the marines the previous day.

AIR WAR: Two U.S. planes accidentally bomb a friendly Vietnamese village, killing 48 civilians and wounding 55 others. An American civic action team is immediately dispatched to the scene, and a later investigation discloses that a map-reading error by South Vietnamese officers is responsible.

October 31

AIR WAR: U.S. planes destroy three antiaircraft missile sites and a highway bridge during a raid 35 miles northeast of Hanoi.

November

USA – MILITARY: The U.S. Air Force deploys its 3rd Tactical Fighter Wing to Bien Hoa for combat operations in III Corps, and 12th Tactical Fighter Wing to Cam Ranh Bay for combat operations in II Corps.

November 2

USA – DOMESTIC: As a war protest, Norman Morrison, a 32-year-old Quaker from Baltimore, immolates himself in front of the Pentagon.

November 4

GROUND WAR: Two U.S. helicopters crash in mid-air near An Khe, killing all nine crew members and passengers on both aircraft.

November 5

USA – DOMESTIC: At a Los Angeles news conference, Senator Robert Kennedy (D-N.Y.) defends "the right to criticize and the right to dissent" from U.S. policy in Vietnam and claims that donating blood to North Vietnam is "in the oldest tradition of this country." Former senator Barry Goldwater disagrees, stating that Kennedy's remarks were "close to treason."

November 5–8

AIR WAR: During a series of raids against North Vietnam, U.S. fighter-bombers from the aircraft carrier *Oriskany* damage or destroy nine antiaircraft sites, five missile launchers, and several support buildings; two planes are shot down.

November 9

USA – GOVERNMENT: In a memorandum prepared by Ambassador Alexis Johnson, the State Department urges the administration to reject Defense Secretary McNamara's recent proposal for a bombing pause. McNamara has proposed a bombing pause several times during previous months, envisioning such a pause to provide Hanoi sufficient time to respond to diplomatic initiatives and, if they did not, to clear the way for an increase in the tempo of the air war when resumed.

USA – DOMESTIC: In the second such anti-war incident within a week, Roger Allen LaPorte, a 22-year-old member of the Catholic Worker movement, immolates himself in front of UN headquarters in New York. Before dying the next day, LaPorte declared that "I'm against wars, all wars. I did this as a religious act."

November 10–20

GROUND WAR: The U.S. 1st Cavalry Division and ARVN troops launch Operation Silver Bayonet in Pleiku Province, II Corps, a follow-on operation to the clash at the Plei Me Special Forces camp. The purpose of the operation is to seek out and destroy Communist forces operating in the Ia Drang Valley. The operation will include two major battles, fought November 14–16 and November 17. Casualties for the entire operation are: U.S.: 239 KIA, 307 WIA; NVA: 1,224.

November 12

USA – GOVERNMENT: Reporting on the fighting in the Ia Drang Valley, McNamara describes how the 1st Cavalry Division has blunted a Communist offensive designed to cut South Vietnam in two. He also announces an increase in troop levels but gives no definite figures, saying that he does not want to tip off the enemy. He also reports that, despite a 100 percent increase in casualties since a similar period in 1964, VC forces have continued to increase in number.

November 14–16

GROUND WAR: During Operation Silver Bayonet, in one of the fiercest battles of the entire war, 1st Battalion, 7th Cavalry, from the U.S. 1st Cavalry Division, battles the entire 66th NVA Regiment at Landing Zone X-Ray, near the base of the Chu Pong Massif in the Ia Drang Valley. Only artillery fire, tactical air support, and the tenacity of the 1st Cavalry troopers prevent the NVA from overrunning the American positions. U.S. casualties during the battle are 79 KIA, 125 WIA; North Vietnamese: 834 KIA, with another 500 estimated killed.

November 16

GROUND WAR: Enemy troops overrun Hiep Duc, a district headquarters 25 miles west of Tam Ky. Although two ARVN battalions will later retake the town, General Thi, commander of South Vietnamese forces in I Corps, is forced to abandon it because he has too few regulars to leave any men there.

November 17

USA – DOMESTIC: The 48th general assembly of Reform Judaism's Union of Hebrew Congregations adopts a resolution urging President Johnson to order an immediate cease-fire in Vietnam, so that peace talks can be arranged.

GROUND WAR: During Operation Silver Bayonet, the 2nd Battalion, 7th Cavalry, from the U.S. 1st Cavalry Division, while en route to recon a site for Landing Zone Albany, is ambushed by a battalion from the 66th NVA Regiment five miles northwest of LZ X-Ray. Losses from this short battle are staggering: U.S.: 151 killed, 121 WIA; NVA:

400. West of Tam Ky, three battalions from the 1st VC Regiment overrun the Regional Forces garrison at Hiep Duc.

November 19
GROUND WAR: Using string bows, VC guerrillas fire arrows dipped in rancid animal fat at U.S. troops guarding the air base at Qui Nhon.

November 21–late December
GROUND WAR: Elements of the U.S. 1st Infantry Division and 173rd Airborne Brigade join with a battalion from the Royal Australian Regiment in Operation New Life-65, a counterinsurgency operation meant to break the hold of the Viet Cong on Binh Tuy Province, III Corps.

November 22
USA – GOVERNMENT: The chairman of the House Armed Services Committee, L. Mendel Rivers (R-S.C.), calls for the bombing of Haiphong and Hanoi, saying that it is "a folly to let the port of Haiphong and military targets of Hanoi remain untouched while war supplies being used against our troops are pouring into port."

November 22–23
GROUND WAR: In an assault on the town of Thach Tru, the 18th NVA Regiment encounters stiff resistance from a South Vietnamese Ranger battalion supported by naval gunfire from two U.S. destroyers and marine tactical aircraft. The U.S. 7th Marines arrive by helicopter the next day, driving enemy forces from the area.

November 24
GROUND WAR: U.S. casualty statistics reflect the intensified fighting in the Ia Drang Valley and other parts of the Central Highlands. A record 240 troops were killed and another 470 were wounded during the previous week.

November 26
SEA WAR: Two nuclear-powered ships, the aircraft carrier USS *Enterprise* and the guided missile frigate USS *Bainbridge,* join the Seventh Fleet and take position off South Vietnam.

November 27
USA – MILITARY: The Pentagon recommends that President Johnson increase U.S. troop strength in South Vietnam during the coming year from 120,000 to 400,000 men so that General Westmoreland can conduct the major sweep operations he deems necessary to destroy enemy forces.

USA – DOMESTIC: Nearly 35,000 war protesters circle the White House for two hours before moving on to the Washington Monument where they are addressed by Dr. Benjamin Spock, Mrs. Martin Luther King, Jr., Norman Thomas, and other speakers.

POWs: The VC release two U.S. Special Forces soldiers captured two years earlier during a battle at Hiep Hoa, 40 miles southwest of Saigon. At a news conference in Phnom Penh three days later, the two Americans, Sergeant George Smith and Specialist Fifth Class Claude McClure, declare that they oppose U.S. actions in Vietnam and will campaign for the withdrawal of U.S. troops. Although Smith later denies having made the statement, U.S. authorities announce that the two men will face court martial for cooperating with the enemy.

November 27–28

GROUND WAR: VC guerrillas from the 271st VC Regiment attack a South Vietnamese regiment on the Michelin rubber plantation in III Corps, inflicting heavy casualties on two ARVN battalions and killing several American advisers; further casualties result when U.S. planes accidentally bomb a South Vietnamese relief unit.

November 28

THE PHILIPPINES: President-elect Ferdinand Marcos of the Philippines states that he will send troops to South Vietnam.

November 30

USA – GOVERNMENT: In a memorandum to President Johnson following a recent visit to South Vietnam, Defense Secretary McNamara reports that the Ky government "is surviving, but not acquiring wide support," while the Viet Cong appear to be getting stronger. He says that U.S. policymakers face two options: to seek a compromise settlement and keep further military commitments to a minimum, or continue to press for a military solution, which will require substantial bombing of North Vietnam. In conclusion, McNamara warns that there is no guarantee of U.S. military success, saying that now "U.S. killed in action can be expected to reach 1000 a month and the odds are even that we will be faced in early 1967 with a 'no-decision' at an even higher level." Nevertheless, his overall evaluation is "that the best chance of achieving our stated objectives lies in the deployments" previously discussed.

November 30–December 2

DIPLOMACY: British foreign secretary Michael Stewart visits Moscow in an effort to enlist Soviet assistance in restarting the Geneva conference on Indochina. Andrei Gromyko, the Soviet foreign minister, rebuffs him, saying that peace talks cannot begin until America withdraws all troops and ceases its bombing of North Vietnam.

December

USA – MILITARY: The U.S. 3rd Brigade, 25th Infantry Division, deploys to Vietnam from Hawaii for combat operations in II Corps (initially).

December 2

USA – GOVERNMENT: U.S. secretary of state Dean Rusk announces that the United States will be willing to attend an international conference on Southeast Asia. UN head U Thant announces that he favors the American proposal, but he is rebuffed by Hanoi.

December 3

USA – GOVERNMENT: In a confidential memorandum to Defense Secretary McNamara, Assistant Secretary John McNaughton recommends a bombing pause to use as a "ratchet" against the North Vietnamese, which the analyst likens to "the device which raises the net on a tennis court, backing off tension between each phase of increasing it." This pause would give the North Vietnamese an opportunity to respond favorably and, if they do not, the tempo of the air war can be readily increased. The memorandum also outlines the conditions the United States should insist upon before a permanent bombing halt.

USA – DOMESTIC: In the United States, the general board of the National Council of Churches issues a statement approving the administration's commitment to unconditional negotiations and urging new peace initiatives.

December 4

USA – DOMESTIC: Fifty Catholic college students from Fordham University, protesting the "suppression" of three priests who actively opposed U.S. policy in Vietnam, picket the New York City chancery of Francis Cardinal Spellman.

TERRORISM: Viet Cong commandos explode a bomb at a Saigon hotel housing U.S. servicemen, killing one U.S. Marine, a New Zealand soldier, and six South Vietnamese civilians; another 137 persons are injured in the blast.

December 7

USA – GOVERNMENT: In a memorandum to President Johnson, Defense Secretary McNamara states that U.S. troop strength must be substantially augmented "if we

Marines from the 7th Regiment move along a rice paddy in pursuit of the Viet Cong, December 1965. *(National Archives)*

are to avoid being defeated there," but cautions again that such deployments will not ensure military success.

December 8–9

AIR WAR: In some of the heaviest air raids of the war, 150 U.S. Air Force and Navy planes launch Operation Tiger Hound, a major air campaign aimed at interdicting troops and supplies moving along the Ho Chi Minh Trail in the southern panhandle of Laos.

December 8–20

GROUND WAR: USMC and South Vietnamese forces join to conduct Operation Harvest Moon/Lien Ket-18, an operation intended to clear Viet Cong forces from the Que Son Valley in Quang Nam and Quang Tin Provinces, I Corps. In heavy fighting, Allied troops, supported by B-52 strikes, overcome stiff resistance and accomplish their objective, but the casualties are high: U.S.: 51 KIA, 256 WIA; ARVN: 90 KIA, 141 WIA, 91 MIA; NVA/VC: 407, 33 POWs.

December 9

USA – DOMESTIC: An article in the *New York Times* mirrors a Defense Intelligence Agency (DIA) report admitting that U.S. air attacks in Operation Rolling Thunder have neither destabilized North Vietnam's economy, nor appreciably reduced the flow of arms and men into South Vietnam. According to the DIA, to believe that the bombings will ever accomplish this is a "colossal misjudgment." Despite the report, the bombing campaign continues for three more years.

December 10

USA – DOMESTIC: Senator Ernest Gruening (D-Alaska) states that the conflict in Vietnam is a civil war that poses no threat to U.S. security interests. He declares that, despite the president's repeated assertion that he is continuing a commitment made by previous administrations, the United States has made no "solemn pledge" to support South Vietnam.

December 11

USA – MILITARY: To prepare for an anticipated expansion of its role in Vietnam, the United States begins emergency construction of additional military installations in Thailand.

December 12

USA – GOVERNMENT: Seventeen Democratic members of the House of Representatives sign a statement supporting President Johnson's refusal to bomb Hanoi and Haiphong.

USSR: Article in *Pravda* accuses Chinese leaders of refusing to cooperate with efforts by other Communist nations to defeat the United States in Vietnam.

December 14

USA – DOMESTIC: The Opinion Research Corporation releases a poll showing that only 20 percent of Americans believe the United States should have withdrawn from Vietnam before its troops became involved in combat.

December 15

AIR WAR: In the first raid on a major North Vietnamese industrial target, U.S. Air Force planes destroy a thermal power plant at Uong Bi, 14 miles north of Haiphong. The plant reportedly supplies about 15 percent of North Vietnam's total electric power.

December 16

USA – MILITARY: General Westmoreland submits a new troop request to Defense Secretary McNamara, stating that he needs a total of 443,000 men by the end of 1966.

December 18

RIVER WAR: U.S. Navy forms the River Patrol Force (Task Force 116) which will launch Operation Game Warden to interdict North Vietnamese and Viet Cong bases and lines of communication in inland waterways in III and IV Corps Tactical Zones in April 1966.

December 18–19

SOUTH VIETNAM: Montagnard tribesmen, seeking autonomy from the South Vietnamese government, stage a series of uprisings in the Central Highlands.

December 19

TERRORISM: A recent increase in Viet Cong bombings prompts U.S. authorities to impose a daily curfew on U.S. forces stationed in Saigon.

December 21

USA – DOMESTIC: Representative Emmanuel Cellar (D-N.Y.) charges the Selective Service director, Lieutenant General Lewis Hershey, with "demeaning the draft act" by reclassifying students who participate in antiwar protests. Hershey denies the accusation.

December 22

CHINA: Beijing issues a statement asserting that "So far, a great part of the Soviet equipment supplied to Vietnam consisted of obsolete equipment discarded by the Soviet armed forces or damaged weapons cleaned out from the warehouse."

December 23

AIR WAR: A U.S. C-123 transport plane crashes into a mountain 240 miles north of Saigon, killing four U.S. crewmen and 81 South Vietnamese soldiers.

December 24

USA – GOVERNMENT: President Johnson suspends Operation Rolling Thunder, the bombing of North Vietnam, to encourage the leaders in Hanoi to agree to conduct negotiations; the bombing pause will last 37 days, until January 31, 1966.

December 26

GROUND WAR: Heavy VC attacks force Allied military authorities to abandon efforts to extend the Christmas truce.

December 27

DIPLOMACY: In conjunction with a bombing pause that began three days earlier, the United States initiates a massive peace drive, as international missions conducted by

General Westmoreland thanks entertainer Bob Hope for his many years of service to U.S. troops in the field, December 1965. *(National Archives)*

UN ambassador Goldberg, Ambassador-at-Large Harriman, Vice President Humphrey, and presidential assistant McGeorge Bundy depart for various world capitals. Their purpose is to explore the possibilities of attaining a negotiated settlement.

December 30
DIPLOMACY: The administration's current diplomatic campaign makes some headway when Poland, Yugoslavia, and Italy agree to aid U.S. peace efforts.

December 31
YEAR-END SUMMARY: Total U.S. strength in South Vietnam is 184,300; 1,369 American military personnel have been killed in action to date and more than 7,000 wounded. In the Rolling Thunder operation, 171 aircraft have been lost to date. There are 22,420 Free World Military Forces now in Vietnam. South Vietnamese military strength remains at 514,000, with a reported 11,000 killed, 22,600 wounded, and 7,400 missing during the previous year's fighting. An estimated 34,500 North Vietnamese and Viet Cong were killed during 1965. South Vietnam's government appears as unstable as ever, and in the United States, protests and demonstrations against the war are increasing.

1966

January 1
USA – MILITARY: Advance elements of the 1st Regiment, 1st Marine Division, arrive in Vietnam from Camp Pendleton, California, to conduct combat operations in I Corps; the rest of the division will follow by the end of March.

January 1–8

GROUND WAR: Paratroopers from the 173rd Airborne Brigade and Australian troops conduct Operation Marauder, a search and destroy operation in Hau Nghia Province, III Corps.

January 1–19

GROUND WAR: Elements of the 1st Cavalry Division conduct Operation Matador in Kontum and Pleiku Provinces, II Corps, to provide security for the incoming 3rd Brigade of the 25th Infantry Division. Casualties are U.S.: 6 KIA, 41 WIA; NVA/VC: 4 KIA, 6 POWs.

January 3

CAMBODIA: In a letter to the UN's secretary-general U Thant, the Cambodian government warns that if Allied forces violate its territory or airspace, it will seek aid from other nations and conduct armed attacks into South Vietnam. The letter also requests that the International Control Commission (ICC) expand its border patrols to investigate reports of arms shipments from Cambodia into South Vietnam, as well as charges that U.S. and ARVN units are attacking Khmer villages.

January 4

NORTH VIETNAM: The Foreign Ministry in Hanoi finally acknowledges the bombing pause in a statement calling recent U.S. diplomatic efforts "a large scale deceptive peace campaign coupled with the trick of 'temporary suspensions of air attack.'" Hanoi asserts that the United States is preparing to double its strength in South Vietnam, while intensifying air attacks over Laos and sending American troops into central Laos and Cambodia.

USA – DOMESTIC: Returning from a recent trip to South Vietnam, Senator George McGovern (D-S.D.) contends that U.S. peace proposals have little chance of success, because the administration refuses to recognize that the conflict is primarily a civil war between the Saigon regime and the National Liberation Front. McGovern asserts that any talks that exclude either of these parties are doomed to failure.

January 5

DIPLOMACY: U.S. ambassador to the UN Arthur Goldberg circulates a letter asking that UN members help "advance the cause of a peaceful settlement" in Vietnam. He states that the United States is "prepared for discussions or negotiations with no prior conditions whatsoever."

January 6

USA – DOMESTIC: John Lewis, chairman of the Student Nonviolent Coordinating Committee, issues a policy statement attacking U.S. actions in Vietnam and announcing SNCC's support of the men "who are unwilling to respond to a military draft."

GROUND WAR: VC forces employ 120 mm mortars for the first time in an attack on the Special Forces camp near Khe Sanh in Quang Tri Province.

January 8

USA – GOVERNMENT: In a report to the Senate Foreign Relations Committee following a recently completed fact-finding tour of Vietnam, Senate Majority Leader Mike Mansfield (D-Mont.) provides a gloomy assessment, observing that the military situation is no better than it had been "at the outset." Senate Majority Leader Everett Dirksen of Illinois expresses opposition to President Johnson's offer of "negotiations without prior conditions" in a statement asserting that total military victory must precede any peace talks. He further urges that the war be extended by blockading North Vietnam.

January 8–14
GROUND WAR: In Operation Crimp/Buckskin, a massive search and destroy operation in III Corps, U.S. forces from the 173rd Airborne Division and other elements of the 1st Infantry Division, supported by troops from Australia and New Zealand, converge on the "Iron Triangle," a stronghold area northwest of Saigon. The Allied forces uncover and destroy a huge tunnel network before pulling out of the area. Casualties are NVA/VC: 107 KIA, 9 POW.

January 12
USA – GOVERNMENT: In his State of the Union speech, President Johnson reveals that, during the previous year, administration officials engaged in "300 private talks for peace in Vietnam with friends and adversaries throughout the world."

January 14
USSR: Moscow issues a communiqué pledging increased military aid to North Vietnam. The statement also reaffirms Soviet support of Hanoi's four-point peace formula as "the only correct basis for solving the Vietnamese problem."

January 16
USA – DOMESTIC: Sixteen Harvard University professors and 13 other scientists condemn the use of crop-destroying defoliation agents in Vietnam.

January 17
TERRORISM: After ambushing his car, VC guerrillas kidnap Douglas Ramsey, a U.S. aid mission representative in Hau Nghia Province. He will not be released until February 12, 1973.

January 18
USA – GOVERNMENT: John McNaughton, assistant secretary of defense, prepares a paper titled "Some Observations About Bombing North Vietnam," which reflects a very pessimistic assessment of the bombing campaign against North Vietnam, concluding that "the program so far has not successfully interdicted infiltration of men and materiel into South Vietnam." Despite the pessimism of his analysis, McNaughton goes on to recommend "more effort for pacification, more push behind the Ky government, more battalions . . . and intensive interdiction bombing."

January 19–February 21
GROUND WAR: Troops from 1st Brigade, 101st Airborne Division, the Republic of Korea's 2nd Marine Brigade, and ARVN forces conduct Operation Van Buren, a combined security effort to protect the rice crop in Phu Yen Province, II Corps. Casualties are NVA/VC: 679.

A Viet-Nam soldier
prepares to bury
his infant son,
slain
by the Viet Cong

'liberation' or conquest ?

THE STRUGGLE IN SOUTH VIETNAM

The cover of a pamphlet that purports to describe the truth about the nature of the insurgent cause in South Vietnam, 1966 *(National Archives)*

January 20

USA – GOVERNMENT: In a speech at Independence, Missouri, President Johnson says that Hanoi is holding up peace because the North Vietnamese leaders hope the United States will quit and urges Hanoi to respond positively to the bombing pause and peace campaign by agreeing to begin peace talks. In testimony before a joint session of the Senate Armed Services and Appropriations Committee, General Earle

Wheeler warns that a permanent bombing halt will deprive the United States of an important bargaining chip in any negotiations that might be arranged.

January 21
GROUND WAR: Viet Cong forces violate a cease-fire called in observance of the Vietnamese Tet holiday.

January 23
USA – MILITARY: The newly renamed Military Airlift Command (MAC) completes Operation Blue Light, the airlift of the 3rd Brigade, 25th Infantry Division, from Hawaii to Pleiku, South Vietnam, to offset the buildup of Communist forces there. The airlift began on December 23, 1965, and its 231 C-141 sorties have moved approximately 3,000 troops and 4,700 tons of equipment.

January 24
NORTH VIETNAM: Ho Chi Minh attacks American peace overtures in a statement demanding that Washington recognize the National Liberation Front "as the sole representative of the people of South Vietnam" and adopt Hanoi's four-point peace formula as a basis for ending the war.

USA – GOVERNMENT: In a memorandum to President Johnson, Defense Secretary McNamara recommends raising the number of U.S. troops in Vietnam to more than 400,000 by year's end, but warns that planned deployments and increased bombing will not ensure military success and the United States may be faced with a "standoff" by 1967 that requires the deployment of even more troops.

January 25
USA – GOVERNMENT: President Johnson strongly suggests that he has decided to resume bombing at a joint White House meeting of the National Security Council with a bi-partisan group of congressional leaders. The administration also releases intelligence reports showing that North Vietnam is using the bombing pause to increase shipments of war supplies along the Ho Chi Minh Trail, infiltrate additional troops into South Vietnam, and repair bridges and other transport facilities damaged by U.S. bombings.

January 25–March 6
GROUND WAR: In Operation Masher/White Wing/Thang Phong II, the largest search-and-destroy operation to date, the U.S. 1st Cavalry Division (Airmobile), South Vietnamese, and Korean forces sweep through Binh Dinh Province in the central lowlands along the coast of II Corps. The operation includes a bloody three-day battle in a small village eight miles north of Bong Son against two battalions of the 22nd NVA Regiment and a 12-day battle in the Kim Son Valley. Casualties are U.S.: 228 KIA, 834 WIA; NVA/VC: 1,342 KIA, 633 POWs.

January 26
USA – GOVERNMENT: In testimony before the House Foreign Affairs Committee, Secretary of State Rusk declares that, despite the bombing suspension, VC terrorists are still conducting bombings and assassinations in South Vietnam. Speaking

at a New York luncheon the same day, special presidential adviser Maxwell Taylor (formerly ambassador to South Vietnam) states that the reasons for halting the raids have been "exhausted." Meanwhile, an Associated Press poll of 50 senators shows that 25 favor a resumption of the bombing.

January 28
USA – MILITARY: Defense Secretary McNamara receives a message from General Westmoreland stating that, in addition to the 443,000 troops already requested, he needs another 16,000 men by year's end.

January 28–February 19
GROUND WAR: A U.S. Marine force of more than 5,000 conducts Operation Double Eagle, a companion operation to the 1st Cavalry's Masher/White Wing. The operation is designed to trap the enemy between the two attacking U.S. forces in Quang Ngai and Binh Dinh Provinces. Casualties are U.S.: 24 KIA, 156 WIA; NVA/VC: 312 KIA, 9 POW.

January 30
SOUTH VIETNAM: In honor of Tet, the Vietnamese lunar new year, the Saigon government releases 21 North Vietnamese Army POWs.

January 31
USA – GOVERNMENT: In a televised address to the nation, President Johnson announces a resumption of Operation Rolling Thunder after a 37-day pause. The president also discloses that he has instructed Ambassador Arthur Goldberg to ask the UN Security Council to arrange an international conference to end the conflict.

February
USA – MILITARY: The U.S. Air Force's 460th Tactical Reconnaissance Wing deploys to South Vietnam for combat operations.

February 1
NORTH VIETNAM: In an article in the January issue of the North Vietnamese Communist Party journal, *Hoc Tap,* General Vo Nguyen Giap asserts that U.S. military efforts have failed "to stabilize the very critical position of the puppet army and administration" of the South Vietnamese government. Moreover, Giap adds, U.S. commitments elsewhere limit the number of men that can be sent to Vietnam. Also this day, Hanoi issues a statement declaring that, because "consideration of the United States war acts in Vietnam fall within the competence of the 1954 Geneva conference," any U.S. Security Council resolution for "intervening in the Vietnam questions would be null and void."

February 2
USA – GOVERNMENT: Defense Secretary McNamara reveals that retired lieutenant general James Gavin's proposal that U.S. troops limit their activities to coastal enclaves was considered by senior Pentagon officials, but all had rejected it. Such a withdrawal would allow enemy forces to consolidate their hold on large areas of South Vietnam and leave ARVN units open to decimation.

February 3

NORTH VIETNAM: An article by Le Duc Tho in the North Vietnamese Communist Party newspaper *Nhan Dan* indicates that not all party members agree with Hanoi's war policy. Tho charges that some comrades "have made an incorrect assessment of the balance of power between the enemy and us and of the enemy ruses. Now they entertain subjectivism and pacifism, slacken their vigilance and fail to get ideologically ready for combat."

February 6–9

USA – GOVERNMENT: President Johnson meets with Nguyen Cao Ky and Nguyen Van Thieu in Honolulu; Johnson announces renewed emphasis on "The Other War," the attempt to provide the South Vietnamese rural population with local security and economic and social programs to win their active support. The talks conclude with issuance of a joint declaration in which the United States promises to help South Vietnam to "prevent aggression," develop its economy, and establish "the principles of self-determination of peoples and government by the consent of the governed." The president declares, "We are determined to win not only military victory but victory over hunger, disease, and despair." In his final statement on the discussions, President Johnson warns conference participants that he will be monitoring their efforts to build democracy, improve education and health care, resettle refugees, and reconstruct South Vietnam's economy.

February 7

SOUTH VIETNAM: Rural Pacification Minister Nguyen Duc Thang reveals that current Saigon pacification efforts reach only about 1,900 of the country's 15,000 hamlets; he further observes that it would require five to six years to place a typical province under government control.

February 8

USA – GOVERNMENT: In testimony before the Senate Foreign Relations Committee, retired lieutenant general James Gavin declares that U.S. foreign policy in Vietnam is "alarmingly out of balance." Gavin also cautions that any further large increases in U.S. troop strength could prompt Chinese intervention and even reopen the Korean front.

February 10

USA – GOVERNMENT: Former ambassador to Russia and presidential adviser George Kennan tells the Senate Foreign Relations Committee that "preoccupation with Vietnam" has caused the United States to neglect more important problems elsewhere. Kennan is particularly concerned about the war's impact on U.S.-Soviet relations.
CHINA: China accuses the USSR of conspiring with the United States to force North Vietnam to the negotiating table. Beijing issues a statement charging that Soviet leaders are allied with the United States against China and that the principal purpose of Soviet aid to North Vietnam is "to sow dissention in Sino-Vietnamese relations and to help the United States to realize its peace talk plot."

February 10–March 2

GROUND WAR: The U.S. 1st Infantry Division and a battalion from the Royal Australian Regiment conduct Operation Rolling Stone to provide security for road building crews working on highways in Binh Duong Province, III Corps. Casualties are NVA/VC: 173.

February 11
USA – GOVERNMENT: President Johnson discloses that additional U.S. forces will be sent to Vietnam to augment the 205,000 troops already serving there, but indicates that the buildup will be gradual.

February 14
TERRORISM: Land mines kill 56 South Vietnamese peasants in three separate blasts along a road near Tuy Hoa, 225 miles northeast of Saigon.

February 15
FRANCE: In a response to a letter from Ho Chi Minh asking that he use his influence to "prevent perfidious new maneuvers" by the United States in Southeast Asia, President Charles de Gaulle states that France is willing to do all that it can to end the war and outlines the French position on Vietnam—that the Geneva agreements should be enforced, that Vietnam's independence should be "guaranteed by the non-intervention of any outside powers," and that the Vietnamese government should pursue a "policy of strict neutrality."

February 16
INTERNATIONAL: The Central Committee of the World Council of Churches adopts a resolution proposing an immediate cease-fire in Vietnam.

February 17
USA – GOVERNMENT: In testimony before the Senate Foreign Relations Committee, General Maxwell Taylor states that a major U.S. objective in Vietnam is to demonstrate that "wars of liberation" are "costly, dangerous and doomed to failure." Discussing the American air campaign against North Vietnam, Taylor declares that its primary purpose is "to change the will of the enemy leadership."

February 20–March 1
GROUND WAR: A U.S. Marine task force conducts Operation Double Eagle II, a follow-on operation to Double Eagle I in Quang Tin and Quang Nam Provinces, I Corps. Casualties are U.S.: 6 KIA, 136 WIA; NVA/VC: 125 KIA, 15 POW.

February 21–27
GROUND WAR: The U.S. 1st Infantry Division conducts Operation Mastiff, a search and destroy mission in Tay Ninh Province, III Corps. During the course of the operation, three VC camps and an arms factory are destroyed in the Boi Loi Woods.

February 22
GROUND WAR: A U.S. Marine patrol rescues 23 men and seven women from a Viet Cong prison camp 350 miles northeast of Saigon.

February 23
SOUTH VIETNAM: According to an Allied spokesman in Saigon, 90,000 South Vietnamese deserted in 1965—twice the number in 1964 and almost 14 percent of

ARVN troop strength. By contrast, best estimates indicate that fewer than 20,000 VC defected during the previous year.

February 25
GROUND WAR: Elements of the U.S. 1st Infantry Division uncover and destroy three VC camps and an arms factory during an operation in the Boi Loi Woods.

February 27–March 3
GROUND WAR: The 2nd Battalion, 1st U.S. Marines, conducts Operation New York, an assault against well-entrenched VC positions northeast of Phu Bai in Thua Thien Province, I Corps. Casualties are U.S.: 17 KIA, 37 WIA; NVA/VC: 122 KIA, 7 POW.

March
SOUTH VIETNAM: Buddhist-led anti-government demonstrations begin in Hue, Danang, and Saigon and will last until June.
USA – MILITARY: The U.S. Air Force's 366th Tactical Fighter Wing and 315th Air Commando Wings are deployed to Vietnam for combat operations. U.S. II Field Force Vietnam is established to coordinate U.S. Army combat operations in III Corps and IV Corps.

March 1
USA – GOVERNMENT: The Senate passes an emergency war funds bill, but rejects an amendment repealing the Tonkin Gulf Resolution proposed by Senator Wayne Morse (D-Oreg.).

March 2
USA – GOVERNMENT: Secretary of Defense McNamara announces that American forces in South Vietnam now total 215,000, with another 20,000 en route. He denies charges that Vietnam requirements have overextended U.S. military resources and asserts that the nation has the capacity to support a major buildup in Vietnam and remain "fully capable of meeting our commitments elsewhere in the world."

March 3
AIR WAR: In response to intelligence that the North Vietnamese are concentrating supplies, USAF jets pound various Red River Valley transport facilities, 40 miles from the Chinese border.

March 3–6
GROUND WAR: The U.S. 1st Infantry Division conducts Operation Cocoa Beach in Binh Duong Province, III Corps. Casualties are U.S.: 10 KIA, 25 WIA; NVA/VC: more than 200 KIA (estimated).

March 4–8
GROUND WAR: Operation Utah/Lien Ket-26 is conducted by more than 7,000 U.S. Marine and ARVN troops in vicinity of Quang Ngai City in I Corps; the operation is launched in response to an ARVN force's call for help. Casualties are U.S.: 98 KIA, 278 WIA; ARVN: 30 KIA, 120 WIA; NVA/VC: 632 KIA.

March 7

AIR WAR: In the heaviest air raids since the bombing began in February 1965, U.S. Air Force and Navy planes fly an estimated 200 sorties against North Vietnam, hitting an oil storage area 60 miles southeast of Dien Bien Phu and a staging area 60 miles northwest of Vinh.

March 7–23

GROUND WAR: Elements of the U.S. 1st Infantry Division, 173rd Airborne Brigade, and the 10th ARVN Division conduct Operation Silver City in War Zone D, Binh Duong Province, III Corps. Casualties: NVA/VC: 303 KIA.

March 9

USA – GOVERNMENT: The State Department issues a 52-page document contending that U.S. intervention in Vietnam is legally justified under international law, the UN Charter, and the U.S. Constitution.

SOUTH VIETNAM: Announcement is made that, as part of an effort to deny food to Viet Cong guerrillas, South Vietnamese pilots flying U.S. aircraft have destroyed 20,000 acres of crops.

March 9–11

GROUND WAR: VC troops overrun a U.S. Special Forces camp at A Shau near the Laotian border after two days of savage fighting. A Marine helicopter manages to lift out 12 of the 17 Green Berets and 172 of the 400-man Vietnamese garrison, but three UH-34 helicopters are shot down.

March 12

SOUTH VIETNAM: Air Vice-Marshal Nguyen Cao Ky, acting as premier, removes the powerful and semiautonomous commander of I Corps, General Nguyen Chanh Thi, a leading Buddhist and potential rival to Ky. Buddhist monks and students quickly join demonstrations supporting General Thi and attacking the Ky regime.

USA – DOMESTIC: After a White House orientation on the war, 38 state governors endorse a resolution declaring that they are fully committed to administration policies in Vietnam and "believe the vast majority of Americans are, too."

March 16

USA – GOVERNMENT: Reporting on his observations during a visit to Vietnam, Representative Clement Zablocki (D-Wis.) claims that for every VC guerrilla killed in recent search and destroy missions, six civilians have died.

March 19

SOUTH KOREA: The South Korean assembly votes to send 20,000 additional troops to Vietnam; 21,000 ROK troops are currently serving in the war zone.

March 19–23

GROUND WAR: U.S. Marines and ARVN troops conduct Operation Oregon in Thua Thien Province, I Corps. Casualties are U.S.: 11 KIA, 45 WIA; NVA/VC: 48 KIA, 8 POW.

March 19–24

GROUND WAR: U.S. Marines and ARVN troops conduct Operation Texas/Lien Ket-26 to retake An Hoa outpost in Quang Ngai Province, I Corps. Casualties are U.S.: 99 KIA, 212 WIA; NVA/VC: 280 to 405 KIA (estimated).

March 22

USA – GOVERNMENT: In a memorandum to Defense Secretary Robert McNamara, Assistant Secretary John McNaughton contends that, although air raids against North Vietnam bolster South Vietnamese morale and provide a bargaining chip for future negotiations, there is no evidence that "they meaningfully reduce either the capacity or the will for the DRV to support the VC." He recommends that the bombings be restricted to a narrow "interdiction and verification zone" in Laos and that steps be taken to construct a physical anti-infiltration barrier.

March 23

CHINA: Beijing rejects a Soviet invitation to a Communist Party congress and reiterates its charges that Soviet leaders are collaborating in a U.S. "plot" to impose peace talks on North Vietnam.

March 25

USA – DOMESTIC: At a New York City rally sponsored by Veterans and Reservists to End the War in Vietnam, 15 veterans from both world wars and the Korean conflict burn their discharge and separation papers.

March 25–April 8

GROUND WAR: Elements of the U.S. 1st Cavalry and a brigade of the 25th Infantry Division conduct Operation Lincoln in Darlac, Kontum, and Pleiku Provinces, II Corps. Casualties are U.S.: 51 KIA, 136 WIA; NVA/VC: 522 KIA, 18 POW.

April

USA – MILITARY: The remainder of the U.S. 25th Infantry Division deploys from Hawaii to Vietnam to join the division's 2nd Brigade in the conduct of combat operations in III Corps; the division will be headquartered at Cu Chi, Hau Nghia Province. The 1st Signal Brigade deploys to Vietnam from Fort Gordon, Georgia, to provide signal support for U.S. forces in Vietnam. The 44th Medical Brigade deploys to Vietnam from Fort Sam Houston, Texas, to provide medical support for U.S. forces in Vietnam. The 5th Marine Regiment, 1st Marine Division, deploys to Vietnam from Camp Pendleton, California, for combat operations in I Corps. The USAF 35th Tactical Fighter Wing deploys to Vietnam for service in II Corps. Headquarters U.S. Naval Forces Vietnam is formed to coordinate naval activities in Vietnam.

RIVER WAR: U.S. Navy TF116 (River Patrol Force) begins Operation Game Warden, the interdiction of enemy traffic in South Vietnamese inland waterways.

April 1

USA – GOVERNMENT: Walt Rostow replaces McGeorge Bundy as national security advisor to the president.

TERRORISM: Viet Cong commandos set off 200 pounds of explosives at a Saigon hotel housing U.S. troops, heavily damaging the nine-story building and killing three Americans and four South Vietnamese.

AIR WAR: Seventh Air Force Headquarters at Tan Son Nhut air base in Saigon is activated as a subcommand of Pacific Air Forces to coordinate USAF activities in Vietnam.

April 4

AIR WAR: U.S. F-4C Phantom fighter-bombers pound the main supply link between North Vietnam and Nanning, China, striking the Phu Lang Thuong railroad bridge, 25 miles northeast of Hanoi; in a related raid, U.S. planes destroy the Phu To railroad bridge northwest of Hanoi.

April 7

GROUND WAR: VC forces overrun a South Vietnamese outpost 25 miles south of Saigon.

April 9

USA – GOVERNMENT: Concern over the confrontation between the regime in Saigon and the Buddhists prompts the administration to conduct a reassessment of Vietnam policy. Undersecretary of State George Ball urges that the United States cut its losses and "halt the deployment of additional troops, reduce the level of air attacks on the North, and maintain ground activity at the minimum level required to prevent the substantial improvement of the Viet Cong position." Other advisers, including CIA analyst George Carver, Assistant Secretary of State William Bundy, and Defense Secretary McNamara recommend a continuation of current policies. However, there is little optimism, even among those who endorse present administration efforts.

USA – GOVERNMENT: The administration publicly concedes for the first time that political turmoil in South Vietnam has begun to disrupt military operations by restricting the activities of ARVN forces.

USA – MILITARY: The U.S. Air Force announces a new policy limiting pilots and crews stationed in Vietnam to a 12-month tour or 100 combat missions over North Vietnam; the Marine Corps and Navy state that they will retain their current policy of no limit on the number of missions pilots fly over North or South Vietnam.

April 12

GROUND WAR: Viet Cong guerrillas launch a mortar attack against Tan Son Nhut air base. During the attack, seven U.S. soldiers and South Vietnamese civilians are killed, 160 U.S. and ARVN troops are wounded, two transport aircraft are destroyed, and 23 helicopters and three planes are destroyed.

AIR WAR: U.S. B-52s from Anderson Air Base in Guam bomb North Vietnam for the first time, in a raid on the Mu Gia Pass, about 85 miles north of the border, the main route used to send supplies and infiltrators into South Vietnam through Laos.

CHINA: Beijing claims to have downed a U.S. attack plane over the Liu Chow Peninsula, north of Hainan island. Although the U.S. Department of Defense will not confirm the incident, it acknowledges that a tanker plane, flying from the Philippines to rejoin the carrier *Kitty Hawk,* is "overdue."

April 13
USA – DOMESTIC: The Southern Christian Leadership Council adopts a resolution urging that the United States "desist from aiding the military junta against the Buddhists, Catholics and students, whose efforts to democratize their government are more in consonance with our traditions than the policy of the military oligarchy."

April 14
SOUTH VIETNAM: Premier Ky and Chief of State Thieu pledge to dissolve the current ruling junta and hold elections for a constituent assembly with legislative powers. The statement mollifies Buddhist leaders, and its issuance signals an uneasy truce between Saigon and anti-government Buddhists.

April 16
USA – GOVERNMENT: At a National Security Council meeting, Assistant Secretary of State William Bundy presents a draft paper entitled "Basic Choices in Vietnam" that supports the option of continuing along current policy lines in South Vietnam. However, he warns that "the war could well become an albatross around the Administration's neck at least equal to what Korea was for President Truman in 1952."

April 17
SOUTH VIETNAM: Speakers at a Bien Hoa protest march involving thousands of Vietnamese Catholics demand that the government discipline Buddhist rioters.
AIR WAR: In the closest raids to Hanoi and Haiphong since the bombing began, U.S. planes destroy two missile sites and damage the main railroad bridge between the two cities.

April 18
USA – GOVERNMENT: In a speech to the Senate, majority leader Mike Mansfield (D-Mont.) declares that the current political crisis in Vietnam makes it urgent that the United States engage in direct talks with North Vietnam, Communist China, "and such elements in South Vietnam as may be essential to the making and keeping of a peaceful settlement" of the war. Beijing rejects the proposal.

April 21
SOUTH VIETNAM: The South Vietnamese government expels a group of six American pacifists for seeking to stage anti-war demonstrations in Saigon.
USA – DOMESTIC: In a lecture at the Johns Hopkins University School of Advanced International Studies, Senator William Fulbright (D-Ark.) warns that the United States is "succumbing to the arrogance of power."

April 23
USA – DOMESTIC: Appearing at the annual convention of the Americans for Democratic Action, Vice President Humphrey states that the administration is willing

"to talk to anyone" at a Vietnam peace conference and would cooperate with "any government the people of South Vietnam freely choose."

AIR WAR: U.S. Air Force F-4C Phantom jets shoot down two MiGs in an air clash over North Vietnam involving at least 16 MiGs and 14 American planes,.

April 26

AIR WAR: In an air battle 20 miles from the Chinese border, a USAF F-4C pilot is flying escort for F-105 Thunderchiefs when the flight is attacked; he shoots down a MiG-21, the most advanced Soviet-made fighter plane in the North Vietnamese air force, with an AIM-9 Sidewinder missile.

April 28

USA – GOVERNMENT: The air force announces that it is sending a team to Vietnam to investigate the efficiency and tactical usefulness of U.S. missiles, after receiving a report that American pilots fired 11 missiles without scoring a hit during the recent clash with two MiG-21s.

April 29

GROUND WAR: U.S. 1st Infantry Division troops uncover and destroy a huge cache of enemy war materiel during an operation in Tay Ninh Province, III Corps.

USSR: An article in the Soviet newspaper *Pravda* asserts that the television program *Batman* is brainwashing American children into becoming "murderers" in Vietnam.

May

USA – MILITARY: The U.S. 1st Aviation Brigade is organized in Vietnam to provide army aviation support for U.S. forces throughout Vietnam.

May 1

GROUND WAR: U.S. forces shell Communist targets in Cambodia.

May 2

USA – GOVERNMENT: In a speech before the U.S. Chamber of Commerce, Defense Secretary McNamara reports that North Vietnamese infiltration into the South is up to 4,500 men a month—three times the 1965 level.

May 3

SOUTH VIETNAM: The Reverend Hoang Quynh, leader of South Vietnam's Roman Catholics, warns against early elections, because the Ky government is estimated to control only 10 percent of the country's territory.

May 5

SOUTH VIETNAM: A 32-member committee, with representatives from all of South Vietnam's major religions, begins drafting a new election law.

May 6

USA – GOVERNMENT: In a memorandum to Secretaries Rusk and McNamara, presidential adviser Walt Rostow contends that on the basis of U.S. experience in Germany during World War II, a "systematic and sustained" bombing of North

Troops of the 173rd Airborne Brigade dash to helicopters under heavy fire during an operation 30 miles north of Saigon, May 1966. *(Texas Tech University Vietnam Archive)*

Vietnamese oil storage facilities could seriously cripple the enemy war effort. However, he warns that "If we take this step we must cut clean through POL system—and hold the cut—if we are looking for decisive results . . ."

May 8
SOUTH VIETNAM: Thich Thien Manh, co-chairman of the leadership committee of the Unified Buddhist Church's Institute of Religious Affairs, issues a statement warning that Vietnamese Buddhists will launch another protest movement if the government does not hold elections as promised.

AIR WAR: A U.S. military spokesman in Saigon reports that recent U.S. air strikes have cut four major railroad links serving Hanoi, including a vital route to Nanning, China; reconnaissance photos also show that the raids have severed two main highways that share bridges with two of the rail lines.

May 10–July 30
GROUND WAR: The U.S. 25th Infantry Division and ARVN troops conduct Operation Paul Revere/Thang Phong 14, a border-screening and area-control mission in Pleiku Province, II Corps. Casualties are U.S.: 10 WIA; NVA/VC: 546 KIA.

May 11
AIR WAR: U.S. Navy A-4 Skyhawk fighter-bombers destroy a surface-to-air missile site 10 miles northeast of Haiphong, as U.S. air raids move increasingly closer to major North Vietnamese population centers.

May 13

CHINA: Beijing charges that five U.S. planes "flagrantly intruded" over China's Yunnan Province and downed a "Chinese plane in training flight."

May 15–June 22

SOUTH VIETNAM: Premier Ky dispatches 1,500 troops to Danang, which has been in a state of virtual rebellion since General Thi's dismissal on March 10. The arrival of the troops touches off another wave of violent protest by Buddhist dissidents. During the next week, the Unified Buddhist Church issues a communiqué predicting that Ky's action will "surely lead to civil war." Besides deploying troops to troubled locales, the government also enters into negotiations with Buddhist leaders, and on June 6 the ruling National Leadership Committee of 10 generals is expanded to include 10 civilians. Two weeks later Premier Ky signs a decree setting September 10 as the date for the election of a constituent assembly with powers to appoint a civilian government. Meanwhile, on June 22, a force of 300 pro-government troops takes control of Quang Tri, the last remaining anti-government Buddhist stronghold.

May 17

USA – GOVERNMENT: Speaking at a Democratic Party fund-raiser in Chicago, President Johnson lashes out at critics of administration policy in Vietnam.

May 18

USA – DOMESTIC: Representative Melvin Laird (R-Mich.) states that a "credibility gap" is developing because the Johnson administration is not providing the American public with precise and candid information on planned troop deployments to Vietnam.

May 19

USA – MILITARY: A U.S. spokesman in Saigon reports that for only the third time since January 1961, more American than South Vietnamese soldiers were killed during the past week; the spokesman also discloses that the week's 6.1 to 1 kill ratio is the most favorable rating in nine months.

May 22

USA – MILITARY: In a television interview, Air Force Secretary Harold Brown reveals that President Johnson opposes widening the air war against North Vietnam, because such a move would not completely cut off North-South movement and might prompt Chinese intervention.

May 24

DIPLOMACY: UN Secretary-General U Thant states that the United Nations does not possess sufficient influence to compel the warring states in Vietnam to begin negotiations. Thant also urges that the NLF be allowed to participate in any peace talks which might be arranged.

May 30

CHINA: Beijing charges that U.S. planes killed three persons during an attack on Chinese fishing boats north of the Gulf of Tonkin in international waters.

May 30–31

AIR WAR: In the largest raids since air attacks on North Vietnam began in February 1965, U.S. planes destroy five bridges, 17 railroad cars, and 20 buildings in the Vinh-Thanh Hoa area. Other planes hit Highway 12 in four places north of Mu Gia Pass and inflict heavy damage on the Yen Bay arsenal and munition storage area, 75 miles northeast of Hanoi.

June

USA – MILITARY: The U.S. 3rd Naval Mobile Construction Brigade (Seabees) is formed at Danang to support navy and marine operations in I Corps.

AUSTRALIA/NEW ZEALAND: The 1st Battalion, Royal Australian Regiment, returns to Australia.

June 2–21

GROUND WAR: The 1st Brigade of the U.S. 101st Airborne Division joins with ARVN units to conduct Operation Hawthorne/Dan Thang-61 in Kontum Province, II Corps. Casualties are NVA/VC: 531 KIA.

June 2–July 13

GROUND WAR: The U.S. 1st Infantry Division and ARVN 5th Division launch Operation El Paso II against the VC 9th Division in Binh Long Province, III Corps. Casualties are NVA/VC: 855 KIA.

Actor John Wayne visits with marines at Chu Lai, June 1966. *(National Archives)*

June 4

USA – DOMESTIC: The Ad Hoc Universities Committee for the Statement on Vietnam takes a three-page advertisement in the *New York Times,* urging the administration to cease all offensive military operations and "evaluate seriously whether self-determination for the Vietnamese as well as our own national interest would not be best served by termination of our military presence."

June 9

GROUND WAR: During the third day of a battle in Kontum Province, Captain William S. Carpenter of the 101st Airborne Division calls for air strikes on his own position to prevent North Vietnamese attackers from wiping out his company; he is recommended for the Congressional Medal of Honor.

USA – MILITARY: In a speech at Nashville, Major General Ben Sternberg, commander of the 101st Airborne Division, states that an additional 500,000 men are needed to seal off South Vietnamese borders to enemy infiltration.

June 11

USA – GOVERNMENT: Defense Secretary McNamara discloses that another 18,000 troops will be sent to Vietnam, raising the U.S. commitment to 285,000 men.

June 15

GROUND WAR: Intelligence sources report that two fresh NVA regiments have moved into the Central Highlands from Laos to serve as the vanguard of a coming enemy offensive.

June 17

SOUTH VIETNAM: In an effort to stabilize the economy and boost official morale, the South Vietnamese government devaluates its currency, lifts some controls on business transactions, and raises the salaries of military and civil servants.

June 18

USA – MILITARY: The JCS receives a new request from General Westmoreland for an additional 111,588 men, saying he will need a total of 542,588 troops for 1967.

June 19–July 1

GROUND WAR: Elements of the U.S. 1st Cavalry Division and 1st Brigade, 101st Airborne, conduct Operation Nathan Hale, a search and destroy mission to clear and secure the Tuy Hoa Valley in Phu Yen Province, II Corps. Casualties are U.S.: 66 KIA, 353 WIA; NVA/VC: 459 KIA, 35 POW.

June 21

NORTH VIETNAM: Hanoi reiterates its demand that an unconditional bombing halt precede negotiations, rejecting a new American proposal for the opening of peace talks.

June 21–27

AIR WAR: U.S. planes strike North Vietnamese petroleum storage facilities in a series of devastating raids.

June 23
SOUTH VIETNAM: Government troops seize Buddhist headquarters at Saigon, bringing to an end a wave of protest that had begun in March with agitation against military rule.

USA – DOMESTIC: The American Baptist Association unanimously endorses a resolution denouncing "the rash of protests and demonstrations" against U.S. policy in Vietnam.

June 24
USA – GOVERNMENT: On a trip to Saigon to help develop civic action programs, presidential adviser Robert Komer declares that pacification efforts should be given top priority. Komer's mission reflects renewed concern among U.S. policymakers about the stability of the South Vietnamese government.

June 29
AIR WAR: U.S. bombers attack fuel storage installations near Hanoi and Haiphong, destroying an estimated 50 percent of North Vietnam's fuel supply. These are the first raids in the immediate vicinity of the two cities and constitute a major escalation of the air war over North Vietnam.

June 30
USA – GOVERNMENT: The Hanoi-Haiphong air strikes are both applauded and denounced in Congress. In voicing his approval, Senator Richard Russell (R-Ga.) states that the raids will reduce American casualties. Sixteen Democratic representatives issue a joint statement declaring that the expanded air strikes commit the United States to "a profoundly dangerous policy of brinkmanship" that challenges China.

CHINA: Beijing calls the Hanoi-Haiphong raids a serious escalation of the war, warning that it is prepared for any eventuality.

July 1
NORTH VIETNAM: Authorities decide to evacuate all persons from Hanoi "except those who have tasks of production or fighting, to assure the defeat of the United States war escalation."

INTERNATIONAL: The World Council of Churches in Geneva sends a cable to President Johnson saying that the latest bombing of North Vietnam is causing a "widespread reaction" of "resentment and alarm" among many Christians. In India, mobs protest the air raids on the Hanoi-Haiphong area with violent anti-American demonstrations in several cities. The Greek Orthodox Church of North America expresses "wholehearted" support for the United States stand against all aggressors, particularly in Vietnam.

July 1–5
AIR WAR: U.S. Air Force and Navy jets carry out another series of raids on fuel installations in the Hanoi-Haiphong area. China reacts by calling the bombings "barbarous and wanton acts that have further freed us from any bounds of restrictions in helping North Vietnam."

July 4

USA – DOMESTIC: The national convention of the Congress of Racial Equality (CORE) votes to adopt two resolutions on the Vietnam War. One calls for the withdrawal of U.S. troops; the other attacks the draft as placing "a heavy discriminatory burden on minority groups and the poor."

July 4–October 28

GROUND WAR: U.S. Marines and ARVN troops conduct Operation Macon, a security operation to protect the An Hoa industrial complex in Quang Nam Province, I Corps. Casualties are U.S.: 24 KIA, 172 WIA; NVA/VC: 380 KIA.

July 5

USA – GOVERNMENT: During a press conference, President Johnson expresses his disappointment at the reaction of a "few" U.S. allies. In New York, Australian prime minister Harold Holt says that he agrees with Johnson that the bombing of the Hanoi-Haiphong area is a "military necessity."

July 5–7

USA – DOMESTIC: State and territorial governors meeting in Los Angeles adopt a resolution expressing "support of our global commitments, including our support of the military defense of South Vietnam against aggression." The resolution passes with a vote of 49–1, with Governor Mark Hatfield (R-Oreg.) the only dissenter.

July 6

INTERNATIONAL: The seven active members of the Communist bloc's Warsaw Pact Treaty military alliance announce their readiness to send "volunteers" to aid North Vietnam in its fight against American "aggression," but only if Hanoi requests them.

July 6–7

AIR WAR: U.S. jets fly 80 missions against petroleum facilities in the Hanoi-Haiphong area. Pentagon officials report that 80 percent to 90 percent of North Vietnam's fuel facilities have come under air attack and 55 percent have been destroyed.

July 6–9

POWs: Hanoi Radio reports that several captured U.S. pilots have been paraded through Hanoi and that angry mobs have demanded punishment for the "American air pirates." On July 7 and July 9, statements are broadcast in which captured pilots allegedly confess their "crimes" against North Vietnam.

July 7

GREAT BRITAIN: The House of Commons defeats a Conservative motion (331–230) that would have committed Britain to support U.S. policy on Vietnam without reservation. A government motion upholding Prime Minister Harold Wilson's support of American policy, but dissociating Britain from the U.S. raids on the Hanoi-Haiphong area, is adopted 299–230.

July 7–August 3

GROUND WAR: A force of more than 8,500 U.S. Marines and 2,500 South Vietnamese conducts Operation Hastings/Lam Son-289 in Quang Tri Province, I Corps, to drive the North Vietnamese 324-B Division back across the DMZ and preempt and

Viet Cong antiaircraft gunners shoot at allied aircraft in Thua Thien Province. *(Texas Tech University Vietnam Archive)*

disrupt enemy plans to mass and attack Quang Tri and Thua Thien. Casualties are U.S.: 126 KIA, 446 WIA; VNMC: 21 KIA, 40 WIA; NVA/VC: 882 KIA, 17 POW.

July 8
SOUTH VIETNAM: Premier Ky calls for sterner military measures, including a land invasion of North Vietnam.

July 9–August 5
USSR: The Soviet Union sends a note to the U.S. embassy in Moscow charging that the air strikes on the port of Haiphong endangered four Soviet ships that were in the harbor. The United States rejects the Soviet protest on July 23, claiming that "Great care had been taken to assure the safety of shipping in Haiphong." A second Soviet note, charging that a Russian ship had been hit by bullets during the raid on August 2, is also rejected by the U.S. embassy, on August 5.

July 11
USA – DOMESTIC: A Harris survey taken shortly after the Hanoi-Haiphong raids shows that 62 percent of those interviewed favor the raids, 11 percent are opposed, and 27 percent are undecided. Of those polled, 86 percent feel the raids will hasten the end of the war.

AIR WAR: Officials in Saigon report increased air attacks in Laos to interdict North Vietnamese infiltration. More than 100 strikes a day are being carried out (this contrasted with fewer than 50 a day six months ago).

July 12–23
POWs: The National Committee for a Sane Nuclear Policy (SANE) and U.S. Social-ist Norman Thomas appeal to North Vietnam's President Ho Chi Minh on behalf

of captured American pilots. On July 15, 18 U.S. senators generally opposed to President Johnson's Vietnam policy sign a statement calling on North Vietnam to "Refrain from any act of vengeance against American airmen." Next day the UN secretary-general urges North Vietnam to exercise restraint in the treatment of American prisoners. Statements by North Vietnamese ambassadors in Beijing and Prague assert on July 19 that the Americans will go on trial, but Ho gives assurances of a humanitarian policy toward the prisoners in response, he says, to the appeal he received from SANE and Norman Thomas.

July 15

AIR WAR: U.S. aircraft fly a record 121 missions against North Vietnam targets, focusing on missile-launching sites in the Hanoi area. Navy jets strike at a fuel dump two miles from Vinh.

July 16–18

GROUND WAR: A U.S. Marine Battalion Landing Team conducts Operation Deckhouse II, amphibious and helicopter assaults to block North Vietnamese routes of entry into Quang Tri Province, I Corps. Casualties are NVA/VC: 24 KIA.

July 21–September 5

GROUND WAR: Troops from the U.S. 4th Infantry Division, the 1st Brigade of the 101st Airborne Division, and the 47th ARVN Regiment conduct Operation John Paul Jones, a mission to secure the Vung Ro Pass in Phu Yen Province, II Corps. Casualties are U.S.: 23 KIA, 132 WIA; NVA/VC: 209 KIA, 40 POW.

July 22

SOUTH VIETNAM: The government lodges a formal protest with the ICC accusing North Vietnam of using the DMZ to infiltrate troops into Quang Tri Province. Specific mention is made of the North Vietnamese 324-B Division, the force engaged in Operation Hastings.

USA – DOMESTIC: Senator J. William Fulbright (D-Ark.) charges that President Johnson is following a policy of "the United States taking on the role of policeman and provider for all non-Communist Asia."

July 30–August 5

AIR WAR: For the first time, U.S. planes intentionally bomb targets in the DMZ. The 15 B-52 jet bombers fly from Guam and strike a Communist camp and supply area a mile north of the Ben Hai River, returning five days later to strike it again.

July 31–August 13

CAMBODIA: Cambodia accuses the United States of bombing border villages and killing several people. A U.S. spokesman first denies that the villages were in Cambodia, then admits that they were. The second raid (August 2) takes place as representatives of the ICC are en route to the area to inspect damage inflicted on Thlok and another village. The damage is confirmed, but a U.S. embassy spokesman in Saigon says on August 12 that all "maps available to us show the two targets are in South Vietnam." The statement expresses "regret" for the error. Prince Sihanouk, Cambodian chief of state, cancels a scheduled September meeting with Ambassador-at-Large W. Averell Harriman to discuss U.S.-Cambodian diplomatic relations.

August

GROUND WAR: The U.S. 4th Infantry Division deploys to Vietnam from Fort Carson, Colorado, to conduct combat operations in II Corps; 196th Light Infantry Brigade deploys to Vietnam from Fort Devens, Massachusetts, to conduct combat operations in III Corps, with headquarters at Tay Ninh.

THE PHILIPPINES: Manila deploys a 2,000-man Philippine Civic Action Group (PHILCAG) to Vietnam for noncombatant operations in III Corps.

August 1–25

GROUND WAR: The U.S. 1st Cavalry Division (Airmobile), South Korean, and ARVN forces conduct Operation Paul Revere II, a border screening/surveillance and area control operation in Darlac and Pleiku Provinces, II Corps. Casualties are U.S.: 80 KIA, 272 WIA; ROK/ARVN: 97 KIA, 431 WIA; NVA/VC: 861 KIA, 119 POW.

August 2

AIR WAR: U.S. bombers attack Haiphong's fuel installations for the third time; Hanoi protests to the ICC.

August 3

AIR WAR: U.S. planes bomb a military headquarters 25 miles northeast of Haiphong.

August 3–January 31, 1967

GROUND WAR: Eleven battalions of U.S. Marines conduct Operation Prairie, a sequel to Operation Hastings, which involves a sweep just south of the DMZ against three battalions of the North Vietnamese 324-B Division. An additional 1,500 marines land from Seventh Fleet ships off Quang Tri Province on September 15 to assist in the operations. The key battle is fought along Mutter's Ridge. Casualties are U.S.: 239 KIA, 1,214 WIA, 1 MIA; NVA/VC: 1,397 KIA, 27 POW.

August 4–6

INDIA: India proposes an expansion of the ICC in the DMZ to prevent the spread of the fighting there. The United States and Canada accept the proposal, but South Vietnam says its acceptance is contingent on Hanoi's agreement.

August 6

USA – DOMESTIC: The 21th anniversary of the bombing of Hiroshima is marked by anti-war demonstrations across the United States.

SOUTH VIETNAM: Thich Thien Hoa, acting chairman of the Secular Affairs Institute of the United Buddhist Church, appeals for international aid to halt what he calls religious persecution of the South Vietnamese people by the Ky regime.

August 6–22

GROUND WAR: U.S. Marines and ARVN forces conduct Operation Colorado/Lien Ket-52 to drive the North Vietnamese from the Que Son Valley in Quang Nam and Quang Tin Provinces, I Corps. Casualties are U.S.: 14 KIA, 65 WIA; NVA/VC: 674 KIA.

August 8

AIR WAR: Three USAF F-105 Thunderchief fighter-bombers are shot down by North Vietnamese ground fire. Major James H. Kasler, regarded by many as one of the leading pilots of the war, bails out and is captured.

August 9

AIR WAR: U.S. warplanes attack two South Vietnamese villages, Truong Trung and Truong Tay, by mistake, killing 63 and wounding 100.

August 10

GROUND WAR: Troops of the 1st Battalion, 5th Marines, fight a bitter battle against NVA forces in Quang Tin Province, 60 miles west of Tam Ky.

AIR WAR: A U.S.-built air base is opened at Sattahib, Thailand. This ceremony marks the first public acknowledgment of U.S.-Thai cooperation in the war.

August 11

AIR WAR: U.S. jets fly 118 missions against targets in the Haiphong area, to include the Uong Bi power plant and 14 oil depots and storage areas.

August 13

CAMBODIA: Prince Sihanouk criticizes the United States over the attack on Thlock, a Cambodian village close to the South Vietnamese border.

USA – GOVERNMENT: In the United States, General William Westmoreland meets with President Johnson at his ranch in Texas to discuss the general's personal assessment of Allied progress in the war.

August 16–19

USA – GOVERNMENT: The House Un-American Activities Committee investigates Americans who have given aid to the Viet Cong with a view toward introducing legislation to make such activities illegal. The hearings are almost immediately disrupted by demonstrators. Before the hearings are over, more than 50 people will be arrested for disorderly conduct. The chairman of the subcommittee, Representative J. R. Pool (D-Tex.) announces that the hearings have revealed that key leadership of groups supporting the Viet Cong are comprised of revolutionary, hard-core Communists.

August 18–19

GROUND WAR: In III Corps area, a company from the 6th Battalion of the Royal Australian Regiment is on patrol near the village of Long Tan when it encounters a much larger Viet Cong force moving to attack the Australian base at Nui Dat. For almost three hours, in darkness and pouring rain, the company fights off repeated attacks until a relief force gets through. Eighteen Australians are killed and 25 wounded. An estimated 245 Viet Cong are killed in the intense fighting.

August 19

USA – MILITARY: After studying classified documents, CIA analyst, Sam Adams will conclude that the irregular enemy forces (those besides the VC mainforce and North Vietnamese army units) are at least double the U.S. military estimates. This will trigger a debate that pits the CIA's analysts and conclusions against U.S. military intelligence.

August 23–29
SEA WAR: The American cargo ship *Baton Rouge Victory* strikes a mine laid by the Viet Cong in the Long Tao River, 22 miles south of Saigon. The half-submerged ship blocks the route from the South Vietnamese capital to the sea. Seven crewmen are killed.

August 24
DIPLOMACY: Secretary of State Rusk sends a letter to French foreign minister Maurice de Murville, outlining U.S. proposals for ending the war, with the hope that President Charles de Gaulle will use the proposals in his discussions with North Vietnamese during his upcoming trip to Asia. The French dismiss the letter as "containing nothing new."

August 26–January 20, 1968
GROUND WAR: The U.S. 1st Cavalry Division conducts Operation Byrd, a pacification operation in Binh Thuan Province, II Corps. Casualties are U.S.: 23 KIA, 278 WIA; NVA/VC: 849 KIA.
AIR WAR: U.S. warplanes fly a record 156 missions against targets along North Vietnam's southern coast and in the panhandle region.

August 28
SOUTH VIETNAM: Nguyen Huu Tho, the president of the National Liberation Front, invites other political groups to join the NLF in a broad and democratic coalition government for South Vietnam, enumerating three points as the basis for a political solution in Vietnam. Chief among these is the withdrawal of all U.S. troops.
USSR: It is reported in three Soviet newspapers that North Vietnamese pilots are undergoing training at a secret Soviet airbase to fly supersonic interceptors against U.S. aircraft.

August 29
CHINA: Beijing charges that U.S. warplanes sank a Chinese merchant ship and damaged another in raids on the Gulf of Tonkin. The Chinese claim that nine crewmen were killed and seven others wounded.

August 30
NORTH VIETNAM: Hanoi Radio announces that Deputy Premier Le Thanh Nghi has signed an agreement with Beijing whereby China will provide additional economic and technical aid to North Vietnam.

September
USA – MILITARY: The U.S. 11th Armored Cavalry Regiment deploys to Vietnam from Fort Meade, Maryland, to conduct combat operations in III Corps. The 18th Military Police Brigade deploys to Vietnam from Fort Meade, Maryland, to provide military police support for U.S. forces in Vietnam.
SOUTH KOREA: The ROK 9th Infantry Division is deployed to Vietnam for combat operations in II Corps.

September 1
NORTH VIETNAM: Soviet leaders assure Ho Chi Minh that Soviet aid is being geared to "the new phase of the war."

September 1–2
CAMBODIA: In a speech before 100,000 in Phnom Penh, Cambodia, President de Gaulle of France denounces U.S. policy in Vietnam and urges the U.S. government to pull its troops out of Southeast Asia. He says that negotiations toward a settlement of the war could begin as soon as the United States commits to withdrawing its troops by a certain date. He and Prince Norodom Sihanouk sign a declaration calling for noninterference in the Indochinese peninsula by foreign nations.

September 4
USA – GOVERNMENT: Assistant Secretary of State William Bundy on NBC-TV's *Meet The Press* rejects de Gaulle's proposal of September 1, saying that the United States intends to withdraw its forces when "the North Vietnamese get out." He also reveals that the United States now has 25,000 military personnel in Thailand, principally to support U.S. Air Force operations.

September 6
SOUTH VIETNAM: Thien Hoa of the United Buddhist Church issues an appeal to his followers to start a three-day hunger strike on September 8, protesting the elections to be held in South Vietnam on September 11.

AIR WAR: B-52 bombers strike twice at infiltration routes and Communist base camps in the southern section of the DMZ.

September 6–9
USA – MILITARY: Three U.S. soldiers who have refused to serve in Vietnam are court-martialed at Fort Dix, New Jersey. The court rejects their defense attorney's argument that the war is illegal and immoral.

September 9
USA – MILITARY: It is revealed in Saigon that the United States intends to step up its destruction of crops in VC-occupied areas by threefold.

September 11
SOUTH VIETNAM: A 117-member constituent assembly is elected to develop a new constitution and pave the way for a restoration of civilian government by 1967. Approximately 81 percent of registered voters take part despite VC intimidation and a widespread boycott by Buddhists, who charge that the election is "completely crooked." The Viet Cong try to disrupt the election by terrorist attacks against civilians and government installations.

September 12
AIR WAR: In the heaviest air raids of the war to date, approximately 500 USAF aircraft strike at a mixture of targets in the North, including coastal installations, transportation lines, and supply areas.

September 14

SOUTH VIETNAM: Journalists report that the South Vietnamese village of Lien Hoa has been razed to the ground by U.S. troops from the 1st Cavalry Division. Inhabitants had been warned to leave the village before it was burned and there were no civilian casualties.

September 14–November 24

GROUND WAR: In the largest operation to date, more than 20,000 U.S. and ARVN troops from the U.S. 1st Infantry Division, a brigade from the 9th Infantry Division, the 173rd Airborne Brigade, the 11th Armored Cavalry Regiment, several ARVN units, and eventually the newly arrived U.S. 196th Light Infantry Brigade conduct Operation Attleboro in War Zone C, 50 miles north of Saigon in Tay Ninh Province, III Corps. The purpose of the operation is to locate and eliminate all enemy troops west of the Michelin rubber plantation. Communist troops are identified as major elements of the 9th VC Division, the guerrillas' best trained and best equipped unit, and the 101st NVA Regiment. Communist resistance is strong, because Tay Ninh Province sector is thought to be the site of the principal VC command center for guerrilla operations in South Vietnam and the central office of the NLF. Casualties are U.S.: 155 KIA, 494 WIA; NVA/VC: 2,130 KIA.

U.S. Army's 145th Combat Aviation Battalion picks up soldiers of the 25th ARVN Division, 1966. *(Texas Tech University Vietnam Archive)*

September 16–19

CHINA: Beijing accuses U.S. aircraft of violations of airspace and attacks against villages and border crossings near the Munan Kwan Pass and in the Kwangsi-Chung region. Secretary of State Dean Rusk announces on the 16th that U.S. planes encountered MiG fighters on September 9 about 30 miles south of the Chinese border. A State Department official admits on September 19 the possibility that there had been some violations of Chinese territory.

September 19

USA – GOVERNMENT: House Republicans issue a white paper that warns that the United States is becoming "a full-fledged combatant" in a war that is becoming "bigger than the Korean War." The paper urges the president to end the war "more speedily and at a smaller cost, while safeguarding the independence and freedom of South Vietnam."

USA – DOMESTIC: Twenty-two U.S. scientists, including seven Nobel laureates, urge President Johnson to halt the use of anti-personnel and anti-crop chemical weapons.

INTERNATIONAL: Pope Paul VI, in the encyclical *Christi Matri*, appeals to world leaders to end the Vietnam War.

September 19–23

AIR WAR: U.S. B-52s conduct extensive bombing raids against a mixture of targets in the DMZ and the area north of it, to include infiltration trails, troop concentrations, supply areas, and base camps.

DIPLOMACY: Secretary-general U Thant proposes again his three-point plan for peace in Vietnam, including cessation of U.S. bombing of the North, de-escalation of the ground war in South Vietnam, and inclusion of the NLF in peace talks. UN ambassador Arthur Goldberg responds in an address to the General Assembly, saying that the United States is prepared to halt the bombing of the North and begin de-escalation when "assurances" are given of a North Vietnamese cutback.

September 23

USA – MILITARY: U.S. command in Saigon announces that its planes are defoliating the jungle south of the DMZ to prevent the North Vietnamese from using it as cover.

September 27

AIR WAR: Village of Hom Be, five miles from Quang Ngai, is attacked in error by two Marine jets, and at least 35 civilians are killed. The United States halts air strikes against the southeastern corner of the DMZ to allow the ICC to resume patrols in the area.

September 30

USA – DOMESTIC: Former president Dwight D. Eisenhower tells newsmen in Chicago that he favors using "as much force as we need to win the war in Vietnam."

October

USA – MILITARY: The U.S. Air Force 834th Air Division and 483rd Tactical Airlift Wing deploy to Vietnam. U.S. Navy begins Operation Sea Dragon to interdict enemy supply vessels in coastal waters off North Vietnam.

October 1

AIR WAR: The U.S. bombing of the North Vietnamese city of Phu Ly, 35 miles south of Hanoi, results in the destruction of all homes and buildings and kills approximately 40 civilians. After the bombing, Phu Ly is visited by Harrison Salisbury, assistant managing editor of the *New York Times*, who is in North Vietnam with the authorization of both Hanoi and Washington. He will report on December 25 about the damage he observed while in North Vietnam.

October 1–24

GROUND WAR: Operation Irving is conducted by the U.S. 1st Cavalry Division, ARVN, and ROK units against the North Vietnamese 610th Division in Binh Dinh Province, II Corps. The operation is a follow-up to Operation Thayer I and its goal is to clear enemy troops from the Phu Cat area, 28 miles northwest of Qui Nhon. Casualties are U.S.: 19 KIA, 26 WIA; NVA/VC: 681 KIA, 690 POW.

October 2–3

USSR: The Soviet Defense Ministry newspaper, *Krasnaya Zuezda*, reports that Russian military experts have come under fire during U.S. raids against North Vietnamese missile sites while training the North Vietnamese in the use of Soviet-made antiaircraft missiles. This is the first public acknowledgment that the Soviets have trained North Vietnamese missile crews and observed them in action.

October 3

USSR: Soviet deputy premier Vladimir N. Novikov announces that he has negotiated an economic and military aid agreement with North Vietnam by which the Soviet Union will provide an undisclosed amount of military and economic assistance.

October 4

AIR WAR: U.S. B-52 bombers attack supply and staging areas in the DMZ, destroying 25 structures.

INTERNATIONAL: Pope Paul VI addresses 150,000 people in St. Peter's Square in Rome and calls for an end to the war in Vietnam through negotiations.

October 6–11

DIPLOMACY: At a Labour Party Conference in London, Foreign Secretary George Brown outlines a plan, largely a restatement of previous British proposals, to end the war in Vietnam. Brown renews the suggestion that the Soviet Union, as co-chairman of the 1954 Geneva Conference, join Britain in reconvening the conference to seek an end to the war.

October 7

USA – GOVERNMENT: Speaking in Washington at a Democratic fund-raising event, President Johnson declares that he will hold fast in Vietnam and will not try to gain cheap popularity "by renouncing the struggle in Vietnam or escalating it to the red line of danger." He asserts that the effort in Vietnam "leads to a more secure America and a free Asia."

October 10–13

USA – GOVERNMENT: Secretary of Defense McNamara goes on his eighth fact-finding visit to South Vietnam to assess General Westmoreland's latest troop request. He confers with Westmoreland, Lodge, various military leaders, and South Vietnam's Premier Ky and Chief of State Thieu. At a news conference in Saigon on October 13, McNamara says that he finds military operations have "progressed very satisfactorily since 1965," but concedes that "progress is very slow indeed" in the pacification program.

October 13

USA – GOVERNMENT: President Johnson, speaking in Washington, rules out any cessation of the bombing in North Vietnam in connection with a conference planned in Manila.

AIR WAR: A record 173 sorties are flown over North Vietnam's panhandle region, bombing radar sites, storage areas, transportation facilities, and missile centers.

October 14

USA – GOVERNMENT: Secretary of Defense McNamara, upon his return to Washington from his trip to Vietnam, details his assessment of the situation there in two long memorandums to President Johnson and for the first time recommends against filling additional troop requests from General Westmoreland. He recommends a "five-pronged course of action": (1) stabilize U.S. force levels in Vietnam;

(2) install a barrier along the DMZ; (3) stabilize the Rolling Thunder bombing program against the North; (4) pursue a vigorous pacification program; and (5) press for negotiations. Reflecting his growing disenchantment, McNamara concludes: "The prognosis is bad that the war can be brought to a satisfactory conclusion within the next two years." Forewarned of McNamara's memos, the Joint Chiefs of Staff responds to his assessment with a memo in which it takes issue with McNamara's pessimistic assessment and his recommendation that there be no increase in the bombing effort.

October 17

Ground War: Units of the 196th Infantry Brigade arrive in Vietnam to join the ongoing Operation Attleboro in III Corps.

Air War: The United States resumes air strikes in the southeastern DMZ, which had been halted on September 27. A U.S. official attributes the resumption of the bombing to the fact that the Hanoi regime has "consistently rebuffed" efforts by the ICC observers to enter and patrol that sector of the zone.

October 17–November 2

USA – Government: Johnson leaves Washington for a 17-day trip to visit seven Asian and Pacific nations and attend a conference scheduled in Manila. En route to Manila, Johnson visits New Zealand and Australia. In Melbourne, he encounters anti-war demonstrators. In Manila, he meets with other Allied leaders October 24–25. Pledging that they will withdraw their troops within six months "if North Vietnam withdraws its forces to the north and ceases infiltration of South Vietnam,"

President Lyndon B. Johnson greets American troops in Vietnam, 1966. *(National Archives)*

the United States, Australia, New Zealand, South Korea, South Vietnam, and the Philippines sign a joint communiqué that includes a four-point "Declaration of Peace" that stresses the need for a "peaceful settlement of the war in Vietnam and for future peace and progress" in the rest of Asia and the Pacific. The president flies to South Vietnam on October 26 for a surprise 2½-hour visit with U.S. troops at Cam Ranh Bay.

October 18–December 30
GROUND WAR: The newly arrived U.S. 4th Infantry Division and elements of the 25th Infantry Division and 1st Cavalry Division (Airmobile) conduct Operation Paul Revere IV, a continuation of ongoing screening and surveillance operations along the Cambodian border in Pleiku Province. Casualties are U.S.: 62 KIA, 158 WIA; NVA/VC: 977 KIA, 18 POW.

October 21
TERRORISM: VC operatives explode a mine in the marketplace of Tra On, a town in the Mekong Delta 75 miles southeast of Saigon, killing 11 persons and wounding 54.

October 24
TERRORISM: A bus detonates a VC mine on a road 18 miles north of Hue, killing 15 Vietnamese civilians and injuring 19.

October 25–November 23
SEA WAR: U.S. Navy Sea Dragon anti-shipping operations off the North Vietnamese coast intensify in the Dong Hoi area. After a gunnery duel between U.S. destroyers and shore batteries, the navy begins a four-week series of attacks that result in the sinking of more than 230 communist vessels.

October 25–February 12, 1967
GROUND WAR: The U.S. 1st Cavalry Division conducts Operation Thayer II in Binh Dinh Province, II Corps, in the rich northern coastal plain and the valleys to the west. The operation will include the Battle of LZ Bird, in which more than 700 soldiers of the 22nd NVA Regiment will attack the 1st Cavalry's base at LZ Bird in the Kim Son Valley. The attack is finally broken by intense, close air support and the first use of Bee Hive artillery rounds fired point-blank into massed enemy infantry. Casualties for entire operation are U.S.: 184 KIA, 747 WIA, 2 MIA; NAV/VC: 1,757 KIA.

October 26
SEA WAR: Fire breaks out on board the 42,000-ton U.S. aircraft carrier *Oriskany* when a locker filled with night illumination magnesium flares bursts into flames. The fire spreads quickly through most of the ship, resulting in 43 crew members dead and a further 16 injured. Three hundred bombs are thrown overboard and four bombers and two helicopters are lost, but after three hours, the fire is brought under control.

October 27
BRITAIN: In London an estimated 50,000 demonstrators take part in a protest against the Vietnam War.

CHINA: The Communist Chinese news agency, Hsinhua, assails the decisions reached at the Manila conference and calls the Allies' troop-withdrawal proposal "out and out blackmail and shameless humbug."

October 27–November 9

DIPLOMACY: Ambassador-at-Large Averell Harriman visits 10 nations to explain the results of the Manila conference and provide the current U.S. assessment of the situation in Southeast Asia. Harriman, acting as Johnson's personal emissary, visits leaders in Ceylon, Indonesia, India, Pakistan, Iran, Italy, France, West Germany, Britain, and Morocco.

October 30

SOUTH VIETNAM: A South Vietnamese government announcement says that the national police have smashed a guerrilla plot to blow up U.S. and Vietnamese buildings in Saigon during National Day celebrations on November 1.

October 31

RIVER WAR: U.S. Navy patrol boats and helicopters prevent a VC flotilla from crossing the Mekong River near My Tho, sinking 51 junks and sampans.

November

USA – MILITARY: The 199th Light Infantry Brigade deploys to Vietnam from Fort Benning, Georgia, for combat operations in III Corps.

November 1

TERRORISM: Viet Cong stage two separate guerrilla attacks in Saigon to coincide with celebrations for South Vietnam's National Day. In the first incident, a 75 mm recoilless rifle is fired at a crowd of civilians waiting for the start of a parade celebrating the South Vietnamese holiday. In the second incident, a VC grenade is thrown at a crowded bus terminal in the city's central market. At least eight persons are killed in the two attacks.

November 3

USA – MILITARY: Defense Department drafts plans for intensified bombing of North Vietnam aimed at forcing Hanoi to negotiate and hindering their efforts to transport materiel to units in South Vietnam. Pentagon leaders admit that attacks on oil facilities have done little to slow down the passage of arms and supplies into the South.

GROUND WAR: Elements of 1st and 25th Infantry Divisions, the 196th Light Infantry Brigade, and the 173rd Airborne Brigade, joined by two ARVN battalions, fight one of the war's largest battles. The battle, a part of Operation Attleboro, takes place in Tay Ninh Province against the 9th VC Division and the 101st North Vietnamese Regiment.

USA – DOMESTIC: Former vice president Richard Nixon criticizes the Manila conference, particularly the pledge to withdraw military forces from Vietnam if North Vietnam withdraws its forces.

November 4

USA – GOVERNMENT: Reacting to Nixon's criticism, President Johnson claims that Nixon confuses rather than clarifies issues and does not "serve his country well" by criticism. Johnson also cautions Hanoi against interpreting the results of the congressional elections as a test of administration policy on Vietnam.

SEA WAR: Fire breaks out aboard the carrier *Franklin D. Roosevelt,* five decks below the flight deck, killing eight sailors.

November 5

USA – GOVERNMENT: At a news conference in Johnson City, Texas, Secretary of Defense McNamara, who has been conferring with the president on his ranch, says that "no sharp increases" are planned in the number of air strikes over Vietnam (current monthly average is 25,000 sorties). He also reveals that America will increase its troop presence in 1967, but at a rate "substantially less" than the 200,000 men added in 1966.

November 7

USA – GOVERNMENT: Defense Secretary McNamara faces a storm of student protests when he visits Harvard University to address a small group of students. As he leaves a dormitory, about 100 anti-administration demonstrators shout at him and demand a debate. When McNamara tries to speak, supporters of the Students for a Democratic Society shout him down. McNamara then tries to leave, but 25 demonstrators throw themselves under his automobile. Police finally escort the secretary of defense from the campus.

November 11

USA – MILITARY: Secretary of Defense McNamara tells the Joint Chiefs of Staff that the new U.S. troop strength goal in Vietnam will be 469,000 men in the field by June 30, 1968.

USA – GOVERNMENT: Ambassador-at-Large Averell Harriman, who has returned from visiting 10 nations to explain the results of the Manila conference, reports to the president and says later, at a news conference, that "Every country in the world wants to see peace with the exception of Red China and North Vietnam." There are indications, though, "that Hanoi is willing to talk provided we do certain things."

DIPLOMACY: The British Council for Peace in Vietnam opens in London, and a letter sent to a council member, Lord Brockway, on October 19 is made public. In it, Secretary-general of the United Nations U Thant calls for a final and unconditional halt in U.S. air attacks on the North and disagrees with the conditional proposal advanced by Ambassador Goldberg at the United Nations on September 22.

November 12

USA – DOMESTIC: A report in the *New York Times* claims that 40 percent of all U.S. aid to Vietnam fails to reach its proper destination due to theft, corruption, black marketeering, and waste. The report notes that at least 400 U.S. servicemen and civilians face charges of corruption and black-market activities.

November 13

USA – DOMESTIC: Freedom House issues a document titled "A Crucial Turning Point in Vietnam," signed by 138 prominent Americans, urging "men of stature in the intellectual, religious and public service communities" to withdraw their support for critics of American policy in Vietnam who have failed to make "the distinction between responsible dissent and unfounded attacks upon our society."

November 14

USA – MILITARY: Captain Archie C. Kuntze (USN) is found guilty by a general court-martial in California on a charge of "conduct unbecoming of an officer and gentleman" while stationed in Saigon. He had been commander of Naval Support Activity in Saigon, where he was known as the "American Mayor of Saigon."

November 15

USA – DOMESTIC: General Earle Wheeler, chairman of the Joint Chiefs of Staff, addresses a gathering at Brown University. Some 60 students walk out to protest his defense of the U.S. involvement in Vietnam. Some of those who remain shout and heckle Wheeler, and others storm the stage. Outside, over 100 students continue the protest.

November 17

USA – GOVERNMENT: A secret report to the president from Secretary of Defense McNamara challenges General Westmoreland's strategy of attrition. McNamara says that the increased number of U.S. troops has not brought about a significant rise in enemy casualties and advises against a further large-scale reinforcement to Vietnam. He concludes by saying that there is "no evidence that more troops than the 470,000 [already recommended] . . . would substantially change the situation." Additionally, he asserts that the bombing campaign has made "no significant impact on the war in the South." McNamara's pessimism is not shared by most of the president's closest advisers, and his recommendations are rejected by the president.

November 18

USA – DOMESTIC: The American National Conference of Catholic Bishops, meeting in Washington, confirms its support for the Johnson administration, saying that the U.S. "presence in VN is justified."
SEA WAR: Two U.S. destroyers shell a North Vietnamese radar site two miles north of the DMZ in the Dong Hoi area.

November 23

SEA WAR: Two U.S. destroyers bombard a flotilla of Communist supply barges off the southern coast of North Vietnam, sinking or damaging 47 out of 60.

November 30–December 1

CHINA: Beijing claims that U.S. bombers attacked a fleet of Chinese fishing boats in international waters off the Gulf of Tonkin, killing 14 sailors and sinking five boats. A second raid takes place the following day.

November 30–December 14, 1967

GROUND WAR: Operation Fairfax/Rang Dong is initiated by three battalions—one each from the U.S. 1st, 4th, and 25th Infantry Divisions—in and around Saigon, III Corps; purpose of the operation is to clear and pacify the area surrounding Saigon. It will be taken over by the U.S. 199th Light Infantry Brigade in January

1967. Upon withdrawal of the 199th, responsibility for the area of operation will
be turned over to the ARVN 5th Ranger Group. Casualties are U.S.: 26 KIA, 75
WIA; NVA/VC: 77 KIA.

November 30–December 22

SOUTH VIETNAM: The South Vietnamese Constituent Assembly draws up draft articles for a new constitution. On December 15, the assembly approves the proposal
for the future civil regime to be headed by a popularly elected president, also a proposal empowering the president, rather than the legislature, to appoint a premier.
On December 21, the assembly approves the establishment of a bicameral legislature made up of a senate and a house of representatives.

December

USA – MILITARY: The 9th Infantry Division deploys to Vietnam from Fort Lewis,
Washington, to conduct combat operations in III Corps (initially), establishing
its initial headquarters at Bearcat, near Bien Hoa. The 31st Tactical Fighter Wing
deploys to Vietnam to support combat operations in II Corps.

December 1

GROUND WAR: In the wake of VC terrorist attacks on the outskirts of Saigon, an
American force of several battalions and a battalion of South Vietnamese Rangers
begins guarding Saigon. Elements of the U.S. 25th Infantry Division are employed
to prevent the VC from entering the rice growing areas near the Ho Bo and Boi Loi
Woods in III Corps.

December 2

AIR WAR: A truck-park five miles south of Hanoi is hit by navy jets in the closest
raid to the city since June 29. The Ha Gia fuel storage depot, 14½ miles north of
Hanoi, is bombed by 50 to 60 U.S. F-4C Phantom jets. Escort jets destroy four radar
missile sites and an antiaircraft emplacement. About 40 miles northeast of Hanoi,
other navy pilots hit a second fuel dump. During the day, eight U.S. planes are
downed, a record for a single day. The number of planes lost over North Vietnam
is now 435.

December 2–14

DIPLOMACY: Ambassador Henry Cabot Lodge asks Janusz Lewandowski, Polish representative on the International Control Commission, to inform Hanoi
of the United States' willingness to meet with North Vietnamese officials. On or
about December 4, Polish foreign minister Adam Rapacki discloses that Hanoi has
accepted the proposal to take part in talks at the ambassadorial level. Hanoi does not
repeat its usual demand for a cessation of U.S. raids on the North as a condition for
entering the talks. However, North Vietnam will refuse to attend after U.S. planes
carry out raids in the Hanoi area on December 13–14.

December 4

GROUND WAR: Under cover of a 4½-hour mortar attack, a VC unit penetrates the
13-mile defense perimeter around Saigon's Tan Son Nhut Air Base. U.S. and South

Vietnamese security guards finally drive off the attackers, killing 18 of them. A U.S. RF-101 reconnaissance jet is badly damaged. The guerrillas return that same night and resume the attack, until security guards kill 11 more Viet Cong and repel the others.

AIR WAR: U.S. fighter-bombers strike the Yen Vien railroad yard six miles northeast of Hanoi and the Ha Gia fuel storage depot, 14½ miles north of the city.

December 5

SEA WAR: The U.S. destroyer *Ingersoll* exchanges fire with a North Vietnamese coastal battery 11 miles northeast of Dong Hoi and is slightly damaged.

December 6

GROUND WAR: U.S. military headquarters at Kontum is attacked.

USA – GOVERNMENT: The Johnson administration discloses that it will need an additional US $9 to 10 billion in supplemental funding to pay for the war in Vietnam during the current fiscal year.

December 7

TERRORISM: Tran Van Van, a prominent member of the South Vietnamese Constituent Assembly, is shot to death by two Viet Cong terrorists while driving to an assembly meeting in Saigon.

December 8

USA – MILITARY: Air Force Secretary Harold Brown releases a detailed assessment of the American air war over North Vietnam, stating that the strikes have caused "serious manpower, supply and morale problems" for North Vietnam but are still not severe enough to persuade Hanoi to enter peace talks.

December 8–9

POWs: The International Red Cross announces in Geneva that North Vietnam has rejected a proposal by President Johnson for joint discussion of fair treatment and possible exchange of war captives held by both sides. Johnson first broached the plan on July 20 at a news conference, and the IRC submitted the proposal to Hanoi in July. The U.S. State Department confirms the next day that the IRC had acted as Washington's intermediary.

December 8–14

DIPLOMACY: Pope Paul VI proposes that two separate 48-hour cease-fires for Christmas and Tet be merged "into a single continuous period of time" to bring about an armistice that will be followed by "sincere negotiations which will lead to peace." On December 14, White House press secretary Bill Moyers says that the United States is willing to discuss the proposal if the Communists show interest.

December 9

USA – DOMESTIC: The General Assembly of the National Council of Churches, meeting in Miami Beach, approves a statement urging the administration to consider a halt in air strikes on North Vietnam.

December 10

USA – DOMESTIC: California governor-elect Ronald Reagan (Republican) declares he favors "an all-out total effort" in Vietnam.

December 12

USA – GOVERNMENT: Walt Rostow, special assistant for national security, says in a memorandum to the president that he has found the Allied military position "greatly improved" in 1966 and envisions a dominant—even potentially victorious—position by the end of 1967.

December 13–14

AIR WAR: U.S. planes bomb the Yen Vien railroad yard, six miles northeast of Hanoi, and attack a truck depot two miles south of the city. International reaction to the raids, especially from Communist countries, is immediate. The Soviet Union and East German news agencies report that for the first time U.S. planes are bombing residential areas in the city of Hanoi and causing civilian casualties. TASS, the Soviet news agency, says that U.S. planes have bombed workers' districts along the Red River embankment. The Hanoi correspondent of the French press agency reports that the village of Cau Dat, outside Hanoi, has been "completely destroyed by bombs and fire." A spokesman at the U.S. embassy in Saigon says on December 14 "If by some remote chance Hanoi was struck by bombs, it was an accident."

December 14–16

USA – GOVERNMENT: Robert J. McCloskey of the U.S. State Department meets with newsmen and at first denies that U.S. planes have bombed Hanoi. He then adds, "I took the question to mean that these are civilian targets or population centers . . . which one generally associates when talking about a city." When asked whether these targets were inside Hanoi's limits, McCloskey replies, "I don't know . . . how one defines what the city limits are." On December 15, the State Department reaffirms its position that "There is no fixed geographical definition which can be called the city limits of Hanoi." On December 16, General Westmoreland issues a statement from Saigon that says, "A complete review of the December 13–14 air strikes on Van Dien and Yen Vien showed that all ordnance expended by U.S. air-strike aircraft was in the military target areas. None fell in the city of Hanoi."

December 16

USA – GOVERNMENT: The White House announces the appointment of David E. Lilienthal to head the American section of a joint Unites States-South Vietnam effort to map long-range plans for South Vietnam's economy.

December 18–20

AIR WAR: Guam-based B-52s bomb North Vietnamese supply bases and staging areas just south of the DMZ, where the reorganized North Vietnamese 324-B Division is believed to be massing for a drive south.

December 20

CHINA: The Chinese Communist Party newspaper, *Jenmin Jih Pao,* calls on North Vietnam and the Viet Cong to spurn negotiations with the United States and to continue the war. The paper charges that the Soviet Union, "in collusion with the United States," is "resorting to dirty tricks by forcing peace talks by coercion, inducement or persuasion . . . with the aim of compelling the Vietnamese people to lay down their arms and give up the struggle!"

December 23

AIR WAR: U.S. intelligence sources confirm reports that North Korean pilots are in North Vietnam, presumably to train North Vietnamese pilots. A previous report had indicated the presence of 100 new MiGs in North Vietnam, increasing the MiG force there to about 200.

December 23–28

USA – DOMESTIC: The Roman Catholic archbishop of New York and military vicar of the U.S. armed forces for Roman Catholics, Francis Cardinal Spellman, visits U.S. servicemen in South Vietnam. In an address at a mass in Saigon, Spellman says that the Vietnamese conflict is "a war for civilization—certainly it is not a war of our seeking. It is a war thrust upon us—we cannot yield to tyranny." Anything "less than victory is inconceivable." On December 26, Spellman tells U.S. soldiers that they are in Vietnam for the "defense, protection, and salvation not only of our country, but . . . of civilization itself." Next day, Vatican sources express displeasure with Spellman's statements in Vietnam. One source says, "The Cardinal did not speak for the Pope or the Church."

December 24

AIR WAR: A U.S. cargo plane en route from Japan crashes in the village of Hoa Vang, near the Danang air base, killing over 100 civilians and all four crewmen.

December 25–26

USA – DOMESTIC: Harrison Salisbury, assistant managing editor of the *New York Times*, files a report describing the destruction from U.S. bombing in several North Vietnamese cities. Salisbury, who had gone to North Vietnam with the authorization of both Hanoi and Washington, visits the sites of several U.S. air strikes that were conducted on October 1. He reports on the destruction in the towns of Phu Ly and Nam Dinh, saying that all the homes and buildings in Phu Ly (population 20,000) were destroyed. Salisbury's press reports cause a stir in Washington. Pentagon officials contend that he is exaggerating the damage to civilian areas, but admit that it is "sometimes impossible to avoid all damage to civilian areas."

December 26

USA – MILITARY: A Defense Department spokesman insists that bombing raids are carried out only against military targets, but that "it is sometimes impossible to avoid all damage to civilian areas" and that bombs may have "accidentally struck civilian areas while attempting to bomb military targets."

December 27

GROUND WAR: The 1st Cavalry Division defends LZ Bird in the Kim Son Valley, sustaining 58 killed in bitter fighting, which is part of operation Thayer II that began October 25.

December 27–31

GROUND WAR: A combined U.S./ARVN joint-service operation takes place against a Viet Cong stronghold in the U Minh Forest in the Mekong Delta, considered one of the best-fortified Viet Cong strongholds in South Vietnam. The forest is bombed and napalmed in preparation for the assault, in which an estimated 1,200 South Vietnamese paratroopers are dropped from Allied air force planes. Some 6,000 combined South Vietnamese troops attack a Viet Cong force in the forest. On December 29, the U.S. destroyer *Herbert J. Thomas* shells suspected Viet Cong positions in the area for seven hours. The operation ends on December 31 with 104 VC reported killed and 18 captured.

December 29

USA – MILITARY: Assistant Secretary of Defense Arthur Sylvester says that the North Vietnamese city of Nam Dinh has been hit by U.S. planes 64 times since mid-1965, and that the air strikes were directed only against military targets: railroad yards, a warehouse, petroleum storage depots, and a thermal power plant. He denounces *New York Times* correspondent Harrison Salisbury's reports on the Nam Dinh air raids as "misstatements of fact."

USA – DOMESTIC: Student body presidents from 100 U.S. colleges and universities sign an open letter to President Johnson expressing anxiety and doubt over U.S. involvement in Vietnam; they warn that many loyal youths may prefer prison to participation in the war.

December 30

DIPLOMACY: British foreign secretary George Brown proposes an international peace conference to end the war in Vietnam.

AIR WAR: Hanoi charges that U.S. planes have bombed North Vietnamese residential and industrial targets in Vinh Lin, Ha Tianh, Nghe An, Thanh Hoa, and Nam Ha, and that U.S. warships shelled residential areas in the Quang Binh Province town of Quang Trac.

December 31

SOUTH VIETNAM: A New Year's truce begins and will extend to January 2, 1967. Both North and South Vietnam will charge each other with many violations during the truce.

USA – GOVERNMENT: President Johnson responds to the controversy over North Vietnamese civilian casualties during U.S. bombing raids by saying that there has been no change in orders "to bomb only military targets."

DIPLOMACY: UN Secretary-general U Thant, in a New Year's message, renews his plea to the United States for an unconditional cessation of the bombing of North Vietnam; in reply to Ambassador Goldberg's request that Thant use his position to obtain a cease-fire, he urges extension of the New Year's truce.

YEAR-END SUMMARY: There are 385,300 U.S. military personnel in Vietnam; 5,008 U.S. servicemen were killed and 30,093 wounded in the fighting in 1966, for a total of 6,664 Americans killed and 37,738 wounded since January 1, 1961. Allied forces include 52,500 Free World Military Forces personnel. Total South Vietnamese armed forces strength increases to 735,900, with 47,712 killed in action to date. NVA/VC losses for the year are placed at 61,631 KIA.

In Operation Rolling Thunder, the total number of individual flights in 1966 was 148,000; the total bomb tonnage was 128,000; the number of aircraft lost was 318; and direct operational costs are $1,200,000,000. The CIA will produce a study in January 1967 that estimates that North Vietnamese casualties from the bombing raids to be 24,000—of which 80 percent are civilian. It is estimated that the bombing is costing the United States nearly $10 for every dollar's worth of damage done to North Vietnam.

1967

January 1
USA – MILITARY: Two brigades from the U.S. 9th Infantry Division, a total of 5,000 soldiers, arrive at Vung Tau.

NORTH VIETNAM: The Communists propose that the Tet truce be extended until February 15.

FRANCE: President Charles de Gaulle, in a New Year's message, calls on the United States to withdraw its troops and end its "detestable intervention in Vietnam."

January 1–April 5
GROUND WAR: Units from the U.S. 4th and 25th Infantry Divisions conduct Operation Sam Houston, a continuation of border surveillance and interdiction operations in Pleiku and Kontum Provinces in the Central Highlands, II Corps, to prevent the movement of North Vietnamese troops and equipment into South Vietnam from Communist sanctuaries in Cambodia and Laos. Casualties are U.S.: 169 KIA; NVA/VC: 733 KIA.

January 2
USA – MILITARY: The New Year's truce, which began at 0700 on December 31, 1966, ends at 0700. The U.S. headquarters in Saigon announces the resumption of normal operations.

AIR WAR: In the biggest air battle of the war to date, U.S. Air Force F-4 Phantom jets down seven communist MiG-21s over North Vietnam. The Phantoms were flying cover for F-105 Thunderchiefs attacking surface-to-air missile sites in the Red River Valley. During this battle, Colonel Robin Olds shoots down one of the MiGs, becoming the first and only U.S. Air Force ace with victories in both World War II and Vietnam.

January 3
NORTH VIETNAM: In an interview in the *New York Times,* Premier Pham Van Dong, in an apparent shift from his previous position, says that the North Vietnamese four-point plan for ending the war "constitutes the basis for a settlement but should not be considered conditions." This raises international speculation that Hanoi is modifying its conditions for ending the war.

January 4
NORTH VIETNAM: In an interview with Harrison Salisbury of the *New York Times,* Nguyen Van Tien, a member of the National Liberation Front's Central Committee,

insists on the NLF's right to participate in any peace talks, describing the front as a military and political force independent of North Vietnam. The same day, Hanoi rejects a British proposal for an international peace conference to end the war, attacking the plan because it fails to include the NLF in proposed negotiations.

January 6–15
GROUND WAR: The U.S. 1st Battalion, 9th Marines, and South Vietnamese Marine Brigade Task Force Bravo launch Operation Deckhouse V, which includes amphibious operations in Kien Hoa Province in the Mekong Delta, located 62 miles south of Saigon. The target area, called the Thanh Phu Secret Zone, is reported by U.S. intelligence sources to contain ammunition dumps, ordnance and engineering workshops, hospitals, and indoctrination centers. Casualties are U.S.: 7 KIA, 35 WIA; NVA/VC: 21 KIA.

January 8
GROUND WAR: Ten children are killed and 25 other civilians wounded when two VC companies in Kien Hoa Province try to shield their advance behind civilian hostages during an exchange of gunfire with an ARVN Ranger company.

January 8–26
GROUND WAR: About 16,000 U.S. soldiers from the 1st and 25th Infantry Divisions, 173rd Airborne Brigade, and 11th Armored Cavalry Regiment join 14,000 South Vietnamese troops in the conduct of Operation Cedar Falls, the first corps-sized operation in the war. The purpose of the operation is to find and eliminate the VC Military Region 4 headquarters and to clear enemy troops from the Thanh Dien Forest Preserve and the Iron Triangle, a 60-square-mile area of jungle believed to contain Communist base camps and supply dumps. U.S. infantrymen discover a vast tunnel complex, apparently a headquarters for guerrilla raids and terrorist attacks on Saigon. Ben Suc, a village reported as hostile, is leveled after its 3,800 inhabitants are removed from the area for resettlement in a camp 20 miles to the south. The National Liberation Front later claims that over 2,500 U.S. soldiers were killed in the 18-day operation, during which 1,229 bombing sorties are flown by U.S. planes in support of the assault. Actual casualties are U.S.: 72 KIA, 337 WIA; ARVN: 11 KIA, 8 WIA; NVA/VC: 750 KIA, 280 POW.

January 9
USA – GOVERNMENT: The U.S. Agency for International Development (USAID) attempts to respond to reports in the American media of widespread corruption and thievery of commodities sent to South Vietnam by the United States. In a report to the president, USAID officials assert, "No more than 5-6 percent of all economic assistance commodities delivered to Vietnam were stolen or otherwise diverted."

January 10
USA – GOVERNMENT: President Johnson, in his annual State of the Union message to Congress, asks for enactment of a 6 percent surcharge on personal and corporate income taxes to help support the Vietnam War for two years, or "for as long as the unusual expenditures associated with our efforts continue." Congress will delay for almost a year, but eventually pass the surcharge. The U.S. expenditure in Vietnam for fiscal year 1967 will be $21 billion.

DIPLOMACY: During a press conference, UN Secretary-general U Thant urges an unconditional halt to U.S. bombing of North Vietnam. He says he has three basic differences with U.S. policy in Vietnam: (1) the NLF is an independent entity and not a "stooge" of Hanoi; (2) the so-called domino theory is not credible; and (3) "South Vietnam is not strategically vital to Western interests and Western security."

January 15

AIR WAR: U.S. planes resume air strikes against the Hanoi area for the first time since December 1966, with a 37-plane mission to destroy railroads, highways, bridges, and surface-to-air missile sites 15 miles from Hanoi.

January 18

USA – GOVERNMENT: Senator John C. Stennis (D-Miss.), chairman of the influential Senate Preparedness Subcommittee, declares that General Westmoreland's troop requests should be met, "even if it should require mobilization or partial mobilization."

January 18–26

AUSTRALIA/NEW ZEALAND: South Vietnamese premier Ky, in a visit to Australia and New Zealand, thanks the leaders of both countries for their aid in the war. The tour is marked by violent antiwar demonstrations.

January 19

CHINA: Beijing joins North Vietnam in issuing a second warning to Thailand against any military intervention in the Vietnam War, threatening stern measures against Thailand if it permits the United States to base B-52s on its territory.

January 20

USA – DOMESTIC: Harry Ashmore, former editor of the *Arkansas Gazette,* arrives in Los Angeles after a visit to North Vietnam and says that the damage inflicted by U.S. bombing there is offset by the raids' unifying influence on the North Vietnamese people and their morale.

January 25

USA – MILITARY: In what appears to be a reaction by the Johnson administration to the controversy over civilian bombing casualties, the Joint Chiefs of Staff issues an order barring American pilots from bombing within a five-mile radius of the center of Hanoi. Planes will be permitted to penetrate the zone only to chase attacking aircraft.

GROUND WAR: A 1,000-man battalion of the U.S. 9th Infantry Division is permanently assigned to the Mekong Delta as part of a plan to put a 30,000-man force in the area to wrest control of the delta from the VC.

January 26

USA – GOVERNMENT: Secretary of Defense McNamara testifies before a Senate committee, saying that there are some 275,000 Communist troops, including 45,000 North Vietnamese regulars, in South Vietnam.

January 26–March 23
GROUND WAR: U.S. Marines and ARVN troops conduct Operation De Soto to relieve an ARVN outpost and clear an area 25 miles south of Quang Ngai City, I Corps. Casualties will be U.S.: 76 KIA, 573 WIA; NVA/VC: 383 KIA, 9 POW.

January 28–29
GROUND WAR: During an operation against the VC in the Mekong Delta, U.S. helicopters accidentally kill 31 Vietnamese civilians and wound 38. The civilians, apparently mistaken for VC, are attacked as they are crossing the Bassac River in 200 sampans at 2345 hours in violation of curfew.

NORTH VIETNAM: Hanoi demands an end to Operation Rolling Thunder before it will agree to negotiations.

January 28–May 31
GROUND WAR: The U.S. 9th Infantry Division conducts Operation Palm Beach in Dinh Tuong Province, IV Corps. Purpose of the operation is to provide security for the construction of the division base camp at Dong Tam. Casualties will be NVA/VC: 570 KIA (estimated).

January 30
USA – DOMESTIC: The U.S. Court of Appeals for the 2nd Circuit rules unanimously in New York City that draft boards cannot punish registrants who publicly protest the war in Vietnam and the draft by reclassifying them to 1-A status.

January 31
USA – DOMESTIC: Approximately 2,000 members of the National Committee of Clergy and Laymen Concerned About Vietnam demonstrate in front of the White House, demanding that President Johnson order a halt to the bombing of North Vietnam.

January 31–March 18
GROUND WAR: The U.S. 3rd Marine Division conducts Operation Prairie II, a continuation of operations in the DMZ area, Quang Tri Province, I Corps. Casualties are U.S.: 93 KIA, 483 WIA; NVA/VC: 694 KIA, 20 POW.

February 1
USA – GOVERNMENT: Speaking with five British journalists, Secretary of State Rusk questions the NLF's claim to independence, saying, "The leadership of the Viet Cong in the south is made up of North Vietnamese generals . . . so we're not very much impressed with this alleged difference between the Liberation Front and Moscow."

GROUND WAR: U.S. Marine artillery and planes accidentally hit a South Vietnamese hamlet 12 miles southwest of Danang, killing eight civilians and wounding 18.

February 1–16
GROUND WAR: Nearly 10,000 U.S. troops from the 9th Infantry Division and 173rd Airborne Brigade launch Operation Big Spring, a drive against the 273rd VC Regiment in War Zone D, a Communist stronghold near the Cambodian border.

February 2–21

GROUND WAR: To disguise preparations for an upcoming operation and to block both the infiltration and exfiltration routes in and out of War Zone C toward the Cambodian border, 6,000—8,000 troops of the U.S. 4th and 25th Infantry Divisions carry out Operation Gadsden in Tay Ninh Province, III Corps. Casualties are U.S.: 15 KIA, 123 WIA; NVA/VC: 36 KIA, 2 POW.

February 5

GROUND WAR: South Vietnamese and Allied forces begin defoliation of jungle growth in the southern part of the DMZ because of alleged "flagrant violations" of the buffer area by North Vietnamese troops.

USA – DOMESTIC: Leaders of 15 politically diverse student organizations get together in Washington and sign a resolution calling for the end to the draft and urging establishment of a voluntary military service.

February 6

USA – GOVERNMENT: Senator Robert Kennedy (D-N.Y.) returns to the United States after holding informal discussions in Vietnam with Western leaders. Kennedy says American participation in the Vietnam War has resulted in the undermining of U.S. prestige abroad. After reporting to President Johnson on his visit, Kennedy denies a *Newsweek* magazine story reporting that he has received North Vietnamese peace proposals for ending the war.

February 7

USA – GOVERNMENT: President Johnson sends a proposal to Prime Minister Harold Wilson calling for an "assured stoppage" of North Vietnamese infiltration in return for a bombing halt and no further augmentation of U.S. forces in South Vietnam.

February 8

DIPLOMACY: In London, Prime Minister Wilson, acting on behalf of President Johnson, meets with Soviet premier Aleksey Kosygin in an effort to negotiate an end to the bombing of North Vietnam and begin peace talks.

February 8–10

USA – DOMESTIC: The National Committee of Clergy and Laymen Concerned About Vietnam sponsors a three-day "Fast for Peace" by Christians and Jews across the United States.

February 8–12

AIR WAR: The United States halts the bombing of North Vietnam during the Tet holiday.

February 10

USA – GOVERNMENT: Washington insists that the formula for talks presented by Prime Minister Wilson to Premier Kosygin requires that North Vietnamese infiltration stop before a bombing halt, not afterward, as Wilson has suggested orally.

GROUND WAR: MACV reports a massive supply buildup in North Vietnam during the first three days of the Lunar New Year truce and the suspension of American bombing raids.

February 11

GROUND WAR: As the Tet holiday cease-fire ends, Allied forces launch 16 operations. Among these is Operation Stone, conducted by the U.S. 1st Marines in Quang Nam Province. Farther to the south, Operation Lam Son-67 is carried out by the U.S. 1st Infantry Division to clear guerrillas from villages in an area 13 miles south of Saigon.

February 11–January 21, 1968

GROUND WAR: The U.S. 1st Cavalry Division, assisted by elements of the 25th Infantry Division, the 22nd ARVN Division, and the ROK Capital Division conduct Operation Pershing in Quang Ngai and Binh Dinh Provinces, I and II Corps. The year-long operation will include a number of bitterly fought battles at LZ Pat, An Quang-Dam Tra O Lake, LZ Geronimo, Tam Quan, Bong Son, and the Nui Mieu cave complex. Casualties will be U.S.: 852 KIA, 4,119 WIA, 22 MIA; NVA/VC: 5,401 KIA, 2,059 POW.

February 13

USA – GOVERNMENT: The bombing of North Vietnam is resumed. The president, ignoring appeals for an extension of the Tet truce from Pope Paul VI, Secretary-general U Thant, and other world leaders, says he has based his decision to resume the bombing on what he terms the unparalleled magnitude of the North Vietnamese supply effort.

GROUND WAR: A U.S. artillery shell accidentally hits a 1st Cavalry Division position, killing seven soldiers and wounding four.

February 13–March 11, 1968

GROUND WAR: The U.S. 9th Infantry Division and South Vietnamese forces conduct Operation Enterprise in Long An Province, III Corps. The year-long operation is aimed at defeating organized enemy forces, eliminating enemy infrastructure, and conducting pacification operations. Casualties will be U.S.: 74 KIA, 380 WIA; NVA/VC: 2,107 KIA reported.

February 14–21

GROUND WAR: Operation Tucson in Binh Duong Province, III Corps, masks the movement of the U.S. 1st Infantry Division in preparation for Operation Junction City. Casualties are U.S.: 3 KIA, 59 WIA; NVA/VC: 8 KIA.

February 15

USA – GOVERNMENT: Secretary of Defense McNamara, during a press conference, says that air raids on military targets in the North are accomplishing their objectives and are also raising morale in South Vietnam. According to McNamara, the Communist buildup in the South has "levelled off" as a result of these raids and North Vietnam has been forced to divert 300,000 persons to repair supply lines.

February 16

GROUND WAR: Communist ground fire downs 13 U.S. helicopters, a record number for a single day; nine are downed during one operation in the Mekong Delta. Four Americans are killed and eight wounded in the loss of 13 helicopters.

U.S. troops examine drugs and equipment found in an underground Viet Cong hospital in War Zone C during Operation Junction City, 1967. *(Texas Tech University Vietnam Archive)*

February 21

GROUND WAR: Writer and historian Bernard B. Fall is killed by a VC mine on Highway 1 about 14 miles northeast of Hue while gathering material for his eighth book on Vietnam; a U.S. Marine photographer is also killed in the blast.

February 22

GROUND WAR: The U.S. command says that American artillery opened fire on North Vietnamese antiaircraft positions just north of the DMZ, using 175 mm guns based near Camp Carroll after a U.S. spotter plane was shot at. This is the first time that land-based artillery has fired across the DMZ.

USA – DOMESTIC: Hundreds of students at the University of Wisconsin demonstrate against the presence of Dow Chemical Company representatives on campus. Dow manufactures the napalm used in Vietnam. Released this day, a Harris survey indicates that 55 percent of those polled favor continued military pressure on North Vietnam; 67 percent support continued bombing. President Johnson's approval rating is 43 percent, with 57 percent of respondents disapproving of the way he is handling the Vietnam War.

February 22–May 14

GROUND WAR: Operation Junction City, largest Allied offensive operation to date, is conducted by 22 U.S. battalions and four ARVN battalions (nearly 25,000 troops). Participating units include elements of the U.S. 1st, 4th, and 25th Infantry Divisions, the 196th Light Infantry Brigade, 11th Armored Cavalry Regiment, and 173rd Airborne Brigade. The purpose of the operation is to clear enemy base areas in War Zone C (in Tay Ninh Province near the South Vietnam-Cambodia border, III Corps) and locate and destroy the Central Office for South Vietnam, the headquarters used by the North Vietnamese to control their military and political efforts in the South. As part of this operation, during the war's only U.S. combat jump, 845 paratroopers of the 2nd Battalion, 503rd Infantry, and Battery A, 3rd Battalion, 319th Artillery Regiment, 173rd Airborne Brigade, drop at Katum. The first day's action is supported by 575 aircraft sorties, a record number for a single day in South Vietnam. The second phase of the operation will begin on March 21. Casualties are U.S.: 282 KIA, 1,576 WIA; NVA/VC: 2,728 KIA.

February 24

USA – GOVERNMENT: Secretary of Defense McNamara denies that he disagrees with Secretary of State Dean Rusk on the bombing of North Vietnam, saying, "I can't recall a single instance when the Secretary of State and Secretary of Defense have differed on bombing policy." Privately, McNamara is increasingly questioning the efficacy of the bombing campaign.

February 26

SEA WAR: U.S. cruisers and destroyers of the Seventh Fleet shell North Vietnamese supply routes along a 250-mile stretch between the DMZ and Thanh Hoa.

February 27

GROUND WAR: The Viet Cong shell the U.S. air base at Danang, killing 12 Americans; due to fires that sweep the adjacent village of Ap Do, more than 150 buildings are destroyed and 35 South Vietnamese civilians are killed.

AIR WAR: The U.S. command discloses that U.S. planes have dropped "a limited number of . . . non-floating mines in rivers in southern North Vietnam."

February 28

RIVER WAR: The Commander, Naval Forces, Vietnam, establishes the Mobile Riverine Force (Task Force 117) to support U.S. 9th Infantry Division in the conduct of operations in the Mekong Delta area.

March 1–4

GROUND WAR: The U.S. 1st Infantry Division, fighting in Tay Ninh Province as part of ongoing Operation Junction City, suffers heavy casualties while killing 150 enemy troops. The U.S. 173rd Airborne Brigade is ambushed near the Cambodian border, with additional heavy casualties.

March 2

USA – GOVERNMENT: Senator Robert Kennedy (D-N.Y.) proposes a three-point plan to help end the war in Vietnam. It includes suspension of U.S. bombing of North Vietnam, and the gradual withdrawal of U.S. and North Vietnamese troops from South Vietnam, with replacement by an international force. Secretary of State Dean Rusk rejects Kennedy's proposal.

AIR WAR: The village of Lang Vei, 15 miles south of the DMZ, is accidentally hit by bombs dropped by two U.S. F-4C Phantom jets, killing at least 83 civilians and wounding 176.

March 7

GROUND WAR: South Korean forces launch Operation Oh Jac Kyo I, their largest operation to date, which involves a linkup between forces along the central coastal area of II Corps.

March 8

USA – GOVERNMENT: Both houses of Congress pass the Mansfield Resolution backing President Johnson's efforts to prevent expansion of the war and his attempts to gain a negotiated peace.

USA – GOVERNMENT: The U.S. chiefs of mission of the East Asian and Pacific areas meet in Baguio, the Philippines, and issue a statement supportive of the administration's policies, concluding: "Any slackening of the collective military effort or the policy and programs in non-military fields would slow down the drive to achieve a stable and honorable peace."

March 9
THAILAND: For the first time, Thailand acknowledges the use of Thai bases by U.S. planes for air raids on North Vietnam.

March 10
SOUTH VIETNAM: The Republic of Vietnam's Council of Ministers approves a new constitution for South Vietnam.

March 10–11
AIR WAR: U.S. planes bomb the Thai Nguyen iron and steel complex, 38 miles north of Hanoi, in the first bombing raid on major industrial installations in North Vietnam. U.S. sources in Saigon concede that this constitutes an escalation of the war.

March 11
GROUND WAR: U.S. 1st Infantry Division troops kill 210 North Vietnamese soldiers in one of the heaviest battles of Operation Junction City.

March 13
USA – GOVERNMENT: The House Appropriations Committee releases secret testimony given on February 20, 1967, by General Wheeler, chairman of the Joint Chiefs of Staff, who said that the North Vietnamese "don't expect to win a military victory in South Vietnam," but "expect to win a victory in the war right here in Washington, D.C."

March 15
USA – GOVERNMENT: President Johnson addresses the Tennessee General Assembly in Nashville and defends his policy of continuing the bombing of North Vietnam. He announces that Ellsworth Bunker will replace Henry Cabot Lodge as ambassador to South Vietnam and that Robert W. Komer will head the pacification and economic assistance programs in Vietnam.

USA – MILITARY: The Defense Department announces an increase in purchases of herbicides and defoliants in fiscal year 1967 to triple destruction of crops and defoliation of jungles in Viet Cong areas.

March 18
SOUTH VIETNAM: The South Vietnamese Constituent Assembly adopts the draft of a new constitution that provides for a democratically elected civilian government, including a president, a vice president, and a bicameral legislature. Provisions of the constitution call for local village elections during four subsequent Sundays. The presidential election will be held in September.

March 18–April 19
GROUND WAR: U.S. Marines conduct Operation Prairie III, a continuation of the Prairie series of search and destroy operations in Quang Tri Province, I Corps. Casualties are U.S.: 56 KIA, 530 WIA; NVA/VC: 252 KIA, 4 POW.

March 19–20

GROUND WAR: During Operation Junction City, the 173rd VC Regiment attacks a troop from the 3rd Battalion of the 5th Cavalry near Ap Bau Bang and Soui Tre, 35 miles north of Saigon. Three Americans are killed and 63 are wounded. VC losses are reported at 227 KIA and three captured. Also this day, a force of more than 2,500 VC attacks elements of the 4th Infantry Division at FSB Gold. A battle ensues in which point-blank artillery fire and hand-to-hand combat finally turn back the human wave attacks launched by the VC. U.S. losses include 30 KIA and 187 WIA; 423 NVA/VC are killed in the battle.

March 20–21

USA – GOVERNMENT: President Johnson and major administration officials, including Dean Rusk and Robert McNamara, meet with Nguyen Cao Ky and Nguyen Van Thieu in Guam to discuss military and political aspects of the war. Premier Ky introduces a plan calling for a 100-mile fortified defensive zone to halt infiltration from North to South Vietnam.

March 20–April 1

GROUND WAR: The Special Landing Force, 1st Battalion, 4th Marines, goes ashore four miles south of the DMZ near Gio Linh to help in Operation Prairie III. Before the landing forces re-embark on April 1, 29 marines are killed and 230 wounded.

March 21

NORTH VIETNAM: The North Vietnamese press agency reports that an exchange of notes took place in February between President Johnson and Ho Chi Minh. The agency says that Ho rejected a proposal made by Johnson for direct talks between the United States and North Vietnam on ending the war, on grounds that the United States "must stop definitely and unconditionally its bombing raids and all other acts of war against North Vietnam." The U.S. State Department confirms the exchange of letters and expresses regret that Hanoi has divulged this information, since the secret letters were intended as a serious diplomatic attempt to end the conflict.

GROUND WAR: Operation Junction City produces what General Westmoreland describes as "one of the most successful single actions of the year" when U.S. forces kill 606 Viet Cong in War Zone C.

March 22

USA – MILITARY: Washington officials announce that Thailand has agreed to the stationing of B-52s on its territory for bombing raids against targets in North and South Vietnam.

March 25

USA – GOVERNMENT: The Senate Preparedness Subcommittee recommends that the United States escalate the air war against North Vietnam by lifting restrictions on bombing targets. The report,

U.S. Air Force makes supply drop during Operation Junction City, 1967. *(Texas Tech University Vietnam Archive)*

based on a subcommittee staff investigation in Vietnam in October 1966, contends that curbing the raids has resulted in heavy losses for proportionately limited gains.

USA – DOMESTIC: The Reverend Martin Luther King, Jr., leads a march of 5,000 antiwar demonstrators in Chicago. Speaking to the demonstrators, King declares that the war in Vietnam is "a blasphemy against all that America stands for."

March 28

USA – DOMESTIC: The *Phoenix*, a private U.S. yacht with eight American pacifists aboard, arrives in Haiphong, North Vietnam, with $10,000 worth of medical supplies for the North Vietnamese. The trip, financed by a Quaker group in Philadelphia, is made in defiance of a U.S. ban on American travel to North Vietnam.

March 30

SOUTH VIETNAM: President Nguyen Van Thieu dismisses six more province chiefs as part of his campaign to eliminate corruption and inefficiency.

March 31

USA – GOVERNMENT: The House Committee on Un-American Activities (HUAC) charges that two antiwar demonstrations scheduled for April 15, 1967, have been proposed by Communists, and that many of the organizations involved are infiltrated or dominated by Communists. The Reverend James L. Bevel, national director of Spring Mobilization Committee to End the War in Vietnam, charges that the HUAC and its chairman, Representative Edwin E. Willis (D-La.) are "liars" and "spreaders of trash."

March 31–April 1

GROUND WAR: In one of the bloodiest battles of Operation Junction City, U.S. troops from the 1st Battalion, 26th Infantry, 1st Infantry Division, fight a fierce battle with 2,500 soldiers from the 271st VC Regiment near Ap Gu, 28 miles northwest of Tay Ninh City. More than 600 enemy are KIA, while U.S. losses are 10 killed and 62 wounded. Heavy artillery and tactical air support help turn the tide of battle in favor of the Americans.

April

NORTH VIETNAM: The Central Committee of the Lao Dong Party passes Resolution 13 at its 13th Plenum in Hanoi, calling for a "spontaneous uprising [in the South] in order to win a decisive victory in the shortest possible time."

GROUND WAR: The 26th Regiment of the U.S. 5th Marine Division is attached to the 1st Marine Division for combat operations in I Corps.

AUSTRALIA: Australia deploys its 7th Battalion, Royal Australian Regiment, to Vietnam to join the 1st Australian Tactical Force for combat operation in III Corps.

April 2

SOUTH VIETNAM: As provided for in the new constitution, effective April 1, local village elections are held. Balloting for legislative people's councils is held in 984 villages with a total population of 5 million.

USA – GOVERNMENT: U.S. officials express fear that the North Vietnamese may be brainwashing U.S. prisoners of war to get anti-American propaganda statements from them.

April 4

USA – DOMESTIC: The Reverend Martin Luther King, Jr., head of the Southern Christian Leadership Conference, indicates that a link is forming between the civil rights and peace movements. Delivering his antiwar speech "A Time to Break Silence," King proposes that the United States (a) stop all bombing of North and South Vietnam; (b) declare a unilateral truce in the hope that it will lead to peace talks; (c) set a date for withdrawal of all troops from Vietnam; and (d) give the National Liberation Front a role in negotiation.

April 5–October 12

GROUND WAR: Two brigades of the U.S. 4th Infantry Division conduct Operation Francis Marion, a follow-on operation to Sam Houston in the western highlands of Pleiku Province. The purpose of the operation is to preclude North Vietnamese infiltration through the Ia Drang Valley, II Corps. Casualties will be NVA/VC: 1,203.

April 6

GROUND WAR: About 2,500 Viet Cong and North Vietnamese troops carry out four closely coordinated attacks on the city of Quang Tri, 15 miles south of the DMZ. U.S. sources say 125 South Vietnamese troops are killed and 180 wounded. Four U.S. Marines are killed and 27 wounded. South Vietnam charges that the Communist attackers had infiltrated from the DMZ, and attribute the success of the Quang Tri raid to aid given to the Communists by disloyal South Vietnamese soldiers. A North Vietnamese force carries out the war's first attack across the bridge spanning the Ben Hai River at the 17th parallel; the South Vietnamese protest to the ICC.

April 7

USA – MILITARY: Secretary of Defense McNamara announces plans to build a fortified barrier just south of the eastern end of the DMZ to curb the flow of arms and troops from North Vietnam into South Vietnam.

USA – DOMESTIC: Republican governor George Romney of Michigan announces his position on the Vietnam war, which coincides with President Johnson's, saying that "It is unthinkable that the United States withdraw from Vietnam."

April 9

USA – DOMESTIC: Former Republican presidential candidate Barry Goldwater praises the administration's policy on Vietnam in a TV interview, saying: "I think the President is now determined to win this war and end it, and all of us are behind him."

April 11

USA – GOVERNMENT: U.S. officials report that Communist China and the Soviet Union have reached an agreement on speeding the shipment of Soviet military supplies to North Vietnam across Chinese territory.

April 12

GROUND WAR: Task Force Oregon is formed in response to MACV's need for reinforcements in I Corps. The task force is stationed at Chu Lai in Quang Tin Province. It will include 15,000 soldiers and will be made up of a brigade each from the U.S. 25th Infantry and 101st Airborne Divisions, the 196th Light Infantry Brigade, and a squadron from the 11th Armored Cavalry Regiment.

April 13

GROUND WAR: Communist forces blow up two bridges between Danang and Quang Tri on Highway 2, the major supply route to U.S. forces along the DMZ.

April 15

SOUTH VIETNAM: South Vietnamese premier Nguyen Cao Ky announces the start of construction on a fortified barrier south of the DMZ to halt infiltration from North Vietnam.

USA – DOMESTIC: Massive parades to protest policy in Vietnam are held in New York and San Francisco. In New York, police estimate that 100,000 to 125,000 people hear speeches by Martin Luther King, Jr., Floyd McKissick, Stokely Carmichael, and Dr. Benjamin Spock. Prior to the march, nearly 200 draft cards are burned by youths in Central Park. The San Francisco march is led by black nationalists, but most of the marchers, estimated at 20,000 by the police, are white.

AIR WAR: Two U.S. Air Force F-100 Super Sabre jets drop bombs off-target, hitting an ARVN battalion position 23 miles northeast of Qui Nhon, killing 41 South Vietnamese troops and wounding 50.

April 18

SOUTH VIETNAM: An agreement is signed in Saigon for an additional $150 million worth of U.S. economic aid to South Vietnam, raising the total amount of assistance in 1967 to a record $700 million.

USA – MILITARY: General Westmoreland notifies the Joint Chiefs of additional troop needs. Concerned about the enemy buildup in sanctuaries in Laos, Cambodia, and parts of South Vietnam as well as the threat posed by large North Vietnamese forces just north of the DMZ, Westmoreland says he needs four and two-thirds divisions—201,250 more troops—to boost the total strength of U.S. forces in Vietnam to 671,616 men. He maintains that this is an "optimum force" needed to contain the enemy threat and maintain the "tactical initiative."

April 19

AIR WAR: Over North Vietnam, Major Leo K. Thorsness (USAF), 357th Tactical Fighter Squadron, along with his electronic warfare officer, Captain Harold E. Johnson, destroys two enemy SAM sites, then shoots down a MiG-17 before escorting search and rescue helicopters to a downed aircrew. Although his F-105 is very low on fuel, Major Thorsness attacks four MiG-17s in an effort to draw the enemy aircraft away from the area. Awarded the Medal of Honor for action this day, Maj. Thorsness will not receive his medal until 1973, because he will be shot down on April 30, 1967, and spend the next six years as a POW.

April 19–21
USA – GOVERNMENT: The United States proposes that the six-mile-wide DMZ be extended 10 miles on each side and that troops on both sides be withdrawn behind the wider buffer. North Vietnam rejects the proposal on the grounds that it does not include Hanoi's principal condition for peace talks—an end to air attacks against North Vietnam.

April 19–September 20
GROUND WAR: Newly formed Task Force Oregon conducts Operation Baker to deny the North Vietnamese the use of the lowlands near Duc Pho in Quang Ngai Province, I Corps. Casualties will be U.S.: 32 KIA, 70 WIA; NVA/VC: 371 KIA, 3 POW.

April 20
USA – MILITARY: The Joint Chiefs transmits General Westmoreland's request for 200,000 additional troops to Secretary of Defense McNamara, "strongly" recommending approval. This confronts the administration with a difficult decision on whether to escalate or level off the U.S. effort.

AIR WAR: For the first time, U.S. planes bomb Haiphong, attacking two power plants inside the city. The raids are carried out by 86 planes from the aircraft carriers *Kitty Hawk* and *Ticonderoga.*

April 20–May 31
GROUND WAR: U.S. Marines and ARVN troops conduct Operation Prairie IV, a continuation of the Prairie series of operations in Quang Tri Province, I Corps. The purpose of this operation is to ease the pressure on the Khe Sanh Combat Base. The operation includes a bloody two-day battle in which the marines capture Hill 174, a heavily fortified North Vietnamese position five miles southwest of Con Thien. Casualties are U.S.: 164 KIA, 1,240 WIA; NVA/VC: 489 KIA, 9 POW.

April 21–May 17
GROUND WAR: The 1st U.S. Marine Division conducts Operation Union to eliminate Communist strongholds between Chu Lai and Danang Quang Nam, and Quang Tin Provinces, I Corps. Casualties are U.S.: 110 KIA, 473 WIA, 2 MIA; NVA/VC: 865 KIA.

April 22
USA – DOMESTIC: Senator Charles Percy (R-Ill.) denounces the Johnson administration as unrealistic in its Vietnam policy and calls for Viet Cong participation in peace talks.

April 22–May 12
GROUND WAR: U.S. troops from the 1st Infantry Division, reinforced by a brigade from the 25th Infantry Division, 11th Armored Cavalry Regiment, and a South Vietnamese Ranger battalion, conduct Operation Manhattan, a search and destroy mission in the Iron Triangle of Binh Duong Province, III Corps. Casualties are U.S.: 15 KIA, 133 WIA; NVA/VC: 123 KIA, 7 POW.

April 24
USA – GOVERNMENT: In response to disagreements within the administration created by General Westmoreland's request for additional troops, Undersecretary

of State Nicholas Katzenbach, acting in Secretary Rusk's absence, orders an intra-agency review of two major options facing the administration. The first option is to provide General Westmoreland with 200,000 more troops with "possible intensification of military actions outside of South Vietnam, including invasion of North Vietnam, Laos, and Cambodia." The second option is to confine troop increases "to those that could be generated without calling up the reserves," plus "a cessation of the bombing of North Vietnam areas north of 20 degrees." This study indicates that resistance to military proposals for escalation is growing among civilian officials in the State Department.

AIR WAR: U.S. planes bomb two MiG bases north of Hanoi in what appears to be a further relaxing of restrictions on air raids around the Hanoi and Haiphong areas.

April 24–30

USA – MILITARY: General Westmoreland arouses controversy by saying that the enemy has "gained support in the United States that gives him hope that he can win politically that which he cannot win militarily." He adds that the GI in Vietnam is "dismayed, and so am I, by recent unpatriotic acts at home."

April 24–May 11

GROUND WAR: In fierce fighting, U.S. Marines defeat North Vietnamese troops from the 325C Division on three hills near the airstrip at Khe Sanh in Quang Tri Province—less than 10 miles from the Laotian border. During the 12-day battle, U.S. forces lose 160 men KIA, with an additional 746 wounded, representing half the combat strength of the two battalions of the 3rd Marine Regiment. The marines capture the last hill on May 5. In a diversionary action, a North Vietnamese force of about 300 moves down from the hills three miles west of Khe Sanh and attacks a comparable South Vietnamese force and a U.S. Special Forces camp. The fighting with the North Vietnamese forces in the high ground surrounding Khe Sanh will last through the second week of May and will become known as "the Hill Fights." Total casualties are U.S.: 155 KIA, 424 WIA; NVA/VC: 940 reported KIA.

April 25

USA – DOMESTIC: Senator George McGovern (D-S.D.) makes a major speech in the Senate attacking administration policies in Vietnam. Democratic senators Robert Kennedy (N.Y.), Frank Church (Ida.), and Ernest Gruening (Alas.) join in the attack.

AIR WAR: U.S. Navy jets from the carriers *Kitty Hawk* and *Bonhomme Richard* attack a cement plant a mile from the center of Haiphong, an oil depot, and an ammunition dump. North Vietnamese officials report that the British freighter *Dartford* is hit by bullets during the raid, wounding six British seamen.

CHINA: Beijing Radio reports that two U.S. F-4 Phantom jets were shot down April 24 after intruding into Chinese air space.

April 26

AIR WAR: U.S. planes from Thailand attack a five-span bridge four miles north of the center of Hanoi in the hope of severing North Vietnam's rail links with Communist China. An electrical transformer station seven miles north of Hanoi is also attacked.

April 27

USA – GOVERNMENT: General Westmoreland returns to the United States to make a speech and put his case for additional troops to the president. Accompanied by the chairman of the Joint Chiefs, General Earle Wheeler, Westmoreland tells Johnson that without the extra troops, "we will not be in danger of being defeated but it will be nip and tuck to oppose the reinforcements the enemy is capable of providing." Wheeler wants the president to call up the reserves to meet Westmoreland's requested troop increase. The president makes no decision at this time, but urges his generals to "make certain we are getting value received from the South Vietnamese troops."

April 28

USA – GOVERNMENT: General Westmoreland addresses a joint session of Congress and evokes a standing ovation by declaring that "Backed at home by resolve, confidence, patience, determination, and continued support, we will prevail in Vietnam over the Communist aggressor."

AIR WAR: Waves of U.S. planes drop hundreds of bombs near the Dan Phuong highway, 12 miles west of Hanoi, and on the Gia Lam railroad repair yards, in one of the heaviest attacks of the war. Hanoi's power station in the northern outskirts is another target.

May

GROUND WAR: U.S. Special Forces begin Operation Daniel Boone, covert intelligence missions into Cambodia to recon the Ho Chi Minh Trail and enemy staging areas. The operations are part of MACV's Special Operations Group Program (SOG) Shining Brass/Prairie Fire. Prairie fire is the code name for Laotian missions.

May–September

USA – MILITARY: A debate develops between the CIA and U.S. military leaders on the issue of how to measure the strength of Communist forces in Vietnam. Brigadier General Joseph A. McChristian, Westmoreland's chief of intelligence, shows his superior a CIA report that estimates available Communist forces at 400,000. Westmoreland feels this gives a distorted impression by lumping regular troops with guerrillas and including even those paramilitary forces engaged primarily in political work. This debate will result in MACV reducing estimated every strength figures from those provided by the CIA.

May 1

USA – GOVERNMENT: Secretary of State Dean Rusk charges that the North Vietnamese have rejected at least 28 peace proposals presented by the United States and other nations. Rusk asserts that the rejection of those proposals by Hanoi "throw[s] a light ... upon the question of who is interested in peace and who is trying to absorb a neighbor by force." Also on this day, Assistant Secretary of State Bundy in a memorandum to Undersecretary Nicholas Katzenbach says he is "totally against" ground operations against North Vietnam, asserting that "the odds were 75 to 25 that it would provoke Chinese Communist intervention."

USA – MILITARY: U.S. military strength in South Vietnam reaches 436,000.

May 1–4

USA – DOMESTIC: The publication of a Republican white paper on Vietnam reveals a wide division in the party. Questioning the administration's policy in Vietnam, the paper asks Republicans to address such questions as: "Does the Republican Party serve America best by saying that politics stops at the water's edge? Must we rally behind the President? Does bipartisanship mean Democratic mistakes are Republican responsibilities?" A number of Republican senators refute the paper.

May 2

AIR WAR: Communist MiG bases at Kep, 37 miles northeast of Hanoi, and Hoa Lac, 19 miles west of Hanoi, are bombed for the third time. Pilots report heavy damage to the targets.

May 2–10

INTERNATIONAL: An "International Tribunal on War Crimes," created by opponents of U.S. policy in Vietnam, opens in Stockholm on May 2. The tribunal hands down a decision accusing the United States of aggression and "widespread, deliberate and systematic bombing of civilian objectives."

May 3

CHINA: Chinese officials claim that four United States aircraft bombed the southern Chinese town of Nin Mong, 20 miles north of the North Vietnamese border, on May 2. The U.S. Defense Department denies the incident.

May 4

USA – GOVERNMENT: Alain C. Enthoven, assistant secretary of defense for systems analysis, sends Secretary McNamara a memorandum entitled "Force Levels and Enemy Attrition." He argues, contrary to General Westmoreland's expectations, that "the size of the force we deploy has little effect on the rate of attrition of enemy forces."

USA – DOMESTIC: The newspaper *Newsday* quotes Senator J. William Fulbright (D-Ark.) as saying he "no longer believes" statements on Vietnam by President Johnson, Secretary Rusk, or Secretary McNamara. He also charges that some leading congressional supporters of the war are influenced by their interest in defense industries in their home states. Later, Fulbright apologizes for "any embarrassment the *Newsday* article may have caused members of Congress."

May 5–6

USA – GOVERNMENT: Assistant Secretary McNaughton sends Secretary of Defense McNamara a recommendation for cutting back the air war to the 20th parallel to reduce U.S. pilot and aircraft losses over heavily defended Hanoi and Haiphong. This is the first recommendation within the administration of a reduction in the bombing campaign. On May 6, McNaughton expresses concern to McNamara about this memorandum, because it had also recommended giving General Westmoreland 80,000 more men. Limiting the troop request to 80,000 men, adds McNaughton, "does the very important business of postponing the issue of a reserve call-up . . . but postpone is all it does."

May 5–10

USA – GOVERNMENT: The State Department discloses a report that was sent to Britain denying that U.S. planes were responsible for damage inflicted on the British freighter *Dartford,* saying that the damage was probably caused by antiaircraft missile debris. This version is supported by a British seaman aboard a nearby ship, but *Dartford* crewmen insist their vessel was strafed by U.S. aircraft.

May 6

POWs: Three U.S. pilots shot down during a raid over Hanoi are paraded through the streets of the capital city.

SOUTH VIETNAM: Ambassador Ellsworth Bunker, in a report to President Johnson, describes an encouraging turnout in recent village council elections. He estimates that 77 percent of eligible voters in participating villages cast votes.

May 8

USA – GOVERNMENT: Walt Rostow, generally described as a "strong bombing advocate," sends a memo to President Johnson recommending a bombing cutback. In the memo, dated May 6, Rostow rejects proposals for mining North Vietnam harbors and bombing port facilities, recommending that the bombing be concentrated on supply routes in southern North Vietnam.

Protesters demonstrate against the Vietnam War in Wichita, Kansas, 1967. *(Texas Tech University Vietnam Archive)*

USA – DOMESTIC: Senator Edward Kennedy (D-Mass.) says that the civilian casualty rate in Vietnam is over 100,000 a year, based on a probe conducted by a Senate subcommittee.

GROUND WAR: The marine base at Con Thien just south of the DMZ comes under a three-hour attack. The assault, backed by mortars, is repulsed after 179 North Vietnamese soldiers and 44 U.S. Marines are killed in bitter fighting. North Vietnam mortar crews also carry out additional attacks on nearby marine camps at Dong Ha, Gio Linh, and Camp Carroll.

May 9

GROUND WAR: A North Vietnamese force attacks a 3rd Marine Regiment unit nine miles northwest of Khe Sanh. In the five-hour clash, the marines suffer 24 casualties.

May 10

USA – GOVERNMENT: The Johnson administration establishes the Civilian Operations and Revolutionary Development Support (CORDS) organization to coordinate the pacification effort in South Vietnam and puts it under military control. Ambassador Robert W. Komer is named head of this program and becomes General Westmoreland's deputy for CORDS.

USA – DOMESTIC: U.S. policy in Vietnam is assailed in a nationwide "teach-in" staged at more than 80 colleges.

May 11

SOUTH VIETNAM: Nguyen Cao Ky informs the cabinet that he will run for president on September 3. Nguyen Van Thieu says it is "entirely possible" that he will run against him.

DIPLOMACY: UN secretary-general U Thant expresses fear that the world is witnessing the initial phase of World War III, saying, "If the present trend continues, I am afraid direct confrontation, first of all between Washington and Beijing, is inevitable." In a statement issued later, Ambassador Arthur Goldberg reaffirms U.S. policy—that the United States will cease "all bombing of North Vietnam the moment we are assured privately or otherwise that this step will be answered promptly by a corresponding and appropriate de-escalation on the other side."

May 11–August 2

GROUND WAR: Task Force Oregon conducts Operation Malheur I-II in Quang Ngai Province, I Corps. The purpose of the operation is to keep Route 1 open to the Binh Dinh Provincial border and to assist in the area's revolutionary development programs. Casualties will be NVA/VC: 869 KIA, 80 POW.

May 12

USA – GOVERNMENT: A CIA report characterizes the mood in North Vietnam after prolonged bombing as one of "resolute stoicism with a considerable reservoir of endurance still untapped."

May 13

AIR WAR: For the second time, pilots of the 8th Tactical Fighter Wing, stationed at Ubon Royal Thai Air Force Base, shoot down seven MiGs in a single day's action over North Vietnam.

May 14–16
CHINA: The *Chicago Daily News* reports that Premier Chou En-lai and four other Chinese officials, during an interview in late February, threatened to send troops into North Vietnam if U.S. troops invade the North. The article quotes Chou as saying that China "was ready tomorrow as need be to send a volunteer army into North Vietnam if Hanoi made such a request." The Chinese Foreign Ministry denies that the interview ever took place.

May 14–December 7
GROUND WAR: The U.S. 25th Infantry Division conducts Operation Kole Kole, a search and destroy operation in Hau Nghia Province, III Corps. Casualties will be U.S.: 144 KIA, 876 WIA; NVA/VC: 797 KIA, 150 POW.

May 15
AIR WAR: The U.S. Defense Department reports that a U.S. F-105 Thunderchief might have crashed in Communist China. The plane is hit during a raid on the Kep area in North Vietnam.

May 15–23
GROUND WAR: U.S. forces just south of the DMZ come under heavy fire, as marine positions between Dong Ha and Con Thien are pounded by North Vietnamese artillery. More than 100 Americans are killed or wounded during heavy fighting along the DMZ. On May 17 and 18, Con Thien base is shelled heavily. Dong Ha, Gio Linh, Cam Lo, and Camp Carroll are also bombarded. On May 18, a force of

Marines from 5th Regiment fire at the enemy near the DMZ, May 1967. *(National Archives)*

5,500 U.S. and South Vietnamese troops invades the southeastern section of the DMZ to smash a Communist buildup in the area and to deny the zone's use as an infiltration route into South Vietnam. On May 19, the U.S. State Department says the offensive in the DMZ is "purely a defensive measure" against a "considerable buildup of North Vietnam troops." The North Vietnamese government on May 21 calls the invasion of the zone "a brazen provocation" that "abolished the buffer character of the DMZ as provided by the Geneva agreements."

May 17

USA – DOMESTIC: Sixteen Senate critics of administration policy on Vietnam issue a statement, drafted by Senator Frank Church (D-Ida.), warning Hanoi that while they might be critical of the administration's handling of the war, they oppose unilateral U.S. withdrawal.

May 18–28

GROUND WAR: U.S. Marines conduct Operation Hickory, the western prong of a multiforce offensive aimed at clearing the area southeast of the DMZ in I Corps in preparation for the construction of the Strong Point Obstacle System, which will become known as "The McNamara Line." This is the first major marine incursion into the DMZ and involves the relocation of more than 10,000 civilians from the buffer zone to Cam Lo refugee area.

May 19

USA – GOVERNMENT: Secretary of Defense McNamara sends a memo to President Johnson that recommends a cutback of the bombing to the 20th parallel and the deployment of only 30,000 more troops for General Westmoreland. He also advocates a considerably more limited overall U.S. objective in Vietnam, saying, "Our commitment is only to see that the people of South Vietnam are permitted to determine their own future. . . . This commitment ceases if the country ceases to help itself."

AIR WAR: U.S. planes bomb a power plant in Hanoi.

May 20

USA – GOVERNMENT: Secretary of Defense McNamara orders a new study of bombing alternatives.

AIR WAR: Colonel Robin Olds (USAF), pilot, and 1st Lieutenant Steven Croaker, his weapons systems officer, down two MiG-17s over the Bak Le rail yards, giving Olds four aerial victories in Vietnam. He had also recorded 12 victories in World War II, making him the only ace to down enemy aircraft in nonconsecutive wars.

May 21

USA – MILITARY: General Earle Wheeler, chairman of the Joint Chiefs of Staff, says that the United States "has no intention of invading North Vietnam."

May 22

USA – GOVERNMENT: President Johnson issues a proclamation designating Memorial Day as a day of prayer and peace. He pledges to continue to resist aggression, but to hold open the door to an honorable peace.

May 23–October 18

USA – GOVERNMENT: A public controversy over the M-16, the basic combat rifle in Vietnam, begins after Representative James J. Howard (D-N.J.) reads to the House of Representatives a letter in which a marine in Vietnam claims that almost all Americans killed in the battle for Hill 881 died as a result of jamming by their new M-16 rifles. U.S. Marine after-action reports following the battles in the hills surrounding Khe Sanh indicate an estimated 50 percent failure rate for the M-16 rifles used by the marines. The Defense Department acknowledges on August 28 that there has been a "serious increase in frequency of malfunctions in the M-16."

May 24

USA – MILITARY: In response to Secretary of Defense McNamara's order for a new study on bombing alternatives on May 20, the Joint Chiefs of Staff submits three memoranda renewing earlier recommendations for more than 200,000 new troops and for air attacks on Haiphong, the mining of Haiphong harbor, and raids on eight major railways leading to China. "It may ultimately become necessary," they said, to send American troops into Cambodia and Laos and take "limited ground action in North Vietnam."

May 25

AIR WAR: After a 24-hour truce in honor of the Buddha's birthday, air raids over North Vietnam resume with attacks on two rail-lines carrying supplies from Communist China to Hanoi.

May 25–27

GROUND WAR: As part of Operation Hickory, elements of two U.S. Marine battalions assault a North Vietnamese position on Hill 117, three miles west of the base at Con Thien. The marines lose 14 KIA and 92 wounded, but kill 41 NVA soldiers.

May 25–June 5

GROUND WAR: The U.S. 1st Marine Division and ARVN troops conduct Operation Union II against North Vietnamese forces in Quang Nam and Quang Tin Provinces, I Corps. Casualties are U.S.: 110 KIA, 241 WIA; NVA/VC: 711 KIA, 23 POW.

May 28–31

GROUND WAR: As part of Operation Prairie IV, two companies from the 4th Marines make heavy contact with an NVA force in bunkers and trenches five miles southwest of Con Thien. The two-day battle to take Hill 174 costs the lives of 10 marines, while 99 others are wounded. Only 20 enemy bodies are found after the fight.

May 30–June 2

GROUND WAR: As part of Operation Union II, elements of the 5th Marines assault a heavily fortified enemy position in the hills along the southern rim of the Que Son Valley, near the Vinh Huy village complex (5.2 miles southeast of Que Son). The marines report killing 540 North Vietnamese soldiers while suffering 73 killed and 139 wounded.

May 31

USA – MILITARY: The Joint Chiefs issues a sharp rebuttal to the 19 May McNamara-McNaughton memorandum, contending that "the drastic changes" in American policy advocated by McNamara "would undermine and no longer provide a complete rationale for our presence in South Vietnam or much of our efforts over the past two years." The JCS also asserts that the McNamara-McNaughton memorandum "fails to appreciate the full implications for the free world of failure" in Vietnam.

June 1

AUSTRALIA: Prime Minister Holt gives President Johnson a pledge of Australia's support in the Vietnam conflict.

June 1–July 26

GROUND WAR: The 2nd Brigade, 9th Infantry Division, and the Mobile Riverine Force conduct Operation Coronado, their first major operation in the Mekong Delta; 500 VC are killed and 75 are captured.

June 2–3

USA – MILITARY: Captain Howard Levy (USA), 30, a dermatologist from Brooklyn, is convicted by a general court-martial at Fort Jackson, South Carolina, of willfully disobeying orders and making disloyal statements about U.S. policy in Vietnam. Levy had refused to provide elementary instruction in skin disease to Special Forces medics on grounds that the Green Berets would use medicine as "another tool of political persuasion."

GROUND WAR: A marine patrol is ambushed by elements of a 2,900-man North Vietnamese regiment near Tam Ky, 30 miles southwest of Danang. The U.S. 5th marines sustain 73 killed and 139 wounded and report 540 North Vietnamese killed.

USSR: The Soviet Union charges that U.S. planes bombed the Soviet merchant ship *Turkestan* in the port of Cam Pha, 50 miles north of Haiphong, and files a protest claiming two crewmen were wounded. The Soviets warn that "appropriate measures" will be taken to ensure the safety of other ships. On June 3, the United States attributes damage to antiaircraft fire.

June 8

USA – GOVERNMENT: Undersecretary of State Nicholas Katzenbach proposes that the United States add 30,000 ground troops "in small increments over the next 18 months" and "concentrate bombing on lines of communication throughout" North Vietnam but shift away from strategic targets around Hanoi and Haiphong.

June 10

GROUND WAR: Two separate Communist mortar attacks strike Pleiku in the Central Highlands, killing 27 people; most of the shells are directed against a pacification school for Montagnard tribesmen.

June 12

CHINA: The Chinese armed forces claim they have shot down a pilotless U.S. reconnaissance plane over the southern part of the Kwangsi Chuang autonomous region.

June 12–26

GROUND WAR: Troops of the U.S. 1st Infantry Division conduct Operation Billings, a drive into War Zone D, 50 miles north of Saigon, in an effort to trap three Viet Cong battalions. On June 13, the Americans kill 60 guerrillas in a four-hour battle. On June 17, in the same area U.S. troops kill at least 196 soldiers. A Viet Cong ambush costs the lives of 31 Americans, with 113 wounded. Total casualties for the operation are U.S.: 57 KIA, 197 WIA; NVA/VC: 347 KIA, 1 POW.

June 14

GROUND WAR: In an all-day battle fought in the Mekong Delta 10 miles southwest of Can Tho, a South Vietnamese force of about 1,000, assisted by armed U.S. helicopters, overwhelms a 450-man Viet Cong battalion.

June 15

SOUTH VIETNAM: Premier Nguyen Cao Ky says informal contacts have been made with Laos to extend into Laos the proposed barrier against infiltration.

June 16

NLF: National Liberation Front Radio warns that captured Americans will be executed if "the U.S. Aggressors and their Saigon stooges" execute "three Vietnamese patriots" sentenced to death by a special military tribunal in Saigon.

June 19–20

RIVER WAR: On the Rach-Hui River, 19 miles south of Saigon, U.S. Navy river assault boats and about 800 men of the U.S. 9th Infantry Division kill 169 Viet Cong. U.S. losses are 28 killed and 126 wounded.

June 20

USA – GOVERNMENT: The United States apologizes to the Soviet Union for what it calls an inadvertent U.S. air attack on the Soviet ship *Turkestan* on June 2.

June 21

FRANCE: In a policy statement to his cabinet, French president Charles de Gaulle links the Middle East conflict to U.S. intervention in Vietnam. He sees no chance of a peaceful settlement in the present world situation, unless the Vietnam War is ended through "termination of foreign intervention."

June 22

GROUND WAR: An NVA ambush virtually wipes out a 130-man company of the 173rd Airborne Brigade near Dak To, Kontum Province. Seventy-six paratroopers are killed and 34 wounded before help can arrive. North Vietnamese body count is 106 dead. American troops entering the battleground the next day find that most of the American dead were killed execution style—point-blank gunshots to the head.

June 23–25

DIPLOMACY: President Johnson and Soviet premier Aleksey Kosygin meet in Glassboro, New Jersey, to discuss world problems.

June 26

AIR WAR: An unarmed U.S. F-4 Phantom jet strays off course and is shot down by Chinese pilots near Hainan island. The two crewmen parachute from the plane and are rescued unhurt from the China Sea by a U.S. Navy helicopter.

June 28

SOUTH VIETNAM: General Duong Van Minh, in exile in Bangkok, announces that he will be a candidate for the presidency in September. The government in Saigon forbids Minh to return.

June 30

SOUTH VIETNAM: The Armed Forces Council resolves rival claims to the presidency in favor of Nguyen Van Thieu, chief of state. Nguyen Cao Ky, who had announced on May 11 that he would run for president, is forced to accept second place on the presidential ticket.

AIR WAR: Several sources report attacks by U.S. planes on foreign ships in Haiphong harbor. The Soviet government charges that a second Russian merchant vessel, *Mikhail Frunze,* was bombed by U.S. planes in Haiphong on June 29. A protest is delivered to the U.S. embassy in Moscow on June 30. The North Vietnamese News Agency reports that two other foreign ships have been struck in Haiphong Harbor.

July 2–14

GROUND WAR: Four battalions of U.S. Marines conduct Operation Buffalo south of the DMZ in Quang Tri Province, I Corps. This operation is launched in response to North Vietnamese efforts to attack Con Thien, one of the key points in the Strong Point Obstacle System. In the first major battle of this operation, a company from 1st Battalion, 9th Marines, is ambushed by 500 troops of the North Vietnamese 90th Regiment about 1½ miles northeast of Con Thien, just south of the DMZ. Reinforcements are rushed to the scene by both sides, and the fighting increases in intensity. Several other sharp battles are fought during the operation. Total casualties are U.S.: 159 KIA, 345 WIA; NVA/VC: 1,281 KIA, 2 POW.

July 4–6

GROUND WAR: North Vietnamese mortars, rockets, and artillery fire 300 rounds in eight separate attacks on U.S. positions at Con Thien and Dong Ha. One of the artillery shells scores a direct hit on a marine outpost, killing nine men and wounding 21.

July 6

INTERNATIONAL: A four-day conference on Vietnam, arranged by several organizations of the international peace movement and the Swedish Society for Peace and Arbitration, begins in Stockholm.

July 7

NORTH VIETNAM: The Central Committee of the Lao Dong Party in Hanoi decides to go ahead with the general offensive-general uprising in South Vietnam. The funeral for General Nguyen Chi Tanh is held in Hanoi. The official obituary of the senior NVA general who had been in charge of the war in the South says that he died in Hanoi of a heart attack, but it was later wrongfully rumored that he died in the south during a U.S. bombing attack.

USA – GOVERNMENT: Congress' Joint Economic Committee issues a report stating that the Vietnam War has created "havoc" in the U.S. economy during 1966 and predicts that the war will cost $4 billion to $6 billion more in 1967 than the $20.3 billion requested by President Johnson.

July 7–12

USA – MILITARY: Secretary of Defense McNamara, accompanied by General Earle Wheeler, chairman of the Joint Chiefs of Staff, travels to Vietnam for a firsthand assessment of the situation, reportedly with instructions from President Johnson to review with General Westmoreland his request for additional troops and "reach an agreement on a figure well below the 200,000 he had requested." On McNamara's final evening in Saigon, he and Westmoreland agree on a 55,000-man troop increase, which will bring the total American commitment to 525,000 troops. Johnson will approve the compromise on August 4.

July 9
USA – GOVERNMENT: Presidential adviser Walt W. Rostow, on *Meet the Press,* states that North Vietnam's strategy has "shifted from a posture of trying to win the war to keeping the war going."

July 10
GROUND WAR: Outnumbered South Vietnamese troops repel an attack by two battalions of the 141st North Vietnamese Regiment on a military camp in Binh Long Province five miles east of An Loc and 60 miles north of Saigon. Communist forces capture a third of the base camp before they are thrown back with the assistance of U.S. and South Vietnamese air and artillery strikes.

July 10–11
GROUND WAR: U.S. forces suffer heavy casualties in two separate battles in the Central Highlands. In the first action, about 400 men of the 173rd Airborne Brigade come under heavy fire from North Vietnamese machine guns and mortars during a sweep of the Dak To area near Kontum. American casualties include 26 KIA and 49 wounded. In the second Highlands clash, 35 soldiers of the U.S. 4th Infantry Division are killed and 31 wounded five miles south of Duc Co.

July 10–October 31
GROUND WAR: U.S. Marines conduct Operation Fremont in Thua Thien Province, I Corps, with the aim of screening the western approaches to Hue and Phu Bai. Casualties are U.S.: 17 KIA, 260 WIA; NVA/VC: 123 KIA.

July 11
USA-GOVERNMENT: It is reported that Secretary of Defense McNamara has said that resources now available in Vietnam are not being well used. Despite the presence of 464,000 American troops in South Vietnam, only 50,000 are available for offensive ground operations.

USA – DOMESTIC: Disagreement over the administration's policies in Vietnam grows in Congress. Senator Mike Mansfield (D-Mont.) warns against further escalation of the war and urges an alternative to expansion by putting the entire question before the United Nations, and containing the conflict by building a defensive barrier south of the DMZ separating North from South Vietnam. Senator George Aiken (R-Vt.) suggests that the administration pay more attention to its Senate leaders than to "certain military leaders who have far more knowledge of weapons than they have of people." Republican leader Everett Dirksen of Illinois, asked if he favors an increase in U.S. troops in Vietnam, replies "If General Westmoreland says we need them, yes, sir."

July 12

CHINA: Beijing claims that its planes chased four U.S. jets after they attacked a Chinese frontier post near Tun Ghing with missiles.

July 13

USA – GOVERNMENT: President Johnson declares in a press conference that "we are very sure we are on the right track" militarily in Vietnam, but acknowledges that more troops will be needed. This announcement comes amid renewed reports that some in the administration disagree with Westmoreland and other U.S. commanders in Vietnam who have requested a substantial increase in U.S. troops.

July 15

GROUND WAR: The U.S. air base at Danang is struck by 50 Communist rockets during a 45-minute attack in which 12 Americans are killed and 40 wounded.

USA – DOMESTIC: The AFL-CIO conducts a survey of its membership and reports that 42 percent are uneasy about the war, but the majority believe that President Johnson is doing the best he can.

July 16–October 31

GROUND WAR: The U.S. 3rd Marine Division conducts Operation Kingfisher in the area south of the DMZ to screen enemy movement into Quang Tri Province, I Corps. The operation includes a number of pitched battles between the marines and North Vietnamese forces. Total casualties will be U.S.: 340 KIA, 1,461 WIA; NVA/VC: 1,117 KIA, 5 POW.

July 17

POWs: The White House calls on the National Liberation Front and North Vietnam to permit an impartial inspection of U.S. POWs.

July 19

USA – GOVERNMENT: In Washington, Secretary of State Rusk tells a news conference that the enemy is "hurting badly" but that he sees a "still tough, long job ahead."

NORTH VIETNAM: A Hanoi delegation headed by Deputy Premier Le Thanh Nghi leaves for Beijing on first leg of trip to secure additional weapons and other aid from Communist countries.

July 20

USA – GOVERNMENT: President Johnson is reported to have added 16 targets to the approved bombing list for North Vietnam, including an airfield, a railroad yard, two bridges, and 12 barracks and a supply area, all within the restricted circles around Hanoi and Haiphong. This represents a markedly different strategy from that of de-escalation recently urged by Defense Secretary McNamara.

July 22–August 3

USA – GOVERNMENT: General Maxwell Taylor, now a consultant to President Johnson, and presidential adviser Clark Clifford, tour South Vietnam, Thailand, Australia, New Zealand, and South Korea to sound out Allied opinion on the possibility of another summit conference and, reportedly, to seek additional Allied troops for the war. During their visit to South Vietnam, Clifford and Maxwell deliver a personal message to the South Vietnamese leaders: "If there was any one act on their part which would be calculated to alienate the American people, it would be to have a rigged election in South Vietnam." On their return, they report no major disagreements on any aspect of the war.

July 23

GROUND WAR: In a five-hour battle, the U.S. 4th Infantry Division virtually wipes out a North Vietnamese company four miles south of Duc Co in the Central Highlands, killing at least 148 of the 400-man battalion.

July 29

USA – GOVERNMENT: According to U.S. intelligence, the number of non-Communist ships calling at North Vietnamese ports has increased from 20 during July–December 1966 to 39 during January–June 1967.

GROUND WAR: A battalion of U.S. Marines is ambushed after penetrating the southern part of the DMZ.

SEA WAR: Fire sweeps the aircraft carrier *Forrestal* off the coast of North Vietnam in the Gulf of Tonkin in the worst U.S. naval disaster in a combat zone since World War II. The accident takes the lives of 134 crewmen and injures 62. Of the carrier's 80 planes, 21 are destroyed and 42 damaged.

July 30

USA – DOMESTIC: The Most Reverend Fulton J. Sheen, Roman Catholic archbishop of Rochester, New York, appeals to President Johnson to "Withdraw our forces immediately from South Vietnam for the sake of reconciliation." A Gallup Poll reports that 52 percent of the American people disapprove of the president's handling of the Vietnam war; 41 percent think the United States made a mistake in sending troops to Vietnam in the first place. Over half, 56 percent, think the United States is losing the war or that progress is stalled.

Late July 1967

GROUND WAR: Viet Cong commanders meet in Cambodia to begin planning for the general offensive-general uprising.

August 1

DIPLOMACY: The U.S. State Department reports that Cambodia rejected a May 27 suggestion for talks as a step toward preventing the use of Cambodian territory by North Vietnamese troops. The Communist troops will continue to use Cambodian territory for base camps and as a sanctuary from which to strike into South Vietnam.

August 2

GROUND WAR: In combat operations in the Mekong Delta, two U.S. helicopters return fire against a group of Viet Cong in the village of Phu Vinh, 60 miles south of Saigon, killing 40 South Vietnamese civilians and wounding 36.

August 3

USA – GOVERNMENT: President Johnson announces that he will raise the U.S. troop ceiling in Vietnam to 525,000 and calls for a 10 percent surtax on individual and corporate income.

GROUND WAR: A captured VC internal document describes "new situation and mission" that will lead to the climax of the war and "split the sky and shake the earth."

AIR WAR: U.S. warplanes fly a total of 197 missions, the highest total for a single day since October 14, 1966, hitting targets ranging from the Hanoi-Haiphong area south to the DMZ.

August 4

USA – GOVERNMENT: The U.S. Court of Military Appeals in Washington upholds the 1965 court-martial of Second Lieutenant Henry H. Howe, who was sentenced to dismissal from the service and a year of hard labor for participating in an antiwar demonstration.

August 5

CHINA: The PRC signs a new aid pact with North Vietnam in a ceremony in Beijing.

USA – GOVERNMENT: Johnson adviser Clark Clifford and retired general Maxwell Taylor return from a trip to the capitals of America's Asian Allies; Clifford reports that the Allies unanimously agree that bombing North Vietnam should be continued at present or even higher levels.

August 6–8

SOUTH VIETNAM: The election campaign opens amid opposition charges that the military slate headed by Nguyen Van Thieu and Nguyen Cao Ky is deliberately impeding the campaign efforts of the 10 civilian presidential candidates.

August 7

USA – MILITARY: General Harold K. Johnson, army chief of staff, reports the "smell of success" in the Allied war effort, marking the beginning of the president's "success campaign."

NORTH VIETNAM: The North Vietnamese newspaper *Nhan Dan* reports that Communist China has signed an agreement to give Hanoi an undisclosed amount of aid in the form of an outright grant.

GROUND WAR: The VC shoot down five U.S. helicopters along the Saigon River four miles from Saigon.

August 8

USA – DOMESTIC: House Republican leader Gerald Ford of Michigan attacks the Johnson administration for "pulling punches" in bombing North Vietnam while sending more Americans to die in the ground war.

AIR WAR: President Johnson approves the extension of Operation Rolling Thunder to include the approval to bomb previously prohibited targets in North Vietnam.

August 9

GROUND WAR: Troops of the 1st Cavalry Division land near a fortified North Vietnamese position in the Song Re Valley, 25 miles west of Duc Pho, Quang Ngai Province, I Corps; five U.S. helicopters are shot down during the operation.

August 9–25

USA – GOVERNMENT: The Senate Preparedness Subcommittee holds closed hearings on the conduct of the war. This subcommittee is known for its hard-line views and military sympathies. Testimony is given by high-ranking military officers, all of whom emphasize the need to continue and even expand the air war against North Vietnam. Secretary McNamara, on August 25, will offer a dissenting view, asserting that bombing of North Vietnam has (1) not reduced the movement of enemy supplies into South Vietnam; (2) not seriously damaged the economy of North Vietnam; and (3) not broken the morale of the North Vietnamese.

August 11
NORTH KOREA: In a ceremony in Pyongyang, North Korea signs a military pact with North Vietnam.

August 11–14
AIR WAR: For the first time, U.S. pilots are authorized to bomb road and rail links in the Hanoi-Haiphong area, formerly on the prohibited target list. This permits U.S. aircraft to bomb targets within 25 miles of the Chinese border and to engage other targets with rockets and cannon within 10 miles of the border.

August 11–28
GROUND WAR: The 1st Marine Division conducts Operation Cochise, a continuation of search and destroy operations in the old Union II area in the Que Son valley, Quang Tin Province, I Corps. Casualties are U.S.: 10 KIA, 93 WIA; NVA/VC: 156 KIA, 13 POW.

August 13–19
AIR WAR: B-52s bomb North Vietnamese positions north of the DMZ in strikes that continue for seven days. The bombings are directed against North Vietnamese troops and installations in the DMZ and just north of the buffer area. On August 19, a record 209 missions are flown against coastal shipping and infiltration traffic.

August 15
USA – DOMESTIC: An article by Robert Pisor of the *Detroit News* reports concern in Saigon about "a massive country-wide military strike" by the Communists to improve their positions prior to the commencement of peace talks.

August 16–23
USA – GOVERNMENT: The Senate Foreign Relations Committee holds hearings on U.S. foreign commitments. Senator William Fulbright (D-Ark.), who feels that Johnson has no mandate to conduct the war on the present scale, attacks President Johnson's broad interpretation of the Gulf of Tonkin Resolution.

August 18
USA – GOVERNMENT: In a news conference, President Johnson says that "Congress could rescind the resolution if it thought we have acted unwisely or improperly."
USA – DOMESTIC: In a speech, Governor Ronald Reagan of California proclaims, "my idea of honorable disengagement is that you win the war. I can't technically say how you'd do it, but some experts have said too many qualified targets have been put off limits to bombing."

August 19

SOUTH VIETNAM: Presidential candidate Thieu seeks to dispel any idea that the military would oppose the accession of a civilian regime.

August 20

USA – DOMESTIC: An Associated Press survey reports that U.S. Senate support for the president's war policy has drastically eroded; of senators replying to the survey, only 44 generally support war politics, while 40 disapprove.

USA – MILITARY: The 20th Engineer Brigade deploys to Vietnam from Fort Bragg, North Carolina, to provide engineer support for U.S. forces.

August 21

AIR WAR: Two U.S. Navy A-6A Intruder jet fighter-bombers from the carrier *Constellation* are pursued by North Vietnamese MiG fighters and stray over the Chinese border, where they are shot down. Beijing claims that its air force downed the American planes.

August 22

USA – GOVERNMENT: Chief of staff of the air force, General John P. McConnell, states before a Senate subcommittee that adopting a graduated bombing policy in 1965, rather than launching a massive blow to destroy 94 targets in 16 days, was a mistake.

USA – DOMESTIC: Former vice president Richard M. Nixon, in an interview with the *Christian Science Monitor,* calls for "massive pressure" short of nuclear weapons to shorten the war.

August 25

NORTH VIETNAM: Hanoi's Administrative Committee orders all workers in light industry and all craftsman and their families to leave the city; only persons vital to the city's defense and production are to remain.

August 25–27

USA – GOVERNMENT: Secretary of Defense McNamara, testifying before the Senate Preparedness Subcommittee, concedes that the U.S. bombing campaign has had little effect on the North's "war making capability." This is the most pessimistic appraisal of the bombing campaign to date. Several senators reply that the United States may as well "get out" if McNamara is correct.

August 26

SOUTH VIETNAM: Presidential candidate Thieu denies that he and vice presidential candidate Ky are trying to rig the elections and promises again that, if he is elected, he will suspend bombing for a week as a "good-will gesture."

AIR WAR: Badly injured after his North American F-100F is shot down over North Vietnam, Major George E. Day (USAF) is captured and severely tortured. He manages to escape and eventually makes it to the DMZ. After several attempts to signal U.S. aircraft, he is ambushed, recaptured, and later moved to a prison in Hanoi, where he continues to offer maximum resistance to his captors. Finally released in

1973, Major Day will be awarded the Medal of Honor for his conspicuous gallantry while a POW.

August 27

GROUND WAR: The Viet Cong launch an offensive in South Vietnam; the heaviest hit areas are Can Tho in the Mekong Delta and Hoi An, 30 miles south of Hue in Thua Thien Province. A total of 355 South Vietnamese are killed.

AIR WAR: The *New York Times* reports that Communist Chinese territory is being used by North Vietnamese MiGs "to escape air clashes with U.S. planes."

August 28

USA – DOMESTIC: Reverend Thomas Lee Hayes, speaking for the National Mobilization Committee, announces that there will be a massive protest march on October 21 in Washington. In the Senate, Mike Mansfield (D-Mont.) makes a proposal endorsed by 10 other senators to bring a peace plan before the United Nations.

August 29

NORTH VIETNAM: Writing in a communist newspaper, General Vo Nguyen Giap says that President Johnson is engaging "backwards logic" in thinking that bombing the North would ease the pressure on the South. This is in response to a claim by Admiral U.S. Grant Sharp that the U.S. bombing is causing Hanoi "mounting logistic, management and morale problems." Giap vows to match every phase of U.S. military escalation.

August 30

GROUND WAR: VC forces attack a radio monitoring station at the Phu Bai marine helicopter base. This station is a secret facility manned by Chinese Nationalists, who monitor North Vietnamese and Chinese Communist communications. Eighteen helicopters are damaged; 10 marines are killed and 30 wounded. South Vietnamese losses are 55 killed and 61 wounded.

August 31

USA – GOVERNMENT: The Senate Preparedness Investigating Committee issues a call to step up bombing against the North, declaring that McNamara has "shackled" the air war against Hanoi and calling for "closure, neutralization, or isolation of Haiphong."

September

GROUND WAR: U.S. Marines establish a base at Khe Sanh, near the Laotian border in I Corps, to serve as a potential launch point for ground operations to cut the Ho Chi Minh Trail.

THAILAND: Thailand deploys its "Queen's Cobra" Regiment to Vietnam for combat operations in III Corps.

September 1

USA – GOVERNMENT: President Johnson, in a news conference, says there is no "deep division" within his administration concerning the bombing of North Vietnam.

NORTH VIETNAM: Premier Pham Van Dong declares that "U.S. imperialism is aggressive and warlike by nature. All it wants is war." He promises that Hanoi will "continue

U.S. Navy and South Vietnamese Navy river patrol boats provide a screening force for USS *Okanogan* as she brings 1,500 Royal Thai Army volunteer troops up the Long Tao shipping channel to Saigon. *(Texas Tech University Vietnam Archive)*

to fight." He reiterates his government's position that an unconditional halt in U.S. raids on the North is Hanoi's prerequisite for negotiations.

September 1–October 31

GROUND WAR: North Vietnamese artillery and mortars pound the U.S. Marine base at Con Thien, five miles below the DMZ, initiating what will become a siege by North Vietnamese regulars. The adjacent bases of Dong Ha, Camp Carroll, and Cam Lo are also shelled regularly during this period. Since August 13, B-52s have struck 83 times along the DMZ, helping, along with U.S. artillery, to relieve pressure on Con Thien.

September 2

SOUTH VIETNAM: On the same day that President Thieu touts his country's attitude toward free speech, two opposition newspapers are shut down. In addressing election observers from 24 nations, he says he will abide by the results of the national election.

September 3

SOUTH VIETNAM: In the national election, Nguyen Van Thieu wins a four-year term as president of South Vietnam with Premier Ky as vice president. They receive 35 percent of the votes cast, with the rest divided among the other 10 candidates; peace candidate Truong Dinh Dzu wins second highest presidential vote.

September 4

GROUND WAR: The siege of Con Thien continues when two companies of the 4th Marines clash with a company of NVA regulars a half-mile south of the fire base. Six marines are killed and 47 are wounded; 38 NVA soldiers are killed and one is captured.

USA – DOMESTIC: Governor George Romney, in a Detroit television interview, says "brainwashing" in Saigon by U.S. generals and diplomats brought about his previous support of the war.

September 4–5

SOUTH VIETNAM: There are allegations of corruption in the national election, but a favorable impression of the election process is reported by 22 prominent Americans who are in Vietnam as election observers.

September 4–15

GROUND WAR: Task Force X-Ray from the 1st Marine Division conducts Operation Swift in Quang Nam and Quang Tin Provinces, I Corps. Purpose of the operation is to prevent enemy disruption of the national elections. The heaviest fighting in this operation is a fierce four-day battle in the Que Son Valley, 35 miles south of Danang. Casualties for the entire operation are U.S.: 127 KIA, 362 WIA; NVA/VC: 517 KIA, 8 POW.

September 5

GROUND WAR: The ROK 2nd Marine Brigade begins Operation Dragon Fire in Quang Ngai Province, I Corps.

September 7

USA – MILITARY: Secretary of Defense McNamara announces plans to build a fortified barrier, with hi-tech listening devices, to block the flow of Communist arms and troops into South Vietnam from the north at the eastern end of the DMZ. The concept is criticized by Westmoreland and marine commanders who dislike the idea of a static defense.

USA – DOMESTIC: Eleven Democratic senators propose that the war be discussed in the United Nations. The U.S. ambassador to the United Nations admits that he has discussed a new peace plan that involves some concessions by the United States.

September 9

USA – DOMESTIC: Governor George Romney attempts to correct the apparent damage to his presidential prospects arising from his September 4 reference to what he called his "brainwashing" by senior military and civilian leaders in the Johnson administration. He charges that the administration has "kept the American people from knowing the facts about the Vietnam war and its full impact on our domestic and foreign affairs."

September 10

AIR WAR: The first U.S. air raid on North Vietnamese ports occurs when the port area of Cam Pha, 46 miles northeast of Haiphong, comes under attack by U.S. aircraft.

September 11

AIR WAR: U.S. warplanes carry out raids on Haiphong and its suburbs in a major effort to isolate the area from the rest of the country. All rail traffic from the port and most road movement from Haiphong is reportedly halted, but several foreign ships in the harbor are damaged.

September 11–November 11

GROUND WAR: Task Force Oregon conducts Operation Wheeler in Quang Tin Province, I Corps. TF Oregon is redesignated 23rd Division (American) on September 25. Casualties are U.S.: 126 KIA, 498 WIA; NVA/VC: 1,103 KIA, 50 POW.

September 12–October 8

GROUND WAR: The Mobile Riverine Force and South Vietnamese troops conduct Operation Coronado V, a search and destroy mission in the Mekong Delta 47 miles southwest of Saigon. Casualties are NVA/VC: 540 KIA.

September 14–15

DIPLOMACY: News reports from French and Canadian sources suggest that North Vietnam can be persuaded to come to the negotiating table. An *Agence France-Presse* dispatch from Hanoi quotes "reliable sources" as saying that peace talks could begin three to four weeks after the cessation of U.S. bombing attacks. The second report, from Canadian external affairs minister Paul Martin, says that officials in Hanoi have indicated that they are interested in opening discussions to end the war, but that suspension of the bombing is still a precondition. U.S. State Department officials express doubt that North Vietnam's position has changed.

September 14–16

NORTH VIETNAM: Defense Minister Vo Nguyen Giap, in several Hanoi radio broadcasts, endorses a strategy of protracted war but declares that "our fight will be more violent in the days ahead." In an analysis of the war that also appears in the newspaper *Quang Doi Nhan Can*, Giap says that the Allied pacification program for winning control of the South Vietnamese countryside has failed because the U.S. troops needed to make it effective had to be shifted to the area below the DMZ to reinforce U.S. Marines under heavy attack there. Giap says the United States has two choices: to expand the ground war by invading North Vietnam, or to continue increasing military pressure with a limited number of troops.

September 15–16

Colonel Robin Olds (USAF) and his men celebrate his return from his 100th combat mission over North Vietnam, September 1967. *(National Archives)*

RIVER WAR: VC attack the U.S. Navy's Mobile Riverine Force on the Rach Ba River in the Mekong Delta. Soldiers from the 2nd Brigade, the 9th Infantry Division respond. Fighting continues for two days with 69 VC killed while U.S. forces sustain 21 killed.

September 17

AIR WAR: U.S. aircraft carry out a bombing raid within seven miles of the Chinese border, targeting the That Khe bridge, the closest that U.S. bombing has yet come to the Communist Chinese frontier.

USA – DOMESTIC: President Johnson is accused of "effectively and brutally cancelling" a private peace initiative begun by U.S. journalist Harry Ashmore. *Centre* magazine alleges Johnson sent a negative letter to Ho Chi Minh after Ashmore had negotiated with Ho. Commenting on the story, Senator William Fulbright says that it shows that U.S.-North Vietnamese negotiations could have begun had the United States been more flexible.

September 18–January 31, 1969

GROUND WAR: The 173rd Airborne Brigade and 1st Air Cavalry Division conduct Operation Bolling/Dan Hoa in Khanh Hoa and Phu Yen Provinces, II Corps. The purpose of the operation is the conduct of search and destroy operations to protect the rice crop. Casualties are NVA/VC: 715 KIA, 30 POW.

SOUTH VIETNAM: The Nationalist Chinese embassy in Saigon is heavily damaged by a bomb explosion.

September 21

SOUTH VIETNAM: General Westmoreland welcomes 1,200 Thai troops upon their arrival in Saigon. The arrival of the Thai force brings to six the number of Allied countries that have sent troops to Vietnam.

AIR WAR: U.S. Navy planes return to Haiphong and destroy the last intact bridge on the Kie Nan highway leading from the city.

DIPLOMACY: Ambassador to the United Nations Arthur Goldberg addresses the UN General Assembly saying that the UN has a "right and duty to concern itself with the Vietnam problem."

September 22

DIPLOMACY: In a speech before the General Assembly, Andrei Gromyko, the Soviet foreign minister, responds to Ambassador Goldberg's speech the previous day by charging that "the most serious threat to peace in the world is the United States."

September 23

USSR: The Soviet Union signs a new aid agreement with North Vietnam in a Moscow ceremony.

September 24

USA – DOMESTIC: The Americans for Democratic Action (ADA) adopts a resolution condemning the administration's position in Vietnam and charging that in Vietnam the United States is "in league with a corrupt and illiberal government supported by a minority of the people."

SOUTH VIETNAM: In Saigon, Hue, and Danang there are demonstrations against the election of Thieu and Ky; the militant Buddhist faction charges that the elections were rigged and demand that the Constituent Assembly cancel the results.

September 25

GROUND WAR: MACV redesignates Task Force Oregon as the 23rd Infantry Division (Americal). The new division is based at Chu Lai in Quang Tin Province, I Corps. It initially consists of the 196th Light Infantry Brigade, but the soon-to-arrive 11th and 198th Light Infantry Brigades will join the Americal by the end of the year.

September 26

USA – DOMESTIC: The *Christian Science Monitor* reports that support for President Johnson's Vietnam policy is eroding in the U.S. House of Representatives, of 205 House members responding to a survey, 43 say they have recently shifted position from support for the administration policies on the war to an emphasis on finding a way out.

USA – MILITARY: The Court of Military Appeals upholds the court-martial convictions of three army privates who had refused to go to Vietnam.

Two navy A-6A Intruder attack aircraft return to aircraft carrier USS *Kitty Hawk* after bombing raids over North Vietnam. *(National Archives)*

AIR WAR: Carrier-based Grumman A-6 Intruder bombers attack two key bridges near the center of Haiphong. USAF pilots pound the Thanh Moi railroad yard northeast of Hanoi.

LAOS: Laotian premier Souvanna Phouma expresses opposition to any extension of the "McNamara line" into Laos. To permit the barrier, he says, would "enlarge the Vietnam conflict at a time when we are trying to limit and contain it."

September 27

USA – DOMESTIC: Senator Thurston B. Morton (R-Ky.) says that President Johnson has been "brainwashed" by the "military-industrial complex" into believing a military victory can be achieved in Vietnam. Also on this day, an advertisement headed "A Call To Resist Illegitimate Authority," signed by over 320 influential people (professors, writers, ministers, and other professionals), appears in the *New Republic* and the *New York Review of Books,* asking for funds to help youths resist the draft.

September 27–November 19

GROUND WAR: The U.S. 1st Infantry Division conducts Operation Shenandoah II in Binh Duong Province and the Loc Ninh area of Binh Long Province, III Corps. One of the main purposes of the operation is to secure Highway 13, also known as "Thunder Road." Casualties will be U.S.: 70 KIA, 114 WIA (partial count only); NVA/VC: 956 KIA.

September 28

GROUND WAR: A Viet Cong Military Region 4 directive secretly orders intensification of political and military action in the Saigon area.

AIR WAR: U.S. Navy pilots from the carrier *Coral Sea* attack and partially destroy the bridge that carries the only major road and rail line out of Haiphong. This makes four bridges in Haiphong that have been destroyed since September 11 when a concerted drive was launched to cut off the port area from the rest of North Vietnam.

September 29

USA – GOVERNMENT: In a Texas speech that becomes known as the "San Antonio Formula," President Johnson declares that the United States will stop bombing North Vietnam if Hanoi agrees to negotiations. In language loaded with veiled criticism of U.S. opponents of the war, Johnson asserts that "protest will not produce surrender" because the United States will "provide all that our brave men require to do the job that must be done: and that job's going to be done." However, he modifies his earlier position by saying that the United States is willing to stop all bombing if the halt "will promptly lead to productive discussions."

SOUTH VIETNAM: In Saigon, a new U.S. embassy is dedicated.

September 30

AIR WAR: Navy planes bomb the Loi Dong trans-shipment point on the Cua Cam River estuary four miles northeast of Haiphong. Other planes pound the Kie Nan MiG base, the Ke Pha army barracks, and the Phuc Loi petroleum storage area near Vinh.

September 30–October 3

SOUTH VIETNAM: While 2,000 students demonstrate outside, the Constituent Assembly meets to discuss whether to legalize the election results. There have been a reported 2,724 cases of irregularities affecting over 1 million of the 5,853,251 votes cast. However, if these votes are discarded, Thieu's margin over his nearest rival would actually increase. On October 3, an assembly vote of 58–43 validates the national election results.

Late September

GROUND WAR: The Hue City Committee of the National Liberation Front orders development of grassroots organizations and plans for future occupation of the city.

October

GROUND WAR: People's Army of Vietnam forces begin attacks near the U.S. Marine base at Khe Sanh. The U.S. 198th Infantry Brigade deploys to Vietnam from Fort Hood, Texas, to join the Americal Division for combat operations in I Corps.

USA – DOMESTIC: U.S. public opinion on the war shifts when polls reveal that more Americans now oppose than support the war.

October 2

AIR WAR: According to State and Defense Department officials, the increased U.S. aerial offensive against North Vietnam that began August 11 has slowed the flow of war supplies from Communist China to Hanoi; the bombing of bridges has halted the movement of military materiél on the key rail line from Dong Dang, near the Chinese border, to Hanoi. However, U.S. officials concede that Communist military equipment is reaching Hanoi by other means.

USA – DOMESTIC: Senator John Sherman Cooper (R-N.Y.) urges the United States to take the "first step" toward negotiations with an "unconditional cessation" of the bombing of North Vietnam. Senator Gale McGee (D-Wy.) defends administration policy, saying the "stake is not only Vietnam but all the nations in Southeast Asia."

October 3

AIR WAR: U.S. aircraft strike key bridges at Loc Binh and Cao Bang in North Vietnam only 10 miles from the Chinese border.

USA – DOMESTIC: Senate Republican Whip Thomas Kuchel (Calif.) warns that a unilateral halt in bombing would be of "enormous value to the North Vietnamese" by permitting them to supply their forces in the South with no impediment. However, Senator Stuart Symington (D-Mo.) proposes that the United States stop all military action in South Vietnam and pressure Saigon to enter into negotiations with the National Liberation Front.

October 4–November 11

GROUND WAR: Troops from the U.S. 1st Cavalry Division and 196th Light Infantry Brigade conduct Operation Wallowa in southern I Corps. The purpose of the operation in Quang Tin Province is to reinforce III MAF and relieve pressure on the marines, who are fighting a heavy series of engagements along the DMZ. Operation

Wallowa merges with Wheeler on November 11. Casualties (through October 31) are U.S.: 46 KIA, 480 WIA; NVA/VC: 675 KIA, 17 POW.

October 4
GROUND WAR: The Communist shelling of Con Thien ends after heavy U.S. air strikes target NVA gun positions north of the DMZ.
AIR WAR: U.S. aircraft again strike the Lang Son railway bridge and the Chien Chiang highway bridge close to the Chinese border.

October 5
AIR WAR: U.S. planes strike the Kep, Kie Nan, and Hoa Lac MiG bases and pound a petroleum storage area two miles northwest of the center of Haiphong. Hanoi's Minister of Education Nguyen Van Huyen charges that a U.S. air raid on a North Vietnamese school on September 20 killed 33 children and wounded 28.
USA – DOMESTIC: Senator Charles Percy (R-Ill.), with the support of 22 other senators, introduces a resolution urging President Johnson to intensify efforts to have the free nations of Asia make a greater contribution of economic and military aid to the South Vietnamese cause.

October 6
AIR WAR: U.S. Navy pilots fly 34 missions as they again strike the Chien Chiang and the Lang Son bridges near the Chinese border, a bridge 39 miles northeast of Hanoi, a rail yard near Mo Trang, and two antiaircraft sites south of Dong Hoi. Also attacked are the Nam Dinh power plant, 45 miles southwest of Haiphong, a railway and highway bridge 24 miles southeast of Hanoi, and eight buildings in the Yen Bac military storage area.

October 7
AIR WAR: U.S. planes strike at Soviet-built helicopters on the ground 30 miles west of Hanoi.
USA – GOVERNMENT: At a Democratic fund-raising event, President Johnson says he will hold fast in Vietnam because that way "leads to a more secure America and a free Asia."

October 8
USA – DOMESTIC: A *New York Times* survey reports that U.S. political and congressional support for the Vietnam War is waning.

October 11
USA – DOMESTIC: Speaker John W. McCormick (D-Mass.) defends administration policy, declaring, "If I was one of those [whose dissent heartened the enemy], my conscience would disturb me the rest of my life."

October 11–20
GROUND WAR: The 3rd Marine Division, in conjunction with ARVN troops and elements of the Marine Special Landing Force (SLF), conducts Operation Medina/Bastion Hill/Lam Son 138 targeted at the enemy's Base Area 101 in the rugged Hai Lang National Forest, southern Quang Tri Province. Casualties are U.S.: 35 KIA, 174 WIA; NVA/VC: 64 KIA.

October 12

USA – GOVERNMENT: At a news conference, Secretary of State Dean Rusk makes controversial comments in which he says that congressional proposals for peace initiatives, which include a bombing halt or limitation, UN action, and a new Geneva conference, are futile because of Hanoi's opposition. Without the pressure of the bombing, "where would be the incentive for peace," he asks. He further says that the Vietnam War is a test of Asia's ability to withstand the threat of "a billion Chinese . . . armed with nuclear weapons." Critics claim he has invoked the "yellow peril" of Chinese power.

October 12–14

AIR WAR: U.S. Navy aircraft conduct heavy strikes against shipyards and docks in Haiphong. Australian Communist correspondent Wilfred Burchett files an eyewitness report October 14 saying that these attacks were directed against a large hospital complex, which was almost completely destroyed. Burchett says he visited the port area after the raid and found no evidence of air damage. He quotes the Haiphong mayor as saying that a third of the city's residential areas have been destroyed, principally since the heavy raids started September 1.

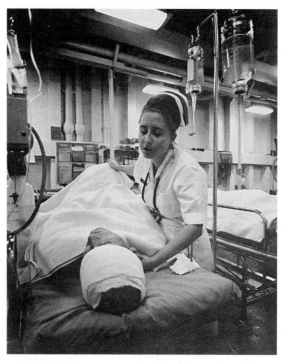

A nurse attends a patient in the intensive care ward of the hospital ship USS *Repose,* steaming off the coast of Vietnam, October 1967. *(National Archives)*

October 12–January 31, 1969

GROUND WAR: The U.S. 4th Infantry Division, in conjunction with the 173rd Airborne Brigade and ARVN units, conducts Operation MacArthur/Binh Tay as one of a series of continuing operations designed to contest North Vietnamese troop and logistical build-ups in the western highlands, II Corps.

October 13–14

GROUND WAR: Con Thien, just below the DMZ, and a nearby marine base at Gio Linh come under increasingly heavy North Vietnamese shelling. The next day Communist troops, following a 130-round mortar barrage, attempt to penetrate the marine positions at Con Thien, but they are thrown back in fierce hand to hand combat.

October 14

USA – DOMESTIC: Senator J. William Fulbright (D-Ark.) charges Secretary of State Rusk with carrying on a "McCarthy-type Crusade" against those who do not agree with the war and the administration's handling of it.

AIR WAR: U.S. jets bomb several targets in the Hanoi-Haiphong area that hitherto have been spared. The planes pound a barge building and repair yard 1½ miles west of Haiphong and an early warning radar station at Kie Nan.

October 16–21
USA – DOMESTIC: Antiwar activists hold demonstrations against the draft throughout the United States; the largest occurs outside the Army Induction Center in Oakland, California, where 125 protesters are arrested.

October 17
NORTH VIETNAM: Hanoi Radio reports that the NLF has formed a new organization designed to spur antiwar sentiment in the United States.
USA – GOVERNMENT: In a televised press conference, President Johnson denies the charge that he is "trying to label all criticism of his Vietnam policy as unpatriotic." Saying that while he doesn't question the motives of the dissenters, he does "question their judgment."

October 19
NORTH VIETNAM: Hanoi rejects the Johnson terms for negotiations expressed in his San Antonio statement of September 29.
USA – DOMESTIC: Senator Henry Jackson (D-Wash.) cautions against the "negative" tone of anti-administration criticism, saying that he is speaking out because he fears "that our frustrations are showing."

October 20
USA – DOMESTIC: *Life* magazine, in an editorial shift, calls for a pause in the bombing of North Vietnam and declares that "homefront support for the war is eroding."

October 20–22
NLF: A special enlarged plenum of the NLF's Central Committee meets to assess the battlefield situation.

October 21–23
USA – DOMESTIC: In Washington, D.C., an estimated 50,000 people protest U.S. policy in the Vietnam War; the demonstrators march in an orderly fashion to the Pentagon where they hold a rally and vigil that continues until the early hours of October 23. The Pentagon is protected by 10,000 troops. The Washington antiwar protest is paralleled by similar demonstrations in Japan and Western Europe.

October 22
USA – DOMESTIC: Representative Morris K. Udall (D-Ariz.) says in a speech that the United States is on "a mistaken and dangerous road" in Vietnam and should stop escalation and start "bringing this war back to the Vietnamese."
AIR WAR: For the first time U.S. Navy jets bomb the North Vietnamese naval base at Nui Dong, seven miles northeast of Haiphong.

October 23–30
AIR WAR: U.S. aircraft conduct heavy raids in the Haiphong-Hanoi region. Targets include some attacked for the first time, and range from bridges and airfields to the largest electrical plant in the North (bombed August 26). The U.S. command in Saigon acknowledges the loss of 13 aircraft, but the North Vietnamese report downing 35.

USA – DOMESTIC: General Lewis B. Hershey, the director of the U.S. draft program, is heavily criticized after he tells local boards to conscript anti-draft activists as early as possible.

October 24–25

AIR WAR: In a combined air force, navy, and marine strike, more than 65 U.S. planes attack North Vietnam's largest airbase, Phuc Yen, 18 miles northwest of Hanoi. The next day, the planes return and bomb the airfield again.

USA – DOMESTIC: Demonstrations are held on two university campuses against the Dow Chemical Company, a manufacturer of napalm used in Vietnam.

October 25

NORTH VIETNAM: Resolution 14 is passed by the Central Committee of the Lao Dong (Worker's) Party in Hanoi, ordering a "general offensive–general uprising" (*tong cong kich–tong khoi nghia*).

USA – GOVERNMENT: Senator Mike Mansfield (D-Mont.) and 54 co-sponsors introduce a resolution in the Senate urging the president to ask the UN Security Council to consider a U.S. proposal to discuss the Vietnam conflict.

October 25–30

AIR WAR: U.S. planes carry on a sustained attack on targets in the Hanoi-Haiphong area. On 25 October, jets bomb the Long Bien bridge, Hanoi's only rail and road link with Haiphong and the Chinese border. The following day navy planes bomb a 32,000-kilowatt thermal power plant about a mile north of the center of Hanoi. Air force planes from Thailand bomb targets three miles south of Hanoi on 27 October. The Long Bien bridge and other targets are hit on 28 October. On successive days, U.S. planes pound the Kie Nan, Kep, and Hoa Lac MiG bases and the Yen Bai airfield.

October 27

GROUND WAR: North Vietnamese 88th Regiment attacks the South Vietnamese base at Song Be in Phuoc Long Province, near the Cambodian border.

October 29–November 3

GROUND WAR: Fierce fighting flares up around Loc Ninh, a rubber plantation town in Binh Long Province, north of Saigon, and the site of a Special Forces camp. NVA and VC troops from the 273rd Regiment attempt to take and hold the town, but are repulsed by a force of 1,400 ARVN and U.S. 1st Infantry Division troops after bitter house to house fighting. Allied losses are about 50; communist losses are reported at "over 1000." This battle is particularly significant because it is the first time that a large NVA and VC force attempts to capture and hold an urban area.

October 30

NORTH VIETNAM: In Hanoi, the National Assembly standing committee approves a decree on punishment for counter-revolutionary activity.

October 31

SOUTH VIETNAM: President Thieu and Vice President Ky are sworn in. A following reception in the Independence Palace is marred by the explosion of three mortar shells on the lawn.

NORTH VIETNAM: Hanoi appeals to the international community to put pressure on the United States to bring the bombing of North Vietnam to an end. The statement claims that "the furious attacks on the area in recent days have killed or wounded 200 civilians and destroyed or set fire to more than 150 homes."

November 1
USA – GOVERNMENT: Defense Secretary McNamara secretly recommends termination of U.S. bombing of North Vietnam and limitation of ground involvement in South Vietnam.

November 1–December 1
GROUND WAR: In some of the bloodiest fighting in the Central Highlands since the Ia Drang Valley battles of 1965, heavy casualties are sustained by both sides in bitter action around Dak To about 280 miles north of Saigon near the Cambodian border. The 1,000 U.S. troops there are reinforced with 3,500 troops of the U.S. 4th Division and the 173rd Airborne Brigade as part of ongoing Operation MacArthur. They face four communist regiments of about 6,000 troops. The climax of the operation comes in a savage battle November 17–23 for Hill 875, 12 miles southwest of Dak To. The 173rd forces the North Vietnamese to abandon their last defensive line on the ridge of Hill 875, but suffers the loss of 158 men, 42 of whom die as a result of an accidental U.S. air strike on U.S. positions on November 19. Casualties for the Battle of Dak To are U.S.: 192 KIA, 642 WIA; NVA/VC: 5,731 KIA reported.

November 1–February 28, 1968
GROUND WAR: The U.S. 3rd Marine Division conducts Operation Kentucky in the Con Thien area south of the DMZ. This is a follow-on to Operation Kingfisher and is designed to prevent enemy interference with the construction of Strong Point A-3 of the Strong Point Obstacle System. Casualties will be U.S.: 478 KIA, 2,698 WIA; NVA/VC: 3,921 KIA.

November 1–March 31, 1968
GROUND WAR: Elements of the U.S. 3rd Marine Division conduct Operation Scotland in the westernmost part of Quang Tri Province to help support and defend the base at Khe Sanh. During this period, beginning in January, the base will be besieged for 77 days. Total casualties for the operation will be U.S.: 205 KIA, 1,668 WIA; NVA/VC: 1,602 KIA. The marines and air force estimate that an additional 10,000–15,000 NVA are killed due to the massive bombings around Khe Sanh during the siege.

November 2
USA – GOVERNMENT: President Johnson convenes a meeting of senior unofficial advisers, known as the "Wise Men," which includes former secretary of state Dean Acheson, General of the Army Omar Bradley, Ambassador-at-Large W. Averell Harriman, and former ambassador to Vietnam Henry Cabot Lodge. Johnson asks them for advice on "How do we unite the country?" The conclusion they reach is that the administration must offer "ways of guiding the press to show the light at the end of the tunnel." In effect, they decide that the American people must be given more optimistic reports.

USA – GOVERNMENT: Selective Service director Lewis B. Hershey confirms that there is a policy to require early induction of draft-eligible persons interfering with draft procedures.

DIPLOMACY: U.S. Ambassador to the United Nations Arthur Goldberg says that the Johnson administration will support the participation of the NLF in UN Security Council discussions or in a reconvened Geneva conference on ending the war.

November 6

AIR WAR: USAF aircraft from Korat Air Base in Thailand bomb the Gia Thuong storage complex, three miles from the center of Hanoi, a target hitherto on the restricted list.

November 7

AIR WAR: U.S. planes bomb rail facilities 21 miles from the Chinese border. Other planes attack the An Ninh Goia shipyard and repair facilities 12 miles west of Haiphong, the first time these targets have been attacked.

November 8

AIR WAR: While attempting to rescue an army reconnaissance team, Captain Gerald O. Young's Sikorsky HH-3E is shot down in Laos. Badly burned, he gives aid to a crew member who also escapes from the wreckage. After 17 hours of leading enemy forces away from his injured crewman, and himself evading capture, the two are rescued. Captain Young will later be awarded the Medal of Honor for his actions.

USA – MILITARY: General Westmoreland publicly declares that the aim of the NVA attack at Dak To is to steal the thunder of the recent inauguration of Thieu as South Vietnamese president.

November 9

SOUTH VIETNAM: President Thieu announces the formation of a new 19-member cabinet. U.S. officials in Saigon express disappointment that Thieu does not include at least some of the defeated civilian candidates so as to form a government of national unity. With the exception of two new officials, the cabinet is made up entirely of ministers who had served in the previous government.

POWs: While on a flight over Laos, Captain Lance P. Sijan (USAF) ejects from his disabled McDonnell-Douglas F-4C and successfully evades capture for more than six weeks. He is caught, but manages to escape. Recaptured and tortured, he will contract pneumonia and die. For his conspicuous gallantry as a POW, Captain Sijan will posthumously be awarded the Medal of Honor.

November 10

NORTH VIETNAM: President Ho Chi Minh signs a decree on counter-revolutionary crimes.

November 11

USA – GOVERNMENT: President Johnson begins a Veterans Day tour of eight military installations to shore up support for the war. During one stop, the president declares that "our statesmen will press the search for peace to the corners of the earth," and suggests that negotiations should be held aboard a neutral ship at sea. Hanoi will reject these latest American overtures four days later.

POWs: Three U.S. POWs, two of them African Americans, are released by the Viet Cong in a ceremony in Phnom Penh, Cambodia. The three men are turned over to Tom Hayden, a "new Left" activist and member of the U.S. committee formed to help the three men. U.S. officials in Saigon say that the released prisoners have been "brain-washed," but the State Department denies this. The VC announce that the release is a response to antiwar protests in the United States and a gesture toward the "courageous struggle" of blacks in the United States.

November 11–12
USA – DOMESTIC: Senator Eugene McCarthy (D-Minn.) addresses a convention of the College Young Democratic Club of America and asserts that Democrats who oppose administration policy on Vietnam "have an obligation to speak out and party unity is not a sufficient excuse for their silence." The next day the convention approves a resolution condemning the administration's Vietnam policy.

November 11–November 11, 1968
GROUND WAR: The Americal Division conducts Operation Wheeler/Wallowa, search and destroy operations to clear the enemy out of Quang Nam and Quang Tin Provinces, I Corps. This is an extension and enlargement of Operation Wallowa, which was launched by the 1st Cavalry Division on October 4. Total casualties for the combined Wheeler/Wallowa operations will be U.S.: 682 KIA, 3,995 WIA; NVA/VC: 10,008 KIA, 184 WIA.

November 13–30
GROUND WAR: The 7th Marine Regiment and Marine Special Landing Force Bravo carry out Operation Foster/Badger Hunt in retaliation for Viet Cong raids in the Dai Loc and An Hoa areas, Quang Nam Province, I Corps. Casualties are U.S.: 25 KIA, 137 WIA; NVA/VC: 125 KIA, 8 POW.

November 13–17
USA – GOVERNMENT: President Johnson is briefed on the situation in Vietnam by Westmoreland, Ambassador Bunker, and the head of the CORDS program, Robert W. Komer. The optimistic picture that they paint leads Johnson to state on television on November 17 that, while much remains to be done, "We are inflicting greater losses than we're taking . . . We are making progress."

November 14
GROUND WAR: Major General Bruno Hochmuth, commander of the 3rd Marine Division, is killed when the helicopter carrying him is shot down. He is the most senior U.S. officer to be killed in action in the war to date.

USA – DOMESTIC: Antiwar demonstrators clash with police in New York during a rally in protest against Secretary of State Rusk who is attending a dinner of the Foreign Policy Association.

November 16
USA – MILITARY: General Westmoreland tells the House Armed Services Committee that U.S. military withdrawal from Vietnam can begin within two years if progress continues. He is reportedly brought home from Vietnam by President Johnson

to revive flagging morale throughout the country and help convince the American people that progress is being made in the war. During his visit, his message on U.S. military prospects in Vietnam is continuously optimistic.

November 17

GROUND WAR: The NLF proclaims a three-day cease-fire for both Christmas and New Year's and a seven-day cease-fire for the upcoming Tet (Lunar New Year) holiday.

November 19

GROUND WAR: U.S. forces in Quang Tin Province capture a Communist Party document ordering a "General Offensive and General Uprising."

USA – GOVERNMENT: The Senate Foreign Relations Committee approves 14–0 a resolution to curb the commitment of U.S. armed forces and to urge the president to take the initiative to have the Vietnamese conflict brought before the UN Security Council.

November 19–24

CAMBODIA: AP correspondents George McArthur and Host Faas file stories from Phnom Penh in which they claim to have been to a VC camp in Cambodia. The Cambodian government asserts on November 21 that the reports of a new military complex constructed by the VC in Cambodia are "grotesque and a challenge to good sense." In retaliation for the press reports, on November 24 Prince Sihanouk states that "from now on the door of Cambodia is hermetically sealed to all American journalists."

November 20–21

USA – DOMESTIC: In California, on the campus of San Jose State, the police attack students demonstrating against the Dow Chemical Company after they refuse to disperse. The next day the students defy Governor Ronald Reagan's warning against further demonstrations and again stage an anti-Dow demonstration.

November 21

USA – MILITARY: At a speech at the National Press Club, General Westmoreland reports that progress is being made in the war and that the war has entered the final phase "when the end begins to come into view"; he predicts that U.S. troop withdrawals can begin in two years, saying, "I am absolutely certain that whereas in 1965 the enemy was winning, today he is certainly losing."

November 22

USA – MILITARY: General Westmoreland briefs officials at the Pentagon and says that the battle around Dak To was "the beginning of a great defeat for the enemy." He reveals that a document removed from the body of a dead NVA soldier on November 6 said that the Dak To battle was to be the beginning of a winter/spring offensive by the B-3 Front.

November 24

USA – MILITARY: MACV officially reduces its estimate of Communist strength in South Vietnam from 294,000 to 223,000–248,000 men. This is a controversial move that causes consternation among many in the intelligence community.

November 25

USA – DOMESTIC: The Very Reverend Edward Swanstrom, auxiliary Roman Catholic bishop of New York and head of Catholic Relief Services, writes in the weekly magazine *Ave Maria*, dated December 2, that the overseas relief agency of the Roman Catholic Church in the United States has provided funds for medical supplies and hospital equipment to be sent to North Vietnam.

November 26

USA – DOMESTIC: Senator Robert F. Kennedy (D-N.Y.) says President Johnson has shifted war aims set out by President Kennedy before his assassination and that these war aims have seriously undermined the moral position of the United States.

November 29

USA – GOVERNMENT: President Johnson announces that Robert McNamara will step down as secretary of defense to become president of the World Bank.

November 30

USA – DOMESTIC: Antiwar Democrat Eugene McCarthy (Minn.) announces that he will enter primaries to challenge President Johnson for the Democratic presidential nomination in 1968, running on a platform advocating a negotiated settlement of the war in Vietnam.

December

NORTH VIETNAM: Hanoi reiterates its position that the United States must stop bombing before serious negotiations can begin.

USA – MILITARY: The 11th Light Infantry Brigade deploys to Vietnam from Hawaii to join the American Division in Quang Ngai Province, I Corps. The 101st Airborne Division (Airmobile) deploys to Vietnam from Fort Campbell, Kentucky, to join its 1st Brigade elements already in-country for combat operations in II Corps.

AUSTRALIA/NEW ZEALAND: Australia deploys 3rd Battalion, Royal Australian Regiment, to join First Australian Task Force for combat operations in III Corps. New Zealand deploys an infantry company to Vietnam to join the Aussies in III Corps.

December 1–7

SOUTH VIETNAM: South Vietnamese police arrest a Viet Cong representative on his way to meet with U.S. embassy officials. He is identified on December 2 as Nguyen Van Huan and is reportedly intercepted after the CIA had arranged a meeting between him and Ambassador Bunker. South Vietnamese deputy Phan Xuan Huy charges that the incident represents a "flagrant act of American interference in the internal affairs of South Vietnam." A Washington report concedes that U.S. and South Vietnamese officials have been in touch with NLF representatives in previous months, but says the contacts have dealt with prisoners and similar matters and not negotiations. In a related matter, the *Washington Post* reports on December 1 that the NLF had sought to send representatives to the United Nations in October to discuss the Vietnamese conflict with the General Assembly.

December 1–January 8, 1968

GROUND WAR: The 1st Brigade, 101st Airborne Division, and a battalion from the 1st Cavalry Division conduct Operation Klamath Falls in Binh Thuan and Lam Dong Provinces, II Corps. The purpose of the operation is to eliminate the headquarters of the enemy's Military Region 6 and all enemy forces in the area of operations. Casualties are U.S.: 25 KIA, 130 WIA; NVA/VC: 156 KIA, 8 POW.

December 2

THAILAND: Officials in Bangkok report that Thailand has received U.S. ground-to-air missiles to protect itself against possible retaliation for permitting the United States to use Thai airbases for the launching of U.S. air strikes against North Vietnam.

December 4

SOUTH VIETNAM: In Saigon, General Westmoreland and General Cao Van Vien, chief of the Republic of Vietnam Joint General Staff, begin discussion of Christmas, New Year's, and Tet cease-fires.

GROUND WAR: The U.S. 9th Infantry Division's riverine force and 400 South Vietnamese in armored troop carriers engage Viet Cong forces in the Mekong Delta. In a coordinated action with the Vietnamese, U.S. troops surround and attack a Viet Cong battalion. They are reinforced by another battalion from the 9th Infantry Division, brought in by helicopters. After the battle, U.S. officials report that 235 of the 300-member Viet Cong battalion were killed in the fighting.

December 4–8

USA – DOMESTIC: A coalition of about 40 antiwar organizations stage four days of "Stop the Draft Week" demonstrations in New York; among the 585 protesters arrested is renowned pediatrician Dr. Benjamin Spock.

December 5

USA – DOMESTIC: Republican leaders Senator Everett Dirksen and Representative Gerald Ford say that the Johnson administration has not done all it could to negotiate a settlement of the war.

December 6–8

GROUND WAR: U.S. and South Vietnamese troops engage the North Vietnamese 3rd Division in a fierce battle near Bong Son, 140 miles south of Danang. U.S. losses are 16 killed and 90 wounded while the North Vietnamese lose 252 soldiers.

December 7

USA – GOVERNMENT: Vice President Hubert Humphrey suggests that there might be non-Communist members in the NLF who would agree to talk with the South Vietnamese.

December 8–10

GROUND WAR: South Vietnamese troops assisted by U.S. aerial rocket artillery trap two Viet Cong battalions near Vi Thanh, 100 miles southwest of Saigon. The South Vietnamese forces claim 365 Communists killed, but U.S. officers question the claim.

December 8–February 24, 1968
GROUND WAR: The U.S. 25th Infantry Division conducts Operation Yellowstone in War Zone C, Tay Ninh Province, III Corps. Casualties will be U.S.: 137 KIA, 1,085 WIA; NVA/VC: 1,170 KIA, 182 POW.

December 10
GROUND WAR: A U.S. artillery base camp 50 miles north of Saigon repels a North Vietnamese/Viet Cong attack, killing 124.

DIPLOMACY: The NLF's proposals for a peace settlement in South Vietnam are rebuffed by the United States when they are placed before the United Nations. The proposals include a coalition government, free elections, and land reform.

December 14–19
AIR WAR: U.S. planes bomb rail yards at Yen Vien, six miles east of Hanoi. A North Vietnamese report claims that homes in the northeastern section of Hanoi were destroyed in the attack. On December 19, it is reported that U.S. pilots have been granted permission to fly through the two previously restricted target areas in North Vietnam—the 25-mile strip along the Chinese Communist border and the outer, 20-mile circle around Hanoi. However, White House permission is still required to bomb targets in both sections.

December 15
GROUND WAR: MACV turns over responsibility for Saigon's defense to South Vietnamese armed forces.

December 15–16
GROUND WAR: Renewed fighting breaks out in the Bong Son area resulting in the deaths of 219 Communist soldiers.

December 16
GROUND WAR: Six battalions from the 101st Airborne Division arrive in Vietnam from Fort Campbell, Kentucky. They will be assigned operational areas of responsibility in III Corps.

December 17
GROUND WAR: The ROK Capital Division launches Operation Maeng Ho 9 in Binh Dinh Province, II Corps. By the end of the operation, there will be 749 reported enemy casualties.

December 17–March 8, 1968
GROUND WAR: The U.S. 199th Light Infantry Brigade conducts Operation Uniontown in Bien Hoa Province, III Corps. The purpose of the operation is to prevent rocket and mortar attacks on the Bien Hoa-Long Binh complex. Casualties are NVA/VC: 922 KIA.

December 18
USA – MILITARY: General Earle Wheeler, chairman of the Joint Chiefs of Staff, tells the Detroit Economic Club "we are winning the war," but warns that the Commu-

nists may try a last desperate effort similar to the Battle of the Bulge in World War II; President Johnson rejects McNamara's plan to halt South Vietnam bombing and limit U.S. participation in the war.

USA – MILITARY: The 1st Battalion of the 20th Infantry, 11th Light Infantry Brigade, arrives in Vietnam to join the Americal Division; the battalion will be stationed at Duc Pho, Quang Ngai Province, I Corps.

USA – DOMESTIC: General David M. Shoup, retired U.S. Marine commandant, says that it is "pure unadulterated poppycock" to believe the U.S. presence is necessary in South Vietnam to prevent a Communist invasion of the United States. Shoup derides the administration's efforts to keep people worried about Communists "crawling up the banks of Pearl Harbor or crawling up the Palisades or crawling up the beaches of Los Angeles."

December 18–19
USA – DOMESTIC: About 750 antiwar demonstrators try to block the armed forces induction center in Oakland; police arrest some 268 demonstrators.

December 19
GROUND WAR: The 11th Light Infantry Brigade, part of the 23rd Infantry Division (Americal), officially arrives in South Vietnam and is stationed at Duc Pho in I Corps.

December 19–June 10, 1968
GROUND WAR: Americal Division conducts Operation Muscatine in Quang Ngai Province, I Corps. The objective of the operation is the relief of the ROK 2nd Marine Brigade and support of the pacification programs in the province. During this operation, in March, a platoon of the 1st Battalion, 20th Infantry, will massacre between 200 and 500 unarmed civilians while conducting a sweep of the village of Son My, better known as My Lai. Casualties for Operation Muscatine will be U.S.: 186 KIA, 417 WIA; NVA/VC: 1,129 KIA.

December 20
USA – MILITARY: General Westmoreland cables Washington that Communists have decided on an intensified countrywide effort to win the war.

December 20–24
USA – GOVERNMENT: President Johnson attends a memorial service for Australian prime minister Harold Holt and then visits Vietnam, Thailand, and the Vatican. In a taped television interview, President Johnson says talks between the Saigon government and members of the National Liberation Front "could bring good results" and praises Thieu's flexible and "statesmanlike position" in agreeing to hold informal talks with members of the National Liberation Front. President Thieu and Johnson meet in Canberra on December 21 and later issue a joint communiqué affirming that Thieu is ready "to discuss relevant matters with any individual now associated with the NLF" but the front will not be recognized as an independent organization by the Saigon government. That day, Johnson, speaking to the Australian cabinet, warns that "kamikaze" attacks are coming in South Vietnam. Continuing his trip,

he visits Korat air base in Thailand December 23 where he tells U.S. pilots that the United States and its allies are "defeating this aggression." The president next visits U.S. combat troops at Cam Ranh Bay in South Vietnam and tells them that the enemy "knows that he has met his master in the field." Johnson then flies to Rome and meets with Pope Paul VI for over an hour with only interpreters present. A Vatican statement says that the Pope had advanced proposals toward attaining peace in Vietnam in his conversations with the president.

December 21–24
GROUND WAR: To thwart plans for what Hanoi calls "the winter-spring offensive," U.S. Marines launch Operation Fortress Ridge in and around the DMZ. An estimated 35,000–45,000 Communist troops are located in or just above the zone. USAF B-52s carry out raids on Communist positions inside the DMZ on December 22.

December 23
NORTH VIETNAM: Ho Chi Minh addresses a national rally in Hanoi, calling for increased efforts in both North and South Vietnam to win the war.

December 24–25
GROUND WAR: Ground action is largely halted and air operations suspended because of a Christmas truce. North Vietnam charges that the United States violated the truce by carrying out air strikes against eight targets.

December 25
GROUND WAR: Viet Cong commanders reconnoiter assigned objectives in Saigon during the Christmas cease-fire in preparation for renewed combat operations.

December 26–27
GROUND WAR: South Vietnamese troops, backed by U.S. artillery and air strikes, encounter the 416th VC Battalion during a search-and-destroy mission aimed at providing security for pacification teams in Quang Tri Province. South Vietnam claims 203 enemy killed.

CAMBODIA: The U.S. State Department discloses that a note has been sent to Cambodia assuring the Phnom Penh regime that it has "no hostile intentions toward Cambodia or Cambodian territory." The note is made public after Cambodia broadcasts the text of its reply, which says that Cambodian territory is not being used as a base for Communist forces involved in Vietnam. Cambodia further charges that U.S. and South Vietnamese forces have committed "flagrant violations of international law through daily incursions into Cambodia territory for purposes of sabotage and assassination." The United States again disavows intentions of expanding the Vietnam War. Prince Sihanouk warns that if U.S. troops invade Cambodia in search of North Vietnamese and Viet Cong forces, his government will ask China, Russia, and "other anti-imperialistic powers" for new military aid.

December 26–29
LAOS: Laotian premier Souvanna Phouma reports that North Vietnamese troops have started a general offensive against government forces in southern Laos. Laotian

sources report at least one battle is being waged near Pha Lane, but say that Laotian troops appear to be in control of the situation. North Vietnam on December 29 denies that its forces have begun a drive in Laos.

December 26–January 2, 1968
GROUND WAR: Operation Badger Tooth is launched to clear the "Street Without Joy" area near the coastal village of Thon Tham Khe on the border of Quang Tri and Thua Thien Provinces. As part of this operation, about 1,000 marines land by boat and helicopter along the coast of Quang Ngai Province and exchange fire with entrenched Communists. U.S. Marines battle NVA troops and 48 marines are killed and 81 wounded during this operation; an estimated 140 enemy troops are killed in the fighting.

December 29
CAMBODIA: Prince Norodom Sihanouk announces approval for the United States to pursue Communists into Cambodia under "certain circumstances."

December 30
NORTH VIETNAM: Messengers deliver Ho Chi Minh's Tet poem to officials and diplomats in Hanoi; Foreign Minister Nguyen Duy Trinh announces that North Vietnam will enter into negotiations with the United States if bombing and other acts of war against the North are stopped.

Marines interrogate Viet Cong suspect during Operation Badger Tooth, December 1967. *(National Archives)*

SOUTH VIETNAM: South Vietnam announces a 36-hour New Year's truce. A Viet Cong cease-fire also goes into effect. Ho Chi Minh extends New Year's greetings to Americans opposed to U.S. policies in Vietnam.

December 31

YEAR-END SUMMARY: U.S. troop levels have reached 485,600, with 16,021 American combat deaths to date. Another 99,742 U.S. servicemen were wounded in action during the year. There are 59,300 Free World Military Forces personnel in Vietnam. South Vietnamese armed forces strength has increased to 798,000 (including Regional and Popular Forces), with 60,428 South Vietnamese personnel killed in action to date. Estimated NVA/VC losses for the year are 90,400 KIA with total losses since 1965 estimated at over 186,000 (however, it is becoming general knowledge that these "body counts" are greatly inflated).

In the air war since February 1965, the U.S. and South Vietnamese air forces have dropped more that 1,500,000 tons of bombs on North and South Vietnam, and it is estimated that these attacks have cut North Vietnam's electrical generating capacity by 85 percent. However, during this year alone, the United States has lost 328 airplanes over North Vietnam, bringing the total number of planes lost to 779 since Rolling Thunder began. Additionally, the United States has lost 225 other planes over South Vietnam since 1961 (this number does not include 500 helicopters lost in combat during the same period). The costs for the war to date exceed $21 billion.

1968

January

RIVER WAR: U.S. Navy begins Operation Clearwater to interdict enemy bases and lines of communication on inland waterways in I Corps.

January 1

USA – MILITARY: In his end-of-year progress report, Admiral U.S. Grant Sharp, commander-in-chief, Pacific, declares that Operation Rolling Thunder has been successful not only in terms of material destroyed, but also in forcing North Vietnam to divert considerable manpower from industrial and agricultural production to military tasks, thus compelling Hanoi to seek ever greater amounts of aid from its Communist allies.

January 2

SOUTH VIETNAM: Saigon expels *Newsweek* reporter Everett Morton for writing articles critical of the South Vietnamese army.

January 3

USA – DOMESTIC: Senator Eugene McCarthy (D-Minn.) enters the New Hampshire primary.

January 4

CAMBODIA: The Cambodian government announces that it has accepted military aid from Communist China, repeating claims that it feels threatened by the United States.

USSR: The Soviet Union charges that U.S. planes damaged a Russian merchant ship during raids on Haiphong and demands that those responsible be punished. The United States expresses its regret, but adds that it is impossible to eliminate such risks.

January 5
NORTH VIETNAM: Foreign Minister Nguyen Duy Trinh announces for the first time that North Vietnam "will hold talks with the United States" after it has "unconditionally" halted bombing and "other acts of war" against North Vietnam.

USA – DOMESTIC: Dr. Benjamin Spock and three others are indicted for counseling draft resistance.

January 6
GROUND WAR: Major Patrick Brady (USA), a medical evacuation pilot, flies three missions and rescues 51 severely wounded soldiers from positions where other aircraft had failed or been shot down. For this action, Brady will later receive the Medal of Honor.

January 8
SOUTH VIETNAM: South Vietnamese national police arrest 100 peasants in Danang for protesting against the U.S. presence in Vietnam. Saigon government officials assert that the demonstration was part of a VC campaign to destabilize the Saigon regime.

January 9
GROUND WAR: VC forces overrun a U.S. airfield at Kontum, killing seven Americans and wounding 25.

USA – MILITARY: Brigadier General William R. Desobry, retiring as senior U.S. adviser in the Mekong Delta, says Viet Cong in the region are "poorly motivated and poorly trained" and that "ARVN now has the upper hand completely."

January 10
GROUND WAR: General Westmoreland, after consultation with Lieutenant General Frederick C. Weyand, commander of II Field Force, orders redeployment of U.S. forces from border areas to positions closer to Saigon.

January 11–21
GROUND WAR: The U.S. 9th Infantry Division conducts Operation AKRON V in Bien Hoa Province, III Corps, to eliminate enemy forces in Base Area 303. Casualties are U.S.: 8 KIA, 84 WIA; NVA/VC: 39 KIA.

January 12
CAMBODIA: Following talks between Ambassador to India Chester Bowles and Prince Sihanouk, the United States and Cambodia announce substantial agreement on measures designed to isolate Cambodia from the war.

January 13
USA – MILITARY: The U.S. Air Force announces that it will begin training 100 South Vietnamese pilots at a Louisiana base.

USA – DOMESTIC: In a statement denouncing administration fiscal policies, a group of 320 economists from 50 colleges and universities opposes any tax increases and asserts that the war is the major cause of U.S. economic problems.

LAOS: Royal Lao troops suffer a major defeat when a combined North Vietnamese–Pathet Lao force captures the town of Nam Bac, a government supply center 60 miles north of the royal capital of Luang Prabang.

January 14

SOUTH VIETNAM: A group of South Vietnamese intellectuals issues a call for elections, with National Liberation Front participation.

January 15

USA – MILITARY: General Westmoreland warns of Communist attacks before or after Tet at a U.S. Mission Council meeting in Saigon.

USA – DOMESTIC: Republican presidential candidate George Romney of Michigan states that the Vietnam War will be his principal campaign issue in the New Hampshire primary.

NLF: NLF presidium begins two-day meeting to discuss impending military action.

January 17

USA – GOVERNMENT: In his State of the Union message, President Johnson declares that the bombing would "stop immediately if talks would take place promptly and with reasonable hopes that they would be productive. And the other side must not take advantage of our restraint."

January 18

USA – DOMESTIC: Singer Eartha Kitt at White House luncheon blames crime and race riots on Vietnam War.

CAMBODIA: The Cambodian government charges that Allied forces pushed 200 yards into its territory and killed three Cambodians; the United States acknowledges that an Allied patrol did make a limited incursion and expresses regret about the casualties.

AIR WAR: Operation Niagara, a joint U.S. Air Force, Navy and Marine Corps air campaign launched in support of the marines manning the base at Khe Sanh, begins with an intensive intelligence and surveillance effort in the area around the marine base. Using sensors installed along the nearby DMZ and reconnaissance flights to pinpoint targets, 24,000 tactical fighter-bomber sorties and 2,700 B-52 strategic bomber sorties will be flown between the start of the operation and March 31, 1968, when it will be terminated.

January 19

USA – GOVERNMENT: President Johnson names Clark Clifford to succeed McNamara as secretary of defense effective March 1, 1968.

January 20–April 14

GROUND WAR: One of the most publicized and controversial battles of the war begins at Khe Sanh with a brisk firefight involving the 3rd Battalion, 26th Marines, and a North Vietnamese battalion entrenched between two hills northwest of the base. The base will be surrounded for 77 days, while intense fighting continues on the surrounding hills. The siege will be lifted on April 14.

January 20–January 31, 1969
GROUND WAR: The U.S. 173rd Airborne Brigade conducts Operation McLain, a reconnaissance-in-force operation in support of pacification efforts in Binh Thuan Province, II Corps. Casualties are NVA/VC: 1,042 KIA.

January 21
GROUND WAR: NVA forces overrun the village of Khe Sanh, and North Vietnamese long-range artillery begin to shell the marine base itself, hitting its main ammunition dump and detonating 1,500 tons of explosives.

January 21–November 23
GROUND WAR: Several battalions from the 3rd Marine Division conduct Operation Lancaster II, a search and clear operation in western Quang Tri Province, I Corps. Casualties are U.S.: 359 KIA, 1,713 WIA; NVA/VC: 1,801 KIA.

C-130 lands at Khe Sanh under fire, February 1968. *(Texas Tech University Vietnam Archive)*

January 22
GROUND WAR: The military command of the NLF issues orders calling for the "annihilation" of all pacification teams and any forces supporting them.
CAMBODIA: In a joint communique, Prince Sihanouk and Yugoslav president Josip Tito express full support for North Vietnam and the NLF.

January 22–February 29
GROUND WAR: Elements of the U.S. 1st Cavalry Division conduct Pershing II, a clearing and pacification operation in the coastal lowlands of Binh Dinh Province, II Corps. Casualties are NVA/VC: 614 KIA.

January 22–March 31
GROUND WAR: Elements of the U.S. 1st Cavalry Division conduct Operation Jeb Stuart, the division's first operation in I Corps. This operation is a large-scale reinforcement of the marines in the area and focuses on clearing enemy Base Areas 101 and 114. During the operation, a combined force of U.S. and South Vietnamese soldiers turns back a North Vietnamese attack on Quang Tri. Casualties will be U.S.: 291 KIA, 1,735 wounded, 24 MIA; NVA/VC: 3,268 KIA, 119 POW.

January 23
USA – MILITARY: North Korea seizes the U.S. intelligence ship *Pueblo* and its 84-man crew in waters off Korea. The ship, allegedly in violation of the 12-mile territorial limit claimed by North Korea, has been on the same type Operation De Soto patrol that the *Maddox* had been on during the Gulf of Tonkin incident August 2–4, 1964.

January 24
USA – GOVERNMENT: Ambassador Bunker and General Westmoreland cable Washington that the Communists may break the Tet truce and urge the South Vietnamese government to cancel truce in I Corps Tactical Zone.

January 25

USA – MILITARY: General Westmoreland reports that the situation at Khe Sanh is critical and may represent the turning point of the Vietnam War.

USA – GOVERNMENT: President Johnson calls 14,787 reservists to active duty in the Korea crisis and orders the nuclear carrier *Enterprise* toward Korea.

LAOS: North Vietnamese troops strengthen their position in the northwest corner of South Vietnam by capturing an outpost inside the Laotian border nine miles west of Khe Sanh.

January 26

GROUND WAR: VC units move to villages on the outskirts of Can Tho and Vinh Long in the Mekong Delta.

SOUTH VIETNAM: Major General Nguyen Duc Thang quits his position as head of South Vietnam's pacification program. In honor of Tet, the Vietnamese lunar new year, President Thieu grants amnesty to nearly 500 prisoners, including many political detainees; Saigon's nighttime curfew is also lifted.

January 27

GROUND WAR: Communist seven-day cease-fire for Tet begins; ARVN troops are restricted to their posts and all leaves are canceled under last-minute orders.

USA – MILITARY: In General Westmoreland's 1967 year-end assessment, delivered this day, the general says that Allied air efforts "had imposed significant difficulties" on North Vietnam and the year "ended with the enemy increasingly resorting to desperation tactics."

January 29

USA – GOVERNMENT: In his annual budget message, President Johnson asks for $26.3 billion to continue the war in Vietnam and announces an increase in taxes.

GROUND WAR: In South Vietnam, the Allied Tet cease-fire is cancelled in the I Corps Tactical Zone, but the cease-fire takes effect in the rest of South Vietnam at 1800 hours.

January 30

GROUND WAR: In the first attacks of what will become the Communist Tet Offensive, VC and North Vietnamese troops launch surprise attacks on Danang, Pleiku, Nha Trang, and nine other cities in I Corps and II Corps; but commanders in Viet Cong Region 5 have started the Tet Offensive 24 hours too early, apparently because they are following the lunar calendar in effect in South Vietnam, rather than a new lunar calendar proclaimed by Hanoi for all of Vietnam. As a result of these premature attacks, Allied commanders cancel the Tet cease-fire throughout all of South Vietnam, and MACV orders all U.S. units on "maximum alert."

USA – GOVERNMENT: Senate confirms Clark Clifford to be secretary of state.

January 31

GROUND WAR: In the early hours of the first day of the Tet holiday truce, Viet Cong forces, supported by large numbers of North Vietnamese troops, launch a country-wide offensive, simultaneously attacking Saigon and other major cities, provincial

ARVN soldier fires at Viet Cong positions in Cholon area during the 1968 Tet Offensive fighting in Saigon. *(Texas Tech University Vietnam Archive)*

capitals, and Allied installations from the Delta to the DMZ. The timing and scope of the attacks finds Allied forces alert but unprepared for an offensive of such magnitude. In one of the most spectacular attacks, a 19-man suicide squad seizes the ground floor of the U.S. embassy and holds it for six hours until an assault force of U.S. paratroopers lands by helicopter on the building's roof and kills or captures the attackers. Nearly a thousand VC troops have infiltrated the capital city and it will take a week of bitter fighting to defeat them. Some of the most intense fighting is in Cholon, the Chinese section of the city. In I Corps, North Vietnamese and VC forces capture Hue, the imperial capital. U.S. Marines and ARVN forces counterattack to recapture the city. President Thieu declares countrywide martial law as Allied forces fight to turn the Communists back all over the country.

USA – DOMESTIC: The American news media is dominated by accounts of the Tet Offensive, which includes some of the heaviest fighting of the Vietnam War; CBS and NBC present 30-minute special reports on the Tet Offensive.

NORTH VIETNAM: In Hanoi, children and old people are evacuated to the countryside in preparation for the anticipated U.S. bombing attacks.

February 1–25
GROUND WAR: VC and North Vietnamese troops massacre 2,800 civilians in Hue.

February 1
USA – DOMESTIC: Richard M. Nixon announces his candidacy for the presidency.

February 2

GROUND WAR: Heavy fighting continues in South Vietnam although the number and intensity of attacks begin to ebb. MACV reports 12,704 Communist troops killed in action since the Tet Offensive began; U.S. battle deaths are listed as 318 and those of the South Vietnamese forces as 661 in the same period.

USA – GOVERNMENT: President Johnson, in a White House press conference, declares that the Tet Offensive is "a complete failure." As for a "psychological victory," the president says that "when the American people know the facts," they will see that here, too, the enemy has failed.

February 2–March 2

GROUND WAR: U.S. Marines and South Vietnamese forces supported by elements of the 1st Cavalry and 101st Airborne Divisions conduct Operation Hue City, the retaking of the imperial capital. The bitter fighting results in the destruction of a large part of the city and heavy loss of life on both sides. Casualties are U.S.: 119 KIA, 961 WIA; ARVN: 363 KIA, 1,242 WIA; NVA/VC: 5,000 KIA (estimated), 15 POW; Civilians: 5,800 KIA/MIA, 116,000 homeless.

February 3

GROUND WAR: Heavy fighting continues in Saigon, Hue, Kontum, Pleiku, Dalat, Phan Thiet, and several other cities; MACV lists enemy losses at 15,595 killed in action with 415 U.S. and 905 ARVN killed in the fighting since the offensive started.

Walter Cronkite of CBS News conducts an interview with the commanding officer of the 1st Battalion, 1st Marines, during the Battle of Hue City, February 1968. *(National Archives)*

In Saigon, Brigadier General Ngoc Loan, chief of the South Vietnamese National Police, shoots a VC suspect in the head at point-blank range. News cameras record the incident and the pictures and video shown on the nightly news stun Americans who see it.

USA – MILITARY: The Joint Chiefs requests that Secretary of Defense McNamara reduce the area prohibited from bombing in North Vietnam to reduce "enemy capability for waging war in the South." General Wheeler cables Westmoreland in Saigon saying that the president has asked him to see "if there is any reinforcement or help that we can give you."

NLF: Central Committee calls for Liberation Army and people to strike "even harder, deeper, and on a wider front."

USA – DOMESTIC: Given the ferocity of the Tet Offensive, Senator Eugene McCarthy (D.-Minn.) accuses the Johnson administration of deceiving itself and the American people about the progress of the war.

February 4
USA – GOVERNMENT: Administration officials appear on television interview programs to defend Johnson's war policy.

February 5
NORTH VIETNAM: *Nhan Dan,* official newspaper of Lao Dong Party in Hanoi, declares, "The once-in-a-thousand year opportunity has come. The bugle has sounded victory."

February 5–17
GROUND WAR: South Vietnamese forces conduct Operation Tran Hung Dao in the Saigon area, with six South Vietnamese marine, four Ranger and five airborne battalions to defeat the forces who had attacked the capital city at the beginning of the new offensive. By the end of the operation, 953 enemy casualties will be reported.

February 6
USA – MILITARY: MACV reports that fighting has diminished throughout most of South Vietnam, but heavy fighting continues in Cholon and Hue; in an official statement, General Westmoreland claims that Allied forces have killed more enemy troops in the past seven days than the United States has lost in the entire war. A spokesman in Saigon reports 21,330 enemy troops killed since Tet began.

NLF: The Communist Party Current Affairs Committee in Can Tho Province in the Mekong Delta declares that the general offensive is a long-term project that may last three or four months, not just a few days.

USA – DOMESTIC: In Washington, 2,000 persons led by Reverend Martin Luther King, Jr., march through Arlington National Cemetery to protest the "cruel and senseless" war.

February 7–8
GROUND WAR: After an 18-hour siege, Lang Vei Special Forces camp, five miles west of Khe Sanh, falls to North Vietnamese troops using Soviet-built PT-76 light tanks;

M113 armored personnel carriers stand by as Vietnamese refugees evacuate the village of My Tho in Dinh Tuong Province during the Tet Offensive, 1968. *(National Archives)*

more than 300 defenders are killed in the attack, including eight U.S. Special Forces personnel.

February 8
USA – MILITARY: General Wheeler, chairman of the U.S. Joint Chiefs of Staff, offers Westmoreland additional men from the 82nd Airborne Division and a U.S. Marine division, telling him that if he needs more troops to "ask for them." Westmoreland responds the next day, asking that the additional troops be deployed.

USA – DOMESTIC: Senator Robert F. Kennedy (D-N.Y.), speaking in Chicago, says that the Tet Offensive has shattered official illusions about the war in Vietnam.

February 9
GROUND WAR: U.S. forces from the 199th Light Infantry Brigade land by helicopter to clear Communist troops in the area around the Phu Tho racetrack in Saigon. In I Corps, a company from the 4th Infantry Division fights a major battle with an enemy force of 250–300 near Hoi An, 10 miles southeast of Danang. Casualties are U.S.: 10 KIA, 33 WIA; NVA/VC: 200 KIA (estimated).

SOUTH VIETNAM: President Thieu announces partial mobilization of South Vietnam.

USA – GOVERNMENT: Secretary of Defense McNamara asks the Joint Chiefs of Staff to prepare plans for General Westmoreland's emergency reinforcement. Also this day, Secretary of State Dean Rusk, in a background briefing, demands of journalists aggressively questioning the administration's handling of the war, "Whose side are you on?"

February 10
AIR WAR: U.S. planes raid Haiphong area for first time in a month.
GROUND WAR: Communist Party committee in Bien Hoa Province near Saigon says in secret report that "the people's spirit for uprising is still very weak."

February 11
SOUTH VIETNAM: The Saigon government announces the call-up of 65,000 more men in response to the new enemy offensive.

February 12
USA – MILITARY: The Joint Chiefs of Staff submits to Secretary McNamara three plans for reinforcing General Westmoreland, but argues against dispatching any reinforcements at this time because it would seriously deplete the strategic reserve; it appears that they hope to force the president to call up the reserves. They recommend, however, that measures be taken for possible deployment of the 82nd Airborne Division and two-thirds of the marine division air wing.
GROUND WAR: In Hue, U.S. Marines, having secured the "new city" on the south side of the Perfume River, cross to the north side to begin the battle to retake the citadel from Communist forces.
USA – DOMESTIC: A Louis Harris poll reports U.S. public support for the war has increased in wake of Tet attacks.

February 13
USA – DOMESTIC: A Gallup poll reports that 50 percent of Americans disapprove of President Johnson's handling of the war.
USA – MILITARY: Secretary of Defense McNamara authorizes the deployment of 10,500 troops—a brigade of the 82nd Airborne Division and the 27th Marine Regimental Landing Team—to cope with threats of a second offensive. The Joint Chiefs of Staff immediately sends McNamara a memorandum asking that 46,300 reservists and former servicemen be activated.

February 14
AIR WAR: In the heaviest aerial attacks against North Vietnam in six weeks, U.S. planes bomb targets near Hanoi, hitting a bridge, two airfields, and several missile sites.
USA – GOVERNMENT: President Johnson flies to Fort Bragg, North Carolina, to visit reinforcements departing for Vietnam, and then flies to the carrier *Constellation* at sea in the Pacific to visit with the crew.
USA – DOMESTIC: Senator Stuart Symington (D-Mo.) reports that the cost of the Vietnam War for fiscal year 1969 was $32 billion.

February 15
AIR WAR: A U.S. Air Force F-4 Phantom shot down over Hanoi becomes the 800th U.S. aircraft lost in the three-year air war over North Vietnam.
USA – DOMESTIC: Republican presidential candidate George Romney of Michigan states that the Vietnam War will be his principal campaign issue in the New Hampshire primary.

February 16

USA – GOVERNMENT: President Johnson, in a surprise press conference, says that rumors that Westmoreland may be relieved of command are false and may have originated abroad; he also announces that additional troops will be approved for Vietnam as needed.

SOUTH VIETNAM: U.S. officials in Saigon report that, in addition to the 800,000 listed as refugees prior to January 30, the Tet Offensive has created 350,000 new refugees.

GROUND WAR: ROK Capital Division launches Operation Maeng Ho 10 in Binh Dinh Province, II Corps.

AIR WAR: To bolster Allied defenses around Khe Sanh, U.S. command deploys the AC-130 gunship to Vietnam. This specialized propeller-driven attack aircraft is armed with a variety of guns and equipped with electronic sensors capable of locating the enemy despite fog, darkness, and jungle.

POWs: Hanoi turns over three U.S. pilots shot down during the previous fall to representatives of the American Mobilization Committee Against the War. They are the first prisoners freed by Hanoi; in late March the United States reciprocates by releasing three North Vietnamese sailors.

February 17

GROUND WAR: A record weekly total of U.S. casualties is set during the preceding seven days, with 543 killed and 2,547 wounded.

February 18

GROUND WAR: Communist gunners shell 45 cities and bases, including Tan Son Nhut air base and Saigon; ground attacks are launched against four cities.

USA – MILITARY: The 3rd Brigade, 82nd Airborne Division, arrives in Vietnam after deploying from Fort Bragg, North Carolina. The brigade is stationed at Hue-Phu Bai in Thua Thien Province, I Corps.

February 20

USA – GOVERNMENT: The Senate Foreign Relations Committee begins hearings on American policy in Vietnam. Early sessions focus on the 1964 Gulf of Tonkin incident. Senators J. William Fulbright (D-Ark.) and Wayne Morse (D-Oreg.) charge the Defense Department with withholding information on U.S. naval activities in the gulf that provoked North Vietnam, leading to the charge of a "credibility gap." At issue is whether the administration had provided Congress with truthful data at the time it was seeking passage of the Tonkin Gulf Resolution in August 1964, which considerably broadened the president's war-making authority in Southeast Asia.

February 21

USA – DOMESTIC: In a major policy statement, the National Council of Churches calls for an immediate bombing halt as a prelude to peace talks.

SEA WAR: The aircraft carrier *Bonhomme Richard* arrives in Vietnam for its fourth combat deployment.

February 23

USA – MILITARY: General Wheeler, chairman of the Joint Chiefs of Staff, departs for South Vietnam to confer with General Westmoreland. During their subsequent talks,

Wheeler tells Westmoreland that the administration might mobilize the reserves and allow Allied forces to move into Laos and Cambodia. Westmoreland replies that the expanded war effort would require an additional 206,000 troops. Meanwhile, there is a basic disagreement developing between the American and South Vietnamese commands regarding enemy military objectives during the recent Tet Offensive. General Westmoreland and his staff believe that Saigon and Khe Sanh are the major enemy targets; ARVN general Cao Van Vien contends that the enemy's primary goal is to split South Vietnam. This disagreement will influence future troop deployments. Back in the United States, the Department of Defense announces a Selective Service call for 48,000 men, the second-highest number of the Vietnam War.

GROUND WAR: At Khe Sanh, Communist gunners bombard the marine defenders with 1,307 artillery rounds, the heaviest shelling of the siege.

February 24

GROUND WAR: South Vietnamese troops storm the former imperial palace in the citadel in Hue, tearing down the National Liberation Front flag and replacing it with the Republic of Vietnam flag. Although the Battle of Hue is not officially declared over for another week, this is the last major engagement of the main phase of the Tet Offensive. Also this day, the U.S. command in Saigon admits for the the first time that pacification efforts have suffered a severe setback as a result of the Tet Offensive.

AIR WAR: U.S. planes bomb the Red River wharves and warehouses of Hanoi for the first time.

DIPLOMACY: UN Secretary-general U Thant issues a statement asserting that if the United States unconditionally halts its bombing of North Vietnam, "meaningful talks will take place much earlier than is generally supposed." Reacting to Thant's declaration, Senator Mike Mansfield (D-Mont.) calls for a trial suspension of the bombing.

February 25

GROUND WAR: U.S. and South Vietnamese troops retake control of Hue; there are 5,113 reported enemy casualties during the course of the bitter fighting there.

February 26

SOUTH VIETNAM: Hundreds of bodies are found in several mass graves in Hue; more bodies will be found later in the year, providing additional evidence of VC massacre of Republic of Vietnam supporters in the city.

February 26–September 12

GROUND WAR: The U.S. 1st Marine Division conducts Operation Houston in the Thua Thien and Quang Nam areas of I Corps. Purpose of the operation is to secure Highway 1 and the Hai Van Pass while providing security for crews working on the railroad between Hue and Danang. Casualties will be U.S.: 121 KIA, 848 WIA; NVA/VC: 702 KIA.

February 27

USA – DOMESTIC: CBS news anchorman Walter Cronkite, who has just returned from Saigon and Hue, tells Americans during his evening broadcast that he is certain "the bloody experience of Vietnam is to end in a stalemate" and asserts that it is time for the United States to seek a negotiated end to the war.

February 28

USA – MILITARY: In a White House meeting, General Wheeler, just back from his recent round of talks with General Westmoreland, delivers a written report to the president, which begins by saying that General Westmoreland has frustrated the enemy's objective of provoking a general uprising, but goes on to say that the offensive has been "a very near thing" for the Allies and that, despite heavy casualties incurred during the Tet Offensive, North Vietnam and Viet Cong forces now have the initiative and are "operating with relative freedom in the countryside." To meet the new enemy threat and regain the initiative, Wheeler says that Westmoreland will need more men and asks the president for an additional 206,000 soldiers "for a proposed ceiling of 731,756." Rather than make an immediate decision on what would be a major increase in the U.S. commitment, President Johnson orders secretary of defense-designate Clark Clifford to form a task force to conduct a complete review of U.S. policy in Vietnam, to include the increased troop request.

February 29

GROUND WAR: North Vietnamese forces launch three attacks against the 37th ARVN Ranger Battalion at Khe Sanh, but are turned back each time.

USA – DOMESTIC: Representative L. Mendel Rivers (D-S.C.), chairman of the House Armed Services Committee, declares that the United States should use either tactical nuclear weapons at Khe Sanh or withdraw from the base.

February 29–December 9

GROUND WAR: U.S. Marines conduct Operation Napoleon/Saline along the Cua Viet River to keep this critical supply line open to the port facility in the Dong Ha area of Quang Tri Province, I Corps. The operation will account for 3,495 reported enemy casualties.

Late February

USA – MILITARY: The 27th Marine Regiment of the 5th Marine Division deploys to Vietnam to join the 1st Marine Division for combat operations in I Corps.

March 1

USA – GOVERNMENT: Clark Clifford is sworn in as the new secretary of defense, replacing Robert McNamara.

SOUTH VIETNAM: President Thieu dismisses seven provincial chiefs in an unprecedented move that many consider a major step toward carrying out his promise to combat corruption and inefficiency.

USSR: Asked to assess how the Soviet Union would react to various measures being considered by U.S. policy makers, Ambassador to Moscow Llewellyn Thompson reports that "any serious escalation except in South Vietnam would trigger [a] strong Soviet response."

March 1–July 30

GROUND WAR: Operation Truong Cong Dinh is launched by ARVN forces and elements of the U.S. 9th Infantry Division in Dinh Tuong and Kien Tuong Provinces in the Mekong Delta to provide security for Highway 4 and My Tho. On May 21, it will combine with Operation People's Road. Casualties will U.S.: 197 KIA, 1,094 WIA; NVA/VC: 2,246 KIA, 134 POW.

March 2

GROUND WAR: In what is described as one of the costliest ambushes of the war, 48 U.S. troops are killed and 28 wounded four miles north of Tan Son Nhut Air Base.

SOUTH VIETNAM: Pacification teams begin returning to hamlets abandoned a month earlier during the opening days of the Tet Offensive.

March 4

USA – GOVERNMENT: In a draft memorandum to the president, the recently formed Clifford group, which includes outgoing secretary of defense Robert McNamara, Deputy Secretary of Defense Paul Nitze, CIA director Richard Helms, General Maxwell Taylor, Assistant Secretary of State for Far Eastern Affairs William Bundy, and Paul Warnke, head of the Pentagon's politico-military policy office, recommends the immediate dispatch of 22,000 more U.S. troops to Vietnam, a reserve call-up of 250,000 men, increased draft calls, and further study of the developing situation. However, the group advises that the deployment of the remaining 185,000 men requested by General Westmoreland remain contingent on future developments. President Johnson asks that the memorandum be sent to General Westmoreland, who, in a reply four days later, welcomes the additional 22,000 troops, but insists that he still needs the full 206,756 reinforcement by year's end.

March 7

USA – GOVERNMENT: Senator J. William Fulbright (D-Ark.), chairman of the Senate Foreign Relations Committee, and other senators interrupt a debate on civil rights to publicly demand that President Johnson consult Congress before making any new troop increases in Vietnam.

AIR WAR: The U.S. Navy deploys a new plane, the A-7 Corsair II, to help repel enemy troops threatening Khe Sanh.

March 8

USA – MILITARY: In a cablegram to the president, General Westmoreland welcomes the additional 22,000 men proposed by the Clifford group, but says he sticks by his request for the full 206,756-man reinforcement by the end of 1968.

March 8–May 17

GROUND WAR: The American Division, the 3rd Brigade of the 82nd Airborne Division, elements of the 1st Brigade, 101st Division, and troops from the ARVN 1st Infantry Division conduct Operations Carentan I-II in Quang Tri and Thua Thien Provinces, I Corps. Casualties will be U.S.: 193 KIA, 1,190 WIA, 11 MIA; NVA/VC: 1,892 KIA, 69 POW.

March 9

USA – DOMESTIC: A Gallup poll reports a new wave of pessimism among Americans about the war in Vietnam.

March 10

USA – DOMESTIC: The *New York Times* breaks the story of Westmoreland's 206,000 troop request, saying that it has stirred controversy within administration ranks. President Johnson is reportedly "furious" at the leak, which gives his political adversaries more ammunition for their attacks on his administration.

SOUTH VIETNAM: In Saigon, Vice President Nguyen Cao Ky declares that the recent enemy offensive has made a general mobilization necessary.

March 11–April 7

GROUND WAR: Operation Quyet Thang (Resolve to Win), largest operation to date, is conducted in the Saigon area and five surrounding provinces of III Corps by elements of the U.S. 1st, 9th, and 25th Divisions and the ARVN 5th and 25th Divisions, an airborne battalion, and South Vietnamese Marine Corps Task Forces—22 U.S. and 11 South Vietnamese battalions. The purpose of the operation is to eliminate a persisting threat to the capital city. Casualties are U.S.: 79 KIA (only partial number); NVA/VC: 3,387 KIA, 36 POW.

March 12

USA – DOMESTIC: President Johnson narrowly defeats Senator Eugene McCarthy (D-Minn.) by 300 votes in the New Hampshire Democratic primary. McCarthy, an outspoken critic of the war in Vietnam, wins 42 percent of the vote to Johnson's 48 percent. A Harris poll later shows that anti-Johnson, rather than anti-war, sentiment provided the basis for McCarthy's performance.

March 14

GROUND WAR: North Vietnamese troops are sighted for the first time in the Mekong Delta.

USA – GOVERNMENT: Senator Robert Kennedy and Theodore Sorenson meet with Secretary of Defense Clifford to discuss a possible U.S. commission to reverse the government's Vietnam policy, but Johnson rejects the plan.

March 15

USA – GOVERNMENT: Former secretary of state Dean Acheson, in a private report to President Johnson, says U.S. victory in Vietnam is not feasible within the limits of public tolerance.

March 16

USA – DOMESTIC: Senator Robert F. Kennedy (D-N.Y.), encouraged by the results of the New Hampshire primary, announces his candidacy for the Democratic presidential nomination; polls indicate Kennedy is now more popular than President Johnson.

WAR CRIMES: In what will become the most publicized war atrocity committed by U.S. troops in Vietnam, between 200 and 500 Vietnamese civilians are massacred in My Lai hamlet by members of a platoon from Charlie Company, 1st Battalion, 20th Infantry, while participating in an assault against suspected Viet Cong encampments in Quang Ngai Province. Although the platoon does not receive any opposing fire as it approaches the hamlet, the platoon leader, Lieutenant William Calley, orders his men to go in shooting. During the resulting massacre, the platoon indiscriminately shoots people and then systematically rounds up the surviving villagers, forces them into a ditch and then executes them. Several old men are bayoneted, some women and children praying outside the local temple are shot in the back of the head, and at least one girl is raped before being killed. The massacre will not come to light until early 1969.

March 17–July 30

GROUND WAR: The U.S. 9th Infantry Division and ARVN 7th Division conduct Operation Duong Cua Dan ("People's Road") to provide security for engineers working on Route 4, the main route between Saigon and the Mekong Delta in IV Corps. On May 21, this operation is combined with Operation Truong Cong Dinh. Total combined casualties will be U.S.: 225 KIA, 1,299 WIA, 1 MIA; NVA/VC: 2,477 KIA, 178 WIA.

March 19

USA – GOVERNMENT: The House of Representatives passes a resolution calling for an immediate congressional review of U.S. policy in Southeast Asia.

AIR WAR: Much to the embarrassment of U.S. military officials, two North Vietnamese defectors report that North Vietnam's intelligence agencies provide as much as 24 hours notice of U.S. B-52 raids.

March 20

GROUND WAR: Pressure on the marine combat base at Khe Sanh lessens; Bru tribesmen report that North Vietnamese artillery units have withdrawn into Laos.

USA – MILITARY: Retired USMC commandant David Shoup estimates that up to 800,000 men are required just to defend South Vietnamese population centers. He further states that the United States can achieve military victory only by invading North Vietnam, but argues that such an operation would not be worth the cost.

USA – DOMESTIC: The *New York Times* publishes excerpts from General Westmoreland's classified end-of-year report, which indicates that the U.S. command did not believe the enemy capable of any action approximating the Tet Offensive.

March 22

GROUND WAR: The Khe Sanh combat base receives 1,100 rounds of rocket and mortar fire.

AIR WAR: U.S. Air Force F-111s fly their first combat mission against targets in North Vietnam.

USA – GOVERNMENT: President Johnson announces that General Westmoreland will become army chief of staff in mid-1968 and that General Creighton Abrams will assume command of Military Assistance Command, Vietnam.

March 23

USA – MILITARY: General Wheeler secretly flies to meet with Westmoreland at Clark Field in the Philippines and tells him that President Johnson will approve only 13,500 additional soldiers out of the original 206,000 requested; Wheeler also instructs Westmoreland to urge the South Vietnamese to expand their own war effort.

March 25

USA – DOMESTIC: A Harris poll reports that in the past six weeks, "basic" support for the war among Americans declined from 74 percent to 54 percent; it also reveals that 60 percent of those questioned regard the Tet Offensive as a defeat of U.S. objectives in Vietnam.

SOUTH VIETNAM: An outbreak of bubonic plague in Tay Ninh Province has reached epidemic proportions and is beginning to spread toward Saigon.

March 25–26

USA – GOVERNMENT: After being told by Defense Secretary Clark Clifford that the Vietnam war is a "real loser," President Johnson is still uncertain about his future course of action; he convenes the "Wise Men," a nine-man panel of retired presidential advisers which includes the respected generals Omar Bradley and Matthew Ridgway, distinguished State Department figures like Dean Acheson and George Ball, and McGeorge Bundy, former National Security Advisor in both the Kennedy and Johnson administrations. After two days of deliberation the group reaches a consensus and advises the president against any further troop increases and recommends that the administration seek a negotiated peace. Johnson is reportedly furious at their conclusions, since this group had previously recommended that he stay the course in Vietnam.

March 30

GROUND WAR: U.S. Marines and PAVN troops engage in a three-hour battle near Khe Sanh, the last major ground combat of the 77-day siege.

USA – DOMESTIC: A Gallup poll reports that 63 percent of those polled disapprove of President Johnson's handling of the war, an all-time low in public approval of his performance.

March 30–January 31, 1969

GROUND WAR: Elements of the U.S. 173rd Airborne Brigade, the 4th and Americal Divisions, and 22nd ARVN Division conduct Operation Cochise Green/Dan Sinh, a search and destroy operation in Binh Dinh Province, II Corps. Casualties will be U.S.: 114 KIA, 187 WIA; NVA/VC: 929 KIA, 25 POW.

March 31

USA – GOVERNMENT: In a televised speech to the nation, President Lyndon Johnson announces that he has "unilaterally" ordered a halt to air and naval bombardments of North Vietnam "except in the area north of the DMZ where the continuing enemy build-up directly threatens allied forward positions." He also states that he is sending 13,500 more troops to Vietnam and will request further defense expenditures, a total of $2.5 billion in fiscal year 1968 and $2.6 billion in fiscal year 1969, to finance recent troop buildups, reequip the South Vietnamese army, and meet "our responsibilities in Korea." In closing, Johnson shocks the nation with an announcement that in effect concedes that his own presidency has become another casualty of the war, saying, "I shall not seek, and I will not accept, the nomination of my party for another term as your President."

GROUND WAR: There are now 50 U.S. combat battalions operating in I Corps—a total of 170,000 troops, an increase of 30,000 in the last three months.

AIR WAR: Operation Niagara ends; during the operation, U.S. Air Force, Navy and Marine Corps aircraft dropped more than 110,000 tons of bombs, including some 76,000 tons by B-52s, on North Vietnamese forces besieging the marines at the Khe Sanh combat base.

April 1

SOUTH VIETNAM: President Thieu declares that the Tet Offensive has "completely failed."

April 1–15

GROUND WAR: The U.S. 1st Cavalry Division (Airmobile) in conjunction with U.S. Marine and ARVN airborne troops, a total of 17 U.S. and four ARVN battalion, conducts Operation Pegasus/Lam Son-207 to reopen Route 9 to the marine base at Khe Sanh, I Corps. The base is officially relieved by elements of the 1st Cavalry Division on April 8, ending the 77-day siege. Casualties are U.S.: 92 KIA, 667 WIA; South Vietnamese: 33 KIA, 187 WIA; NVA/VC: 1,044 KIA, 9 POW.

April 2

AIR WAR: Following widespread criticism in reaction to continuing air strikes deep within North Vietnamese territory, the administration explains that the bombing limitation applies only to the region north of the 20th parallel—an "area of North Vietnam containing almost 90 percent of its population and three-quarters of its land."

April 3

NORTH VIETNAM: At the end of a government message broadcast by Hanoi Radio denouncing the bombing limitation as a "perfidious trick" intended "to appease public opinion," Hanoi declares its "readiness" to meet with U.S. representatives to discuss "the unconditional cessation of the U.S. bombing raids and all other acts of war against the Democratic Republic of Vietnam so that talks may start." In his response, President Johnson chooses to ignore the statement's abusive features and simply announces that "we will establish contact with representatives of North Vietnam."

April 4

USA – DOMESTIC: Martin Luther King, Jr., is assassinated in Memphis.

April 8–May 31

GROUND WAR: A combined force from ARVN III Corps and U.S. II Field Force units conducts Operation Toan Thang (Complete Victory), largest operation to date, to destroy VC and North Vietnamese forces within the Capital Military District, III Corps; 42 U.S. and 37 South Vietnamese battalions are involved. Casualties are U.S.: 208 KIA, 1,210 WIA, 1 MIA (partial count); NVA/VC: 3,542 KIA (reported).

April 8–November 11

GROUND WAR: The U.S. 198th Infantry Brigade and other elements of the Americal Division conduct Operation Burlington Trail, a combat sweep in Quang Tin Province along the Quang Nam Province border in I Corps. Casualties will be U.S.: 129 KIA, 965 WIA; NVA/VC: 1,931 KIA.

April 10–12

GROUND WAR: In three days of intense fighting, U.S. troops recapture the Special Forces camp at Lang Vei, are driven out by NVA counterattack, but then retake the camp a second time.

April 11

USA – GOVERNMENT: At his first Pentagon press conference, Defense Secretary Clifford announces a call-up of 24,500 military reservists to serve as support forces in Vietnam and to replenish the army's Strategic Reserve. He also states that the troop ceiling for U.S. strength in Vietnam has been raised to 549,000.

DIPLOMACY: The United States rejects a North Vietnamese proposal that preliminary talks be held in Warsaw, insisting that, on "serious matters of this kind, it is important to hold talks in a neutral atmosphere, fair to both sides."

April 13

LAOS: U.S. officials in Vientiane report that a recent North Vietnamese-Pathet Lao offensive, resulting thus far in the virtual encirclement of the two provincial capitals of Saravane and Attopeu in southern Laos, suggests that the enemy has adopted a new strategy of "attacking towns and taking terrain."

April 15, 1968–February 28, 1969

GROUND WAR: U.S. Marines and soldiers from the 1st Cavalry Division conduct Operation Scotland II as a follow-on to Operation Pegasus in I Corps. The objective of the operation is to clear North Vietnamese forces out of Quang Tri Province. Casualties will be U.S.: 435 KIA, 2,395 WIA; NVA/VC: 3,304 KIA, 64 POW.

Men of the 1st Battalion, 4th Marines, board Marine CH-46s at the start of Operation Scotland II, April 1968. *(Texas Tech University Vietnam Archive)*

April 16

USA – GOVERNMENT: At a series of meetings in Honolulu, President Johnson discusses recent Allied and enemy troop deployments with U.S. military leaders. He also confers with South Korean president Park Chung Hee to reaffirm U.S. military commitments to Seoul and assure Park that his country's interests will not be compromised by a Vietnamese peace agreement.

April 18

USA – MILITARY: The U.S. command in Saigon discloses figures showing that the South Vietnamese government lost control over 1.1 million people as a result of the Tet Offensive.

April 19–May 17

GROUND WAR: Elements of the U.S. 1st Cavalry Division, 101st Airborne Division, and 196th Light Infantry Brigade plus the ARVN 1st Division and Airborne Task Force Bravo conduct Operation Delaware/Lam Son-216 in the A Shau Valley to preempt enemy preparations for another pending attack on the Hue area of I Corps. Casualties are U.S.: 142 KIA, 731 WIA, 47 MIA; NVA/VC: 869 KIA.

April 21

GROUND WAR: A high-ranking NVA defector exposes enemy plans to conduct a second wave of attacks on Saigon beginning April 22.

April 22

USA – GOVERNMENT: Defense Secretary Clifford declares that the South Vietnamese have "acquired the capacity to begin to insure their own security [and] they are going to take over more and more of the fighting." This is the first public announcement of a policy that, under the Nixon administration, will become known as "Vietnamization."

April 23–30

USA – DOMESTIC: Student protesters occupy several buildings at Columbia University until forcibly removed by police.

April 26

USA – DOMESTIC: More than 200,000 people demonstrate against the war in New York City. Students in various universities around the world cut classes as part of an antiwar strike organized by the Student Mobilization Committee to End the War in Vietnam.

AIR WAR: F-111 raids resume, after suspected technical malfunctions had caused the planes to be grounded for three weeks.

April 27

USA – DOMESTIC: Vice President Hubert Humphrey announces his candidacy for the Democratic presidential nomination. In an interview, he says he supports the current U.S. policy of sending troops "where required by our own national security."

April 28

NORTH VIETNAM: Hanoi sources report the formation of a new political organization in South Vietnam, the Alliance of National, Democratic, and Peace Forces, which is prepared to conduct peace talks with the United States. Although the alliance reportedly represents non-Communist South Vietnamese nationalists, the U.S. State Department refuses to recognize the group.

April 29

SOUTH VIETNAM: Opposition and independent members in the lower house of South Vietnam's National Assembly issue a statement calling for a change of government, because of corruption in high places.

April 30

GROUND WAR: The U.S. embassy in Saigon reports that, during the Tet Offensive in Hue, NVA and Viet Cong forces executed more than 1,000 civilians and buried them in mass graves, 19 of which have recently been uncovered.

May 1–December 17

GROUND WAR: Task Force Funston from the U.S. 9th Infantry Division conducts Operation Kudzu in Dinh Tuong Province, IV Corps. The objective of the operation is to provide security for the division base at Dong Tam. Casualties are U.S.: 28 KIA, 336 WIA; NVA/VC: 187 KIA, 41 POW.

May 3–4

NEGOTIATIONS: President Johnson announces that, after 34 days of discussion, the United States and North Vietnam have agreed to begin formal negotiations in Paris on May 10 or shortly thereafter. Hanoi discloses that ex-foreign minister Xuan Thuy will head the North Vietnamese delegation at the talks. W. Averell Harriman is named as his U.S. counterpart. The North Vietnamese Communist Party newspaper *Nhan Dan* declares that Hanoi's four-point program and the NLF's political program remain "the correct basis for a political solution of the Vietnam problem." Secretary of State Rusk asserts that the United States regards an end to Communist infiltration of South Vietnam and neighboring countries as vital for "an honorable peace in Southeast Asia."

May 3–10

GROUND WAR: In the highest weekly hostile fire casualty toll of the war, 562 U.S. military personnel are killed in action.

May 4–August 24

GROUND WAR: U.S. Marine Corps units conduct Operation Allen Brook west of Hoi An City in southern Quang Nam Province, I Corps. Casualties will be U.S.: 172 KIA, 1,124 WIA; NVA/VC: 1,917 KIA.

May 5–13

GROUND WAR: What turns out to be the second phase of the Tet Offensive begins with the simultaneous shelling of 119 cities, town, and military barracks. Heavy fighting continues for a week in what becomes popularly known as "Mini-Tet." The principal enemy target is Saigon where, following a major ground assault, the fighting quickly spreads to Cholon, the Phu Tho racetrack, and Tan Son Nhut air base. The battle climaxes on May 12, when U.S. jets, dropping napalm and high-explosive bombs, pound a vital Viet Cong stronghold in the slum district around the Y bridge, preparing the way for an assault by U.S. infantry troops. According to Allied sources, 5,270 North Vietnamese are killed in the offensive,

ARVN forces take on enemy troops in Gia Dinh, some three miles northeast of the presidential palace in Saigon, May. 1968. *(Texas Tech University Vietnam Archive)*

compared with 152 Americans and 326 South Vietnamese killed in just eight days of fighting.

May 9

SOUTH VIETNAM: President Thieu declares that his government will never recognize the National Liberation Front, even if the United States should negotiate an end to the war.

USA – MILITARY: The U.S. Army announces that in order to bolster its firepower and mobility, the 101st Airborne Division will be converted into an airmobile division. It also discloses that separate reconnaissance squadrons will be attached to each of the five remaining infantry divisions in Vietnam.

May 9–17

GROUND WAR: The 1st Cavalry Division conducts Operation Concordia in Quang Tri Province, I Corps. Casualties are U.S.: 28 KIA, 116 WIA; NVA/VC: 349 KIA.

May 10–12

GROUND WAR: Elements of the American Division conduct Operation Golden Valley, the evacuation of 1,400 personnel from the Kham Duc Special Forces camp, 60 miles west of Chu Lai in Quang Tin Province, I Corps. During the evacuation, a battalion from the 1st Infantry fights a major battle with soldiers from the North Vietnamese 2nd Division. Casualties are U.S.: 20 KIA, 116 WIA; NVA/VC: 345 KIA.

May 11

GROUND WAR: As part of the ongoing "Mini-Tet," Communist forces shell 159 cities, towns, and military bases throughout South Vietnam, including Saigon and Hue, in the largest number of attacks since the earlier Tet offensive. Fourteen persons are reported killed and about 100 wounded in a series of terrorist attacks near Saigon. Initial reports claim at least 500 Communists killed in the fighting.

NEGOTIATIONS: Delegates from the United States and North Vietnam hold their first formal meeting at the Majestic Hotel in Paris. They agree that, for the time being, participation will be restricted to representatives of the United States and North Vietnam.

May 12

AIR WAR: Lieutenant Colonel Joe M. Jackson (USAF), flying an unarmed Fairchild C-123 transport, lands at a forward outpost at Kham Duc, South Vietnam, in a rescue attempt of a combat control team. After a rocket-propelled grenade fired directly at his aircraft proves to be a dud, Colonel Jackson takes off with the team on board and lands at Danang. He will later be awarded the Medal of Honor for his actions.

May 15–19

NEGOTIATIONS: To break an impasse at the Paris peace talks, the United States asks that the meeting be moved into secret session.

May 17–November 3

GROUND WAR: Operation Jeb Stuart III is conducted as a continuation of U.S. 1st Cavalry Division and ARVN rice denial and cordon operations along the border of Quang Tri and Thua Thien Provinces, I Corps. Casualties will be U.S.: 212 KIA, 1,512 WIA; NVA/VC: 2,016 KIA, 251 POW.

May 17–February 28, 1969
GROUND WAR: The U.S. 101st Airborne Division conducts Operation Nevada Eagle, a continuation of earlier cordon and search operations in central Thua Thien Province, I Corps. Casualties will be U.S.: 175 KIA, 1,161 WIA; NVA/VC: 3,299 KIA, 853 POW.

May 18
SOUTH VIETNAM: Newly appointed premier Tran Van Huong declares his opposition to negotiations with the National Liberation Front in a statement asserting that the peace talks should be between Saigon and Hanoi, rather than the United States and North Vietnam.

May 18–October 23
GROUND WAR: The U.S. 1st Marine Division conducts Operation Mameluke Thrust in central Quang Nam Province, I Corps. Casualties will be U.S.: 267 KIA, 1,730 WIA; NVA/VC: 2,728 KIA.

May 21
SOUTH VIETNAM: The Allied command in Saigon announces the start of a new program, Operation Hearts Together, designed to resettle Saigon families made homeless by the fighting.

May 22
NEGOTIATIONS: Xuan Thuy, chief North Vietnamese delegate to the Paris peace talks, declares that negotiations will remain deadlocked until the United States unconditionally terminates all bombing raids on North Vietnam. If the talks should collapse, Thuy adds, "the American side would bear the full and entire responsibility." Ambassador Harriman replies that a bombing halt must be accompanied by mutual troop withdrawals along the DMZ, but Thuy rejects the proposal, charging that it is the United States, not North Vietnam, that has violated the buffer zone.
AIR WAR: The U.S. Marine Corps makes its first use of the North American OV-10A "Bronco," a light observation aircraft.

May 23
SOUTH VIETNAM: At the conclusion of an experimental civic affairs program in Long An Province, John Paul Vann and other U.S. advisers issue a report recommending widespread changes in the pacification effort. The report states that Saigon has little understanding of its people's needs and has consistently failed to provide adequate funds and services for grass-roots programs. As a result, the Viet Cong continue to collect taxes and recruit troops from many hamlets that the government claims it has pacified.

May 25
SOUTH VIETNAM: Premier Tran Van Huong announces the formation of a new 19-member cabinet in which a faction supporting Vice President Ky is given only one post. In the previous 17-member cabinet, the Ky faction had controlled seven ministries.

May 25–June 4, 1968

GROUND WAR: The Viet Cong launch their third major assault of the year on Saigon, actually a part of the overall Tet Offensive that will extend into the fall. The heaviest fighting occurs during the first three days of June, and again centers on Cholon, where U.S. and South Vietnamese forces use helicopters, fighter-bombers, and tanks to dislodge deeply entrenched Viet Cong infiltrators. A captured enemy directive, which the U.S. command makes public on May 28, indicates that the Viet Cong see the offensive as a means of influencing the Paris peace talks. More than 700 U.S. soldiers and marines die in this fighting.

May 27

THAILAND: Premier Thanom Kittikachorn announces that, at President Johnson's request, his country will send 5,000 more troops to Vietnam.

May 28–June 19

GROUND WAR: The USMC's Task Force Hotel conducts Operation Robin North/ Robin South to prevent enemy attacks on Khe Sanh and northern Quang Tri Province, I Corps. Casualties are NVA/VC: 725.

May 30

SOUTH VIETNAM: Information Minister Ton That Thien issues a directive lifting press censorship, which has been in effect since the beginning of the Tet Offensive.

June

AUSTRALIA: Australia deploys its 4th Battalion, Royal Australian Regiment, to Vietnam to replace the regiment's 2nd Battalion and conduct combat operations in III Corps.

June 1

SOUTH VIETNAM: Recent government directives on pacification indicate that, since the Tet Offensive, the program's focus has shifted from school-building, health care, and providing other forms of aid to an emphasis on training self-defense teams and bolstering hamlet security.

June 1–February 16, 1969

GROUND WAR: U.S. and South Vietnamese units conduct Operation Toan Thang II, a continuation of post-Tet Offensive operations throughout III Corps to maintain pressure on the enemy.

June 3

NEGOTIATIONS: Le Duc Tho, a member of the North Vietnam Communist Party's Politburo, joins the North Vietnamese negotiating team as a special counselor.

June 5

USA – DOMESTIC: Senator Robert Kennedy (D-N.Y.), a leading critic of administration policy in Vietnam, is shot after announcing his victory in California's Democratic presidential primary; he dies the next day.

June 10

USA – MILITARY: General Westmoreland turns over his command to General Creighton Abrams. At a press conference, Westmoreland defends his attrition policy, declaring that it will ultimately make continued fighting "intolerable to the enemy." He also explains that, because it is impossible to "cut a surface line of communication with other than ground operations," Washington's ban on ground attacks to interdict Communist infiltration through Laos precludes the achievement of military victory. Westmoreland denies, however, that the military situation is stalemated.

SOUTH VIETNAM: Information minister Ton That Thien declares that the U.S. impact on Vietnamese culture, religion, and politics has been "devastating" and "disintegrating."

June 13

SOUTH VIETNAM: Open arms minister Phan Quang Dan is dismissed for suggesting that the government hold direct talks with the National Liberation Front.

June 14

USA – DOMESTIC: A federal district court jury in Boston convicts Dr. Benjamin Spock and three others of conspiring to aid, abet, and counsel draft registrants to violate the Selective Service Law.

June 19

SOUTH VIETNAM: In a public ceremony at Hue, President Thieu signs a general mobilization bill, which decrees that men between the ages of 18 and 43 will be subject to induction into the regular armed forces. Men between the ages of 44 and 50 and 16- and 17-year-old youths will be eligible to serve part-time in the civilian People's Self Defense Organization. An estimated 90,000 17-year-olds in the People's Self Defense Organization may be transferred to the regular army. It is believed that, by the end of 1968, the law will provide for the induction of an additional 200,000 men.

June 26

SOUTH VIETNAM: Speaking on behalf of the South Vietnam's House of Representatives, Duong Van Ba demands that Saigon be given a role in the Paris peace talks, asserting that "we should tell the United States government and the United States people that we suspect that there is now a plot to sell out South Vietnam to the Communists."

NEGOTIATIONS: Cyrus Vance, deputy U.S. delegate to the peace talks, seeks to break a continuing impasse in the negotiations by appealing to North Vietnam for some sign that it is taking steps to scale down the level of military violence. Although this is the first time that U.S. negotiators have urged military reciprocity in such broad terms, Xuan Thuy rejects the initiative and repeats Hanoi's demand that all U.S. bombing raids on North Vietnam be unconditionally terminated. Thuy also insists that the Saigon government be replaced by a coalition regime committed to a neutral foreign policy and eventual reunification.

June 27

GROUND WAR: U.S. Marines evacuate the combat base at Khe Sanh. MACV announces that U.S. forces are departing the military base and attributes the pull-back to a change in the military situation. To cope with increased NVA infiltration and activity in the DMZ area, Allied forces are adopting a more "mobile posture," thus making retention of the outpost at Khe Sanh unnecessary.

June 28

USA – MILITARY: Lieutenant Colonel Richard A. McMahon denounces the "body count" as a "dubious and possibly dangerous" method of determining the enemy's combat potential.

LAOS: Prince Souvanna Phouma declares that the United States should continue to reject Hanoi's demands for a bombing halt until North Vietnam agrees to withdraw its forces from Laos.

June 29

SOUTH VIETNAM: South Vietnamese premier Tran Van Huong expresses concern that, because of its impatience to end the war, the United States is making too many concessions at the peace talks, behavior that he believes the North Vietnamese interpret as a sign of weakness.

GROUND WAR: For the second time in three days, South Vietnamese forces patrolling the Saigon area uncover a huge arms cache containing rockets and other weapons. MACV believes that capture of the materiel has caused the Viet Cong to postpone plans for another assault on Saigon.

June 30

SOUTH VIETNAM: Socialist Phan Ba Cam announces the formation of a new South Vietnamese political party, Vietnam People's Force, committed to ending the war peacefully, unifying North and South Vietnam, and building a socialist economy.

July 1

USA – MILITARY: The 1st Brigade, 5th Infantry Division (Mechanized), deploys to Vietnam from Fort Carson, Colorado, for combat operations in I Corps under the operational control of III MAF.

AIR WAR: U.S. B-52 bombers resume raids north of the DMZ.

July 2

USA – GOVERNMENT: At President Johnson's request, Congress passes a $6 billion supplemental appropriations bill to sustain U.S. operations in Vietnam.

President Johnson listens to a tape sent by Captain Charles Robb, his son-in-law, from Vietnam, July 1968. *(Texas Tech University Vietnam Archive)*

July 3

USA – MILITARY: General Westmoreland replaces General Harold K. Johnson as army chief of staff. In Saigon, MACV releases figures showing that more Americans were killed during the first six months of 1968 than in all of 1967.

GROUND WAR: U.S. troops conducting a sweep near Saigon uncover an enemy arms cache containing 56 Soviet and Chinese rockets; three more caches are discovered two days later west and northwest of the capital.

July 4

GROUND WAR: In a 2½-hour-long battle, U.S. infantrymen from the 25th Infantry Division repulse a combined North Vietnamese and Viet Cong attack on their base at Dau Tieng, 40 miles northwest of Saigon.

SOUTH VIETNAM: At a formal ceremony inaugurating the formation of a new multi-party pro-government political grouping, the People's Alliance for Social Revolution, President Thieu praises the organization as a "major step toward grass roots political activity." An alliance manifesto asserts that it is "determined to wipe out corruption, do away with social inequalities, and rout out the entrenched forces of militarists and reactionaries who have always blocked progress."

July 8

SOUTH VIETNAM: President Thieu announces that the possibility of another enemy offensive has caused him to postpone a planned visit to the United States.

CAMBODIA: A formal complaint to the United Nations charges that Allied helicopters killed 14 Cambodians working in their rice fields more than 6,000 yards from the border.

July 9

NLF: Le Quang Chanh, a member of the NLF Central Committee, reaffirms the NLF's goal of overthrowing the present Saigon regime in a statement asserting that no elections can be held to form a postwar government in South Vietnam until all U.S. and Allied forces have withdrawn.

NEGOTIATIONS: Bui Diem, chief South Vietnamese observer at the Paris peace talks, reiterates Saigon's call for direct negotiations between North and South Vietnam. His statement reflects a growing fear on the part of the Saigon government that the United States and North Vietnam might conclude a settlement inimical to the South's interests.

July 13

USA – DOMESTIC: Governor Nelson Rockefeller of New York, a Republican presidential candidate, reveals a four-stage peace plan, which, he argues, could end the war in six months if North Vietnam agrees to it. The proposal calls for a mutual troop pullback and interposition of a neutral peacekeeping force, followed by the withdrawal of all North Vietnamese and most Allied units from South Vietnam, free elections under international supervision, and direct negotiations between North and South Vietnam on reunification.

July 14–18

USA – GOVERNMENT: Defense Secretary Clifford visits South Vietnam to confer with U.S. and South Vietnamese leaders. Upon his arrival in Saigon, Clifford states that the United States is doing all that it can to improve the fighting capacity of the South Vietnamese army and intends to provide all ARVN units with M-16 automatic rifles.

July 16
USA – MILITARY: A senior U.S. military source in Saigon reveals that enemy units have withdrawn toward the west, indicating that an attack on the capital has been postponed.

July 18–20
USA – GOVERNMENT: President Johnson meets President Thieu in Honolulu to discuss relations between Washington and Saigon. Johnson reaffirms his administration's commitment "to defend South Vietnam." Thieu states that he has "no apprehensions at all" concerning the U.S. commitment. In a joint communiqué, Thieu further asserts that his government is determined "to continue to assume all the responsibility that the scale of forces of South Vietnam and their equipment will permit," thus tacitly accepting current U.S. efforts to "Vietnamize the war." The two presidents also agree that South Vietnam "should be a full participant playing a leading role in discussions concerning the substance of a final settlement" to the conflict.

July 20
SOUTH VIETNAM: South Vietnam observes National Shame Day, the anniversary of the 1954 Geneva Accords.
NORTH VIETNAM: Ho Chi Minh marks the anniversary of the Geneva Accords by issuing an appeal to step up the war of resistance against U.S. imperialism.

July 21
SOUTH VIETNAM: The widows of six South Vietnamese military officers and government officials killed during a tour of the Saigon battlefront on June 2—by what U.S. authorities say was a misdirected U.S. helicopter rocket—charge that the United States deliberately murdered their husbands, all of whom were political allies of Vice President Ky, who was then seeking to assume control of the Saigon military district. Three days later, a joint U.S.-South Vietnamese investigating board will confirm that a malfunctioning rocket was responsible for the deaths.

July 22
NEGOTIATIONS: Nguyen Thanh Le, North Vietnamese spokesman at the Paris peace talks, tells reporters that the Honolulu conference has revealed that "the position of the United States remains infinitely obstinate" and that apparently the United States is still determined to support the "puppet government" in Saigon.

July 24
GROUND WAR: Task Force South is organized by combining a battalion from the 173rd Airborne Brigade and one from the 101st Airborne Division with logistics, aviation, and artillery units. TF South is stationed at Dalat in Tuyen Duc Province and Phan Tiet in Binh Thuan Province, II Corps.

July 26

SOUTH VIETNAM: Truong Dinh Dzu, a peace candidate in the September 1967 presidential elections, is sentenced to five years at hard labor for urging the formation of a coalition government as a step toward ending the war. This is the first time that a major political figure has been tried and convicted under a 1965 decree ordering the prosecution of persons "who interfere with the government's struggle against Communism."

August 2

POWs: Three U.S. pilots released by Hanoi arrive in Laos and report that they have been well treated. Five days later, Ambassador Averell Harriman informs North Vietnamese negotiators in Paris that the United States will reciprocate by turning over 14 North Vietnamese seamen. Harriman also states that he hopes that more prisoner exchanges can be arranged in the future.

August 2–April 24, 1969

GROUND WAR: The ARVN 54th Regiment conducts Operation Lam Son-245 in Thua Thien; it will report 636 enemy killed by the end of the operation.

August 4–20

GROUND WAR: A combined U.S.-ARVN task force conducts Operation Somerset Plain/Lam Son-246 in the A Shau Valley, Thua Thien Province, I Corps. Casualties are U.S.: 19 KIA, 104 WIA, 2 MIA; ARVN: 15 KIA, 57 WIA, 2 MIA; NVA/VC: 171 KIA, 4 POW.

August 4–December 31, 1969

GROUND WAR: Elements of the U.S. 9th Infantry Division, Mobile Riverine Force, and Vietnamese marines conduct Operation Quyet Chien in Kien Giang Province, IV Corps. Casualties are U.S.: 131 KIA, 997 WIA; NVA/VC: 2,248 KIA, 191 POW.

August 5–8

USA – DOMESTIC: The Republican National Convention opens in Miami. The Vietnam plank adopted during the convention calls for an honorable negotiated peace and "progressive de-Americanization" of the war. During the convention, Richard M. Nixon and Spiro T. Agnew are chosen as the presidential and vice presidential nominees for the upcoming election. In his speech accepting the nomination, Nixon promises to "bring an honorable end to the war in Vietnam" and to inaugurate "an era of negotiations" with leading Communist powers, while restoring "the strength of America so that we shall always negotiate from strength and never from weakness."

August 8

GROUND WAR: During efforts to repel three Viet Cong ambushes, U.S. troops from the 9th Infantry Division accidentally kill 72 civilians and wound 240 in the Mekong Delta town of Cai Reng.

August 9

GROUND WAR: Ninety-six Americans are reported killed for the previous week. This is the lowest weekly U.S. death toll since August 12, 1967.

August 10

AIR WAR: A U.S. Air Force F-100 Super Sabre jet accidentally strafes a unit of the 101st Airborne Division in the A Shau Valley, killing eight and wounding five.

August 12–13

GROUND WAR: Heavy fighting erupts again in the Mekong Delta between VC and Allied troops, who are part of a 75-battalion force guarding infiltration routes into Saigon. The action results in 181 Viet Cong killed.

August 15

USA – MILITARY: The XXIV Corps is established to coordinate U.S. Army combat operations in I Corps.

GROUND WAR: Heavy fighting intensifies in and around the DMZ, as ARVN and U.S. troops engage a North Vietnamese battalion. In a 7½-hour battle, 165 enemy troops are killed. At the same time, U.S. Marines attack three strategic positions just south of the DMZ, killing 56 North Vietnamese soldiers.

SOUTH VIETNAM: President Thieu denounces the Paris talks as a North Vietnamese "trick" and declares that peace will become possible only when "our armed forces can achieve an absolute victory in the future."

August 17

USA – MILITARY: The Defense Department reports that U.S. aircraft have flown 117,000 missions over North Vietnam since February 1965, dropping over 2.5 million tons of bombs and rockets, but men and supplies continue to pour into South Vietnam.

August 18

GROUND WAR: The North Vietnamese and Viet Cong launch a limited offensive with 19 separate attacks throughout South Vietnam. In the heaviest fighting in three months, Communist troops attack key positions along the Cambodian border in Tay Ninh and Binh Long provinces, northwest of Saigon. In Tay Ninh, 600 Viet Cong, supported by elements of two North Vietnamese divisions, attack the provincial capital, capturing several government installations. U.S. reinforcements from the 25th Infantry Division are rushed to the scene and after a day of house-to-house fighting expel the Communists from the city.

August 19

USA – GOVERNMENT: President Johnson, in a major speech at the Veterans of Foreign Wars convention in Detroit, challenges Hanoi to respond to his limitations of the bombing campaign, but he refuses to curtail other military activities in Southeast Asia, saying that "there are some among us who appear to be searching for a formula which would get us out of Vietnam and Asia on any terms, leaving the people of South Vietnam and Laos and Thailand . . . to an uncertain fate."

USA – DOMESTIC: A Harris survey indicates that 61 percent of those polled are against calling a halt to the bombing.

August 21

GROUND WAR: The 25th Infantry Division clashes with Viet Cong near Saigon and reports 700 Communist killed.

August 22

GROUND WAR: For the first time in two months, Viet Cong forces launch a rocket attack on Saigon, killing 18 and wounding 59. Administration officials denounce this attack as a direct repudiation of President Johnson's peace overture of August 19.

August 23–25

GROUND WAR: Communist forces launch rocket and mortar attacks on numerous cities, provincial capitals, and military installations. The heaviest shelling is on the U.S. airfield at Danang and the cities of Hue and Quang Tri. North Vietnamese forces numbering between 1,200 and 1,500 troops attack the U.S. Special Forces camp at Duc Lap, 130 miles northeast of Saigon, near the Cambodian border. The camp falls but is retaken by an Allied relief column led by U.S. Special Forces troops on August 25. A reported 643 North Vietnamese troops are killed in the battle.

August 24–September 9

GROUND WAR: Elements of the ARVN 23rd Division conduct Operation Tien Bo in Quang Duc Province, II Corps, claiming 1,091 North Vietnamese and Viet Cong killed or wounded.

August 26–29

USA – DOMESTIC: The Democratic Party National Convention opens in Chicago. There is an immediate conflict over the party's Vietnam platform between those who support the Johnson administration's handling of the war and applaud the president's efforts to scale down the war and begin peace talks, and an anti-war faction led by Senators Eugene McCarthy (D-Minn.) and George McGovern (D-S.D.). On the 28th, this confrontation results in a contentious three-hour debate inside the convention hall while a full-scale riot erupts outside the convention hall, where anti-war protesters battle with police and National Guardsmen. The melee begins after 150 policemen attack a protester encampment in Lincoln Park. Inside the convention hall, the administration plank is adopted and ultimately the delegates choose Vice President Hubert Humphrey and Senator Edmund Muskie from Maine as the party nominees for the upcoming election.

August 30

GROUND WAR: The NLF proclaims that a new offensive is being launched. Over 30 U.S. troops from the 101st Airborne Division are killed during a Viet Cong attack at Ap Trung Dau. Other paratroopers, acting on information gleaned from a North Vietnamese defector, attack and destroy a Communist regimental headquarters 12 miles south of Hue, killing 176 enemy troops and capturing seven antiaircraft guns and 435 other weapons. North Vietnamese forces overrun a U.S. Special Forces camp at Ha Thanh, 14 miles west of Quang Ngai, but Allied troops will retake the outpost three days later.

September

GROUND WAR: The U.S. 27th Marines of the 5th Marine Division, attached to the 1st Marine Division, leaves South Vietnam.

September 1

AIR WAR: Lieutenant Colonel William A. Jones III (USAF) leads a rescue mission of a downed pilot near Dong Hoi, North Vietnam. Finding the downed pilot, Colonel Jones attacks a nearby gun emplacement. On his second pass, Colonel Jones's aircraft is hit and the cockpit of his Douglas A-1H is set ablaze. He tries to eject, but the extraction system fails. He then returns to base and reports the exact position of the downed pilot (who is rescued the next day) before receiving medical treatment for his burns. Colonel Jones will die in an aircraft accident in the United States before he can be presented with the Medal of Honor for his actions the day of the attempted rescue.

September 2

AIR WAR: The U.S. command orders the heaviest bombing in weeks along infiltration routes leading into Saigon. The increased raids reflect Allied concern that North Vietnam will celebrate its annual National Day with another assault on the capital.

September 4–24

GROUND WAR: Troops from the Americal Division and 2nd ARVN Division conduct Operation Champagne Grove in Quang Ngai Province, I Corps. Action results in a major battle with a regiment from the 3rd NVA Division three miles northwest of Quang Ngai City. Casualties are U.S.: 43 KIA, 172 WIA; NVA/VC: 378 KIA.

September 8

GROUND WAR: Brigadier General Truong Quang An becomes the first ARVN general killed in action when his aircraft is shot down near Duc Lap.

September 10

USA – GOVERNMENT: In a speech before the American Legion convention, President Johnson states that, according to General Abrams, if the bombing of the North Vietnamese panhandle is terminated without reciprocal de-escalation on Hanoi's part, "the military capacity of the enemy to hurt our forces would greatly increase." At another point in the speech, the president reveals his concern over the mounting cost of the war.

September 10–20

GROUND WAR: A battalion from the 101st Airborne Division joins with the 54th ARVN Regiment and the 7th ARVN Cavalry in Operation Vinh Loc, a cordon and search of Vinh Loc Island, 15 miles east of Hue, I Corps. Captured VC tell their interrogators that more than 80 percent of the Communist infrastructure on the island was wiped out during the operation. Casualties are U.S.: 2 KIA, 9 WIA; NVA/VC: 154 KIA, 126 POW.

September 11–16

GROUND WAR: About 1,500 VC and PAVN troops launch a major attack on Tay Ninh in III Corps Tactical Zone. The next day, 2,000 ARVN reinforcements are sent in to aid the local garrison; after a four-day battle, the North Vietnamese are driven out of the city. Also on September 16, a convoy from the U.S. 25th Infantry Division is ambushed nine miles southeast of Tay Ninh.

September 11–April 24, 1969
GROUND WAR: The 1st ARVN Division conducts Lam Son-261 in Thua Thien and Quang Tri Provinces, I Corps, reporting 724 enemy casualties.

September 13
GROUND WAR: Major General Keith L. Ware, commander of the 1st Infantry Division and Medal of Honor recipient in World War II, is killed in a helicopter crash near the Cambodian border in Binh Long Province, III Corps. Seven other Americans die in the crash.

September 13–October 1
GROUND WAR: The largest sustained operation inside the DMZ opens when ARVN and U.S. infantry and armored troops from the 1st Brigade, 5th Infantry Division, supported by close air support, artillery, and naval gunfire, conduct a preemptive strike by moving two miles into the buffer zone to relieve enemy pressure on Allied bases along the 40-mile stretch of South Vietnam's northern frontier and to prevent an anticipated offensive by two NVA divisions thought to be currently operating within the DMZ. On September 17, 2,000 marines are airlifted into the area and B-52s, striking for the first time in a month, hit targets on both sides of the Ben Hai River, part of the demarcation between North and South Vietnam. Ten days later, an additional 4,000 marines attack into the buffer zone in a coordinated pincer movement designed to trap remaining Communist forces. The operation results in 742 NVA killed, while American losses include 65 killed and 77 wounded.

September 18
SOUTH VIETNAM: In an article in *Foreign Affairs*, Major General Duong Van Minh argues that only the introduction of participatory democracy at the village level can restore unity in South Vietnam and create a political system capable of defeating the Communists.

September 20
USA – MILITARY: MACV defends the use of defoliants in Vietnam at a news conference in Saigon, claiming that their use in selected areas in South Vietnam has neither appreciably altered the country's ecology, nor produced any harmful effects on human or animal life.

September 23
DIPLOMACY: A heated argument develops in the United Nations, when Secretary-general U Thant seems to encourage an anti-U.S. resolution.

September 26
DIPLOMACY: In his annual report to the UN General Assembly, U Thant characterizes the Vietnam War as a nationalist struggle and declares that major powers should "let the Vietnamese themselves deal with their own problems." He also reiterates his earlier appeal for a bombing halt and asserts that the parties to the Paris talks should

seek to reunify North and South Vietnam and neutralize the entire Indochinese peninsula.

September 28
USA – MILITARY: MACV discloses that the enemy has substantially increased its use of Cambodia as a staging area and sanctuary. Recent intelligence reports indicate that NVA-VC military activity in the region nearest Saigon has "increased three-fold" since November 1967.

September 28–October 19
GROUND WAR: A battle begins for the Special Forces camp at Thuong Duc, 20 miles southwest of Danang. The Communists briefly capture the base before being driven out by air and artillery strikes. They then besiege the base, but the marines launch Operation Maui Peak on October 6 to relieve the base. By October 19, the road to Thuong Duc is once again open. Casualties are U.S.: 28 KIA, 100 WIA; NVA/VC: 353 KIA.

September 30
USA – DOMESTIC: Apparently trying to distance himself from Johnson's policies, Hubert Humphrey announces that, if elected, he will halt the bombing of the North if there is any "evidence, direct or indirect, by deed or word" of Communist willingness to restore the DMZ between North and South Vietnam.
AIR WAR: The 900th U.S. aircraft is shot down over the North.
SEA WAR: The USS *New Jersey,* the world's only active battleship, arrives in Vietnamese waters and goes into action, shelling North Vietnamese positions in the DMZ with its 16-inch guns.

U.S. battleship *New Jersey* off the coast of Vietnam *(Texas Tech University Vietnam Archive)*

October 1

CHINA: Foreign Minister Chou En-lai offers China's support for "heroic Vietnamese people."

October 3

USA – DOMESTIC: General Curtis E. LeMay, running mate of independent presidential candidate George Wallace, causes a storm of controversy by seeming to advocate using nuclear weapons in Vietnam.

GROUND WAR: Twenty-four U.S. personnel die when a U.S. Army CH-47 helicopter collides with a U.S. C-7 Caribou transport aircraft over Camp Evans, 11 miles north of Hue. All aboard both aircraft perish in the crash.

AIR WAR: In the heaviest raid over North Vietnam since July 2, U.S. planes destroy 45 supply craft and 31 trucks and sever roads in more than 20 places.

October 4

GROUND WAR: U.S. Marines reoccupy the abandoned base at Khe Sanh to establish an artillery position to support ongoing search and destroy operations in the area.

October 5

NORTH VIETNAM: A statement issued by the North Vietnamese Water Conservation Ministry charges that the United States is intensifying its air strikes against dikes, dams, and other water management projects.

October 8

RIVER WAR: Operation Sealords (Southeast Asia Lake, Ocean, River, and Delta Strategy), a U.S. Navy-South Vietnamese navy operation, is launched with the objectives of cutting enemy supply lines from Cambodia and disrupting enemy base areas in the Mekong Delta and other inland waterways. Operations will be conducted in conjunction with the U.S. 9th Infantry Division's Riverine Assault Force, ARVN, and South Vietnamese marines. The U.S. Navy's participation in the operations will cease in 1971, when the operation will become a South Vietnamese navy responsibility.

October 9–14

NEGOTIATIONS: Sounding out the United States, a North Vietnamese representative in Paris asks Ambassador Harriman whether the United States would "stop the bombing if we give you an affirmative clear answer to the question of Saigon participation" in the talks. Harriman immediately relays the proposal to President Johnson, who turns to General Abrams and Ambassador Ellsworth Bunker in Saigon for their assessment of the query. When they respond that they "interpret the exchange to mean that Hanoi is ready for a shift in tactics from the battlefield to the conference table," Johnson instructs Bunker to present the matter to President Thieu. The South Vietnamese leader agrees to a bombing halt, but insists that Allied military pressure in South Vietnam be continued.

October 10

SOUTH VIETNAM: After rumors of an attempted coup, President Thieu asserts on national television that his government is under no threat. On the previous day, however, ARVN troops in the capital were put on a state of maximum readiness.

October 11

USA – DOMESTIC: In San Francisco, 7,000 protesters, including 200 soldiers, 100 reservists, and 700 veterans, take part in a protest march, the first of its kind to be organized and led by servicemen.

October 12

USA – DOMESTIC: In an address to a symposium at De Pauw University, former presidential adviser McGeorge Bundy advocates an unconditional bombing halt and a substantial withdrawal of U.S. forces from South Vietnam.

October 14

USA – MILITARY: U.S. Defense Department officials announce that the army and Marine Corps will be sending about 24,000 men back to Vietnam for involuntary second tours, citing the length of the war, high turnover of personnel resulting from one-year duty tours, and a tight supply of experienced officers.

October 15

USA – MILITARY: After a decrease in communist military activity, MACV reports that NVA regular troops appear to have been withdrawn to border areas to regroup and that infiltration into the South has declined. Although U.S. officials believe that the enemy is using the current battlefield lull to prepare for another offensive, they do not reject the possibility that this is a political signal intended to break the present impasse in the Paris negotiations.

October 16

NEGOTIATIONS: Ambassador Harriman, aware that a breakthrough in the talks may be imminent, attempts to sweeten the pot by suggesting that Hanoi would be eligible for various forms of economic aid if a negotiated settlement can be reached.

October 16–22

SOUTH VIETNAM: In a series of meetings with Ambassador Bunker, President Thieu insists that North Vietnam agree to three conditions prior to a bombing halt: that it respect the neutrality of the DMZ, stop shelling South Vietnamese cities and towns, and agree to South Vietnamese participation in the Paris talks. He also demands that the NLF be excluded from the negotiations.

October 16–April 24, 1969

GROUND WAR: The ARVN 2nd Regiment conducts Operation Lam Son-271 in Quang Tri Province. There are 603 enemy casualties by the end of the operation.

October 17

USA – DOMESTIC: The *New York Times* reveals a U.S. plan to halt the bombing of North Vietnam if Hanoi makes concessions.

October 18

USA – DOMESTIC: Rumors that the administration will soon announce a bombing halt send sales volume on the New York Stock Exchange soaring; U.S. bond prices also climb.

October 21
POWs: The United States releases 14 North Vietnamese sailors.

October 22
SOUTH VIETNAM: Appearing to soften his previous stance somewhat, President Thieu states that he is no longer against a cessation of bombing.

October 24–December 6
GROUND WAR: The U.S. 5th Marine Regiment conducts Operation Henderson Hill, a continuation of Operation Mamaluke Thrust, as part of a search and clear effort in Quang Nam Province, I Corps. Casualties are U.S.: 35 KIA, 231 WIA; NVA/VC: 700 KIA.

October 26–29
GROUND WAR: In the first major enemy ground assault in over a month, U.S. 1st Infantry Division troops are attacked in Tay Ninh Province, 59 miles north of Saigon near the Cambodian border. U.S. B-52s conduct 22 strikes in the Tay Ninh area in an effort to disperse a reported massing of North Vietnamese forces.

October 27
BRITAIN: An estimated 50,000 persons march through the streets of London protesting the Vietnam War.

October 28
GROUND WAR: The U.S. Army's 1st Cavalry Division begins its move from I Corps Tactical Zone to an area northwest of Saigon in III Corps.

October 29
USA – GOVERNMENT: General Abrams secretly returns to Washington and in talks with President Johnson states that, given current battlefield conditions, he can accept the military consequence of a complete cessation of the bombing of North Vietnam. This represents a significant change in Abrams's previous stance.

October 31
USA – GOVERNMENT: Five days before the presidential election, President Johnson announces on national television that, due to favorable developments in the Paris talks, he has ordered a complete halt to the bombing and naval bombardment of North Vietnam. He further discloses that Hanoi has agreed to allow the South Vietnamese government to participate in the peace talks, while the United States has consented to a role for the NLF, though the latter concession "in no way involves recognition of the National Liberation Front in any form." Domestically, the president's action draws widespread acclaim with both major presidential candidates expressing their full support. The reaction in Saigon, however, is much more subdued; President Thieu issues a communique declaring that the United States has acted unilaterally in its decision to halt the bombing.

AIR WAR: With President Johnson's announcement of a bombing halt, Operation Rolling Thunder comes to an end. After three years and nine months, the results of the bombing campaign are unimpressive. A total of 304,000 sorties have been flown over North Vietnam with very little appreciable impact on the war in the South.

November

AIR WAR: U.S. Air Force launches Operation Commando Hunt, a joint-service effort to interdict enemy supply lines along the 1,700-mile length of the Ho Chi Minh Trail.

GROUND WAR: Operation Phoenix begins. The program focuses on identifying, infiltrating, and destroying the VC infrastructure—the upper echelon of NLF political cadres and party members. It becomes one of the most controversial operations undertaken by U.S. personnel in Vietnam, but the North Vietnamese will later admit that the program was very effective in targeting the VC infrastructure.

November 1

USA – GOVERNMENT: U.S. officials in Washington disclose that there will be a three-fold increase in the number of air strikes along the Ho Chi Minh trail in Laos to compensate for the bombing cessation over North Vietnam. It is believed that President Johnson has approved the intensified attacks on enemy infiltration routes to obtain support from U.S. military commanders for his decision to terminate air raids against the North.

USA – MILITARY: The U.S. mission in Saigon initiates the Le Loi program, an intensified civic action campaign intended to repair the damage done by the enemy's 1968 offensive and to return control of the rural population to pre-Tet levels.

November 2

SOUTH VIETNAM: In a speech before the South Vietnamese National Assembly, President Thieu states that South Vietnam will boycott the Paris talks because the NLF has been admitted as a separate delegation. It is later revealed that a prominent Nixon supporter influenced Thieu and Ky by offering them better terms after Nixon was elected if they refused to participate. Vice President Ky supports Thieu's decision, telling a group of legislators that President Johnson's decision to terminate the bombing indicates that "We can trust the Americans no longer—they are just a band of crooks."

November 2–7

GROUND WAR: Elements of the U.S. 1st Cavalry Division and the 1st ARVN Division conduct Operation Comanche Falls III, a combined sweep of an area approximately 20 miles northwest of Hue in Thua Thien Province, I Corps. Casualties are U.S.: 20 KIA, 57 WIA, 2 MIA; ARVN: 21 KIA, 102 WIA; NVA/VC: 4,242 KIA, 37 POW.

November 6

USA – DOMESTIC: Eight years after losing the presidential election in 1960 to John F. Kennedy, Richard M. Nixon makes a comeback, narrowly defeating Hubert Humphrey in the 1968 presidential election, promising to bring the war to an end and achieve "Peace with Honor."

November 7–April 2, 1969

GROUND WAR: The U.S. 1st Cavalry Division, 11th Armored Cavalry Regiment, and two ARVN Ranger battalions conduct Operation Sheridan Sabre in Binh Long, Phuoc Long, and Tay Ninh Provinces, III Corps. The objective of the operation is to block North Vietnamese infiltration from Cambodia. Casualties will be U.S.: 219 KIA, 1,387 WIA, 6 MIA; NVA/VC: 2,898 KIA, 53 POW.

November 8

SOUTH VIETNAM: As a condition for South Vietnamese participation in the expanded Paris talks, President Thieu proposes a two-sided conference: "Each side is to consist of a single delegation headed by the principal party. Our side—the victims of aggression—will be headed by South Vietnam. Our delegation will include the United States and, if necessary, our other allies. The other side is the side of the Communist aggressors, to be headed by North Vietnam. Their delegation can include members of Hanoi's auxiliary forces, labeled as the NLF." Both Washington and Hanoi reject the proposal.

November 8–9

AIR WAR: U.S. B-52s conduct air strikes against a suspected enemy force of 35,000 men about five miles from the Cambodian border, in Tay Ninh Province.

November 9

SOUTH VIETNAM: The Saigon government files a protest with the International Control Commission charging that enemy forces have shelled population centers in 14 provinces since the bombing halt.

November 10

GROUND WAR: North Vietnamese guns, firing from inside the DMZ, shell U.S. Marine positions just south of the buffer zone for the first time since President Johnson announced the bombing halt; a marine air and artillery counterattack destroys 10 enemy bunkers.

November 11

USA – GOVERNMENT: President-elect Richard Nixon is briefed at the White House by key members of the Johnson administration. He promises that he will let Johnson speak for him on the war until he assumes office in January 1969.

November 12

USA – GOVERNMENT: Speaking at a news conference in Washington, Defense Secretary Clifford warns that, if South Vietnam does not agree soon to participate in the talks, the United States may conduct negotiations without them.

November 13

USA – GOVERNMENT: The Johnson administration charges that recent North Vietnamese artillery strikes from inside the DMZ have violated the agreement upon which the bombing halt is based. A North Vietnamese official in Paris later denies the accusation in a statement asserting that the United States has violated the buffer zone with naval and ground fire. The spokesman also contends that U.S. reconnaissance flights over the North constitute further violations.

November 14

SOUTH VIETNAM: The South Vietnamese government closes down a Saigon newspaper for publishing a detailed account of Defense Secretary Clifford's criticisms of the Thieu regime. It is the 10th newspaper that the government has suspended or shut down in the past three weeks.

November 15
USA – MILITARY: MACV announces that recent intelligence reveals that the movement of military vehicles in southern North Vietnam has increased by 300 percent since the bombing ended, while NVA troop and supply movements north of the DMZ have quadrupled. Aerial observations also reveal that work crews have repaired all bombed-out bridges between the 17th and 19th parallels.

November 16
DIPLOMACY: There are sharp diplomatic exchanges between Washington and Hanoi over alleged NVA activity in the DMZ.

November 17
CAMBODIA: The Cambodian government charges that South Vietnamese patrol boats shelled the village of Prek Koeus in Kampot Province, killing 12 civilians and wounding another 12.

November 19
USA – GOVERNMENT: At a White House ceremony, President Johnson presents Medals of Honor to Capt. James Taylor, Spec. 4 Gary G. Wetzel, Sgt. Sammy L. Davis, Spec. 5 Dwight H. Johnson, and Chaplain Angelo J. Liteky.

November 20–December 9
GROUND WAR: U.S. Marines conduct Operation Meade River, a cordon and search operation in support of the Le Loi, or "accelerated pacification," program in Quang Nam Province, I Corps. Operating 10 miles south of Danang between the La Tho and Ky Lam Rivers, the U.S. 9th Marines place a cordon of troops around an area believed to contain 1,400 enemy troops and then move in to engage the trapped NVA and VC forces. Casualties are U.S.: 107 KIA, 385 WIA; NVA/VC: 841 KIA, 182 POW.

November 23
USA – MILITARY: MACV reports that 210 "indications of enemy activity and presence" inside the DMZ, ranging from sightings of enemy vehicles to artillery strikes, have been recorded since the bombing halt.

November 26
SOUTH VIETNAM: After intense U.S. pressure, South Vietnamese foreign minister Tran Chanh Thanh announces that, following several weeks of discussion with U.S. officials, his government has decided to take part in the Paris peace talks despite the presence of the NLF.
GROUND WAR: Responding to intelligence reports that NVA troops 500 yards inside the DMZ pose a threat to the marine base at Con Thien, U.S. and ARVN forces enter the buffer zone for the first time since the bombing halt and drive the enemy back from its advance positions.

November 29
NLF: Hanoi Radio broadcasts an NLF directive calling for a new offensive to "utterly destroy" Allied forces. The broadcast adds that the operation is particularly concerned

with eliminating the "Phoenix Organization" units, which are targeting the VC infrastructure in the South.

December 1
USA – DOMESTIC: The National Commission on Causes and Prevention of Violence issues a report, *Rights in Conflict,* characterizing the behavior of the Chicago police during the Democratic National Convention as "gratuitous and mindless."

December 1–May 31, 1969
GROUND WAR: Elements of the U.S. 9th Infantry Division, including the Mobile Riverine Force, conduct Operation Speedy Express in the Mekong Delta south of Saigon. Casualties (through January 31 only) are U.S.: 40 KIA, 312 WIA; NVA/VC: 10,889 KIA.

December 7–March 8, 1969
GROUND WAR: The U.S. 1st Marine Division conducts Operation Taylor Common in the An Hoa Basin in Quang Nam Province, I Corps. Casualties will be U.S.: 151 KIA, 1,324 WIA; NVA/VC: 1,398 KIA, 29 POW.

December 8–February 10
GROUND WAR: The ARVN 1st Ranger Group conducts operation Le Loi I in Quang Nam Province, claiming 695 enemy casualties by the end of the operation.

December 11
GROUND WAR: The U.S. mission in Saigon issues a statement declaring that 73.3 percent of the South Vietnamese live in relatively secure areas controlled by the

William Colby, head of CORDS, visits RF/PF troops. *(Texas Tech University Vietnam Archive)*

Saigon government; the report also claims an increase of 3.5 percent in Saigon-controlled areas since the interception of the Le Loi and Phoenix programs.

December 12

NEGOTIATIONS: Responding to North Vietnamese and NLF demands that the four delegations to the Paris negotiations be seated at separate tables, Nguyen Cao Ky refuses to consent to any seating plan that will place the NLF on an equal footing with Saigon. The issue is one of several procedural points, to include the shape of the table, that will deadlock the talks.

December 12–13

AIR WAR: In South Vietnam, U.S. B-52s pound numerous targets north of Saigon in an apparent effort to disrupt an expected enemy offensive.

December 15

USA – GOVERNMENT: Defense Secretary Clifford states that the United States has no "obligation" to keep 540,000 troops in Vietnam until a final political settlement is concluded and suggests that the administration and the North Vietnamese arrange a de-escalation once the expanded talks begin.

December 15–February 28, 1969

GROUND WAR: The Americal Division conducts Operation Fayette Canyon in Quang Nam Province, I Corps. Casualties will be U.S.: 2 KIA, 17 WIA; NVA/VC: 327 KIA, 4 POW.

December 16

USA – DOMESTIC: In a decision concerning an appeal by 57 military reservists, the Supreme Court refuses to review the federal government's constitutional right to send reservists to Vietnam in the absence of an official declaration of war.

December 17

USA – DOMESTIC: Senator George McGovern (D-S.D.) characterizes Nguyen Cao Ky as a "little tinhorn dictator" in a statement complaining that Saigon is deliberately trying to delay the peace talks. A Gallup Poll indicates that the majority of Americans are now ready to let South Vietnam take over the fighting and assume a leading role in the peace talks.

December 18

USA – DOMESTIC: Dr. Henry Kissinger, in an article published in *Foreign Affairs*, proposes that the peace talks proceed on two tracks: the United States and North Vietnam arranging a mutual withdrawal of forces in one set of negotiations, while South Vietnam and the NLF forge a political settlement in separate discussions. He further asserts that the United States can accept neither military defeat nor an externally imposed change in the South Vietnamese government, but that, once North Vietnam has withdrawn its forces from the South, the United States has no obligation to maintain the Saigon government by force.

December 23

NEGOTIATIONS: Tran Buu Kiem, NLF representative in Paris, rejects any direct negotiations between the NLF and Saigon, adding that "if one wants to settle a conflict, one settles it between the direct adversaries," which in this case are the United States and the Viet Cong.

December 27

GROUND WAR: MACV reports that there were 140 enemy-initiated violations of the Christmas truce. The Saigon government issues a statement dismissing 30 members of its 80-man peace delegation for a "violation of national discipline."

December 30

GROUND WAR: Allied forces announce that they will not observe a 72-hour New Year's cease-fire unilaterally declared by the Viet Cong.

December 31

YEAR-END SUMMARY: U.S. military personnel in Vietnam number 536,100; 14,314 U.S. military personnel have been killed during this year, bringing the total American losses since 1959 to 30,610. An additional 200,000 Americans were wounded during the year. There are 65,600 Free World Military Forces personnel now in Vietnam; 978 FWMF personnel were killed during the year. South Vietnamese strength has increased to 820,000 with 20,482 South Vietnamese troops killed during 1968, bringing to 88,343 the total number of South Vietnamese military personnel killed in action to date. Estimated NVA/VC losses for the year are 35,774 KIA, bringing the total number of reported killed since 1961 to 439,000.

1969

January 1–August 31

GROUND WAR: Elements of U.S. 9th Infantry Division and ARVN 5th Regiment conduct Operation Rice Farmer in the Mekong Delta, IV Corps; operation will result in 1,860 enemy soldiers reported killed.

January 1–December 31

GROUND WAR: The U.S. 9th Infantry Division and the ARVN 7th, 9th, and 21st Divisions conduct Operation Quyet Thang, a multi-division yearlong search and clear operation in support of pacification programs in the Mekong Delta, IV Corps. Casualties will be U.S.: 178 KIA, 1,836 WIA; NVA/VC: 37,874 KIA, 500+ POW.

January 2

GROUND WAR: The New Year 72-hour cease-fire proclaimed by the Viet Cong ends. **NEGOTIATIONS:** U.S. and North Vietnamese negotiators meet in Paris for four hours in an attempt to break the impasse in the peace talks, which have stalled due to a controversy over the shape of the conference table.

January 4

USA – GOVERNMENT: President-elect Nixon announces that he will ask Ellsworth Bunker to remain at his post as ambassador to South Vietnam.

January 5

USA – GOVERNMENT: President-elect Nixon names Henry Cabot Lodge to succeed W. Averell Harriman as chief U.S. negotiator at the Paris peace talks. Lawrence

Edward Walsh, a New York lawyer and deputy attorney general, is named deputy chief negotiator to replace Cyrus R. Vance.

RIVER WAR: The U.S. Navy announces that it has established the final link of interlocking water patrols along a 150-mile stretch of the Cambodian–South Vietnamese border; more than 100 vessels are involved.

January 6

SOUTH VIETNAM: Le Minh Tri, education minister in the government of South Vietnam, dies 10 hours after a bomb is thrown in his car. The police refuse to specifically blame the VC as Tri had made many enemies in fighting corruption in the educational system and had received many death threats.

January 10

GROUND WAR: The VC ambush and wipe out a nine-man U.S. patrol near Dong Tam in the Mekong Delta; the VC also mortar several town and military bases elsewhere in the region.

DIPLOMACY: Sweden announces it will establish full diplomatic relations with North Vietnam.

January 11

CAMBODIA: A U.S. helicopter is shot down by Cambodian antiaircraft gunners. One crew member is killed and three are rescued. Prince Norodom Sihanouk charges that the helicopter intruded into Cambodian territory.

January 13

SOUTH VIETNAM: In preparation to counter an anticipated enemy offensive, all special leaves for South Vietnamese troops are cancelled.

January 13–February 9

GROUND WAR: In the largest amphibious assault of the war, U.S. Marines and troops from the 2nd ARVN Division land on the Batangan Peninsula, as part of Operation Bold Mariner, a cordon and search mission in Quang Ngai Province, I Corps. Casualties are U.S.: 5 KIA, 32 WIA; NVA/VC: 60 KIA, 26 POW.

January 13–July 21

GROUND WAR: U.S. Marines, soldiers from the American Division, and South Vietnamese troops will take into custody 470 Viet Cong suspects during the conduct of Operation Russell Beach, a complementary operation to Bold Mariner meant to clear guerrilla forces from the Batangan Peninsula. During the course of Bold Mariner and Russell Beach, more than 12,000 civilians are checked out and relocated off the Batangan Peninsula to the Quang Ngai City area of I Corps. Combined casualties will be U.S.: 56 KIA, 268 WIA; NVA/VC: 158 KIA, 104 POW.

January 14

USA – GOVERNMENT: In a combined State of the Union address and final message to the nation, President Johnson urges the country to press its "quest for peace" in Vietnam.

GROUND WAR: U.S. forces from the 25th Infantry Division kill 122 enemy troops while beating back an attack on a supply convoy northwest of Saigon; seven Americans are killed and 10 wounded.

SOUTH VIETNAM: A government spokesman proposes that U.S. forces start a "gradual, phased withdrawal" from South Vietnam.

January 15

USA – GOVERNMENT: President Johnson sends his final budget to Congress calling for Vietnam war-related expenditures of $25,733,000,000 for the fiscal year 1970. This includes a $3,500,000,000 reduction in spending for the war, the first since the United States entered the conflict in Vietnam.

January 16

NEGOTIATIONS: An agreement is reached in Paris for the opening of expanded peace talks; it is agreed that representatives of the United States, South Vietnam, North Vietnam, and the National Liberation Front will sit at a circular table without nameplates, flags or markings. This compromise allows the United States and South Vietnam to speak only of two sides, while allowing North Vietnam and the NLF to speak of four sides.

January 17

NEGOTIATIONS: At a Paris news conference, Tran Hoai Nam, chief spokesman for the National Liberation Front, says that the NLF will participate in the talks as a "fully independent and equal party."

January 18

SOUTH VIETNAM: President Thieu confirms that he has requested the withdrawal of some U.S. troops from South Vietnam in 1969.

NEGOTIATIONS: The expanded Paris peace talks open; negotiators agree to hold the first plenary session on substantive issues early the following week.

January 20

USA – GOVERNMENT: Richard Milhous Nixon is inaugurated as president of the United States and says during his speech that "after a period of confrontation, we are entering an era of negotiation." William Rogers replaces Dean Rusk as secretary of state. Melvin Laird replaces Clark Clifford as secretary of defense. Henry Kissinger replaces Walt Rostow as national security advisor.

January 22

GROUND WAR: U.S. troops find 56 Viet Cong and 100 women and children in a tunnel complex on the Batangan Peninsula.

January 22–March 19

GROUND WAR: The U.S. 9th Marine Regiment (Reinforced) conducts Operation Dewey Canyon north of the A Shau and Da Krong valleys in Quang Tri and Thua Thien Provinces, I Corps. The purpose of the operation is to disrupt enemy logistics and base areas threatening Hue. Casualties are U.S.: 130 KIA, 920 WIA; NVA/VC: 1,617 KIA, 5 POW.

January 24
SOUTH VIETNAM: Saigon city government bans firecrackers during the lunar new year because the VC used firecracker noise during Tet in 1968 to conceal its attack.

January 25
NEGOTIATIONS: The first fully attended meeting of the formal Paris peace talks is held. Ambassador Henry Cabot Lodge, the chief negotiator for the United States, urges an immediate restoration of a genuine DMZ as the first "practical move toward peace." Lodge also suggests a mutual withdrawal of "external" military forces and an early release of prisoners of war.
GROUND WAR: A force of 800 Americans, after a six-day battle, finally succeeds in entirely seizing a village seven miles northwest of Quang Ngai, which had been occupied by about 200 Communist troops.

January 29
GROUND WAR: The VC proclaim a week's cease-fire, February 15–22, for Tet, the Vietnamese lunar new year.

January 30
NEGOTIATIONS: At the second plenary session, Tran Buu Kiem and Xuan Thuy, heads of the National Liberation Front and North Vietnamese delegations respectively, reject Lodge's proposals and condemn American "aggression." They demand that a reduction in the fighting must be tied to a political settlement.

January 31–February 1
INTERNATIONAL: The UN Secretariat receives documents and charges made by the Cambodian government that U.S. and South Vietnamese forces killed and wounded civilians on Cambodian territory on December 14 and during three raids in November 1968.

February 1
SOUTH VIETNAM: A three-month pacification program ends as officials report that one million South Vietnamese have been added to those under the "relatively secure" control of the Saigon government. U.S. officials claim that, as of mid-January, 76.3 percent of the population is "relatively secure." A goal is set for the remainder of 1969 to bring 90 percent of the South Vietnamese population under government control.
NORTH VIETNAM: Le Duan, first secretary of the Communist Party, speaking at a celebration in Hanoi marking the 40th anniversary of the party, warns the North Vietnamese people that they "must be prepared to fight for many more years" to force the withdrawal of U.S. forces from Vietnam.
RIVER WAR: The U.S. Navy turns over 25 heavily-armed river boats to the South Vietnamese navy.

February 6
USA – GOVERNMENT: President Nixon, at a news conference, says that while an American troop reduction in Vietnam is high on his list of priorities, there will have to be progress in the peace talks before he can announce any reduction.

NEGOTIATIONS: In Paris, there is a restatement of earlier proposals and positions. The United States and South Vietnam urge North Vietnam and the NLF to reconsider their proposal to take military steps to reduce the fighting; North Vietnam and NLF negotiators restate their earlier rejection and accuse the United States of trying to separate the military questions from the political problems.

February 7

GROUND WAR: U.S. officials announce that the military operation on the Batangan Peninsula in Quang Ngai Province is a success and report 200 enemy killed and 251 captured since the operation began on January 13.

February 10

NEGOTIATIONS: South Vietnamese vice president Nguyen Cao Ky, political adviser to the delegation from South Vietnam, says his government will negotiate a political settlement with the Viet Cong after North Vietnam withdraws its troops from South Vietnam. Ky states that he would like to see the United States and North Vietnam agree on a mutual withdrawal of forces while leaving the settlement of political issues to the South Vietnamese government and the NLF. On leaving Paris for Hanoi, Le Duc Tho, political adviser to the North Vietnamese delegation, says that the Nixon administration is "pursuing the same policy as the administration of President Johnson."

February 14

USA – DOMESTIC: A Gallup poll indicates that the number of people who want the United States to pull out of Vietnam immediately has risen from 21 to 35 percent of the population.

February 15

GROUND WAR: The seven-day Tet cease-fire proclaimed by the Viet Cong begins. Allied forces announce that they will observe a 24-hour Tet truce.

USA – MILITARY: There are now 539,000 American soldiers in South Vietnam as Allied troop strength reaches an all-time high of 1,610,500.

February 17–October 31

GROUND WAR: In an effort to maintain pressure on the enemy following the 1968 Tet Offensive, U.S. and South Vietnamese forces conduct Operation Toan Thang III, multiple search and destroy operations throughout III Corps. Casualties will be U.S.: 886 KIA, 3,805 WIA (partial total); NVA/VC: 12,051 KIA, 406 POW.

February 22–23

GROUND WAR: The Tet cease-fire ends when Communist forces launch the so-called "post-Tet" offensive, firing rocket and mortar rounds into Saigon and approximately 115 other cities and Allied positions, including Danang, Hue, and the U.S. base at Bien Hoa. Approximately 100 U.S. servicemen are killed during the first 15 hours of fighting; enemy losses are estimated at 1,000.

SWEDEN: More than 200 U.S. draft evaders and military deserters are given refuge in Sweden.

February 23
USA – GOVERNMENT: President Nixon, responding to the new series of enemy attacks, orders a full investigation to determine whether the attacks violate the accord that was responsible for the U.S. bombing halt of North Vietnam on November 1, 1968.

February 24
GROUND WAR: It is reported that nearly 200 Americans have been killed since the "post-Tet" offensive began. Communist forces continue shelling towns and military bases, but the attacks diminish as only about 60 targets are struck.

February 24–March 10
GROUND WAR: The ARVN 2nd Division conducts Operation Quyet Thang-22 in Quang Ngai Province, I Corps. By the end of the operation, 777 enemy casualties will be reported.

February 25
GROUND WAR: Communist troops assault two major installations near Saigon and shell more than 50 towns and bases in the fourth consecutive day of attacks. Near Bien Hoa Air Base, 150 enemy soldiers are reported killed. The 25th Infantry Division headquarters base at Cu Chi is hit by sappers, leaving 38 U.S. dead. Meanwhile, two U.S. positions just south of the DMZ come under heavy attack. Thirty-six U.S. Marines are killed during one attack by an NVA suicide squad. The U.S. losses are described as the highest in a single battle in nearly six months.
NORTH VIETNAM: In a Hanoi radio broadcast, the Foreign Ministry asserts that the "South Vietnamese people" have a right to attack U.S. forces "at any place on Vietnamese territory." North Vietnam also denies that it agreed to any conditions in return for a bombing halt.

February 27
GROUND WAR: U.S. sources put American losses in the current offensive in which the Communists have shelled 30 military installations at between 250 and 300 compared with enemy casualties totalling 5,300. South Vietnamese officials report 200 civilians killed and 12,700 made homeless.
NEGOTIATIONS: At the sixth plenary session of the peace talks in Paris, the United States argues that the post-Tet attacks, particularly the shelling of population centers in South Vietnam, violate the U.S.-North Vietnamese understanding that led to a halt of the bombing of North Vietnam.

February 27–May 8
GROUND WAR: U.S. Marines conduct Operation Purple Martin in Quang Tri Province, I Corps. The operation is aimed at driving North Vietnamese troops back across the DMZ. Casualties will be U.S.: 79 KIA, 268 WIA; NVA/VC: 374 KIA, 4 POW.

February 27–June 20
GROUND WAR: The ARVN 1st Ranger Group conducts Operation Quang Nam in Quang Ngai Province, I Corps; 688 enemy casualties will be reported by the end of the operation.

February 28
GROUND WAR: U.S. troops fight a day-long battle near Saigon.

March 1
SOUTH VIETNAM: President Thieu states that the ongoing Communist offensive has been a "complete failure" and enemy troops "no longer have the ability to sustain themselves."

March 1–April 14
GROUND WAR: The U.S. 4th Infantry Division conducts Operation Wayne Grey in Kontum Province, II Corps; casualties are NVA/VC: 608 KIA.

March 1–August 14
GROUND WAR: Troops from the U.S. 101st Airborne Division and 1st ARVN Division conduct Operation Kentucky Jumper, a continuation of Nevada Eagle aimed at eliminating enemy base areas, lines of communication, and infiltration routes in Thua Thien Province, I Corps. Casualties are U.S.: 58 KIA, 94 WIA (partial count); NVA/VC: 1,675 KIA, 41 POW.

March 2
USA – GOVERNMENT: President Nixon meets in Paris with Ambassador Lodge and South Vietnamese vice president Nguyen Cao Ky.

March 4
USA – GOVERNMENT: President Nixon declares that the United States "will not tolerate" additional attacks and warns that an appropriate response will be made.

March 5
GROUND WAR: Communist forces fire seven rockets into Saigon, resulting in 22 civilians killed and a large number of wounded.

March 6
USA – MILITARY: Secretary of Defense Melvin Laird and Chairman of the Joint Chiefs of Staff General Earle Wheeler arrive in South Vietnam for a five-day visit.

GROUND WAR: MACV reports that 453 Americans were killed during the first week of the post-Tet offensive and 2,593 were wounded. There were 251 South Vietnamese and 6,752 enemy soldiers reported killed during the fighting.

NEGOTIATIONS: The seventh plenary session is broken off when South Vietnam's chief negotiator, Pham Dang Lam, requests to adjourn because an "atmosphere favorable to useful discussion does not exist." Ambassador Lodge reminds North Vietnam and the NLF that the understanding that led to the bombing halt is still in effect.

CAMBODIA: Prince Norodom Sihanouk says he will release four U.S. pilots, captured after their observation plane was downed on February 12, but protests the violation of Cambodian airspace.

March 8
GROUND WAR: Communist gunners increase the attacks on military targets, striking about 50 locations as ground fighting also increases. A North Vietnamese attack on

the 1st Cavalry Division's Firebase Grant, 45 miles northwest of Saigon is turned back when the defenders fire their artillery pieces directly into the attacking troops.
LAOS: U.S. military sources report an incursion of about 100 U.S. Marines into Laos. Elsewhere in I Corps, marines seize about a dozen hilltops just north of Dong Ha, as part of Operation Dewey Canyon, begun in late January.

March 9
GROUND WAR: Communist gunners shell 35 military positions and six civilian communities.

March 12
SOUTH VIETNAM: President Thieu establishes five new cabinet posts and fills several other government positions in a further consolidation of power.
DIPLOMACY: Four U.S. pilots, captured by Cambodian forces, arrive in Thailand after a letter from President Nixon to Prince Sihanouk brings them freedom.

March 13
GROUND WAR: MACV reports 336 U.S. soldiers killed during the second week of the offensive and 1,694 wounded. There are 259 South Vietnamese soldiers, 4,063 enemy soldiers, and 72 civilians reported killed.

March 14
USA – GOVERNMENT: At a news conference, President Nixon says that there is no prospect for a U.S. troop reduction in the foreseeable future because of the enemy offensive. He states that the prospects for withdrawal will hinge on the level of enemy activity, progress in the Paris talks, and the ability of the South Vietnamese to defend themselves.

March 15
GROUND WAR: U.S. Marines move about one mile into the southern section of the DMZ, the first U.S. military force in the area since November 1968. Fighting breaks out three miles north of Gio Linh after a U.S. patrol observes Communist rocket emplacements firing into South Vietnam.

March 15–May 2
GROUND WAR: Troops from the U.S. 5th Infantry Division (Mechanized), U.S. Marines, 2nd ARVN Regiment, and 7th ARVN Cavalry conduct Operation Maine Crag in the southwest corner of Quang Tri as a complementary operation to Dewey Canyon. Casualties will be U.S.: 17 KIA, 104 WIA; NVA/VC: 207 KIA.

March 16
NORTH VIETNAM: Ho Chi Minh urges the Vietnamese people and armed forces to press the fight until the United States is defeated.

March 17
USA – GOVERNMENT: Senator George McGovern (D-S.D.) accuses President Nixon of continuing the "tragic course" of the Johnson administration. The Nixon administration, says McGovern, rather than seeking a military disengagement and

settlement, seems intent on pursuing a "policy of military attrition and moral disaster." Other Senate leaders, notably Senate Majority Leader Mike Mansfield (D-Mont.), say that Nixon should be given "a further chance."

CUBA: Cuba establishes formal diplomatic relations with the National Liberation Front.

March 18

AIR WAR: The United States begins the covert and illegal bombing of Cambodia by U.S. Air Force B-52 bombers striking staging areas and troop concentrations in eastern Cambodia to a depth of five miles from the Vietnam border. The first mission targeting Base Area 353, formally designated Operation Breakfast, was approved by President Nixon at a meeting of the National Security Council on March 15. Additional missions targeting other base areas are code-named Supper, Lunch, Dessert, and Snack. The series of B-52 strikes inside Cambodia become known as the "Menu" bombings. A total of 3,630 flights over Cambodia will drop 110,000 tons of bombs over a 14-month period through April 1970. This bombing and all subsequent "Menu" operations are kept secret from the American public and the U.S. Congress until the *New York Times* reveals their existence in a May 1970 article.

March 19

USA – GOVERNMENT: Secretary of Defense Laird, appearing before the Senate Armed Services Committee, asks for $156,000,000 for a program to increase the capability of South Vietnamese troops so they can replace U.S. forces even before all outside forces have been withdrawn by mutual agreement.

March 20

USA – DOMESTIC: A federal grand jury, under anti-riot provisions of the 1968 Civil Rights Act, indicts eight persons on charges of conspiracy to incite riot during the 1968 Democratic convention in Chicago. Eight policemen are also indicted, seven of them on charges of assaulting demonstrators.

GROUND WAR: MACV reports 351 Americans killed from March 9 to 15, the third week of the enemy offensive. Also reported killed are 325 South Vietnamese soldiers and 4,137 enemy soldiers.

March 20–31

GROUND WAR: Operation Quyet Thang-25 is conducted by the ARVN 4th Regiment in Quang Ngai Province, I Corps.

March 22

USA – DOMESTIC: A Gallup poll of 1,500 Americans indicates that 32 percent favor greatly escalating the war or "going all-out," 26 percent favor pulling out, 19 percent favor a continuation of the current policy, and 21 percent have no opinion. In Washington, D.C., nine antiwar demonstrators, including five Roman Catholic clergymen, are arrested after ransacking the Dow Chemical offices.

March 24

USA – MILITARY: President Nixon names Lieutenant General William B. Rosson as deputy commander of U.S. forces in Vietnam and nominates him for a fourth star.

March 26

USA – DOMESTIC: Women Strike for Peace demonstrators picket Washington, D.C., in the first large antiwar demonstration since Nixon's inauguration.

March 28

GROUND WAR: U.S. officials find a mass grave near Hue containing at least 57 bodies of civilians presumably killed by the Communists in last year's Tet Offensive. More such graves will be found.

March 29

GROUND WAR: U.S. deaths for the week of March 23–29 raise the total to 33,641 KIA—12 more than in the Korean War.

March 30–May 29

GROUND WAR: The U.S. 7th and 26th Marine Regiments conduct Operation Oklahoma Hills to clear North Vietnamese troops from the area southwest of Danang in Quang Nam Province, I Corps. Casualties are U.S.: 44 KIA, 439 WIA; NVA/VC: 596 KIA.

April 1

USA – MILITARY: Secretary of Defense Laird announces that B-52 bomber raids in South Vietnam will be decreased by more than 10 percent as a result of further cuts in next year's defense budget.

NLF: The Liberation News Agency, the news organ of the National Liberation Front, claims that the ongoing offensive has "shattered" the strategic plan conceived by General Abrams following the 1968 Tet offensive.

April 2

SOUTH VIETNAM: A government spokesman announces that the Viet Cong assassinated 201 civilians in the last week of March, bringing the total for the first three months of the year to almost 2,000.

April 3

USA – GOVERNMENT: Secretary Laird announces that the United States is moving to "Vietnamize" the war as rapidly as possible, but warns it does not serve the United States' purpose to discuss troop withdrawals while the enemy is conducting an offensive.

GROUND WAR: U.S. combat deaths for the week of March 23–29 raise the toll to 33,641 Americans killed in eight years of U.S. involvement in Vietnam, 12 more than fell during the Korean War.

April 5–6

USA – DOMESTIC: Antiwar demonstrations occur in several U.S. cities. Thousands of antiwar demonstrators march in New York City demanding that the United States withdraw from Vietnam. The weekend of antiwar protests ends with demonstrations and parades in San Francisco, Los Angeles, Washington, D.C., and other cities.

U.S. MAT advisers train RF platoon. *(Texas Tech University Vietnam Archive)*

April 7

SOUTH VIETNAM: President Thieu, in a State of the Union address to the opening session of the National Assembly in Saigon, offers the enemy a policy of "national reconciliation" in which former Viet Cong members would enjoy full political rights in exchange for the withdrawal of North Vietnamese troops from South Vietnam, Laos, and Cambodia. Thieu stresses that Viet Cong members will be able to participate in South Vietnamese politics only as individuals and not as members of the NLF or any other official Communist party.

April 8

NEGOTIATIONS: A Viet Cong spokesman in Paris rejects Nguyen Van Thieu's proposals.

AIR WAR: MACV reports that five waves of B-52s hit suspected enemy camps near the Cambodian border.

April 9

USA – DOMESTIC: The Chicago Eight, who were indicted on March 20 on federal charges of conspiracy to incite riot at the 1968 Democratic convention in Chicago, plead not guilty. Also on this day, the results of a Gallup poll conducted March

28–31 report that 44 percent approved of the way Nixon was handling the situation in Vietnam, 30 percent reserved judgment or gave no opinion, while 26 percent disapproved.

GROUND WAR: Workers uncover 65 bodies from a grave near Hue, apparent victims of Viet Cong execution squads in the city during the 1968 Tet offensive.

April 10–11
GROUND WAR: The Communist offensive continues with 45 mortar and rocket attacks during the night. Increased ground fighting is reported in the Mekong Delta and in the area northwest of Saigon. The town of Vinh Long, 60 miles southwest of Saigon, suffers the heaviest mortar attack on a provincial capital since the offensive began when it is struck by 100 mortar rounds; 15 persons are reported killed and 103 wounded.

April 14
GROUND WAR: U.S. troops kill 198 Communist soldiers in a massive enemy attack against a firebase 33 miles northwest of Saigon. Thirteen Americans are killed and three wounded.

April 15, 1969–January 1, 1971
GROUND WAR: The U.S. 173rd Airborne Brigade and 4th Infantry Division conduct Operation Washington Green I-II as part of a pacification operation in the An Lao Valley of Binh Dinh Province, II Corps. Casualties will be U.S.: 142 KIA, 1,342 WIA; NVA/VC: 1,957 KIA.

Helicopters of the 170th and 189th Helicopter Assault Companies await the loading of troops in the Central Highlands, April 1969. *(National Archives)*

April 16

DIPLOMACY: In a message to Prince Sihanouk of Cambodia, President Nixon says that the United States "recognizes and respects the sovereignty, independence, neutrality and territorial integrity of the kingdom of Cambodia within its present frontiers." Sihanouk reports that he is ready to resume diplomatic relations with the United States.

April 17

NEGOTIATIONS: At the 13th plenary session, the Paris talks continue to show no progress as Communist negotiators reject Allied proposals for mutual troop withdrawals and repeat their earlier demand that U.S. forces must leave unconditionally and at once.

April 18

USA – GOVERNMENT: President Nixon, at a news conference, says he feels the prospects for peace have "significantly improved" since he took office, largely because of what he terms the greater political stability of the Saigon government and improvement in the South Vietnamese armed forces.

April 18–December 31

GROUND WAR: The ARVN 22nd Division conducts Operation Dan Thang-69 in Binh Dinh Province, II Corps. Enemy casualties are reported at 507 killed and wounded.

April 19

AIR WAR: The United States turns over the first 20 of 60 jet fighter-bombers to be transferred to the South Vietnamese air force.

April 20

SOUTH VIETNAM: A new political party is formed in Saigon opposed to both communism and critical of President Thieu. The party is officially called the Progressive Nationalist Movement and is headed by Dr. Nguyen Ngoc Huy, a member of South Vietnam's delegation to the Paris talks.

April 22–September 22

GROUND WAR: The U.S. 4th Infantry Division conducts Operation Putnam Tiger, a continuation of screening efforts along the South Vietnam/Cambodian border in Kontum and Pleiku Provinces, II Corps. Casualties will be NVA/VC: 563 KIA.

April 23

GROUND WAR: U.S. Marines and North Vietnamese forces clash between Cam Lo and "The Rockpile" in Quang Tri Province, I Corps. Eight Marines are killed and 17 wounded; 14 North Vietnamese soldiers are killed.

April 24–25

AIR WAR: In two days of the heaviest bombing raids of the war, almost 100 B-52 bombers, based in Thailand and Guam, drop close to 3,000 tons of bombs on a border area 70 miles northwest of Saigon.

April 26

GROUND WAR: U.S. forces report killing 213 enemy troops near the Cambodian border, 45 miles northwest of Saigon, in one of the bloodiest battles fought in almost a year, but only one American is killed and one wounded. U.S. planes and artillery attack North Vietnamese gun positions in Cambodia near the border following a Communist assault on a U.S. artillery base on the frontier.

April 27

GROUND WAR: Heavy fighting erupts near the Cambodian border for the second consecutive day as U.S. forces turn back an attack by 300 enemy troops; 100 Communist soldiers and 10 Americans are reported killed.

April 30

DIPLOMACY: Prince Sihanouk withdraws his assent to the resumption of diplomatic relations with the United States because the United States fails to mention its stand regarding the status of a group of offshore islands, including Dao Phu Duoc, claimed by both Cambodia and South Vietnam.

GROUND WAR: The peak U.S. troop strength in Vietnam is achieved—543,482.

April 30–July 16

GROUND WAR: The U.S. 9th Marine Regiment of the 3rd Marine Division conducts Operation Virginia Ridge to prevent further infiltration across the DMZ in northern Quang Tri Province, I Corps. Casualties will be U.S.: 106 KIA, 475 WIA; NVA/VC: 558 KIA, 9 POW.

May 1

USA – GOVERNMENT: In a speech on the floor of the Senate that is widely regarded as the end of a self-imposed moratorium on criticism that senators have been following since the Nixon administration took office, George Aiken (R-Vt.), senior member of the Senate Foreign Relations Committee, urges the Nixon administration to begin an immediate "orderly withdrawal" of U.S. forces from South Vietnam.

May 3

CHINA: Beijing charges that four U.S. jets bombed the southern Chinese town of Nin Mong, 20 miles north of the North Vietnamese border, on May 2. The U.S. Defense Department denies the incident.

May 5

GROUND WAR: Communist soldiers attack a U.S. military camp 65 miles northwest of Saigon; 125 enemy soldiers are reported killed and four are captured. American losses are nine killed and 59 wounded.

May 6

GROUND WAR: A U.S. helicopter crashes and burns 75 miles north of Saigon, killing 34 soldiers in what is believed to be the worst helicopter disaster of the war. To date 2,595 helicopters have been reported lost.

May 8

NEGOTIATIONS: At the 16th plenary session of the Paris talks, the NLF presents a 10-point program for an "overall solution" to the war, calling for an unconditional withdrawal of U.S. and Allied troops from Vietnam, the establishment of a coalition government and the holding of free elections, South Vietnam to settle its own affairs "without foreign interference," and the eventual reunification of North and South Vietnam.

May 9

USA – DOMESTIC: William Beecher, military correspondent for the *New York Times,* authors a page-one dispatch from Washington, "Raids in Cambodia by U.S. Unprotested," which accurately describes the first of the secret B-52 bombing raids in Cambodia. Within hours, Henry Kissinger, presidential assistant for national security affairs, contacts J. Edgar Hoover, the director of the Federal Bureau of Investigation, asking him to find the governmental sources of Beecher's article. During the next two years, General Alexander Haig, a key Kissinger assistant, coordinates the FBI wire tapping of the telephones of a number of reporters and National Security Council staff members.

SOUTH VIETNAM: The Foreign Ministry in Saigon says South Vietnam is prepared to discuss, in private or at a plenary session, three of the NLF's 10 points: the exchange of captives, the restoration of the neutrality of the DMZ and the application of the 1962 agreement on Laos.

May 9–12

GROUND WAR: The U.S. 5th Marines, in an effort to defend the area's rice and corn fields, engages North Vietnamese troops near Hill 67 in the "Arizona" area, about five miles northeast of An Hoa. Six Americans are killed and 12 are wounded; 233 NVA/VC are reported killed in the fighting.

May 10–June 7

GROUND WAR: The U.S. 9th Marine Regiment, 3rd Marine Division, and elements of the 101st Airborne Division (Airmobile) conduct Operation Apache Snow in western Thua Thien Province, I Corps. The purpose of the 2,800-man sweep of the A Shau Valley is to cut off the North Vietnamese there and stop any infiltration from Laos that threatens Hue to the northeast and Danang to the southeast. Total casualties for the operation are U.S.: 113 KIA, 627 WIA; NVA/VC: 977 KIA, 5 POW.

May 10–20

GROUND WAR: As part of Operation Apache Snow, U.S. paratroopers, pushing northeast, find a large number of Communist forces entrenched on Ap Bia Mountain (Hill 937). In fierce fighting against the 29th NVA Regiment, directed by Major General Melvin Zais, the mountain comes under heavy Allied air strikes, artillery barrages, and 10 bloody infantry assaults. Friendly fire from two Cobra gunships kills two and wounds 35 at command post of the 3rd Battalion, 187th Infantry. The Communist stronghold is captured in the 11th attack when 1,000 troops of the 101st Airborne Division and 400 South Vietnamese soldiers fight their way to the summit of the mountain. There are 630 North Vietnamese reported killed. U.S. casualties are listed as 70 killed and 373 wounded. Due to the intense fighting and the high loss of life, the battle for Ap Bia Mountain is dubbed "Hamburger Hill." U.S. forces will abandon the hill on May 27 and U.S. intelligence will report on June 17 that more than 1,000 North Vietnamese have reoccupied the hill.

May 11–12

GROUND WAR: Communist forces shell 159 cities, towns, and military bases throughout South Vietnam, including Saigon and Hue, in the largest number of attacks since the 1968 Tet Offensive. The headquarters of five of nine U.S. divisions were targets. In a series of attacks near Saigon, 14 persons are reported killed and about 100 wounded. Initial reports claim at least 500 Communist soldiers killed.

May 13

GROUND WAR: In a Communist attack on a U.S. camp near the Laotian border, 20 Americans are killed and 65 wounded; 20 North Vietnamese are reported killed.

May 14

USA – GOVERNMENT: In his first full-length report to the American people on the Vietnam War, President Nixon responds to the 10-point plan offered by the National Liberation Front. Nixon proposes a phased, mutual withdrawal of major portions of U.S., Allied, and North Vietnamese forces from South Vietnam over a 12-month period, with the remaining non-South Vietnamese forces withdrawing to enclaves and abiding by a cease-fire until withdrawals are completed. Nixon also insists that North Vietnamese forces withdraw from Cambodia and Laos at the same time and recommends internationally supervised elections for South Vietnam. Nixon's offer of a "simultaneous start on withdrawal" represents a revision of the last formal proposal offered in October 1966, known as the "Manila formula," in which the United States stated that the withdrawal of U.S. forces would be completed within six months after the North Vietnamese leave South Vietnam.

NEGOTIATIONS: Tran Buu Kiem, speaking at a luncheon in Paris, says the 10-point program put forth by the NLF "forms a whole" and says that he is opposed to only partial acceptance of the NLF program.

GROUND WAR: Communist forces shell Danang as 22 South Vietnamese are reported killed and 21 are wounded.

DIPLOMACY: Prime Minister Lee Kuan Yew of Singapore meets with President Nixon at the White House and cautions against hasty U.S. withdrawal from Vietnam.

May 15–June 7

USA – GOVERNMENT: Eight Democratic members of the House of Representatives introduce legislation asking President Nixon to withdraw 100,000 troops unconditionally and to call for a cease-fire.

GROUND WAR: The ARVN 42nd Regiment and 22nd Ranger Group conduct Operation Dan Quyen 38-A ("People's Rights") in Ben Het-Dak To area of II Corps, claiming 945 enemy killed by the end of the operation.

May 16–August 13

GROUND WAR: Elements of the Americal and 101st Airborne Divisions conduct Operation Lamar Plain southwest of Tam Ky in Quang Tin Province, I Corps. Casualties will be U.S.: 105 KIA, 333 WIA; NVA/VC: 524 KIA, 11 POW.

May 18

GROUND WAR: More than 1,500 Communist troops attack U.S. and South Vietnamese camps near Xuan Loc, 38 miles east of Saigon in III Corps. The attackers are driven off after five hours of intense fighting. At the U.S. camp, 14 Americans are killed and 39 wounded; 24 enemy soldiers are killed. At the South Vietnamese camp, four South Vietnamese are killed and 14 wounded, with 54 Communist soldiers reported killed and nine captured. In another battle near the Laotian border, 12 Americans are killed and 79 wounded, with enemy casualties reported at 125 KIA.

May 20

USA – DOMESTIC: As part of a growing outcry over U.S. military policy in Vietnam, Edward Kennedy (D-Mass.), in a Senate speech, scorns the military tactics of the Nixon administration, in particular the battle for Ap Bia Mountain, as "senseless and irresponsible."

May 21

GROUND WAR: A MACV spokesman in Saigon defends the battle for Ap Bia Mountain as necessary to stop enemy infiltration and protect Hue.

May 22

GROUND WAR: In Phu Bai, Major General Melvin Zais, commander of the 101st Airborne Division, which took Ap Bia Mountain, says his orders were "to destroy enemy forces" in the A Shau Valley and says that he did not have any orders to reduce casualties by avoiding battle. The U.S. military command in Saigon states that the recent battle for Ap Bia was an integral part of the policy of "maximum pressure" that has been pursued for the last six months and confirms that no orders had been received from President Nixon to modify the basic strategy.

NEGOTIATIONS: Ambassador Lodge, at the 18th plenary session of the Paris talks, says he finds common ground for discussion in the proposals of President Nixon and the NLF. In reply, Nguyen Thanh Le, spokesman for the North Vietnamese, says the programs are "as different as day and night."

May 24

NEGOTIATIONS: Xuan Thuy, head of the North Vietnamese delegation, says that while there are "points of agreement" between the proposals of President Nixon and the NLF, it is necessary for the United States to abandon its support of the South Vietnamese government for the conference to progress.

May 25

SOUTH VIETNAM: President Thieu assumes personal leadership of the National Social Democratic Front at its inaugural meeting in Saigon, saying the group is "the first concrete step in unifying the political factions in South Vietnam for the coming political struggle with the Communists," and emphasizing that the new party will not be "totalitarian or despotic."

May 27

GROUND WAR: U.S. troops abandon Ap Bia Mountain. A spokesman for the 101st Airborne Division says that U.S. troops "have completed their search of the mountain, and are now continuing their reconnaissance-in-force mission throughout the A Shau valley." When this is reported in the United States, there is much dismay that this terrain will be abandoned after the bloody battle to capture it has resulted in great loss of life.

May 30

SOUTH VIETNAM: President Thieu, concluding a four-day visit to South Korea, says at a news conference that he will "never" agree to a coalition government with the NLF. Regarding the role of the NLF in possible elections, Thieu says that "if the Communists are willing to lay down their weapons, abandon the Communist ideology and abandon atrocities, they could participate in elections."

June 1

GROUND WAR: A U.S. Special Forces camp is cut off for a month; by the end of the siege U.S. casualties will total 100 KIA and WIA.

June 3

DIPLOMACY: South Vietnamese president Thieu, on a four-day state visit to Taiwan, issues a joint communiqué with Chiang Kai-shek declaring that the "absurd demand" for "a coalition government must be resolutely rejected."

June 5

AIR WAR: American planes make the first raids against North Vietnam since the bombing halt of November 1, 1968, in retaliation for the shooting down of a reconnaissance aircraft.

June 5–7

GROUND WAR: In Tay Ninh and Binh Long Provinces, allied officers report finding the bodies of 447 Communist soldiers strewn over 11 battlefields after two nights of fighting along the Cambodian border in III Corps. Five Americans are killed-in-action and 21 are wounded. In another battle, 10 U.S. Marines are killed and 24 wounded near Khe Sanh. During the night 65 Communist shellings are reported. Danang is struck by 45 rockets in three separate attacks in which four U.S. airmen are killed and 37 wounded.

June 8

USA – GOVERNMENT: While meeting at Midway island in the Pacific with President Thieu, President Nixon announces the planned withdrawal of 25,000 American combat troops before the end of August. Nixon and Thieu underscore the point that U.S. forces will be replaced by South Vietnamese forces. This is the official announcement of "Vietnamization," a new program designed to turn the war over to the South Vietnamese as U.S. troops are withdrawn.

June 8–August 14

GROUND WAR: The 101st Airborne Division and 3rd ARVN Regiment conduct Operation Mont-

Soldiers of the Royal Thai Black Panther Division display enemy weapons captured after a battle with the Viet Cong in Binh Long Province in June 1969. *(Texas Tech University Vietnam Archive)*

gomery Rendezvous, a follow-on operation to Apache Snow to deny the North Vietnamese use of the A Shau Valley in Thua Thien Province, I Corps. Casualties will be 451 NVA/VC: 451 KIA, 8 POW.

June 9

SOUTH VIETNAM: President Thieu, in a televised news conference in Saigon, attempts to counter the pessimism following President Nixon's announcement at Midway on the previous day by saying "this is a replacement, not a withdrawal. Withdrawal is a defeatist and misleading term."

NEGOTIATIONS: An NLF spokesman says that the refusal of Nixon and Thieu to accept a coalition government for South Vietnam is "an obstacle to progress" in the Paris negotiations.

June 10

USA – GOVERNMENT: President Nixon says the Midway meeting has "opened wide the door to peace" and invites North Vietnam "to walk with us through that door." Nixon challenges North Vietnam to begin withdrawing forces or to begin serious negotiations or both.

SOUTH VIETNAM: The NLF and other opponents of the Saigon regime form the Provisional Revolutionary Government (PRG) of South Vietnam. The position of the PRG is declared to be no different in substance from NLF policy. The formation of the PRG is seen as a challenge to the Thieu government for political control of South Vietnam.

June 11

GROUND WAR: Communist forces stage heavy ground attacks on two U.S. bases south of Danang. Viet Cong troops cut through the defense perimeter and fight the defenders in hand-to-hand combat at a base at Tam Ky, 35 miles south of Danang. Sixteen Americans are killed and 62 Communist soldiers are reported KIA in the bitter fighting.

NEGOTIATIONS: In Paris, the Provisional Revolutionary Government presents a 12-point "program of action" at a news conference. The program is basically the same as that set forth by the NLF in its earlier 10-point program. Under the new political arrangement, the NLF would remain the "organizer and leader" of the resistance to the "aggression" by the United States, while the PRG will be responsible for internal and foreign policy.

June 12–15

DIPLOMACY: Bulgaria, Cambodia, China, Cuba, Czechoslovakia, East Germany, Hungary, Mongolia, North Korea, North Vietnam, Poland, Rumania, Syria, the Soviet Union, and Yugoslavia recognize the Provisional Revolutionary Government.

June 13

USA – GOVERNMENT: The U.S. government discloses it used wiretapping devices to eavesdrop on the "Chicago Eight," antiwar activists who were indicted for inciting riots during the 1968 Democratic national convention. The government contends that it had the right to eavesdrop without court approval on members of an organization it believed to be seeking to attack and subvert the government.

LAOS: Premier Souvanna Phouma acknowledges publicly for the first time that U.S. planes regularly carry out bombing raids in Laos and says the bombing will continue as long as North Vietnam uses Laotian bases and infiltration routes.

AIR WAR: B-52 bombing missions over the Ho Chi Minh Trail in southern Laos will rise to 5,567 in 1969, up from 3,377 in 1968, according to Pentagon statistics. The B-52s, no longer permitted to bomb North Vietnam since the November 1968 bombing halt, are increasingly diverted to Laos and, in secret, to Cambodia. Nearly 160,000 tons of bombs will be dropped on the Ho Chi Minh Trail in 1969, a 60 percent increase from 1968. The total number of bombing sorties by U.S. land- and sea-based warplanes will rise to 242,000 in 1969.

June 14

USA – MILITARY: In accordance with Nixon's Midway speech, MACV announces that three combat units are to be withdrawn; they include the 1st and 2nd Brigades, 9th Infantry Division, and Regimental Landing Team 9, 3rd Marine Division, a total of about 13,000–14,000 men. The remainder of the 25,000 to be withdrawn are support troops.

June 14–15

GROUND WAR: North Vietnamese forces twice attack 3rd Brigade headquarters of the 101st Airborne Division atop a 2,000-foot peak just east of Ap Bia Mountain. Eighty-one North Vietnamese are reported killed. U.S. losses are 18 killed and 47 wounded.

June 16

GROUND WAR: Troops of Thailand's Black Panther Division repel 500 Viet Cong attackers who assault their base 20 miles east of Saigon three times. The defenders, aided by U.S. close air support, attack helicopters, and artillery, report killing 212 enemy soldiers while losing six killed and seven wounded.

June 17

USA – MILITARY: U.S. intelligence reports that an estimated 1,000 North Vietnamese troops have reoccupied Ap Bia Mountain.

GROUND WAR: U.S. officials disclose the launching of a combined U.S.-South Vietnamese search-and-destroy operation on June 8 in the A Shau Valley, 28 miles southwest of Hue. Twenty-one Americans have been killed and 130 wounded thus far in Operation Montgomery Rendezvous, a follow-on to Apache Snow, which included the Battle of Hamburger Hill.

June 17–21

GROUND WAR: MACV reports increased fighting below the DMZ. An estimated 250 enemy troops are reported killed during the five-day period, while 30 Americans are killed and 71 wounded.

June 19

USA – DOMESTIC: Former secretary of defense Clark Clifford, writing in the journal *Foreign Affairs,* proposes a timetable for withdrawal from Vietnam that calls for the removal of 100,000 combat troops in 1969 and an additional 100,000–150,000 troops by the end of 1970. President Nixon, speaking at a news conference after the publication of the article, expresses the "hope that we could beat Mr. Clifford's timetable."

GROUND WAR: Communist forces shell 12 targets near the city of Tay Ninh, 50 miles northwest of Saigon and 12 miles from the Cambodian border, followed by six attacks on the city itself and its surrounding villages. About 1,000 civilians flee their homes as Allied and Communist troops fight in the city streets. It is reported that 146 Communist soldiers are killed. Americans losses are three killed and 14 wounded. Elsewhere in the same province, VC units ambush a U.S. convoy.

June 21
GROUND WAR: Approximately 600 Communist soldiers storm a U.S. base near Tay Ninh. Seven Americans are killed and 18 wounded. Communist losses around Tay Ninh in the last two days are estimated at 194 killed.

June 23
GROUND WAR: Ben Het, a U.S. Special Forces camp located six miles from the junction of the Cambodian, Laotian, and South Vietnamese borders, is besieged and cut off by 2,000 North Vietnamese troops using artillery and mortars. The base is defended by 250 U.S. soldiers and 750 South Vietnamese Montagnards.

June 25
RIVER WAR: The U.S. Navy turns over to the South Vietnamese navy 64 river patrol gunboats valued at $18.2 million in what is described as the largest single transfer of military equipment in the war thus far. The transfer raises the total number of boats in the South Vietnamese navy to more than 600.

June 26
GROUND WAR: A force of 180 South Vietnamese troops is airlifted into Ben Het to help relieve the beleaguered garrison there. A U.S. military spokesman reports that 100 U.S. servicemen have been killed or wounded at Ben Het since June 1.

June 27
GROUND WAR: A total of 445 artillery shells strike Ben Het, more than double the total for any previous day.

USA – DOMESTIC: In a pictorial article entitled "Vietnam—One Week's Dead," *Life* magazine publishes the photographs of the 242 American military personnel killed in Vietnam during the week of May 28–June 3, 1969.

June 28
GROUND WAR: A 1,500-man South Vietnamese force begins new sweeps around Ben Het. U.S. units remain in an advisory role and supply only air and artillery support. MACV reportedly considers the Ben Het campaign a test of the ability of the South Vietnamese forces to stand up against the North Vietnamese and Viet Cong. Meanwhile, U.S. sources in Saigon report that North Vietnamese infiltration into South Vietnam in January–May was 40 percent lower than in the corresponding 1968 period.

USA – DOMESTIC: A Gallup poll shows 42 percent of the American people favor a faster withdrawal of U.S. troops than that ordered by President Nixon, while 16 percent favor a slower rate; 29 percent favor a total withdrawal, 61 percent are opposed, and 10 percent undecided.

July 2

SOUTH VIETNAM: Ninety-two of 135 South Vietnamese house deputies sign a letter to President Thieu asking him to dismiss Premier Tran Van Huong.

USA – DOMESTIC: Senator George McGovern (D-S.D.) reveals that he met privately with the chief North Vietnamese and National Liberation Front negotiators in Paris on May 22. McGovern says that he is convinced that fruitful negotiations cannot begin unless the United States agrees to "unconditional withdrawal" from Vietnam and discontinues its "unqualified embrace" of the Thieu-Ky government.

GROUND WAR: A convoy of South Vietnamese armored personnel carriers reaches Ben Het over a road from Dak To that has been blocked for a week by North Vietnamese troops. Allied commanders report that the siege of Ben Het has been broken, as combat activity in the last 24 hours declines to its lowest level in a month.

July 3

GROUND WAR: The U.S. military command in Saigon reports that three North Vietnamese regiments (about 7,500 men) have withdrawn across the DMZ during the past three weeks.

July 7

USA – MILITARY: The first U.S. troops to be withdrawn from South Vietnam depart Saigon. Eight hundred men of the 3rd Battalion, 60th Infantry, 9th Infantry Division, leave for home. They will land at McChord Air Base in Washington the next day. The unit will be stationed at nearby Fort Louis.

July 9

USA – DOMESTIC: David Dellinger, a member of the Chicago Eight and chairman of the National Mobilization Committee to End the War in Vietnam, arrives in Paris

Troops from the 9th Infantry Division depart from Saigon airport on 7 July 1969 as part of the first increment of the U.S. troop withdrawal. *(Texas Tech University Vietnam Archive)*

at the invitation of the North Vietnamese delegation to arrange the release of three U.S. prisoners-of-war with the encouragement of the State Department.

July 10
GROUND WAR: MACV announces the lowest casualty figures in six months for the week ending July 5; 153 soldiers are reported killed and 722 wounded as a battlefield lull moves into its third week. During this period, 247 South Vietnamese soldiers are killed and 586 wounded.

USA – DOMESTIC: David Dellinger announces that a team of U.S. pacifists will fly to Hanoi to bring home three U.S. prisoners-of-war.

July 11
SOUTH VIETNAM: President Thieu, in a televised speech, makes a "comprehensive offer" for a political settlement that challenges the National Liberation Front to participate in free elections organized by a joint electoral commission and supervised by an international body. Following the speech, Foreign Minister Tran Chanh Thanh clarifies the Thieu proposal, saying that the Communists can never participate in elections in South Vietnam "as communists" nor have any role in organizing elections and that only the South Vietnamese government can organize elections.

USA – DOMESTIC: The U.S. First Circuit Court of Appeals in Boston reverses the 1968 conviction of Dr. Benjamin Spock on charges of conspiracy to counsel evasion of the draft.

July 12
GROUND WAR: Communist gunners shell a U.S. 9th Division center processing troops to be returned home. Two are killed and 21 wounded.

July 13
USA – DOMESTIC: George Wallace criticizes President Nixon for his handling of the war and says he favors an all-out military victory if the Paris talks fail to produce peace soon.

USA – MILITARY: The 4th Battalion, 47th Infantry, 9th Infantry Division, departs from South Vietnam.

July 14
USA – MILITARY: The 1st Battalion, 9th Marines, 3rd Marine Division, departs from South Vietnam.

July 15
NEGOTIATIONS: President Nixon sends a secret letter to Ho Chi Minh declaring that he solemnly desires "to work for a just peace." Defending his proposal of May 14 as "fair to all parties," Nixon says that "there is nothing to be gained by waiting." At the same time Jean Sainteny, a retired French diplomat, after conferring with Nixon and Henry Kissinger, relays a U.S. proposal for holding secret negotiations to Xuan Thuy, the chief North Vietnamese representative to the Paris talks, for transmittal to Hanoi. Hanoi will ultimately accept the secret proposal.

USA – GOVERNMENT: Secretary of Defense Laird, testifying before a Senate committee, says there has been no change in the battlefield orders to U.S. commanders to maintain "maximum pressure" on the enemy. Laird, however, admits that the present military strategy is under review.

USA – DOMESTIC: A U.S. federal appeals judge overrules a lower court judge, allowing antiwar activist Rennie Davis, under federal indictment on charges of having conspired to incite disorder during the 1968 Democratic convention, to fly to Hanoi to aid in the release of three U.S. prisoners of war.

SOUTH VIETNAM: Vice President Nguyen Cao Ky, in a speech made during his first public appearance in five months, says President Thieu's offer of July 11 challenging the NLF to participate in free elections constitutes a "grave step backward" in the national policy of anti-communism.

July 16–September 25

GROUND WAR: The U.S. 3rd Marine Regiment conducts Operation Idaho Canyon, a series of sweeps of the northern Quang Tri-DMZ area in I Corps. Casualties will be U.S.: 78 KIA, 366 WIA; NVA/VC: 565 KIA and 5 POW.

July 17

NEGOTIATIONS: At the 26th plenary session of the Paris talks, the Communist delegations formally reject President Thieu's offer of July 11 calling for free elections in South Vietnam with nonorganized Communist participation.

July 17–20

USA – MILITARY: General Wheeler, chairman of the Joint Chiefs of Staff, conducts four days of conferences and inspections with U.S. commanders in South Vietnam in an effort to assess the battlefield lull, determine the progress of the South Vietnamese armed forces, and to discuss future strategy.

July 18

USA – MILITARY: The 3rd Battalion, 47th Infantry, 9th Infantry Division, departs South Vietnam.

July 19

NORTH VIETNAM: Ho Chi Minh, marking the anniversary of the 1954 Geneva Accords, says no free elections can be held in South Vietnam while U.S. troops remain there and the Thieu government remains in power.

July 20

USA – GOVERNMENT: A top-secret plan, commissioned by presidential assistant Henry Kissinger, is completed by the office of the chief of naval operations. Code-named Duck Hook, the study proposes measures for military escalation against North Vietnam. The military options include a massive bombing of Hanoi, Haiphong, and other key areas of North Vietnam; a ground invasion of North Vietnam; the mining of harbors and rivers; and a bombing campaign designed to sever the main railroad links to China. Altogether 29 major targets in North Vietnam are pinpointed for destruction in a series of air attacks planned to last four days and to be renewed until Hanoi capitulates.

GROUND WAR: A VC force of unknown size attacks the U.S. 9th Infantry Division headquarters at Dong Tam in the Mekong Delta, IV Corps. Six American soldiers are wounded in the attack.

July 21–September 21

GROUND WAR: Troops from the U.S. 1st Infantry Division and 8th ARVN Regiment conduct Operation Strangle in Binh Duong Province, III Corps. The objective of the operation is to neutralize enemy forces in the "Iron Triangle" and "Trapezoid" areas. Casualties will be NVA/VC: 365 KIA, 35 POW.

July 22

USA – GOVERNMENT: As President Nixon begins a trip to Asia, he meets with Secretary of Defense Laird and General Earle Wheeler, who has just returned from South Vietnam. Wheeler reports that the situation there is "good" and that the program to improve the South Vietnamese armed forces is on schedule.

July 23

GROUND WAR: U.S. troops of the 1st Brigade, 9th Infantry Division, departing for the United States, turn over a fire support base at Cai Lay in the Mekong Delta to the ARVN 7th Division.

July 25

USA – GOVERNMENT: In a briefing in Guam for the news media accompanying him on his trip to Asia, President Nixon discusses at length the future role the United States should play in Asia and the Pacific after the conclusion of the Vietnam War. The president's remarks are quickly labeled as the "Nixon Doctrine" and are interpreted to mean that, while the United States will have primary responsibility for the defense of allies against nuclear attack, the noncommunist Asian nations must bear the responsibility for their own defense against conventional attack, as well as their own internal security.

July 26

SOUTH VIETNAM: President Thieu says his proposal of free elections with Viet Cong participation is "the final solution we can afford to offer."

GROUND WAR: U.S. combat deaths drop to 110 for the week of July 20–26. This is the lowest weekly total since January 1 and the fourth lowest in two years.

July 28

GROUND WAR: In the biggest battle since the combat lull began, more than 1,000 U.S. troops from 2nd Brigade, 25th Infantry Division, supported by tanks and armored personnel carriers, surround an enemy stronghold known as "the Citadel" in Hau Nghia Province, about 25 miles north of Saigon. In daylong fighting the Americans struggle through hedgerows and bunkers before overwhelming a Viet Cong force identified as elements of two battalions of the 268th Viet Cong Regiment; 53 enemy KIA are reported. U.S. losses total three dead and 14 wounded.

July 29

GROUND WAR: In III Corps, elements of the 2nd Brigade, 25th Infantry Division, reinforce a Special Forces CIDG camp under fire near the Plain of Reeds. U.S. casualties include eight KIA and nine WIA; enemy losses are reported as 65 KIA.

July 30

USA – GOVERNMENT: President Nixon makes an unscheduled 5½ hour visit to South Vietnam, where he meets with President Thieu and privately discusses U.S.

troop withdrawals and possible changes in military tactics with U.S. commanders. Nixon also visits U.S. troops of the 1st Infantry Division at Di An, 12 miles south of Saigon.

July 31

USA – GOVERNMENT: President Nixon visits India and discusses the Vietnam war with Prime Minister Indira Gandhi. Nixon says he visited South Vietnam to demonstrate his solidarity with President Thieu and praises Thieu as one of the four or five best leaders in the world.

August 1

AIR WAR: It is announced that the 27 aircraft lost in the previous week bring total losses for the conflict to date to 5,690.

August 4

POWs: Radio Hanoi announces the release of three U.S. prisoners of war. The POWs (Captain Wesley Rumble, Lieutenant Robert Frishman, and Seaman Douglas Hegdahl) are to be turned over to the custody of a pacifist group led by Rennie Davis; they are the first U.S. prisoners freed by the North Vietnamese since August 2, 1968.

NEGOTIATIONS: First secret session takes place between Henry Kissinger and North Vietnamese representative Xuan Thuy at the apartment of Jean Sainteny in Paris. Kissinger reiterates the May 14 proposal calling for a mutual withdrawal of North Vietnamese and U.S. troops and also warns that if no progress is made by November 1 toward ending the war, the United States will consider measures of "grave consequences." Xuan Thuy replies that North Vietnam considers the National Liberation Front's 10-point proposal to be the only "logical and realistic basis for settling the war." The negotiations end with only the agreement to keep open the new, secret channel of communications.

President Richard Nixon shakes hands with troops during a brief visit to Vietnam, July 1969. *(Texas Tech University Vietnam Archive)*

August 6

WAR CRIMES: The U.S. Army announces that Colonel Robert Rheault and seven other Green Berets have been charged with premeditated murder and conspiracy to commit murder of a South Vietnamese national whom they suspected of being a double agent. The officers are confined in Long Binh military prison, 12 miles northeast of Saigon.

August 7

GROUND WAR: A VC raid on the U.S. hospital at Cam Ranh Bay leaves two U.S. personnel dead and 99 injured, of whom 53 are patients. Before withdrawing, the

Communist commandos destroy 10 wards, damage three others, and blow up the hospital's water tower and officer barracks. In a separate incident, several explosions rip through the South Vietnamese air force school in Saigon, killing eight and injuring 62, including four Americans.

August 8

GROUND WAR: Fourteen Americans and 17 South Vietnamese are killed in military actions ranging from the DMZ to the Saigon area. The heaviest combat occurs near the DMZ where 102 enemy soldiers are reported killed. In the same action 164 Americans and 51 South Vietnamese are wounded.

August 8–20

GROUND WAR: U.S. and South Vietnamese forces clash with the North Vietnamese in a series of battles in northern Binh Long Province, III Corps. In one fierce battle near Loc Ninh, elements of the U.S. 11th Armored Cavalry Regiment and ARVN Rangers kill 77 enemy soldiers.

August 9

GROUND WAR: In military action near Danang, 600 U.S. troops go to the aid of two U.S. units. There are 138 Communist soldiers reported killed. U.S. losses are 15 killed and more than 50 wounded. In a separate action, about 50 B-52 bombers hit

Paratroopers from 1st Battalion, 501st Infantry, treat wounds received during action east of Tam Ky, August 1969. *(National Archives)*

North Vietnamese troop concentrations 70 miles north of Saigon, along the Cambodian border. After being forced from cover, a North Vietnamese force of about 100 soldiers comes under ground attack by U.S. infantry, resulting in a total of 64 Communists killed and six captured.

August 10
GROUND WAR: North Vietnamese soldiers attack two U.S. Marine bases 1,500 meters apart near the DMZ. During the bitter fighting that ensues, 17 marines are killed and 83 wounded. Seventeen enemy bodies are found inside the perimeter of one marine camp.

August 12
GROUND WAR: Communist forces launch a new offensive with attacks on 150 cities, towns, and bases. The heaviest attacks are aimed at the area adjacent to the Cambodian border northwest of Saigon, where an estimated 2,000 Communists attack Tay Ninh, Quan Loi, Loc Ninh, and An Loc. Farther north, North Vietnamese commandos fight their way into the U.S. 1st Marine Division headquarters compound in Danang, but are eventually driven out by the marines who kill 40 Communist soldiers while sustaining five killed and 23 wounded in the process.

August 12–14
GROUND WAR: U.S. Marines and NVA regulars fight an intense battle in the "Arizona Territory," in Quang Nam Province. U.S. casualties include 22 KIA and 100 wounded, while North Vietnamese losses total 255 killed.

August 13
GROUND WAR: MACV headquarters reports 1,450 enemy killed during the previous 24 hours in the heaviest fighting in three months. Ninety Americans and 107 South Vietnamese are killed during the action.

August 14
USA – MILITARY: In response to congressional criticism, the Department of Defense concedes that the number of U.S. troops in Vietnam has actually increased since President Nixon took office, but attributes the increase to troop arrivals scheduled during the Johnson administration.

August 14–15
GROUND WAR: U.S. troops kill 96 enemy soldiers when Communist forces unsuccessfully attempt to storm U.S. camps in Hau Nghia, Tay Ninh, and Binh Long Provinces in III Corps.

August 15
USA – MILITARY: The Department of Defense releases figures revealing that U.S. troop strength in Vietnam currently stands at 534,200.

August 17–26
GROUND WAR: U.S. troops from the American Division report killing at least 650 North Vietnamese in a bitter battle in the Que Son Valley, 30 miles south of Danang.

More than 60 Americans are reported killed in the fighting. During the height of the battle on August 24, Company A of the 196th Light Infantry Brigade refuses the order of its commander to continue combat operations; they have made repeated unsuccessful attempts to reach a downed U.S. helicopter and told their lieutenant that they had "simply had enough." After the battalion executive officer talks to the troops, they move out, reaching the helicopter only to find all eight men aboard dead. Neither the soldiers nor their lieutenant are disciplined, but the officer is transferred to another assignment in the division.

August 21–22

USA – GOVERNMENT: President Nixon and South Korean president Park Chung Hee meet in San Francisco. In his welcoming address, Nixon notes that South Korea has "more fighting men in South Vietnam than any other nation" except the United States and South Vietnam. The United States will spend $250 million in 1969 to maintain South Korea's 50,000-man contingent in South Vietnam.

A soldier in Vietnam, 1969 (National Archives)

August 22

USA – GOVERNMENT: The United States and Thailand agree to begin negotiations on the reduction of the 49,000-man American presence in Thailand. These forces are primarily involved in conducting air operations against Communist troops in Laos and South Vietnam.

August 23

SOUTH VIETNAM: President Thieu chooses Deputy Premier and Interior Minister Tran Thien Khiem, a close and powerful friend, to replace Tran Van Huong as premier. A new cabinet is to be presented to the South Vietnamese people on September 1.

August 24

GROUND WAR: U.S. troops battle Communist soldiers for more than seven hours 28 miles north of Saigon. A total of 28 enemy troops are reported killed. Another 30 Communist soldiers are reported killed in three other clashes near the city. Two Americans are killed and five wounded in the fighting. Communist forces again shell the U.S. hospital at Camn Ranh Bay.

August 25–December 31

GROUND WAR: The ARVN 4th Regiment conducts Operation Lien Ket-414 in Quang Ngai Province, I Corps. There are 710 enemy casualties reported by the end of the operation.

August 26

USA – MILITARY: MACV announces that the departure of troops in the next two days will complete the 25,000-man withdrawal announced by President Nixon at Midway on June 8.

August 26–December 31

GROUND WAR: The ARVN 5th Regiment launches Operation Lien Ket-531 in Quang Tin Province, I Corps. There are 542 enemy casualties by the end of the operation.

August 27

USA – MILITARY: The 1st and 2nd Brigades of the U.S. 9th Infantry Division depart Vietnam. The 3rd Brigade remains in-country and is reassigned to the 25th Infantry Division.

August 28

GROUND WAR: Sharp fighting again erupts in the Danang area. Communist losses are reported at 18. U.S. losses are 13 marines killed and 42 wounded. The Department of Defense reports that 93,653 Communist soldiers were killed during the first half of the year, January 1–June 30. This number is down from the 119,000 Communist troops reported killed during the same period the previous year.

August 30

NORTH VIETNAM: Ho Chi Minh's reply to President Nixon's letter of July 15 is received in Paris. Ho accuses the United States of a "war of aggression" against the Vietnamese people, "violating our fundamental national rights" and warns that "the longer the war goes on, the more it accumulates the mourning and burdens of the American people." Ho says he favors the National Liberation Front's 10-point plan as "a logical and reasonable basis for the settlement of the Vietnamese problem." Ho demands that the United States "cease the war of aggression," withdraw its troops from Vietnam, and allow self-determination for the Vietnamese people. President Nixon will not reveal this communication until his speech to the nation on November 3.

September 1

SOUTH VIETNAM: President Thieu and Premier Tran Thien Khiem name a new 31-member cabinet, strong in technicians and soldiers but lacking political leaders. Khiem, in a ceremony at the presidential palace, says that there will be no radical changes in policy. The cabinet does not include any representatives of the noncommunist opposition, leaders of religious groups, or any leaders of the factions of the pro-government National Social Democratic Front.

September 3

Ho Chi Minh dies in Hanoi at the age of 79.

September 4–5

HANOI: Radio Hanoi announces the death of Ho Chi Minh and says that the NLF will halt military operations for three days, September 8–11, in mourning for Ho.
NORTH VIETNAM: Premier Zhou Enlai (Chou En-lai) and a delegation from China hold talks with First Secretary Le Duan and other members of the North Vietnamese

Politburo. The Chinese leaders assure the North Vietnamese of their continued support in the war against the United States.

September 5

WAR CRIMES: Lieutenant William Calley is charged with six specifications of premeditated murder in the deaths of 109 Vietnamese civilians at My Lai in March 1968.

GROUND WAR: North Vietnamese gunners shell Danang and nearby installations. At least 13 civilians are killed. In a Communist attack on a bridge south of Danang, three U.S. Marines are killed and 30 wounded. A Viet Cong rocket attack sets fire to tons of food at a U.S. Navy storage area east of the city. Communist ground forces attack nine other Allied bases. About 140 Communist soldiers are reported killed. Twenty Americans and 30 South Vietnamese are also killed.

September 6

NORTH VIETNAM: The Communist Party newspaper *Nhan Dan* and Radio Hanoi announce that Ho Chi Minh is to be succeeded by a committee consisting of Le Duan, first secretary of the party; Truong Chin, member of the Politburo and chairman of the National Assembly; General Vo Nguyen Giap, defense minister; and Premier Pham Van Dong.

GROUND WAR: Three battles rage in the jungles north of Saigon as Communist gunners shell 40 targets during the night. In the fighting, 91 Communist soldiers, 35 Americans, and 68 South Vietnamese are reported killed.

September 9

NORTH VIETNAM: Funeral services, attended by 250,000 mourners, are held for Ho Chi Minh in Hanoi's Ba Dinh Square. Among those in attendance are Soviet premier Aleksey Kosygin, Chinese vice-premier Li Hsien-nien, and Prince Norodom Sihanouk of Cambodia.

GROUND WAR: A South Vietnamese military spokesman says government troops have increased their offensive operations during the Viet Cong-proclaimed cease-fire. U.S. and Communist forces curtail their military activity. Nearly all U.S. bombers in South Vietnam are grounded.

September 10

CAMBODIA: Norodom Sihanouk expresses support for the "just stand" of the North Vietnamese and calls on the United States to withdraw from South Vietnam.

GROUND WAR: As Communist forces shell more than 30 Allied military installations, the U.S. forces resume military operations at the same level as before the cease-fire.

September 10–November 15

GROUND WAR: Elements of the U.S. 1st Infantry Division and the 3rd Brigade, 82nd Airborne Division, conduct Operation Yorktown Victor in Binh Duong Province, III Corps. This is the last operation for the 3rd Brigade, 82nd Airborne, which will subsequently redeploy from South Vietnam.

CORDS advisers meet with hamlet chief in Binh Dinh Province, 1969. *(Texas Tech University Vietnam Archive)*

September 13
SOUTH VIETNAM: After President Thieu proposes elections to include the NLF, Vice President Ky warns that any coalition with the NLF will provoke a coup within 10 days.

GROUND WAR: Allied forces report killing 113 Communist soldiers in the course of repulsing a heavy attack on a village near Quang Ngai. Damage to the village includes 260 houses destroyed and eight civilians killed.

USA – MILITARY: In response to increasing Communist attacks, the White House announces the resumption of B-52 raids following a 36-hour suspension.

September 14
GROUND WAR: North Vietnamese troops are reported to be in the Mekong Delta for the first time in the war. This movement is reported to have taken place in the four weeks since U.S. troops departed the region as part of President Nixon's withdrawal plan.

September 15
GROUND WAR: A regular North Vietnamese unit, 2,000 men from the 18th Regiment, attacks a government training center six miles north of Tri Ton in the Mekong Delta, but the attack fails, with a reported loss of 83 enemy troops killed.

September 16

USA – GOVERNMENT: President Nixon announces a plan to withdraw an additional 35,000 troops.

GROUND WAR: U.S. helicopter gunships mistakenly open fire on a group of civilians in the Mekong Delta, killing seven and wounding 17. South of the DMZ in I Corps, 25 U.S. Marines are killed and 63 wounded in fighting with North Vietnamese forces.

September 17

GROUND WAR: NVA troops assault two U.S. Marine outposts just below the DMZ, killing 23 Americans and wounding 24 from the 3rd Regiment, 3rd Marine Division. A total of 23 North Vietnamese soldiers are reported killed during the fighting.

September 18

USA – MILITARY: MACV announces that two Marine Corps regiments stationed along the DMZ and an army airborne brigade assigned to guard Saigon, a total of 19,500 men, will make up the combat contingent of the next increment of the U.S. troop withdrawal program, which had been announced by President Nixon two days earlier.

USA – DOMESTIC: It is disclosed that antiwar protesters will be organizing a 36-hour "March Against Death" to take place in Washington in November; at the same time, there will be another rally in San Francisco. This effort is led by Dr. Benjamin Spock and 10 other representatives of the New Mobilization Committee to End the War in Vietnam.

September 19

USA – GOVERNMENT: President Nixon announces the cancellation of the draft calls for November and December, previously scheduled for 32,000 and 18,000 respectively.

September 21

AIR WAR: Thirty-five U.S. B-52s drop more than 1,000 tons of ordnance on an NVA troop concentration north of the Rockpile, a U.S. Marine base near the DMZ, following attacks there September 17.

September 23

USA – DOMESTIC: The trial of eight antiwar activists, who become known as the Chicago 8, opens in Chicago as 1,000 young people demonstrate outside the courthouse.

GROUND WAR: A company of more than 130 South Vietnamese troops, led by U.S. Green Berets, suffers more than 50 percent casualties in heavy fighting six miles from the Cambodian border, about 65 miles northwest of Saigon. Seven ARVN soldiers are killed and 62 wounded. The enemy suffers 35 killed after U.S. fighter-bombers are called in to support the ARVN troops.

September 24

USA – MILITARY: MACV reports that all 62 South Vietnamese aboard an Air Vietnam DC-4 and two people on the ground are killed when the DC-4 collides with a U.S. jet at Danang airport. The U.S. jet landed safely.

September 25

TERRORISM: Nineteen die in two terrorist incidents near Danang. VC commandos throw a grenade into a meeting place, killing four civilians and one policeman; 26 civilians are wounded. A bus strikes a mine 95 miles southeast of Danang killing 14 civilians.

USA – GOVERNMENT: Senator Charles Goodell (R-N.Y.) proposes legislation that would require the withdrawal of U.S. troops from Vietnam by the end of 1970.

September 26

USA – GOVERNMENT: President Nixon, speaking at a news conference, cites "some progress" in the effort to end the Vietnam War and says "we're on the right course in Vietnam." He urges the American people to give him the support and time he needs to end the war honorably, saying, "If we have a united front, the enemy will begin to talk." Nixon brands the attitude of Senator Goodell and others like him in Congress as "defeatist."

USA – DOMESTIC: Twenty-four liberal Democratic congressmen hold a caucus in which they decide to endorse the nationwide protest scheduled for October 15 and press in Congress for resolutions calling for an end to the war and a withdrawal of U.S. troops.

GROUND WAR: MACV discloses that a U.S. helicopter mistakenly attacked a group of civilians near Tan Ky, killing 14.

CHINA: In Beijing, North Vietnam and China sign a new agreement of military and economic aid for an undisclosed sum for 1970.

September 27

SOUTH VIETNAM: President Thieu says his government entertains no "ambition or pretense" to take over all fighting by the end of 1970, but given proper support South Vietnamese troops can replace the "bulk" of U.S. troops in 1970. Thieu says his agreement on any further U.S. troop withdrawals will hinge on whether his requests for equipment and funds for ARVN forces are granted.

September 29

USA – MILITARY: Stanley Resor, secretary of the army, announces that the U.S. Army, conceding that it is helpless to enlist the cooperation of the CIA to gather evidence in the case, is dropping the murder charges of August 6 against Colonel Robert Rheault and seven other Green Berets accused of killing a Vietnamese national.

September 29–December 31

GROUND WAR: The ARVN 32nd Regiment begins Operation Quyet Thang-21/38 in An Xuyen Province, IV Corps.

September 30

USA – MILITARY: The U.S. and Thai governments announce a planned withdrawal of 6,000 Americans, mostly airmen, from Thailand, to be completed by July 10, 1970.

People's Self-Defense Forces prepare for operations in Thua Thien Province, 1969. *(Texas Tech University Vietnam Archive)*

October

POWs: An *Air Force* magazine cover story, "The Forgotten Americans of the Vietnam War," ignites national concern for the prisoners of war and the missing in action. It is reprinted in condensed form as the lead article in the November 1969 issue of *Reader's Digest*, and read in its entirety on the floor of Congress and inserted into the *Congressional Record* on six different occasions. This article stirs the conscience of the nation and rallies millions to the cause of the POWs and MIAs.

October 1

USA – GOVERNMENT: President Nixon allows draft deferments for graduate students.

October 3

USA – MILITARY: MACV announces that the U.S. military effort is being shifted from battlefield support to military and technical training in the ongoing campaign to turn the responsibility for the war over to the South Vietnamese armed forces.

October 4

USA – MILITARY: General Wheeler, chairman of the Joint Chiefs of Staff, visits Vietnam to check on the progress of Vietnamization.

October 7

USA – GOVERNMENT: President Nixon, in a meeting at the White House with Premier Souvanna Phouma of Laos, gives assurances that the United States will insist on a withdrawal of North Vietnamese forces from Laos and Cambodia as part of any settlement of the Vietnam War. The Laotian leader requests increased American military aid.

USA – MILITARY: At his departure following a four-day inspection trip in South Vietnam, General Wheeler reports that "progress in Vietnamization is being steadily and realistically achieved," but U.S. forces will have to assist the South Vietnamese "for some time to come."

October 8

USA – DOMESTIC: Members of Students for a Democratic Society (SDS) clash with Chicago police during a demonstration outside the site of the "Chicago 8" trial; 40 demonstrators are arrested.

October 9

USA – MILITARY: Secretary of Defense Laird, reporting on General Wheeler's trip to Vietnam at a news conference, announces that U.S. commanders in Vietnam have been given new orders aimed at placing the "highest priority" on shifting the burden of the fighting to the ARVN forces. Laird describes the new tactics as "protective reaction," but says that the new orders do not forbid U.S. commanders from seeking out and attacking enemy troops that pose threats. Other government sources announce that only 64 Americans were killed in the week of September 28–October 4, the lowest weekly total since the end of 1966.

USA – DOMESTIC: The National Guard is called in as demonstrations continue in Chicago outside the trial of the Chicago 8.

October 10

USA – Military: The U.S. Navy transfers 80 river patrol boats to the South Vietnamese navy in the largest single transfer of naval equipment since the war began.
Ground War: South Vietnamese armed forces assume responsibility for the defense of Saigon as the last U.S. combat contingent in the city is moved to an area 20 miles away.

October 11

USA – Domestic: A Gallup poll reports that 57 percent of Americans say they would like to see Congress pass legislation that calls for the withdrawal of all U.S. troops by the end of 1970.

October 15

USA – Domestic: "National Moratorium" demonstrations attract huge crowds in Washington, D.C., and other major cities involving hundreds of thousands of people. The demonstrations range from rallies to prayer vigils and involve a broad spectrum of the population. The protest, as a nationally coordinated antiwar demonstration, is considered unprecedented.

October 16

USA – Military: Secretary of Defense Laird announces U.S. plans to keep a "residual force" of some 6,000 to 7,000 troops in South Vietnam after hostilities end there.

October 19

Ground War: Communist military activity intensifies. It is reported that South Vietnamese troops successfully engaged North Vietnamese forces in two major battles in the U Minh Forest of the Mekong Delta, killing 116 North Vietnamese soldiers. ARVN losses are six killed and 16 wounded. In another battle 85 miles northeast of Saigon, U.S. troops kill a reported 14 enemy troops while suffering five dead.

October 21

Ground War: Seven Americans are killed and 20 wounded in six short but sharp battles north and west of Saigon. A total of 46 Communist soldiers are reported killed. Two more Americans are killed when their spotter plane is downed by enemy ground fire.

October 22

Ground War: U.S. field commanders contend that there has been no basic change in their orders on military strategy and tactics. The officers do admit, however, that there are restrictions, such as no ground assaults against fortified areas. The commanders deny that they have been ordered to keep casualties down and say that the battlefield situation does not even remotely resemble a cease-fire. The commanders add that they had never even heard of Secretary of Defense Laird's phrase "protective reaction."

October 24

USA – Military: The U.S. Army Blackhorse base near Xuan Loc, 38 miles northeast of Saigon, headquarters of the U.S. Army's 11th Armored Cavalry, is turned over to ARVN's 18th Division to be used as an infantry regiment base and training center.

GROUND WAR: Units of the U.S. 25th Infantry Division fight one of the biggest battles in some time 28 miles north of Saigon. Forty-seven Communist soldiers are killed. American losses include 10 killed and 12 wounded.

October 29

USA – DOMESTIC: Chicago 8 defendant Bobby Seale is gagged and chained to his chair at his trial for conspiracy to incite riot. The judge's order comes after Seale repeatedly shouts accusations and insults at the judge and prosecution. In November, Seale's conduct will force the judge to try him separately, and the remaining defendants will become known as the Chicago Seven.

October 31

AIR WAR: U.S. B-52s bomb the Central Highlands to protect U.S. Special Forces camps at Duc Lap and Bu Prang from North Vietnamese forces, which are reported concentrating near the Cambodian border for a future attack.

November 1–December 28

GROUND WAR: The ARVN 23rd Division conducts Operation Dan Tien-33D in Quang Duc Province, II Corps. There are 746 enemy casualties reported by the end of the operation.

November 3

USA – GOVERNMENT: President Nixon makes a major televised speech on his Vietnam policy, appealing for national unity and promising that U.S. troops will be pulled out according to an "orderly scheduled timetable." To gather support for his policies in Vietnam and in an attempt to blunt the renewed strength of the antiwar movement, he appeals to the "silent majority" that favors his Vietnamization plan of gradual American withdrawal from Vietnam. As he spoke, dispatches from South Vietnam revealed that a force of 5,000 North Vietnamese troops was increasing the pressure in the Central Highlands.

November 4

USA – DOMESTIC: A Gallup poll survey conducted in the wake of the president's speech indicates that 77 percent of those asked are in support of Nixon's policy in Vietnam. Congressional reaction to the president's speech is also overwhelmingly favorable. A bipartisan group of 50 Democrats and 50 Republicans in the House of Representatives introduces legislation supporting the president.

GROUND WAR: In the biggest battle in four months, South Vietnamese infantry units, supported by U.S. planes and artillery, clash with North Vietnamese troops for 10 hours at Duc Lop near the Cambodian border. Eighty North Vietnamese soldiers are reported killed. South Vietnamese losses are 24 killed and 38 wounded.

November 6

GROUND WAR: U.S. troops are withheld from the developing battle at Duc Lop to gauge how well ARVN forces can cope on their own.

November 7

GROUND WAR: Saigon's outer defenses come under heavy attack for the first time since May 1968 as an estimated 100 Viet Cong fire at two government police posts.

November 8
GROUND WAR: Allied spokesmen report North Vietnamese troops have assaulted a South Vietnamese navy-marine task force headquarters in the Mekong Delta for the second time in three days. South Vietnamese troops report killing 80 Communist soldiers in a day-long battle 15 miles from the base. Eight South Vietnamese are killed and 43 wounded.

November 9
GROUND WAR: North Vietnamese forces maintain pressure on Duc Lop and three other Allied outposts along the Cambodian border, setting off a day-long fight. The U.S. military command still offers no infantry support to the South Vietnamese, giving only air and artillery support.

November 11
SWEDEN: Foreign Minister Torsten Nilsson announces that Sweden will begin a three-year, $45 million program of economic aid to North Vietnam on July 1, 1970. This reverses a previous decision to provide only humanitarian assistance while the war is in progress.

November 12
WAR CRIMES: Investigative reporter Seymour Hersh breaks the story on the My Lai massacre in the *New York Times*. In a cable filed through Dispatch News Service and picked up by more than 30 newspapers the following day, Hersh reveals the extent of the U.S. Army's charges against Lieutenant William Calley. Hersh writes that: "the Army says he deliberately murdered at least 109 Vietnamese civilians during a search-and-destroy mission in March 1968, in a VC stronghold known as 'Pinkville.'"

USA – GOVERNMENT: With massive protests and demonstrations due to take place November 14–15 in Washington, the federal government begins to assemble 9,000 troops to assist the police and National Guard. The Defense Department announces that the troops are being made available at the request of the Justice Department and will augment 1,200 National Guardsmen and a 3,700-man police force.

November 12–December 28
GROUND WAR: The ARVN 23rd Division launches Operation Dan Tien-40 in Quang Duc Province, II Corps. There are 1,012 reported enemy casualties by the end of the operation.

November 13
USA – GOVERNMENT: President Nixon pays extraordinary separate visits to the House of Representatives and the Senate to convey his appreciation to those who support his Vietnam policy and to ask for understanding and "constructive criticism" from those congressional members who oppose him. Also this day, Vice President Spiro Agnew criticizes the news media, particularly television, for its coverage of the president's Vietnam policies and the demonstrations and protests aimed at them.

USA – DOMESTIC: The second moratorium opens as organizers concentrate on mass demonstrations in Washington, D.C., and San Francisco. The antiwar demonstrations commence with a symbolic "March Against Death," which begins at Arlington

National Cemetery and continues past the White House. The march is headed by relatives of servicemen killed in Vietnam and contains 46,000 marchers.

GROUND WAR: MACV reports 122 North Vietnamese troops killed in two days of fighting six miles southwest of an Allied outpost at Con Thien near the DMZ. U.S. losses are 22 killed and 53 wounded. In other clashes near Danang, 130 Communist soldiers are reported killed while 17 Americans are killed and 60 wounded.

November 14

USA – DOMESTIC: Washington D.C., police resort to tear gas to break up a demonstration when 2,000 protesters attempt to march on the South Vietnamese embassy. At least 20 demonstrators are arrested and seven policemen are injured.

GROUND WAR: In fighting between Communist and South Vietnamese troops in the Central Highlands, Vietnamese air force planes strike both enemy and ARVN soldiers, killing 20 ARVN troops and wounding 53 more. Communist losses are reported at 95 killed.

November 15

USA – DOMESTIC: Over 250,000 demonstrators rally in Washington as part of the "Moratorium," sponsored by the New Mobilization Committee to End the War in Vietnam ("New Mobe"). The police once again use tear gas as radicals split off from the main rally to march on the Justice Department in a demonstration led by members of the Youth International Party ("Yippies") and supporters of the "Chicago Eight" defendants. Almost 100 demonstrators are arrested. Protests also take place elsewhere in the United States.

INTERNATIONAL: Major protests are held in a number of European cities, including Frankfurt, Stuttgart, West Berlin, and London, designed to coincide with the moratorium demonstrations in Washington and San Francisco. The largest overseas demonstration occurs in Paris, where 2,651 persons are arrested; there are similar demonstrations in 42 other cities in France.

WAR CRIMES: Survivors of the My Lai massacre, interviewed by reporters at a relocation hamlet in Song My village, allege that U.S. personnel slaughtered 567 Vietnamese men, women, and children on March 16, 1968.

GROUND WAR: Twenty helicopters are destroyed in an attack on the U.S. 4th Infantry Division's Camp Radcliff at An Khe, 260 miles northeast of Saigon.

November 16–17

GROUND WAR: Allied bombers and artillery attack North Vietnamese positions inside Cambodia that have shelled Allied camps at Bu Prang and Duc Lop. MACV explains the raids on Cambodian territory as an exercise of the "inherent right of self-defense against enemy attacks."

November 18

GROUND WAR: South Vietnamese troops lose 60 men killed or wounded in a clash with North Vietnamese forces in the Mekong Delta, the first major action in the northern delta since the U.S. 9th Division was withdrawn. North Vietnamese losses are put at 14 killed. A South Vietnamese spokesman says the high ARVN casualties are "due to bad fighting on our part."

November 20

NEGOTIATIONS: Ambassador Henry Cabot Lodge and his assistant, Lawrence E. Walsh, resign as the chief U.S. delegates to the Paris peace talks effective December 8. Philip C. Habib will be named the acting head of the delegation.

USA – DOMESTIC: The *Cleveland Plain Dealer* publishes photographer Ron Haeberle's explicit photos of the My Lai massacre. Seymour Hersh files a second My Lai story based on interviews with Michael Terry and Michael Bernhardt, who served under Lieutenant William Calley. The American public is stunned.

November 24

USA – MILITARY: The 3rd Recon Battalion of the 3rd Marine Division departs from South Vietnam. The 35,000-man troop withdrawal announced September 15 is reached three weeks prior to the December 15 deadline.

WAR CRIMES: The army announces that Lieutenant William Calley will be court-martialed for the premeditated murder of 109 Vietnamese civilians at My Lai. Army Secretary Stanley Resor and Army Chief of Staff William C. Westmoreland announce the appointment of Lieutenant General William R. Peers to "explore the nature and scope" of the original investigation of the My Lai slayings in April 1968. The initial probe, conducted by members of the 11th Infantry Brigade, the unit involved in the affair, concluded that no massacre had occurred and that no further action was warranted.

November 25

GROUND WAR: Communist forces step up attacks against U.S. troops shielding Allied installations near the Cambodian border. Ten Americans are killed and 70 wounded. U.S. troops report killing 115 enemy soldiers. North Vietnamese troops destroy more than a dozen tanks and tons of ammunition at a U.S. base near the Cambodian border.

November 28

GROUND WAR: A 300-man ARVN unit is ambushed in the Mekong Delta, losing 36 KIA. A counterattack in the same area, 72 miles southwest of Saigon, results in 45 Communist soldiers reported killed.

November 30

USA – MILITARY: The U.S. 3rd Marine Division officially departs South Vietnam.

GROUND WAR: Five U.S. personnel die and four are injured when four helicopters are shot down by North Vietnamese gunners about 10 miles from Song Be near the Cambodian border.

December 1

USA – GOVERNMENT: The first draft lottery since 1942 is held at Selective Service System headquarters. Those 19-year-olds whose birthdate is September 14 and whose last name begins with a "J" will be the first to be called.

December 3

GROUND WAR: Communist troops attack the town of Tuyen Binh in the Mekong Delta and are repelled by defenders and U.S. close air support. Fifteen civilians are killed and 30 are wounded. A total of 108 Communist soldiers are reported killed in the action.

December 4

USA – DOMESTIC: A Louis Harris survey reports 46 percent of those polled indicate sympathy with the goals of the November Moratorium demonstrations; 45 percent disagree.

December 7–8

GROUND WAR: Communist forces launch 44 attacks throughout South Vietnam. Allied soldiers report killing 88 North Vietnamese troops in two clashes near Tay Ninh. One American is killed and four are wounded.

December 7–March 31, 1970

GROUND WAR: The U.S. 101st Airborne Division (Airmobile), in coordination with the ARVN 1st Infantry Division, conducts Operation Randolph Glen, a search and clear mission in support of pacification efforts in the populated lowlands of Thua Thien Province, I Corps. Casualties will be U.S.: 123 KIA, 257 WIA; NVA/VC: 721 KIA, 19 POW.

December 8

USA – GOVERNMENT: President Nixon, at a news conference, says that the Vietnam War is coming to a "conclusion as a result of the plan that we have instituted," which calls for replacing U.S. troops with South Vietnamese forces.

Soldiers carry a wounded comrade through a swampy area, 1969. *(National Archives)*

December 9

GROUND WAR: A Viet Cong force attacks a national police field force training center in Dalat, killing 13 police and wounding 25.

December 11

USA – MILITARY: The headquarters and three subordinate infantry battalions of the U.S. 3rd Brigade, 82nd Airborne Division, are withdrawn from Vietnam.

NEGOTIATIONS: North Vietnamese chief negotiator Xuan Thuy boycotts the Paris talks in protest against what the North Vietnamese delegation insists is the "sabotage" and "downgrading" of the talks by the U.S. failure to name a replacement for Henry Cabot Lodge.

December 12–20

SOUTH VIETNAM: The Philippine army's 1,350 noncombatant Civic Action Group, which has been in-country since September 1966, withdraws from South Vietnam.

December 13

GROUND WAR: Eleven American soldiers are killed and 27 wounded in scattered attacks that leave 130 Communist soldiers reported dead. Bien Hoa air base is hit by Communist rocket attacks. The Americal Division reports killing 53 enemy soldiers in a battle two miles southeast of My Lai.

December 14

GROUND WAR: U.S. troops of the 3rd Brigade, 1st Cavalry Division, report a total of 1,177 enemy soldiers killed in the fighting near the Cambodian border since September 24.

December 15

USA – GOVERNMENT: President Nixon announces the beginning of the third phase of the troop reductions in Southeast Asia, promising that an additional 50,000 American troops will be withdrawn from South Vietnam by April 15, 1970. This withdrawal will bring the total reductions so far to 115,000.

GROUND WAR: Operation Danger Forward II begins with elements of the 1st Infantry Division and 5th ARVN Division conducting offensive operations to neutralize enemy forces in the area northwest of Saigon, which includes the "Trapezoid" and the Michelin rubber plantation.

December 16

USA – GOVERNMENT: Secretary of Defense Laird reports draft calls will be reduced by about 25,000 men next year as a direct result of plans to withdraw 50,000 troops from Vietnam.

GROUND WAR: South Vietnamese troops are airlifted into the Mekong Delta to confront a Communist troop concentration. During the fighting, 17 ARVN soldiers are killed and 61 wounded. Enemy losses are reported as 83 KIA.

December 18

USA – GOVERNMENT: Congress passes legislation to prohibit the use of current Department of Defense appropriations to introduce ground troops into Laos or Thailand.

December 21

THAILAND: The government in Bangkok announces plans to withdraw its 12,000-man contingent from South Vietnam.

December 24

GROUND WAR: A Viet Cong-proclaimed three-day Christmas truce begins at 0100 hours.

December 25

GROUND WAR: Allied military forces suspend combat activity for 24 hours beginning at 1800 hours.

December 27

GROUND WAR: In their fiercest battle in six weeks, U.S. forces report killing more than 70 NVA soldiers in a day-long battle nine miles northwest of Loc Ninh, near the Cambodian border about 80 miles north of Saigon.

December 28

GROUND WAR: Seven Americans are killed and five are wounded when explosive charges are thrown into a 25th Infantry Division base camp near Lai Khe, 25 miles northwest of Saigon.

December 30

GROUND WAR: A Viet Cong-proclaimed three-day New Year's truce begins at 0100.

NEGOTIATIONS: In Paris, Philip Habib, acting head of the U.S. delegation to the peace talks, hands over to the Communist side a list of 1,406 names of U.S. servicemen missing in action as of December 24. Habib says that he hopes the other side will indicate, as a "matter of humanitarian concern for their families," which men are prisoners and which are known dead.

December 31

GROUND WAR: Allied military forces suspend combat activity for 24 hours starting at 1800.

USA – MILITARY: In Washington, the U.S. Army announces that it will court-martial Staff Sergeant David Mitchell on charges of assault with intent to murder 30 South Vietnamese civilians at My Lai.

YEAR-END SUMMARY: U.S. troop strength in South Vietnam declines to 475,200; so far, some 60,000 American troops have returned home. U.S. combat deaths in 1969 total 9,414, bringing the total number of U.S. military personnel killed in action to date to 40,024, with another 260,000 wounded and some 1,400 listed as missing or captured;. Free World Military Forces personnel in Vietnam now number 70,300. During this year South Vietnamese armed forces strength has increased to 897,000, while 110,176 South Vietnamese military personnel have been killed in action to date. Estimated NVA/VC losses for the year exceed 45,000, bringing total estimated enemy losses since 1965 to over 400,000. The growing casualty list, coupled with the knowledge that U.S. troops are being withdrawn, is beginning to lead to a demoralized U.S. fighting force in which drug use is on the rise and "fragging" incidents are increasing. In the previous year, there were 117 convictions in the U.S. Army for "mutiny and other acts involving wilful refusal" to follow orders (compared with 82 such convictions in 1968).

1970

January 2
GROUND WAR: The U.S. command reports 65 Americans killed in action during the past week.

January 3
GROUND WAR: North Vietnamese troops attack a U.S. camp near Duc Pho, south of Quang Ngai, killing seven Americans and wounding 11.

January 6
GROUND WAR: Three North Vietnamese sapper teams attack and penetrate a U.S. 7th Marine Regiment base in the Que Son Valley, killing 13 Americans and wounding 63. Reported NVA losses are 38 killed.

January 8
SOUTH VIETNAM: President Thieu states that it will be "impossible and impractical" to withdraw all U.S. combat troops in 1970. Thieu says further U.S. withdrawals will depend on the "critical question" of whether the United States supplies South Vietnam with adequate equipment and funds to modernize its armed forces. Although Thieu says that he has been assured by the Nixon administration of the necessary assistance, he contends that U.S. troop withdrawals will have to be phased over a number of years.
WAR CRIMES: Private Gerald Smith and Sergeant Charles Hutto, both due to leave the U.S. Army next week, are charged with murder and sexual offenses in connection with the killing of civilians at My Lai; 11 more members of the Americal Division will be charged with complicity in the killings.

January 8–9
GROUND WAR: U.S. troops, supported by armor, artillery, and air strikes, report killing 109 Communist soldiers near Tay Ninh; U.S. losses are two killed and 10 wounded.

January 16
TERRORISM: A Viet Cong force moves into a refugee camp in the village of Chau Thuan on the Batangan Peninsula, hurling dynamite charges into houses and killing 16 civilians and wounding 21.

January 18
TERRORISM: Mines planted by the Viet Cong explode at the Thu Duc Officers Training School, 12 miles northeast of Saigon, killing 18 persons, including 16 South Vietnamese officer cadets and their instructor, and wounding 33.

January 19–July 22

GROUND WAR: Troops from the U.S. 1st Brigade, 5th Infantry Division (Mechanized), and 1st ARVN Division conduct Operation Greene River in Ouang Tri Province, I Corps, to support provincial pacification programs. Casualties will be Allied: 68 KIA, 967 WIA; NVA/VC: more than 400 KIA.

January 22

GROUND WAR: A combined force of North Vietnamese and VC attack a South Vietnamese marine brigade command post in the Mekong Delta, killing 15 and wounding 41. The Communist losses are reported at 72. At an artillery base, 55 miles north of Saigon, 13 U.S. soldiers are killed and three wounded in an ammunition explosion.

January 26

GROUND WAR: MACV reports increased combat activity in all four corps regions as Communist forces shell 29 targets. The Communists report 75 killed in various actions; nine Americans are killed and five wounded.

POWs: Lieutenant Everett Alvarez, Jr., (USN) spends his 2,000th day in captivity in Southeast Asia. First taken prisoner when his plane was shot down on August 5, 1964, he is the longest-held POW in North Vietnam.

January 28

AIR WAR: A flight of U.S. fighter-bombers attacks an antiaircraft missile site 90 miles inside North Vietnam after missiles are fired at an unarmed U.S. reconnaissance plane and its jet escorts. One F-105 is brought down by Communist ground fire. A rescue helicopter sent to search for the jet's two missing pilots is shot down by a MiG-21 near the North Vietnamese-Laotian border. The downed helicopter's six-man crew is also listed as missing. These reconnaissance missions have been conducted daily since the November 1968 bombing halt.

USA – DOMESTIC: A Gallup poll shows 65 percent of those interviewed approve of President Nixon's handling of the war, his highest approval rate to date.

January 30

USA – GOVERNMENT: President Nixon, at a news conference, states that "the policy of Vietnamization is irreversible," even without any progress at the Paris peace talks. Nixon warns that if North Vietnam steps up its military activity in South Vietnam during U.S. withdrawals, he will deal with the situation "more strongly than we have dealt with anything in the past."

AIR WAR: In announcing the combat action over North Vietnam involving the attack on an antiaircraft missile base and the downing of a U.S. jet, the White House denies the incident signals any change in U.S. policy. In Saigon, MACV acknowledges that there have been periodic air-to-ground engagements in North Vietnam since the bombing halt that were not made public because they were considered "insignificant."

NEGOTIATIONS: In the Paris peace talks, U.S. representatives affirm that the United States sends reconnaissance planes over North Vietnam with fighter escorts, but denies this violates the bombing halt understanding. The North Vietnamese delegation charges that U.S. planes bombed and strafed several populated areas.

January 31–February 1

GROUND WAR: Communist forces carry out more than 100 rocket, mortar, and ground attacks against Allied bases and towns ranging from the DMZ to the Mekong Delta. Nineteen Americans are killed and 119 wounded. South Vietnamese losses are 11 killed and 86 wounded. More than 400 Communist soldiers are reported killed.

February

AIR WAR: Operation Good Luck is initiated by the U.S. Air Force to strike North Vietnamese and Pathet Lao forces in the Plain of Jars.

February 2

USA – DOMESTIC: Antiwar protesters file suit against the Dow Chemical Company in a Washington, D.C., court. The plaintiffs are trying to force the company to disclose all government contracts to prove that the company is still making napalm.

AIR WAR: U.S. fighter-bombers attack North Vietnamese missile and antiaircraft gun positions for the second time in a week after an unarmed reconnaissance jet comes under intense antiaircraft fire. The action takes place in the area of the Ban Karai Pass, an infiltration route leading into Laos through North Vietnamese mountains, 20 miles north of the DMZ.

February 3

USA – GOVERNMENT: The Senate Foreign Relations Committee reopens hearings on the Vietnam War. Senator Charles Goodell (R-N.Y.) says that Vietnamization has been "a great public relations success." Senators Harold Hughes (D-Ida.), Thomas Eagleton (D-Mo.), and Alan Cranston (D-Calif.) speak in support of a Senate resolution calling for the termination of the American commitment to South Vietnam unless the Saigon government takes steps to broaden its cabinet, reduces press censorship, and release political prisoners.

GROUND WAR: Viet Cong gunners shell Bien Hoa Air Base. U.S. helicopter gunships respond by killing 23 enemy soldiers. Another 52 Communist soldiers are reported killed by U.S. forces in two battles north of Saigon.

February 5

GROUND WAR: In an accidental attack by a U.S. helicopter gunship, 275 miles northeast of Saigon, eight South Vietnamese soldiers are killed and 31 wounded.

February 10

USA – MILITARY: Arriving in South Vietnam, Defense Secretary Laird announces that he is satisfied with the current pace of Vietnamization. However, he also says that ways to improve it and push it forward are being examined.

LAOS: Souvanna Phouma states that he will take no action against Communist supply activity along the Ho Chi Minh Trail if North Vietnam will withdraw combat troops from Laos.

February 11

USA – GOVERNMENT: Secretary of Defense Laird says that U.S. warplanes will continue to take whatever steps are necessary to protect themselves during reconnaissance flights over North Vietnam.

February 12

GROUND WAR: A U.S. Marine unit is ambushed by elements of the 31st NVA Regiment near FSB Ross, about 10 miles west of Hiep Duc in Quang Nam Province, I Corps. A battalion from the Americal Division is sent to reinforce the Marines. Thirteen Americans are killed in the fighting and 13 wounded.

February 14

USA – DOMESTIC: A Gallup poll shows that 55 percent of those polled continue to oppose an immediate withdrawal of U.S. troops from Vietnam, but that the number of those who favor such a withdrawal has risen from 21 percent in a November poll to 35 percent since a poll conducted in November 1968. Also this day, during the trial of the Chicago Seven (formerly the Chicago Eight—one defendant is now being tried separately) conspiracy trial, Julius Hoffman charges four defendants with contempt of court after numerous violent outbursts in the courtroom.

GROUND WAR: In an ambush by North Vietnamese soldiers near the Cambodian border, eight U.S. servicemen are killed and 30 wounded; 31 Communist soldiers are reported killed in the fighting.

February 15

USA – DOMESTIC: As the jury continues to deliberate in the trial of the Chicago Seven, defense attorneys William Kunstler and Leonard Weinglass and three more defendants are sentenced to prison for contempt of court.

GROUND WAR: South Vietnamese soldiers, with the aid of an armored brigade and U.S. artillery and close air support, kill 145 Communist soldiers belonging to a battalion apparently planning to attack Danang; South Vietnamese losses are four killed and 26 wounded.

February 17–18

AIR WAR: B-52 raids in South Vietnam are halted for 36 hours while the bombers attack North Vietnamese and Pathet Lao forces threatening the Plain of Jars in northern Laos. The expansion of the B-52 bombing missions to northern Laos is carried on U.S. military records as routine missions over South Vietnam or southern Laos, where bombing along the Ho Chi Minh Trail has been conducted on a near-daily basis and fully reported.

February 19

USA – MILITARY: The raids over northern Laos are made public, provoking a new wave of congressional criticism regarding the policies of the Nixon administration in Indochina.

WAR CRIMES: A five-man U.S. Marine patrol enters the small village of Son Thang, 8.5 miles northeast of Hiep Duc, and, after being spooked by a woman who attempts to run away, begins firing and kills five women and 11 children. The unit commander tries to cover up the tragedy but fails, and the five members of the patrol will be charged with premeditated murder; two will be eventually convicted.

USA – DOMESTIC: The Chicago Seven are acquitted of conspiracy charges, but on the following day five will receive the heaviest possible sentences—five years imprisonment and $5,000 fines plus court costs—after being found guilty of inciting to riot.

February 20

GROUND WAR: Fourteen U.S. soldiers die and 29 are injured when an armored unit of the U.S. 196th Light Infantry Brigade, Americal Division, is ambushed by North Vietnamese forces south of Danang in the Que Son Valley, I Corps.

February 21

NEGOTIATIONS: Henry Kissinger begins secret talks with Le Duc Tho, the fifth-ranking member of the Hanoi Politburo, at a villa outside Paris. Tho states that the North Vietnamese position continues to be an unconditional U.S. withdrawal on a fixed date and the abandonment of the Thieu government as a precondition for further progress in the stalled negotiations. The North Vietnamese reject Kissinger's proposals for a mutual withdrawal of military forces, the neutralization of Cambodia and a mixed electoral commission to supervise elections in South Vietnam. The other two meetings, in which there will be a similar lack of progress, will be held on March 16 and April 4.

LAOS: Following an offensive launched in northern Laos on 12 February, 3,000 North Vietnamese troops capture the airfield at Xieng Khouong, 100 miles northeast of the capital of Vientiane, the last military stronghold of the Laotian government in the Plain of Jars area.

February 26

USA – GOVERNMENT: Defense Secretary Laird, responding to strident criticism over U.S. military activity in Laos, states that U.S. air operations there are confined to cutting off North Vietnamese supply lines through Laos into South Vietnam.

February 28

TERRORISM: Ten South Vietnamese civilians die and 15 are wounded when a bus strikes a mine near Danang. Eleven other civilians are wounded by grenades thrown at a truck in the same area.

March

USA – MILITARY: The 26th Marine Regiment of the 5th Marine Division conducts its last patrol, stands down, and departs Vietnam.

March 2

USA – MILITARY: U.S. officials announce a new method for measuring progress in pacification programs in which district advisers answer 139 "more or less" objective questions about the state of the program in their respective districts. A computer then interprets the information and marks a scorecard. In the first month of operation using the new methods, the number of hamlets reported to be relatively pacified is reduced from 92.7 percent to 89.9 percent.

March 9

USA – MILITARY: The U.S. Marines turn over control of the I Corps area to the U.S. Army, and Lieutenant General Melvin Zais, commanding general, XXIV Corps, assumes command of the 150,000 troops in the five northernmost provinces of South Vietnam.

March 10

USA – MILITARY: The U.S. Army accuses Captain Ernest Medina, Lieutenant William Calley's company commander, and four other soldiers of committing crimes at My Lai in March 1968 that range from premeditated murder to rape and the "maiming" of a suspect under interrogation.

March 11

CAMBODIA: An estimated 20,000 demonstrators, protesting the presence of Communist forces in Cambodia, assault the embassies of the Provisional Revolutionary Government and North Vietnam in Phnom Penh, causing heavy damage to both.

March 12–13

CAMBODIA: The Cambodian government announces the cancellation of a trade agreement with North Vietnam that allows them to use the port of Sihanoukville as a source of supply for their military forces in Cambodia and South Vietnam. Premier Lon Nol apologizes for the attacks on the Vietnamese embassies, but also issues an ultimatum that their troops must leave Cambodia in 72 hours. Cambodian demonstrators continue to rampage in the streets of Phnom Penh, attacking Vietnamese shops and homes.

March 16

USA – DOMESTIC: The New Mobilization Committee to End the War in Vietnam ("New Mobe") sponsors a national "anti-draft week."

DIPLOMACY: North Vietnamese, NLF, and Cambodian officials meet in Phnom Penh to discuss the presence of Communist military forces in Cambodia.

March 17

WAR CRIMES: The U.S. Army, following an investigation by a panel headed by Lieutenant General William Peers, accuses 14 officers of suppressing information relating to the incident at My Lai in March 1968. The charges include dereliction of duty, failure to obey lawful regulations, and false swearing. The report says that U.S. soldiers committed individual and group acts of murder, rape, sodomy, maiming, and assault that took the lives of a large number of civilians and concludes that "a tragedy of major proportions" occurred at My Lai. The Peers report says that each successive level of command received a more watered-down account of what actually happened at My Lai; the higher the report went, the lower was its estimate of civilians allegedly killed by Americans. American Division headquarters, where accounts of the incident stopped, received information that only 20 to 28 civilians had been killed.

March 18

CAMBODIA: General Lon Nol, premier and defense minister, assisted by First Deputy Premier Prince Sisowath Sirik Matak, seizes power in Cambodia, deposing Prince

Norodom Sihanouk (en route back to Cambodia after visiting Moscow and Beijing at the time).

March 19

CAMBODIA: The National Assembly grants "full power" to Premier Lon Nol, declares a state of emergency, and suspends four articles of the constitution, permitting arbitrary arrest and banning public assembly.

March 20

GROUND WAR: In the first coordinated Allied-Cambodian military operation of the war, a Cambodian army commander calls in a U.S. spotter plane and South Vietnamese artillery to help repel a 150-man NVA attack on an outpost about 10 miles north of the South Vietnamese district capital of An Phu.

March 21

DIPLOMACY: Pham Van Dong, prime minister of North Vietnam, flies secretly to Beijing and meets with Chinese premier Zhou Enlai (Chou En-lai) and deposed Cambodian head of state Norodom Sihanouk. Sihanouk agrees to accept the leadership of the Cambodian Communists.

March 22

TERRORISM: At Hoc Man, seven miles northwest of Saigon, VC explode a bomb at a Buddhist meeting, killing 14 women and children and wounding 20 others.

March 23

DIPLOMACY: In Beijing, Norodom Sihanouk issues a public call for arms against the Lon Nol government in Phnom Penh and the establishment of a National United Front of Kampuchea (FUNK). North Vietnam, the NLF, and the Pathet Lao immediately pledge their support to the new organization.

March 25

DIPLOMACY: North Vietnam announces it is recalling its diplomats from Cambodia.

March 27–28

GROUND WAR: Following several days of consultations with the Cambodian government, South Vietnamese troops, supported by advance artillery and air strikes, launch their first major military operation into Cambodia. The South Vietnamese encounter a 300-man Viet Cong force in Kandal Province and report killing 53 communist soldiers. Two teams of U.S. helicopter gunships take part in the action. Three South Vietnamese soldiers are killed and seven are wounded. U.S. and South Vietnamese officials disavow any knowledge of the operation.

March 28

USA – GOVERNMENT: The White House announces for the first time that U.S. troops, depending on the judgment of their field commanders, are permitted to cross the Cambodian border in response to enemy threats. U.S. officials contend that this does not mean a widening of the war, but that it merely represents a restatement of the rules promulgated by the Pentagon and already in force.

March 29
GROUND WAR: North Vietnamese troops attack an American base near the Cambodian border, killing 13 and wounding 30. Communist losses are reported as 75 killed.

April
AIR WAR: U.S. Air Force launches Operation Patio to strike targets in Cambodia in support of U.S. ground operations.

April 1
GROUND WAR: The intensity of the war increases when Communist forces launch ground assaults or artillery attacks at 115 installations throughout South Vietnam.

USA – WAR CRIMES: The U.S. Army formally charges Captain Medina of being "responsible" for the murder of Vietnamese civilians killed by members of his infantry company at My Lai. Medina, speaking at a news conference, discloses that the army has accused him of premeditated murder of not less than 175 civilians and denies having participated in or ordered or seen any mass killings at My Lai.

AIR WAR: In the first such action reported since the November 1968 bombing halt, a U.S. military spokesmen reports that a U.S. Navy F-4 Phantom shot down a North Vietnamese MiG-21 while flying reconnaissance escort on March 28 near Thanh Hoa, about 85 miles south of Hanoi.

USA – MILITARY: Headquarters, U.S. Marine Corps, announces that it will no longer accept draftees and reinstitutes voluntary enlistments to fill its ranks.

April 1–September 5
GROUND WAR: In I Corps, the U.S. 101st Airborne Division conducts Operation Texas Star, a follow-on to Operation Randolph Glen in Quang Tri and Thua Thien Provinces. One brigade of the division retains responsibility for pacification and development support in Thua Thien Province, while the other two brigades conduct offensive operations in the western portions of Quang Tri and Thua Thien Province. Casualties will be U.S.: 386 KIA, 1,978 WIA, 7 MIA; NVA/VC: 4,138 KIA, 49 POW.

April 2
USA – DOMESTIC: Massachusetts governor Francis Sargent signs a bill challenging the legality of the Vietnam War.

April 3
GROUND WAR: Communist forces shell 60 targets as heavy attacks continue for the third consecutive day. U.S. troops pursuing a Communist battalion toward the Cambodian border meet heavy resistance; 10 Americans and 62 Communist soldiers are reported killed during the action.

April 4
USA – DOMESTIC: In the largest prowar demonstration held in Washington, D.C., since America's involvement in Vietnam began, about 15,000 people march up Pennsylvania Avenue to rally at the Washington Monument in support of President Nixon's conduct of the war and "victory over the Communists in Vietnam."

April 4–5
GROUND WAR: MACV reports the heaviest fighting along the DMZ involving U.S. troops in nearly five months; in combat centered four miles southwest of Con Thien

and one mile south of the 17th parallel, six Americans are killed and 40 wounded. Additionally, there are new clashes farther to the south, where two South Vietnamese battalions push 10 miles into Cambodia.

April 6–7
CAMBODIA: Communist forces attack Cambodian troops at Chiphu, near the eastern end of Svay Rieng Province. Cambodian losses are listed as 20 killed, 30 wounded, and 30 missing.

April 7–8
GROUND WAR: Nine infantry battalions from the 1st U.S. Infantry Division depart South Vietnam.

April 8
GROUND WAR: Allied military officials announce 754 South Vietnamese soldiers were killed the week of March 29–April 4, the second highest South Vietnamese casualty toll for a week in the war. U.S. losses for the same period are 138 dead, the highest since September 1969.

April 9
CAMBODIA: Cambodia withdraws all of its military forces from Svay Rieng Province, also known as the "Parrot's Beak," abandoning it to the Vietnamese Communists. One-half of the province's population, about 30,000 civilians, also withdraws westward. Most of those remaining are ethnic Vietnamese.

April 10
CAMBODIA: Cambodian troops massacre hundreds of ethnic Vietnamese in the village of Prasot in Svay Rieng Province. The Cambodian government reports the deaths of 89 villagers due to "crossfire."
USA – MILITARY: Two battalions from the U.S. 4th Infantry Division depart from South Vietnam.

April 11
USA – DOMESTIC: A Gallup poll shows 48 percent of those polled approve of President Nixon's policy in Vietnam, while 41 percent disapprove. This figure reflects a decline from the president's 65 percent approval rating in January.

April 14
CAMBODIA: President Lon Nol appeals for foreign military assistance.
GROUND WAR: Two thousand South Vietnamese troops, operating with a token Cambodian force, attack a North Vietnamese base camp one mile inside Cambodia. South Vietnamese headquarters reports 179 Communist soldiers killed and claims that the operation took place entirely in South Vietnam. President Thieu denies South Vietnamese troops crossed the border.

April 15
USA – MILITARY: The 1st Infantry Division officially departs from Vietnam, bound for duty in Germany and Fort Riley, Kansas. A force of 12,900 U.S. Marines departs South Vietnam to complete the third phase of U.S. troop withdrawals announced by President Nixon. There are now 429,200 U.S. troops in Vietnam.

GROUND WAR: MACV reports 25 Americans killed and 54 wounded yesterday in one of the year's highest one-day casualty tolls. The casualties include 14 Americans killed and 32 wounded in an explosion of a U.S. artillery shell rigged as a Viet Cong booby-trap near Duc Pho, 105 miles south of Danang. Tactical air support called in during a firefight between a company from the 1st Battalion, 5th Marines, and North Vietnamese forces accidentally kills 30 civilians in the village of Le Bac, approximately nine miles northwest of An Hoa in I Corps.

April 16

CAMBODIA: Rampaging Cambodian troops kill at least 1,000 ethnic Vietnamese civilians at Takeo, 50 miles south of Phnom Penh.

April 19

USA – DOMESTIC: The Vietnam Moratorium Committee announces that it is disbanding because its sources of funding have run dry and President Nixon's withdrawal policy has undermined the nonradical opposition to the war.

April 20

USA – GOVERNMENT: President Nixon pledges to withdraw 150,000 more U.S. troops over the next 12 months based entirely on the "progress of Vietnamization."

GROUND WAR: South Vietnamese troops move into Cambodia in their third major cross-border offensive in the past week. South Vietnamese sources report killing 144 Communist soldiers. Twenty South Vietnamese soldiers are killed and 70 wounded.

CAMBODIA: Following reports by Cambodian military authorities that Communist forces have more than doubled their area of control, including Svay Rieng Province, Premier Lon Nol sends a personal appeal to President Nixon asking for military aid.

April 22

AIR WAR: An AC-130 gunship is shot down over Saravan, Laos, resulting in the loss of 10 airmen from the 16th Special Operations Squadron.

April 24–25

DIPLOMACY: China sponsors a conference near Canton attended by Norodom Sihanouk; Prince Souphonouvong, leader of the Pathet Lao; Nguyen Huu Tho, president of the Provisional Revolutionary Government of South Vietnam; and North Vietnamese prime minister Pham Van Dong. The leaders of the four Communist movements pledge joint action to expel the United States and other forces that oppose them in Indochina. Chinese Premier Zhou Enlai (Chou En-lai) attends the final session of the conference and gives it his endorsement.

April 28

USA – DOMESTIC: President Nixon gives his formal authorization to commit U.S. combat troops, in cooperation with South Vietnamese units, against Communist troop sanctuaries and base areas in Cambodia. Secretary of State William Rogers and Secretary of Defense Melvin Laird, who had been excluded from the decision to use U.S. troops, are informed for the first time. General Wheeler cables General Abrams, informing him of the decision that a "higher authority has authorized certain military actions to protect U.S. forces operating in South Vietnam." Three National Security Council staff members and key aides to presidential assistant Henry Kissinger resign in protest over the planned invasion of Cambodia.

GROUND WAR: Two U.S. Marine Skyhawk jets accidentally bomb a South Vietnamese outpost during a battle in Quang Ngai province, killing 10 South Vietnamese soldiers and wounding 20 others.

April 29

GROUND WAR: In what becomes known as the Cambodian incursion, 13 major ground operations (two of which involve U.S. ground campaign units) are launched to clear North Vietnamese sanctuaries in Cambodia. As 6,000 ARVN soldiers commence an attack into the Parrot's Beak area of Cambodia, supported by U.S. warplanes and artillery, the United States announces that it will provide combat advisers, tactical air support, medical evacuation teams, and supplies to the South Vietnamese forces.

April 30

USA – GOVERNMENT: President Nixon, in a nationally televised speech, announces he is sending U.S. combat troops into Cambodia to destroy Communist sanctuaries and supply bases. Nixon says the objective of the U.S. forces is the Fishhook area,

President Richard Nixon conducts a press conference to explain the Cambodian incursion, April 1970. *(National Archives)*

50 miles northwest of Saigon, which the president calls the "key control center" for the enemy and its "headquarters for the entire communist military operation in South Vietnam." Nixon says the purpose of the military action is not to occupy Cambodian territory and insists "this is not an invasion of Cambodia" since the border areas are "completely occupied and controlled by North Vietnamese forces." In defending his decision, Nixon argues that "plaintive diplomatic protests" no longer are sufficient since they will only destroy American credibility in areas of the world "where only the power of the United States deters aggression." Nixon warns that "if, when the chips are down, the world's most powerful nation, the United States of America, acts like a pitiful, helpless giant, the forces of totalitarianism and anarchy will threaten free nations and free institutions throughout the world." Widespread protests follow on college campuses across America.

May
AIR WAR: U.S. Air Force launches Operation Freedom Deal to strike targets in Cambodia in support of Cambodian army.

May 1
GROUND WAR: The military operation into the Fishhook area of Cambodia is launched by a combined force of 8,000 U.S. and 2,000 South Vietnamese soldiers. The purpose of the operation is to eliminate enemy forces and locate and eliminate COSVN, the command headquarters for Communist activities in South Vietnam.

May 1–2
AIR WAR: Heavy bombing raids are carried out against supply depots and other targets in North Vietnam. One raid involves at least 128 U.S. warplanes against targets in Quang Binh and Nghe An Provinces. A Hanoi Radio broadcast charges that more than 100 planes attacked targets in two provinces, killing or wounding many civilians. On May 2, U.S. spokesmen confirm the raids.

May 2
USA – GOVERNMENT: Alexander Haig, deputy to presidential assistant Henry Kissinger, requests FBI wiretaps on *New York Times* reporter William Beecher; Robert Pursley, Secretary of Defense Laird's military assistant; Richard Peterson, the State Department counselor; and William H. Sullivan, an assistant secretary of state. Beecher will report the following day on the intensive bombing raids against North Vietnam. The wiretaps will remain in effect until February 10, 1971.

USA – GOVERNMENT: Senators George McGovern (D-S.D.), Mark Hatfield (R-Oreg.), and Charles Goodell (R-N.Y.) announce they will offer an amendment to a pending military procurement authorization bill to cut off funds for all U.S. military action in Southeast Asia.

GROUND WAR: Fighting continues for the third day in the northernmost zone of South Vietnam with the military action focused on the town of Hiep Duc, 40 miles south of Danang, where North Vietnamese troops have firm control of three hamlets. South Vietnamese troops report killing 219 enemy soldiers. Seven Americans and 12 ARVN soldiers are killed.

USA – Domestic: Ohio National Guardsmen and police subdue students on the campus at Kent State University after the ROTC building is attacked and burned to the ground. Student strikes spread to a number of campuses to protest the expansion of the war into Cambodia.

Cambodia: More than 2,000 well-armed Cambodian mercenaries, serving in units in South Vietnam operated by the U.S. Special Forces, are flown into Cambodia to reinforce the Cambodian army.

May 3

USA – Military: A U.S. military spokesman acknowledges the resumed bombing of North Vietnam.

May 4

USA – Domestic: At Kent State in Ohio, 100 National Guardsmen open fire on a group of students, killing four and wounding 11. President Nixon issues a statement deploring the deaths and saying the incident should serve as a reminder that "when dissent turns to violence it invites tragedy." The National Student Association and former Vietnam Moratorium Committee leaders call for a national university strike of indefinite duration, beginning immediately, to protest the war. At least 100 colleges and universities pledge to strike. The presidents of 37 universities sign a letter urging President Nixon to clearly show his determination to end the war.

Ground War: About 20 miles north of the Fishhook area, U.S. troops from the 11th Armored Cavalry Regiment reach the site of what is believed to be the largest Vietnamese base in the area, known as "the City." Communist forces launch heavy attacks in the area around Phnom Penh as North Vietnamese and Viet Cong units cut the Phnom Penh–Saigon highway at a point 29 miles from the Cambodian capital.

USSR: In a rare public news conference, Soviet Premier Aleksey Kosygin personally criticizes President Nixon for sending U.S. troops into Cambodia.

May 5

USA – Government: President Nixon meets with congressional committees at the White House and gives the legislators a "firm commitment" that U.S. troops will be withdrawn from Cambodia in three to seven weeks. Nixon also pledges that he will not order U.S. troops to penetrate deeper than 21 miles into Cambodia without first seeking congressional approval.

Ground War: A U.S. force of over 100 tanks from the 11th Armored Cavalry Regiment captures Snoul, Cambodia, 20 miles from the tip of the "Fishhook," virtually leveling the village, which had been held by the North Vietnamese.

May 6

USA – Domestic: More than 100 colleges and universities across the nation shut down as thousands of students join a nationwide campus protest. Governor Ronald Reagan closes down the entire California university system until May 11, involving more than 280,000 students on 28 campuses. Pennsylvania State University, with 18 campuses, is closed down for an indeterminate period. A National Student Association spokesman reports that students from more than 300 campuses are boycotting classes.

GROUND WAR: In Cambodia, three new fronts are opened, bringing to nearly 50,000 the number of Allied troops in Cambodia (31,000 of them American). One U.S. spearhead, by troops of the 25th Infantry Division, moved across the border from Tay Ninh Province, between the Fishhook and Parrot's Beak areas. In another U.S. thrust, the 1st Cavalry Division (Airmobile) is airlifted into the jungle 23 miles west of Phuoc Binh, South Vietnam, northeast of the "Fishhook" area.

May 6–16
GROUND WAR: Elements of U.S. 4th Infantry Division and 40th ARVN Regiment conduct Operation Binh Tay I to clear enemy Base Area 702 in Pleiku Province, II Corps. Casualties are U.S.: 43 KIA, 118 WIA; NVA/VC: 212 KIA, 7 POW.

May 8
SOUTH VIETNAM: President Thieu says he and Premier Lon Nol of Cambodia have worked out "agreements in principle" for South Vietnamese troops to conduct continuing military operations in eastern Cambodia. Thieu makes it clear that South Vietnamese troops will not be bound by the restrictions President Nixon has placed on the use of U.S. forces and says that there is no deadline or limits to the South Vietnamese operations in Cambodia.

USA – GOVERNMENT: President Nixon, at a news conference, defends the U.S. troop movement into Cambodia, saying the operation will drive the enemy back, providing additional time for the training of South Vietnamese forces and thus shortening the war for Americans. Nixon reaffirms his promise to withdraw 150,000 U.S. soldiers by next spring. Also this day, more than 250 State Department and foreign aid employees sign a letter to Secretary of State Rogers criticizing U.S. military involvement in Cambodia.

USA – DOMESTIC: College students across the nation intensify their antiwar protests with marches, rallies, and scattered incidents of violence. About 400 schools are affected by strikes, with more than 200 colleges and universities closed completely. In New York City, helmeted construction workers break up a student antiwar demonstration on Wall Street in New York City, attacking demonstrators in a melee that leaves more than 70 persons injured.

May 9
USA – DOMESTIC: Between 75,000 and 100,000 young people, mostly from college campuses, demonstrate peaceably in Washington, D.C., at the rear of a barricaded White House, opposing the Cambodian invasion and demanding the withdrawal of U.S. military forces from Vietnam and other Southeast Asian nations. Afterward, a few hundred militants spread through surrounding streets, causing some damage. Police attack the most threatening crowds with tear gas. Elsewhere, protests continue on more than 400 college campuses.

RIVER WAR: Thirty U.S. gunboats join a flotilla of 110 South Vietnamese craft in a thrust up the Mekong River in an attempt to neutralize enemy sanctuaries along a 45-mile stretch of river between the South Vietnamese border and Phnom Penh. The U.S. vessels move no farther north than Neak Luong, in compliance with the U.S. policy of limiting U.S. penetration of Cambodia to 21.7 miles.

May 12

SOUTH VIETNAM: South Vietnamese vice president Ky announces that Allied naval vessels have begun blockading a 100-mile stretch of the Cambodian coastline to prevent Communist forces from resupplying by sea. The blockade extends from Kompong Som, formerly Sihanoukville, to the South Vietnamese border.

USA – GOVERNMENT: Defense Secretary Laird, testifying before the Senate Armed Services Committee, says that the Vietnamization program is going so well that the U.S. will have no ground fighting troops in Vietnam after June 30, 1971.

May 14

USA – DOMESTIC: Police kill two African-American students and wound 12 others during student protests at Jackson State College in Mississippi.

GROUND WAR: Allied military officials announce 863 South Vietnamese were killed the week of May 3–9. This is the second highest weekly death toll of the war for the South Vietnamese.

May 15

USA – GOVERNMENT: Congress is virtually buried under an avalanche of mail, telegrams, and petitions heavily opposed to the use of U.S. troops in Cambodia.

May 17

GROUND WAR: A force of 10,000 South Vietnamese troops, supported by 200 U.S. advisers, aircraft, and logistical elements, moves into Cambodia and reaches Takeo in a 20-mile thrust. The Communists report 211 killed.

May 19

GROUND WAR: Communist forces shell more than 60 Allied positions to commemorate the 80th anniversary of Ho Chi Minh's birth.

May 20

USA – DOMESTIC: More than 100,000 construction workers, dockmen, and office workers lead a parade in New York City supporting the policies of President Richard Nixon and attacking Mayor John Lindsay and other opponents of the Vietnam War.

GROUND WAR: About 2,500 South Vietnamese soldiers, supported by U.S. airpower and advisers, open a new front in Cambodia, 125 miles north of Saigon, bringing the number of South Vietnamese troops in Cambodia to 40,000. South Vietnamese forces link up with Cambodian forces 25 miles north of Takeo after a cross-country drive in which they report killing 400 Communist soldiers.

May 22

USA – GOVERNMENT: The White House announces that the United States is prepared to continue air cover, if needed, for South Vietnamese forces that are considered almost certain to remain in Cambodia after U.S. troops are withdrawn.

SOUTH VIETNAM: South Vietnam announces a halt in the repatriation of Vietnamese refugees in Cambodia. About 50,000 to 80,000 refugees have already been moved to South Vietnam since the start of evacuation efforts on May 10. Seventy thousand more refugees remain stranded in refugee camps. Pham Huy Ty, head of South Vietnam's permanent liaison mission in Phnom Penh, says the halt is due to greater security measures for Vietnamese residents being instituted by the Cambodian government. The increasing presence of South Vietnamese troops in Cambodia has inflamed the traditional animosities between the two countries.

May 23–24

GROUND WAR: A large South Vietnamese force led by Khmer Krom, ethnic Cambodian mercenaries assigned to the Cambodian army, attacks Cambodia's largest rubber plantation in Chup, about 50 miles northeast of Phnom Penh, which accounts for 50 percent of Cambodia's rubber production. An NVA regiment is reported to have retreated into the 70-square-mile plantation. In the subsequent fighting, 12 Khmer Rouge soldiers are reported killed and 15 captured, but 15 civilian workers are killed and 80 others wounded.

May 26

NORTH VIETNAM: Norodom Sihanouk arrives in Hanoi and is greeted at the airport by Premier Pham Van Dong, Defense Minister Vo Nguyen Giap, and Foreign Minister Nguyen Duy Trinh. Sihanouk urges the people of Indochina to unite in their fight against foreign intervention.

May 27

DIPLOMACY: Following three days of talks in Saigon, South Vietnamese and Cambodian representatives sign agreements reestablishing diplomatic relations (broken since 1963), providing for economic and military cooperation and dealing with the treatment of Vietnamese residents in Cambodia.

May 31

GROUND WAR: About 75 Communist soldiers, who had seized key outposts in the resort city of Dalat, 145 miles northeast of Saigon, slip past 2,500 South Vietnamese militiamen and soldiers who had surrounded their positions. In earlier fighting, 47 Communist soldiers are reported killed; South Vietnamese losses are 16 killed and two wounded.

June 1–3

GROUND WAR: In heavy fighting 21 miles south of the DMZ, North Vietnamese sappers overrun part of a South Vietnamese fire base, but are beaten back after inflicting heavy losses. On June 3, fresh South Vietnamese troops relieve the base. The Communists report 83 killed; South Vietnamese losses are 50 killed and 119 wounded.

June 3

USA – GOVERNMENT: President Nixon, in a televised speech, claims the Allied drive into Cambodia is the "most successful operation of this long and difficult war," and that he is now able to resume the withdrawal of U.S. troops from South Vietnam. Nixon reaffirms earlier pledges to bring the Cambodian operation to an end by June 30 with "all our major military objectives" achieved and reports that 17,000 of the

31,000 U.S. troops in Cambodia have returned to South Vietnam. After June 30, says Nixon, "all American air support" for Allied troops fighting in Cambodia will end, with the only remaining American activity being attacks on enemy troop movements and supplies threatening U.S. forces in South Vietnam. Nixon promises that 50,000 of the 150,000 troops, whose withdrawal from Vietnam he had announced April 20, "will be out by October 15."

June 3–8
GROUND WAR: Communist forces attack Cambodian troops at Kompong Thom, 87 miles north of Phnom Penh, and at Siem Reap, 80 miles to the northwest of the capital. Communist troops capture Kompong Thom and the nearby town of Am Leang on June 7, but are driven out on June 8. Cambodian officials report 128 Communist soldiers killed around both centers. Cambodian losses are officially listed as nine killed and 23 wounded.

June 6
SOUTH VIETNAM: Vice President Ky, in a speech to the Cambodian parliament, says South Vietnam has no territorial ambitions in Cambodia and will send military forces to help Cambodia wherever and whenever Phnom Penh asks.

June 8
NORTH VIETNAM: In a speech delivered in Hanoi, Norodom Sihanouk pledges Cambodians will fight with the Vietnamese Communists to defeat U.S. "imperialism."

June 8–13
GROUND WAR: U.S. troops battle Communist forces within an 11-mile radius of Memot in the Fishhook region of Cambodia. U.S. losses are 13 killed and 60 wounded. Nine Communist soldiers are reported killed.

June 11
GROUND WAR: A force of 200 Viet Cong guerrillas shoots its way through the hamlet of Thanh My, 17 miles southeast of Danang, firing mortars and rifles, and throwing satchel charges and grenades into civilian homes. An estimated 114 civilians are killed and 316 homes destroyed.

June 12–16
GROUND WAR: In the deepest penetration that South Vietnamese forces have made into Cambodia yet (50 miles), a force of 4,000 ARVN and 2,000 Cambodian soldiers battles 1,400 Communist troops for the provincial capital of Kompong Speu, 30 miles southwest of Phnom Penh. The town is captured by the Communists on June 13, but retaken by Allied forces on June 16. South Vietnamese officials report 183 enemy soldiers killed, while losing four killed and 22 wounded. Civilian casualties in Kompong Speu are estimated at 40–50 killed.

June 15
GROUND WAR: South Vietnamese forces report 110 NVA soldiers killed in three battles around Prey Veng, 30 miles east of Phnom Penh. Thirteen South Vietnamese are killed and 37 wounded.

June 16–21

CAMBODIA: North Vietnamese attacks almost completely isolate Phnom Penh. The principal fighting rages in and around Kompong Thom, about 90 miles north of the capital. On June 17, Cambodia's last working railway line, which runs to the border with Thailand, is severed when Communist troops seize a freight train with 200 tons of rice and other food supplies at a station at Krang Lovea, about 40 miles northwest of Phnom Penh. On June 18, Communist forces sever Highway 1, linking Phnom Penh with Saigon, 30 miles southeast of the capital and Highway 4, leading southwest to the port of Kompong Som.

June 22

RIVER WAR: The U.S. Navy turns over 273 combat boats to the Vietnamese navy in ceremonies in Saigon.

June 24

USA – GOVERNMENT: On an amendment offered by Senator Robert Dole (R-Kans.) to the Foreign Military Sales Act, the Senate votes, 81–10, to repeal the Tonkin Gulf Resolution. The Nixon administration takes a neutral stance on the vote, denying that it relies on the Tonkin resolution as the basis for its war-making authority in Southeast Asia.

USA – GOVERNMENT: U.S. embassy in Phnom Penh discloses that the United States has stepped up the shipment of arms of Cambodia and that all of the $7.9 million in military aid promised for the current fiscal year either has arrived or will arrive shortly.

June 26

USA – GOVERNMENT: Secretary of State Laird affirms the U.S. plans to continue bombing raids inside Cambodia after June 30. Laird makes clear the "primary emphasis" of the raids will be the denial of routes for enemy troops and supplies, but refuses to rule out air support for Allied ground combat troops.

June 27

CAMBODIA: All Cambodian troops are reported to have withdrawn from Ratanakiri Province, leaving the northeastern part of the country under the virtual control of the Khmer Rouge and their North Vietnamese allies.

June 29–30

GROUND WAR: The final withdrawal of U.S. ground combat troops from Cambodia is completed, ending two months of operations in Cambodia. Military officials report 338 Americans killed and 1,525 wounded in the operation. The South Vietnamese report 866 killed and 3,724 wounded. About 34,000 South Vietnamese troops remain in Cambodia. Allied forces claim 11,000 enemy casualties.

June 30

USA – GOVERNMENT: President Nixon, in a written report on the U.S. operation in Cambodia, pronounces it a "successful" operation. Ruling out the use of U.S. troops there in the future, Nixon says that Cambodia's defense will be left largely to Cambodia and its allies. Regarding the use of U.S. airpower in Cambodia, Nixon states that the United States will not provide air or logistical support for South Vietnamese forces in Cambodia, but will continue bombing enemy personnel and supply concentrations "with the approval of the Cambodian government." Nixon notes that more than a year's supply of weapons and ammunition was captured and that 11,349 enemy soldiers were killed by Allied forces.

USA – GOVERNMENT: The Senate votes, 58–37, to adopt the Cooper-Church amendment to limit presidential power in Cambodia. The amendment bars funds to retain U.S. troops in Cambodia after July 1 or to supply military advisers or mercenaries or to conduct "any combat activity in the air above Cambodia in direct support of Cambodian forces" without congressional approval. The amendment represents the first limitation ever voted on the president's powers as commander-in-chief during a war situation. The House of Representatives rejects the amendment July 9 and it is eventually dropped from the Foreign Military Sales Act.

July 1
USA – GOVERNMENT: President Nixon announces the appointment of David K. E. Bruce to head the U.S. delegation to the Paris peace talks.

July 1–23
GROUND WAR: In the costliest single battle of the year, elements of the 101st Airborne Division withstand heavy rocket, mortar, and ground attacks by the 803rd NVA Regiment on Fire Base Ripcord, 25 miles west of Hue.

July 2
SOUTH VIETNAM: President Thieu incorporates both the Regional Forces and the Popular Forces into the South Vietnamese Army, and redesignates the corps tactical zones as Military Regions.

July 3
TERRORISM: South Vietnamese civilian passengers are killed when a river boat strikes a Communist floating mine on the Cua Viet River near Dong Ha, about nine miles south of the DMZ.

July 7
GROUND WAR: Major General George W. Casey, commander of the 1st Cavalry Division, and six other army personnel are killed in a helicopter crash while flying from Tay Ninh to Cam Ranh to visit troops in the hospital.

July 8
GROUND WAR: Helicopter gunships from the 101st Airborne Division kill an estimated 150–200 enemy soldiers of the North Vietnamese 304th Division trying to cross the border into South Vietnam from Laos near Khe Sanh in I Corps.

July 9–15
GROUND WAR: Elements of the U.S. 5th Infantry Division (Mechanized), the 101st Airborne Division, and the 3rd ARVN Regiment conduct Operation Clinch Valley, an airmobile assault into the border area near Khe Sanh to exploit the enemy sightings from July 8. Casualties are U.S.: none reported; NVA/VC: 226 KIA.

July 15
SOUTH VIETNAM: President Thieu, in a speech honoring South Vietnamese troops who participated in the Cambodian operation, vows to "beat to death" those of his countrymen who call for an "immediate peace" with the Communists.

July 23

GROUND WAR: U.S. troops abandon Fire Base Ripcord north of the A Shau Valley after heaving bombing strikes and artillery barrages fail to stop a North Vietnamese build-up around the base. In three weeks of fighting at the base, U.S. losses are 61 killed and 345 wounded.

July 26

GROUND WAR: A force of 2,500 South Vietnamese troops move into Cambodia from Dan Phuc, in South Vietnam's western Mekong Delta, raising the number of South Vietnamese soldiers in Cambodia to 20,000. In initial fighting, 35 Communist soldiers are reported killed.

July 31

SOUTH VIETNAM: President Thieu declares South Vietnam's conditions for peace are unchanged and once again rules out any coalition government with the Communists, except one that might result from internationally supervised elections. Thieu puts the Communist side and those urging a more flexible negotiating position on notice that U.S. negotiators have no new proposals approved by the South Vietnamese government.

August 4

GROUND WAR: In a battle in the Mekong Delta, South Vietnamese forces kill 44 Communist soldiers. Six South Vietnamese are killed and 29 are wounded.

August 6

USA – GOVERNMENT: In response to eyewitness reports that U.S. warplanes are flying direct combat support missions for Cambodian ground troops, Secretary of Defense Laird says that recent U.S. bombings are part of a general interdiction campaign to protect U.S. forces in South Vietnam. He makes it clear that the Nixon administration's definition of interdiction encompasses virtually all of Cambodia.
NEGOTIATIONS: U.S. chief negotiator David Bruce attends his first session of the Paris talks. The Communist negotiators declare that the positions of both sides appear as intractable as ever.

August 8

AIR WAR: Confidential orders are issued to all U.S. unit commanders telling them to say that U.S. air raids in Cambodia are for interdiction purposes, to protect the remaining U.S. troops in South Vietnam, and to aid the process of Vietnamization.

August 11

GROUND WAR: As part of the Vietnamization effort, South Vietnamese troops relieve U.S. units of their responsibility for guarding the Cambodian and Laotian borders along almost all of the South Vietnamese frontier.

August 15

GROUND WAR: South Vietnamese officials report that regional forces have killed 308 Communist troops in four days of heavy fighting along a coastal strip south of the DMZ. This is one of the biggest victories of the war for the regional forces in the war.

August 19

CAMBODIA: Cambodia and the United States sign a $40 million military aid agreement, which will provide training funds and a wide array of military equipment and weapons, to include small arms, ammunition, communications equipment, and spare parts. The aid package will be provided for the fiscal year ending June 30, 1971.

August 21

USA – MILITARY: Defense Secretary Laird announces the "Total Force" policy, leading to much greater reliance by the services on Guard and Reserve units.

GROUND WAR: Viet Cong mortars shell the Mekong Delta village of Bu Chuc in Chau Duc Province, killing 11 persons and wounding 42.

August 24

AIR WAR: U.S. B-52s carry out heavy bombing raids along the DMZ.

USA – DOMESTIC: Four antiwar protesters set off a bomb that kills one at the University of Wisconsin. The bomb, set off at 3:42 A.M., is intended to destroy the Army Math Research Center housed on the second through fourth floors of Sterling Hall, but causes massive destruction to other parts of the building as well. It results in the death of Robert Fassnacht, a physics researcher, and injures four others, none of whom are affiliated with the Math Center.

August 26

GROUND WAR: Thirty-four U.S. servicemen are killed when two helicopters are shot down in separate incidents. A total of 3,998 helicopters have been lost by this time in the war, 1,777 of them to enemy ground fire.

August 27

SOUTH VIETNAM: Vice President Spiro Agnew meets with South Vietnamese president Thieu in Saigon. In a speech at Ton Son Nhut air base, Agnew praises the South Vietnamese people for suffering "so much in freedom's cause" and promises that "there will be no lessening of U.S. support."

GROUND WAR: MACV reports that 52 Americans died in combat during the week of August 16–22; 358 soldiers were wounded. This is the lowest casualty toll since the week of December 3–9, 1966.

August 28

THAILAND: Thailand announces that it plans to withdraw its 11,000-man force from South Vietnam, but no timetable is given for the withdrawal.

August 29

TERRORISM: Communist forces attack a Buddhist orphanage and temple south of Danang, killing 15 and wounding 45.

August 30

SOUTH VIETNAM: An estimated six million South Vietnamese cast ballots for 30 seats at stake in the senate elections. While the voting is going on, Communist forces attack at least 14 district towns, a provincial capital, and several polling places. Fifty-five civilians are reported killed and 140 wounded.

August 31

SOUTH VIETNAM: Anti-government Buddhist candidates win 10 of 30 senate seats contested in the previous day's election. However, the senate as a whole remains in the firm control of conservative, pro-government supporters. Catholics still hold 50 percent of the senate seats, even though they constitute only 10 percent of the population of South Vietnam.

August 31–May 7, 1971

GROUND WAR: Troops from the Americal Division join U.S. Marines for the conduct of Operation Imperial Lake, an attempt to clear North Vietnamese forces from the Que Son Mountains south of Danang, I Corps. The operation begins with 10 marine artillery batteries pounding the mountains in one of the largest preparatory artillery strikes of the war; shells rain down on 53 separate targets for six hours. The artillery strikes are followed by two hours of tactical air strikes. Casualties will be U.S.: 24 KIA, 205 WIA; NVA/VC: 305 KIA.

September 1

USA – GOVERNMENT: Senators George McGovern (D-S.D.) and Mark Hatfield (D-Oreg.) make an unsuccessful attempt to obtain a Senate resolution setting a deadline for all U.S. troops to be out of Vietnam. The Senate rejects the McGovern-Hatfield amendments by 55–39. The amendment would have set a deadline of December 31, 1971, for complete withdrawal of American troops from South Vietnam. The Senate also turns down 71–22 a proposal forbidding the army from sending draftees to Vietnam. Also on this day, a bipartisan group of 14 senators, including both the majority and minority leaders, sign a letter to President Nixon asking him to propose a comprehensive standstill cease-fire for South Vietnam at the Paris peace talks.

September 3

NEGOTIATIONS: North Vietnamese chief negotiator, Xuan Thuy, who walked out of the talks in December 1969 returns to the negotiations, declaring that the position of North Vietnam remains unchanged. Thuy demands that the United States must agree to withdraw unconditionally and "renounce" the Saigon government.

September 4

GROUND WAR: In a strike directed against South Vietnam's pacification program, VC guerrillas attack a civil defense training center in Binh Dinh Province; 14 South Vietnamese are killed and 26 wounded.

September 5–October 8, 1971

GROUND WAR: The 101st Airborne Division (Airmobile), in coordination with the ARVN 1st Infantry Division, conducts Operation Jefferson Glen, a search and clear mission to prevent a North Vietnamese buildup and to support pacification operations in Thua Thien Province, I Corps. This will be the last major military operation in which U.S. ground forces take part. Casualties will be NVA/VC: 2,026 KIA.

September 7

CAMBODIA: A major attack by Cambodian loyalist forces commences, but makes little progress.

NEGOTIATIONS: In Paris, Henry Kissinger holds the first of two clandestine meetings with North Vietnamese representatives in Paris. Le Duc Tho does not attend either meeting; North Vietnam is represented by Xuan Thuy. A second meeting will be held September 27. There will be no progress at either session.

September 8

GROUND WAR: More than 200 Communist troops attack the Tra Bong district headquarters and Ranger camp south of Danang, killing 24 South Vietnamese and wounding 42. One U.S. adviser is also killed.

September 10

GROUND WAR: A 2,000-man South Vietnamese force completes its military operations in the Parrot's Beak area of Cambodia. Fifty-eight enemy soldiers are reported killed.

September 12

GROUND WAR: Communist troops launch a new assault against South Vietnamese troops near Fire Base O'Reilly just below the DMZ. Farther to the south in the Mekong Delta, South Vietnamese forces report killing 73 enemy soldiers.

September 17

NEGOTIATIONS: Nguyen Thi Binh, foreign minister of the Provisional Revolutionary Government, attending the peace talks for the first time in three months, outlines an eight-point program, which is similar to another program first presented in May 1969. In exchange for the withdrawal of all U.S. and Allied forces by June 30, 1971, Communist forces will refrain from attacking the departing troops and offer to begin immediate negotiations on the release of POWs, once the withdrawal is agreed to. The PRG statement demands the purge of South Vietnam's top three leaders: President Thieu, Vice President Ky, and Premier Tran Thien Khiem.

GROUND WAR: MACV reports Communist forces have downed and destroyed nine U.S. helicopters in the last six days and have damaged eight others, killing four Americans and wounding six. U.S. troops report killing 54 enemy soldiers in four actions near Danang.

September 19

RIVER WAR: A force of 200 South Vietnamese vessels and 1,500 marines begins naval operations 35 miles southeast of Phnom Penh aimed at destroying Communist base areas and infiltration corridors between the Bassac and Mekong Rivers.

September 20

GROUND WAR: North Vietnamese gunners down a U.S. helicopter during the insertion of a reconnaissance team and then shell an armored relief force attempting to reach the scene, one mile south of the DMZ. Eleven Americans are killed and 11 are wounded.

September 21

SOUTH VIETNAM: The revised "Hamlet Evaluation System" used by U.S. officials to measure progress in the pacification effort indicates that 92.8 percent of the population of South Vietnam is pacified and under control of the government. However, the report says that 996,600 people live in areas where neither the Communists nor the government has control.

September 26

USA – DOMESTIC: A Gallup poll indicates that 55 percent of the population of the United States favor the recently defeated McGovern-Hatfield amendment calling for U.S. troops to be pulled out of Vietnam by the end of 1971 if there is no declaration of war; 36 percent are opposed.

SOUTH VIETNAM: Vice President Ky says he has decided not to attend a pro-war rally scheduled for October 3 in Washington, D.C.

September 27

GROUND WAR: Twelve U.S. soldiers are killed and five wounded in accidents involving helicopter collisions and the accidental triggering of mines.

September 28

RIVER WAR: It is announced that the recent South Vietnamese operations along the Bassac and Mekong Rivers in Cambodia claimed 233 enemy casualties.

October 3

USA – DOMESTIC: More than 20,000 people gather at the Washington Monument for a Vietnam victory rally, which is addressed by Tran Khoa Hoc, a junior South Vietnamese embassy aide, in the absence of Vice President Ky who was originally to have attended the event. The speaker pleads for continued assistance by Americans and other peoples of the world for South Vietnam in its struggle against communism.

October 4

USA – GOVERNMENT: President Nixon confers privately in Dublin, Ireland, with the U.S. negotiators to the Paris talks, David Bruce and Philip Habib. Following the meeting, Nixon says that European leaders on his recent tour showed a more sophisticated understanding of U.S. aims in Vietnam than they did when he toured Europe early in 1969.

GROUND WAR: As Communist forces shell 19 targets, 15 South Vietnamese are killed and seven wounded in two terrorist incidents north of Saigon. In the Mekong Delta, ARVN troops report killing 19 enemy soldiers.

October 5

GROUND WAR: As the surge in Communist activity continues, 20 civilians are killed and 40 wounded in an attack on a refugee camp 280 miles northeast of Saigon.

October 6

GROUND WAR: Intensified Communist shellings continue for a third consecutive day, most of them in the coastal provinces of the central and northern parts of South Vietnam. Seven refugees are killed and 52 wounded in an attack on a resettlement center near Phu My on the central coast.

GROUND WAR: South Vietnamese military headquarters in Saigon announces the end of a three-month operation in southeastern Cambodia and the withdrawal of the task force involved. During the operation 453 enemy soldiers have been reported killed. South Vietnamese losses are 93 killed and 642 wounded.

October 7

USA – GOVERNMENT: In a televised speech, President Nixon announces five-point proposal to end the war, based on a "standstill" cease-fire in place in South Vietnam, Laos, and Cambodia. He proposes eventual withdrawal of U.S. forces, unconditional release of prisoners of war (POWs), and political solutions reflecting the will of the South Vietnamese people. Nixon rejects the Communist proposals for the ouster of Nguyen Van Thieu, Nguyen Cao Ky, and Tran Thiem Khiem as "totally unacceptable." Nixon's proposals are well received at home, but will be rejected by the Communists.

October 8

USA – GOVERNMENT: The United States publicly urges the Soviet Union to use its "considerable influence" with the Communists to persuade them to accept President Nixon's new proposals. The Senate adopts a resolution expressing support for President Nixon's October 7 initiative, calling the proposals "fair and equitable."
NEGOTIATIONS: The Communist delegation in Paris rejects President Nixon's October 7 proposal as "a maneuver to deceive world opinion," and continues to demand an unconditional and total withdrawal of U.S. forces from Indochina and the overthrow of the "puppet" leaders in Saigon.

October 11

GROUND WAR: A U.S. helicopter gunship accidentally fires 12 rockets at South Vietnamese troops in the Mekong Delta, 132 miles southwest of Saigon, killing eight and wounding 23.
USA – MILITARY: The 3rd Brigade, 9th Infantry Division, departs South Vietnam.

October 11–12

USA – MILITARY: The 199th Light Infantry Brigade and its four subordinate battalions depart South Vietnam for Fort Benning, Georgia, where the units will be deactivated.

October 12

USA – GOVERNMENT: Nixon announces that the United States will withdraw a further 40,000 troops before Christmas.

October 13

USA – GOVERNMENT: In a report prepared at the request of President Nixon, British counterinsurgency expert Sir Robert Thompson explains that smashing the VC is a prerequisite for solving the political troubles of South Vietnam. After a five-week secret mission to South Vietnam in September and early October, Thompson reports that U.S. and Allied intelligence and police efforts have failed to destroy the Communists' subversive apparatus in South Vietnam. His report concludes that success in other areas of pacification cannot solve the basic political problems of South Vietnam after the withdrawal of the bulk of U.S. forces so long as the VC apparatus remains virtually intact.

GROUND WAR: In two days of fighting in Quang Ngai Province, 10 Americans are killed and 24 wounded. Communist losses are put at 13 killed.

October 14
NEGOTIATIONS: Hanoi releases a statement officially rejecting President Nixon's peace proposal of October 7; he calls on the United States to reply to the "concrete proposals" advanced by the Provisional Revolutionary Government on September 17.
GROUND WAR: Nine U.S. soldiers and 15 South Vietnamese soldiers are killed and five Americans are wounded by a VC booby trap, 66 miles southeast of Danang.

October 15
USA – GOVERNMENT: President Nixon announces that a further 40,000 American troops will be withdrawn from South Vietnam by the end of the year.
NEGOTIATIONS: The Communist delegations in Paris declare that their rejections of the recent peace proposals by President Nixon are "firm, total, and categorical." The Communists reject the proposal on troop withdrawals because they say Nixon refuses to set a date for the withdrawal of U.S. forces and continues to insist on mutual withdrawal.

October 18
AIR WAR: A U.S. warplane mistakenly drops two 500-pound bombs on a South Vietnamese troop base at Thien Ghon, near the Cambodian border, leaving 18 ARVN soldiers dead and seven others wounded.

October 21
GROUND WAR: In combat centered around the district town of Thuong Duc and a nearby Special Forces camp, 26 miles south of Danang, the Allied command reports killing 163 VC and capturing 20 in two days of fighting. Many of the Communist soldiers are killed by close air support, helicopter gunships, and artillery.

October 23
USA – MILITARY: U.S. sources disclose that the Americal Division has violated an April order prohibiting the use of defoliating agents. An investigation reveals that troops used the chemical to strip away enemy cover and destroy crops "on several occasions."

October 24–25
CAMBODIA: ARVN forces begin two new drives into Cambodia.

October 25
GROUND WAR: Fourteen Americans are reported killed in mine and booby trap explosions in Quang Tin and Quang Nan Provinces. In other action, as part of a South Vietnamese offensive in Quang Tin Province, Allied forces report killing 37 Communist soldiers without suffering any casualties.

October 28
GROUND WAR: In various actions, 41 VC are reported killed; elsewhere four South Vietnamese are killed and nine are wounded in VC shellings of two Mekong Delta towns.

South Vietnamese soldiers from the 1st ARVN Division move along a trail during an operation near File Support Base O'Reilly in 1 Corps, October 1970. *(National Archives)*

October 30–November 1

GROUND WAR: Fighting in the five northernmost provinces comes to a virtual halt as the worst monsoon rains in six years strike the region. The resultant floods kill 293 people and leave more than 200,000 homeless.

October 31

SOUTH VIETNAM: President Thieu delivers a speech on the state of the nation before a joint session of the National Assembly, asserting that pacification has now reached 99.1 percent of the population. He declares that the Communists view negotiations merely as a way to gain time and "to achieve victory gradually." Thieu says that he will never accept a coalition government with the Communists, citing "countless past experiences" that show it would not bring peace. Contending that pacification has worked, he says that a military victory is close at hand and that "we are seeing the light at the end of the tunnel."

November 2

GROUND WAR: In their first attack on the capital since July 20, Communist forces fire four rockets into Saigon, killing seven civilians and wounding 25.

November 4

USA – MILITARY: The United States hands over an air base in the Mekong Delta to the Vietnamese air force as part of the Vietnamization program. Secretary of the Air Force Robert Seamans and General Abrams attend the ceremony. The air base will become the home of two South Vietnamese helicopter squadrons, with the United States providing 62 aircraft, 31 of which are turned over with the air base.

November 5

GROUND WAR: MACV reports the lowest weekly death toll in five years (since the week ending October 25, 1965); 24 Americans died in combat during the week of October 25–31, making it the fifth consecutive week in a row in which the U.S. death toll is under 50. Nevertheless, the fighting continues in the northern provinces as U.S. troops report killing seven NVA in a battle 17 miles southeast of Danang. In another firefight, U.S. Marines report killing 20 NVA while losing one of their own killed.

November 6

GROUND WAR: ARVN troops launch a new offensive aimed at cleaning out border sanctuaries and blocking the movement of North Vietnamese forces into South Vietnam, advancing across a 100-mile-wide front in the southeastern part of Cambodia.

November 8

GROUND WAR: The U.S. 2nd Brigade, 25th Infantry Division, becomes a separate command, allowing the bulk of the division to prepare to depart South Vietnam.

November 9

USA – GOVERNMENT: The Supreme Court refuses to hear a challenge by the state of Massachusetts regarding the constitutionality of the Vietnam War. By a six to three vote, the justices reject the effort of the state to bring a suit in federal court in defense of Massachusetts citizens who claim protection under a state law that allows them to refuse military service in an undeclared war.

November 10–11

GROUND WAR: For the first time in five years, there are no U.S. combat fatalities in Indochina.

November 11
GROUND WAR: The 6,000-man South Vietnamese task force pulls out of Cambodia after failing to find new Communist troop sanctuaries. Forty-one enemy soldiers are reported killed in the operation.

November 13
AIR WAR: North Vietnamese gunners shoot down a manned but unarmed U.S. reconnaissance aircraft 42 miles south of Vinh in North Vietnam. The two crewmen are apparently killed. It is the 13th U.S. plane shot down over North Vietnam since the November 1, 1968, bombing halt.

USA – GOVERNMENT: Defense Secretary Laird, speaking at a press conference, denounces the shooting down of the unarmed plane as a violation of "certain understandings" between the United States and North Vietnam. He hints at escalation in retaliation, saying that the United States is "ready to take appropriate action in response" to such attacks. Also on this day, Vice President Spiro Agnew accuses network TV news of bias and distortion.

November 14
NORTH VIETNAM: The North Vietnamese continue to insist that they are bound by no agreement relating to the cessation of bombing on November 1, 1968, denying once again that they had accepted any conditions for the bombing halt. Nguyen Thanh Lee, spokesman for the North Vietnamese delegation at the Paris talks, insists that "there is absolutely no tacit accord" between the United States and North Vietnam and, instead, refers to "acts of provocation" by the Nixon administration designed as a pretext for the expansion of the war.

GROUND WAR: North Vietnamese troops attack two U.S. units in the northern jungles, killing four Americans and wounding 25 others. Other action reported raises U.S. casualties in the northern sector to eight killed and 49 wounded in the previous 24 hours.

November 15
GROUND WAR: Booby traps and land mines kill nine Americans and wound 10.

November 16
DIPLOMACY: South Vietnamese vice president Ky, speaking at the U.S. Military Academy at West Point, New York, says that Cambodia would be overrun by Communist forces "within 24 hours" if South Vietnamese troops, currently operating there, are withdrawn. Ky describes the Cambodian operation of last May as the "turning point" of the war and said that as a result the enemy was forced to revert to low-level guerrilla warfare. Ky reports that his government is concerned that the Nixon administration might be yielding to the "pressure of the anti-war groups" and pulling out the remaining U.S. troops too quickly.

November 17
WAR CRIMES: The army court-martial of Lieutenant William L. Calley, charged with killing civilians at My Lai, begins at Fort Benning and will last until March 1971.

GROUND WAR: Communist forces shell Bien Hoa air base, killing three Americans and two South Vietnamese. Fourteen civilians are wounded in the attack.

THAILAND: Premier Thanom Kittikachorn says that his country will withdraw all of its 12,000 troops from South Vietnam by 1972.

November 18

USA – GOVERNMENT: President Nixon asks Congress for supplemental funds for the Cambodian government of Premier Lon Nol. Nixon asks for $155 million in new funds—$85 million for military assistance, mainly in the form of ammunition—as well as $100 million to restore funds taken from other foreign appropriations during the year by "presidential determination" and given to Cambodia.

GROUND WAR: In Vietnam, a U.S. marine helicopter returning from a rescue mission crashes into the Que Son Mountains, 22 miles southwest of Danang, killing 15 marines, including members of the patrol that were rescued.

November 19

TERRORISM: Nine civilians are killed and 43 are wounded when a Vietcong grenade is thrown into an open-air movie at Cong Thanh, 20 miles northeast of Saigon.

November 20

USA – GOVERNMENT: Backing up the president's recent appeal to Congress for more money for Cambodia, Defense Secretary Laird states that failure to vote the funds could delay the U.S. pull-out and argues that the aid is a "good investment."

WAR CRIMES: Sergeant David Mitchell is acquitted in Fort Hood, Texas, of intent to murder 30 South Vietnamese civilians at My Lai in March 1968.

November 21

COVERT WAR: A combined air force and army team of 40 Americans, led by Colonel "Bull" Simon (USA), conducts a heliborne assault of a prison camp at Son Tay, 23 miles west of Hanoi, in an attempt to free 70–100 Americans suspected of being held there. U.S. warplanes provide escort and attack North Vietnamese troop installations and antiaircraft sites within two miles of the camp. However, the team finds no POWs and has to fight its way out, killing 25 guards in a 40-minute fight at the camp while sustaining no casualties.

AIR WAR: Approximately one hour after the Son Tay raid, U.S. aircraft (200 fighter bombers and 100 support aircraft) inflict the most severe bombing raids in two years on North Vietnam as retaliation for the shooting down of U.S. reconnaissance aircraft.

NORTH VIETNAM: Hanoi Radio reports that "wave after wave" of U.S. bombers attacked targets in North Vietnam and says that the planes struck at targets ranging from Haiphong to Hoa Binh Province, southeast of Hanoi.

USA – GOVERNMENT: Secretary of Defense Laird issues a statement confirming reports of U.S. bombing raids against North Vietnam, saying that the raids all took place below the 19th parallel and that they were in response to continued attacks on U.S. reconnaissance planes

November 22

POWs: Nineteen South Vietnamese POWs are sprung from a VC prison camp in the Mekong Delta by a combined U.S. and South Vietnamese rescue squad made up of

15 U.S. Navy SEALs and 19 South Vietnamese commandos. No friendly casualties are reported.

GROUND WAR: North Vietnamese forces attack the headquarters of a South Vietnamese task force operating just inside the Cambodian border near Krek. South Vietnamese losses are 10 killed and 20 wounded.

November 23

USA – MILITARY: Secretary of Defense Laird discloses the November 21 U.S. raid on the North Vietnamese prison camp at Son Tay, emphasizing that it was the only operation that took place north of the 19th parallel.

NEGOTIATIONS: The Communist delegations to the Paris talks say they will not attend the next session of the talks to protest the recent U.S. bombing raids against North Vietnam. Xuan Thuy says that as an excuse for "acts of war," the United States has "invented the so-called understanding" permitting reconnaissance missions over North Vietnam.

November 24

USA – GOVERNMENT: Secretary of Defense Laird, in testimony before the Senate Foreign Relations Committee, says he will recommend to President Nixon the resumption of full-scale air attacks on North Vietnam if Hanoi engages in major violations of the tacit understanding with the United States regarding the halt in the bombing of North Vietnam. Laird notes these violations include the firing at unarmed U.S. reconnaissance planes, the shelling of major South Vietnamese population centers, and troop movements through the DMZ.

GROUND WAR: In Vietnam, a helicopter carrying South Vietnamese soldiers collides with a U.S. light plane in the Mekong Delta; 13 South Vietnamese and four Americans are killed.

November 26

NORTH VIETNAM: Nguyen Thanh Le, spokesman for the North Vietnamese delegation to the Paris talks, claims 49 civilians were killed and 40 wounded in the recent U.S. bombing raids. Of this total, 28 are reported to have died in the bombing of a restaurant in Ha Tinh, just below the 19th parallel.

November 27

SOUTH VIETNAM: A U.S. Air Force C–123 transport plane is reported missing with six Americans and 73 South Vietnamese aboard. On December 7, the wreckage will be found in the Central Highlands, but there are no survivors.

GROUND WAR: A South Vietnamese task force, operating in southeastern Cambodia, comes under North Vietnamese attack near the town of Krek. The South Vietnamese command reports repelling the assault and killing 48 enemy soldiers. The South Vietnamese command also reports killing 33 Viet Cong in the Rung Sat Special Zone, 23 miles southeast of Saigon.

USA – GOVERNMENT: In Washington, Daniel Henkin, an assistant secretary of defense for public affairs, acknowledges that U.S. aircraft struck military targets near Hanoi during the attempted prisoner-of-war rescue mission at Son Tay.

November 29

SOUTH VIETNAM: A U.S. Air Force C-123 transport plane enroute to the United States, carrying 32 Americans and 12 South Vietnamese, crashes into a mountain near Cam Ranh Bay; only two American airmen survive the crash.

AIR WAR: MACV announces that a U.S. fighter-bomber has attacked a North Vietnamese antiaircraft position, five and a half miles north of the DMZ, near the Laotian border. The raid is termed another "protective reaction" attack.

November 30

NEGOTIATIONS: The Provisional Revolutionary Government announces that its forces in South Vietnam will observe three truces, from midnight December 24 to midnight December 27; for New Year, from midnight December 31 to January 3, 1971; and for Tet, from midnight January 26 to midnight January 30, 1971.

GROUND WAR: The Allied commands announce that there is an increase in fighting throughout South Vietnam. Five Viet Cong guerrillas are killed in a battle 100 miles southeast of Saigon; five more are killed in a skirmish 31 miles northeast of the capital. Near the city of Dalat, in the Central Highlands, the South Vietnamese report killing enemy soldiers in several clashes, while losing seven KIA and 22 wounded.

December 1

GROUND WAR: A 7,000-man South Vietnamese force launches a major drive against a suspected Communist force of 3,000 soldiers in the U Minh Forest in the southern part of the Mekong Delta.

December 2

GROUND WAR: Communist forces fire rocket barrages against 22 towns and military bases throughout South Vietnam. Nearly 100 attacks have been reported in the last four days.

December 4

GROUND WAR: South Vietnamese forces push deeper into the U Minh Forest and report killing 59 Viet Cong in the first three days of the operation. South Vietnamese troops report killing 35 Viet Cong in three small engagements.

December 5

NORTH VIETNAM: A North Vietnamese army newspaper, replying to warnings by U.S. Secretary of Defense Laird regarding the bombing of North Vietnam, declares that the country will not be intimidated by U.S. bombing threats and says U.S. reconnaissance planes will be downed, antiaircraft installations will be set up anywhere, and troops will be massed in any sector.

December 7

USA – MILITARY: The 4th Infantry Division (less its 3rd Brigade) and 1st Logistical Command depart South Vietnam.

December 8

USA – MILITARY: The 25th Infantry Division (less 2nd Brigade) departs South Vietnam.

GROUND WAR: South Vietnamese troops continue their drive in the U Minh Forest and report killing 144 Viet Cong in the first eight days of the operation. Eight South Vietnamese have been killed and 71 wounded. Elsewhere, South Vietnamese and Communist forces clash in the Fishhook area of Cambodia.

December 9

SOUTH VIETNAM: South Vietnamese government announces that it will observe only one-day truces for Christmas and New Year's.

GROUND WAR: A force of 200 North Vietnamese, using mortars and rockets, attacks a South Vietnamese force in the Fishhook area just inside Cambodia. Thirty South Vietnamese are killed and 41 are wounded.

December 10

NORTH VIETNAM: The North Vietnamese government and the Communist Party issue an extraordinary appeal to the North Vietnamese people and army for redoubled efforts to win the war. The North Vietnamese high command calls for the armed forces to heighten their preparedness and determination "to fight victoriously."

USA – GOVERNMENT: President Nixon, holding his first news conference in four months, warns that if North Vietnam increases "the level of fighting in South Vietnam . . . I will order the bombing of military sites in North Vietnam . . . That is the reaction that I shall take." Nixon defends his request for an additional $250 million in foreign assistance, mostly military aid, for Cambodia as "probably the best investment in foreign assistance that the United States has made in my life-time." He notes that if the army of Premier Lon Nol were not fighting 40,000 NVA soldiers inside Cambodia, the North Vietnamese would "be over killing Americans" in South Vietnam.

WAR CRIMES: The defense opens its case in the murder trial of Lieutenant William Calley. Defense attorney George Lattimer cites "superiors' orders" as one of several reasons why noncombatants were killed. Other reasons included the poor training of the platoon, the rage of the men who had seen buddies killed, and the expectation of fierce resistance. Lattimer contends that Captain Ernest Medina, company commander, told the men that at long last they were going to fight the enemy and ordered "every living thing" killed. Lattimer also charges that the whole episode was observed by higher commanders, both on the ground and in the air, including Lieutenant Colonel Frank Barker, task force commander, and General Samuel W. Koster, commanding officer of the Americal Division.

December 14

USA – MILITARY: The 44th Medical Brigade withdraws from Vietnam.

GROUND WAR: Six of eight Americans in an infantry patrol are killed when they inadvertently enter an old U.S. minefield south of the DMZ.

December 17

WAR CRIMES: The trial of William Calley adjourns until January 11, 1971.

December 18–January 19, 1971

GROUND WAR: The U.S. 1st Marines and 51st ARVN Regiment conduct Operation Hoan Dieu-101 in Quang Nam Province, I Corps. Casualties are U.S.: 5 KIA, 87 WIA; NVA/VC: 690 KIA (estimated), 87 POW.

December 19

GROUND WAR: U.S. troops report killing 10 enemy soldiers south of the DMZ. South Vietnamese forces report killing 26 Communist soldiers in the U Minh Forest and 39 Communist soldiers in two other engagements in the Mekong Delta.

December 20

GROUND WAR: Communist forces, observing the 10th anniversary of the founding of the National Liberation Front, bombard four Allied positions, down four U.S. planes, and ambush a U.S. convoy. Five Americans are killed and six wounded. The Allied command reports killing 99 Communist soldiers in weekend actions ranging from the DMZ to the U Minh Forest.

December 22

NORTH VIETNAM: Defense Minister Vo Nguyen Giap affirms that U.S. unarmed reconnaissance flights over North Vietnam will be shot down and says that the United States has no right to make such flights.

December 22–29

USA – GOVERNMENT: Congress adopts legislation that denies funds for the introduction of ground troops into Cambodia and Laos, but does not include a proposed ban on further operations elsewhere in Southeast Asia.

December 23

USA – GOVERNMENT: Secretary of State Rogers acknowledges that President Nixon is going beyond the 1968 understanding in threatening to renew the bombing of North Vietnam if it steps up the level of fighting in South Vietnam. Rogers, however, contends that this is because the situation has been changed by U.S. troop withdrawals.

December 24

GROUND WAR: Two hours before the start of the Allied Christmas cease-fire, a U.S. artillery battery fires a 105 mm shell into a group of soldiers of the 1st Brigade, 101st Airborne Division, killing nine American soldiers and wounding nine others. The incident takes place 11 miles south of Hue.

December 26–27

GROUND WAR: South Vietnamese troops report killing 38 more enemy soldiers in the U Minh Forest in the Mekong Delta.

December 27

NORTH VIETNAM: The Communist Party newspaper *Nhan Dan,* commenting on U.S. Secretary of State Rogers's news conference, says President Nixon will "invite upon himself heavier setbacks" unless he learns from President Johnson's "failure." The newspaper says Nixon's proposal for a standstill cease-fire is not the "key" to a settlement.

December 29

USA – GOVERNMENT: Congress adopts legislation that denies funds for the introduction of ground combat troops into Laos or Thailand but does not ban further operations elsewhere in Southeast Asia.

December 30

USA – MILITARY: The U.S. Navy ends its four-year role in inland waterway patrol, turning over 125 U.S. vessels to the South Vietnamese navy. This brings the total number of vessels turned over to the South Vietnamese to 650. About 17,000 Americans will remain with the South Vietnamese navy as advisers in shore positions and aboard South Vietnamese vessels.

December 31

USA – GOVERNMENT: Congress repeals the Tonkin Gulf Resolution.

YEAR-END SUMMARY: U.S. military strength in South Vietnam has declined to 334,600; nearly 200,000 troops have returned home so far. American losses for the year include 4,204 killed, bringing the total number of U.S. military personnel killed in action since 1959 to 44,228. Free World Military Forces personnel in Vietnam have declined to 67,700; South Vietnamese armed forces strength has increased to 986,000. Total South Vietnamese military personnel killed in 1970 is now 20,914, bringing the total number killed since 1965 to 133,522. In Paris, the peace talks are stalled, as all parties make demands that the others will not accept—and none will make concessions.

1971

January 1

USA – GOVERNMENT: Congress passes legislation forbidding the use of U.S. ground troops in Cambodia and Laos, but not the use of U.S. airpower in those countries.

January 2–25

CAMBODIA: Cambodian and South Vietnamese forces continue a drive to clear the Communist blockade of the strategic Route 4 between Phnom Penh and Kompong Som, the nation's sole port facility.

January 3

GROUND WAR: Despite the New Year cease-fire, fighting continues intermittently, reaching a climax on this day when South Vietnamese troops enter the southern part of the DMZ in pursuit of North Vietnamese forces that attacked an ARVN patrol deployed just south of the DMZ. After a 10-hour battle, the South Vietnamese troops withdraw from the DMZ.

AIR WAR: A large force of B-52 bombers and some 300 fighter-bombers attack Communist supply and infiltration routes along the Ho Chi Minh Trail in Laos and Cambodia.

January 6

USA – MILITARY: MACV announces a program to combat widespread drug use by U.S. soldiers. This action is taken after a Defense Department report cites drug use as a cause for breakdown in military discipline and order.

WAR CRIMES: The army drops charges of a cover-up in the My Lai massacre against four officers, making a total of 11 people who have been cleared of responsibility during the My Lai trials.

January 7
USA – DOMESTIC: The *New York Times* reports on MACV's estimate that some 65,000 U.S. soldiers and marines were involved with drug abuse in 1970.

January 7–11
USA – MILITARY: Accompanied by Admiral Thomas Moorer, chairman of the Joint Chiefs of Staff, Defense Secretary Laird arrives in South Vietnam to assess the military situation and check on the progress of the "Vietnamization" effort. Laird announces that U.S. "combat responsibility" will end by midsummer, but later warns President Nixon and his cabinet of "some tough days ahead."

January 8
AIR WAR: U.S. jets hit two North Vietnamese missile bases north of the DMZ in "protective reaction" strikes.

USA – DOMESTIC: Opposing a scientific study made under Dr. Matthew Meselson, professor of biology at Harvard University, the Department of Defense denies that the U.S. defoliation program has completely destroyed nearly 250,000 acres of mangrove forest in South Vietnam, and defends the program by citing the advantages of cleared land for small Vietnamese farmers and for the lumber industry.

January 12
USA – DOMESTIC: The Reverend Philip F. Berrigan, serving a six-year prison term on charges of destroying draft records, and six others are indicted by a grand jury on charges of conspiring to kidnap presidential adviser Henry Kissinger and of plotting to blow up the heating tunnels of federal buildings in Washington. The "Harrisburg Seven," as they come to be known, deny the charges and denounce them as a government effort to destroy the peace movement.

WAR CRIMES: In a Washington news conference, representatives of the antiwar Concerned Officers Movement, four army officers and a navy officer, formally request a military court of inquiry to investigate reported war crimes by U.S. soldiers in Vietnam, citing 300 pages of testimony by Vietnam veterans given in December 1970 and holding as precedent the Nuremberg and Japanese war crimes trials.

January 15–17
AIR WAR: B-52 bombers escorted by U.S. fighter-bombers strike Communist missile sites in North Vietnam along the Vietnam-Laotian border.

January 17
CAMBODIA: Led by South Vietnamese lieutenant general Do Cao Tri, and with U.S. air support and advisers, some 300 South Vietnamese paratroopers raid a Communist prisoner of war camp near the town of Mimot in Cambodia on information that 20 U.S. prisoners are being held there. They find the camp empty but capture 30 enemy soldiers and sustain no casualties.

January 18
USA – DOMESTIC: In a televised speech, Senator George S. McGovern (D-S.D.) begins his antiwar campaign for the 1972 Democratic presidential nomination

by vowing to bring all U.S. soldiers home from
Vietnam.

January 20

NORTH VIETNAM: A Hanoi communiqué accuses
the United States of almost daily bombing raids on
North Vietnam, to include defoliation missions.
The Defense Department denies the charges, citing the use of "protective reaction" strikes only.

January 21

USA – GOVERNMENT: Amid reports of U.S. air and
ground presence in the Cambodian fighting, 64
Democratic congressmen present legislation to deny
funds to "provide U.S. air or sea combat support for
any military operations in Cambodia." The Democrats also introduce a resolution to end at once "all
offensive action by the United States in Southeast
Asia" and the removal of all U.S. troops by June.
NEGOTIATIONS: The third straight session of the
Paris peace talks continues, but there is still a stalemate. This session marks the 100th meeting since
the talks began on January 25, 1969.

South Vietnamese
Air Force personnel
prepare to assume
control of Soc Trang
airfield in January
1971 as part of
President Nixon's
Vietnamization
program. *(Texas Tech
University Vietnam
Archive)*

January 22–24

CAMBODIA: Communist gunners shell central
Phnom Penh for the first time and simultaneously
penetrate the nation's major airport, destroying much of Cambodia's military fleet.
U.S. air operations are greatly stepped up; later in the week, after fresh Communist
terrorist attacks on the capital, Cambodian forces will clash with them in several
battles outside Phnom Penh.

January 25

SOUTH VIETNAM: Saigon reports the withdrawal of 5,300 troops from Cambodia, where they had been fighting alongside Cambodian soldiers to open Route 4
between Phnom Penh and Kompong Som.

January 26–30

GROUND WAR: The two sides declare separate truces in observance of Tet, the Vietnamese lunar new year. Despite at least 53 reported violations during the truce
(January 26–27), the Allied commands term it the quietest in recent years. The
Communists interrupt their own cease-fire (January 26–30) with a grenade explosion in a Binh Dinh theater that kills 10 South Vietnamese and a marketplace bomb
blast that kills nine others.

January 30–February 7

GROUND WAR: About 9,000 U.S. troops from the 1st Brigade, 5th Infantry Division (Mechanized), the American Division, and the 101st Airborne Division conduct

Operation Dewey Canyon II in the vicinity of Khe Sanh. The action starts with an armored/engineer task force from Fire Support Base Vandegrift clearing Route 9 to Khe Sanh. The objective of the operation is to secure a launch site for the initial phase of Lam Son-719, the South Vietnamese invasion of Laos that will commence on February 8.

February 3–4
GROUND WAR: In what is proclaimed a new campaign to eradicate Communist border sanctuaries, a force of 1,500 ARVN troops crosses the frontier into Cambodia's Kompong Cham Province, already occupied by some 7,500 ARVN troops. The drive is assisted by U.S. air support and 7,500 Cambodian troops. The 9th NVA Division headquarters at Chup is the primary objective of the operation. In a related development, the first gasoline convoy in over two months reaches Phnom Penh from Kompong Som.

February 8
CAMBODIA: Premier Lon Nol suffers a paralyzing stroke and turns his duties over to Deputy Premier Sisowath Sirik Matak. Still debilitated by the stroke, he will resign on April 20, but a week later he will withdraw his resignation, staying on in a figurehead role as Deputy Premier Sisowath Sirik Matak continues to run the government pending his recovery.

Hueys from the Americal Division prepare for operations at their base in Chu Lai, January 1971. *(Texas Tech University Vietnam Archive)*

February 8–April 6

GROUND WAR: ARVN forces begin Operation Lam Son-719, when 12,000 South Vietnamese troops advance from Khe Sanh along Route 9 into Laos to interdict the Ho Chi Minh Trail and attack North Vietnamese base areas. The objective is to seize Tchepone and destroy North Vietnamese supply dumps in the area. U.S. ground forces are prohibited from entering Laos in accordance with a U.S. congressional ban, but they provide logistical support, with some 2,600 helicopters to airlift Saigon troops and supplies, in addition to artillery fire into Laos from U.S. fire bases located along the border in South Vietnam. The drive on Hanoi's supply routes and depots is described as the "bloodiest fighting" of the Indochina war by some observers. Enemy resistance is light at first as the spearhead of the South Vietnamese force thrusts its way across the border toward Tchepone, a major enemy supply center on Route 9. However, resistance stiffens in the second week and the push bogs down during the last week in February, some 16 miles from the border, after bloody fighting in which Communist troops overrun two ARVN battalions.

South Vietnamese soldiers move through thick jungle vegetation in Laos during Operation Lam Son 719 in 1971. *(Texas Tech University Vietnam Archive)*

February 10

GROUND WAR: Four journalists, including Larry Burrows of *Life* magazine, Kent Potter of UPI, Henri Huett of AP, and Keisaburo Shimamoto of *Newsweek* are killed in a South Vietnamese helicopter accident in Laos.

February 12

GROUND WAR: Cambodian brigadier general Neak Sam is killed during a battle with the Communists.

February 17

USA – GOVERNMENT: In his first major news conference since the beginning of the Laotian operation, President Nixon refuses to set limits on the use of U.S. airpower, barring only the use of tactical nuclear weapons. He also insists that Americans will remain in South Vietnam as long as U.S. POWs remain in the hands of the North Vietnamese.

February 20

SOUTH VIETNAM: According to the U.S. embassy in Saigon, the United States will give $400,000 to construct 288 isolation cells in the South Vietnamese political prison on Con Son island.

February 20–23

AIR WAR: U.S. aircraft bomb antiaircraft artillery and missile sites near the border with Laos in renewed "protective reaction" strikes. According to MACV, this action is taken after Soviet-built surface-to-air missile (SAM) firings are directed at U.S. aircraft bombing Ho Chi Minh Trail supply lines.

February 21

USA – DOMESTIC: In a Gallup poll taken following the Laotian offensive, President Nixon's approval rating falls to the lowest point thus far in his term of office.

February 22

GROUND WAR: The South Vietnamese advance into Laos comes to a standstill 16 miles over the frontier.

USA – DOMESTIC: Former senator Eugene McCarthy introduces an antiwar teach-in at Harvard University, in which concerned students are urged to employ political tactics instead of violent confrontation. On the same day at Yale University, former head of the U.S. Paris peace talk delegation, W. Averell Harriman, leads another teach-in.

February 23

GROUND WAR: The commander of South Vietnamese forces in Cambodia, Lieutenant General Do Cao Tri, dies in a helicopter crash along with François Sully, a *Newsweek* correspondent. Tri's death stalls the offensive in Cambodia for several weeks, as his replacement, General Nguyen Van Minh, reformulates military strategy for the operation.

February 25

USA – GOVERNMENT: In both houses of Congress, legislation is initiated to forbid U.S. military support of any South Vietnamese invasion of North Vietnam without

Phuong Hoang (Phoenix) team conducts operations in Tay Ninh Province, 1969. *(Texas Tech University Vietnam Archive)*

congressional approval. The Foreign Relations Committee chairman, Senator J. William Fulbright (D-Ark.), declares the Laotian invasion illegal under the terms of the repeal of the Gulf of Tonkin Resolution, which allowed the president only the mandate to end the war. Also on this day, President Nixon, in his State of the World address, emphasizes the "grave risk" of U.S. underinvolvement if the burden of the war is shifted too swiftly to the South Vietnamese.

February 27
GROUND WAR: Operation Phoenix is expanded to include the jailing and selective assassination of Viet Cong suspects and sympathizers.
NEGOTIATIONS: The North Vietnamese delegation in Paris condemns the decision to permit the rescue of U.S. airmen from Laos by U.S. ground forces.

March 1
USA – DOMESTIC: A bomb explodes in the Capitol Building in Washington, D.C., causing an estimated $300,000 in damages but hurting no one. A group calling itself the Weather Underground claims credit for the bombing as a protest of the U.S.-supported Laos invasion.

March 2
CAMBODIA: North Vietnamese gunners shell Kompong Som's oil refinery, destroying 80 percent of the nation's main fuel storage facility.

March 3
USA – MILITARY: The 5th Special Forces Group departs South Vietnam.

March 5
USA – MILITARY: The 11th Armored Cavalry Regiment, less its 2nd Squadron, departs South Vietnam.

March 5–8
CHINA: Premier Zhou Enlai (Chou En-lai) visits Hanoi and, in a March 10 communiqué with North Vietnamese premier Pham Van Dong, vows all-out Chinese support for the North Vietnamese struggle against the United States.

March 6–15
GROUND WAR: Operation Lam Son-719 continues as reinforced South Vietnamese forces push into Tchepone, the main North Vietnamese supply deport on the Ho Chi Minh Trail. They find the base deserted and almost completely destroyed as a result of American bombing raids. Fighting near the Vietnam border intensifies, and in the second week of March Saigon troops abandon four fire bases in Laos and more than 6,000 of 21,000 ARVN soldiers are withdrawn as casualties soar on both sides. Allied officials declare that the offensive is still going according to plan, but fierce Communist counterattacks are seen as the reason for the Allied pullback. On March 15, the operation's support base at Khe Sanh comes under relentless Communist mortar and rocket fire.

March 10
INTERNATIONAL: A group of 171 pacifists meets in Paris with all delegations to the peace talks to determine the "requisites for peace."

AUSTRALIA: John Gorton is ousted as the nation's prime minister, following a crisis in which Defense Minister Malcolm Fraser resigns, and after a dispute with the army over Vietnam policy.

March 15
GROUND WAR: Operation Dewey Canyon II's rear support base at Khe Sanh comes under relentless Communist mortar and rocket fire. Sappers penetrate the perimeter. Three U.S. personnel are killed and 14 wounded.

March 17
NEW ZEALAND: Partial withdrawals are set for New Zealand's Vietnam combat force of 264 men.

March 20
GROUND WAR: In Operation Lam Son-719, near the Laotian border, 53 men of the 1st Cavalry, Americal Division, disobey orders and refuse to retrieve a disabled helicopter and an armored vehicle from a battle zone. The soldiers are reassigned, with no disciplinary action taken, and their commanding officer is relieved of his position. Another armored unit rescues the equipment the next day.

March 21–22
AIR WAR: North of the DMZ, U.S. jets attack North Vietnamese missile emplacements, destroying three. In a related incident, for the first time in two years, a North Vietnamese missile downs a U.S. Air Force F-4 jet 35 miles inside North Vietnam. The two crewmen will be rescued on March 23.

March 22–24
GROUND WAR: Some 3,000 North Vietnamese and Pathet Lao troops attack government positions near Luang Prabang after an intensive two-day shelling of the Laotian capital's airport. On March 24, three Laotian battalions push back the Communists.

March 24
GROUND WAR: Although Operation Lam Son-719 does not officially end until April 6, the operation is effectively over as the last South Vietnamese units pull out under heavy Communist pressure. The human toll for the 45-day operation is high for both sides. Saigon lists 1,160 killed, 4,271 wounded, and 240 missing. An AP dispatch, citing privileged information, reports much higher casualty figures of nearly 50 percent–3,800 dead, 5,200 wounded, and 775 missing. According to the South Vietnamese report the U.S. losses include 450 dead, 104 helicopters downed, 608 damaged, and five planes destroyed. Saigon claims 13,688 Hanoi troops killed and 167 taken prisoner, along with 6,657 weapons captured, 120 tanks and 297 trucks destroyed, and tons of ammunition, food, and equipment taken. However, the South Vietnamese forces also lose massive amounts of equipment, including tanks, artillery, and helicopters, during the fighting. Essentially, both sides incur heavy casualties and loss of equipment, but continue to claim "complete victory." Traffic on the Ho Chi Minh Trail is soon back to its previous levels, and only the annual monsoons will slow it down.

March 25

AIR WAR: Citing the violation of the DMZ's neutrality by the massing of North Vietnamese antiaircraft and artillery emplacements in the northern end of the buffer zone, the U.S. State Department warns of retaliatory air strikes.

NEGOTIATIONS: Hanoi and Viet Cong chief delegates boycott the March sessions in Paris to protest U.S. bombing and what they say are U.S. "threats of war."

March 27

USA – MILITARY: The 5th Battalion, 7th Cavalry; 1st Battalion, 8th Cavalry; and 2nd Battalion, 12th Cavalry, of the 1st Cavalry Division depart from South Vietnam.

March 28–31

GROUND WAR: The South Vietnamese district capital of Duc Duc is overrun by two North Vietnamese regiments. Reportedly, some 100 civilians are left dead, 150 wounded, and 800 houses burned. Elsewhere, in a one-hour battle, Communist forces partly overrun a U.S. artillery base in northern Quang Tin Province, leaving 33 Americans dead and 76 wounded. They are driven off by artillery and air strikes, leaving behind 12 enemy dead.

March 29

WAR CRIMES: Lieutenant William L. Calley is found guilty of premeditated murder at My Lai in U.S. Army court-martial proceedings at Fort Benning, Georgia.

March 29–30

CAMBODIA: The Communists again seize control of a 10-mile stretch of Route 4, near Phnom Penh, as North Vietnamese and Viet Cong troops push back a Cambodian convoy of several battalions. The fight for the strategic road will continue until April.

March 30

AIR WAR: U.S. planes conduct raids on North Vietnamese positions in the DMZ.

March 31–April 1

GROUND WAR: With U.S. air support, South Vietnamese commandos raid North Vietnamese positions inside Laos. On April 6, some 200 South Vietnamese commandos carry out a 10-hour raid in the same area, destroying fuel supplies, weapons, food supplies, and storage huts.

March 31–April 12

GROUND WAR: A battle rages around Fire Base 6, a South Vietnamese stronghold in the Central Highlands, as Communist troops press a continuous assault against the garrison of 5,000–6,000 men while U.S. bombers pound the heavy Hanoi troop concentrations around the base. In an effort to break the siege, on April 12, U.S. C-130 cargo transports begin dropping 1,500-pound bombs.

April

USA – MILITARY: The 1st Marine Division withdraws from Vietnam.

April 1

USA – GOVERNMENT: Charging some Democrats with "giving comfort to the enemy," Senate Republican leader Hugh Scott (R-Pa.) denounces critics of the war on the floor of Congress. Vice President Agnew calls the war critics "home-front sniper," insisting that the majority of citizens believe the U.S. soldiers in Vietnam have acted patriotically, but that the antiwar activists have garnered all the publicity, and thus have made veterans feel guilty for having fought for what these critics call an immoral cause.

April 3
WAR CRIMES: President Nixon orders Lieutenant William Calley, Jr. removed from the Fort Benning stockade and promises to personally review Calley's court martial for the murders at My Lai.

April 6
GROUND WAR: Operation Lam Son-719 officially ends.

April 7
USA – GOVERNMENT: President Nixon announces that 100,000 American troops will leave South Vietnam by the end of the year.

April 7–8
USA – MILITARY: Nine of the 1st Infantry Division's normally assigned infantry battalions depart.

April 13
USA – MILITARY: The 1st Marines cease all offensive operations.

April 14
USA – MILITARY: The 1st Marine Division and III Marine Amphibious Force depart South Vietnam.

April 14–October
GROUND WAR: In a follow-up to Operation Lam Son-719, some 5,000 South Vietnamese begin Lam Son-720, a push into the Communist-held A Shau Valley along the Laotian border, but make no major contact along the Communist infiltration route. Some 400 U.S. troops also participate. On April 21, U.S. helicopters airlift 1,500 South Vietnamese marines north of the valley, following two days later with 525 more troops. Saigon newspapers describe the A Shau operation as only a "training exercise" for the replacement of those troops lost in Lam Son-719. Brigadier General Vu Van Giai, commander of Lam Son-720, announces that the operation will extend until October.

April 16
GROUND WAR: The South Vietnamese command announces that the siege of Fire Base 6, which has been in effect since March 31, has been broken by 400 ARVN reinforcements airlifted in, although the 6,000 to 10,000 North Vietnamese surrounding the base do not yet allow reinforcements to arrive by foot. During the week that follows, South Vietnamese forces will launch a counteroffensive to clear the surrounding area of NVA troops.

April 18
SOUTH VIETNAM: Vice President Nguyen Cao Ky says that the recently concluded Operation Lam Son-719 was no victory. He also reports that Vietnamization is

going very slowly; and he denounces U.S. Democratic presidential aspirant George McGovern for his stated interest in investigating charges that Ky is implicated in opium smuggling.

April 18–23

AIR WAR: U.S. jets carry out the 30th raid since January 1 against missile sites and aintiaircraft positions inside North Vietnam, in the heaviest six-day period of raids since the November 1968 bombing halt. In one of the deepest penetrations of North Vietnam since November 1970, two sites 125 miles south of Hanoi are hit.

April 19–26

USA – DOMESTIC: As a prelude to a massive antiwar protest, Vietnam Veterans Against the War begin a five-day demonstration in Washington, D.C. The generally peaceful protest, called Dewey Canyon III, after the February–March operation in I Corps, ends on April 23 with some 1,000 veterans throwing their combat ribbons, helmets, uniforms, and toy weapons on the Capitol steps. Earlier they had lobbied with their congressmen, laid wreaths in Arlington National Cemetery, and staged mock "search and destroy" missions. On April 24 a massive rally of some 200,000 takes place on the Mall. A simultaneous protest by 150,000 in San Francisco, described as the largest such rally to date on the West Coast, is disrupted by radical groups and militant Mexican Americans who charge that the peace movement is "a conspiracy to quench the revolution." Washington's week of orderly demonstrations ends on April 26 as militant leaders take over and the tactics are changed to aggressive "people lobbying," with the avowed purpose of "shutting down the government." But some 5,000 Washington police, backed by 12,000 troops, outmaneuver them.

April 20

USA – MILITARY: The Pentagon releases figures confirming that fragging incidents are on the rise. In 1970, 209 such incidents caused the deaths of 34 men, as compared to 1969 when there were 96 such incidents.

April 22–28

USA – GOVERNMENT: Veterans Against the War testimony before various congressional panels reveals that G Company, 7th Battalion, 9th Marine Regiment, participated in Operation Lam Son-719 inside Laos, contrary to the congressional ban, for a two-week period in February. They also charge that officially reported U.S. battle death tolls are lower than actual casualties and that U.S. soldiers participated in various specific war crimes against the enemy as well as against South Vietnamese civilians.

April 23

DIPLOMACY: A meeting of Allied ministers reaches an agreement that New Zealand, Australia, South Korea, and the United States will keep some forces in South Vietnam when the bulk of their combat troops are withdrawn.

April 24–27

GROUND WAR: Hostilities resume as NVA troops hit Allied installations throughout South Vietnam. In the most devastating attack, the ammunition depot at Qui Nhon is blown up. On the 27th the aviation fuel tanks at Danang air base explode when hit by

Communist fire. In the three-day period, 54 South Vietnamese soldiers and civilians are killed and 185 wounded. The United States lists seven dead and 60 wounded.

April 26
USA – MILITARY: MACV announces that the U.S. force level in Vietnam is at its lowest since July 1966, having dropped to 281,400 men.

April 29
USA – MILITARY: U.S. casualty figures for April 18–24 are released. The 45 dead bring total U.S. losses for the Vietnam War since 1961 to 45,019, making Indochina losses fourth only to Americans killed in the Civil War, World War II, and World War I. On May 17, the Defense Department issues figures showing a drop in the combat death rate for black soldiers in 1970 from the previous years. This serves to allay somewhat the controversy over whether disadvantaged social groups have borne an unfairly heavy combat burden.

USA – MILITARY: The 1st Cavalry Division (Airmobile), less 3rd Brigade, departs South Vietnam for Fort Hood, Texas. The remaining brigade becomes a separate command with four infantry battalions and associated support units.

WAR CRIMES: Captain Eugene Kotouc is found not guilty in the court martial relating to the My Lai massacre of March 1968.

April 30
USA – MILITARY: I Field Force Vietnam is disestablished and the 2nd Brigade, 25th Infantry Division, departs South Vietnam for Hawaii.

May 2
USA – MILITARY: Headquarters II Field Force Vietnam is disestablished.

May 3–5
USA – DOMESTIC: The militant antiwar demonstrations in Washington end as police, assisted by U.S. Marines from Quantico and Camp Lejeune, arrest 12,614 protesters, a record high for arrests in a civil disturbance in the nation's history. Due to inadequate detention facilities, most of those arrested are held 24 hours and then released, with the charges against them subsequently dropped.

May 8
USA – DOMESTIC: In Washington, D.C., the Reverend Carl McIntire leads some 15,000 demonstrators carrying U.S. flags and Bibles in support of a military victory in Vietnam. Members of the Veterans of Foreign Wars and New York Ironworkers Local 361 (the "hardhat movement") also participate. McIntire urged President Nixon to repeal his Vietnam policy and "use the sword as God intended."

May 8–10
GROUND WAR: During the truce marking Buddha's birth, Allied forces accuse the North Vietnamese of 66 violations of the cease-fire.

May 10–18
AIR WAR: U.S. jets hit North Vietnamese antiaircraft sites, reportedly destroying 13 emplacements around the Mu Gia Pass, 75 miles north of the DMZ.

May 11–15

CAMBODIA: South Vietnamese troops conduct two drives. On the 11th, a force of some 5,000 soldiers with U.S. air support sweeps from Kandol Chrum south to Kandol Trach in an attempt to clear out Communist headquarters and training sites used for attacks inside South Vietnam west of Saigon. On May 15, over 1,000 South Vietnamese troops, with the aid of 320 U.S. helicopter gunship missions and 32 bombing raids, sweep the Parrot's Beak area of southeastern Cambodia.

May 12

LAOS: The Pathet Lao Patriotic Front announces its preconditions for peace, which include the end of U.S. intervention and bombing in Laos. Laotian premier Souvanna Phouma is receptive to immediate peace talks, but does not comment on the Communist demand for a U.S. bombing halt.

May 12–13

GROUND WAR: The first major battle of Operation Lam Son-720 takes place when North Vietnamese forces hit the same South Vietnamese 500-man marine battalion twice in the same day. Each time the Communists are pushed back after heavy fighting. Earlier, the South Vietnamese reportedly destroyed a North Vietnamese base camp and arms production facility in the A Shau Valley. On May 19, a six-hour battle rages in which thousands of South Vietnamese troops engage the Communists, and three Allied helicopters and a reconnaissance plane are downed. Ground fighting, air strikes, and artillery fire continue in the A Shau Valley through May 23; the South Vietnamese claim the capture of more Communist bunker networks and the destruction of large amounts of supplies and ammunition.

May 13

NEGOTIATIONS: Still deadlocked, the Vietnam peace talks enter their fourth year.

May 16

USA – MILITARY: MACV acknowledges that heroin addiction among the troops in South Vietnam has reached epidemic proportions. The official estimate is that 10–15 percent of all lower-ranked enlisted men are addicts, amounting to some 37,000 soldiers.

May 16–18

LAOS: After bitter fighting, North Vietnamese forces obtain control of the Boloven Plateau in southern Laos by taking the government strongpoints of Pak Song and Ban Houei Sai. North Vietnamese forces destroy 75 percent of Dong Hene, the Laotian military headquarters.

May 19

USA – MILITARY: The army disciplines two generals for failing to conduct an adequate investigation of My Lai, demoting Major General Samuel W. Koster from two-star to one-star rank. At the same time, both Koster and Brigadier General George H. Young, Jr., his assistant division commander at the time of the massacre, are stripped of their Distinguished Service Medals, and letters of censure are placed in their files.

May 19–22

GROUND WAR: North Vietnamese forces put pressure on U.S. positions along the DMZ with heavy rocket and mortar attacks. The assault on Fire Base Charlie 2 results in a direct hit on a bunker, killing some 30 soldiers.

May 23

GROUND WAR: North Vietnamese demolition experts infiltrate the major U.S. air base at Cam Ranh Bay, blowing up six aviation fuel tanks, for a loss of some 1.5 million gallons.

May 24

USA – MILITARY: At Fort Bragg, North Carolina, an antiwar newspaper advertisement signed by 29 U.S. soldiers supporting the Concerned Officers Movement results in controversy. But no official action is taken against the military dissidents.

May 26–31

CAMBODIA: Some 1,000 North Vietnamese capture the strategic rubber plantation town of Snoul, driving out some 2,000 South Vietnamese as U.S. air strikes support the Allied forces. Snoul gives the Communists control of parts of Routes 7 and 13 leading into South Vietnam, as well as large amounts of military equipment and supplies abandoned by the ARVN. On May 31, Cambodia calls for peace talks, but demands that all North Vietnamese and Viet Cong forces withdraw. The Communists refuse.

May 27

SWEDEN: Foreign Minister Torsten Nilsson reveals increased Swedish assistance to the Viet Cong, including some $550,000 worth of medical supplies. Similar aid is to go to Cambodian and Laotian civilians affected by the Indochinese fighting.

May 30

GROUND WAR: The North Vietnamese conduct a series of 48 attacks during a 24-hour period, including attacks against five Allied bases along the DMZ and the U.S. air base at Danang.

May 31

GROUND WAR: As North Vietnamese attacks along the DMZ continue for a 17th day, some 2,500 South Vietnamese begin a drive south of the zone to clear Communist infiltration routes. In Saigon, a bomb blast levels a government building, leaving three civilians dead and 12 wounded.

June 1

USA – DOMESTIC: In support of the Nixon administration's conduct of the war, a group named the Vietnam Veterans for a Just Peace declares it represents the majority of U.S. Vietnam veterans, and calls the protests and congressional testimony of Vietnam Veterans Against the War "irresponsible."

June 2

WAR CRIMES: The army announces that Brigadier General John Donaldson, a former brigade commander in South Vietnam, has been charged with killing six Vietnamese and assaulting two others. The 43-year-old West Point graduate, a top planner for the Joint Chiefs of Staff, is the highest ranking officer to be accused of killing civilians in the war, and the first general to be charged with a war crime since the Philippine insurrection 70 years before. He is charged in connection with an incident in Quang Ngai Province in March 1969. Lieutenant Colonel William McCloskey, his operations officer in Vietnam, is accused of murdering two Vietnamese in a separate incident.

CAMBODIA: A 2,000-man South Vietnamese force begins a drive to block Communist infiltration into the western part of the Mekong Delta region.

June 5–6

GROUND WAR: As part of the increased North Vietnamese DMZ attacks, a fierce battle develops around South Vietnam's Fire Base Charlie, 12 miles southeast of Khe Sanh. Supported by U.S. helicopter gunships, the South Vietnamese inflict over 200 killed on the North Vietnamese attackers.

June 7

USA – GOVERNMENT: In an unusual secret U.S. Senate session to review the American military role in Laos, several senators, including Stuart Symington (D-Mo.), J. William Fulbright (D-Ark.), and Edward Kennedy (D-Mass.), attack Nixon administration policies in that country's ongoing war. Chief among their concerns are $350 million in annual military aid and the employment of 4,800 CIA-financed Thai troops. The State Department defends the use of "volunteer" Thai soldiers in Laos as predating the 1970 congressional ban on the use of mercenaries.

June 8–12

CAMBODIA: Communist troops wage an intensive battle to gain control of the strategic Vi Hear Suor marshes. On June 9, the North Vietnamese capture Srang, 25 miles southeast of Phnom Penh, killing many government troops in the 10-hour assault.

June 9

USA – MILITARY: An army first lieutenant en route to Vietnam goes absent without leave and becomes the first U.S. officer to request asylum in Sweden. According to estimates, some 500 U.S. war resisters and deserters have sought sanctuary in Sweden to date.

June 12

GROUND WAR: Operation Lam Son-720 continues in the A Shau Valley, as 6,000 South Vietnamese troops move north to unite with two Saigon marine brigades just south of the DMZ to block ever-increasing enemy infiltration through the buffer zone.

June 13–December 30

USA – DOMESTIC: The *New York Times* begins publishing the Pentagon Papers, a secret study of the American involvement in Vietnam that was originally prepared for Secretary of Defense McNamara. Over the next three days, the newspaper, which was given the papers by State Department officer Daniel Ellsberg will publish leaked portions of the 47-volume Pentagon analysis of how the U.S. commitment in Indochina grew over a period of three decades. The publication of the Pentagon Papers, which include closely guarded communiqués, recommendations and decisions on the U.S. military role in Vietnam during the Kennedy and Johnson administrations, along with the diplomatic phase in the Eisenhower years, creates a nationwide furor, with congressional and diplomatic reverberations as all branches of the government debate over what constitutes "classified" material and how much should be made public. The publication of the documents precipitates a crucial legal battle over "the people's right to know" and leads to an extraordinary session of the U.S. Supreme Court to settle the issue.

June 15
GROUND WAR: The three-week siege of Fire Base 5 in the Central Highlands is broken after a 12-hour battle between ARVN paratroopers and the NVA, in which the South Vietnamese capture a large Communist complex 100 yards from the artillery base.

June 16
USA – GOVERNMENT: Two votes in the Senate to set a Vietnam troop withdrawal deadline fail to pass; the next day, a similar measure in the House also fails.
CAMBODIA: Communist commandos attack three naval guard posts inside Phnom Penh, leaving four Cambodian sailors dead.

June 17
JAPAN: After 21 months of hard bargaining, U.S. secretary of state Rogers and Japanese foreign minister Kiichi Aichi sign a treaty returning Okinawa, scene of one of the bloodiest World War II Pacific campaigns, to Japanese rule. Located just 400 miles from Communist China for 25 years, it has been the key center through which U.S. supplies flowed in the Korean and Vietnam wars. It is due to remain the most powerful base in the western Pacific, but under terms of the treaty, nuclear weapons are banned from Okinawa and its use as a staging base for wars in Asia is to be limited.

June 17–18
GROUND WAR: The North Vietnamese renew their attack on Fire Base Sarge, south of the DMZ. The 400 attackers are driven back by the 200-man South Vietnamese garrison, which is reinforced the next day with the arrival of 1,800 fresh troops.

June 22
USA – GOVERNMENT: After setbacks earlier in the month, antiwar forces in Congress make a surprising comeback when, after a bewildering series of parliamentary maneuvers, the Senate passes a measure favoring a complete pullout by the spring of 1972, in a 57 to 42 vote. The legislation is conditional on a U.S.-Hanoi accord on the release of American POWs. A White House statement later in the day says the amendment is not binding and warns that if the Communists were to "assume it to

be U.S. policy," it "could seriously jeopardize the negotiations in Paris." The proposal will be rejected in the House by a vote of 219 to 176.

June 22–28
GROUND WAR: In a major DMZ area engagement, some 1,500 North Vietnamese attack the 500-man South Vietnamese garrison at Fire Base Fuller. Despite U.S. B-52 raids dropping 60 tons of bombs on June 21 and a 1,000-man South Vietnamese reinforcement on June 24, the South Vietnamese have to abandon the base when the North Vietnamese bombardment destroys 80 percent of their bunkers. On June 28, a Saigon spokesman announces that 120 South Vietnamese have reoccupied Fire Base Fuller, but will not rebuild the fortifications. Casualty figures are reported at nearly 500 North Vietnamese dead and 135 wounded.

June 25
NEGOTIATIONS: As announced by the North Vietnamese delegation, the Pathet Lao renew their peace proposal which includes an immediate end to U.S. military involvement and bombing raids in Laos. Laotian premier Souvanna Phouma rejects the plan, calling for Vientiane as the site of any proposed Laotian peace talks and demanding the prior withdrawal of North Vietnamese troops from Laos.

June 26
GROUND WAR: Last U.S. Marine combat unit—the 3rd Amphibious Brigade—departs from Danang, ending six years and three months of U.S. Marine combat operations in Vietnam.

June 30
USA – GOVERNMENT: The Supreme Court rules that articles based on the classified Pentagon material may be published by newspapers.
AIR WAR: In an attempt to knock out Communist rocket emplacements that have been shelling U.S. and South Vietnamese bases south of the DMZ during the past two weeks, 14 U.S. F-4 Phantom fighters hit North Vietnam just above the DMZ.

July 1
USA – GOVERNMENT: The 26th Amendment to the Constitution, granting 18-year-olds the vote, is ratified and becomes law. The Vietnam War, fought mostly by U.S. soldiers too young to vote, is the major cause for this reform, as antiwar activists have pointed to the injustice of asking those who have no voice in the political decision to sacrifice themselves in battle.
USA – MILITARY: In the single largest troop pullout since the phased withdrawal began in 1969, 6,100 U.S. soldiers depart the Central Highlands, beginning the wind-down of the U.S. combat role in that region. The majority of the some 236,000 U.S. troops remaining in Vietnam are in the bitterly contested northernmost provinces of South Vietnam. And by the end of the month, all U.S. Marine units will have departed, with only marine advisers and embassy guards remaining.
GROUND WAR: Fighting again flares up around Fire Base Fuller where 300 Communist attackers are turned away with the help of U.S. and South Vietnamese air power and the insertion of 150 South Vietnamese reinforcements.

NEGOTIATIONS: The Viet Cong present a new seven-point peace plan at the Paris talks, offering release of all U.S. and Allied prisoners of war in North and South Vietnam in return for a U.S. troop pullout by the end of 1971. The plan also calls for the end of Vietnamization and the end of all U.S. political and military intervention in both Vietnams. The initial U.S. and South Vietnamese reaction to the plan is noncommittal, but at the July 8 session, U.S. ambassador David Bruce tells the Communists that the United States "cannot possibly accept" the proposal as it stands; however, conceding that the plan has some new elements, he will ask for a "fresh start" in negotiations.

July 8–15

GROUND WAR: U.S. helicopters airlift some 1,500 South Vietnamese into the Parrot's Beak sector to begin a new drive to block Communist infiltration into the Saigon region. The drive is halted on July 15 and two-thirds of the South Vietnamese withdraw after no contact is made with the enemy. Later in the month, ARVN forces launch four separate drives inside Cambodia.

July 8–9

GROUND WAR: MACV turns over complete responsibility for the defense of the area just below the DMZ to South Vietnamese troops. On July 8, Fire Base Alpha 4 is turned over to the South Vietnamese. The next day, some 500 U.S. forces of the 1st Brigade, 5th Mechanized Division, hand over Fire Base Charlie 2, four miles south of the DMZ, to Saigon troops, completing the transfer of defense responsibilities for the border area. Two separate contingents of 50 U.S. artillerymen remain at each base to monitor radar equipment and to man the artillery pieces.

July 11

AIR WAR: In the 46th protective reaction strike inside North Vietnam since the beginning of the year, two U.S. fighter-bombers destroy an emplacement of antiaircraft guns near the Mu Gia Pass. On the previous day, the North Vietnamese fired three missiles at, but missed, a U.S. reconnaissance plane 45 miles north of the DMZ.

July 13

LAOS: Laotian tribesmen, reportedly led by CIA advisers, take control of the Plain of Jars in a seven-day drive, meeting little resistance. The Defense Department subsequently denies any participation by U.S. advisers.

USA – MILITARY: A U.S. Air Force court-martial in London finds Captain Thomas Culver guilty of participating in a British antiwar demonstration while in civilian clothes.

July 14

CHINA: Concluding a 12-day visit to China, Australian Labour Party leader Gough Whitlam reveals that Premier Zhou Enlai (Chou En-lai) expressed to him China's interest in participating in a new international conference on Indochina, similar to the 1954 Geneva conference. The North Vietnamese, Viet Cong, and the Soviet Union react negatively to the Chinese proposal.

July 15

USA – GOVERNMENT: In a surprise announcement issued simultaneously in Beijing and the United States, President Nixon stuns the world by disclosing that he will visit China before May 1972. Nixon reports that he will go there "to seek normalization of relations between the two countries and to exchange views on questions of concern to both sides."

July 19–28

CAMBODIA: Two thousand Saigon troops sweep the southeastern Cambodian area to block North Vietnamese infiltration into the Mekong Delta. On July 21, some 10,000 South Vietnamese already inside Cambodia, aided by an armored brigade and U.S. artillery and helicopter gunships, sweep a more northeasterly region, engaging the Communists on July 22 between Krek and Minot. On July 26, about 1,000 Saigon troops cross into Cambodia some 90 miles north of Saigon. And on July 28, 3,500 Saigon forces with 80 armored vehicles will begin a drive north of Kampong Trabek near Route 1, the main highway linking Phnom Penh to Saigon.

July 20

LAOS: In a move that indicates Thai troops are permanently occupying a large strip of Sayaboury Province in Laos, they construct several permanent military bases in a 100-mile-deep and 20-mile-wide area, reportedly with CIA assistance.

July 22

USA – DOMESTIC: In Washington, D.C., four relatives of Vietnam POWs accuse Vietnam Veterans Against the War leader John F. Kerry of using the POW issue to further his own political goals.

NORTH VIETNAM: The North Vietnamese announce that they see the forthcoming Nixon visit to China as a divisive attempt by the United States to insert a wedge between Hanoi and Beijing.

July 26

GROUND WAR: In a mission marking the fourth phase of Operation Lam Son-720, U.S. helicopters insert a battalion of 1,600 Saigon troops into the A Shau Valley. They sweep the area over the next two days but meet no enemy.

July 29

NEGOTIATIONS: The chief U.S. delegate to the Paris peace talks, David Bruce, announces that he is resigning as of July 31 for reasons of health. William J. Porter, U.S. ambassador to South Korea, is named to succeed Bruce in Paris. In an interview on the following day, the head of the Viet Cong delegation, Nguyen Thi Binh, proposes to identify all U.S. POWs as soon as the U.S. designates a deadline for the complete withdrawal of all its troops. She also criticizes Porter for brutal policies in the South Vietnamese pacification program when he was deputy U.S. ambassador in Saigon.

August 2

LAOS: The Nixon administration officially acknowledges that the CIA is maintaining a 30,000-man force of "irregulars" fighting throughout Laos. This force has been recruited and is paid directly by the U.S. intelligence agency. According to a once top secret report released by the Defense and State Departments, the extent of U.S. financial involvement in Laos in 1970 comes to a total of $284,200,000. In addition, the report notes greatly increased Chinese road-building activity in northern Laos and the concurrent placement by the Chinese of new long-range, radar-directed antiaircraft guns along the road from Muong Sai toward Dien Bien Phu.

August 3

CAMBODIA: ARVN forces supported by South Vietnamese fighter-bombers and helicopters level two Cambodian villages held by Communist troops in the Parrot's Beak region, killing many of the enemy soldiers. The South Vietnamese forces have been operating inside Cambodia since early spring.

August 6

USA – MILITARY: Last remaining troops of the 4th Battalion, 503rd Infantry, 173rd Airborne Brigade, which had been the first U.S. combat unit to go into action in 1965, are pulled out of the field and begin preparations to leave Vietnam.

August 7

CAMBODIA: Ending an 11-day operation to block an essential Communist infiltration and supply route north of Phnom Penh, Cambodian government forces overrun the strategic town of Prey Kry.

August 12–15

GROUND WAR: North Vietnamese military activity greatly increases along the DMZ. The North Vietnamese conduct three separate assaults against South Vietnamese ground positions. On August 13, the Communists attack Fire Bases Alpha 1 and 2. On August 15, they capture the South Vietnamese marine base at Ba Ho, two miles south of the DMZ. In this action, most of the 180 South Vietnamese defenders are reported as casualties, with Communist losses at 200 dead.

August 15

CAMBODIA: Cambodia demands that South Vietnamese troops be pulled out of the country due to alleged atrocities committed by them against Cambodian civilians.

August 18

AUSTRALIA/NEW ZEALAND: Australia and New Zealand declare that they will withdraw their respective troop contingents from South Vietnam by the end of the year. The Australians have 6,000 men in South Vietnam and the New Zealanders number 264. Both nations agree to leave behind small training contingents. Australian prime minister William McMahon proclaims that the South Vietnamese forces are now able to assume Australia's role in Phuoc Tuy Province, southeast of Saigon, and that Australia will give South Vietnam $28 million over the next three years for civilian projects. During their time in Vietnam, the Australian forces lost 473 dead and 2,202 wounded; the monetary cost of the war was $182 million for military expenses and $16 million in civilian assistance to South Vietnam.

August 20

WAR CRIMES: Lieutenant William Calley's life sentence for the My Lai massacre is reduced to 20 years.

August 20–29
SOUTH VIETNAM: General Duong Van Minh and Vice President Nguyen Cao Ky, fellow candidates for the October presidential election, accuse incumbent President Nguyen Van Thieu of rigging the election and withdraw from the race.

August 21
USA – DOMESTIC: Antiwar protesters associated with the Catholic Left raid draft offices in Buffalo, New York, and Camden, New Jersey, to confiscate and destroy draft records. The FBI and local police arrest 25 protesters.

August 22
AIR WAR: U.S. jets attack two North Vietnamese antiaircraft and missile sites 38 and 115 miles north of the DMZ after the emplacements threaten U.S. planes carrying out bombing missions along the Ho Chi Minh Trail in neighboring Laos.

August 25
USA – MILITARY: The 173rd Airborne Brigade departs from South Vietnam.

August 25–30
GROUND WAR: The Communists launch a new offensive to disrupt the upcoming General Assembly elections in South Vietnam. The height of the new offensive occurs August 28–30 when the Communists launch 96 attacks in the northern part of South Vietnam. U.S. bases also come under attack at Lai Khe, Cam Ranh Bay, where sappers blow up part of the ammunition dump.

August 27
USA – MILITARY: The 1st Brigade, 5th Infantry Division (Mechanized), departs South Vietnam, having operated along the western edge of the DMZ since January 1971.

August 29
SOUTH VIETNAM: President Nguyen Van Thieu retains control of the National Assembly as candidates backing him sweep the opposition in the Mekong Delta with a solid majority in the 159-member lower house.

August 31
THAILAND: Royal Thai Army, less its 2nd Brigade, departs South Vietnam.

September 6–18
GROUND WAR: Some 13,500 ARVN troops with U.S. air support (including B-52s) begin Operation Lam Son-810, aimed at seeking out and destroying NVA bases near the DMZ adjacent to the Laotian border; there are reportedly about 15,000 NVA in the area of operation.

September 9
NEGOTIATIONS: VC and North Vietnamese representatives in Paris turn down new chief delegate William L. Porter's request for secret negotiations to break the deadlock.
SOUTH KOREA: Defense Minister Yoo Jae Heung announces in Seoul that Korea will begin the scheduled pull-out of its 48,000-man force from South Vietnam, which will be completed by mid-1972.

September 14–21

GROUND WAR: South Vietnamese troops launch an operation to destroy a Communist stronghold in the U Minh Forest of the Mekong River Delta. The operation lasts for a week and is characterized by intense fighting, leaving 113 South Vietnamese dead and 183 wounded. There are 400 Communists reported killed. During the fighting, NVA gunners down 11 U.S. helicopters supporting the ARVN operation.

September 15–16

LAOS: Government forces retake Paksong on the Boloven Plateau in a bitter battle. Communist losses are reported at 279 killed and 600 wounded. Laotian casualties include 302 killed, 745 wounded, and 1,995 missing.

September 16

TERRORISM: Fourteen South Vietnamese and one American die when a Saigon nightclub is bombed by a VC terrorist.

September 16–20

GROUND WAR: Communists step up their efforts in the Saigon area. An ambush on the Michelin rubber plantation leaves 15 South Vietnamese soldiers and three U.S. advisers dead. On the 20th, 600 Communist commandos assault the government base near Tay Ninh, 55 miles northeast of Saigon, leaving 21 South Vietnamese soldiers dead and 64 wounded.

September 20

USA – MILITARY: The 18th and 20th Engineer Brigades are withdrawn from Vietnam.

September 21

AIR WAR: In an eight-hour period, 200 U.S. fighter-bombers, protected by 50 escort planes, carry out an intensive series of raids, described as "protective," over an area 35 miles north of the DMZ to knock out the greatly increased number of North Vietnamese antiaircraft and missile emplacements in the DMZ area. The mission is meant to lessen the chance of a large-scale North Vietnamese campaign to disrupt South Vietnam's October presidential elections.

USA – GOVERNMENT: The Senate defeats a liberal-led filibuster against the Selective Service bill in a 61 to 30 vote. The House had passed the compromise version of the two-year draft extension bill in August, which enabled the president to resume military inductions, halted since the expiration of the previous draft law at the end of June. It gives Nixon two years to work toward an all-volunteer army. The bill also contains a record $2.4 billion military pay raise and authorization for the president to drop undergraduate student deferments.

September 22

WAR CRIMES: Captain Ernest L. Medina is found not guilty on all charges in his court-martial relating to the My Lai massacre of March 1968.

September 23

NEGOTIATIONS: The North Vietnamese delegation boycotts the Paris peace talks in opposition to the U.S. raids conducted on September 21.

September 24
NORTH VIETNAM: Hanoi protests that many civilians were killed or wounded in the air attacks of September 21, describing them as an intensification of the war.

September 26–October 9
CAMBODIA: U.S. and South Vietnamese forces stave off Communist assaults along the Cambodian border. The Allies begin a counteroffensive on September 29 to reopen Route 22 between Tay Ninh, South Vietnam, and Krek, Cambodia. The 20,000 South Vietnamese in Cambodia are reinforced by 4,000 more men, as MACV moves 1,500 troops and armored vehicles to the front just inside South Vietnam. U.S. B-52 bombers batter North Vietnamese positions inside Cambodia. During the offensive, Saigon forces are able to lift two Communist sieges of South Vietnamese bases, at Fire Base Tran Hung Dao on October 1 and Fire Base Alpha inside Cambodia on October 9.

September 28
CHINA: China and North Vietnam sign an aid treaty in Hanoi, which is expected to raise Chinese economic assistance over the $200–250 million it currently grants annually to North Vietnam.

September 30
USA – GOVERNMENT: The Senate approves a tough Vietnam pull-out amendment sponsored by Mike Mansfield (D-Mont.) for the second time. Republicans join Democrats for the 57 to 38 vote, backing the rider to the $21 billion military procurement authorization bill calling for withdrawal of U.S. troops from Southeast Asia within six months.

October 2
CAMBODIA: Hostilities in the Mekong Delta flare up near Kien Thien, leaving 16 North Vietnamese and 18 South Vietnamese dead.

October 3
SOUTH VIETNAM: President Thieu is elected to another four-year term in office in an election in which he is the only candidate (all other candidates boycott the election, claiming that it is rigged). He receives 94.3 percent of the votes cast as 87 percent of the nation's eligible voters turn out, according to official accounts. The election is marked by protests from students, veterans, and Buddhist groups. In a campaign designed to disrupt the balloting, Communist gunners fire three rockets into Saigon, killing three civilians. Throughout the country, Communist attacks accompany the election.

October 7
AIR WAR: In the most intensive air strike on NVA bunkers and artillery sites in over a year, U.S. B-52s drop nearly 1,000 tons of bombs on enemy targets near Krek in Cambodia and around the South Vietnamese city of Tay Ninh.

October 8
GROUND WAR: In Thua Thien Province, Operation Jefferson Glen involving the U.S. 101st Airborne Division in coordination with the South Vietnamese 1st Infantry

Division ends after 399 days. It is the last major operation in which U.S. ground forces participate; the Allies report 2,026 enemy casualties during the operation.

POWs: Staff Sergeant John V. Sexton, Jr., becomes the 22nd American prisoner to be freed by the VC in 10 years. As a "reciprocal gesture," the U.S. releases a North Vietnamese officer in Cambodia, in the hope the move will spur the liberation of other U.S. POWs. On the previous day, a U.S. spokesman announced that two-thirds of the 1,618 U.S. servicemen reported missing are assumed dead.

October 11

USA – GOVERNMENT: Washington proposes free elections in South Vietnam to be organized by an independent body representing all political forces in the South, with Thieu resigning one month before elections.

GROUND WAR: Several U.S. soldiers at Fire Support Base Pace near the Cambodian border refuse to go out on a night combat patrol. The command is cancelled when it becomes known that a South Vietnamese unit is already performing the mission.

October 15

USA – GOVERNMENT: Senator Edward Kennedy (D-Mass.) demands that the Pentagon investigate the issues arising from a petition submitted by 65 U.S. soldiers stationed at Fire Support Base Pace who say they had been ordered to carry out border combat missions contrary to stated U.S. policy.

October 16–22

CAMBODIA: General Lon Nol suspends the Cambodian National Assembly and announces that he will rule by executive decree. He says that he is doing so because the "sterile game of democracy" is hampering the war-torn country in its fight against the Communists. On October 22, Lon Nol abolishes constitutional rule after declaring a state of emergency. Despite these moves, the U.S. government declares its continuing support for the Phnom Penh government.

October 18

AIR WAR: A U.S. warplane mistakenly drops two 500-pound bombs on a South Vietnamese troop base at Thieng Hon, near the Cambodian border, leaving 18 ARVN soldiers dead and seven others wounded.

October 20

CAMBODIA: More than 2,500 South Vietnamese troops begin a drive against an estimated 1,600–2,000 Communists north of Krek in Cambodia. On October 28, Saigon will report that the enemy has withdrawn before the ARVN troops and armored units could engage them.

October 27–29

CAMBODIA: Fighting intensifies as Cambodian government forces battle with VC and NVA troops northeast of Phnom Penh; the most significant engagements occur around the provincial capitals of Kompong Thom and Rumlong. The Communists begin a siege of these garrisons after their demolition frogmen destroy a crucial Route 6 bridge, thus severing supply lines for the 20,000 Cambodians on the northeast front. Some 400 government soldiers are reported dead as a result of the combat.

October 29

USA – MILITARY: The total number of U.S. troops remaining in Vietnam drops to 196,700—the lowest level since January 1966.

October 31

SOUTH VIETNAM: Nguyen Van Thieu is sworn in for his second four-year term amid massive security precautions. To mark the occasion, Thieu releases 2,938 VC POWs.

November 2

CAMBODIA: Government forces lift the siege of Prakham, northeast of Phnom Penh. The Communists, who had surrounded the village for over a week, withdraw, leaving behind 291 dead.

November 3

GROUND WAR: A thousand South Vietnamese troops begin a drive against Communist infiltration routes, southwest of Kompong Traket, that lead toward Saigon.

November 7

CAMBODIA: Ten government troops die in a Communist attack on Bam Nal, 70 miles northwest of Phnom Penh.

November 10

CAMBODIA: Communist forces bombard Phnom Penh airport, killing 25 persons and wounding 30. Nine airplanes are damaged in the attack. At the same time, another North Vietnamese unit attacks a radio transmission facility nine miles to the northwest, leaving 19 Cambodians dead.

November 12

USA – GOVERNMENT: President Nixon states that an additional 45,000 American troops will leave South Vietnam during December and January, saying that U.S. ground forces are now in a defensive role and all offensive action is being undertaken entirely by South Vietnamese forces. He further states that 80 percent of the forces in Vietnam when he took office have come home, and that U.S. casualties have dropped to less than 10 a week

November 13

AIR WAR: Predicting a major North Vietnamese drive down the Ho Chi Minh Trail into Laos and Cambodia, Saigon military spokesmen report a massive Communist buildup of supplies near the Ben Karai and Mu Gia passes in North Vietnam. Intelligence photographs also reveal extensive road repair activity and new antiaircraft emplacements. In response to the threat, U.S. B-52s step up air raids against Communist strongholds in Cambodia, Laos, and South Vietnam.

GROUND WAR: At a Central Highlands fire support base near Pleiku, the South Vietnamese defenders ward off an assault by some 600 Communists, killing 163 North Vietnamese and Viet Cong. ARVN losses total 29 dead and 32 wounded.

CAMBODIA: Government forces incur heavy losses as the siege of Rum Long turns into a rout. After almost three weeks of siege, the 400 Cambodian defenders are forced to flee, but only 30 reach safety. The others are either captured or killed. In addition, some 400 other Cambodians die as their two reinforcing battalions make an unsuccessful attempt to break through the Communist encirclement to assist the defenders.

November 16

CAMBODIA: As the fighting gets closer to Phnom Penh, the United States steps up its air activities in support of the Cambodian government. U.S. helicopter gunships strike at North Vietnamese emplacements at Tuol Leap, 10 miles north of Phnom Penh.

November 17

THAILAND: Citing "the increasing threat to national security," Prime Minister Kittikachorn of Thailand seizes complete power, suspending constitutional rule and imposing martial law. Backed by military and civilian leaders described as a "revolutionary council," Kittikachorn pledges to continue Thailand's pro-U.S. and anti-Communist policy.

November 19

CAMBODIA: Cambodians appeal to Saigon for help as Communists get closer to Phnom Penh. Saigon officials reveal that in the previous week, an eight-person Cambodian delegation flew to the South Vietnamese capital to officially request South Vietnamese artillery and engineer support for beleaguered government troops.

USA – DOMESTIC: In Washington, the U.S. National Conference of Catholic Bishops issues its most forceful resolution to date opposing the Vietnam War.

November 22

GROUND WAR: Large-scale South Vietnamese offensive (about 25,000 troops) begins against a reported 5,000 Communists in the Mekong Delta between the U Minh Forest and the Ca Mau Peninsula, but they encounter only light resistance.

CAMBODIA: About 25,000 South Vietnamese troops, aided by 2,500 Cambodians, begin a major offensive against the North Vietnamese around Phnom Penh, as the Khmer Rouge close in on the capital. The drive is aimed at an area near Chup, reportedly the headquarters for three NVA divisions and several supply depots, and encounters only light resistance through November 30.

November 23

CAMBODIA: U.S. B-52 bombers, helicopter gunships, and other aircraft intensify their strikes on Communist targets in support of the major South Vietnamese offensive in Cambodia. Despite a prohibition against any U.S. ground presence in Cambodia, U.S. advisory personnel are sighted in Krek and Phnom Penh.

November 27

GROUND WAR: Some 15,000 South Vietnamese begin a new drive in the Central Highlands aimed at Communist bases there. The United States provides artillery and air support, losing three helicopters to enemy fire.

November 29

USA – MILITARY: The Americal Division, including the 11th Infantry and 198th Infantry Brigades, is deactivated.

December

AUSTRALIA: The last troops of the Royal Australian Regiment depart South Vietnam.

December 1–11

CAMBODIA: The situation worsens as Communists renew their attacks on government positions, forcing the retreat of Cambodian forces from Ba Ray, six miles northeast of Phnom Penh and from nearby Kampong Thmar. As their resistance deteriorates, the Cambodian government issues a plea for intensified U.S. and South Vietnamese air support. On December 2, the North Vietnamese overrun Cambodian forces trying to reopen Route 6. Nearly half of the 20,000-man government contingent flees, as hundreds die. The Communists regain control of a 30-mile stretch of Route 6, cutting off thousands of refugees and some 10,000 government troops in the northern Kampong Thmar area. On December 6, the Cambodian forces abandon the village of Bat Do Cung, 16 miles north of Phnom Penh, leaving some 50 dead. On the same day, Hanoi Radio reports that the Cambodians have lost some 12,000 fighting men in the past week's action. On December 7, Communist gunners renew their shelling of Phnom Penh, firing three rockets into the capital and eight rockets into the international airport. The next day the battle continues nine miles from Phnom Penh as 1,000 government troops try to hold back the North Vietnamese near the hamlet of Sre Ngei. The capital is inundated by refugees from the surrounding villages. Although on December 9 the Cambodian forces are successful in recapturing Kleah Sanday, 10 miles south of Phnom Penh, two days later they are forced to abandon the Pnom Baset garrison overlooking Phnom Penh's northern defense perimeter, eight miles outside the city.

December 6

LAOS: Two North Vietnamese battalions capture the strategic town of Saravane and its air strip at Ban Khot north of the Boloven Plateau.

December 7

CAMBODIA: Communist gunners fire rockets into Phnom Penh.

December 9

NEGOTIATIONS: For the first time since the Paris peace talks began, both sides fail to set another meeting date after the 138th session. The standoff is spurred by the Communist refusal to accept a proposal by chief U.S. delegate William Porter that calls for a week's break in the talks. Both sides announce on December 28 that they will not attend the next scheduled meeting. The cancellation makes it the third meeting to be called off in a month. Earlier, Porter had angered the opposite side by postponing the next session of the conference until December 30, to give Hanoi and the Viet Cong an opportunity to develop a "more constructive approach" at the talks.

CAMBODIA: Refugees from outlying settlements pour into Phnom Penh as the Communists push closer and closer to the capital.

December 14

CAMBODIA: About 6,000 South Vietnamese, aided by 4,000 Cambodian troops and by intensive U.S. activity, capture Chup, a sanctuary for the North Vietnamese 7th and 9th Divisions. The reported 9,000 North Vietnamese stationed there vanish. This achievement follows several days of bloody battle near the hamlet of Dam Be that left a reported 167 Communists dead. Viet Cong radio reports that the South Vietnamese lost 500 men at Dam Be, while Saigon places the total at 14. On December 17, the South Vietnamese abandon Chup, other former Communist bases in the area, and the leveled town of Suong in order to consolidate their position.

December 16
AIR WAR: It is announced that 8,053 U.S. aircraft have now been lost in the conflict.

December 17
CAMBODIA: Government positions in Prak Ham, 40 miles north of Phnom Penh, and their 4,000-man Taing Kauk base are the targets of continuing heavy bombardment by encircling Communist forces. The Prak Ham siege is lifted four days later. As the Communists continue to encircle Phnom Penh in the face of weakened Cambodian resistance, demonstrations inside the capital break out against the Lon Nol regime. The government reacts by banning all such protests, as well as political meetings, and by authorizing police searches of private houses.
WAR CRIMES: Colonel Oran K. Henderson, the highest ranking officer to be tried over the My Lai massacre and subsequent cover-up, is acquitted of cover-up charges.

December 18–19
AIR WAR: In the heaviest single-day loss since December 1967, three U.S. F-4 Phantom jets are lost over northern Laos and North Vietnam. One other jet is downed on the 19th.

December 20–29
LAOS: A force of 15,000 NVA soldiers captures the strategic Plain of Jars, overrunning 6,000–7,000 Laotian defenders assisted by Thai irregulars. Both sides suffer heavy casualties, according to Laotian reports. On the 21st, the Communists begin a drive against the government base of Long Thieng, defended by CIA-recruited Meo tribesmen. On December 28, after a 12-hour mortar and ground attack, the North Vietnamese and their Pathet Lao allies seize the town of Pak Song, thus gaining control of the complete Boloven Plateau. But they leave the next day, and Laotian government forces move back into Pak Song.

December 22
USSR: In a blast that emphasizes the rift between the two Communist super powers, the Soviet Union accuses China of backing U.S. policies in Vietnam.

December 23
LAOS: In Vientiane, American entertainer Bob Hope tries to negotiate with North Vietnamese authorities there for the release of U.S. POWs. His proposal suggests the payment of $10 million to a North Vietnamese children's charity in exchange for the release of Communist-held POWs.

December 23–25
GROUND WAR: Holiday truces go into effect as the Communists unilaterally announce a 72-hour Christmas truce for December 23–25, and the Allies proclaim

a 24-hour truce for December 24–25. According to Saigon sources, the Viet Cong commit 49 violations, and the Viet Cong charge allied forces with 170 violations. U.S. air strikes continue.

December 26–28

USA – DOMESTIC: Flying the U.S. flag upside down from the crown of the Statue of Liberty, 15 antiwar Vietnam veterans barricade themselves inside the monument, but end their occupation early December 28, obeying a federal court order. In Washington on December 28, over 80 antiwar veterans are arrested after clashing with police on the steps of the Lincoln Memorial.

December 26–30

AIR WAR: In reaction to a North Vietnamese buildup, American planes attack airfields and other military targets in the southern part of the country—the most extensive air operations against the Communists since the November 1968 bombing halt. On December 27, Secretary of Defense Melvin Laird justifies the attacks by saying that the Communists have failed to live up to the agreements made prior to the 1968 halt. The raids are part of the effort to disrupt Communist preparations for an anticipated offensive during the Tet holidays of 1972.

December 31

YEAR-END SUMMARY: U.S. military strength has declined to 156,800; more than 177,000 American troops have returned home. American losses for the year are 1,386 KIA, bringing the total number of American personnel killed in action to date to 45,626. Free World Military Forces personnel decline to 53,900. South Vietnamese armed forces strength increases to 1,046,250 personnel; 21,500 South Vietnamese military personnel were KIA this year, bringing the overall total to 156,260 South Vietnamese armed forces personnel killed in action to date. NVA/VC losses for the year are 97,000 KIA; total NVA/VC losses for the war since 1965 are estimated at more than 347,000.

1972

January 1

AIR WAR: U.S. warplanes make over 200 strikes on North Vietnamese supply lines in Cambodia and Laos. These are the initial strikes that will continue throughout the rest of the month. The intensification of the air war is largely an attempt to disrupt Communist preparations for an anticipated Tet (February 15) offensive.

USA – MILITARY: The army reports that between 1969 and 1971, more than 700 fragging incidents have occurred, resulting in 82 deaths and 651 injured.

January 2

USA – GOVERNMENT: President Nixon announces that U.S. forces will continue to withdraw from South Vietnam, but that 25,000–35,000 U.S. troops will remain until the release of all U.S. POWs. He says that North Vietnamese negotiators in Paris "totally rejected" any consideration of POW release before a U.S. troop pullout deadline is announced.

CAMBODIA: Some 10,000 ARVN troops pull out of southeastern Cambodia to back up Saigon defenses for the expected Tet Offensive.

January 3

USA – DOMESTIC: Senator George McGovern (D-S.D.), candidate for the Democratic Party nomination for president, charges that the Nixon administration is using the POW issue to justify bombing of North Vietnam and the continued support of the "corrupt" Thieu regime.

LAOS: Meo tribal forces loyal to the Laotian government evacuate Long Tien base, which has been under North Vietnamese artillery fire since December 31, 1971; more than 500 men on each side have died in the previous month's fighting in the area.

January 6

NEGOTIATIONS: After a one-month lapse, official peace talks resume in Paris. The Communist delegation restates its position that the release of the POWs is dependent upon (1) the pullout of U.S. forces; (2) the withdrawal of U.S. support for the Thieu regime; and (3) cessation of the Vietnamization program, "a plot to withdraw U.S. troops but still continue the war of American aggression by puppet forces under U.S. direction and with U.S. support and supplies."

January 7

GROUND WAR: In the heaviest shelling of U.S. forces in six months, 18 Americans are wounded by a mortar attack on Fire Support Base Fiddler's Green, 20 miles northeast of Saigon.

CAMBODIA: An 1,800-man South Vietnamese force begins an operation in northeastern Cambodia to disrupt Communist bases and capture supplies collected for the anticipated offensive.

DIPLOMACY: India and North Vietnam expand diplomatic relations by upgrading their consulates in Hanoi and New Delhi to embassies. The United States and South Vietnam criticize the Indian action and challenge Indian membership in the International Control Commission (ICC), established at the 1954 Geneva Conference.

January 8

USA – MILITARY: Defense Secretary Melvin Laird states that "from a military standpoint, the Vietnamization program has been completed."

January 10

USA – DOMESTIC: Former vice president Hubert Humphrey criticizes President Nixon, saying that it is taking longer for President Nixon to withdraw U.S. troops from Vietnam than it did to defeat Hitler and calls for an immediate end to the war.

GROUND WAR: Seven militiamen are wounded when Communists attack the Binh Thuan administration office six miles from Saigon. One U.S. soldier is killed and two wounded in the ambush of a patrol 24 miles northeast of Saigon.

January 12

GROUND WAR: With 34 attacks against South Vietnamese military and civilians in the previous 24 hours, Communist attacks become more frequent than at any time since last October. The most serious attack occurs 90 miles southwest of Saigon when VC ambush a 30-man platoon of South Vietnamese militiamen in the Mekong Delta.

January 13

USA – GOVERNMENT: President Nixon announces that 70,000 U.S. troops will leave South Vietnam over the next three months, reducing U.S. troop strength there by May 1 to 69,000 troops. Since taking office, Nixon has withdrawn more than 400,000 American troops from Vietnam. U.S. combat deaths are down to less than 10 per week. Nixon's announcement comes in response to presidential challengers' criticism that the president is pulling out troops but, by turning to airpower, is not ending U.S. involvement in Vietnam.

January 16

USA – DOMESTIC: Religious leaders from 46 Protestant, Catholic, and Jewish denominations meet in Kansas City to discuss Vietnam; ultimately they ask the Nixon administration to withdraw all American troops from Vietnam and refuse aid to the Indochinese governments.

January 17

USA – GOVERNMENT: President Nixon warns President Thieu in a private letter that his refusal to sign any negotiated peace agreement would render it impossible for the United States to continue assistance to South Vietnam.

AIR WAR: Flying more than 200 strikes, U.S. planes hit supply routes and depots in Laos along the Ho Chi Minh Trail, in a continuing campaign against the anticipated Tet Offensive.

January 18

WAR CRIMES: Seymour Hersh, winner of a Pulitzer Prize for his account of the My Lai massacre, reports that a secret investigation by the U.S. Army Criminal Investigation Division has concluded that 347 civilians died at My Lai, a number "twice as large as has been publicly acknowledged." Hersh also charges that the army is covering up an incident in which 90 civilians were murdered in the hamlet of My Khe 4 on the same day as the My Lai massacre.

AIR WAR: In the air war, a U.S. Navy fighter downs the first MiG in 22 months, deep inside North Vietnam. U.S. planes from bases in Thailand, South Vietnam, and aircraft carriers fly 250 sorties against targets in North Vietnam.

January 20

GROUND WAR: In continued efforts to disrupt an anticipated Communist offensive, a contingent of more than 10,000 South Vietnamese troops begins a sweep 45 miles northwest of Saigon to find and destroy enemy forces. There is much speculation that the North Vietnamese will launch such an offensive around the Tet (Chinese New Year) holiday.

THAILAND: Thai government forces totaling 12,000 troops heavily armed with U.S. equipment, begin an operation against 150–200 Communist guerrillas defending a mountain base at Lom Sak in northeast Thailand, about 300 miles from Bangkok.

January 21

GROUND WAR: U.S. soldiers at Fire Base Melanie northeast of Saigon are reportedly angry and confused over administration statements that remaining soldiers in South Vietnam are in a "defensive" posture, not in combat.

AIR WAR: B-52s continue bombing suspected enemy supply dumps in the Central Highlands.

January 25

USA – GOVERNMENT: President Nixon, in response to criticism that his administration has not made its best efforts to end the war, reveals that his National Security Advisor Henry Kissinger has held 12 secret peace negotiating sessions between August 4, 1969, and August 16, 1971, in Paris with Le Duc Tho, a member of Hanoi's Politburo, and/or Xuan Thuy, Hanoi's chief delegate to the formal Paris peace talks.

USA – DOMESTIC: Pulitzer Prize–winning journalist Seymour Hersh claims that members of the army's Americal Division destroyed documents to protect their officers involved in the My Lai murders.

January 26

NORTH VIETNAM: Radio Hanoi announces North Vietnam's rejection of the latest U.S. peace proposal and presents a nine-point counterproposal.

USA – GOVERNMENT: Henry Kissinger asserts that the abrupt removal of U.S. aid would guarantee the collapse of the Saigon regime. Remarks are made in response to North Vietnam's continued insistence that the United States cease all support for the Thieu government and remove all U.S. equipment and arms in the possession of the South Vietnamese army.

AIR WAR: U.S. planes strike a radar and missile site near Dong Hoi, the 19th strike inside North Vietnam since the beginning of the year.

January 27

GROUND WAR: A total of 116 Communist soldiers die during two heavy attacks in the Central Highlands and the Mekong Delta as the level of fighting rises across South Vietnam.

January 28

GROUND WAR: Ten Americans are wounded when a resupply helicopter is badly shot up in fighting 13 miles southeast of Xuan Loc.

AIR WAR: U.S. planes make their 20th strike inside North Vietnam this year.

January 31

NORTH VIETNAM: In a communiqué charging President Richard Nixon and Henry Kissinger with "unilaterally" divulging the substance of the secret talks, creating the impasse at the secret meeting, and distorting the facts, North Vietnam publishes several sensitive documents, including the nine-point plan it submitted during the secret talks, its own version of the eight-point U.S. plan, a seven-point VC plan submitted in 1971, and the text of messages concerning a November 20, 1971, meeting that the United States cancelled. The documents point out two major differences between the U.S. and North Vietnamese plans. Washington wants the withdrawal of all foreign forces from South Vietnam with the condition of an agreement in principle on a final solution, while Hanoi insists on the withdrawal of U.S. and Allied troops from all of Indochina without condition. Hanoi also wants the immediate resignation of the Thieu regime with elections held by a North Vietnamese-South Vietnamese-Viet Cong replacement government.

February
SOUTH KOREA: The ROK Marine Brigade withdraws from Vietnam.

February 1
GROUND WAR: South Vietnamese forces numbering 1,300 chase a 400-man Communist force into Cambodia. South Vietnamese troops make three separate drives into southeastern Cambodia to counter Communist infiltration into South Vietnam and to disrupt preparations for Communist attacks into the Mekong Delta.

February 3
NEGOTIATIONS: The PRG delegation presents a revised version of its seven-point July 1971 peace proposal, calling for South Vietnamese president Thieu's resignation in exchange for immediate discussion of political settlement, a specific date for total U.S. withdrawal from South Vietnam and release of all military and civilian prisoners, and an end to Saigon's "warlike policy."

February 4
THAILAND: A force of 824 soldiers, the last of Thailand's 12,000 troops who served in South Vietnam, departs.

CHINA: A statement affirming Chinese support for the Communist struggle in Indochina quotes Premier Zhou Enlai (Chou En-lai) as saying that China backs the seven-point VC proposal and will support the North Vietnamese and PRG until they achieve total victory.

February 5
NEGOTIATIONS: The North Vietnamese formally reject President Nixon's eight-point peace plan, which was submitted privately to the North Vietnamese delegation in Paris.

February 7
LAOS: About 4,000 Laotian troops supported by U.S. airpower attempt to relieve the pressure on Long Tieng by attacking North Vietnamese forces who have been occupying the Plain of Jars in northern Laos since the end of 1971. After a month the North Vietnamese have the Laotians on the run; nevertheless, Laotian officials call the operation a success.

February 9
AIR WAR: A series of over 100 U.S. air strikes begins against infiltration routes and suspected North Vietnamese buildups in the Central Highlands.

SEA WAR: The aircraft carrier *Constellation* joins the carriers *Coral Sea* and *Hancock* off the coast of Vietnam.

February 10

GROUND WAR: Twenty-five rockets hit the U.S. air base at Danang and the city itself, killing three and wounding 17. At the same time, Communist guerrillas attack at three points 15 to 35 miles south of Danang.

NEGOTIATIONS: Formal weekly peace talks in Paris break down when the U.S. delegation, to protest an antiwar rally set to begin in Versailles the next day, refuses to agree on a date for the next meeting.

February 11

AIR WAR: U.S. and VNAF planes fly over 200 missions against targets in northern South Vietnam and the Central Highlands.

February 12

CAMBODIA: About 6,000 Cambodian troops launch a major operation to recapture the religious center of Angkor Wat from 4,000 North Vietnamese troops entrenched around the famous Buddhist temple complex, seized in June 1970. Fighting continues throughout the month. Even with the addition of 4,000 more troops, the Cambodians are unsuccessful and will eventually abandon their efforts to expel the North Vietnamese.

AIR WAR: The heaviest U.S. air raids in two years strike Communist bases for a fifth day along the South Vietnamese/Laotian border.

February 13

AIR WAR: U.S. B-52s fly 19 missions in 24 hours, the largest number for a 24-hour period since records began to be kept in June 1968. Targets are Communist infiltration routes and bases west of Kontum, particularly North Vietnamese Army Base Area 609.

February 16

USA – DOMESTIC: A Gallup poll finds that 52 percent of those interviewed approve of President Nixon's handling of the war while 39 percent disapprove.

AIR WAR: It is announced that a U.S. "limited duration" air operation has begun to knock out North Vietnamese artillery positions in North Vietnam's southernmost province.

GROUND WAR: John Paul Vann, chief U.S. official in Military Region II, claims that the Tet Offensive has begun in Binh Dinh Province. He estimates Communist strength in the Central Highlands at 35,000–60,000 troops. South Vietnamese and Allied troops in the region number 220,000.

February 17

AIR WAR: Three U.S. planes are shot down by surface-to-air missiles during the 29-hour "limited duration" bombing of North Vietnam.

GROUND WAR: A battalion of the 18th ARVN Division is ambushed near Long Giao in Long Khanh Province. One adviser is wounded.

February 19

POWs: Hanoi allows five U.S. airmen held in the North to send televised messages to their families from the International Club in Hanoi, in the presence of journalists and diplomats.

February 20

GROUND WAR: The Mekong Delta and Danang are the targets for more than 67 Communist attacks over the weekend. These attacks result in heavy South Vietnamese casualties. Two Americans are killed and 10 wounded in attacks at Bien Hoa and Phan Rang air bases.

February 21

DIPLOMACY: President Nixon arrives in Beijing, announcing that this visit to the People's Republic of China is "the week that changed the world." In meeting with Nixon, Prime Minister Zhou Enlai (Chou En-lai) urges early peace in Vietnam, but does not endorse North Vietnam's political demands.

February 24

NEGOTIATIONS: Talks resume in Paris, but the Communists leave after only 17 minutes to protest renewed U.S. bombing raids against the North.

February 25

GROUND WAR: In a five-hour battle around a Communist bunker line 42 miles east of Saigon, U.S. troops clash with Communists in the biggest single engagement in nearly a year, resulting in four dead and 47 wounded, almost half the U.S. weekly casualties.

February 27

DIPLOMACY: In a joint communiqué released by China's Zhou Enlai (Chou En-Lai) and President Nixon during the president's visit to China, the United States reiterates its support of the eight-point proposal advocated by itself and South Vietnam in January and China announces its support of the seven-point proposal presented by the Viet Cong in February. The communiqué itself, although apparently presenting conflicting sides, is reportedly the result of intense negotiations.

February 29

SOUTH KOREA: South Korea pulls 11,000 troops out of Vietnam as part of its ongoing withdrawal program, leaving 37,000 Korean soldiers in South Vietnam.

March 2–3

GROUND WAR: ARVN troops sweep the western Central Highlands to disrupt suspected Communist plans for an offensive; four Americans are wounded in a booby-trap explosion 20 miles northeast of Saigon.

AIR WAR: U.S. planes continue "protective reaction" strikes against antiaircraft batteries and radar sites as far as 120 miles of the DMZ while B-52s continue their fifth straight day of saturation raids against Communist positions in the Central Highlands.

March 6

AIR WAR: More than 20 planes continue raids against antiaircraft installations inside North Vietnam. One MiG is shot down in an air battle over North Vietnam involving about a dozen U.S. planes and MiGs.

March 7

NORTH VIETNAM: Hanoi and VC radio announce that U.S. bombing in the North is striking "many populated areas"; U.S. command replies that all targets are antiaircraft defenses.

AIR WAR: U.S. jets battle five MiGs and shoot one down 170 miles north of the DMZ in the biggest air battle in Indochina in three years. The total of 86 U.S. air raids over North Vietnam to date this year equals the total for all of 1971.

March 8–9

DIPLOMACY: The U.S. government reports that, Chinese premier Zhou Enlai (Chou En-lai) on a secret visit to brief Hanoi on his meetings with President Nixon, declared that he refused to act as an intermediary for the United States in settling the war.

GROUND WAR: Communist rockets and mortar shells hit South Vietnamese bases at 10 points along the DMZ. Eight U.S. soldiers are wounded by a booby-trap nine miles south of Danang.

AIR WAR: U.S. planes hit antiaircraft defenses in North Vietnam and in the DMZ for the eighth straight day and continue to bomb below the DMZ around Danang and in the Central Highlands.

March 10

USA – MILITARY: The 101st Airborne Division officially departs South Vietnam for Fort Campbell, Kentucky.

March 11

LAOS: A 4,500–6,000-man North Vietnamese force threatens Long Tieng, after taking the village of Sam Thong, defended by a 4,000-man Thai force, seven miles to the northwest. Communist artillery closes the Long Tieng airstrip the next day; the opposing forces continue to battle for strategic ground about the base.

March 12

AUSTRALIA: The First Task Force withdraws from Vietnam.

March 16

GROUND WAR: Combined with VC shelling of Quang Ngai and a U.S. base camp the preceding day, Communist forces initiate 41 attacks in 24 hours, most against local militia units.

March 17–18

GROUND WAR: ARVN troops supported by air and artillery kill 180 Communist troops as they push back an attack by hundreds of North Vietnamese in the area between Hue and the A Shau Valley. Over 400 North Vietnamese troops have been killed in the continuing South Vietnamese drive on the eastern edge of the valley. In the mountains west of Hue, ARVN forces succeed in preventing Communist forces from hitting lowland cities from their mountain bases, claiming 513 North Vietnamese killed in two weeks of this totally South Vietnamese operation, in which South Vietnamese troops sustain 86 killed and 186 wounded.

CAMBODIA: A total of 8,000 South Vietnamese troops continue their drive into eastern Cambodia. Although there is no significant engagement, tons of supplies are found. South Vietnamese troop strength in Cambodia will reach 10,000 over the next few days.

March 21
CAMBODIA: More than 100 civilians are killed and 280 wounded as Communist artillery and rockets strike Phnom Penh and environs in the heaviest attack on that city since the beginning of the war in Cambodia in 1970. Following the shelling, a Communist force of 500 men attacks and enters Takh Mau, six miles southeast of Phnom Penh, killing at least 25 civilians.

March 23
NEGOTIATIONS: At the direction of President Nixon the U.S. delegation to the peace talks announces an indefinite suspension of the conference until North Vietnamese and National Liberation Front representatives enter into "serious discussions" on concrete issues determined beforehand. When Washington calls for an end to the Communist offensive in Vietnam as a precondition to continuing the talks, the North Vietnamese and Viet Cong counter with a call for an end to U.S. bombing of both North Vietnam and South Vietnam, but then agree to talk without the cessation of bombing.

March 28
AIR WAR: An AC-130 gunship is shot down over Muang Phine, Laos, resulting in the death of 14 airmen from the 16th Special Operations Squadron.

March 30
GROUND WAR: A major coordinated Communist offensive begins with the biggest North Vietnamese drive since the Tet Offensive of 1968. North Vietnamese troops attack South Vietnamese bases and towns along the DMZ, heralding the eventual participation of 500 tanks and 14 divisions plus 26 separate regiments of North Vietnamese regular troops—150,000 men—as well as thousands of Viet Cong, supported by heavy rocket and artillery fire. The March 30 attacks along the DMZ from Dong Ha to the mountains near Khe Sanh mark the first Communist use of long-range artillery along the DMZ. This action proves to be the opening phase of the Nguyen Hue Campaign or, as it will become more popularly known, the NVA Easter Offensive. Thirty-five South Vietnamese soldiers die and hundreds of civilians and soldiers are wounded.

North Vietnamese troops firing an 82 mm mortar *(Texas Tech University Vietnam Archive)*

March 31
GROUND WAR: The firing of more than 5,000 rockets, artillery, and mortar shells on 12 South Vietnamese positions just below the DMZ precedes and accompanies ground assaults against South Vietnamese positions in Quang Tri Province. The attacks are thrown back, with 87 North

Vietnamese killed, but eventually South Vietnamese firebases Fuller, Mai Loc, Holcomb, Pioneer, and two smaller bases near the DMZ are abandoned as the North Vietnamese push the defenders back toward their rear bases. Attacks against three bases west of Saigon force the South Vietnamese to abandon six outposts.

April

AIR WAR: U.S. planes bomb North Vietnamese troop formations in South Vietnam and north of the DMZ; demonstrations in the United States protest the bombings.

April 1

GROUND WAR: Following three days of the heaviest artillery and rocket bombardment of the war, 12,000–15,000 soldiers of Hanoi's 304th Division, supported by artillery and antiaircraft units equipped with SAM-2 surface-to-air missiles equaling another division, sweep across the DMZ and rout the ARVN 3rd Division, driving them toward their rear bases. The Communist ground objectives are apparently Quang Tri City, capital of Quang Tri Province, and then to advance on Hue and Danang farther to the south. With the new offensive, Hanoi hopes to (1) impress the Communist world and its own people with its determination; (2) capitalize on U.S. antiwar sentiment and possibly hurt President Nixon's chances for reelection; (3) prove "Vietnamization and pacification" a failure; (4) damage South Vietnamese forces and the Thieu regime's stability; (5) gain as much territory as possible before a possible truce; and (6) accelerate negotiations on its own terms.

AIR WAR: The U.S. Navy's last in-country combat unit—Light Attack Squadron 4—withdraws from Vietnam.

April 2–4

GROUND WAR: The 304th NVA Division supported by Soviet tanks and heavy artillery takes the northern half of Quang Tri Province, leaving only Quang Tri City, the combat base, and Dong Ha, all under heavy attack, in South Vietnamese hands. Brigadier General Vu Van Giai, commander of the 3rd ARVN Division, moves his staff out of Quang Tri combat base to the citadel at Quang Tri City. By April 3, Dong Ha is in flames; the next day South Vietnamese troops abandon Fire Base Anne, eight miles southwest of Quang Tri City, and their northern line of defense on the Cua Viet River. Some 20,000–40,000 civilians flee to the south to get away from the heavy fighting.

April 3

AIR WAR: The United States prepares hundreds of B-52s for possible air strikes. President Nixon sends additional B-52s to Anderson Air Base in Guam and orders reinforcement of the Seventh Fleet; the *Kitty Hawk* is the first of four additional aircraft carriers to join the two carriers already on station off Vietnam.

April 5

GROUND WAR: Moving out of eastern Cambodia, North Vietnamese troops open the second front of their offensive with a drive into Binh Long Province, 75 miles north of Saigon, with the 5th VC Division (actually an NVA main force division) attacking the district town of Loc Ninh and to the south while simultaneously cutting Highway 13 between Saigon and An Loc. In I Corps, Communist forces continue to advance on Quang Tri City and Hue. Observers from Hanoi to Washington see the South Vietnamese response as the deciding factor in the success of North Vietnam's offensive. For the most part, ARVN troops have elected to pull back rather than fight, and U.S. advisers are critical of the South Vietnamese "defensive mentality" as the action takes on more and more the quality of a conventional war. In Quang Tri, the South Vietnamese 56th Regiment has apparently deserted to a man, and Hanoi claims that most of the militia in Quang Tri Province has defected. Two ARVN bases south of Hue are attacked as Communist operations spread into Thua Thien Province.

AIR WAR: U.S. Air Force fighter-bombers begin reinforcing the units in Thailand as part of the build-up in response to the new North Vietnamese offensive in South Vietnam.

April 6

AIR WAR: Clear weather for the first time in three days allows U.S. planes and navy warships to begin the sustained air strikes and naval bombardments ordered by President Nixon after meeting with the Special Action Group on April 3–5. Hundreds of U.S. planes, flying 225 missions by April 9, hit North Vietnamese troop concentrations and missile emplacements above and below the DMZ. Two U.S. planes are shot down over North Vietnam by two SAM-2 missiles, a new element in North Vietnamese air defenses.

Marine aircraft begin landing at Danang as part of the U.S. aerial buildup; the chairman of the Joint Chiefs of Staff, Admiral Thomas W. Moorer, announces the resumption of aerial attack and naval bombardment of North Vietnam.

USA – MILITARY: The 2nd Squadron, 11th Armored Cavalry, departs Vietnam.

April 7

GROUND WAR: The North Vietnamese offensive drive in Quang Tri Province slackens as U.S. and South Vietnamese planes take advantage of good weather to bomb Communist positions. In III Corps, Communist troops take Loc Ninh, and move south to surround the 6,000 troops of South Vietnam's 5th Infantry Division in the provincial capital of An Loc which is only 65 miles from Saigon; heavy fighting ensues.

AIR WAR: Saigon reports that U.S. planes on April 5 destroyed Ben Hai bridge in the DMZ, the only road link between North and South Vietnam.

April 8

GROUND WAR: The 2nd NVA Division striking from Laos and Cambodia opens a third front of the Easter offensive in the Central Highlands, cutting the important highway between Kontum and Pleiku at several points. To the south, An Loc is completely surrounded and under siege. Elsewhere, the first attacks of the offensive against U.S. installations leave three Americans dead and 15 wounded at the Cam Ranh air base, and two Americans dead and four wounded at the Nui Ba Den Mountain radio relay station.

April 9

GROUND WAR: North Vietnamese troops are thrown back from a major assault against ARVN positions at Fire Base Pedro, 10 miles southwest of Quang Tri City, losing over 1,000 men and 30 tanks in the operation. South Vietnamese losses are also believed to be heavy. Saigon command orders the 21st ARVN Division, based in the Mekong Delta, to move north and open the road to An Loc where the 5th ARVN Division is still surrounded. Fierce Communist resistance prevents the relief force from getting through. All but two of Hanoi's combat divisions have been committed to battle in the current offensive.

April 10

AIR WAR: U.S. aircraft begin to bomb North Vietnam above the 19th parallel for the first time since the November 1968 bombing halt. MACV acknowledges that B-52s are hitting the north for the first time since November 1967. Target priority is given to SAM-2 missile sites, which have made raids over North Vietnam increasingly hazardous.

SEA WAR: U.S. aircraft carriers *Saratoga* and *Midway* are ordered from Florida and California to join the four other carriers and warships already engaged in the bombardment of North Vietnam.

April 11

GROUND WAR: Fire Base Bastogne in Thua Thien Province, 20 miles west of Hue, is besieged by Communist forces. After five days of heavy fighting, the base's 500 defenders receive supplies by parachute and a few reinforcements by helicopter. Holding Bastogne is critical to the defense of Hue's western flank.

AIR WAR: B-52 strikes against Communist forces attacking ARVN positions in the Central Highlands near Kontum remove any immediate threat to that city. The JCS orders two more squadrons of B-52s to Indochina. Strikes against North Vietnam are again hampered by poor weather.

April 12

GROUND WAR: Fifty of 142 U.S. soldiers of the 196th Infantry Brigade refuse patrol duty around Phu Bai, 42 miles south of the DMZ, shouting, "We're not going; this isn't our war . . . why should we fight if nobody back home gives a damn about us; why the hell are we fighting for something we don't believe in?" The 50 soldiers finally agree to go. Meanwhile, the 1st ARVN Division sets up new artillery positions and brings in a tank battalion and a fresh infantry regiment to secure Route 547, the main artery between Hue and Phu Xuan, which has been under attack for several days.

April 12–13

AIR WAR: U.S. fighter-bombers and B-52s pound Communist troops attacking An Loc west of the city, but fail to halt their advance. B-52s bomb as close as one mile west of the city.

April 13

GROUND WAR: Communist forces from the 9th VC Division (actually a main force North Vietnamese division) launch a major attack on An Loc with 40 tanks and 9,000 men, taking half the city after a day of close combat; but the defenders, supported by B-52s, tactical aircraft, and attack helicopters, hold on to the southern half of the city.

Sea War: U.S. Navy operations in Vietnam are at their highest since 1968.

April 14

Ground War: Communist attacks in South Vietnam—107 in 24 hours—reach their highest level since the 1968 Tet Offensive. Danang and Saigon and many parts of South Vietnam are hit by terrorist attacks; rockets are fired on Saigon and nearby Tan Son Nhut airport. The ARVN 1st Airborne Brigade begins to arrive in An Loc to reinforce the 5th ARVN Division. They are the last reinforcements to reach the city for nearly two months.

Air War: Orders for B-52 strikes against diplomatic, political, and military objectives throughout the 200-mile-long southern panhandle of North Vietnam call for the most extensive use of B-52s thus far in the war.

April 15

Ground War: North Vietnamese forces overrun Fire Base Charlie, 20 miles northwest of Kontum, as their offensive in the Central Highlands continues.

Air War: The United States resumes bombing of Hanoi and Haiphong after a four-year lull.

April 15–20

USA – Domestic: Hundreds of antiwar demonstrators are arrested in incidents across the country as escalation of the bombing in Indochina provokes a new wave of protests.

April 16

Air War: In the first use of B-52s against Hanoi and Haiphong since November 1968, 18 B-52s and about 100 U.S. Navy and Air Force fighter bombers hit supply dumps near Haiphong's harbor. Sixty fighter bombers hit petroleum storage facilities near Hanoi, with another wave of planes striking later in the afternoon. Washington makes it clear that the United States will bomb military targets almost anywhere in Vietnam; Hanoi reports 13 civilians killed in Hanoi and 47 in Haiphong.

Sea War: The U.S. missile frigate *Worden* is damaged in the Tonkin Gulf by radiation-seeking missiles fired from U.S. planes, resulting in one sailor dead and wounding nine. The destroyer *Buchanan* is hit by one round from a North Vietnamese shore battery, resulting in one sailer killed and seven wounded.

April 17

USA – Domestic: The first major antiwar protests of the year begin at the University of Maryland with demonstrations against the Reserve Officers Training Corps (ROTC). Hundreds of students are arrested and 800 National Guardsmen are ordered onto the campus. Significant protests continue across the country in reaction to the increased bombing of North Vietnam.

April 18

USA – Military: Secretary of Defense Laird, testifying before the Senate Foreign Relations Committee, says he does not rule out the possibility of blockading and mining Haiphong harbor. He says that every area of North Vietnam is subject to bombing as long as the current invasion continues, and that the bombing is for the protection of the 85,000 U.S. personnel still in South Vietnam.

April 19

USA – DOMESTIC: Eight Ivy League college presidents and the president of MIT issue a joint statement condemning the renewed bombing of North Vietnam and supporting orderly antiwar demonstrations.

GROUND WAR: Communist attacks throughout the Mekong Delta rise sharply. Most of the regular South Vietnamese troops from the area have been sent to relieve An Loc, where fighting has intensified with another round of NVA tanks and human wave attacks. In the Central Highlands, North Vietnamese forces overrun Hoi An, inflicting heavy casualties.

SEA WAR: U.S. Seventh Fleet warships bombarding the North Vietnamese coast are attacked by North Vietnamese MiGs and patrol boats as Hanoi begins to challenge the U.S. naval presence in the Tonkin Gulf for the first time since 1964. In the heaviest sea action of the war, the U.S. destroyer *Higbee* is badly damaged. The U.S. missile frigate *Sterett* downs one MiG.

April 20

GROUND WAR: North Vietnamese troops cut Route 19, which connects Pleiku and Qui Nhon on the coast, at An Khe Pass. After a week of fierce fighting, South Korean troops clear the pass, losing 51 men in the fighting. Near the DMZ, seven U.S. soldiers are killed trying to rescue two others.

USA – GOVERNMENT: In the House of Representatives, the Democratic Party caucus votes to support legislation that will set a termination date for U.S. involvement in Vietnam, at the same time denouncing both the current bombing of North Vietnam and North Vietnam's invasion of South Vietnam.

USA – DOMESTIC: Classes are canceled at Columbia University after the police are called to control picketing antiwar students.

DIPLOMACY: Henry Kissinger arrives in Moscow to prepare for President Nixon's coming spring visit. He repeats past U.S. offers for a settlement in Vietnam, adding that North Vietnamese invasion troops now participating in the offensive in South Vietnam must be withdrawn.

NEGOTIATIONS: The Communist delegations in Paris formally propose resumption of the peace talks for April 27, whether or not the United States halts its bombing of North Vietnam.

April 22

GROUND WAR: Fighting in the Mekong Delta is the heaviest in 18 months. During the past two weeks Communist forces of up to one battalion in size have taken a large part of important Chuong Thien Province.

USA – DOMESTIC: Antiwar demonstrations prompted by the intensified U.S. bombing in Indochina draw 30,000–60,000 marchers in New York, 30,000–40,000 in San Francisco, 10,000–12,000 in Los Angeles, and smaller gatherings in Chicago and several other U.S. cities.

April 23

GROUND WAR: Tanks and soldiers of the 320th NVA Division push back South Vietnam's 22nd Division at Tan Canh and attack Dak To in the Central Highlands.

The North Vietnamese offensive, now in its fourth week, is temporarily slowed at its two other fronts in Quang Tri and Binh Long Provinces. So far 250,000 civilians have fled from their homes, and at least six U.S. advisers and 3,000 South Vietnamese have been killed. Communist deaths are estimated at 13,000.

CAMBODIA: The town of Kampong Trach near the South Vietnam border falls to Communist forces after a siege by at least 1,500 troops lasting 17 days. During the next three weeks 11 other Cambodian positions fall to the Communists.

April 25

GROUND WAR: The 320th NVA Division drives 5,000 ARVN troops into retreat and traps 2,000–3,000 others in a border outpost northwest of Kontum, appearing to be on the way to cutting South Vietnam in two across the Central Highlands along Highway 19.

CAMBODIA: Communist troops have by now taken control of all Cambodian territory bordering South Vietnam to the east of the Mekong River with the exception of the provincial seat Svay Rieng and a few other government strongholds.

April 26

USA – GOVERNMENT: President Nixon, despite the Communist offensive, announces that another 20,000 U.S. troops will be withdrawn from Vietnam in May and June, reducing authorized troop strength to 49,000. Sea and air support will continue; the U.S. Navy has doubled the number of its fighting ships off Vietnam.

April 27

GROUND WAR: North Vietnamese troops shatter defenses north of Quang Tri and move to within 2.5 miles of the city. Using Russian-built T–54 heavy tanks, they will take Dong Ha, seven miles north of Quang Tri, the next day, continuing to tighten their ring around the provincial capital while shelling it heavily. South Vietnamese troops suffer their highest casualties for any week in the war.

AIR WAR: Four air force fighters, using Paveway I "smart bombs," knock down the Thanh Hoa Bridge in North Vietnam. Previously, 871 sorties had resulted in only superficial damage to the bridge.

NEGOTIATIONS: Official Vietnam peace talks, suspended by the United States on March 23, resume in Paris at the proposal of the Communist delegations, but the session is described as "fruitless."

April 28

GROUND WAR: Fire Base Bastogne, 20 miles west of Hue, falls to the Communists; Fire Base Birmingham, four miles to the east, is also under heavy attack. Much of Hue's population is now fleeing south to Danang. Twenty-thousand North Vietnamese troops converge on Kontum, encircling and cutting it off; U.S. commanders call the defending 22nd Division "inadequate" and describe its survival as "problematical."

April 29–30

GROUND WAR: Almost 10,000 civilians and military personnel are evacuated by plane and helicopter from Kontum to Pleiku as North Vietnamese troops tighten their grip on this key Central Highlands town. In Quang Tri, ARVN troops flee southward and North Vietnamese troops move closer to the city. To the south, An Loc remains under siege.

AIR WAR: U.S. B-52s fly 700 raids over North Vietnam.

May 1

GROUND WAR: North Vietnamese troops capture Quang Tri City, the first provincial capital taken during their offensive, consolidating control of the entire province. Hanoi claims 10,000 South Vietnamese and Allied casualties in the battle. Three districts of Binh Dinh Province also fall, leaving about one-third of the Province under Communist control.

USA – MILITARY: The number of U.S. troops in Vietnam now stands at 66,300, 2,700 fewer than President Nixon's goal of reducing troop strength to 69,000 by this date.

SWEDEN: About 60,000 persons demonstrate in Stockholm to protest U.S. bombing in Vietnam.

May 2

GROUND WAR: The panicking 10,000-man 3rd ARVN Division abandons Quang Tri Province, becoming the second South Vietnamese combat division to collapse within a week. The entire defense of the front north of Hue is left to a brigade of several thousand South Vietnamese marines, as the fleeing 3rd Division troops rush southward.

NEGOTIATIONS: The secret negotiations among Kissinger, Le Duc Tho, and Xuan Thuy resume in Paris. The meeting is unproductive. Kissinger and Tho will meet again in Paris on July 19, August 1, August 14, September 15, September 26–27, and October 8–11.

May 3

GROUND WAR: Lieutenant General Ngo Quang Truong arrives in Danang to assume command of I Corps. The previous corps commander, Lieutenant General Hoang Xuan Lam had been relieved by President Thieu.

May 4

NEGOTIATIONS: The United States and South Vietnam call an indefinite halt to the Paris peace talks after the 149th session, citing a "complete lack of progress." North Vietnam and the Viet Cong will ask the United States and South Vietnam to return to the conference table on May 16, but their proposal will be rejected, as will a June 13 Communist proposal asking the United States to withdraw from Vietnam and return to the conference table.

AIR WAR: The aircraft carrier *Saratoga* is ordered to join the other U.S. carriers now operating off Vietnam, bringing the total number of carriers to six for the first time in the war. Fifty fighter-bombers are ordered to join the nearly 1,000 U.S. combat aircraft currently in Indochina.

May 5

GROUND WAR: Troops of the ARVN 21st Division trying to reach beleaguered An Loc via Highway 13 are again pushed back by elements of the 7th NVA Division, who overrun a supporting South Vietnamese fire base. At Kontum, Route 14, briefly reopened the preceding day, is once again closed as Communist troops repulse South Vietnamese paratroopers. In My Tho Province in the Mekong Delta, Viet Cong guerrillas put the 203rd Civil Guard out of combat, capturing seven prisoners and much materiel.

May 6

USA – DOMESTIC: Sixty presidents of midwestern private colleges issue a statement calling for immediate and total withdrawal of U.S. forces from Indochina. Letters containing this statement are sent to President Nixon and the Democratic presidential aspirants.

GROUND WAR: The survivors of South Vietnam's 5th ARVN Division at An Loc continue to take a daily artillery battering from the Communist forces surrounding the city; by this time, the city, that had previously been home to more than 20,000, lay in ruins. Saigon announces the evacuation of all civilians from Kontum City south to Pleiku.

May 7

NORTH VIETNAM: In a special broadcast commemorating Vietnam's victory over the French at Dien Bien Phu in 1954, Defense Minister Vo Nguyen Giap says that the people of Vietnam have defeated three U.S. administrations and are about to win a complete victory over President Nixon.

May 8

USA – GOVERNMENT: President Nixon orders Operation Linebacker, which includes heavy bombing of North Vietnam's military supply network and the mining of Haiphong harbor as well as other measures to prevent the flow of arms and materiel to the Communists. Foreign ships in North Vietnamese ports will have three days to leave before the mines are activated; the U.S. Navy will then search or seize ships. U.S. aircraft will bomb rail lines from China and take whatever other measures are necessary to stem the flow of materiel to the south. Nixon adds that the mining, search, and seizure of ships and bombing of the north will stop if all American POWs are returned and an internationally supervised cease-fire begins.

May 8–12

USA – DOMESTIC: A wave of antiwar demonstrations stemming from President Nixon's May 8 announcement of the mining of North Vietnamese harbors leads to violent clashes with police and 1,800 arrests on college campuses and in cities from Boston to San Jose, California. Police use wooden bullets and tear gas in Berkeley; three police are shot in Madison, Wisconsin; and 715 National Guardsmen are activated to quell violence in Minneapolis.

May 9

USA – DOMESTIC: U.S. Senate Democrats pass a resolution "disapproving the escalation of the war in Vietnam," and present a modified version of the Case-Church amendment, for the first time voting for a cutoff of war funds.

NEGOTIATIONS: Hanoi's delegation calls Nixon's order for mining and bombing a violation of the 1954 Geneva agreement and of the 1968 assurance that U.S. air strikes against the North would end.

AIR WAR: U.S. bombing in North Vietnam reaches the all-time high levels of 1967–68, when the air war was at its most intense.

May 10

INTERNATIONAL: President Nixon's decision to mine North Vietnamese harbors is castigated by the Soviet Union, China, and their eastern European allies, and receives only lukewarm support from western Europe.

AIR WAR: The United States loses at least three aircraft and the North Vietnamese 10 as 150–175 American planes hit targets over Hanoi, Haiphong, and along rail lines leading from China. Lieutenant Randy Cunningham (USN) and Lieutenant (j.g.) Willie Driscoll (USN), flying an F-4J Phantom off the *Constellation*, shoot down three MiGs in one combat mission. Added to two previous victories, this makes them the first American aces of the Vietnam War (and the only U.S. Navy aces).

USAF Captain Charles B. DeBellevue (WSO), flying with Captain Richard S. Ritchie (pilot) in a McDonnell-Douglas F-4D, records his first aerial kill. Captain DeBellevue, who would go on to be the leading American ace of the Vietnam War, will record four of his victories with Captain Ritchie.

F-4 Phantoms from the 8th Tactical Fighter Wing drop "smart bombs" on the Paul Doumer Bridge, damaging the mile-long highway and rail crossing at Hanoi and putting it out of use. It will not be rebuilt until air attacks on North Vietnam cease in 1973.

May 10–11

GROUND WAR: North Vietnamese forces from the 5th VC Division (actually a main force NVA division) launch a major attack against the besieged ARVN forces in An Loc forging two salients in the South Vietnamese perimeter, but the defenders, with the help of massive U.S. airpower, turn back the assault.

May 11

USA – MILITARY: The Department of Defense estimates that the cost of mining North Vietnamese ports and rivers will total $1.5 billion during the next 13 months, and suggests additional appropriations.

SOUTH VIETNAM: President Thieu declares martial law—the first time it has been necessary since the 1968 Tet Offensive—in an attempt to cope with problems caused by the current Communist offensive. Draft age is lowered to 17 and 45,000 excused draftees are recalled.

USSR: The Soviet Union demands that the United States end the mining and bombing of North Vietnam, accusing the United States of "gross violation of . . . freedom of navigation."

May 13

GROUND WAR: Six U.S. advisers land 1,000 South Vietnamese marines behind North Vietnamese lines in seventeen U.S. helicopters southeast of Quang Tri City in the first South Vietnamese counterattack since the beginning of the Communist offensive. The marines reportedly kill more than 300 North Vietnamese before returning to South Vietnamese-controlled territory the next day. North Vietnamese tanks and troops begin the long-awaited offensive against Kontum.

May 14

Ground War: A force of 4,000 soldiers of the 1st ARVN Division, which has reportedly been engaged in a counterattack for over a week, moves to within half a mile of Fire Base Bastogne. About 110 North Vietnamese are killed, and three tons of ammunition and supplies are uncovered.

Mid-May

Air War: For the first time in the war, U.S. Marines make use of Bien Hoa airfield when Marine Air Group 12 moves in with two A-4 Skyhawk squadrons. The marine planes fly in support of ARVN forces in I and IV Corps and make some sorties into Cambodia.

May 15

USA – Military: Headquarters U.S. Army Vietnam is disestablished.
Ground War: South Vietnamese troops retake Fire Base Bastogne, a matter of strategic importance, as the recapture of the fire base should prevent the Communists from moving their heavy artillery to within shelling distance of Hue.
Sea War: The United States announces that it is sending a seventh aircraft carrier, the *Ticonderoga*, and at least six other destroyer-type warships to Vietnam. The harbors of Haiphong, Cam Pha, Dong Hoi, Hon Gai, Thanh Hoa, Vinh, and Quang Khe, and the Ared River and other rivers and canals of North Vietnam are being mined. U.S. sources call the mining "100 percent effective," but Hanoi reports that the mines are being removed as soon as they are dropped and ships are moving without difficulty.

May 16

Air War: A series of air strikes over the past five days has destroyed all of North Vietnam's pumping stations in the southern panhandle, thereby cutting North Vietnam's main fuel line to the South.

May 17

South Vietnam: All college and universities in South Vietnam are closed to allow for the conscription of students.
Ground War: Preceded by five B-52 strikes, which reportedly kill 300 North Vietnamese to the south, fresh ARVN forces are inserted by helicopter along Highway 13 south of An Loc in a continuing effort to relieve this besieged city.
Sea War: Ten Communist supply boats are sunk and 20 others are damaged off the mouth of the Cua Viet River as U.S. warships continue to shell North and South Vietnamese coastlines.

May 19

Ground War: Elements of the 9th and 21st ARVN Divisions combine with South Vietnamese airborne troops to open new stretches of road near An Loc and reach to within two miles of the besieged city but heavy fighting continues. In II Corps, NVA troops, preceded by a heavy artillery barrage, try unsuccessfully to break through the lines of the 23rd ARVN Division defending Kontum.

May 20

Diplomacy: President Richard Nixon meets with Leonid Brezhnev for summit talks in Moscow. Although Vietnam is discussed, there is no change in the Soviet Union's support of North Vietnam, and both parties are apparently unwilling to risk détente over the topic.

GROUND WAR: A heavy North Vietnamese attack brings to a standstill the South Vietnamese column moving up Route 13 to relieve An Loc.

May 23

GROUND WAR: The 1st NVA Division invades the lower Mekong Delta. Its apparent objective is Chuong Thien Province, known for its weakness in resisting Communist infiltration. Almost all regular ARVN troops have been withdrawn from the Mekong Delta to aid in the battle for An Loc.

AIR WAR: The heavy U.S. air attacks, which began with Nixon's May 8 interdiction order, are widened to include more industrial and nonmilitary sites. In 190 strikes, the United States loses one plane but shoots down four. The strikes concentrate on rail lines around Hanoi and Haiphong, rail lines to China, bridges, pipelines, power plants, troops, and troop training facilities.

May 25

GROUND WAR: NVA troops supported by tanks launch a frontal attack on Kontum, while commandos who had previously slipped into the city block access to the Kontum airfield, the besieged city's only means of supply. Some 148 North Vietnamese are reported killed in heavy fighting in Kontum's northeast sector. B-52s begin bombing North Vietnamese troop concentrations around the city.

May 29

DIPLOMACY: In a joint communiqué issued by the United States and the Soviet Union, following the conclusion of summit talks during President Nixon's visit to Moscow, both countries set forth their standard positions on Vietnam. The United States insists that the future of South Vietnam should be left to the South Vietnamese without interference; and the Soviet Union insists on a withdrawal of U.S. and Allied forces from South Vietnam and an end to the bombing of North Vietnam.

June 2

AIR WAR: Thirty to 40 USAF planes and helicopters fly through heavy fire to rescue Captain R. C. Locher, who has been trapped northwest of Hanoi since his Phantom jet went down May 10.

USA – DOMESTIC: One hundred protesters gather on the White House sidewalk to begin the second year of an anti-Vietnam War vigil. Originally begun by a Quaker group, the vigil outside the White House is sustained by various activists.

June 3

WAR CRIMES: A secret, 260-page army analysis of the My Lai massacre, known as the Peers report and made public by Pulitzer Prize-winning journalist Seymour Hersh, concludes that the entire command structure of the Americal Division, including Brigadier Generals Koster and Young, wittingly and unwittingly suppressed information on the My Lai incident.

June 4

WAR CRIMES: Seymour Hersh further reports that a massacre at My Khe 4, two miles from My Lai, was perpetrated by Bravo Company, Task Force Barker, Americal

Division, on March 16, 1968, the same day as the My Lai massacre. No prosecutions have been made because of a lack of evidence.

GROUND WAR: North Vietnamese troops repeatedly attack Phou My, a district capital in Binh Dinh Province, and are beaten back only after U.S. planes kill 60 soldiers.

June 5
USA – GOVERNMENT: Secretary of Defense Laird, testifying before a joint congressional appropriations committee meeting, says the increase in U.S. military activity in Vietnam could add $3–5 billion to the 1973 fiscal budget, doubling the annual cost of the war.

June 6
GROUND WAR: South Vietnamese forces drive out all but a few of the Communist troops remaining in Kontum, with over 200 North Vietnamese killed in six skirmishes. Several thousand NVA troops remain in the vicinity.

June 7
DIPLOMACY: At the UN Conference on Human Environment in Stockholm, the United States protests Sweden's use of the term "ecocide" in denouncing U.S. use of herbicides in Vietnam.

USA – DOMESTIC: Senator George McGovern (D-S.D.), who has swept the Democratic Party spring primaries and has been one of the earliest and most vocal opponents of U.S. Vietnam War policy, continues to make the war one of the central issues of the campaign by announcing at a news conference that he will go "anywhere in the world" to negotiate an end to the war and a return of POWs and withdrawal of U.S. troops from Southeast Asia.

AIR WAR: U.S. planes continue the heaviest bombing of the war. Munitions used in the intensified bombing of North and South Vietnam account for most of the increased cost of the war.

June 9
GROUND WAR: Part of the relief column composed mainly of 21st ARVN Division troops, which has been trying to reach besieged An Loc from the Mekong Delta since 9 April, finally arrives. These battered units do not significantly reinforce An Loc, and the two-month siege is not lifted. Observers believe that the best hope for An Loc is that the North Vietnamese will run out of shells but the defenders continue to hold. In Military Region II, senior U.S. adviser John Paul Vann is killed in a helicopter crash. Military intelligence reports that the entire North Vietnamese 325C Division has moved into South Vietnam to join the drive against Hue.

AIR WAR: Under President Nixon, the number of USAF fighter-bombers in Southeast Asia has tripled and the total number of B-52s has quadrupled. Six carriers are in the Tonkin Gulf, where before there had been only two, and two more are en route. Because of the air force commitment to close air support in South Vietnam, navy planes are flying two-thirds of the attack sorties against North Vietnam.

June 10
AIR WAR: U.S. Phantom jets destroy the Lang Chi hydroelectric power plant, using laser-guided 2,000-pound bombs. This plant supplied electricity to the Hanoi-Haiphong area.

June 12

USA – MILITARY: General John D. Lavelle, former four-star general and air force commander in Southeast Asia, testifies before the House Armed Services Committee that he was relieved of his post in March and later demoted after repeatedly ordering unauthorized bombing of military targets in North Vietnam. Court-martial charges were brought against him by his subordinates, which also implicated his superiors, particularly General Abrams, but the charges were dropped by the air force because the "interests of discipline" had already been served. Lavelle became the first four-star general in modern U.S. history to be demoted on retirement, although he continued to receive a full general's retirement pay of $27,000 per year.

USA – MILITARY: The Joint U.S. Public Affairs Office (JUSPAO) in Saigon is closed after four years of directing public affairs and psychological warfare in Vietnam. Most of its duties are assumed by the U.S. Information Agency. JUSPAO is declared successful in "winning the hearts and minds" of the Vietnamese people.

CHINA: In its strongest statement against the United States since President Nixon's visit, China for the first time denounces the intensified bombing of North Vietnam, calling the raids, which approach her borders for the first time since 1968, acts of aggression against the Vietnamese people and "grave provocations against the Chinese people."

June 13

GROUND WAR: Large numbers of fresh troops from the 18th ARVN Division are flown into the An Loc area. Although most of the Communist troops have been pushed out of the northern part of the city, North Vietnamese troops still block Route 13 and continue to shell An Loc.

June 14

AIR WAR: U.S. planes, flying a record 340 strikes over North Vietnam, sever the main railway line between Hanoi and Haiphong.

June 17

USA – DOMESTIC: Five men are arrested for breaking into the Democratic National Committee offices at the Watergate complex of apartments and hotel in Washington, D.C.

June 18

GROUND WAR: South Vietnamese troops break the siege of An Loc, begun on April 5. President Thieu flies in to make a surprise visit to the city and congratulate the defenders.

AIR WAR: An AC-130 gunship is shot down southwest of Hue; 12 airmen of the 16th Special Operations Squadron are KIA.

June 19

WAR CRIMES: Calling the My Lai massacre "trifling by comparison," veteran Vietnam correspondent Kevin Buckley in a *Newsweek* article charges that U.S. soldiers deliberately killed thousands of Vietnamese citizens under the guise of "pacification" during Operation Speedy Express conducted by the 9th Infantry Division in the Mekong Delta, December 1968–May 1969.

June 20
USA – Government: President Nixon appoints General Creighton W. Abrams, commander of U.S. forces in Vietnam, to be U.S. Army chief of staff. He will be replaced in Saigon by General Fred Weyand.

Air War: With the new AH-1J Sea Cobra, U.S. Marine unit HMA-369 begins flying armed helicopter strikes from the decks of the *Constellation,* off the coast of South Vietnam. Marine A-6 Intruders of VMA-224, flying from the deck of the USS *Coral Sea,* make most of their missions into Laos and North Vietnam.

June 22
Ground War: The 21st Division, decimated by its attempts to relieve An Loc, is replaced by the 25th ARVN Division which moves up Highway 13 to the besieged city. Large numbers of fresh South Vietnamese troops are flown into the An Loc area; U.S. helicopters insert 18th ARVN Division troops to positions south of An Loc to replace badly battered 9th ARVN Division troops. Although most of the Communist troops within the city itself have been eliminated, North Vietnamese forces still block parts of Route 13 and continue to shell An Loc. Far to the north, ARVN forces successfully defend against a major NVA push, killing 146 and destroying 18 tanks in fighting west of Hue.

June 23
Ground War: U.S. helicopters are required to fly almost all the dangerous missions around An Loc because South Vietnamese crews have panicked under fire. Several U.S. helicopters and their crews have been lost in the last two weeks, causing bitterness among U.S. airmen.

June 26
USA – Domestic: Syndicated columnist Jack Anderson makes public four unpublished volumes of the Pentagon Papers, which cover Johnson administration efforts to get peace talks started. Anderson defends his disclosure, remarking that President Nixon has made public "even more sensitive negotiations." Also on this day, the Democratic National Convention Platform Committee approves a plank making the first order of business for a victorious presidential candidate the immediate withdrawal of U.S. forces from Vietnam.

Air War: The United States establishes a 25-mile-wide buffer zone along Vietnam's border with China within which it will not bomb.

Thailand: The shift of fighter-bomber squadrons—up to 150 U.S. planes and more than 2,000 pilots—from Danang to bases in Thailand is completed. The shift is necessitated by the pending withdrawal of U.S. infantry troops, which provided security for the air base at Danang.

USA – Military: The 3rd Brigade (Separate) of the 1st Cavalry Division (Airmobile), Task Force Garry Owen, departs South Vietnam.

June 27
South Vietnam: President Thieu is granted emergency powers enabling him to rule by decree for six months. The final Senate vote is held after Saigon's curfew, when no opposition members are present, and the Senate will later pass a nonbinding resolution asserting that Thieu has no authority to rule by decree.

June 28

USA – GOVERNMENT: President Nixon announces that no more draftees will be sent to Vietnam unless they volunteer for such duty. A force of 10,000 troops will be withdrawn from Vietnam by September 1, leaving a total of 39,000 U.S. military personnel in-country.

GROUND WAR: Over 10,000 South Vietnamese marines and paratroopers push across the My Chanh River to begin a drive to retake Quang Tri Province. Supported by at least 17 U.S. cruisers and destroyers and 100 B-52s flying the largest number of missions to date against Communist troop positions, the counteroffensive meets with stiff opposition and makes little headway.

June 29

USA – MILITARY: General Frederick C. Weyand replaces General Creighton Abrams as commander, U.S. Military Assistance Command, Vietnam; Abrams will replace Westmoreland as Army chief of staff. The 196th Infantry Brigade, the last U.S. Army ground combat brigade in Vietnam, departs.

NEGOTIATIONS: President Nixon agrees to the resumption of peace talks in Paris "on the assumption that the North Vietnamese are prepared to negotiate in a constructive and serious way." Talks will begin again July 13.

June 30

USA – MILITARY: XXIV Corps is disestablished at Danang and its assets form the basis for its successor, the First Regional Assistance Command (FRAC).

NEW ZEALAND The last of the New Zealand troop contingent withdraws from Vietnam.

GROUND WAR: More South Vietnamese troops arrive in Quang Tri Province by helicopter for the third straight day. Supported by continued U.S. air and naval firepower, the counteroffensive penetrates to six or seven miles from Quang Tri City.

July 2

USA – MILITARY: U.S. military and civilian sources disclose that weather modification techniques, such as seeding the clouds to suppress antiaircraft fire and hinder troop movements, have been used in both Vietnam and Laos since 1963.

July 7

GROUND WAR: South Vietnamese troops advancing on Quang Tri are brought to a standstill at La Van Ngha village about two miles from the city. Heavy Communist shelling of Hue continues; to the south in Binh Long Province, the main highway to An Loc remains blocked in several places.

LAOS: Premier Souvanna Phouma accepts the offer of Pathet Lao leader Prince Souphanouvong to resume talks to end the fighting. Negotiations will begin October 17 and continue throughout the year, but remain fruitless.

July 9

GROUND WAR: At An Loc, an enemy artillery shell kills Brigadier General Richard Tallman (USA) and four other Americans while also wounding two advisers. He and his personal staff had just flown into the city to confer with U.S. advisers.

July 10
GROUND WAR: Although President Thieu claims that his troops have entered Quang Tri, fighting remains deadlocked outside the city. Meanwhile, the situation remains relatively static on South Vietnam's two other fronts, but military action has increased so much in the last 24 hours in the Mekong Delta southwest of Saigon that some believe the Communists are opening a new front there.

July 13
NEGOTIATIONS: The Paris peace talks resume after a 10-week suspension. Both sides restate their positions; central to the talks is the future of the Saigon government.

July 14
USA – DOMESTIC: Six national leaders of the 20,000-member Vietnam Veterans Against the War are indicted by a federal grand jury on charges of conspiring to incite an "armed rebellion" at the Republican National Convention.

July 15
GROUND WAR: South Vietnamese troops trying to retake Quang Tri City finally break through, advancing to within 700 yards of the Citadel, a large walled fortress in the center of town.
AIR WAR: B-52s bombing Communist bunkers around Quang Tri kill 300 soldiers in two raids.

July 17–20
GROUND WAR: South Vietnamese paratroopers fight their way to within 200 yards of the Citadel in Quang Tri City, which is described by observers as a city of "rubble and ash." Citizens emerging from neighborhoods retaken by the paratroopers join the refugees heading south to Hue on Route 1. The fighting to recapture the rest of the city continues.

July 19
NEGOTIATIONS: Washington and Hanoi announce that the secret Paris peace talks have resumed. Henry Kissinger and Le Duc Tho confer for six-and-a-half hours. By mutual agreement, neither side reveals details of the meetings.
GROUND WAR: Opening a counteroffensive in coastal Binh Dinh Province, a large force of South Vietnamese troops moves north toward the district capital at Hoi An. Saigon's forces succeed in taking the city two days later, but will lose the western half one week after that.

July 21
USA – MILITARY: The Defense Department acknowledges unsuccessful attempts to destroy rain forest cover in 1966 and 1967 by starting forest fires, but denies secrecy or any desire to create devastating fire storms. During Operation Pink Rose, an area the size of Philadelphia in the Boi Loi Woods, a dense forest area northwest of Saigon was defoliated and hit with magnesium bombs, but the tropical forest proved too moist for the project, which was undertaken by the Defense Department and U.S. Forest Service.

July 24

USA – Government: The U.S. Senate passes the Cooper amendment to a military aid bill, which stipulates complete U.S. troop withdrawal from Vietnam within four months of Hanoi releasing all U.S. POWs. The overall bill fails to pass, in what is seen as a victory for the Nixon administration.

United Nations: Secretary-General Kurt Waldheim discloses that he has received information that apparently confirms that U.S. planes and naval vessels have deliberately damaged dikes in North Vietnam that are essential to flood control during the rainy season. The North Vietnamese have repeatedly claimed that their dikes have deliberately been bombed since U.S. air and naval attacks resumed above the 20th parallel in May. The U.S. Defense Department, President Nixon, and Secretary of State William P. Rogers claim that any U.S. strikes against dikes were accidental. Nixon calls Waldheim "well-intentioned and naïve," asserting that the dike controversy is a deliberate attempt on the part of the North Vietnamese to create an extraneous issue to divert attention from "one of the most barbaric invasions of history."

Air War: U.S. fighter-bombers attack supply complexes in Hanoi in the first strikes against the capital in a month. Laser-guided bombs are used because their pinpoint accuracy allows them to "hit the target and not the civilians." Laser- and TV-guided bombs, despite a cost that is four to five times as much as conventional bombs, have proven highly successful and accurate, and have, according to one U.S. official, introduced "a whole new magnitude" of warfare.

July 26

Ground War: Although South Vietnamese paratroopers hoist their flag over Quang Tri Citadel, they are unable to hold the Citadel for long or to secure Quang Tri City. Fighting outside the city remains intense. South Vietnamese troops under heavy shelling are forced to abandon Fire Base Bastogne, which protects the southwest approaches to Hue.

July 28

USA – Government: A CIA report made public by the Nixon administration reveals that U.S. bombing has caused accidental minor damage to North Vietnam's dikes at 12 places. The nearly 2,000 miles of dikes on the Tonkin plain and more than 2,000 along the sea make civilized life possible in the Red River Delta. Destruction of the dikes would mean the destruction of centuries of patient work and cause the drowning or starvation of hundreds of thousands of peasants. Bombing the dikes had been advocated by some U.S. strategists since the beginning of U.S. involvement in the war, but was rejected outright by U.S. presidents as an act of terrorism unworthy of the United States.

USSR: The Soviet Union continues to publicize what it calls the two-month U.S. bombing campaign to destroy the dikes and dams of the Tonkin Delta.

July 29

War Crimes: Former U.S. attorney general Ramsey Clark visits North Vietnam as a member of the International Commission of Inquiry into U.S. War Crimes in Indochina, to investigate alleged U.S. bombing of nonmilitary targets in North Vietnam. His visit stirs intense controversy at home. Clark reports over Hanoi Radio that he has seen damage to hospitals, dikes, schools, and civilian areas.

July 31

NORTH VIETNAM: Hanoi challenges the Nixon administration on the dike controversy, claiming that since April there have been 173 raids against the dikes with direct hits in "149 places."

CAMBODIA: Near Kampong Trabek in the Parrot's Beak region of eastern Cambodia, about 2,000 South Vietnamese troops begin an operation designed to cripple a possible Communist operation against Route 4, which links Saigon with the Mekong Delta.

August 1

NEGOTIATIONS: Henry Kissinger meets privately with Le Duc Tho and Xuan Thuy in Paris. The Communists relax somewhat their previous demands that President Thieu abdicate, but the North Vietnamese do not appear to Kissinger to be in any hurry to reach any agreement before the November presidential election, in which they clearly favor George McGovern.

August 2

GROUND WAR: In one of the heaviest artillery bombardments since the North Vietnamese first launched the Nguyen Hue Offensive, 2,000 rounds hit South Vietnamese marines trying to recapture the provincial capital of Quang Tri. Supported by U.S. B-52s, ARVN troops reenter Fire Base Bastogne, lost earlier in the year, only to find it empty of enemy troops.

August 5

SOUTH VIETNAM: President Thieu announces a decree requiring every daily newspaper to deposit $47,000 with the government as a guarantee against possible fines and court charges. The decree also says that the government can shut down any newspaper whose daily issue has been confiscated a second time for "articles detrimental to the national security and public order." Sixteen newspapers and 15 periodicals will eventually cease publication, leaving only two opposition papers in Saigon.

August 7–8

GROUND WAR: North Vietnamese forces attack the Long Thanh rubber plantation 17 miles east of Saigon, inflicting heavy casualties on ARVN troops.

AIR WAR: Seasonal bad weather limits the usual air strikes throughout North Vietnam, often reducing the usual number by one-third except for B-52s, which fly above the clouds.

August 9

CAMBODIA: Over 2,000 South Vietnamese rangers clash with North Vietnamese troops in Cambodia. U.S. warplanes destroyed 14 tanks the day before, near Kampong Trabek. Intelligence reports indicate a large Communist buildup in Cambodia.

August 10

GROUND WAR: North Vietnamese forces block Routes 1, 4, and 13, all major South Vietnamese supply routes to Saigon. For the next two months, Communist forces repeatedly interdict these and other key supply routes critical to Saigon's survival.

August 11

GROUND WAR: The last U.S. ground combat unit in South Vietnam, the 3rd Battalion, 21st Infantry, Task Force Gimlet, is deactivated, along with G Battery, 29th Field Artillery. Delta Company had completed the 3rd Battalion's last patrol on August 5, ending the U.S. infantry war in Vietnam. The unit had been guarding the U.S. air base at Danang. This leaves only 43,500 advisers, airmen, and support troops in-country. This number does not include the sailors of the Seventh Fleet or the air force personnel in Thailand and Guam.

NEGOTIATIONS: Calling Vietnamization the main target of the Communist forces, the chief Viet Cong delegate in Paris maintains that the key issue in the current talks is a political settlement in Saigon.

August 13

GROUND WAR: Viet Cong sappers raid the ammo dump at Long Binh, destroying thousands of tons of ammunition, but the South Vietnamese forces have stabilized battle lines around the country. Some observers say that the Communists may be reverting to guerrilla tactics.

USA – DOMESTIC: Ex-captain J. E. Engstrom (USA) says that a military report he helped prepare in 1971 estimating that 25 percent of the lower-ranking enlisted men in Vietnam were addicted to heroin was suppressed and replaced by a "watered-down" version considered more acceptable to the U.S. command.

August 14

SOUTH VIETNAM: South Vietnam's interior minister denies reports of widespread torture of political prisoners who have been rounded up since the start of the Communist offensive in March. Critics charge that at least 10,000 persons have been imprisoned in reeducation centers, with arrests continuing, and that many prisoners have been taken to Con Son jail by the CIA's Air America helicopters. There are charges that the police have made little distinction between those who had Communist connections and those who were merely opposed to the Thieu regime.

USA – DOMESTIC: Former attorney general Ramsey Clark reports after his tour of North Vietnam with the International Commission of Inquiry into U.S. War Crimes in Indochina that if Democratic candidate George McGovern is elected president in November, all U.S. POWs will be freed by North Vietnam within three months. He reports that the POWs he interviewed during his trip were "unquestionably . . . well treated" and that he saw damage to North Vietnam's dikes in at least six places, and other extensive destruction in nonmilitary areas.

NEGOTIATIONS: Kissinger again meets privately with Le Duc Tho and Xuan Thuy in Paris.

August 16

AIR WAR: U.S. fighter-bombers fly 370 air strikes against North Vietnam, the highest daily total of the year; additionally, there are eight B-52 strikes in the North.

Meanwhile, U.S. warplanes fly 321 missions (including 27 B-52 strikes) in South Vietnam, mostly in Quang Tri Province. Despite this heavy air activity, hopes for an agreement to the war rise as Henry Kissinger leaves Paris to confer with President Thieu and his advisers and North Vietnam's chief negotiator returns to Hanoi.

August 19

USA – DOMESTIC: Democratic candidate George McGovern attacks U.S. pacification techniques of applying "massive firepower and free-fire zones and [clearing] six million people out of their homes."

GROUND WAR: In I Corps, there is major fighting near the northern district capital of Que Son and neighboring Camp Ross. After a heavy bombardment, the North Vietnamese capture both the town and the base, giving the Communists control of most of Quang Nam Province.

August 22

USA – DOMESTIC: Delegates entering the Republican National Convention in Miami Beach are harassed by 3,000 antiwar demonstrators, many painted with death masks. The rest of the convention is marked by demonstrations outside the meeting hall and hundreds of protesters are arrested and some are injured when police use riot-control agents.

GROUND WAR: Bypassing South Vietnamese strongpoints around Hue and Danang, the North Vietnamese open a major new front to the south of Quang Tri, moving in heavy 130 mm artillery without detection.

August 23

USA – DOMESTIC: Richard Nixon and Spiro Agnew are renominated at the Republican National Convention in Miami.

August 26

USA – MILITARY: U.S. officials report that the rate of civilian casualties in South Vietnam has risen more than 50 percent since the beginning of North Vietnam's spring offensive. Some 24,788 civilians have been wounded between March 30 and July 31, an average of 6,197 per month, compared to an average of 2,700 for each of the six preceding months.

August 27

AIR WAR: In the heaviest bombing in four years, U.S. aircraft flatten North Vietnamese barracks near Hanoi and Haiphong. Planes also hit bridges on the northeast railroad line to China.

SEA WAR: Four U.S. warships shell the Haiphong port area after dark from two miles offshore. Cruiser *Newport News* sinks one of two North Vietnamese patrol boats in pursuit, and destroyer *Rowan* sets the other on fire.

August 28

AIR WAR: The U.S. Air Force gets its first ace since the Korean War when Captain Richard S. Ritchie, flying with his Weapons Systems Officer, Captain Charles B. DeBellevue, in an F-4 out of Udorn Air Base in Thailand, shoots down his fifth MiG near Hanoi. Two weeks later, Captain DeBellevue, flying with Captain John A. Madden, Jr., will shoot down his fifth and sixth MiG, making him the leading American ace of the war; all of his victories come in a four-month period. The U.S. Navy already has two aces, Cunningham and Driscoll. By this time in the war, there is only one U.S. fighter-bomber base left in South Vietnam, at Bien Hoa; the rest of the air support is provided by aircraft flying from carriers or U.S. bases in Thailand and Guam.

August 29
GROUND WAR: President Nixon announces withdrawals that will reduce total U.S. strength in South Vietnam to 27,000 by December 1.

August 30
GROUND WAR: North Vietnamese artillery hit South Vietnamese marine positions around Quang Tri with about 2,000 heavy-caliber shells. The shelling demonstrates that the North Vietnamese are experiencing no shortages in Quang Tri despite Allied efforts to cut supply lines.

August 31
GROUND WAR: U.S. weekly casualty figures of five dead and three wounded are the lowest recorded since record-keeping began in January 1965.

September 2
AIR WAR: Phuc Yen, 10 miles north of Hanoi and one of the largest air bases in North Vietnam, is smashed by U.S. bombers. A MiG is shot down during the attack, bringing the total to 47 MiGs shot down since the beginning of the North Vietnamese offensive.

September 5
LAOS: U.S. helicopters evacuate Meo tribesmen who have suffered heavy losses following fighting around the Plain of Jars that began in mid-August.

September 6
GROUND WAR: South Vietnamese troops pull out of Tien Phuoc, 37 miles south of Danang, leaving the Communists in control of two-thirds of Quang Tin Province. In the Mekong Delta, 22 soldiers of the 9th ARVN Division are killed and 176 wounded in an attack on the division forward command post 60 miles from Saigon. The NVA appears to be trying to get Saigon to spread its forces thin.

SOUTH VIETNAM: President Thieu abolishes popular elections in the country's 10,775 hamlets and supersedes a 1968 law establishing the election of hamlet and village officers. The 44 province chiefs, all appointed by Thieu, are ordered to reorganize local government and appoint hamlet officials. Thieu cites the Communist offensive as justification for these measures. He claims that many hamlet chiefs are Communists and provide support for insurgents, but the decree was actually drafted before the offensive began.

September 8
USA – MILITARY: The Defense Department admits that on July 17 the crippled American destroyer *Warrington* may have struck a U.S. mine emplaced during the U.S. mining of North Vietnamese waters.

September 10

GROUND WAR: Communists raid Tan Son Nhut and Bien Hoa air bases near Saigon. Two South Vietnamese are killed, 20 hurt, and five South Vietnamese planes are damaged at Tan Son Nhut. At Bien Hoa, 40 Americans are wounded and one gunship and 50 South Vietnamese helicopters are damaged.

SOUTH VIETNAM: The U.S. embassy in Saigon protests continuing South Vietnamese national radio and TV broadcasts which for four weeks have been calling presidential candidate McGovern a "mad dog" and "enemy of the people."

September 11

NEGOTIATIONS: The PRG delegation announces that any settlement in South Vietnam must reflect "reality" of "two administrations, two armies and other political forces."

September 12

GROUND WAR: U.S. intelligence agencies (CIA and DIA) report to the National Security Council that the North Vietnamese have 100,000 regular troops in the South and can sustain fighting in the South "at the present rate" for two years; that while U.S. bombing has caused heavy casualties and prevented North Vietnam from doubling operations, the overall effects are disappointing because troops and supplies have kept moving south. It is estimated that 20,000 fresh troops have infiltrated into the South in the last six weeks. The number of NVA troops in the Mekong Delta has increased as much as tenfold, up to 30,000 in the last year, and a third oil pipeline, like the others nearly impossible to cut by air strikes, has been completed between North Vietnam and China.

September 15

GROUND WAR: The South Vietnamese recapture Quang Tri City after four days of heavy fighting, claiming that over 8,135 NVA have been killed in the battle. The city has been virtually destroyed by the intense fighting that has raged since NVA forces occupied it in May. Although this is one of the most significant South Vietnamese victories since the beginning of the North Vietnamese Spring Offensive, 977 South Vietnamese perished in the four-and-a-half-month battle. Most of the rest of Quang Tri Province remains in Communist hands. Meanwhile, a new Communist offensive opens in Quang Ngai Province.

September 16

AIR WAR: The U.S. Air Force reports it has destroyed 90 percent of North Vietnam's largest rail yard, 38 miles from Hanoi, on the northeast line running to China.

GROUND WAR: Communist forces begin an offensive with simultaneous attacks on district capitals in southern Quang Ngai Province.

September 17

POWs: Three U.S. pilot POWs are released by Hanoi, the first captives released since 1969; they are turned over to members of the Committee for Liaison with Families of American Servicemen Detained in Vietnam, the American group headed by Cora Weiss, who arranged their release. Hanoi cautions the United States not to force the freed men to "slander" North Vietnam and to avoid any "distortions" about Hanoi's treatment of the POWs.

September 19
AIR WAR: Captain Charles B. DeBellevue (USAF) shoots down his sixth MiG to become the leading ace of the war. He was the first Weapons Systems Officer to be designated an Ace.

September 20
AIR WAR: The air force reveals that U.S. planes have been mining the coastal rivers and canals of northern Quang Tri Province below the DMZ, the first mining of waterways within South Vietnam.

September 22
GROUND WAR: The fighting in Quang Ngai Province moves closer to the provincial capital of Quang Ngai City, forcing South Vietnamese troops to abandon one fire base to the east and one fire base to the west of the city.

September 26
AIR WAR: With the rainy season coming, the United States decides to deploy two squadrons (48 planes) of F-111 attack bombers to Takhli Air Base, Thailand, to give better low-level and all-weather capabilities for the approaching monsoon season in North Vietnam.

September 26–October 7
NEGOTIATIONS: Against a background of rumors of major diplomatic developments, Henry Kissinger and Le Duc Tho, the chief North Vietnamese negotiator, hold the 19th session of their private talks.

September 28
GROUND WAR: Weekly casualty figures contain no U.S. combat fatalities. This has not occurred since March 1965. There is a general lull in heavy ground fighting for the sixth straight day, but the North Vietnamese launch some harassing attacks in Quang Ngai Province.

September 30
AIR WAR: U.S. planes, hitting North Vietnamese air bases in Phuc Yen, Yen Bai, Quan Lang, and Vinh, destroy five MiG fighters on the ground and damage nine others, also on the ground; these represent about 10 percent of the total North Vietnamese air force.

October 1
SEA WAR: Twenty sailors die and 37 are wounded when a shell goes off in the barrel of a gun aboard the U.S. heavy cruiser *Newport News*. Towed to Subic Bay in the Philippines for repairs, she is needed so badly on the gun line that she is returned to action with the damaged center gun turret sealed.

October 3
USA – MILITARY: The Defense Department reports that more than 800,000 tons of "air ammunitions" have been used over Indochina between January 1 and September 30, compared with 763,160 for all of 1971. U.S. planes have dropped 7,555,800

tons of bombs between February 1965 and August 30, 1972—more than three times as much as was used by the Allies during WW II.

October 7

GROUND WAR: South Vietnamese forces come under attack along Route 13 north of Saigon in a new phase of the Communist offensive. In the Mekong Delta, My Tho is hit by a series of light attacks; there have been over 100 Communist attacks during the last 24 hours. Most of the 300,000 persons who fled Quang Tri Province during the spring offensive now live in squalid refugee camps at Danang.

AIR WAR: U.S. B-52s continue heavy raids in Binh Duong Province aimed at preventing Communist infiltration toward Saigon. U.S. planes fly 300 strikes over North Vietnam.

CAMBODIA: In one of the heaviest raids inside Phnom Penh since the beginning of the war, NVA troops blow up a bridge over the Tonle Sap, less than two miles from the center of the city, killing 36 Cambodian soldiers and civilians and losing 28 of their own force.

U.S. Air Force B-52 lands at U Tapao Air Base, Thailand, after returning from a bombing mission over South Vietnam, October 1972. *(National Archives)*

October 8–11

NEGOTIATIONS: Rumors arise that there has been a breakthrough in the secret talks in Paris. North Vietnamese representative Le Duc Tho presents a draft peace agreement proposing that two separate administrations remain in South Vietnam and negotiate general elections. This settlement accepts in substance the U.S. proposals, thus dropping demands for a political solution to accompany a military one. Tho, believing that the Americans are eager for peace in Vietnam before the elections, proposes that the United States and North Vietnam arrange a cease-fire governing all military matters between themselves, leaving the political questions to be settled by the Vietnamese sides, who will be governed by a "National Council of Reconciliation" until a final settlement is reached. Hanoi and Saigon will continue to occupy the territory each presently holds until then. Kissinger, who considers Hanoi's offer a breakthrough, explicitly agrees to North Vietnamese troops remaining in the South. He cables President Thieu "to seize as much territory as possible."

USA – GOVERNMENT: Washington starts Operation Enhance Plus—the transfer of $2 billion worth of military equipment to South Vietnam, including aircraft, tanks, and artillery pieces. This program was designed to complete the Vietnamization process by giving South Vietnam as much equipment as possible before the peace agreement was signed.

October 9

GROUND WAR: Several hundred VC continue to control at least three hamlets within 20 miles of Saigon.

October 11

AIR WAR: U.S. Navy aircraft attacking the Gia Lam rail yard northeast of Hanoi accidentally hit the French, Indian, and Algerian legations in Hanoi, killing Delegate General Pierre Susini.

October 12

SOUTH VIETNAM: Thieu declares that peace will come only when the Communists have been exterminated. He says, in a speech in Saigon, that "coalition with the Communists means death" and that the Communists will have to be killed "to the last man" before there will be peace.

GROUND WAR: The Ben Het Special Forces camp is struck by 1,500 rockets and then taken by the Communists. One U.S. soldier is killed and one wounded in the ambush of an ARVN convoy 25 miles southeast of Saigon. Elsewhere, South Vietnamese troops retake Ba To, south of Danang. The Communists retain their control of at least two hamlets within 20 miles of Saigon.

USA – GOVERNMENT: The U.S. Senate approves the nomination of General Creighton Abrams, commander of U.S. forces in Vietnam since mid-1968, to be army chief of staff. Consideration of his nomination has been sidetracked for months by Senate hearings into unauthorized bombing raids against North Vietnam ordered by General John Lavelle, whose testimony before the House Armed Service Committee appeared at times to implicate Abrams.

NEGOTIATIONS: The 163rd session of the regular peace talks is held in Paris.

October 12–13

SEA WAR: Racial violence flares aboard U.S. Navy ships; 46 sailors are injured in a race riot involving more than 100 sailors on the aircraft carrier *Kitty Hawk* off Vietnam. Twenty-one black crewmen will eventually be charged with assault and rioting and ordered before a court-martial in San Diego. In another racial incident in San Diego in November, 123 mostly black seamen assigned to the aircraft carrier *Constellation* refuse to reboard the ship after shore leave because they "fear for their lives." Late in November, black/white clashes occur among 30 seamen at the naval station on Midway Island in the Pacific and among 33 seamen at the Navy Correctional Center in Norfolk, Virginia.

October 16

USA – MILITARY: General Creighton Abrams assumes the office of U.S. Army chief of staff.

GROUND WAR: Communist attacks concentrate on major roads in the Saigon area, and the shelling disrupts traffic. Nearly 100 harassing attacks have occurred in the last 24 hours.

AIR WAR: U.S. warplanes carry out the heaviest raids of the year against North Vietnam, with at least 370 strikes; B-52s hit Communist positions in Cambodia and Laos.

October 17

NEGOTIATIONS: After another meeting in Paris, Henry Kissinger flies to Saigon for four days of talks with President Thieu, who has for two days denied the requests of

Ambassador Ellsworth Bunker to see him. There is a growing feeling that the secret talks in Paris have reached a critical stage. The U.S. Army chief of staff, General Abrams, is en route to Saigon; the Pacific commander in chief, Admiral Noel Gayler, is also in Saigon. The fact that senior U.S. military and diplomatic personnel are meeting in Saigon fuels the rumor of an imminent cease-fire.

SOUTH VIETNAM: In Saigon, the city's supply of food is restricted and driving outside the city is hazardous due to continued Communist activity against the highways around the capital.

October 18

SOUTH VIETNAM: Thieu rejects Hanoi's proposals, opposing draft treaty provisions that allow North Vietnamese troops to remain in place in the South.

October 19

USA – MILITARY: Faced with growing congressional concern over the unauthorized bombing of North Vietnam, Defense Secretary Laird announces revised command procedures aimed at "further strengthening" civilian control of the military. A new group of inspectors general will conduct regular checks to see if orders from Washington are being carried out, and inspectors general from the various service branches will henceforth report to their civilian service secretaries as well as their military chiefs.

October 20

USA – GOVERNMENT: The United States formally admits that it mistakenly dropped a bomb that "inadvertently struck" the French embassy in Hanoi on October 11. The United States had previously asserted that the damage was done by a North Vietnamese SAM-2 antiaircraft missile. Many Frenchmen consider the incident a result of the United States using the bombing of North Vietnam to test new weapons.

October 21

NEGOTIATIONS: North Vietnam's Premier Pham Van Dong announces that Hanoi will accept a cease-fire as the first step to a peace settlement. According to Dong's proposal, the cease-fire would be followed by the withdrawal of U.S. forces, with all POWs to be released when the settlement is agreed upon. It is also stipulated that Saigon and the VC will join in a coalition followed by general elections within six months. President Thieu's status is not mentioned.

October 22

NEGOTIATIONS: Henry Kissinger meets with President Thieu in Saigon to try to secure Thieu's agreement to the cease-fire draft, particularly to Viet Cong participation in postwar Vietnam. Thieu, who wishes South Vietnam to be recognized as a sovereign state, accuses the United States of conspiring with China and the Soviet Union to undermine his regime, and rejects the proposed accord almost point for point. He presents Kissinger a list of 129 demands that includes recognition of the DMZ and South Vietnamese sovereignty, the withdrawal of all North Vietnamese forces from the South, and the acknowledgment of the existing governmental structure in South Vietnam. Kissinger, who is due to initial the draft in Hanoi at the end of the month, cables President Nixon that Thieu's terms "verge on insanity" and flies home to confer with the president.

GROUND WAR: Bien Hoa airport is hit by a barrage of Communist rockets; South Vietnamese commanders report that they do not feel that the peace talks have affected military action.

AIR WAR: U.S. B-52s continue bombing Communist positions in an arc north of Saigon; U.S. planes fly 220 missions over North Vietnam.

LAOS: Increased fighting erupts as both Communist and government forces attempt to gain ground before an anticipated Indochinese cease-fire. Government troops begin a drive to retake the southern village of Saravane, and will succeed six days later; but the village will change hands four more times by the end of the year.

October 23

NEGOTIATIONS: A U.S. message to Hanoi requests further negotiations, citing difficulties with Saigon.

October 24

AIR WAR: As a sign of good faith, Nixon temporarily suspends the Linebacker raids north of the 20th parallel. Interdiction raids in South Vietnam continue.

NEGOTIATIONS: According to Nixon administration officials, the principal obstacle to a cease-fire is in Saigon, where President Thieu broadcasts a denunciation of the cease-fire treaty, calling all peace proposals discussed by Kissinger and Hanoi in Paris unacceptable, and urging his troops to wipe out the Communist presence in the South "quickly and mercilessly."

October 26

NORTH VIETNAM: Radio Hanoi announces that secret talks in Paris have produced a tentative agreement to end the war. It broadcasts a summary of the nine-point cease-fire draft treaty agreement, accusing the United States of trying to sabotage it by claiming difficulties in Saigon.

USA – GOVERNMENT: Hoping to reassure the North Vietnamese of U.S. sincerity and President Thieu of U.S. determination to see the treaty through, Henry Kissinger announces at a White House press conference that "peace is at hand." "We believe that an agreement is in sight." In his first report on the secret peace talks, Kissinger confirms Hanoi's announcement that a breakthrough occurred on October 8, with both sides reaching an overall agreement on a nine-point peace plan. Although denying that the United States agreed to sign the document by October 31, Kissinger says that he believes that a final agreement can be reached in one more meeting with the North Vietnamese lasting "not more than three or four days."

NEGOTIATIONS: In Paris at a news conference, Xuan Thuy announces that Hanoi and the United States reached an agreement on October 17 on all but two points: the release of POWs and post-cease-fire arms shipments. He claims that since North Vietnam decided to accept the U.S. proposals on these points, the United States refusal to sign the treaty on October 31 and its request for more talks creates an "extremely serious situation."

October 29

SOUTH VIETNAM: It is decreed in Saigon that all South Vietnamese houses must have a national flag displayed on pain of arrest and that the possession or display of a VC flag will be punishable by death. Additionally, President Thieu is still working on a decree that would make being a Communist or associating with a Communist punishable by death.

NEGOTIATIONS: The United States announces that the peace accord will definitely not be signed by October 31, although optimism is expressed concerning early settlement of the remaining details.

GROUND WAR: Communists are steadily taking over settlements around Saigon, occupying 17 hamlets within 40 miles of the city. Route 1 is cut east and west of Saigon. One hundred thirty-eight Communist attacks occur throughout South Vietnam, the highest number for any single day in 1972.

AIR WAR: U.S. B-52s and fighter-bombers hit North Vietnam below the 20th parallel. U.S. B-52s fly 23 missions and fighter bombers make 313 strikes against Communist positions in South Vietnam.

October 31

GROUND WAR: Hoping to expand their control of South Vietnamese territory before a truce goes into effect, several thousand North Vietnamese troops move out of sanctuaries in Cambodia and into South Vietnam's Mekong Delta and the area surrounding Saigon, leaving the burden of fighting Cambodian government troops to the Khmer Rouge.

November 1

SOUTH VIETNAM: Continuing his objections to the draft peace treaty developed in Paris, President Thieu makes public his opposition to the tentative Kissinger-Tho agreement, denouncing it as a "surrender of the South Vietnamese people to the Communists" and "only a cease-fire to sell out Vietnam."

NEGOTIATIONS: Xuan Thuy, in a television interview in Paris, asserts that the problem with the peace settlement is not one of major or minor points, as the United States claims, but the seriousness of the United States altogether. Hanoi does not object to another Kissinger-Le Duc Tho meeting; what Hanoi desires, he says, is that the United States keep its word.

GROUND WAR: In a CH-47 Chinook helicopter crash near My Tho in the Mekong Delta, 22 U.S. personnel are killed.

AIR WAR: Heavy U.S. bombing concentrates on North Vietnamese base areas in Laos and Cambodia.

LAOS: Two hundred Laotian troops die when their garrison is overrun by North Vietnamese and Pathet Lao forces, forcing another 300 soldiers and 1,000 civilians into Thailand as they overrun the Nam Thorn Buk Kwang garrison, about 90 miles east of Vientiane. This operation is part of an offensive launched October 28 to gain ground before the expected cease-fire.

November 2

NEGOTIATIONS: President Nixon announces that there will be no signing of the draft truce agreement until all remaining issues are resolved. Radio Hanoi announces that the U.S. delay in signing forces North Vietnam to increase fighting on all fronts.

GROUND WAR: There have been 142 attacks in South Vietnam in the previous 24 hours.

USA – GOVERNMENT: The White House discloses that the South Vietnamese air force will receive hundreds more aircraft than previously agreed upon. This increase is seen as another attempt to coax President Thieu into early acceptance of the cease-fire.

November 7

USA – DOMESTIC: Richard Nixon defeats Senator George McGovern and is reelected president of the United States. Nixon carries all states but Massachusetts for a total of 97 percent of the electoral vote; but only 55 percent of the electorate votes in the election, the lowest turnout since 1948. The Democrats widen their majority in Congress, picking up two Senate seats. Nixon pledges to secure "peace with honor in Vietnam."

AIR WAR: B-52s set a record for concentrated bombing of a single province—Quang Tri—in a single day.

USA – MILITARY: The 1st Signal Brigade departs Vietnam.

November 8

SOUTH KOREA: South Korean troops withdraw from the fighting and retire to rear bases. The 37,000 troops of the ROK's original 48,000-man presence who remain are scheduled to depart in December.

November 10–12

SOUTH VIETNAM: There are reports that hard-line Communist troops in the South led by General Le Vinh Khoa have rebelled in protest over the pending negotiated settlement. Hanoi denies reports of a rebellion, calling them examples of CIA psychological warfare.

November 11

GROUND WAR: The massive Long Binh U.S. military base, once the largest U.S. installation outside the continental United States, is handed over to the South Vietnamese. This effectively marks the end of direct U.S. participation in the war. About 29,000 U.S. soldiers remain in South Vietnam, most of them advisers with ARVN troops, helicopter crewmen, and maintenance, supply, and office staff. The United States and Hanoi continue to move supplies into South Vietnam in preparation for a cease-fire. Communist shelling around Quang Tri City is the heaviest in the area since the summer.

November 14

USA – GOVERNMENT: One week after his reelection, President Nixon extends to President Thieu his "absolute assurance" that the United States will "take swift and severe retaliatory action" if Hanoi violates the pending cease-fire once it is in place. He instructs Kissinger to present Le Duc Tho with 69 amendments to the treaty draft submitted by Thieu, despite Kissinger's protestations that the changes are "preposterous" and may wreck the treaty.

President Richard Nixon meets at Camp David with Henry Kissinger (left) and General Alexander Haig to discuss the Vietnam situation, November 1972. *(National Archives)*

November 15

SOUTH VIETNAM: Willard E. Chambers, chief of the U.S. pacification effort in South Vietnam, quits "in sheer disgust," expressing extreme dissatisfaction with those running the war effort. Chambers says that, although he always supported the U.S. policy of preventing a Communist takeover in South Vietnam, those in charge have been unequal to the task: a "parade of overranked non-entities whose actions reflect their own ignorance of Vietnam, of the peculiarities of a people's war and of the requirements of counterinsurgency."

AIR WAR: U.S. planes make over 800 tactical air strikes in North Vietnam's southern panhandle, one of the heaviest days of raids in the war.

November 20–21

NEGOTIATIONS: Henry Kissinger and Le Duc Tho hold the 21st round of secret peace talks in Paris. Kissinger presents new demands by President Thieu. Besides these demands, there are still two major differences between the two sides. The first concerns the nature of the international supervisory force (Canada, Hungary, Indonesia, and Poland) that will monitor the agreement. The United States envisions a force of several thousand; North Vietnam sees this force as one of no more that 250. The other issue is South Vietnam's sovereignty, which President Thieu insists upon. Le Duc Tho rejects the list of Thieu's demands.

November 22

NEGOTIATIONS: In response to Thieu's demands, Le Duc Tho presents a set of new demands of his own. He withdraws the previously offered concession that American POWs would be released before political prisoners held by Saigon are freed and demands that all American civilian technicians depart along with the U.S. military personnel when they withdraw.

SOUTH VIETNAM: A captured North Vietnamese directive signed by Le Duan orders Communist forces in South Vietnam to observe a cease-fire scrupulously for the first 60 days, and repeats instructions to take as much territory as possible before the cease-fire begins. The directive predicts that South Vietnam will violate the cease-fire with arrests and attempts to retake territory.

AIR WAR: The United States loses the first B-52 to be brought down by a North Vietnamese surface-to-air missile (SAM) near Vinh on the day when B-52s fly their heaviest raids of the war over North Vietnam. The Communists claim 19 B-52s shot down to date.

November 23–25

NEGOTIATIONS: Secret talks resume in Paris, but appear to be hopelessly deadlocked. When the talks break up with no resumption scheduled before December 4, there is speculation that the talks have reached an impasse. The most significant issues are the implementation of the international supervisory force and Saigon's insistence on the withdrawal of all North Vietnamese troops from South Vietnam.

November 27

SOUTH VIETNAM: Sources in Saigon reveal that U.S. officials have been secretly building up U.S. civilian personnel under Department of Defense contracts. About 10,000 U.S. advisers and technicians have been instructed to stay in South Vietnam after a cease-fire, essentially taking over the role of the departing military advisers.

GROUND WAR: There is heavy fighting in northern South Vietnam, in the foothills around Quang Tri. The North Vietnamese have lately relied on artillery, mortar, and rocket attacks, possibly reflecting a loss of personnel during the lengthy fighting.

November 30

USA – GOVERNMENT: White House press secretary Ron Ziegler says that no more public announcements concerning U.S. troop withdrawals from Vietnam will be made now that the level of the U.S. presence has fallen to 27,000 men.

USA – MILITARY: Defense Department sources say that there will not be a full withdrawal of U.S. forces from Vietnam until a final truce agreement is signed, and that such an agreement will not affect the 54,000 U.S. servicemen in Thailand or the 60,000 aboard Seventh Fleet ships off the Vietnamese coast.

GROUND WAR: Bad weather slows attempts by South Vietnamese troops to regain complete control of Quang Tri Province before the expected cease-fire.

AIR WAR: B-52s bomb Quang Tri Province and North Vietnam's southern panhandle; U.S. fighter-bombers fly 40 strikes despite bad weather, which slows attempts by South Vietnamese forces to regain control of Quang Tri Province before the expected cease-fire.

NEGOTIATIONS: In two separate meetings, President Nixon and Henry Kissinger meet with the Joint Chiefs of Staff to brief them on the Paris talks; Kissinger expresses the belief that a final agreement is near.

December 4
NEGOTIATIONS: Secret talks resume after a nine-day recess. Commenting on the problematical negotiations, Kissinger says that the North Vietnamese have changed their position on all of the principal points agreed to by November 20. Contradictory rumors about concessions, agreements, pressures, and plans continue to rise around the talks.
GROUND WAR: The second rocket attack in four days hits Bien Hoa air base. The rockets are directed at pre-cease-fire stockpiling of U.S. aircraft.

December 6
NEGOTIATIONS: Secret talks resume in Paris after a 24-hour break during which U.S. negotiators receive new instructions from the White House.
GROUND WAR: Tan Son Nhut Air Base near Saigon is hit by the heaviest Communist rocket attack in four years. One U.S. rescue helicopter is destroyed and a fuel dump is set ablaze. U.S. planes bomb suspected Communist positions within 10 miles of the air base; the strikes are followed by ARVN attacks against the area from which the rockets were fired. Heavy fighting continues around Quang Tri.

December 7
USA – GOVERNMENT: The State Department announces that 100 Foreign Service officers are on the alert to go to South Vietnam after a truce, to report their observations to the U.S. government, and to relay possible truce violations to the international supervisory commission.
NEGOTIATIONS: Key issue at the secret Paris talks is currently Saigon's insistence that all North Vietnamese troops be withdrawn from South Vietnam. Communist delegates at the formal talks renew their demand that the United States sign the October 17 draft agreement without any changes.
AIR WAR: B-52s drop in excess of 600 tons of bombs in and around the DMZ; 85 of the 242 strikes flown in the previous 24 hours hit South Vietnam's northern military region.

December 9
AIR WAR: Heavy bombing of Communist troops and supply depots along the DMZ continues for the third straight day. U.S. fighter-bombers fly 60 missions over North Vietnam and 208 in support of South Vietnamese troops in the South.

December 10
NEGOTIATIONS: Technical experts of both sides begin to work on the language of the accord, giving rise to expectations that a final agreement is close.
USA – GOVERNMENT: General Alexander Haig, who has been in Washington, briefing President Nixon on the Paris talks is alerted to fly to Saigon with the accord, so that President Thieu can sign at the same time as the United States and Hanoi in Paris.

GROUND WAR: Fighting continues near Tam Ky and Quang Tri City, although Communist ground attacks are down countrywide.

AIR WAR: U.S. B-52s bomb both sides of the DMZ for the fourth straight day; fighter-bombers make 90 strikes in North Vietnam and 218 in South Vietnam.

December 12

LAOS: The Pathet Lao propose an immediate truce to be supervised by a commission formed by representatives of both sides and the existing International Control Commission (ICC). The Laotian government will respond with a counterproposal on December 19 that will be rejected by the Pathet Lao, whose own cease-fire proposal includes the withdrawal of all U.S. and foreign troops within 90 days and the formation of a coalition government, which the Laotian government rejects as unconstitutional.

December 13

NEGOTIATIONS: After Kissinger meets with Le Duc Tho for six hours, the talks are deadlocked; Le Duc Tho breaks off the talks, saying he must return to Hanoi for consultation. Kissinger flies to the United States to confer with President Nixon. However, both parties agree to resume negotiations at a future date. The central issues of political power in South Vietnam and President Thieu's demand that Hanoi withdraw its troops or at least recognize Saigon's sovereignty over South Vietnam, which would make North Vietnam's presence illegal, remain unsettled. Kissinger suggests to President Nixon that he step up bombing of North Vietnam now or defer such action for one more try at negotiations in January, resuming aggressive bombing should new talks fail.

GROUND WAR: Fighting is heavy in Pleiku and in Quang Tri Province.

AIR WAR: In the air war, B-52s strike at 100 tanks and several thousand North Vietnamese troops heading south over the Ho Chi Minh trail in Laos. Heavy rains limit tactical air strikes in North Vietnam to 20, although 323 are flown in support of troops in South Vietnam in the last 24 hours.

December 14

USA – GOVERNMENT: President Nixon issues a demand that North Vietnam begin talking "seriously" or suffer "grave consequences," at the same time directing the chairman of the Joint Chiefs of Staff, Admiral Thomas Moorer, to prepare plans for the most intense bombing of the war against military sites in and around Hanoi and Haiphong. The Joint Chiefs of Staff have long lobbied for permission to bomb this area.

NEGOTIATIONS: Teams of experts from each side meet to discuss technicalities and protocols. During these discussions, the North Vietnamese representatives submit a Vietnamese text of the protocol on prisoners containing several important changes that Hanoi failed to join in the main negotiating sessions.

December 15

THAILAND: The publication of a new interim constitution ends 13 months of absolute rule by Field Marshal Thanom Kittikachorn, who led the coup of November 17,

1971. Not much changes; martial law continues and Kittikachorn becomes premier, minister of defense, and minister of foreign affairs in a government dominated by military men.

December 16

NEGOTIATIONS: North Vietnam once again criticizes the United States for breaking the agreement to maintain silence on the secret talks and "stone-walled from beginning to end" in the technical talks. The PRG delegation to the formal Paris talks blames the United States for preventing a final agreement by proposing the withdrawal of North Vietnamese troops from South Vietnam and the re-establishment of the DMZ. The Communists refuse to set a date for the resumption of negotiations. Henry Kissinger breaks his silence on the secret talks and announces at a news conference in Washington that the talks have failed to achieve what President Nixon regards as "just and fair agreement to end the war." The deadlock centers on the nature of the international supervisory team and U.S. insistence on Saigon's sovereignty over South Vietnam. Kissinger charges that Hanoi is to blame for the failure to reach an agreement, and asserts that the United States will not be blackmailed, stampeded, or charmed into an agreement.

THAILAND: In Thailand, Premier Thanom Kittikachorn gives approval, and MACV and Seventh Air Force Headquarters announce that planning has been completed for relocation of MACV from Saigon to Nakom Phanom Air Base in Thailand once the cease-fire is enacted. MACV will be renamed Military Assistance Command Southeast Asia (MACSEA).

December 18–31

USA – GOVERNMENT: The Nixon administration announces the resumption of bombing and mining of North Vietnam, saying that the full-scale raids will continue until "such time as a settlement is arrived at." Strikes are ordered at targets not previously bombed. White House press secretary Ronald Ziegler says that the bombing will end only when all U.S. POWs are released and an internationally recognized cease-fire is in force.

AIR WAR: Operation Linebacker II commences. It is designed to force the North Vietnamese back to the negotiating table. U.S. aircraft, including both B-52s and fighter-bombers, will conduct the most concentrated air offensive of the war. During this operation, also called the "Christmas Bombing," which lasts for eleven days these planes will drop 40,000 tons of bombs, mostly over the densely populated area between Hanoi and Haiphong.

In a throwback to past aerial combat, Staff Sergeant Samuel O. Turner, the tail gunner on a Boeing B-52D bomber, downs a trailing MiG-21 with a blast from .50 caliber machine guns near Hanoi. Six days later, Airman First Class Albert E. Moore, also a B-52 gunner, will shoot down a second MiG-21 after a strike on the Thai Nguyen rail yard. These will be the only aerial gunner kills of the war.

GROUND WAR: In Vietnam, heavy fighting continues for the third day around Quang Tri City, where South Vietnamese paratroopers supported by U.S. B-52s have been battling for control of Fire Base Anne, eight miles southwest of Quang Tri City. Over 150 North Vietnamese reportedly are killed in the fighting.

AUSTRALIA/NEW ZEALAND: Australia's involvement in the Vietnam war ends with the withdrawal of a final group of about 60 military advisers from Saigon. The Australian combat role ended in November 1971.

December 19

NORTH VIETNAM: Hanoi's foreign ministry, calling the new B-52 raids against Hanoi, Haiphong, and six provinces "extremely barbaric," accuses the United States of premeditated intensification of the war and calls the action insane.

NEGOTIATIONS: North Vietnam's negotiator Xuan Thuy rebuts Henry Kissinger's assertion that additional demands by Hanoi stalled the talks, claiming that the United States wrecked the talks when Kissinger brought 126 changes of the October draft to the November 20 meeting.

AIR WAR: MACV reports three B-52s and two fighter-bombers lost since the resumption of the bombing and mining above the 20th parallel. Fifteen flyers are listed as missing. More than 100 B-52s from Guam and Thailand and hundreds of fighter-bombers participate in the raids. An estimated 185 surface to air missiles are fired at the B-52s over the Hanoi-Haiphong area.

SEA WAR: The USS *Goldsborough*, shelling North Vietnam, is hit by return fire, which kills two and wounds three.

December 19–20

INTERNATIONAL: Italy, the Netherlands, and Sweden officially condemn the resumption of American bombing above the 20th parallel, as do China and the Soviet Union. *Le Monde* compares the attacks to the bombing of Guernica during the Spanish Civil War; the *Manchester Guardian* calls the bombing "the action of a man blinded by fury or incapable of seeing the consequences of what he is doing." Pope Paul VI and Secretary-general Kurt Waldheim both express concern for world peace.

December 20

NORTH VIETNAM: Hanoi Radio reports 215 persons killed and 325 wounded in Hanoi by the U.S. raids of December 18 and 19; 45 killed and 131 wounded in Haiphong on December 18. Thousands of homes and civilian buildings are destroyed or damaged. Nixon administration officials claim that the raids have caused heavy damage to military targets.

December 21

NEGOTIATIONS: The Communist delegations walk out of the formal Paris peace talks in protest over the bombing of North Vietnam, calling for another session on December 28. Citing reports of heavy casualties and a million new refugees, Thich Nhat Hahn, chief of the Vietnamese Buddhist peace delegation to Paris, says Buddhists are astonished to read that most Americans think the war is over, when suffering in Vietnam is at its worst in 10 years.

GROUND WAR: Although ground action elsewhere is relatively light, major fighting continues in the Quang Tri City region.

AIR WAR: Linebacker II raids continue. The Cuban and Egyptian embassies are hit in Hanoi, as one Russian and Chinese freighters in Haiphong. Over Ban Laongam,

Laos, an AC-130 gunship is shot down, resulting in the loss of 14 airmen from the 16th SOS.

CAMBODIA: Cambodian and South Vietnamese troops join in an operation to clear insurgents from an area of southeast Cambodia 35 miles south of Phnom Penh.

December 22

AIR WAR: Linebacker II continues. Bach Mai, Hanoi's largest hospital, is hit by U.S. planes; the Indian embassy in Hanoi is damaged. Ten B-52s, each costing $8 million, have been lost since December 18, along with at least 55 flyers listed as missing, a number equal to 13 percent of the POWs held by Hanoi before the raids.

USA – GOVERNMENT: Washington announces that the bombing of North Vietnam will continue until Hanoi agrees to negotiate "in a spirit of good will and in a constructive attitude."

USA – DOMESTIC: Forty-one U.S. religious leaders issue a pastoral letter condemning the bombing of North Vietnam. The intensified bombing has revived antiwar protests.

December 23

AIR WAR: The East German embassy and the Hungarian commercial mission in Hanoi are hit in the seventh day of U.S. bombing; reports persist that a POW camp has been hit, with U.S. POWs killed and wounded.

USA – MILITARY: USAF officials, announcing that 97 percent of U.S. B-52s make it through Hanoi's Russian SAM-2 bomber defense system—designed as a defense against B-52s—say this proves that B-52s can penetrate Russian defenses.

December 24

SOUTH VIETNAM: Comedian Bob Hope gives what he says is his last Christmas show to U.S. servicemen in Saigon. The show marks his ninth consecutive Christmas appearance in Vietnam. Hope endorses President Nixon's bombing of North Vietnam to force it to accept U.S. peace terms, and receives South Vietnam's highest civilian medal for his "anti-Communist zeal."

AIR WAR: U.S. officials report the loss of an 11th B-52 and announce a temporary Christmas halt to the bombing, to roughly correspond with the 24-hour Christmas truce being observed by South Vietnam and the Communists on the ground in the South.

December 25

USA – MILITARY: U.S. military strength in South Vietnam is reduced by 700 men this week, to a total of 24,000, the lowest total in almost eight years.

Master Sergeant Louis E. LeBlanc, a crewman on a B-52 shot down over Hanoi during Operation Linebacker II, is captured by militiamen in Ha Tay Province, northwest of Hanoi, December 22, 1972. *(Texas Tech University Vietnam Archive)*

GROUND WAR: Communist forces shell the Danang air base and surrounding areas, damaging five U.S. helicopters.

AIR WAR: Intense U.S. bombing is resumed above the 20th parallel after a 36-hour lull because, according to U.S. officials, Hanoi has sent no word that it is ready to resume peace talks. The amount of bombs dropped on North Vietnam between December 18 and December 24 equals half the tonnage dropped on England during World War II.

December 26

NEGOTIATIONS: Nguyen Thanh Le, spokesman for the North Vietnamese delegation at the formal Paris peace talks, says Hanoi is willing to resume negotiations once the United States stops bombing above the 20th parallel.

AIR WAR: U.S. planes, including 120 B-52s, stage the most violent attack of the war on Hanoi, raining bombs on downtown Hanoi for more than 40 minutes and losing at least five B-52s.

December 27

SOUTH VIETNAM: President Thieu, on the day before the expiration of his special powers, signs a decree that will eliminate virtually all of South Vietnam's political parties except for his own Democratic party, which was formed in November.

GROUND WAR: Fighting in the Quang Tri area continues, with the South Vietnamese command reporting 56 Communist ground attacks in the last 24 hours.

AUSTRALIA: Australia ends its military aid to South Vietnam and its training program for Cambodian troops. Some observers feel that this surprise aid cut will adversely affect Nixon administration efforts to obtain military aid from Congress.

December 28

NORTH VIETNAM: Hanoi announces heavy damage and destruction of densely populated civilian areas in Hanoi, Haiphong, and their suburbs.

GROUND WAR: More than 1,900 mortar and artillery shells hit South Vietnamese troops in Quang Tri Province. North Vietnamese troops beat back a South Vietnamese attempt to recapture Firebase November in the Central Highlands.

December 29

INTERNATIONAL: Italy, the Netherlands, Sweden, Belgium, and Austria officially protest the U.S. bombing of North Vietnam. England, France, and West Germany maintain official silence despite public demands for official condemnation.

December 30

USA – GOVERNMENT: Washington announces that negotiations between Kissinger and Le Duc Tho will resume on January 2. In response to the scheduled resumption of the peace talks, President Nixon orders a halt to Linebacker II, but bombing below the 20th parallel continues. A total of 20,000 tons of bombs have been dropped on North Vietnam during the most intense U.S. bombing operation of the Vietnam War. Fifteen B-52s and 11 other U.S. aircraft were lost, along with 93 flyers downed or killed, missing, or captured. Many government officials believe that the bombing and naval bombardment of North Vietnam has been counterproductive because of heavy U.S. losses, international opposition, and growing congressional opposition. Nixon supporters maintain that the bombing has brought the Communists back to the negotiating table.

December 31

NEGOTIATIONS: In a statement issued in Paris, the Hanoi delegation to the regular peace talks asserts that the U.S. bombing did not succeed in "subjugating the Vietnamese people," and calls attention to the losses of U.S. planes and the unfavorable world reaction to the raids.

YEAR-END SUMMARY: By this date, U.S. military strength has declined to 24,200 from 159,000 at the start of the year. A total of 4,300 U.S. servicemen were killed during 1972, bringing the total number of U.S. military personnel killed in action to date to 45,926. South Vietnamese troop strength at the end of 1972 is 1.1 million men and women under arms. A total of 39,587 South Vietnamese military personnel died in 1972, for a total of losses to date of 195,847 KIA.

1973

January 5

USA – GOVERNMENT: President Nixon promises President Thieu privately that the United States will respond with "full force" if Hanoi violates the diplomatic settlement.

January 8

AIR WAR: Captain Paul D. Howman (pilot) and First Lieutenant Lawrence W. Kullman (WSO), flying in a McDonnell Douglas F-4D, shoot down a MiG-21 near Hanoi, the last recorded aerial victory in the Vietnam War.

January 8–19

NEGOTIATIONS: National Security Advisor Henry Kissinger and Hanoi's Le Duc Tho resume negotiations in Paris. An agreement is reached on January 9, and a joint U.S.-North Vietnamese announcement issued January 18 says Kissinger and Tho will meet again on January 23 "for the purpose of completing the text of an agreement."

January 15

NEGOTIATIONS: Citing "progress" in the Paris negotiations between Kissinger and Le Duc Tho, President Nixon halts the most concentrated bombing of the war, as well as mining, shelling, and all other offensive actions against North Vietnam. The cessation of hostilities against North Vietnam does not extend to South Vietnam, where the fighting continues.

USA – GOVERNMENT: President Nixon threatens to cut aid to South Vietnam if Thieu does not comply with the peace proposals being worked out by Kissinger and Le Duc Tho.

January 18–26

GROUND WAR: In the South, heavy fighting breaks out as both sides scramble to gain as much territory as possible before the cease-fire goes into effect.

AIR WAR: Between January 17 and 25, U.S. planes make nearly 3,000 strikes in South Vietnam.

January 20

USA – GOVERNMENT: President Nixon sends another ultimatum to President Thieu regarding signing of the peace settlement, demanding an answer by January 21.

January 23

NEGOTIATIONS: President Nixon announces that Henry Kissinger and Le Duc Tho have initialled a peace agreement in Paris "to end the war and bring peace with honor in Vietnam and Southeast Asia." This agreement is very similar to the one they had agreed to in October. The agreement calls for a cease-fire that will begin at 0800 hours, January 28, Saigon time (1900 hours, January 27, Eastern Standard Time). Under the provisions of the agreement, all POWs will be released within 60 days.

January 24

NEGOTIATIONS: National Security Advisor Henry Kissinger announces that a truce is also expected in Laos and Cambodia.

January 27

NEGOTIATIONS: The United States, South Vietnam, the PRG, and North Vietnam formally sign "An Agreement Ending the War and Restoring Peace in Vietnam" in Paris. Due to South Vietnam's unwillingness to recognize the Viet Cong's Provisional Revolutionary Government, all references to it are confined to a two-party version of the document signed by North Vietnam and the United States. In order to get the South Vietnamese to sign the agreement, they are presented with a separate document that does not make reference to the PRG, due to Saigon's long-time refusal to recognize the Viet Cong as a legitimate participant in the discussions to end the war. The settlement includes an in-place cease-fire throughout Vietnam. In addition, the United States agrees to the withdrawal of all U.S. troops and advisers (now totaling about 23,700) and the dismantling of all U.S. bases within 60 days. In return, the North Vietnamese agree to release all U.S. and other prisoners of war. Nixon calls it "peace with honor," but fighting continues in Vietnam.

USA – GOVERNMENT: Secretary of Defense Melvin Laird announces the end of the draft.

GROUND WAR: The last U.S. serviceman to die in combat in Vietnam, Lieutenant Colonel William B. Nolde, is killed by an artillery shell in An Loc at 2100 hours, 11 hours before the truce is to go into effect. Four Americans are killed in the last week of the war.

SOUTH VIETNAM: Saigon controls about 75 percent of South Vietnam's territory and 85 percent of its population. The South Vietnamese army is well-equipped via last-minute deliveries of U.S. weapons, and will continue to receive U.S. aid after the cease-fire; the South Vietnamese air force is now the fourth largest in the world. The CIA estimates that there are about 145,000 North Vietnamese soldiers in South Vietnam, about the same as the year before.

January 28
NEGOTIATIONS: A cease-fire goes into effect at 8 A.M., Saigon time (midnight on January 27, Greenwich Mean Time). This proves to be only a momentary lull, as the fighting renews almost immediately with both the ARVN and NVA jockeying for key positions.
CAMBODIA: Lon Nol proposes a cease-fire, but his proposal will be rejected by Prince Sihanouk on April 9.

January 30
USA – GOVERNMENT: Melvin Laird resigns as secretary of defense and is succeeded by Elliott Richardson.

February 1
USA – GOVERNMENT: In a secret letter to North Vietnamese premier Pham Van Dong, President Nixon pledges to contribute to "postwar reconstruction in North Vietnam" in the "range of $3.25 billion" over five years.

February 5
NEGOTIATIONS: Direct talks begin between the Provisional Revolutionary Government and the South Vietnamese government, but there is little progress.
AIR WAR: A U.S. EC–47Q aircraft is shot down over Saravan, Laos; eight airmen from the 56th Special Operations Wing are killed.

February 6
NEGOTIATIONS: In accordance with the Paris Peace Accords, supervisors from the International Commission of Control and Supervision (ICCS), who have been delegated to oversee the cease-fire in place, start to take up their positions; they are from Canada, Hungary, and India.

February 7
DIPLOMACY: Canada becomes the first Western nation to recognize North Vietnam.

February 12–27
POWs: The return of U.S. POWs as part of the peace settlement begins with North Vietnam's release of 142 of 587 U.S. prisoners at Hanoi's Gia Lam airport. The first 20 POWs arrive at Travis Air Force Base in California on February 14. The release program will continue after a delay on February 27, when North Vietnam accuses the United States of "encouraging" Saigon to make difficulties for the Four Party Joint Military Commission and claims that Saigon had conducted 20,000 military operations since the beginning of the cease-fire.

February 15
NEGOTIATIONS: Following four days of talks between Henry Kissinger and Pham Van Dong in Hanoi, the United States and North Vietnam issue a joint communiqué agreeing to establish a joint economic commission to develop economic relations, particularly with regard to U.S. contribution to reconstruction and "healing the wounds of war" in North Vietnam.

February 16

NEGOTIATIONS: The Four-Party Joint Military Commission with representatives from among the recent combatants, appeals to both sides in South Vietnam to respect the cease-fire and reaffirms prohibition on air combat missions.

GROUND WAR: Specialist Fifth Class James L. Scroggins is mortally wounded when his CH–47C helicopter of the 18th Aviation Company, is shot down south of An Loc. He will die on February 23.

February 20

AIR WAR: U.S. warplanes begin a series of missions over Cambodia in support of Lon Nol's military forces, being pressed hard by the Khmer Rouge and their North Vietnamese allies.

February 21

LAOS: Souvanna Phouma's government and the Pathet Lao announce they have reached a cease-fire agreement, ending 20 years of war despite some continued fighting. The agreement provides for cessation of all military activities in Laos, including that by the United States and North Vietnamese.

February 23

USA – MILITARY: Last U.S. air cavalry units depart Vietnam.

March

RIVER WAR: U.S. Navy Operations Market Time, Game Warden, and Clearwater are discontinued.

NORTH VIETNAM: General Tran Van Tra, one of the leading Communist commanders in the South, is summoned back to Hanoi to attend a high-level meeting. Spurred by the absence of U.S. B-52s, Hanoi launches a huge logistical program to prepare for future military operations in the South. An all-weather road is built from Quang Tri to the Mekong Delta, and work begins on a 3,000-mile oil pipeline from Quang Tri to Loc Ninh, the major headquarters 75 miles northwest of Saigon. Allied officials meanwhile report that Communist forces are building up supplies and military equipment in the border province of Tay Ninh, northwest of Saigon.

THAILAND: The last of the Royal Thai Army Volunteer Force departs from South Vietnam.

March 10

SOUTH KOREA: The ROK Capital Division departs from South Vietnam.

March 15

USA – GOVERNMENT: President Nixon hints that the United States might intervene again in Vietnam to prevent Communist violations of the truce. Nixon has previously assured President Thieu that "We will respond with full force should the settlements be violated by North Vietnam."

March 16

SOUTH KOREA: The ROK 9th Infantry Division withdraws from Vietnam.

March 17

CAMBODIA: A Cambodian pilot bombs the presidential palace in Phnom Penh in an unsuccessful attempt to kill Lon Nol.

March 27

USA – GOVERNMENT: The White House announces that bombing of Cambodia at the request of Cambodian president Lon Nol will continue until Communist forces end military operations there and agree to a cease-fire.

March 28

SOUTH VIETNAM: The 60-day, first phase of Vietnam's cease-fire ends with continued fighting.

USA – MILITARY: The 1st Aviation Brigade departs Vietnam. This date is announced as the cut-off date for award of the Vietnam Service Medal and the Republic of Vietnam Campaign Medal.

March 29

USA – MILITARY: The last U.S. troops leave South Vietnam, ending nearly 10 years of U.S. military presence in that country. U.S. Military Assistance Command Vietnam headquarters is disestablished. Only a defense attaché office and a few marine guards at the Saigon American embassy remain, although some 8,500 U.S. civilians stay on.

POWs: Hanoi releases the last 67 of its acknowledged POWs, bringing the total number released to 590. They arrive at Clark Air Base, Philippines, on April 1.

The Vietnam War is over for the United States. The cost of the war has been staggering. More than 3,000,000 Americans served in Vietnam; 47,253 were killed in action or died as a result of combat; and 10,449 died of nonbattle injuries. Some 313,919 Americans were wounded in action; 153,300 of these were classified as "seriously" wounded, while 1,340 Americans are listed as missing in action. A total of 4,865 helicopters and 3,720 fixed-wing aircraft were shot down or otherwise destroyed. Eight million tons of bombs were expended in the war—four times the total tonnage dropped in all of World War II. For South Vietnam 223,748 military personnel were killed and 499,026 were wounded. It is estimated that nearly a million NVA and VC died in the fighting. And 415,000 civilians were killed and another 935,000 wounded.

April 2

USA – GOVERNMENT: The U.S. Senate approves 88–3 an amendment forbidding any aid to North Vietnam without prior and specific approval by the Congress. In California, President Nixon and President Thieu end a two-day visit with a joint communiqué expressing "full consensus" and a U.S. promise of continuing economic aid to South Vietnam. Thieu says he will never ask the United States to send troops back to South Vietnam. Nixon makes it clear that future aid is dependent upon congressional approval.

April 4

USA – GOVERNMENT: The House of Representatives unexpectedly rejects a White House-sponsored request to increase military aid to South Vietnam.

April 9

CAMBODIA: Prince Sihanouk, acting as spokesman for the Cambodian rebels, rejects Lon Nol's truce proposal.

April 19–August 8

USA – DOMESTIC: Representative Elizabeth Holtzman (D-N.Y.) and four air force officers file suit in federal district court to halt the "secret American bombing of Cambodia." On July 25, Federal District Court Judge Orrin G. Judd rules in favor of their suit, although the White House requests and receives a stay of Judge Judd's decision from the court of appeals two days later. On August 1, Supreme Court Justice William O. Douglas orders the bombing halted on an appeal from Holtzman, but is overruled by a full sitting of the Supreme Court a few hours later. On August 8, the court of appeals finally overturns Judge Judd's initial ruling, which called U.S. bombing in Cambodia "unauthorized and illegal."

April 27–May 2

GROUND WAR: South Vietnamese forces conduct a successful attacks into Svay Rieng Province in Cambodia against Communist base areas. It is the last large-scale ARVN offensive of the war.

June 4

USA – GOVERNMENT: The U.S. Senate approves a bill to block funds for any U.S. military activities in Indochina, and the House of Representatives concurs. Nixon and Kissinger lobby to postpone the ban until August 15, to enable the continued bombing of Cambodia.

June 13

NEGOTIATIONS: A new accord, which becomes known as "Son of Cease-fire," seeks to strengthen the January 27 cease-fire agreement in South Vietnam. Representatives of the original signers of the January 27 cease-fire sign a new 14-point agreement calling for an end to all cease-fire violations in South Vietnam. Coming at the end of month-long negotiations between Kissinger and Tho, the settlement includes an end to all military activities at noon, June 15; an end to U.S. reconnaissance flights over North Vietnam; the resumption of U.S. minesweeping operations in North Vietnamese waters; the resumption of U.S. talks on aid to North Vietnam; and the meeting of commanders of opposing forces in South Vietnam to prevent outbreaks of hostilities. This agreement proves no more effective than the original peace agreement.

June 24

USA – GOVERNMENT: Graham Martin is sworn in as ambassador to South Vietnam, replacing Ellsworth Bunker, who had served in that capacity since 1967.

June 29–30

USA – GOVERNMENT: Congress agrees that bombing in Cambodia can continue until August 15, after which spending for any military activity in Indochina must be approved by Congress.

July

NAVAL WAR: U.S. Task Force 78 completes the clearing of Haiphong and other North Vietnamese harbors of mines laid down by the United States since May 1972, in accordance with the cease-fire agreement of January 27.

July 16–17

USA – GOVERNMENT: The Senate Armed Services Committee begins a probe into allegations that the U.S. Air Force made thousands of secret B-52 raids into Cambodia in 1969 and 1970 at a time when the United States recognized the neutrality of the Sihanouk regime in Cambodia. The Pentagon acknowledges that the raids against Cambodia were authorized by President Nixon and then-secretary of defense Melvin Laird. Sihanouk denies the State Department claim that he requested or authorized the bombing; Laird and Kissinger deny that they knew of or authorized the falsification of records.

August 8

USA – GOVERNMENT: Vice President Agnew brands as "damned lies" reports that he took kickbacks from government contracts in Maryland. He vows never to resign.

August 14

CAMBODIA: After several days of intense bombing in the area around Phnom Penh, Operations Arc Light and Freedom Deal end as the United States ceases bombing Cambodia at midnight in accordance with the deadline previously set by Congress, bringing to an end 12 years of combat activity in Indochina. The United States continues unarmed reconnaissance flights and military aid to Cambodia and Laos, but all direct U.S. military action in Cambodia, Laos, and Vietnam ceases.

August 17

USA – GOVERNMENT: Washington reveals plans to withdraw U.S. troops from Thailand.

August 22

USA – GOVERNMENT: President Nixon announces that Henry Kissinger is to become secretary of state, replacing William P. Rogers, who resigns the same day.

August 26

SOUTH VIETNAM: Candidates supported by President Thieu sweep South Vietnamese national elections, the first since 1972. Thieu maintains a firm grip on the legislature.

August 31

CAMBODIA: After heavy fighting around Kampong Cham, forces loyal to Sihanouk launch a direct attack on the town and make large gains.

September 22

GROUND WAR: Fighting rages at an ARVN base near Pleiku. Le Minh firebase is taken by an NVA force supported by tanks, and an attempt by the ARVN to retake it on October 25 will be bloodily repulsed.

September 29–30

GROUND WAR: Heavy fighting takes place at Kheim Hanh, when an ARVN sweep against North Vietnamese forces backfires and an ARVN battalion is decimated.

September 30

CAMBODIA: Cambodian government forces complete the process of regaining Kampong Cham.

October

NORTH VIETNAM: Pham Van Dong and Le Duan, seeking military aid for North Vietnam, are rebuffed in both Moscow and Beijing.

October 1

SOUTH VIETNAM: President Thieu declares that the Communists are planning a spring 1974 "general offensive" and calls for "preemptive attacks."

October 3–7

GROUND WAR: South Vietnamese forces carry out heavy raids against the PRG zone in Tay Ninh Province in MR III.

October 10

USA – GOVERNMENT: Vice President Spiro T. Agnew pleads no contest to tax evasion and resigns. He is replaced by Gerald R. Ford, Jr.

October 15

GROUND WAR: Leadership of the Communist forces in South Vietnam issues an order to begin counterattacks on South Vietnamese bases and other targets in retaliation for Saigon's earlier operations.

October 16

INTERNATIONAL: Henry Kissinger and North Vietnamese diplomat Le Duc Tho are awarded the Nobel Peace Prize for negotiating the Paris peace accords. Kissinger accepts, but Tho declines the award until such time as "peace is truly established."

October 24

GROUND WAR: U.S. intelligence reports that, since the cease-fire, the North Vietnamese military presence in South Vietnam has increased by 70,000 troops, 400 tanks, at least 200 artillery pieces, 15 antiaircraft artillery sites, and 12 airfields. An all-weather road from North Vietnam to Tay Ninh Province has almost been completed.

USA – GOVERNMENT: Nixon vetoes the War Powers Resolution, which would limit presidential power to commit armed forces abroad without congressional approval. The bill would require the president to report to Congress within 48 hours after commitment of armed forces to foreign combat and would limit to 60 days the time they may stay without congressional approval. Nixon claims that the bill would impose "unconstitutional and dangerous restrictions" on presidential authority.

November

GROUND WAR: North Vietnamese tanks and troops seize two South Vietnamese camps near the Cambodian border in a two-day battle, one of the most savage since the January 28 cease-fire.

November 4–7
GROUND WAR: The fall of three ARVN bases in Quang Duc Province enables the communists to control the main communication route from Kontum and Pleiku to the south.

November 7
USA – GOVERNMENT: Congress overrides President Nixon's veto and passes the War Powers Resolution, which limits presidential authority to send troops into combat abroad.

December 3
GROUND WAR: Viet Cong raiders destroy 18 million gallons of oil in storage tanks near Saigon.

December 6
USA – GOVERNMENT: Gerald Ford is sworn in as the first unelected vice president, succeeding Spiro T. Agnew.

December 15
SOUTH VIETNAM: Communist troops ambush a Joint Military Commission–sanctioned MIA recovery team, killing a U.S. Army officer and wounding four Americans and several South Vietnamese soldiers.

December 31
YEAR-END SUMMARY: The size of the U.S. military contingent in Vietnam is limited to 50, after 46,163 U.S. military personnel killed in action to date. Estimated strength of South Vietnamese forces is 1,110,000, with 223,748 South Vietnamese armed forces personnel killed in action to date.

1974

January 4
GROUND WAR: South Vietnamese troops report that 55 soldiers have been killed in two clashes with Communist forces.
SOUTH VIETNAM: Claiming that the war has "restarted," President Thieu asserts, "We cannot allow the communists a situation in which . . . they can launch harassing attacks against us," and orders his forces to launch a counteroffensive to retake lost territory. The announcement essentially marks the end of attempts to adhere to the agreements of the Paris Peace Accords.

January 15–28
CAMBODIA: Khmer Rouge inflict large number of civilian casualties when shelling Phnom Penh.

January 27
GROUND WAR: The fighting continues in South Vietnam despite the cease-fire that was initiated on January 28, 1973, under the provisions of the Paris Peace Accords and the June 13 "Son of Cease-Fire" agreement. Saigon reports that 13,778 government soldiers, 2,159 civilians, and 45,057 Communist troops have died in the fighting since the 1973 truce.

February

GROUND WAR: ARVN troops begin major offensive against areas controlled by the Provisional Revolutionary Government in central South Vietnam and west of Saigon; intense fighting follows.

February 22

USA – MILITARY: The National Academy of Science reports, in a study ordered by Congress and commissioned by the Pentagon, that the use of chemical herbicides in the Vietnam War by the United States did damage to the ecology of South Vietnam that might last as long as a century.

March 30

SOUTH VIETNAM: Saigon information minister Hoang Duc Nha warns that North Vietnam is planning a general offensive to reconquer South Vietnam. Fighting in the Central Highlands this month between Kontum and Chuong Nghia is the bloodiest since the cease-fire.

April 5

LAOS: A new coalition government is formed with Souvanna Phouma as premier and Prince Souphanouvong, leader of the Pathet Lao, as one of the deputy premiers.

April 5–7

CAMBODIA: Khmer Rouge forces overrun six outposts protecting Phnom Penh.

May

GROUND WAR: North Vietnamese general Tran Van Tra estimates that his forces have recaptured all the territory in the Mekong Delta taken by the South Vietnamese following the cease-fire.

May 6

USA – GOVERNMENT: The U.S. Senate turns down a Nixon administration request for $266,000,000 in military aid for South Vietnam.

May 9–July 30

USA – GOVERNMENT: The House of Representatives Judiciary Committee opens impeachment hearings against President Richard Nixon, voting to impeach him on three counts on July 30.

May 22

USA – GOVERNMENT: The U.S. House of Representatives approves a $474,000,000 cutback in aid to South Vietnam.

July 9

CAMBODIA: Prince Sihanouk rejects another request by Lon Nol for truce talks.

August 5–11

USA – GOVERNMENT: Congress places a $1 billion ceiling on military aid to South Vietnam for fiscal year 1974. This figure is trimmed to $700 million by August 11. Military aid to South Vietnam in fiscal year 1973 was $2.8 billion; in 1975 it will be $300 million.

August 8
USA – GOVERNMENT: Under siege because of revelations of criminal acts connected to the Watergate scandal, Richard Nixon announces that he will resign the office of president at 12 P.M. on August 9.
GROUND WAR: Communist forces continue attacks around Danang. U.S. officials estimate that North Vietnamese forces in the South are stronger than at any previous time in the war.

August 9
USA – GOVERNMENT: Richard Nixon resigns as president; Vice President Gerald R. Ford becomes president.

August 15
GROUND WAR: North Vietnamese tanks break out from Ben Cat and get to within 15 miles of Saigon.

September 4
USA – MILITARY: General Creighton Abrams, U.S. Army chief of staff, dies in office from cancer.

September 8
USA – GOVERNMENT: President Ford pardons former president Richard Nixon.

September 10
SOUTH VIETNAM: South Vietnam protests construction of air bases in the Provisional Revolutionary Government zone on the basis that it has control of all air space over South Vietnam.

September 14
LAOS: A provisional administration is formed in Laos that includes members of both the Communist Pathet Lao and the former Royal Laotian government.

September 16
USA – GOVERNMENT: President Ford offers amnesty to Vietnam-era draft evaders.

September 28
GROUND WAR: In the northern provinces, NVA troops, after a series of successful pushes in July and August, close to within 15 miles of Hue. NVA pressure on the city is maintained throughout October.

October
NORTH VIETNAM: During a Politburo session, Communist political and military leaders, concluding that the United States is unlikely to intervene and cannot save Thieu even if it does, tentatively decide on a major offensive to be launched in 1975.

October 3
USA – MILITARY: General Fred Weyand succeeds General Abrams as the U.S. Army chief of staff.

October 8

GROUND WAR: The PRG calls on public figures and organizations in South Vietnam to work for overthrow of Thieu government and establishment of new regime in Saigon.

November

SOUTH VIETNAM: Following rioting and protests by anti-government demonstrators in Saigon, which lead to violent clashes with police, several leading South Vietnamese opposition members publicly denounce President Thieu and his "repressive" policies.

DIPLOMACY: Kissinger concludes from discussions with Russia and China that both nations consider Saigon doomed and are concentrating on expanding their own spheres of influence—the Chinese in Cambodia and the Russians in Vietnam. The promise of aid from the Soviet Union encourages Hanoi to accelerate plans for military operations.

November 30

CAMBODIA: Lon Nol again proposes a cease-fire in Cambodia.

December 3

SOUTH VIETNAM: South Vietnamese intelligence reports that it has obtained documents indicating that the Communists are planning a sharp increase in fighting for the coming season.

December 13

GROUND WAR: General Tran Van Tra and Pham Hung, head of the Communist Central Office for South Vietnam and political commissar for Communist forces in the South, order the 301st Corps, made up of the 7th Division and newly formed 3rd Division, to attack Phuoc Long Province, north of Saigon. This is to be a test case to determine how the South Vietnamese will respond to a multi-division attack, but more importantly to see how the United States will respond.

December 31

USA – MILITARY: U.S. military strength in Vietnam remains at 50 personnel.

GROUND WAR: South Vietnamese Command reports that 80,000 persons have been killed in fighting throughout the country this year, the highest total for any year of the war.

1975

January 1

CAMBODIA: Khmer Rouge begins final offensive against Phnom Penh.

January 6

GROUND WAR: Phuoc Binh, the capital of Phuoc Long Province, about 60 miles north of Saigon, falls to the North Vietnamese 301st Corps. Phuoc Binh is the first provincial capital taken by the Communists since the fall of Quang Tri on May 1, 1972. Two days later, the North Vietnamese capture the last of the South Vietnamese positions in the region, gaining control of the entire province. There is no response from the United States.

January 8
GROUND WAR: Communist forces seize the remainder of Phuoc Long Province. The United States still does nothing, failing to intervene with airpower as previously promised. This convinces the Politburo in Hanoi that the Americans will not return to Vietnam and encourages Le Duan to urge more aggressive action. The decision is made to launch a new offensive to set the conditions for a general uprising and final victory in 1976.

January 9
NORTH VIETNAM: With the fall of Phuoc Long Province, Hanoi orders a follow-on operation to take advantage of the situation. This is to be a limited offensive into the Central Highlands. It is to be called Campaign 275 and its objective is to set the conditions for a decisive general offensive in 1976.

January 15
USA – GOVERNMENT: President Gerald Ford does not mention Vietnam in his State of the Union address.

January 28
USA – GOVERNMENT: President Gerald Ford asks Congress for an additional $522 million in military aid for South Vietnam and Cambodia. He reveals that North Vietnam now has 289,000 troops in South Vietnam, and tanks, heavy artillery, and antiaircraft weapons "by the hundreds."

February 5
GROUND WAR: North Vietnamese general Van Tien Dung goes south to take command of Communist forces in preparation for Campaign 275.

February 26
USA – GOVERNMENT: A bipartisan congressional delegation arrives in Saigon to make a firsthand assessment of the situation. They meet with Ambassador Martin, receive briefings, make trips to the field, and have dinner and discussions with President Thieu. President Ford had urged the delegation to visit South Vietnam with hopes that they might return and support his request for additional military aid for Saigon. And upon their return, all but Representative Bella Abzug (D-N.Y.) advocate some increase in military and humanitarian aid. In the end, however, Ford's ploy does not work and a week later the Democratic caucus in the House and Senate will vote to oppose any further aid to South Vietnam or Cambodia.

March 10
GROUND WAR: The People's Army of Vietnam begins its Campaign 275 with a three-division attack on Ban Me Thuot, which initiates heavy fighting in the Central Highlands. The North Vietnamese overrun most of the town within hours. Many U.S. analysts feel that this may be the beginning of the end for South Vietnam.

March 11
SOUTH VIETNAM: Meeting with his senior commanders in Saigon, President Thieu directs that South Vietnamese forces focus on defending the "untouchable

heartland" where the majority of South Vietnam's population resides. This area includes the southern half of the country. With regard to the northern half, the less populated area, it will be a matter of "hold what you can."

March 13
GROUND WAR: Ban Me Thuot, capital of Darlac Province, finally falls to the Communists on March 13. Many soldiers of the 23rd ARVN Division desert and try to rescue their families, a recurring phenomenon that will contribute heavily to the collapse of South Vietnamese forces over the next few months.

March 14
SOUTH VIETNAM: Meeting with his senior commanders at Cam Ranh, President Thieu orders the "redeployment" of ARVN forces from Pleiku and Kontum "in such a manner as to reoccupy Ban Me Thuot at all costs." That may have been the idea, but the order will effectively cause the abandonment of those two key cities to the North Vietnamese.

March 16–April 1
GROUND WAR: The withdrawal from Pleiku and Kontum begins, as thousands of civilians join the soldiers streaming down Route 7B toward Tuy Hoa. By March 17, they come under heavy Communist attack. The withdrawal, scheduled to be completed in three days, is still underway on April 1. Only 20,000 of 60,000 soldiers ever reach the coast. Of 400,000 refugees, only 100,000 survive; the fate of the rest is unknown.

March 19
GROUND WAR: With the fall of South Vietnamese forces in the Central Highlands, the North Vietnamese forces attack Quang Tri Province, in I Corps, which rapidly falls to North Vietnamese attack. The highway south from Quang Tri is inundated with fleeing soldiers and refugees.

March 24
GROUND WAR: The "Ho Chi Minh Campaign" begins. Hanoi hands General Dung a new timetable calling for the liberation of the South before the spring rains begin in May. To achieve this, North Vietnamese troops must reach Saigon no later than the last week in April, before South Vietnamese forces can regroup to defend it.

March 25
GROUND WAR: Saigon gives the order to evacuate Hue by sea and abandon it to the Communists. By now more than one million refugees, driven by memories of the Communist slaughter of civilians in Hue during the 1968 Tet Offensive, are streaming toward Danang, which is already under heavy rocket fire.

March 26
GROUND WAR: Hue falls to the North Vietnamese advance with very little resistance.

March 27
USA – GOVERNMENT: President Ford sends General Frederick Weyand, army chief of staff and former MACV commander, to Saigon to make an assessment of the deteriorating situation. Upon arrival, he assures Thieu of Ford's "steadfast support" for South Vietnam.

President Gerald Ford meets in the Oval Office with his advisers to discuss the situation in Vietnam, March 1975 (left to right: Ambassador Graham Martin, General Fred Weyand, Henry Kissinger, and President Ford). *(National Archives)*

March 28
USA – GOVERNMENT: President Ford announces he has ordered U.S. Navy transports and "contract vessels" to assist in the evacuation of South Vietnamese coastal cities.

March 29
GROUND WAR: Danang falls to the North Vietnamese advance. Many citizens die in the general chaos while attempting to escape from the airports, docks, and beaches.

April 1
GROUND WAR: After a brief fight by the ARVN 22nd Division, the cities of Qui Nhon, Tuy Hoa, and Nha Trang are abandoned by the South Vietnamese, yielding the entire northern half of the country to North Vietnamese control with very little fight. More than half of South Vietnam's territory is now controlled by the North Vietnamese. During the first week in April Communist forces coming from the south push into Long An Province, just south of Saigon, threatening to cut Highway 4, Saigon's main link with the Mekong Delta.
CAMBODIA: Lon Nol flees Cambodia.

April 4
SOUTH VIETNAM: A major U.S. airlift of South Vietnamese orphans begins with disaster, when an Air Force C-5A cargo jet crashes shortly after takeoff from Tan Son

Nhut, killing more than 100 children. Two thousand others, most of them orphans of U.S. servicemen, are eventually taken to the United States for adoption.

April 5
USA – MILITARY: After a week-long mission to South Vietnam, General Frederick Weyand, reports to Congress that South Vietnam cannot survive without additional military aid. Questioned later by reporters, who ask if South Vietnam can survive with additional aid, he replies that there is "a chance."

April 6–15
GROUND WAR: Two regiments from the ARVN 2nd Division and one brigade of airborne troops are landed at Phan Rang airport, on April 6, in hopes of mounting a counteroffensive. After three days of relative quiet, the airborne brigade is sent to Xuan Loc on April 10 where a major battle is developing. Subsequently, North Vietnamese troops and tanks overrun Phan Rang and eliminate any significant ARVN presence in the region.

April 7
GROUND WAR: Le Duc Tho arrives at Communist headquarters in Loc Ninh to oversee the final Communist offensive drive. Well over two-thirds of Vietnam is now under Communist control.

April 8–21
GROUND WAR: The ARVN 18th Division in Xuan Loc begins battling two North Vietnamese divisions at the last South Vietnamese defense line before Saigon. It will become the last battle in the defense of the Republic of South Vietnam. During the first week a regiment of the 5th ARVN Division and an airborne brigade arrive as reinforcements, while two more North Vietnamese divisions arrive to join the attackers. The ARVN forces are well dug in and manage to hold out against a number of NVA assaults until they run out of tactical air support and are overwhelmed by sheer numbers, finally abandoning Xuan Loc to the Communists on April 21.

April 9–11
LAOS: Clashes occur between Pathet Lao insurgents and Laos government troops.

April 10
USA – GOVERNMENT: President Ford requests $722 million in supplemental military aid for Saigon, but Congress denies his request, despite a personal plea before a joint session.

April 12
CAMBODIA: The U.S. ambassador to Cambodia and his staff leave Phnom Penh on April 12 as part of Operation Eagle Pull, the aerial evacuation of the U.S. embassy.

April 13
CAMBODIA: The Department of Defense announces that U.S. aircraft are parachuting supplies into Phnom Penh because the airport has been closed by enemy fire.

April 14
South Vietnam: Operation Baby Lift, the American airlift of Vietnamese orphans to the United States from South Vietnam, comes to an end, having evacuated about 2,000 children.

April 16
Cambodia: Phnom Penh falls to the Khmer Rouge, ending five years of war. The People's Assembly headed by Pol Pot, established in December, will institute a draconian agrarian collectivization program that will result in the infamous "Killing Fields" and cause two to four million deaths over the next two years.

April 21–25
South Vietnam: With the fall of Xuan Loc, President Thieu resigns and transfers authority to Vice President Tran Van Huong before any of the several plots against him can be implemented. He flees Saigon on April 25.

April 23
USA – Government: At a speech at Rice University, President Ford says the war is finished, "as far as America is concerned. Today, Americans can regain the sense of pride that existed before Vietnam. But it cannot be achieved by re-fighting a war."

April 28
South Vietnam: Vice President Tran Van Huong transfers authority as chief of state to General Duong Van Minh, who helped overthrow Diem in 1963; Minh is the South Vietnamese official with whom the Communists have indicated they are willing to negotiate.

April 29
South Vietnam: Operation Frequent Wind begins removing the last Americans from Saigon, including Ambassador Graham Martin. In 19 hours, 81 helicopters carry more than 1,000 Americans and almost 6,000 Vietnamese to aircraft carriers waiting offshore. Corporal Charles McMahon, Jr., and Lance Corporal Darwin Judge (USMC) are the last U.S. military personnel killed in action in Vietnam, struck by shrapnel from an NVA rocket while guarding Tan Son Nhut Air Base. Two U.S. servicemen become the last Americans to die in Vietnam when their helicopter crashes near an aircraft carrier taking part in the evacuation.

April 30
Ground War: Communist troops enter Saigon as the last Americans and their dependents rush to evacuate. The final helicopter lifts off from the roof of the American embassy at 7:53 A.M., carrying the last 11 marine guards. The Communist troops meet only sporadic resistance as they move into the city. That morning after tanks crash through the gates of the presidential palace, President Duong Van Minh surrenders unconditionally to the Communists. Colonel Bui Tin, who accepts the surrender from General Minh, explains, "You have nothing to fear. Between Vietnamese there are no victors and no vanquished. Only the Americans have been beaten. If you are patriots, consider this a moment of joy. The war for our country is over."

May

LAOS: The coalition government formed a year ago is close to collapsing, and there is fighting between the Pathet Lao, supported by North Vietnamese troops, and rightist factions. Demonstrations by students and others are increasingly aimed at U.S. buildings and operations. By the end of the month, many of the top right-wing officials of the Laotian government will resign under the steadily mounting pressure from pro-Communist forces.

May 1

VIETNAM: In Saigon, prostitution, dance halls, and "acting like Americans" are banned.

May 7

VIETNAM: A rally in Saigon attended by 30,000 celebrates the capture of the city, and also commemorates the 21st anniversary of Vietnamese victory over the French at Dien Bien Phu in 1954.

USA – GOVERNMENT: President Ford issues a proclamation designating this as the last day of the "Vietnam era" for military personnel to qualify for wartime benefits.

May 12

CAMBODIA: The U.S. merchant ship *Mayaguez*, with 39 seamen aboard, is seized in the Gulf of Siam by the Cambodian Khmer Rouge government, who claim the ship is part of a spy operation. Diplomatic appeals fail to secure the return of the ship and its crew.

May 14–15

CAMBODIA: President Ford orders a military rescue attempt to recover the crew of the *Mayaguez*; U.S. Marines land on Koh Tang Island to free the American freighter and its crew. Thirty-eight Marines die in the operation, with 50 wounded and three missing; the crewmen of the *Mayaguez* are released unharmed the same day.

May 15

VIETNAM: North Vietnamese and Viet Cong troops conduct victory parade in Saigon streets.

May 16

LAOS: Pathet Lao troops seize Pakse.

REFUGEES: Congress appropriates $405 million to fund a refugee aid program and authorizes resettlement of South Vietnamese and Cambodian refugees in the United States. Over 140,000 refugees are flown to the United States under the program in the next few months.

May 20

LAOS: Savannakhet falls to the Pathet Lao.

June

LAOS: Pathet Lao troops seize U.S. embassy property in Vientiane.

June 3
VIETNAM: At a meeting of the National Assembly in Hanoi, Premier Pham Van Dong calls for normalization of relations with the United States, conditioned on U.S. economic aid to Hanoi and a pledge to observe the 1973 Paris cease-fire.

August 23
LAOS: Pathet Lao forces consolidate the Communist takeover of Laos.

November 14
USA – GOVERNMENT: Secretary of State Henry Kissinger announces that the United States is prepared to hold talks with Vietnam and Laos and Cambodia on normalizing relations.

December
CAMBODIA: The Congress of the National United Front of Cambodia approves a new constitution; the state is renamed Democratic Kampuchea.

December 3
LAOS: The Lao coalition headed by Souvanna Phouma is abolished; Laos becomes a Communist state with Sophanouvong as president. The Communist Pathet Lao, now in control of most of the territory and cities of Laos, abolishes the coalition government, ends the 600-year-old monarchy, and establishes the People's Republic of Laos.

December 20
REFUGEES: The last of 140,000 refugees who arrived under the resettlement program leave Fort Chaffee, near Fort Smith, Arkansas the last of four processing centers established in the United States. Since May 2, 50,796 refugees have been processed at Fort Chaffee.

1976

March 20
THAILAND: The Thai government orders the United States to close all its military installations in Thailand and to withdraw all U.S. personnel except for 270 military advisers.

April 25
VIETNAM: All-Vietnam elections are held for a new national assembly; 249 deputies are elected from the North and 243 from the South, 60 seats of the total of 492 being reserved for minorities. The united National Assembly will meet for the first time on June 24.

July 2
VIETNAM: The newly created National Assembly names reunited Vietnam the Socialist Republic of Vietnam. North Vietnamese premier Pham Van Dong becomes prime minister in the new government, and all high offices but one go to former leaders of North Vietnam. Hanoi is declared the capital, and the North Vietnamese

flag, anthem, and emblems are approved as official symbols of the state. The North Vietnamese constitution becomes the national constitution, until a commission appointed by the assembly can draw up a new document. Saigon is renamed Ho Chi Minh City (which includes the surrounding province of Gia Dinh).

November 2

USA – DOMESTIC: Democrat Jimmy Carter defeats Gerald Ford in the U.S. presidential election.

November 15

USA – GOVERNMENT: The United States casts the single Security Council veto on Vietnam's admission to the United Nations, claiming that Hanoi has failed to give an accounting of at least 800 U.S. servicemen still listed as missing in Vietnam. Vietnam asserts that it is impossible to furnish a complete list of those missing in action.

December 14–20

VIETNAM: In Hanoi, the Lao Dong Party convenes its first party congress since 1960. A five-year-plan for 1976–80 provides for extensive expansion of industry and agriculture, foreign trade, and reinvestment, as well as large-scale redistribution of the nation's population. The Lao Dong Party is renamed the Communist Party.

1977

January 21

USA – GOVERNMENT: In his first major presidential act, President Carter pardons almost all draft evaders (about 10,000) of the Vietnam era. Carter says he will immediately address the problem of upgrading the discharging of the nearly 100,000 deserters.

March 20

DIPLOMACY: The first U.S. government mission to Vietnam since the fall of Saigon in 1975 returns with the remains of 12 U.S. pilots and a pledge of assistance from Hanoi to cooperate in discovering the fate of other missing Americans.

May 2–4

DIPLOMACY: The United States and Vietnam open the first round of negotiations in Paris on normalizing relations. The United States promises not to veto Vietnam's admission to the United Nations and to lift its trade embargo against Vietnam once diplomatic relations are established.

May 19

USA – GOVERNMENT: The U.S. State Department releases a classified letter from President Nixon pledging $4.75 billion in U.S. postwar reconstruction aid to North Vietnam. This letter, dated February 1, 1973, will often be cited by Hanoi as constituting a U.S. commitment. On this same day, in a television interview with David Frost, former president Nixon portrays himself as a wartime president who took action to save a nation "torn apart" by dissent. He regrets not moving "stronger, sooner" in Cambodia and Laos.

June 12–19
REFUGEES: The *New York Times* reports in several dispatches that the number of refugees from southern Vietnam and the rest of Indochina is increasing, and that refugees are finding it more difficult to find haven in neighboring Asian countries.

August 8
VIETNAM: Washington reports that heavy fighting raged along the Cambodian-Vietnamese border in May, forcing Vietnam to evacuate two southern border towns on land claimed by the Cambodians.

September 20
VIETNAM: Sponsored by a record number of countries, the Socialist Republic of Vietnam is admitted to the United Nations at its 32nd General Assembly.

October 28
REFUGEES: President Carter signs a bill that opens the way for refugees to apply for U.S. citizenship and extends federal aid programs for refugees who have come to the United States following the 1975 Communist victories in Vietnam, Laos, and Cambodia.

December 31
CAMBODIA: The Cambodian government breaks diplomatic relations with Vietnam, giving "ferocious and barbarous aggression" by Vietnam as the reason. Earlier in December fierce fighting occurred when Vietnam occupied the "Parrot's Beak" area of Cambodia, after a Cambodian raid into Tay Ninh Province killed or injured 2,000 persons.

1978

January 3
VIETNAM: U.S. officials assert that Vietnamese-Cambodian fighting is a "proxy war" between China and the Soviet Union. Vietnamese troops now occupy 400 square miles of Cambodia in the border region of the two countries; China sides with Cambodia in the border dispute.

May 1
CHINA: Hundreds of ethnic Chinese flee Vietnam following the nationalization of privately-owned businesses in Saigon. Beijing accuses Vietnam of abusing and expelling 70,000–90,000 Chinese since 1977, and announces that it is sending ships to evacuate those who have fled.

June 29
VIETNAM: The Socialist Republic of Vietnam joins Comecom (the Council of Mutual Economic Assistance), the Soviet-sponsored East European economic alliance.

July 3
CHINA: Citing Vietnam's treatment of ethnic Chinese, China announces the termination of all economic assistance to Vietnam.

August 15

CHINA: Talks in Hanoi between Vietnam and China collapse when China recalls its delegation. Each side accuses the other of initiating a border clash involving refugees, during which, the Chinese claim, Vietnamese forces occupied Chinese territory.

November 3

VIETNAM: The Socialist Republic of Vietnam signs a 25-year Treaty of Friendship and Mutual Defense with the Soviet Union. This agreement calls for cooperation in the development of Vietnam and for "mutual consultation" in case either nation is attacked. China calls the pact a "threat to the security" of Southeast Asia.

December 4

REFUGEES: Malaysia temporarily reverses policy and announces it will admit Vietnam's "boat people," who fled (or were expelled) from Vietnam in crowded, unseaworthy boats. As in other neighboring Asian countries, there is deep-seated hostility to Vietnamese settlement in any numbers. There are many sinkings, drownings, and even attacks by pirates as the boat people are frequently turned back and refused asylum.

December 15

USA – GOVERNMENT: President Carter announces that full-scale diplomatic relations between the United States and China will begin on January 1, 1979. Formal U.S.-Taiwan ties will be broken the same day.

December 21

CAMBODIA: A major invasion by Vietnamese troops into southern Cambodia halts 40 kilometers from the Mekong River port of Kratie.

1979

January 1

DIPLOMACY: The United States and People's Republic of China establish normal diplomatic relations.

January 7

CAMBODIA: Phnom Penh falls to Vietnamese forces, who remove the Khmer Rouge regime and replace it with a Communist government drawn from the Hanoi-backed Cambodian National United Front for National Salvation; Vietnamese troops remain as an occupying force.

February 17

CHINA: Chinese forces launch an invasion of northern Vietnam in a "punitive attack," largely as retaliation for Vietnam's invasion of Cambodia. More than 200,000 Chinese troops supported by aircraft and artillery attack along most of the common 480-mile frontier. Vietnamese forces put up stiff resistance. While criticizing Vietnam for invading Cambodia, the United States calls for China to withdraw from Vietnam. The Soviet Union warns China to "stop before it is too late," and Vietnam requests the United Nations "to force the Chinese aggressive troops to withdraw from Vietnam."

March 5
CHINA: China announces that all Chinese frontier troops are withdrawing from Vietnam. During this operation, China has penetrated up to 40 miles into Vietnam and taken the provincial capital of Lang Son, ostensibly to punish Vietnam for an alleged 700 armed "provocations" along the border in the last six months. China later claims that 20,000 Chinese and 50,000 Vietnamese troops were killed or wounded in the fighting.

April 18–28
CHINA: Vietnamese and Chinese negotiators fail to agree on a peace settlement that will normalize relations between their nations. China continues to insist that Vietnam withdraw all forces from Cambodia and Laos, a demand that Vietnam steadfastly rejects.

July 21
REFUGEES: At an international conference in Geneva on the dramatically worsening plight of Indochinese refugees, Vietnam promises to stem the flow of these people. The U.S. State Department calculates that the number of people fleeing Vietnam, Cambodia, and Laos has increased almost tenfold during the year, to 300,000. At least 147,000 refugees are in camps in Thailand, 51,000 in Malaysia, and 20,000 in other countries, where most are unwanted for permanent settlement. At least 30,000 Cambodians have been repatriated.

August 5
VIETNAM: Hoan Van Hoang, a close colleague of the late Ho Chi Minh and deputy chairman of Vietnam's National Assembly, defects to China, charging that Vietnam's treatment of its ethnic Chinese is "even worse than Hitler's treatment of the Jews."

September 25
CAMBODIA: Although total victory over Pol Pot forces was claimed on July 22, 180,000 Vietnamese troops in Cambodia launch a new offensive against the Khmer Rouge, whose number is estimated at only 40,000 guerrillas.

October 14
REFUGEES: Arrivals of boat people throughout Southeast Asia have dwindled drastically. Refugee officials report that arrivals from Vietnam during September numbered only 6,600, compared to 55,000 arrivals in June.

October 16
CAMBODIA: The largest Red Cross food shipment to date (1,500 tons) arrives to relieve the famine in Cambodia. Months of effort to relieve widespread starvation have been frustrated by the lack of agreement between various factions.

November 24
USA – DOMESTIC: The U.S. General Accounting Office reports that thousands of U.S. troops deployed in South Vietnam were exposed to Agent Orange herbicide,

despite previous Defense Department denials of such assertions. About 4,800 former Vietnam veterans have asked the Veterans' Administration for treatment of disorders they believe were caused by contact with Agent Orange, which contains a toxic chemical, dioxin.

December 6–January 1, 1980
CAMBODIA: Early in December, the International Red Cross reports that little of the 33,000 tons of food it has delivered to Cambodia has been distributed. Although relief officials blame technical and logistical problems, the United States accuses the Phnom Penh government and Vietnam of deliberately blocking distribution. By January 1 UNICEF director James Grant is able to announce, after a visit to Cambodia, that the thousands of tons of food and medicine piled up in warehouses are finally reaching the people.

1980

March 9
CHINA: Chinese premier Hua Kuo-feng pledges support for Cambodian guerrillas fighting the Vietnamese-supported Cambodian government. Negotiations between China and Vietnam stall again when Vietnam refuses to discuss its invasion of Cambodia.

March 21
CAMBODIA: Despite optimistic pronouncements in preceding months, UNICEF now states that "The prospect of famine [in Cambodia] has significantly increased," due to a second harvest failure and logistical problems.

June 23
REFUGEES: Vietnamese troops in Cambodia cross into Thailand and battle Thai troops for two days near a camp holding some 200,000 Cambodian refugees. The Vietnamese seek to halt the repatriation of Cambodian refugees, many of whom they fear will join the fight against the Vietnamese. Some 100,000 Cambodian refugees are driven into Thailand.

October 22
UNITED NATIONS: The UN General Assembly, voting 97 to 23, with 23 abstentions, approves a resolution calling on Vietnam to withdraw its troops from Cambodia.

November 4
USA – DOMESTIC: Ronald Reagan defeats Jimmy Carter in the U.S. presidential election.

1981

January 28
VIETNAM: Hanoi says it is prepared to withdraw an unspecified number of troops from Cambodia if Thailand stops assisting Cambodian guerrillas opposed to the Vietnam-supported Phnom Penh government. Thailand denies providing any aid to guerrillas.

July

VIETNAM: The Vietnamese government turns over the remains of three Americans to U.S. officials.

December 12

VIETNAM: The Vietnamese government invites a group of U.S. war veterans to discuss such issues as Agent Orange and the fate of U.S. servicemen still missing in action. The four veterans who participate are criticized for serving Vietnamese propaganda purposes.

1982

October 22

USA – GOVERNMENT: President Reagan signs legislation to make it easier for thousands of Asian-born children of U.S. servicemen to enter the United States.

September

VIETNAM: Vietnamese foreign minister Nguyen Co Thach announces agreement to a long-standing U.S. request for regular meetings in Hanoi to resolve the POW/MIA issue.

October

VIETNAM: The government of Vietnam turns over the remains of four Americans and identification data on three others.

November 13

USA – DOMESTIC: The Vietnam Veterans Memorial is dedicated in Washington, D.C., in memory of the 57,939 U.S. soldiers killed or missing in the Vietnam War. The memorial, designed by Yale architectural student Maya Ying Li, consists of two black granite walls forming a shallow "V," listing the names of all the Americans killed in the war. The dedication is attended by more than 100,000 Vietnam veterans.

December

USA – GOVERNMENT: Congress passes a resolution supporting President Reagan's efforts on POW/MIAs.

December 24

USA – DOMESTIC: A group of unemployed Vietnam veterans begins a round-the-clock candlelight vigil at the site of the Vietnam Veterans Memorial in Washington, D.C., to call attention to the U.S. servicemen still missing in action.

1983

January 28

USA – DOMESTIC: President Reagan, at a meeting of the National League of Families of American Prisoners and Missing in Southeast Asia, says U.S. intelligence agencies are "fully focused" on the problem of servicemen still missing and that the goal of full accounting is of "highest national priority."

February
LAOS: A U.S. POW/MIA technical team visits Laos for the first time since the war's end.

March 31
REFUGEES: Vietnamese troops and artillery assault a refugee camp on the Thai-Cambodian border, forcing thousands of Cambodians into Thailand. Red Cross doctors abandon the camp hospital and flee with the refugees.

June
SOUTH VIETNAM: The government of Vietnam returns the remains of nine American servicemen.

July
SOUTH VIETNAM: The Vietnamese government suspends technical talks on the POW/MIA issue, citing "hostile statements" by senior American officials of the administration.

July 5
USA – DOMESTIC: According to documents made public by federal judge George C. Pratt, Jr., the Dow Chemical Company knew as early as the mid-1960s that exposure to dioxin might cause serious illness or death, but the company withheld this knowledge from the government and continued to sell herbicides contaminated by dioxin to the U.S. Army and the public. Judge Pratt is hearing a multi-billion dollar lawsuit by 20,000 Vietnam-era veterans against several chemical companies.

October 29
USA – DOMESTIC: The Reagan administration's sharp curb on press coverage of the Grenada invasion is traced to deep military resentment of Vietnam war reporting, when journalists had virtually free movement in Vietnam war zones.

October 30
VIETNAM: In an article in the *New York Times Magazine* on life in Vietnam, Craig R. Whitney says that Vietnam's leaders seem overwhelmed by the problems of feeding 54 million people without the war's great influx of foreign aid and supplies. Average per capita income in Vietnam is $150 per year.

December
LAOS: At Lao government invitation, a U.S. technical team surveys a U.S. crash site in Southern Laos and proposes a joint excavation effort by both governments.

1984

February
VIETNAM: A U.S. delegation led by Assistant Secretary of Defense Richard Armitage meets with senior Vietnamese officials, who agree to resume technical meetings and accelerate cooperation on the POW/MIA issue. The remains of five Americans are turned over to U.S. representatives.

February 12
CHINA: China accuses Vietnam of shelling Chinese border villages during lunar new year celebrations, killing a farm worker and wounding several others.

April 30
VIETNAM: Vietnam charges that Chinese gunners have fired thousands of artillery rounds into Vietnam's northern provinces this month, and that Chinese reconnaissance squads have penetrated as far as 1.5 miles into Vietnamese territory, raising tensions all along the border. Visits by journalists to the largely undamaged Lang Son Province buttress the contention of some Western diplomats that the fighting is largely "a war of communiqués." It is, however, no less serious for that.

May 7
USA – DOMESTIC: Federal District Judge Jack B. Weinsten announces a $180 million out-of-court settlement against seven chemical companies in a class-action suit brought by 15,000 Vietnam veterans against manufacturers of Agent Orange. At least 40,000 veterans are involved in various suits against manufacturers of the defoliant, with potential claimants in the hundreds of thousands.

May 28
USA – DOMESTIC: On Memorial Day, the only unknown U.S. casualty of the Vietnam War is interred at Arlington National Cemetery at a ceremony attended by 250,000, including congressmen, members of the international diplomatic community, and Vietnam veterans. Many see the burial as a national gesture that lays to rest the polarization of the Vietnam era. President Reagan, named honorary next-of-kin, delivers the eulogy at the hero's funeral, and urges greater efforts to locate the more than 2,400 servicemen still missing.

July
INTERNATIONAL: At a meeting of ASEAN (Association of Southeast Asian Nations) in Indonesia, the region's foreign ministers condemn Vietnam's "illegal occupation" of Kampuchea (Cambodia).
VIETNAM: The Vietnamese government returns the remains of eight persons, six of whom are later identified as Americans.

July 15
VIETNAM: Fighting breaks out along the border between China and Vietnam. The Chinese charge that the Vietnamese invaded first and were repulsed after 10 hours; the Vietnamese charge that the Chinese began the fighting by shelling border villages and then moving troops into Vietnam. Many observers feel that the Chinese continue incursions in northern Vietnam to distract the Vietnamese and prevent them from mounting a full-scale offensive against Chinese-backed guerrillas in Kampuchea.

September 1
REFUGEES: Nearly 10 years after the Communist takeover of Saigon and five years after the Vietnamese invasion of Cambodia, more than 130,000 Indochinese

refugees remain in Thailand awaiting resettlement abroad. The United States has resettled about 300,000 of the 600,000 refugees who have entered Thailand since 1975; hundreds of thousands of refugees also remain in camps in Cambodia and Laos. International refugee officials have worked out a plan to encourage boat captains to rescue "boat people." Previously, captains had refused to pick up Vietnamese refugees at sea because of difficulty in finding ports at which they would be allowed to disembark.

September 11
USA – GOVERNMENT: Secretary of State George Shultz announces that the United States will ask Vietnam to release an estimated 10,000 political prisoners currently held in "re-education" camps for resettlement in the United States over the next two years. Most of these prisoners are anti-Communists who worked for U.S. programs. Shultz also announces that the United States will admit 8,000 Vietnamese children fathered by U.S. servicemen over the next three years.

November 11
USA – DOMESTIC: A statue of three servicemen, added to the Vietnam Veterans Memorial after protests by veterans, is dedicated.

1985

February 22
LAOS: U.S. and Lao technical personnel conduct the first joint crash site excavation.

March 20
VIETNAM: The remains of six American servicemen are repatriated to U.S. officials during ceremonies in Hanoi.

July 7
DIPLOMACY: Indonesian foreign minister relays a message to the United States from Hanoi of an agreement to reenter into high-level discussions with U.S. officials to resolve the POW/MIA issue within a two-year period, beginning January 1, 1986.

August 17
VIETNAM: The government of Vietnam turns over to U.S. officials the remains of 26 Americans, the largest effort of its kind since the end of U.S. involvement in Vietnam.

November 17
VIETNAM: U.S. and Vietnamese technical officials meet in Hanoi to conduct the first joint excavation of a U.S. crash site in that country.

December 7
VIETNAM: The Vietnam government turns over to U.S. technical officials the remains of seven U.S. servicemen.

1986

February 15
VIETNAM: During a meeting in Hanoi with a U.S. delegation, Vietnamese officials reiterate their pledge to investigate live sightings and publicly admit the possibility of Americans being alive in remote areas.

February 17
LAOS: U.S. and Lao technical officials jointly excavate a second crash site in southern Laos to resolve the status of 14 Americans missing in a 1972 incident.

April 10
VIETNAM: The government of Vietnam turns over to U.S. officials in Hanoi 21 remains believed to be U.S. personnel.

July 19
USA – GOVERNMENT: President Reagan thanks the governments of Vietnam and Laos for their renewed efforts to help find MIA remains.

December 15–19
VIETNAM: The Vietnamese Communist Party elects Nguyen Van Linh as general secretary, and war-time leaders, such as Truong Chinh and Pham Van Dong, resign from the Politburo. Soon thereafter, the government in Hanoi announces Doi Moi, a series of economic reforms.

1987

January
USA – GOVERNMENT: Retiring U.S. Army general John W. Vessey, Jr., former chairman of the Joint Chiefs of Staff, is appointed special presidential emissary for POW/MIA affairs.

April 22
USA – GOVERNMENT: The United States says plans to send a special envoy to Hanoi are on hold until that capital indicates an interest in resolving the issue of POW/MIAs.

1988

March 14
VIETNAM: Vietnam and China begin three days of military skirmishes over the disputed Spratly Islands.

1989

September 26
CAMBODIA: Vietnam completes its withdrawal of troops from Kampuchea. Some 23,000 Vietnamese soldiers were killed and 55,000 wounded fighting Pol Pot's forces for 11 years.

December 11–12

REFUGEES: Hong Kong authorities forcibly repatriate 51 Vietnamese refugees. Some 2,000 refugees agree to return to Vietnam voluntarily by year's end.

1990

August

CAMBODIA: Under United Nations auspices, Cambodian factions agree to form a coalition government and to hold national elections.

October

INTERNATIONAL: The European Economic Community (EEC) establishes trade relations with Vietnam.

December 1

VIETNAM: The Communist Party of Vietnam releases its draft platform for the "Building of Socialism in the Transitional Period."

1991

April 21

DIPLOMACY: The United States and Vietnam agree to establish a U.S. office in Hanoi to help determine MIAs' fate. Washington presents Hanoi with a road map for phased normalization of relations and the lifting of the embargo.

August

DIPLOMACY: Vietnam resumes diplomatic relations with China following a visit to Beijing by Vietnamese premier Vo Van Kiet for talks with Chinese premier Li Peng.

October 29

REFUGEES: Britain and Vietnam sign an agreement on the repatriation of Vietnamese refugees from Hong Kong.

1992

January 23

USA – MILITARY: Joint Task Force Full Accounting (JTF-FA) is established to resolve the cases of Americans still unaccounted-for as a result of the Southeast Asia conflict. The JTF will be headquartered in Honolulu with detachments in Vietnam, Cambodia, Laos, and Thailand.

April 13

USA – GOVERNMENT: Washington lifts its embargo on telecommunication links with Vietnam and by the end of April agrees to begin trading such critical items as medicine and food.

June 4

VIETNAM: In a step toward normalizing relations with the United States, the Vietnamese government confirms the release of all former South Vietnamese officials being held in reeducation camps.

September 19
VIETNAM: The Vietnam National Assembly disbands the National Defense Council that played a leading role during the Vietnam War.

October 10
VIETNAM: Following an assurance by the U.S. government of resettlement in the States, guerrillas of Vietnam's United Front for the Liberation of Oppressed Races (FULRO) surrender to United Nations officials, ending their 28-year fight for autonomy.

October 17–19
USA – GOVERNMENT: The U.S presidential envoy, General John Vessey, visits Vietnam and receives that government's promise to search through records and photographs relating to POW/MIAs.

1993

July 2
DIPLOMACY: President Bill Clinton ends U.S. opposition to settlement of Vietnam's $140 million arrears to the International Monetary Fund, clearing the way for the resumption of international lending to Vietnam.

July 15–17
VIETNAM: A U.S. government delegation visits Vietnam and decides to create three temporary posts there for U.S. State Department officials who will help in the search for POW/MIAs.

September 13
USA – GOVERNMENT: President Bill Clinton announces the relaxing of America's trade embargo with Vietnam and says U.S. companies can now bid for Vietnam projects that use funds from international organizations.

November 11
USA – DOMESTIC: Glenna Goodacre's sculpture, "Vietnam Women's Memorial," is dedicated to those women who served during the Vietnam War; it depicts a Vietnam soldier with three nurses, and is positioned near the Vietnam Veteran's Memorial in Washington, D.C.

1994

January 16
USA – MILITARY: Admiral Charles Larson, head of U.S. Pacific Command, visits Vietnam, the highest ranking active-duty U.S. military officer to do so since the war's end. He concludes that lifting the trade embargo will help efforts to account for Americans missing from the war.

January 27
USA – GOVERNMENT: Backed by broad bipartisan support, the Senate approves a nonbinding resolution urging President Clinton to lift the trade embargo on Vietnam, a move that it is hoped will help get a full account of MIAs.

February 3

USA – GOVERNMENT: President Bill Clinton announces the lifting of the 19-year embargo on trade with Vietnam.

February 7

VIETNAM: The Vietnamese government hands over the apparent remains of 12 American soldiers to U.S. authorities.

October 5

USA – GOVERNMENT: The House of Representatives passes a bill saying that MIA accounting should remain central to U.S. policy in Vietnam.

1995

July 11

USA – GOVERNMENT: President Clinton extends U.S. diplomatic recognition to the Socialist Republic of Vietnam; it is agreed that liaison offices will be set up in Hanoi and Washington; James Hall becomes the first consul-general to Vietnam, but the United States desires more information about POW/MIAs before exchanging ambassadors.

April

VIETNAM: Vietnam celebrates the 20th anniversary of the end of the war. Hanoi publishes casualty figures for the war (1954–75) showing that more than 1 million Vietnamese combatants and some 2 million civilians were killed.

1997

April 10

USA – GOVERNMENT: Douglas "Pete" Peterson, Florida congressman and former air force pilot, who was shot down and imprisoned in North Vietnam for six years, is confirmed as the first U.S. ambassador to Vietnam. Vietnam's Le Van Bang is confirmed as Vietnam's ambassador to the United States.

2000

November 17–21

USA – GOVERNMENT: President Clinton visits Vietnam.

KEY INDIVIDUALS IN SOUTHEAST ASIA

Short biographies are provided for most of the key figures who were involved in, or had a primary influence on, the war in Vietnam. The biographies focus on the individual's role in the Vietnam War, and the length of a biography should not be seen as an indication of anyone's overall importance in world history.

Abrams, Creighton Williams (1914–1974)
Commander, U.S. Military Assistance Command, Vietnam, 1968–72 U.S. Army chief of staff, 1972–74

Born in Springfield, Massachusetts, on September 16, 1914, Creighton W. Abrams, Jr., graduated from the U.S. Military Academy in 1936 and was commissioned in the cavalry. He became famous in World War II as one of General George Patton's foremost tank commanders, leading the armored relief column to Bastogne during the Battle of the Bulge. A division and corps commander in the early 1960s, he served as the deputy chief of staff for operations and vice chief of staff of the army before becoming deputy to General William Westmoreland at MACV in 1967; in that position he was responsible for modernizing the Army of the Republic of Vietnam and, in cooperation with Robert W. Komer, managing the pacification program in South Vietnam. When Westmoreland was appointed chief of staff of the army in July 1968, General Abrams assumed command of MACV. He was given the difficult task of implementing Presi-

dent Richard Nixon's Vietnamization policy and, in 1969, the job of overseeing the gradual withdrawal of U.S. forces from Vietnam while keeping North Vietnamese forces at bay. The Cambodian "incursion" in 1970 was part of his plan to take the pressure off the South Vietnamese. In 1972, General Abrams again succeeded General Westmoreland, this time as chief of staff of the army. His main task was rebuilding an army that was in disarray following its withdrawal from Vietnam. General Abrams died in office of lung cancer on September 4, 1974.

Acheson, Dean (1893–1971)
U.S. secretary of state, 1949–53

As undersecretary of state for economic affairs from 1945 to 1947, he helped formulate the containment policy and the Truman Doctrine. After retiring from government service briefly, he returned and served as secretary of state from 1949 to 1953. He began his tenure supportive of Southeast Asian nationalism, but by 1950 he began to see the Viet Minh as a front for Soviet or Chinese communism, and therefore supported former emperor Bao Dai, rather than Ho Chi Minh, and advocated U.S. support for France in the First Indochina War. During the Johnson administration, Acheson, by then a respected elder statesman, was one of the "Wise Men," a group of unofficial advisers to President Johnson.

On March 26, 1968, Acheson sharply repudiated his previous endorsement of the Johnson administration's escalation policy, declaring that the United States could not prevent a North Vietnamese victory and, consequently, should de-escalate and seek to end the war. This position no doubt had an impact on Johnson's subsequent decision not to run for re-election.

Adams, Sam (1933–1988)
Central Intelligence Agency (CIA) analyst, 1963–73
Adams joined the CIA after a two-year stint in the navy and became an analyst. In 1966, after being assigned to the Southeast Asia Branch to work on Vietnam, Adams reviewed agent field reports about the strength of the Viet Cong and People's Army of Vietnam forces and came to the conclusion that the enemy had far more people than U.S. intelligence estimates showed. After more study, he further concluded that the U.S. military intentionally underestimated the number of troops to bolster claims of progress and to justify further escalation. Adams's charges became the basis for a controversial *60 Minutes* television segment that resulted in General William Westmoreland's multimillion-dollar lawsuit against the CBS network (which was eventually settled out of court). Adams died in 1988, but his book, *War of Numbers,* was published posthumously in 1994.

Agnew, Spiro T. (1918–1996)
Governor of Maryland, 1967–69; U.S. vice president, 1969–73
As Richard M. Nixon's vice president, Agnew harshly criticized the Democratic Party, the antiwar movement, and the media. He claimed to speak for decent, conservative Americans against the radicalism that had emerged from the turmoil of the 1960s. He repeatedly attacked the media for its "liberal eastern bias." Agnew's efforts contributed to Nixon's "silent majority" strategy for marshaling support in the wake of antiwar protests. Agnew resigned in October 1973, following allegations of criminal conduct while Baltimore County executive and governor of Maryland. He was succeeded by Gerald R. Ford, Jr.

Argenlieu, Georges Thierry d' (1889–1964)
French high commissioner for Indochina, 1946–47
Appointed by French president Charles de Gaulle, Vice Admiral d'Argenlieu zealously reestablished French authority in Indochina following the end of World War II. He preempted the Fontainebleau Conference by unilaterally and without authority declaring the Republic of Cochin China in southern Vietnam. The bombardment of Haiphong in November 1946, which he ordered, led to open warfare with the Viet Minh in December and so evolved into the First Indochina War. Argenlieu was recalled to Paris in 1947 because of his extreme unpopularity among the Vietnamese, French socialists, and communists.

Ball, George Wildman (1909–1994)
Undersecretary of state, 1961–66
George W. Ball, who served as director of the U.S. Strategic Bombing Survey during World War II, was a respected attorney and government official, who became undersecretary of state in the Kennedy administration. Ball strongly opposed American military involvement in Vietnam, warning in 1961 that sending 8,000 American advisers to Vietnam would lead to having 300,000 U.S. troops there in five years and that the United States would become mired in a hopeless war. In the Johnson administration, Ball continued to argue against U.S. escalation in Vietnam, submitting 18 memoranda and talking papers in which he refuted the arguments for expanding the war, including the decision to launch regular bombing attacks against North Vietnam. In each case, his warnings went unheeded. Convinced that he could not change administration policy and meeting stiff resistance from Dean Rusk, Robert McNamara, and McGeorge Bundy, Ball resigned from the State Department in September 1966 and returned to private law practice. Ball served as U.S. Ambassador to the United Nations for a few months in

1968, but resigned to work for the Hubert Humphrey presidential campaign.

Bao Dai (1911–1997)

Emperor of Annam, 1925, reigned 1932–1945;
last emperor of Vietnam, 1949–55

Born Prince Nguyen Vinh Thuy on October 22, 1913, he succeeded his father, Khai Dinh, to the Nguyen dynasty throne upon his father's death. Educated in France, he was crowned emperor of French-controlled Annam in 1925, taking the name Bao Dai, "Keeper of Greatness." He set out to modernize Vietnam, but he was merely a figurehead under the French and turned to a life of hunting, gambling, and womanizing. In March 1945, Japanese occupation forces invited him to form a supposedly independent government in Vietnam. After the Japanese surrendered and the Viet Minh seized power, he abdicated but served in a symbolic role as "Citizen Prince" under Ho Chi Minh, until he became dissatisfied and fled to Hong Kong and ultimately to the French Riviera in 1946. In 1949, at the request of the French, who had regained power, Bao Dai agreed to return to Vietnam and was reinstalled as a figurehead emperor of the newly proclaimed State of Vietnam, which had resulted from the Elysée Agreements. In 1954, he installed Ngo Dinh Diem as prime minister. Five months later, Diem deposed him in a referendum. Bao Dai then went into permanent exile in France, where he lived until his death.

Bay Vien (unknown–1972)

Leader of Binh Xuyen

Born Le Van Vien, Bay Vien was the leader of Binh Xuyen, Saigon's powerful criminal syndicate in the 1940s and 1950s. Through payoffs to Emperor Bao Dai and with French approval, Bay Vien became a general in the South Vietnamese army and head of the national police. After the Ngo Dinh Diem government defeated the Binh Xuyen in a power struggle in 1955, Bay Vien fled to Paris.

Bradley, Omar N. (1893–1981)

General, U.S. Army; first chairman, Joint Chiefs of Staff, 1947–53

During the Indochina War, General Bradley, noted World War II general, helped to draft Pentagon contingency plans to assist the French in 1952. After retirement, Bradley visited Vietnam in 1967 and declared his full support for the war effort. In 1968, he was one of the few "Wise Men" of President Johnson's special advisory group to advise against withdrawal from Vietnam.

Brown, George Scratchley (1918–1978)

U.S. Air Force general and chairman of the Joint Chiefs of Staff, 1974–78

Appointed air force chief of staff by President Richard Nixon in July 1973, the Senate hearings on Brown's appointment raised the issue of his role in the secret bombing of Cambodia in 1969 and 1970, when he was in command of the Seventh Air Force in Vietnam. Brown explained that the bombing missions had been kept secret for security reasons on orders from higher authority. Brown was confirmed and a year later was appointed chairman of the Joint Chiefs of Staff. Brown took an active role in the Ford administration's final attempts to save South Vietnam in March 1975. The administration advocated sending military aid to South Vietnam in response to the North Vietnamese final offensive, but was constrained by recent congressional legislation, notably the War Powers Act of 1973, limiting the president's authority to act abroad. Brown later linked the collapse of Saigon's forces during the final North Vietnamese offensive to congressional cutbacks in military aid. He stressed that aircraft, tanks, and armored personnel carriers lost in battle had not been replaced by the United States. Terminally ill, General Brown retired from active duty in 1978 and died on December 5.

Brown, Sam (1943–   )

Leader of student antiwar movement

While a student at the Harvard Theological Seminary, Brown organized student volunteers for

Senator Eugene McCarthy's 1968 presidential bid, and in 1969 helped found the Vietnam Moratorium Committee, a group of antiwar activists. Brown chaired the group, which sponsored the largest (to that time) antiwar demonstrations throughout the country on October 15, 1969, and in Washington, D.C., on November 15, 1969.

Bundy, McGeorge (1919–1996)

U.S. special assistant to the president for national security affairs, 1961–66

President John Kennedy appointed Bundy, a former dean at Harvard, his national security advisor in January 1961. From that time until Bundy's departure from office in 1966, he was one of the principal architects of U.S. policy in Southeast Asia under both Kennedy and Johnson. He believed strongly in the support of South Vietnam as a bulwark against the spread of communism in Southeast Asia and was a strong advocate for the dramatic increase in the U.S. military advisory effort in Vietnam under the Kennedy administration. After Kennedy's assassination, Bundy became more pro-war. By late 1964, he advocated that the United States adopt an extensive air campaign, varying the intensity of the bombing raids with the rate of Communist troop infiltration into the South. The bombing campaign, subsequently named Operation Rolling Thunder, began in March 1965. He also supported the use of U.S. ground forces to put pressure on Hanoi to agree to a negotiated settlement to the war. By 1966, however, Bundy began to question the escalation and what he saw as the lack of attention paid to the pacification effort. Ultimately, these concerns led to his resignation after which he became president of the Ford Foundation. He continued to advise Johnson as one of the president's "Wise Men" and in 1968, during a fateful meeting following the Tet Offensive, he advocated de-escalation and eventual U.S. withdrawal.

Bundy, William Putnam (1917–2000)

Central Intelligence Agency, 1951–61; U.S. assistant secretary of defense for international security affairs, 1961–63; U.S. assistant secretary of state for East Asian and Pacific affairs, 1964–68

William Bundy, along with his younger brother, played a significant role in drafting U.S. policy in Vietnam during both the Kennedy and Johnson administrations. Bundy recommended an aggressive program to block Communist expansion in that country. However, Bundy did not initially favor a ground combat role; he instead pushed for air strikes against military and industrial targets in the North. By 1964, Bundy believed that the administration needed congressional approval for further action in Vietnam; he wrote preliminary drafts of what eventually would become the Gulf of Tonkin Resolution in August 1964. In 1964–65, Bundy headed a working group to formulate U.S. policy recommendations. He opposed a large U.S. troop buildup, fearing that the fight would thus become the responsibility of the United States. He argued that bombing was a viable means of bringing North Vietnam to the bargaining table, and that the United States should not cease bombing operations unless Hanoi agreed to limit infiltration of troops into the South and to halt VC operations there. By the spring of 1967, however, Bundy had changed his mind and he opposed continued escalation of the war, claiming that to escalate would have an adverse impact on U.S. allies and would have a limited effect on Hanoi; he walked a line between the pro-war and anti-war factions within the administration. Bundy left government service in 1969.

Bunker, Ellsworth (1894–1984)

U.S. ambassador to South Vietnam, 1967–73

A former U.S. ambassador to Argentina, India, Italy, and Nepal, Bunker was sent to Saigon by President Johnson to replace Henry Cabot Lodge as ambassador to South Vietnam in April 1967. Throughout his tenure there, Bunker was a wholehearted supporter of U.S. policy in Vietnam and of General Westmoreland's methods of fighting it, even at a time when many other officials in the Johnson administration were beginning to have doubts. He strongly supported the Saigon government, and helped revamp the U.S.-South

Vietnamese pacification and counterinsurgency efforts. He openly endorsed President Thieu in the 1967 and 1971 elections. He backed the 1970 incursion into Cambodia, believing that destruction of North Vietnamese bases in that country would give the South Vietnamese armed forces more time to develop as U.S. forces were withdrawn under President Nixon's "Vietnamization" policy. He accompanied Henry Kissinger during the contentious sessions that persuaded Thieu to accept the Paris Peace Accords in 1973. Bunker resigned his post in Saigon in 1973 and, after returning to Washington, became ambassador-at-large. He died on September 27, 1984.

Calley, William Laws, Jr. (1943–   )
Second lieutenant, U.S. Army

William L. Calley was born on June 8, 1943, in Miami, Florida. He was a platoon leader in the 1st Battalion, 20th Infantry Regiment, 23rd Infantry (American) Division. Calley directed his platoon in the massacre of several hundred Vietnamese civilians in the hamlet of My Lai, part of the northern coastal village of Song My, on March 16, 1968. He was court-martialed and charged with killing 109 Vietnamese. In March 1971, he was convicted of the premeditated murder of at least 22 people and was subsequently sentenced to life imprisonment at hard labor, dismissal from the service, and forfeiture of all pay and allowances pending the outcome of an automatic review of his case by another command. After a lengthy review process in both military and civilian courts, his sentence was reduced to 10 years. After serving one-third of his term, he was released on parole in 1974 and given a dishonorable discharge. Other officers and enlisted men were investigated and tried for their roles in the massacre, but Calley was the only one found guilty of a crime at My Lai.

Cao Van Vien (1921–2008)
General, Army of the Republic of South Vietnam; chief, Joint General Staff, 1965–1975

General Cao Van Vien retained the top military post in South Vietnam through many government upheavals. He became an officer under the French in 1949, and in 1953 he was given command of a battalion of the Vietnamese National Army. In 1960, he was appointed to command the Airborne Brigade. He remained loyal to President Ngo Dinh Diem and did not participate in the coup that overthrew Diem in 1963. Nevertheless, he became chief of staff to the Joint General Staff. As commander of III Corps, he belonged to the so-called Young Turks faction that took power in 1964, and he was a close ally of President Nguyen Van Thieu. He became chief of the JGS in September 1965. General William Westmoreland met weekly with Vien, who resisted U.S. pressure to reform the ARVN or to replace corrupt officers. He was long an advocate of a major ground incursion into Laos to cut the Ho Chi Minh Trail, a plan that was eventually executed in 1971 as Operation Lam Son 719. Later, after U.S. troops had been withdrawn, Vien proposed the withdrawal from the Central Highlands that led to communist victory in April 1975. After gaining asylum in the United States, Vien worked at the U.S. Army Center for Military History, where he authored several monographs on the war. He became a U.S. citizen in 1982 and died of sudden cardiac arrest in Annandale, Virginia, on January 22, 2008.

Church, Frank Forrester (1924–1984)
U.S. senator (D-Idaho), 1957–81

As a member of the Foreign Relations Committee, Church was critical of U.S. military involvement in South Vietnam and in 1963 opposed aiding the regime of Ngo Dinh Diem. In June 1965, he called for direct negotiations with the National Liberation Front, free elections in South Vietnam, and a scaling down of the U.S. war effort. In the spring of 1970 Church and Senator John Sherman Cooper (R-Kentucky) introduced an amendment to a foreign military sales bill prohibiting deployment of U.S. ground troops in Cambodia, which passed in the Senate but was rejected in the House by a vote of 237 to 153. A scaled-down version was passed in December as a rider to a defense appropriations bill, which prevented the introduction of ground troops into Laos or Thailand. The adoption of the Cooper-Church amendment represented the first limitation ever voted on the president's power as commander-in-chief during a war. In 1973 Congress passed a bill, sponsored by Church and Senator Clifford Case (R-N.J.), cutting off funds for all U.S. military activity in Indochina. After a strong run for the presidency in 1976, Church lost his bid for reelection to the Senate in 1980. He died of cancer on April 7, 1984.

Clark, Ramsey (1927–)

Assistant U.S. attorney general, 1965–67; U.S. attorney general, 1967–69

As acting attorney general in 1966, Clark opposed a Selective Service System proposal to induct draft resisters quickly into military service in Vietnam. As attorney general, despite pressure from the White House, he resisted policies to repress the antiwar movement, allowing large, potentially violent demonstration, including the 1967 March on the Pentagon. He also criticized police violence toward citizens and refused to use wiretaps except in cases of national security. These positions led to criticism from within the Johnson administration and from conservatives, who labeled him soft on crime. After leaving office in 1969, Clark joined the antiwar movement and in 1972 he visited North Vietnam to investigate reported U.S. bombing of civilian targets. Subsequently he practiced law and continued his political activism, volunteering to defend Saddam Hussein in his trial before the Iraqi Special Tribunal in 2005.

Cleaver, (Leroy) Eldridge (1935–1998)

Leader of the Black Panther Party

Cleaver, with other black-power advocates such as H. Rap Brown, Stokely Carmichael, and Bobby Seale, was critical of the nonviolent disobedience tactics of Martin Luther King, Jr., and supported the radical wing of the antiwar movement. While in exile in Algeria in August 1970, Cleaver made two broadcasts over Radio Hanoi aimed at black servicemen in Vietnam, extolling the cause of the North Vietnamese.

Clifford, Clark McAdams (1906–1998)

U.S. secretary of defense, 1968–69

An attorney and confidante of Democratic presidents beginning with Harry Truman, Clifford joined Undersecretary of State George Ball in advising Lyndon Johnson in 1965 to seek negotiations rather than begin a military escalation in Vietnam that could risk becoming an open-ended commitment in an area of questionable strategic importance. However, after Johnson decided to expand the war by sending U.S. ground troops, Clifford supported the effort, believing that the United States should take all measures to achieve a quick victory. In 1966 and 1967, convinced by optimistic briefings, Clifford advised against bombing halts. As one of President Johnson's "Wise Men," Clifford supported further escalation and urged Johnson to stay the course. When Robert McNamara stepped down as secretary of defense in 1968, Johnson appointed Clifford to the post in the belief that the new secretary would stand firm on continuing the war effort. However, when General Westmoreland requested 206,000 additional troops in the wake of the Tet Offensive, Clifford became convinced that the United States should halt all bombing of North Vietnam and withdraw its forces from Vietnam. He arranged a briefing for Johnson with the "Wise Men," many of whom had come to share the same opinion as Clifford; Johnson felt betrayed by the group, who had originally supported his handling of the war, but their recommendations deeply affected the president. Shortly after the meeting, Johnson denied the military's request for more troops and stunned the nation with his announcement that he would not run for reelection. Clifford spent the last months of Johnson's presidency laying the groundwork for U.S. withdrawal and Vietnamization; he returned to his legal practice in January 1969.

Coffin, William Sloane (1924–2006)

Chaplain, Yale University, 1958–75

A leading opponent of the Vietnam War, Coffin was an important founding member of the group that became Clergy and Laity Concerned About

Vietnam (CALCAV). He was convicted with Dr. Benjamin Spock in 1968 for conspiring to encourage resistance to Selective Service laws, though the verdict was reversed on appeal and charges against both men were dropped.

Colby, William Egan (1920–1996)

Station chief, Central Intelligence Agency (CIA), Saigon, 1959–62; deputy director civil operations and revolutionary development support (CORDS), 1968; director, Phoenix Program, 1969; director, CIA, 1973–76

Colby was commissioned in the U.S. Army in 1941 and was detailed to the Office of Strategic Services (OSS) in 1943 to work with the French underground. When the Korean War broke out, Colby joined the CIA. First posted to Vietnam in 1959, he served as CIA station chief in Saigon until 1962, during which time he was involved in the strategic hamlet program and the recruitment of Montagnard tribesmen by U.S. Special Forces. In 1962, he returned to Washington, D.C., to become head of the CIA's Far Eastern Division, in which he presided over the CIA's programs throughout Southeast Asia. He considered the 1963 coup against President Diem to be a grave error. In 1968 he returned to Vietnam to succeed Robert Komer as deputy to the commander of MACV; in that position he was responsible for the Civil Operations and Rural Development Support (CORDS) program, which included the Phoenix program. He denied charges that the Phoenix program, which was aimed at eliminating the Viet Cong infrastructure, was involved in assassinations, but he and the program became a focus for the antiwar movement. In 1970 and 1971, Colby was called before congressional committees to testify about the program. He pointed out that many of the dead had been killed in battle, but refused to state categorically that there had been no assassinations. Although the program was considered a failure at the time, North Vietnamese officials and former members of the National Liberation Front and Viet Cong have since acknowledged that it had a devastating effect on their war effort. In June 1971, Colby resigned his post because of the serious illness of his daughter. He became executive director-comptroller of the CIA in 1972 and director of the CIA in 1973; his tenure was controversial because he revealed the extensive illegal activities of the CIA during the Vietnam War. Under pressure from President Gerald Ford, who was not pleased when Colby cooperated with congressional investigations, he retired from the agency in 1976 and returned to the practice of law. He died in a boating accident near his home in Rock Point, Maryland, on April 27, 1996.

Collins, James Lawton, Jr. (1917–2002)

U.S. Army general

General Collins served as General William Westmoreland's personal representative responsible for coordinating Allied operations with South Vietnam's Joint General Staff and other allies in May 1965. Collins harshly criticized the ARVN officer corps, later suggesting that the United States should have insisted on removal of corrupt and incompetent officers. Collins wrote two books drawing on his experiences, and became the army's chief of military history after the war.

Collins, Joseph Lawton (1896–1987)

U.S. Army general and adviser to President Eisenhower

Nicknamed "Lightning Joe" by his troops, Collins had been one of Eisenhower's most successful corps commanders in the D-day invasion of Europe in 1944 and later became U.S. Army chief of staff. As president, Eisenhower sent Collins to Saigon in November 1954 to assess the abilities of Ngo Dinh Diem and to set up a military training program for Diem's army. Collins recommended reducing U.S. support because of Diem's refusal to institute democratic reforms. Although many of Collins's perceptions of Diem's weaknesses later proved correct, the Eisenhower administration, at the time, decided to continue its support of Diem as the best available leader in the South. Collins was recalled in 1955 and he retired from the army in 1956.

Conein, Lucien (1919–1998)

CIA officer

Conein, a French-born officer in the U.S. Office of Strategic Services (OSS), fought the Japanese in northern Vietnam in 1945. An expert in demolition and guerrilla tactics, he returned to Vietnam to organize covert operations against the Communists in Northern Vietnam in 1954 under Edward Lansdale's Saigon Military Mission. He went to Saigon in 1962 as an adviser to the South Vietnamese Ministry of the Interior and in 1963 aided the coup that ousted Ngo Dinh Diem.

Cooper, John Sherman (1901–1991)

U.S. senator (R-Kentucky), 1957–73

Cooper voted for the Gulf of Tonkin Resolution in 1964, but became one of the early critics of U.S. involvement in Vietnam. He criticized the bombing of North Vietnam and warned against an escalation of the conflict in the aftermath of the 1968 Tet Offensive. Cooper cosponsored the unsuccessful Cooper-Church amendment with Frank Church. The amendment, a response to the 1970 Cambodian incursion, prohibited the president from spending any funds for U.S. troops fighting in Cambodia after July 1 without the consent of Congress, and also included a number of other restrictions on presidential power with regard to the war in Southeast Asia. The Senate passed the measure, but the House deleted the Cooper-Church amendment from the appropriations bill. Congress later adopted a modified version of the Cooper-Church amendment in December 1970 that prohibited the president from committing U.S. ground forces to combat in Laos and Thailand. Cooper retired from the Senate at the end of his term in 1973.

Cronkite, Walter Leland (1916–   )

CBS Evening News anchor, 1954–81

Joining the Columbia Broadcasting System in 1950, after serving as a war correspondent for United Press International during World War II, Cronkite soon became one of CBS's most important network correspondents and later its chief anchorman. On September 2, 1963, President John F. Kennedy granted Cronkite an exclusive interview in which he stated that the success of the war in Southeast Asia would ultimately be determined by South Vietnamese willingness to pursue the struggle. In the mid-1960s, Cronkite was cautiously optimistic about the war, but after visiting Vietnam during the Tet Offensive in early 1968, Cronkite reported on nationwide television that the war was not working and that the United States might have to accept a stalemate. According to many observers, the defection of Cronkite especially upset President Johnson, who had regarded the anchorman as an administration ally; the president was afraid that Cronkite accurately reflected public opinion.

Cushman, Robert Everton, Jr. (1914–1985)

Commander, III Marine Amphibious Force, Vietnam, 1967–69; commandant of the U.S. Marine Corps, 1972–75

In June 1967, Lieutenant General Cushman, who was awarded the Navy Cross during World War II, assumed command of the III Marine Amphibious Force, in charge of the 1st and 3rd Marine Divisions, as well as all army units engaged in combat in I Corps. During his tour in Vietnam, Cushman oversaw defense of Khe Sanh, the battle for Hue, and the I Corps counteroffensive in the wake of the Tet Offensive. After returning to the United States in 1969, he became deputy director of the CIA and served in that position until 1972, when he was appointed commandant of the Marine Corps. General Cushman retired in 1975 and died on January 2, 1985.

Dellinger, David (1915–2004)

Leader in the antiwar movement

Dellinger was leader of the pacifist War Resisters League. He began lobbying against American participation in Vietnam in 1963, advocating immediate withdrawal of U.S. troops from Southeast Asia. He helped organize the Assembly of Unrepresented People in 1965, which sponsored acts of civil disobedience against the war. Dellinger co-chaired the

Spring Mobilization to End the War in Vietnam in 1966 and in 1968 was involved in the demonstrations at the Democratic National Convention in Chicago. He was among eight leaders of the demonstrations indicted for conspiring and traveling over state lines to incite rioting. Dellinger was acquitted of conspiracy, but found guilty of rioting, a conviction that was overturned on appeal.

Dewey, A. Peter (1917–1945)

U.S. Army officer

Dewey, a U.S. Army lieutenant colonel working for the Office of Strategic Services (OSS), was in Saigon in 1945 helping Americans who had been imprisoned by Japan during World War II. On September 26, 1945, Dewey was killed by Viet Minh machine-gun fire while driving a jeep near OSS headquarters in Saigon, becoming the first American serviceman killed in Vietnam.

Donovan, William J. (1883–1959)

Director, Office of Strategic Services, 1942–45;
U.S. Ambassador to Thailand, 1953–54

As World War II neared its end, Major General "Wild Bill" Donovan dispatched a U.S. OSS team to French Indochina to rescue downed aviators and provide intelligence about Japanese forces in the region. Ho Chi Minh had asked the United States to support Vietnamese independence. The OSS mission, which worked with the Viet Minh against the Japanese, was the first U.S. involvement in Vietnam.

Dulles, Allen (1893–1969)

Director, Central Intelligence Agency, 1953–61

Dulles, brother of John Foster Dulles, was a supporter of Ngo Dinh Diem. He urged President Dwight D. Eisenhower to bolster Diem's government during its early years. He approved the first CIA mission, under Major General Edward G. Lansdale (USAF), that went into South Vietnam on June 1, 1954. Dulles also supported Diem's blocking of the 1956 elections because of his belief that Ho Chi Minh would win.

Dulles, John Foster (1888–1959)

U.S. Secretary of State, 1953–59

Dulles was appointed secretary of state by President Eisenhower in 1953. In the spring of the following year, the French sought U.S. intervention in Vietnam to relieve their beleaguered garrison at Dien Bien Phu. Although Dulles viewed the Viet Minh as another instrument of Communist aggression and believed that the fall of Indochina would lead to the loss of Southeast Asia with disastrous consequences for the United States, he opposed the use of U.S. air strikes in support of the French. Instead, he called for a policy of "united action," a plan for the formulation of a multinational coalition to guarantee the security of Southeast Asia. However, U.S. allies, particularly the British, were unwilling to support such a coalition. At the Geneva Conference of 1954, Dulles opposed a negotiated settlement and on his order the United States did not sign the Geneva Accords, which divided Vietnam and left the Communists in control of the north and a pro-Western government in control of the south. In a unilateral declaration, the United States declared that "it would view any renewal of aggression in violation of the . . . agreements with great concern and as seriously threatening international peace and security," thereby providing the basis for subsequent U.S. involvement in Vietnam. Later that year, Dulles negotiated the Southeast Asia Treaty, which established SEATO. He initially had doubts about Ngo Dinh Diem's ability to lead South Vietnam, but became an enthusiastic supporter and announced that military and economic aid would be sent to South Vietnam, as well as advisers to help Diem solidify his position. Terminally ill with cancer, Dulles resigned in April 1959 and died on May 24.

Duong Van Minh (1916–2001)

General, Army of the Republic of South Vietnam;
Chairman, Revolutionary Military Council, 1963–
64; President of South Vietnam, 1975

"Big Minh," as he became known to the Americans, was a French-trained soldier who first came into prominence in 1955, when, as commander of the colonial garrison in Saigon, he was instrumental in subduing the uprising by the Hoa Hao sect. He initially earned the favor of Ngo Dinh Diem, who promoted him to major general. Over time, Diem became suspicious of Minh's popularity, appointed him "Special Adviser," and removed him from troop command. Disgruntled, Minh was one of the key figures in the plot to overthrow Diem in November 1963, and reportedly the one who gave approval for Diem's assassination. After taking control of the South Vietnamese government as head of the Military Revolutionary Council, Minh was deposed by a countercoup on January 30, 1964. Exiled abroad until 1968, he was seen by some as the leader of a "third force," between President Nguyen Van Thieu and his followers and the Communists. He was a presidential candidate in the South Vietnamese election of 1966, but was disqualified as an exile. He ran again in 1971 but withdrew in protest, complaining that the United States was meddling in the election. In April 1975, Minh again came to the fore as the one most likely able to negotiate with North Vietnamese army forces closing in on Saigon. When President Thieu resigned in favor of Vice President Tran Van Huong, the elderly and sick Huong appointed Minh as the new president on April 28, 1975. Two days later, Minh surrendered Saigon to Communist forces, on April 30, 1975. For years after the war Minh was imprisoned in Communist reeducation camps, until he was released and immigrated to France in 1983. In the last four years of his life, he lived in Pasadena, California, with his daughter. He died on August 5, 2001, at the age of 85.

Durbrow, Elbridge (1903–1997)
U.S. ambassador to South Vietnam, 1957–61
President Eisenhower appointed Durbrow, a career foreign service officer, and U.S. ambassador to Saigon in 1957. He clashed with the Ngo Dinh Diem regime, sharply criticizing corruption and nepotism in Diem's government. At the same time, he faulted Diem's American advisers for not speaking out against Diem's repressive tactics, which he believed were driving the South Vietnamese people to support the Viet Cong. Durbrow reluctantly backed Diem in the failed coup of 1960, but continued pressing him to build popular support with reforms and elections until President Kennedy replaced him with Frederick Nolting in 1961.

Eisenhower, Dwight David (1890–1969)
U.S. president, 1953–61
Eisenhower was born on October 14, 1890, in Denison, Texas. He graduated from the U.S. Military Academy in 1915 and won fame as the Supreme Allied Commander in Europe during World War II. Elected president in 1952, he served two terms. Seeking to contain communism, he supported the French in their war with the Viet Minh (1946–54) with money, arms, and a small contingent of technical personnel. He believed that if Vietnam fell to communism, other Asian nations might collapse in turn, according to his domino theory. Despite this, he decided not to intervene when the Viet Minh surrounded the French at Dien Bien Phu in 1954. Lack of Allied support, especially from Great Britain, lack of congressional support, and the opposition of the U.S. Army chief of staff, General Matthew B. Ridgway, played a major role in this decision. At the 1954 Geneva Conference, the United States supported what was to become the Republic of Vietnam (South Vietnam). After the conference, the administration dispatched economic and military aid to the government of South Vietnam and military advisers to the newly formed South Vietnamese armed forces and took the lead in creating the Southeast Asia Treaty Organization (SEATO) as a bulwark against Communist expansion. The Eisenhower administration provided $1 billion in aid to the Diem government, while urging him to democratize his regime. President Eisenhower returned to private life in 1961. After his presidency, he publicly supported the Vietnam policies of the Kennedy and Johnson administrations, but became increasingly dissatisfied with Johnson's inability to bring the war to a successful conclusion. He died on March 28, 1969.

Ellsberg, Daniel (1931–)

Senior liaison officer, U.S. embassy, Saigon, 1965–66; assistant to the U.S. ambassador to South Vietnam, 1967

After two years in the U.S. Marine Corps, attending Harvard, and working for the RAND Corporation, Ellsberg joined the Defense Department in 1964, where he became one of Secretary of Defense Robert S. McNamara's "whiz kids." Touring Vietnam in 1965, Ellsberg was a strong proponent of the Johnson administration's Vietnam policy. Following his return to the RAND Corporation, Ellsberg participated in a massive study of U.S. involvement in Southeast Asia commissioned by Secretary of Defense Robert S. McNamara in 1967. The study convinced Ellsberg that the war was unjust, the result of several presidents' unwillingness to bear responsibility for the loss of South Vietnam to the Communists. This helped transform him from a stalwart war supporter to an antiwar activist. In 1969, after urging immediate withdrawal from Vietnam in memos, position papers, and magazine articles, he used his top-secret clearance to obtain the Pentagon study and photocopied it. When prominent opponents of the war declined to use it, Ellsberg gave a copy of the study to the *New York Times,* which began publishing excerpts in June 1971. When the Nixon administration sought an injunction against the newspaper, the Supreme Court ruled in favor of the *Times*'s right to publish the documents. Ellsberg was tried twice for theft of government property and espionage, but all charges were dropped because of evidence of government misconduct. Among other abuses, the Nixon administration had organized a clandestine unit, known as the "plumbers," to break into the office of Ellsberg's former psychiatrist. The "plumbers" later became involved in the ill-fated Watergate break-in. After the war ended, Ellsberg became active in the antinuclear movement.

Fall, Bernard B. (1926–1967)

Vietnam scholar

Born in Austria, Fall was a French citizen who first went to Vietnam in 1953 as an associate professor at Howard University in Washington, D.C. A critic of both French and U.S. policy in Vietnam, Fall authored seven well-regarded books about the French and American wars there, becoming acknowledged internationally as an expert on the war. Fall was killed by a Viet Cong booby trap along Highway 1 near Hue in 1967.

Felt, Admiral Harry Donald (USN) (1902–1992)

Admiral, U.S. Navy; U.S. commander in chief, Pacific, 1958–64

More concerned with the Communist threats in Korea, Taiwan, and Laos than in Vietnam, Felt recommended against sending U.S. troops to South Vietnam in 1961. He changed his position and became a vocal supporter of intervention, predicting victory in three years. When journalists questioned his optimism, Felt told them to "Get on the team." The first reports of the insurrection against President Ngo Dinh Diem occurred while Felt was on an official visit to Saigon in November 1963. He rushed out of the presidential palace just prior to the coup. Felt retired and was replaced by Admiral U.S. Grant Sharp, Jr., in June 1964.

Ford, Gerald Rudolph, Jr. (1913–2006)

U.S. congressman, 1949–73; vice president, 1973–74; president of the United States, 1974–77

Ford was born on July 14, 1913, in Omaha, Nebraska. Graduating from the University of Michigan in 1935 and Yale Law School in 1941, he served as a U.S. Navy officer in World War II. He was elected to the U.S. House of Representatives in 1948 and became House minority leader in 1965, criticizing President Lyndon Johnson for not prosecuting the Vietnam War vigorously enough. Ford supported President Richard Nixon's pursuit of détente with the Soviet Union, rapprochement with the People's Republic of China, and Vietnamization of the Vietnam War. Appointed vice president by Richard Nixon when Spiro Agnew resigned from office in 1973, Ford publicly defended the administration's record on Vietnam. Following

Nixon's resignation from office on August 9, 1974, Ford presided over the final stage of the Vietnam War. As president, he tried to bolster the sagging governments in South Vietnam and Cambodia. However, Congress appropriated less than half of the $2 billion in aid for South Vietnam that Ford requested for fiscal year 1975. When the Communists launched their final offensives in Vietnam and Cambodia, Ford asked for supplemental appropriations for South Vietnam's defense. When Congress, convinced that the extra funds would not make any difference, refused the request, Ford said that the decision gravely impaired the chances of survival for South Vietnam. He made two unsuccessful efforts to secure emergency military assistance for Saigon, but finally ordered the evacuation of all remaining U.S. military and embassy personnel from Saigon and Phnom Penh, as Communist forces closed in on the two capital cities. In May 1975, Ford responded with military action when Cambodia seized the U.S. merchant ship *Mayaguez*. He ordered air strikes on Cambodian bases and a rescue mission that cost the lives of 41 Americans even as the ship's crew was being released. In 1976, the American public, disgusted with how the Vietnam War had ended, fed up with political scandals such as Watergate and with the political turmoil that had resulted, elected Jimmy Carter, who promised to restore morality to domestic and foreign policy. After his defeat, Ford returned to private life. He died on December 26, 2006, at his California home.

Fulbright, James William (1905–1995)
U.S. senator (D-Arkansas), 1959–74
Fulbright supported the Eisenhower and Kennedy administrations' containment policies and the U.S. presence in South Vietnam. A friend and political ally of President Lyndon Johnson, he was instrumental in congressional passage of the Gulf of Tonkin Resolution, which gave the president legal authority to expand and Americanize the war. He subsequently shifted his position on the war, deciding that intervention in Vietnam was

not in America's interest and, in fact, threatened to weaken U.S. society, undermine improved relations with the Soviet Union, and might even precipitate a war with China. Calling for de-escalation of the war, he became a major critic of Johnson's policy in Vietnam. He convened hearings in 1966 to give war critics a platform for their views. In 1967 he published *The Arrogance of Power,* a book that offered a cogent liberal intellectual critique of the war that helped legitimize domestic opposition to the war. After Richard Nixon became president, Fulbright continued his staunch opposition to U.S. policy in Vietnam. He opposed Nixon's Vietnamization policy because he saw it as an attempt to avoid serious negotiations with North Vietnam. He denounced the April 1970 Cambodian incursion and worked to enact the Cooper-Church amendment. He played a key role in the passage of the War Powers Act in 1973.

Galbraith, John Kenneth (1908–2006)
Economist; U.S. ambassador to India, 1961–63
Galbraith, a key adviser to President John F. Kennedy, lobbied against U.S. involvement, arguing that the South Vietnamese government was corrupt and that South Vietnam lacked the strategic or economic importance to justify U.S. military involvement. He gave similar advice to President Johnson. In 1967, he led the "Negotiations Now!" petition drive to get one million signatures calling for an end to the U.S. bombing of North Vietnam.

Goldwater, Barry M. (1909–1998)
U.S. senator (R-Arizona), 1953–65, 1969–87;
1964 Republican presidential candidate
By 1960, Goldwater had emerged as the national leader of a growing conservative movement. Beginning in 1963, he became a vocal critic of the Johnson administration. He condemned Johnson's Great Society platform as an expensive and excessive expansion of government power, and he challenged the restrained, advisory approach of U.S. policy in Vietnam. He criticized Johnson for his failure to seek "total victory" by carrying the war

directly and massively to North Vietnam. In 1964, he became the Republican nominee for president. Although he never actually advised using nuclear weapons against the North, the Johnson campaign was able to convey the impression that he had. His doctrinaire domestic views and advocacy of escalation in Vietnam hurt him with voters, many of whom saw him as a trigger-happy extremist, and he received only 39 percent to Johnson's 61 percent in the 1964 voting. He returned to the Senate in 1969. He remained a hawk on the Vietnam War, advising President Richard Nixon to carry the war to North Vietnam. After the war was over, he insisted that it was lost "at home." He served in the Senate until 1987, playing a key role in the passage of the influential Goldwater-Nichols DOD Reorganization act of 1986. He died on May 29, 1998, at the age of 89 of complications from a stroke.

Greene, Wallace M., Jr. (1907–2003)
U.S. Marine Corps commandant, 1964–68

Greene strongly supported John F. Kennedy's policy in Vietnam. In the autumn of 1964, he advocated escalation of the war, to include the bombing of North Vietnam and an increased combat role for the U.S. Marines. Greene subsequently maintained an optimistic view of U.S. prospects in Vietnam, but by early 1966, he was advocating a major change in U.S. policy, shifting the focus from combat against enemy main forces to pacification, while acknowledging that the effort to win the hearts and minds of the Vietnamese people would take approximately 10 years to accomplish. He retired in January 1968, just before the Tet Offensive.

Gruening, Ernest (1887–1974)
U.S. senator (D-Alaska), 1959–69

An early critic of U.S. involvement in Vietnam, Gruening, a Democrat from Alaska, and Senator Wayne L. Morse cast the only votes against the Gulf of Tonkin Resolution in 1964. Gruening subsequently became a vocal critic of the war on the Senate floor, in public appearances, and in the

media. Beginning in May 1965, he voted against every military appropriations bill. Partly because of his position on the war, Gruening was defeated by Mike Gravel in the 1968 Democratic Senate primary.

Haig, Alexander (1924–)
U.S. Army general; White House chief of staff under President Richard Nixon, 1973–74; secretary of state, 1981–82

Haig served in Vietnam and was wounded in 1966 while commanding the 1st Battalion, 26th Infantry Regiment, 1st Infantry Division, and later received the Distinguished Service Cross after the Battle of Ap Gu. In 1969, Haig became military assistant to Henry Kissinger at the National Security Council; in 1970, he was promoted to Kissinger's deputy. Nixon began sending Haig on missions to Vietnam to survey the situation there. In late 1972 and early 1973, Haig was one of the principal emissaries Nixon used to persuade Nguyen Van Thieu to sign the Paris Peace Agreement. In January 1973, he went briefly to the Pentagon as deputy chief of staff of the army, but within months he returned to the White House to replace H. R. Haldeman, who had resigned as a result of the growing Watergate scandal. Haig played a major role in the Nixon administration's efforts to deal with the scandal. After Nixon's resignation in 1974, Haig served as supreme allied commander of the North Atlantic Treaty Organization (NATO) from 1974 to 1978. He was secretary of state from 1981 to 1982.

Halberstam, David (1934–2007)
U.S. journalist

A correspondent in South Vietnam for the *New York Times* in 1962 to 1964, David Halberstam became well known as one of several young journalists to report on the instability and corruption of the Diem government. He went to Vietnam in 1962 supportive of the basic aims of the American effort there. However, he soon began to question the optimistic assessments in official U.S. government reports on the progress of South Vietnam in combating the Viet Cong insurgency. Halberstam's reporting of problems in the Army of the Republic of Vietnam and the success of the Viet Cong forces in the Mekong Delta earned the ire of Secretary of State Dean Rusk, who accused him of trumpeting "communist propaganda." Halberstam shared a Pulitzer Prize in 1964 for his reporting and also gained the unique distinction of having President John Kennedy ask the *New York Times* to transfer him from Vietnam. The *Times* refused. Halberstam wrote several books on or related to the war, including *The Best and the Brightest,* a best-selling critical portrait of America's war leaders, which won the National Book Award in 1973. He died in an automobile accident in Menlo Park, California, on April 23, 2007.

Harkins, Paul Donald (1904–1984)

Commander, U.S. Military Assistance Command, Vietnam, 1962–64

Commissioned in the cavalry, during World War II Harkins served with General George S. Patton's Third Army and later was chief of staff of the Eighth Army in Korea, where he also commanded two infantry divisions. On February 8, 1962, President John F. Kennedy named Harkins the first commander of the U.S. Military Assistance Command, Vietnam (MACV). During the next two years he supervised the buildup of the U.S. support effort in Vietnam, continually providing optimistic and upbeat reports that encouraged Kennedy and his advisers to believe that victory was imminent. He countered any pressure on Ngo Dinh Diem to liberalize his regime and severely disciplined subordinates who criticized Diem. He worked well with U.S. ambassador Frederick Nolting, who was also a Diem supporter, but he soon clashed with Henry Cabot Lodge, who replaced Nolting. He opposed the plotting that led to the overthrow and subsequent assassination of South Vietnamese president Ngo Dinh Diem. In July 1964, he was replaced by his deputy, General William C. Westmoreland, and retired from active duty that year. Harkins died on August 21, 1984.

Harriman, William Averell (1891–1986)

U.S. assistant secretary of state for Far Eastern affairs, 1961–63; undersecretary of state for political affairs, 1963–65; ambassador at large with responsibility for Southeast Asia, 1965–69

Harriman played a key role in shaping U.S. policy in Southeast Asia during the Vietnam War. In 1962, he was instrumental in negotiating the Geneva agreements that resulted in the neutrality of Laos. As the American role in Vietnam expanded in the mid-1960s, Harriman consistently opposed a purely military solution to the war there, believing that a permanent settlement could be achieved only through political and diplomatic means. Harriman became increasingly critical of Diem; in August 1963, he collaborated with Roger Hilsman and Michael Forrestal in drafting a cable that would set in motion the U.S. policy decision not to stand in the way of the coup to overthrow Diem, which was carried out on November 1 by South Vietnamese military officers. In 1965, President Johnson appointed Harriman Ambassador at Large with the principal duty of handling Southeast Asian affairs. In 1966, Johnson dispatched him on a worldwide tour seeking support for U.S. Vietnam policy while sounding out the possibilities for a negotiated settlement of the war. When preliminary peace talks opened in May 1968, Harriman went to Paris as chief U.S. negotiator, a post he would hold until succeeded by Henry Cabot Lodge in January 1969. Later that year, Harriman endorsed the October 15 Moratorium antiwar protest. During the Nixon administration, Harriman pressed for a complete withdrawal of Americans from Vietnam on a fixed schedule. In 1971, he urged Congress to use the power of the purse to end the war.

Hatfield, Mark O. (1922–)

U.S. senator (R-Oregon), 1967–97

Hatfield was a leading antiwar senator during the Vietnam War. In May 1970, when Nixon ordered American troops into Cambodia, Hatfield co-sponsored with Senator George McGovern (D-South Dakota) an amendment to an arms appropriations bill that provided for a cutoff of funds for the Vietnam War after December 31, 1970, and the withdrawal of all U.S. forces from Vietnam. The McGovern-Hatfield amendment became a rallying cry for antiwar activists, but the amendment was rejected by the Senate twice, once in 1970 and again in 1971 (after the cut-off date was changed to December 31, 1971).

Hayden, Tom (1939–   )
Antiwar activist
A founder and the first leader of Students for a Democratic Society (SDS), Hayden went to North Vietnam in 1965 and 1967 with other antiwar activists. In 1968, he was arrested for helping lead the antiwar demonstrations at the Democratic National Convention in Chicago, and became one of the "Chicago Seven" charged, and later acquitted of, conspiracy. Hayden and his future wife, Jane Fonda, led the "Free the Army" campaign, which held meetings at sites near military installations to influence U.S. military personnel to question the Vietnam War.

Helms, Richard M. (1913–2002)
Director, Central Intelligence Agency (CIA), 1966–72
Helms served with the OSS during World War II and worked his way up through the CIA to become the first career officer appointed director of central intelligence (DCI), serving in this position longer than any other man, with the exception of Allen Dulles. In 1966, during the Johnson administration, Helms was at the center of a debate over the appropriate level of U.S. bombing and the number of troops the United States should commit. Helms's position remained consistent throughout the war. The bombing, he believed, had not worked, neither breaking the resolve of the North Vietnamese, nor disrupting their supply lines to the south. Later, Helms became involved in a dispute with the Pentagon over the North Vietnamese Army's order of battle, which widened the existing rift between the CIA and the military. In the late

stages of the war, Helms came under attack from critics protesting covert CIA operations in Southeast Asia. During the Nixon administration, Nixon pressured Helms into involving the CIA in Watergate; the director first agreed, but then disengaged the CIA from the cover-up. Helms believed that Nixon's personal use of the CIA made it vulnerable to congressional attack. President Nixon dismissed Helms in November 1972 but subsequently appointed him U.S. ambassador to Iran, where he served until 1977.

Hersh, Seymour (1937–   )
Journalist
In November 1969, Hersh broke the story on the My Lai massacre, winning the Pulitzer Prize for that reporting. His report was a major factor that led to a lengthy U.S. Army investigation of the incident and its cover-up. Writing for the *New York Times* in 1974, Hersh exposed the CIA's illegal domestic surveillance of opponents of the Vietnam War.

Hilsman, Roger, Jr. (1919–   )
Director, U.S. Department of State, Bureau of Intelligence and Research, 1961–63; assistant secretary of state for Far Eastern affairs, 1963–64
Hilsman influenced U.S. counterinsurgency programs in Vietnam in the early 1960s, arguing for efforts to win the allegiance of the peasants while isolating the Viet Cong from the population through the Strategic Hamlet program. In late 1962, President Kennedy sent Hilsman and Michael Forrestal to Vietnam on a fact-finding mission. The resulting report expressed reservations about U.S. policy in Vietnam, but concluded that it was essentially sound. However, the report questioned the stability of the Ngo Dinh Diem regime. Following Diem's repression of Buddhists in 1963, Hilsman recommended that Kennedy encourage a coup against Diem. Together with Forrestal and W. Averell Harriman, Hilsman prepared a cable instructing Ambassador Henry Cabot Lodge to warn Diem that he had to reform

or lose U.S. support. The cable also instructed Lodge to inform a group of South Vietnamese army generals that the United States would not stand in the way of a coup to remove Diem from office. The military coup was carried out on November 1. Increasingly at odds with President Johnson and Secretary of State Dean Rusk over Vietnam policy, he resigned his State Department post in early 1964 and became a professor at Columbia University in New York. In his 1967 book, he criticized the Johnson administration's escalation of the war.

Ho Chi Minh (b. Nguyen Tat Thanh) (1890–1969)

Leading Vietnamese revolutionary, founder and first president of Democratic Republic of Vietnam, 1945–69

Ho Chi Minh, "He Who Enlightens," was one of the many aliases of Nguyen Tat Thanh, born in 1890 in Nghe An Province in the protectorate of Annam (central Vietnam). Son of an impoverished mandarin, he left Vietnam in 1912 and ended up in France, where, accepting Marxist Leninism because of its anticolonial stance and position of national liberation, under the alias Nguyen Ai Quoc, "Nguyen, the Patriot," he became a founding member of the French Communist Party on December 30, 1920. He went to the Soviet Union in 1923 to work at the headquarters of the Communist International (Comintern). In November of the following year, he arrived in Canton, China, as Comintern agent, assigned to form a Marxist-Leninist revolutionary organization in French Indochina. Ho formed the Vietnamese Revolutionary Youth League in 1925. In 1929–30, he founded the Indochina Communist Party (ICP) in Hong Kong. He was arrested by the British police in Hong Kong in mid-1931, but was released after being held for a year and a half. He returned to Moscow in 1934, continuing to work for the Comintern. He went to China in 1938, and in 1940 he reestablished contact with the ICP in Vietnam. At the end of that year, having changed his name to Ho Chi Minh, he returned to Vietnam for the first time since 1911. In May 1941, he chaired the Eighth Plenum of the Indochinese Communist Party at Pac Bo and formed the Vietnam Doc Lap Dong Minh ("League for Vietnamese Independence"), better known as the Viet Minh. This was a nationalist front organization under Communist leadership created to mobilize the citizenry. Ho traveled to China in 1942 to seek help from the Chinese Nationalist government for operations against the Japanese, but he was arrested by the Chinese as a Communist agent. Upon his release in 1943, he returned to Vietnam. The Viet Minh entered into an alliance with the American Office of Strategic Services (OSS), providing intelligence about the Japanese in Indochina and assisting with the recovery of downed U.S. pilots. After the Japanese surrender in 1945, the Viet Minh seized power in Hanoi during what became known as the August Revolution. On September 2, 1945, Ho declared the independence of Vietnam from French colonial control and announced the formation of the Democratic Republic of Vietnam (DRV). Through clever political maneuvering, he had gained almost total political power by the time the French returned to Vietnam in early 1946. Instead of confronting French power, Ho attempted to work out a compromise position for Vietnam within the French Union, and he traveled to Paris for that purpose in May 1946. The French, determined to reimpose colonial rule over Vietnam, refused to compromise. During the fall of 1946, Ho sought to avoid hostilities, but differences between the Vietnamese and French could not be resolved. In December, fighting between the French and the Viet Minh broke out and the nine-year First Indochina War ensued. Waging guerrilla war against the French, Ho's fortunes ebbed and flowed. The DRV was recognized by most Soviet bloc countries, and thus France was able to cast the conflict in cold war terms, garnering U.S. materiel support in the process. Unable to defeat the Viet Minh after years of bloody stalemate, an exhausted France finally agreed to peace talks in Geneva in April 1954. Shortly thereafter, the French suffered a humiliating defeat at the hands of Ho's military commander, General Vo Nguyen Giap, at Dien Bien Phu, which forced them to give up the fight. A truce was signed on July 20, 1954, and the First Indochina War ended. The truce left Vietnam divided, and Laos and Cambodia became independent. Ho launched a land reform campaign in 1955 to eliminate the "landlords." Thousands were murdered and thousands more sent to Vietnamese gulags. In Ho's own province a revolt broke out against these excesses in November 1956. Ho's troops ruthlessly stamped out the revolt, and 6,000 peasants were killed or imprisoned. Later he apologized for these excesses, and in recent years the North Vietnamese government claimed it was pushed into such brutal measures by "Chinese advisers." From 1956 to 1959, Ho Chi Minh continued to consolidate his power in the North. Although he had organized some 37 armed companies in the South, he discouraged them from armed attacks on the South Vietnamese government, believing that South Vietnam would collapse on its own. In 1959, all this changed. "Political struggle" and armed violence were authorized for the Viet Cong, and assassinations of local village authorities and other government officials soared to over 4,000 a year. After a January 1959 Politburo decision to conquer South Vietnam by force, expansion of the Ho Chi Minh Trail began in May 1959, and in July aid was begun to the Pathet Lao guerrillas in Laos. In December 1960, a front organization—the National Liberation Front—was organized in the South. Ostensibly a nationalist coalition to oversee the Viet Cong, it took its orders directly from the North Vietnamese Politburo. The Second Indochina War had begun. For the next 10 years, Ho Chi Minh mobilized the Vietnam population and never wavered from his goal of reunifying North and South Vietnam under Communist rule. Presiding over the collective leadership of the Lao Dong Party in Hanoi, Ho retained a major voice on diplomacy and on strategy in the struggle for South Vietnam. However, his health began to deteriorate seriously around 1965. Ho did not live to see his country reunited; he died on September 2, 1969, with final victory almost six years away.

Hoffman, Abbie (1936–1989)

Antiwar leader

Hoffman, a flamboyant leader of the Youth International Party (better known as the "Yippies") was one of the "Chicago Seven" antiwar activists indicted for conspiring and traveling over state lines to incite rioting at the August 1968 Democratic National Convention in Chicago. He remained a radical until his death on April 12, 1989, from an apparent suicide.

Humphrey, Hubert (1911–1978)

U.S. Senator (D-Minnesota), 1948–64, 1970–78;
Vice President, 1964–68; Democratic presidential
nominate, 1968

Elected senator in 1948, Humphrey became one of the Democratic Party's leading liberal spokesmen. In 1964, President Johnson chose Humphrey as his vice presidential running mate. After the election, Humphrey irritated the president by arguing against a hard-line policy in Vietnam, and he questioned the effectiveness of trying to bomb North Vietnam into negotiating. Angered by Humphrey's dissent, Johnson excluded him from foreign policy meetings for a year. However, in February 1966 the president sent Humphrey on a tour of nine Asian nations, including South Vietnam. After his return, Humphrey outdid other administration officials in his optimism about the Vietnam War and became a vigorous advocate of the war. In 1968, after Johnson announced that he would not run for reelection, Humphrey won the Democratic Party's nomination for president at the contentious Chicago convention in August of that year. However, bitter disputes inside the convention hall and clashes between police and young antiwar protesters outside the hall intensified rifts within the party and associated the Democrats with violence and chaos in the eyes of the public. The war haunted Humphrey during his presidential campaign because he, as Johnson's vice president, could not effectively distance himself from the president's war policies. Plagued by his identification with an unpopular war, Humphrey presented a more conciliatory position on Vietnam in September, calling for a bombing halt, gradual U.S. disengagement, and a negotiated settlement, but he was unable to break out of Johnson's shadow and was defeated by Richard Nixon, who won by a narrow margin (less than one percent of the popular vote). In 1970, Humphrey won the Senate seat vacated by Eugene McCarthy and was reelected in 1976; he served until his death on January 13, 1978.

Huynh Phu So (1919–1947)
Founder of the Hoa Hao sect

Huynh Phu So declared himself a holy man in 1939, and thereafter was regarded as a prophet by his followers, the Hoa Hao sect, located mainly in the villages of the lower Mekong River Delta. So based the sect on internal faith and simple prayers rather than on elaborate rituals in pagodas, ideas that conflicted with the prevailing hierarchal Confucian view. In the 1940s, the French, fearing that the sect would undermine French colonial control and encourage revolutionary activities, arrested So and committed him to an insane asylum. When the Japanese arrived, they released So and armed the Hoa Hao. Huynh Phu So was assassinated by the Viet Minh in April 1947. Upon the death of their leader, the sect split into three rival factions, but they would eventually reunite in opposition to the Ngo Dinh Diem regime, joining the Binh Xuyen and Cao Dai armies in opposition. This coalition was defeated by Diem's forces in 1955, and the Hoa Hao sect was further crushed in 1956 when Ba Cut, one of its leaders, was captured and publicly executed. Some Hoa Hao remnants joined the National Liberation Front, but most took refuge near the Cambodian border. After Diem's overthrow, many Hoa Hao rallied to the Saigon government and the Hoa Hao became a strongly pro-government force, providing a number of Civilian Irregular Defense Group companies in An Giang, Kien Phong, and Kien Tuong Provinces.

Later, however, Hoa Hao forces would clash with President Nguyen Van Thieu's forces when he refused to tolerate independent Hoa Hao militia forces.

Johnson, Harold Keith (1912–1983)
General, U.S. Army; Chief of Staff, U.S. Army, 1964–1968

A survivor of the infamous Bataan Death March and three years' imprisonment by the Japanese in World War II, President Lyndon Johnson appointed him over 43 more senior generals to replace General Earle Wheeler as army chief of staff. The president sent Johnson to South Vietnam on a fact-finding trip in March 1965 to make an assessment of the situation. Doubtful that bombing could win the war, General Johnson, with some hesitation, recommended sending the first U.S. combat troops, a recommendation he came to regret. He commissioned a study later that year, Program for the Pacification and Long-term Development of South Vietnam (PROVN), which reinforced his misgivings about how the war was being conducted. In the long run, however, General Johnson had little influence on the course of the war in Vietnam and was rarely consulted on operational matters. During the height of the American buildup from June 1965 to June 1966, General Johnson saw the president privately only twice. He retired from active duty in July 1968. General Johnson died on September 24, 1983.

Johnson, Lyndon Baines (1908–1973)
U.S. representative, (D-Texas), 1937–49; U.S. senator (D-Texas), 1949–61; vice president, 1961–63; president of the United States, 1963–69

Born on August 27, 1908, at Stonewall, Texas, Johnson graduated from Southwest Texas State Teachers College in 1930. A Democrat and strong supporter of the New Deal, he was elected to the U.S. House of Representatives in 1937 and served four terms there. When World War II broke out, he joined the military without resigning from Congress. Elected to the U.S. Senate in 1948, he became Senate majority leader in 1954. He tried for the Democratic nomination in the presidential race of 1960, but was defeated by John F. Kennedy, who subsequently chose Johnson as his vice presidential running mate. They won the election by a slight margin over Richard Nixon and Henry Cabot Lodge. In 1961, Kennedy sent Johnson to Vietnam to assure the government of Ngo Dinh Diem that the United States intended to protect South Vietnam from a Communist takeover. Johnson promised Diem technical and financial aid and military supplies, hinting at the possibility of sending U.S. combat troops. Johnson advised against the Kennedy administration endorsement of a military coup that toppled Diem's government and resulted in his murder. Upon Kennedy's assassination on November 22, 1963, Johnson assumed the presidency.

During the first several months of his presidency, Johnson sought to continue the Southeast Asian policy that Kennedy had initiated, but he was much more interested in domestic matters than foreign affairs. However, he was fearful that a Communist victory in Vietnam would open the rest of Southeast Asia to Communist domination, embolden the Soviet Union and China, and give the Republicans a point of attack against his administration. He was determined not to "lose" South Vietnam. He retained Kennedy's top foreign policy advisers—Robert McNamara, Dean Rusk, Maxwell Taylor, Walt Rostow, and McGeorge Bundy. They advocated the "flexible response" doctrine, which called for the gradual application of force to halt Communist aggression wherever and whenever it appeared and urged the new president to stand firm in Vietnam.

As commander-in-chief of U.S. armed forces, Johnson was ultimately responsible for the step-by-step military escalation of the war. Plans to increase U.S. military aid began in late 1963, when it became apparent that the South Vietnamese government was losing ground in its battle against the Viet Cong. Johnson also authorized Oplan 34A, a program of covert attacks against North Vietnam, and contingency planning for a bombing campaign against the North. Johnson resisted implementation of the bombing campaign because he did not want it to affect his coming bid for reelection. Nevertheless, the Gulf of Tonkin incident of August 2–4, 1964, led Johnson to authorize retaliatory bombing of North Vietnam. This allowed him to refute the charges of his Republican opponent, Barry Goldwater, that he was soft on communism in Vietnam. On August 7, at Johnson's request, Congress passed the Tonkin Gulf Resolution, granting the president broad authority to use military force throughout Southeast Asia "to prevent further aggression."

In February 1965, Communist guerrillas attacked the U.S. military installations at Pleiku and Qui Nhon; this, along with reports Johnson received claiming that the VC were expanding their control of the South Vietnamese countryside, prompted the president to initiate Operation Rolling Thunder, a protracted bombing campaign against North Vietnam. Soon thereafter he authorized the landing of two combat-ready U.S. Marine battalions to protect the air base at Danang, and on April 1 approved the use of U.S. ground troops for offensive operations. The gradual expansion of the U.S. forces would continue until early 1968, when some 500,000 American military personnel were in Vietnam.

Between 1965 and 1967, Johnson announced repeatedly that he favored negotiations with the North Vietnamese, and several bombing halts were called, ostensibly to facilitate the start of talks. Hanoi's leaders did not respond to the president's "peace feelers," in part because they insisted upon an unconditional halt to the bombing of the North, but also because they felt they could wear down the American will to carry on the war. In a September 1967 speech delivered at San Antonio, Johnson promised to halt the air war indefinitely if North Vietnam agreed promptly to begin peace negotiations and not to "take advantage of the cessation in bombing to resupply men and materiel to the South." Since there were already some 100,000 North Vietnamese troops in the South, Hanoi rejected the "San Antonio Formula."

As the war continued to rage with very little sign of real progress, public support declined and the antiwar movement grew. In late 1967, in an effort to shore up public support for the war, Johnson launched an information campaign claiming that the Communists were close to defeat. However, the Tet Offensive of February 1968, in which some 90 South Vietnamese cities were attacked by both VC and NVA forces, severely strained the administration's credibility. The offensive, although a military disaster for the Communists, helped convince Johnson to de-escalate the war. Following Tet, General William C. Westmoreland and the Joint Chiefs of Staff asked for more than 206,000 additional troops, about half to be deployed to Vietnam and the rest to strengthen security in other parts of the world. Johnson appointed his new secretary of defense, Clark Clifford, as head of a task force to study the proposal and examine its impact on the budget, public opinion, and future prospects for negotiations with the North Vietnamese. Clifford's report, based upon extensive discussion with senior military and civilian Pentagon officials, called for mobilization of the Reserves but only to meet contingency situations and asserted the belief that additional troops in Vietnam would have no positive effect and might even provoke a "domestic crisis" at home.

On March 25, an informal group of "Wise Men" was assembled at the State Department, including Dean Acheson, George Ball, Matthew Ridgway, and Henry Cabot Lodge. When Johnson asked them for their recommendations, the consensus was to de-escalate. Earlier that month, on March 12, Senator Eugene McCarthy had made a strong showing in the New Hampshire Democratic primary. Just four days later, Senator Robert Kennedy had announced he too would run as an antiwar candidate. The Clifford report and the recommendations of the "wise men" combined with the political developments within his own party to convince Johnson that drastic measures had to be taken.

On March 31, the president went before a nationwide television audience to announce a unilateral halt to air and naval bombardment of North Vietnam except for the area immediately north of the DMZ. He called on North Vietnam "to respond positively and favorably to this new step toward peace." At the close of the broadcast, Johnson shocked the nation by announcing that he would not seek reelection. Three days later, North Vietnam agreed to open negotiations in Paris. Talks began that May.

Johnson returned to his ranch in Texas in 1969, where he began work on his memoirs. He died on January 22, 1973, five days before the Paris Agreement on Ending the War and Restoring Peace in Vietnam was signed.

Jones, David C. (1921–   )

General, U.S. Air Force

A flight instructor in World War II and a bomber pilot in the Korean War, Jones was vice commander and director of operations of the Seventh Air Force in Vietnam in 1969; Jones helped plan Operation Menu, the secret bombing of Cambodia, and kept it concealed from Congress. Promoted to full general in 1971, he left Vietnam to command U.S. Air Forces in Europe. He succeeded General George Brown as U.S. Air Force chief of staff in 1974, and as chairman of the Joint Chiefs of Staff in 1978. Jones retired in 1982.

Katzenbach, Nicholas (1922–   )

U.S. attorney general, 1965–66; undersecretary of state, 1966–69

As attorney general in 1965, Katzenbach supported the war effort and promised to investigate those who protested the draft. As undersecretary of state, Katzenbach testified before the Senate Foreign Relations Committee in 1967, offering a broad interpretation of presidential power to start military action, arguing that the congressional ratification of the Southeast Asia Treaty Organization (SEATO) and the passage of the Gulf of Tonkin Resolution gave the president the authority to prosecute the Vietnam War as he saw fit to include the commitment of U.S. ground troops. Later, however, he came to advocate that the government should resist further increases in U.S. troop levels. By 1968, he had concluded that the U.S. should withdraw from Vietnam. In 1973, Katzenbach charged that President Nixon had exceeded his constitutional powers, and supported the War Powers Act.

Kennedy, Edward M. (1932–   )

U.S. senator (D-Massachusetts), 1962–

During his first six years in office, Kennedy, the younger brother of President John F. Kennedy, focused primarily on domestic issues. He offered limited support to President Johnson's Vietnam policy in January 1966 by not opposing the bombing of North Vietnam. Kennedy visited South Vietnam in 1965 and in 1967 began to criticize America's involvement in the war. Kennedy became openly outspoken against the war after the assassination of his brother, Robert, on June 4, 1968. On August 21, Kennedy outlined a four-point plan to end the war. This plan included an end to the bombing of North Vietnam, negotiations with North Vietnam to remove all foreign troops from South Vietnam, formation of a government in South Vietnam that could survive a U.S. departure, and a decrease in the U.S. military presence to begin in 1968. Along with Senators Eugene J. McCarthy (D-Minnesota) and George McGovern (D-South Dakota), Kennedy sponsored a similar plank at the 1968 Democratic convention, but the delegates voted against it. Kennedy continued as a vocal opponent of President Nixon's war policy, denouncing what he saw as the bloody futility of the battle for Ap Bia (Hamburger Hill) in 1969. He gave a speech at the Boston protest of 100,000 people in the 1969 moratorium, criticizing Nixon's apparent lack of a timetable for ending the war. In 1970, Kennedy sharply condemned the Cambodian incursion and demanded a withdrawal from Vietnam. By 1973 he fully opposed further U.S. involvement in the war in Vietnam.

Kennedy, John Fitzgerald (1917–1963)

U.S. representative (D-Massachusetts), 1947–53;
U.S. senator (D-Massachusetts), 1953–60; president of the United States, 1961–63

Kennedy was born on May 29, 1917, in Brookline, Massachusetts. After graduation from Harvard University in 1940, he served as an officer in the U.S. Navy during World War II. Elected to the U.S. House of Representatives in 1946 and to the Senate in 1952, Kennedy defeated Richard Nixon in 1960 to become the 35th president of the United States.

As a senator, Kennedy had favored U.S. aid to the French in the Indochina War, and as early as 1956 had called South Vietnam "the cornerstone of the Free World in Southeast Asia" and advocated U.S. support for South Vietnam and Ngo Dinh Diem. As president, Kennedy was concerned with containing the spread of communism. Unlike Eisenhower, whose defense policy had revolved around nuclear weapons and "massive retaliation," Kennedy turned to a policy of "flexible response," which included an expanded military establishment with sufficient conventional, nuclear, and counterinsurgency forces to oppose any level of Communist aggression throughout the world.

When Eisenhower left office in 1961, he told Kennedy that the crisis point in Asia would be Laos, where an American-supported right wing regime under Phoumi Nosavan was fighting a coalition of neutralist and Laotian Communist forces supported by North Vietnam and the Soviet Union. A compromise settlement was reached in Geneva, which temporarily decreased the crisis in Laos.

Kennedy's attention then turned to Vietnam, where communist guerrillas were growing stronger and pressuring the Diem regime. Alarmed by reports that the military situation in South Vietnam was deteriorating, Kennedy sent General Maxwell Taylor and National Security Council aide Walt Rostow to Vietnam on a two-week fact-finding mission in the fall of 1961. The Taylor-Rostow report recommended a substantial increase in the U.S. involvement, including the dispatch of some 8,000 U.S. ground troops to Vietnam to indicate America's commitment to Diem and his government. During the administration's discussion of the report's recommendation, the Joint Chiefs of Staff urged the dispatch of regular combat troops. Kennedy was concerned that a commitment of combat units might embroil the United States directly in the Vietnam war, but he also sought to avoid the loss of South Vietnam—and the rest of Southeast Asia—to the Communists. He rejected the combat force option and opted for stepping up the level of military and economic aid and the number of military and civilian advisers, which would surpass 16,000 by the time of his assassination in 1963. As part of this increased military aid, Kennedy dispatched Special Forces troops who, upon arrival, trained and led indigenous troops in combat against the Viet Cong. He also sent both helicopter squadrons and U.S. Air Force pilots, who also found themselves in combat. The administration maintained the pretense that these U.S. military personnel were in Vietnam only as advisers.

Kennedy hoped that these measures would sufficiently bolster the Diem regime and preclude the need for regular U.S. combat troops. With the increased American support, Diem and his military forces appeared to be making some progress against the Viet Cong, but by the end of 1962 the situation had worsened, as the Communist forces expanded and stepped up their insurgency campaign. On the political front, Diem's continued refusal to institute various reforms recommended by U.S. advisers and his suppression of opposing political and religious factions convinced the president and his top advisers that Diem was an impediment to U.S. policy objectives in Vietnam. This realization eventually led the Kennedy administration to give tacit approval to a coup that overthrew the Diem government on November 1, 1963, resulting in the death of Diem and his brother Nhu. Kennedy was assassinated in Dallas on November 22, 1963.

Kennedy, Robert Francis (1925–1968)

U.S. attorney general, 1961–64; U.S. senator (D-New York), 1964–68

After serving as chief counsel of the Senate Rackets Committee in the 1950s, Robert Kennedy became

attorney general after his brother, John, won the 1960 presidential election. He resigned in August 1964, nine months after John Kennedy's assassination, and was elected to the U.S. Senate from New York in November. Kennedy initially supported President Johnson's Vietnam War policy, voting for an additional supplemental appropriations bill in May 1965 for the war. At the same time, in his first major Senate speech, Kennedy articulated three possible options for the United States in Vietnam: withdrawal, military escalation, or "honorable negotiations." In February 1966, however, he broke with the administration, calling for a coalition government in Saigon. He became increasingly critical of the war effort following the president's resumption of the bombing of North Vietnam and continued his attacks on U.S. policy throughout 1967. After Eugene J. McCarthy's surprisingly strong showing in the March 1968 New Hampshire primary, he declared his candidacy for the Democratic presidential nomination. Two weeks later Johnson announced he would not seek reelection. Throughout his campaign, Kennedy made the war the central issue, repeatedly advocating a negotiated settlement to the war. Shortly after midnight on June 5, after defeating Senator McCarthy in the California primary, Kennedy was shot and died.

King, Martin Luther, Jr. (1929–1968)

Civil rights leader; Cochairman, Clergy and Laity Concerned About Vietnam, 1966–68

Born in Atlanta, Georgia, King graduated from Morehouse College in 1948. He became a pastor of a Baptist church in Montgomery, Alabama, in 1954, while still working on his Ph.D. in theology at Boston University. At the end of 1955, he became famous while leading a campaign to end racial segregation of the city buses in Montgomery. In 1957, he helped found the Southern Christian Leadership Conference. In 1960, he helped organize the Student Nonviolent Coordinating Committee. He preached a doctrine of strict nonviolence and by 1963, when he made his famous

"I Have a Dream" speech during a massive demonstration he had organized in Washington, D.C., he was a national leader. King first broke with the Johnson administration over the Vietnam War in July 1965 in a controversial speech opposing escalation and calling for a negotiated settlement. King's speech provoked harsh criticism from several quarters. President Johnson, recently allied with King to gain passage of the Civil Rights Act of 1964 and the Voting Rights Act of 1965, felt betrayed by King's criticism of his Vietnam policy. The *New York Times* and other influential papers chastised King for linking the civil rights and antiwar movements, and the National Association for the Advancement of Colored People (NAACP) passed a resolution calling such linkage a "serious tactical mistake." Set back by such disapproval, King maintained a low profile on the war for the next year, but by late 1966 he decided he could no longer remain silent and became co-chair of Clergy and Laity Concerned About Vietnam. King based his opposition to the Vietnam War on his belief in nonviolence, his concern for the war's cost and its effect on the Great Society, and the racial implications of the war, claiming that a disproportionate number of young black men were fighting and dying in Vietnam. King's criticism of the war became increasingly forceful throughout 1967. He explicitly aligned the civil rights movement with the antiwar movement, renewed his call for civil disobedience, and urged young men to seek conscientious objector status. King was assassinated on April 4, 1968.

Kissinger, Henry Alfred (1923–   )

Assistant to the president for national security affairs, 1968–75; Secretary of State, 1973–77

Henry Kissinger served as a consultant to the Kennedy and Johnson administrations in the areas of arms control and foreign policy. In December 1968, he was named Special Assistant to the President for National Security Affairs by president-elect Richard Nixon. Nixon and Kissinger were determined to avoid a defeat in Vietnam, because they both believed that a defeat would seriously cripple the credibility of the United States on the world stage. Accordingly, Nixon sent Kissinger to Paris, where the ongoing peace talks were making little progress. Through a French intermediary, Kissinger made contact with Le Duc Tho, one of the most powerful members of the Lao Dong Party. Kissinger and Tho began holding secret talks with North Vietnamese diplomats in a suburb outside Paris beginning in August 1969. These talks, initially conducted without the knowledge of the official U.S. delegation to the negotiations being conducted in Paris, became the real venue for meaningful discussion, but the negotiations progressed slowly. Kissinger initially insisted on a mutual withdrawal of troops from South Vietnam, but the North Vietnamese steadfastly refused to agree to remove their troops and demanded the ouster of South Vietnamese president Nguyen Van Thieu.

While conducting the secret talks in Paris, Kissinger supported Nixon's Vietnamization policy and his escalations of the war, to include the secret bombing of Cambodia, the 1970 Cambodian incursion, and the 1971 South Vietnamese push into Laos. With the fighting in Vietnam continuing and the public and private negotiations in Paris making little progress, Kissinger and Nixon were pursuing an alternate route to a settlement of the Vietnam War as part of an overall strategy to exploit strained Sino-Soviet relations. Kissinger went to Beijing in July 1971 to lay the groundwork for a historic visit there by Nixon in February 1972. After his trip to Beijing the president traveled to Moscow in May 1972 for a summit with Soviet leader Leonid Brezhnev. In discussions with North Vietnam's two strongest allies, Nixon made resolution of the Vietnam conflict a high priority.

That spring, the North Vietnamese launched a major conventional offensive that was stymied largely by U.S. bombing. By October of 1972, both sides had moderated their previous positions somewhat, and Kissinger and Le Duc Tho had worked out a peace agreement. Although President Thieu publicly repudiated the agreement,

Kissinger declared, "Peace is at hand," to reassure North Vietnam of America's desire to achieve a peaceful solution, but he was unable to get Hanoi to agree to changes demanded by Saigon and further discussions were deadlocked in December. President Nixon, with Kissinger's backing, ordered Operation Linebacker II, intense bombing of the Hanoi-Haiphong area to pressure the north into resuming negotiations, provoking another storm of condemnation from the press at home and abroad.

In January, Kissinger and Le Duc Tho settled on a peace agreement that was substantially the same as the October agreement. Nixon reassured Thieu of continued U.S. support and advised him to approve the settlement. A formal agreement was signed in Paris on January 27, 1973. Its terms included the withdrawal of U.S. military forces, a prisoner-of-war exchange, and a cease-fire. North Vietnamese troops would be left in place and the Thieu government would remain in power. The agreement proved ineffective and the war continued. In June 1973, Kissinger met again with Le Duc Tho concerning the observance of the January agreement, but to little avail, and the fighting in Vietnam continued. In September 1973, Kissinger was named secretary of state by President Nixon, a post he would hold until the end of the Ford administration. The following month he was awarded the Nobel Peace Prize with Le Duc Tho, who refused to accept it.

Komer, Robert William (1922–2000)

Deputy to commander U.S. Military Assistance Command, Vietnam for Civil Operations and Rural Development Support, 1967–68

Komer graduated from Harvard University in 1942. After service in the U.S. Army in World War II, he returned to Harvard to earn his master's degree in 1947 and then joined the CIA. After service as a Middle East analyst for the CIA, he became a Middle East expert on the National Security Council. Named special assistant to President Johnson in March 1966, he was charged with revitalizing the

effort against the insurgency in Vietnam. In May 1967, he went to Vietnam to assume the role of deputy to the commander of MACV, with the rank of ambassador. He organized the CORDS (Civil Operations and Rural Development Support) program, which was designed to unify all American military and civilian pacification efforts in a single organization under MACV. He initiated the controversial effort to eliminate the Viet Cong infrastructure, known as the Phoenix program. Although the CORDS effort achieved some success under Komer, his very optimistic reports in late 1967 proved somewhat embarrassing when the Communists launched the Tet Offensive early in 1968. In November 1968, President Johnson appointed Komer ambassador to Turkey. He left government service after President Nixon took office in 1969. He worked for the Rand Corporation from 1969 to 1977; while there he wrote a study that criticized the "over-militarization" of U.S. policy in Vietnam.

Kong Le (1934–   )

Leader of neutralist military forces in Laos, 1960–62

Kong Le was an officer in the Royal Lao Army who provided the military forces for the bloodless coup of December 25, 1959, which brought the rightist Phoumi Nosavan to power. However, in August 1960, Kong Le led another coup that overthrew a pro-U.S. regime and returned neutralist Prince Souvanna Phouma as head of the government. Le's coup alarmed U.S. policy makers, who feared the spread of communism in Southeast Asia. By December, rightist Laotians supported by the U.S. Central Intelligence Agency defeated Kong Le's troops and retook the capital city of Vientiane. Kong Le and Souvanna Phouma retreated to the Plain of Jars, where they allied with the Pathet Lao and the People's Army of Vietnam, and began to get aid from the Soviet Union. When the Second Coalition Government was formed in 1962, Souvanna Phouma returned to Vientiane as prime minister. Soviet and PAVN support for Kong Le's forces ceased, and by the end of 1962, he turned to the United States for aid. During the following years, he was weakened by the defection of some of his forces to the Communists and the hostility of rightist elements in Vientiane. He resigned as commander of the neutralist armed forces in November 1966 and fled Laos in 1967. After the fall of Laos to the Pathet Lao in 1975, he tried to organize a resistance movement against the Communist government, cooperating with the government of China in organizing guerrilla groups to be infiltrated into Laos to try to overthrow the government in Vientiane.

Krulak, Victor H. (1913–   )

U.S. Marine Corps general and commander of Fleet Marine Force, Pacific

A 1934 Naval Academy graduate, Krulak had a distinguished combat record in World War II and the Korean War. As a major general, Krulak served as special assistant for counterinsurgency and special activities for the Joint Chiefs of Staff from February 1962 until January 1964. As such he was responsible for the development of counterinsurgency doctrine and policy, especially as it applied to Vietnam. After a fact-finding mission to Vietnam, Krulak told the Kennedy administration that the war was winnable if the United States would support Ngo Dinh Diem, a recommendation that contradicted that of State Department official Joseph Mendenhall, who accompanied Krulak to Vietnam. Promoted to lieutenant general, Krulak assumed command of Fleet Marine Force, Pacific, in March 1964 and served in that post until his retirement in June 1968. In this capacity, he was responsible for the readiness and organization of all marine units in the Pacific, including Vietnam. Although not in the operational chain of command, Krulak strongly influenced marine strategy in South Vietnam's northern provinces. With his emphasis on pacification and focus on protecting the Vietnamese people, he was a proponent of the Combined Action Program, a marine pacification approach and thus a strong dissenting voice against the search-and-destroy tactics and attrition strategy pursued by the operational

commander, General William C. Westmoreland. Krulak believed that the manpower necessary to secure the countryside was sapped by the requirements of a war of attrition.

Laird, Melvin Robert (1922–   )

U.S. secretary of defense, 1969–73

In 1952, Melvin Laird, who served in the U.S. Navy in World War II, was elected to the U.S. House of Representatives and served there until appointed secretary of defense by President Nixon in January 1969. In that office, he pushed hard for the rapid withdrawal of U.S. ground forces, putting him at odds with National Security Advisor Henry Kissinger. He was instrumental in creating the "Vietnamization" program designed to improve the capabilities of South Vietnam's armed forces while withdrawing U.S. forces there. Although initially concerned about the political reaction to the Cambodian incursion in the spring of 1970, Laird backed the operation fully after President Nixon announced it, arguing that it was necessary for the safe withdrawal of American troops from Vietnam. Laird wielded considerable influence early in the Nixon administration, but due to disagreements with Kissinger and the president over Vietnam policy, he later was not always informed of White House decisions. He opposed the secret bombing of Cambodia and the 1972 "Christmas" bombing of North Vietnam. He resigned in March 1973, choosing not to serve in the second Nixon administration, and returned to private life.

Lansdale, Edward Geary (1908–1987)

U.S. Air Force general; assistant air attaché, U.S. embassy, Saigon, 1954–1956; special assistant to U.S. ambassador in South Vietnam, 1965–68

A former advertising man, Lansdale served with the Office of Strategic Services and then in the U.S. Army in the Pacific theater during World War II. In 1947, he joined the newly formed air force. President Eisenhower sent Lansdale to the recently divided Vietnam in June 1954, as chief of the covert-action Saigon Military Mission, which was charged with weakening Ho Chi Minh's Democratic Republic of Vietnam by encouraging immigration to the south, while simultaneously trying to bolster Bao Dai's southern State of Vietnam. Lansdale helped organize the departure of nearly one million Catholic refugees from the north as the Communists took over. During the two years he was in Vietnam, Lansdale became an adviser to Prime Minister Ngo Dinh Diem. Lansdale helped the South Vietnamese government set up plans for the integration of northern refugees into the South and aided in the development of programs to train government administrators in provinces vacated by the Viet Minh. Lansdale became a close personal friend of Diem and supported him during the sect crisis of early 1955. Lansdale left Vietnam in 1956. From 1957 to 1963, Lansdale served as the deputy director of the Pentagon's Office of Special Operations. From 1965 to 1968, Lansdale served as a special assistant to the U.S. ambassador in South Vietnam to work on pacification issues. He tried to reorient the U.S. war effort toward counterinsurgency, but his influence on U.S. policy was limited and he left Vietnam and ended his career with the U.S. government in 1968.

Lavelle, John D. (1916–1979)

U.S. Air Force general; commander, Seventh Air Force, Saigon, 1971–72

Born on September 9, 1916, in Cleveland, Ohio, Lavelle graduated from John Carroll University in 1938 and joined the Army Air Corps in 1939, receiving his pilot wings and a commission in June 1940. A combat fighter pilot in the European theater of operations during World War II, he commanded a supply depot in Japan during the Korean War. Lavelle was assigned as vice commander-in-chief of the Pacific Air Force in Honolulu in September 1970, and in that position he controlled U.S. Air Force strikes against North Vietnam. On July 29, 1971, General Lavelle was appointed commander of the Seventh Air Force and concurrently deputy commander of MACV. Frustrated by the October 1968 policy that suspended

bombing operations over North Vietnam except in retaliation for North Vietnamese attacks on U.S. reconnaissance aircraft, Lavelle began having pilots make false reports of such attacks in order to conduct strikes on North Vietnamese installations under the guise of "protective reaction strikes." When the truth of these illegal missions came out in the fall of 1972, Lavelle was called before the House and Senate Armed Services Committee to explain "secret bombings." During his testimony, General Lavelle said that the missions had been encouraged by both General Creighton Abrams (commander of Military Assistance Command, Vietnam) and Admiral Thomas Moorer (chairman of the Joint Chiefs of Staff), which Abrams denied. Charged with ordering some 28 missions involving 147 sorties against unauthorized targets in violation of existing guidelines, General Lavelle was relieved of command, reduced in rank, and retired from active duty. He died on July 10, 1979.

Le Duan (1908–1986)

Founding member, Indochinese Communist Party; general secretary, Vietnam Workers Party and Vietnamese Communist Party, 1957–86

Born in 1908 in the province of Quang Tri in the French protectorate of Annam, central Vietnam, Le Duan joined Ho Chi Minh's Revolutionary Youth League in 1928 and was a founding member of the Indochinese Communist Party in 1930. He became a member of the Central Committee in Ho Chi Minh's Democratic Republic of Vietnam in 1945. In 1946, largely due to Le Duc Tho's backing, he was given responsibility for leading the resistance against the French in Nam Bo, the southern third of Vietnam. He remained there until 1957. In August 1956, he wrote "The Revolutionary Line in the South," arguing that Ngo Dinh Diem would have to be overthrown by revolution, although the recommendation would not be adopted by the party until 1959. Le Duan, Le Duc Tho, and Pham Hung, who had worked together in the South, were close allies in Hanoi from the late 1950s onward. In 1957, Le Duan became the administrative head of the Lao Dong (Worker's Party) and was officially recognized as party first secretary in September 1960. Le Duan played the major role in the decision of the 15th Plenum in 1959 to initiate guerrilla warfare in the South. He was also instrumental in aligning the DRV with the Chinese. When Ho Chi Minh's health began failing in the mid-1960s, Le Duan emerged as the leader of the government of North Vietnam and he succeeded Ho upon Ho's death in 1969. Working with Pham Van Dong and Vo Nguyen Giap, he directed the war that saw final victory with the capture of Saigon in 1975. Le Duan held the office until his death in 1986.

Le Duc Tho (b. Phan Dinh Khai) (1911–1990)

Chief North Vietnamese negotiator at Paris peace talks, 1968–73

Tho was a founding member of the Indochinese Communist Party in the 1930s and spent six years in a French prison. During the Viet Minh war against France, he headed the resistance movement in southern Vietnam. Elected to the Politburo in 1955, Tho continued as a principal party leader during the war against the Americans. He supervised the war in the south from hidden jungle bases in the 1960s. When the Paris peace talks began in 1968, Le Duc Tho was the principal negotiator for the Democratic Republic of Vietnam. He personally conducted most of the secret negotiations with Henry Kissinger beginning in 1969, holding firm to Hanoi's insistence on combining political and military issues. He worked out the compromises with Kissinger that led to the tentative agreement of October 1972. The two men signed the final Paris Peace Accords on January 27, 1973. He declined the 1973 Nobel Peace Prize, which was to be shared with Kissinger, because, he said, the war in Vietnam continued. When the Politburo decided in March 1975 to launch what was hoped would be the final offensive, Le Duc Tho was sent south to convey the decision to the military commanders there

personally. Working with Pham Hung and Van Tien Dung, he helped supervise the final North Vietnamese assault on Saigon in 1975. He also supervised Vietnam's invasion of Cambodia in 1978–79. He resigned his leadership position and retired in 1986, but remained very powerful until his death in 1990.

LeMay, Curtis (1906–1990)

U.S. Air Force chief of staff, 1961–65

LeMay became an officer in the U.S. Army Air Corps in 1930. As commander of the 20th Bomber Group, he presided over the fire-bombing of Japanese cities in 1945. He commanded the Strategic Air Command from 1948 to 1961. General LeMay believed that air power could achieve most military aims. In late 1963, he advocated a massive bombing campaign against North Vietnam. He gained notoriety with his remark in a 1965 book that the United States should "bomb them [the North Vietnamese] back to the Stone Age." After retiring from the air force, he was George Wallace's vice presidential running mate on the American Independent Party ticket in an unsuccessful bid for the 1968 election. During the campaign, he aroused controversy by saying that, in Vietnam, the United States should "use anything we could dream up, including nuclear weapons."

Lodge, Henry Cabot (1902–1985)

U.S. ambassador to South Vietnam, 1963–64 and 1965–67

Lodge was elected to the U.S. Senate in 1936, resigned his seat to serve with the U.S. Army in Europe during World War II, and was reelected in 1946. Defeated for reelection in 1952 by John F. Kennedy, Lodge was appointed ambassador to the United Nations in 1953 by President Eisenhower. He ran unsuccessfully as Richard M. Nixon's vice presidential candidate in 1960, defeated once again by Kennedy. In June 1963, President Kennedy, seeking bipartisan support for his Vietnam policy, appointed Lodge to replace Frederick Nolting as

U.S. ambassador to South Vietnam. He arrived in Saigon on August 22, in the midst of a crisis precipitated by President Ngo Dinh Diem's repression of the Buddhists. A week after his arrival, Lodge cabled Washington expressing his opinion that the war could not be won with Diem in power. When a group of South Vietnamese generals made it known that a coup was being planned, Lodge was authorized to inform the generals that the United States would do nothing to "thwart a change of government." On November 1, 1963 the generals launched their coup, ousting and killing Diem and his brother Nhu.

In May 1964, Lodge resigned his post and made an attempt to win the Republican nomination for president, but the attempt failed. In July 1965 he began a second tour as ambassador to South Vietnam. He revitalized the pacification program, hoping to create popular support for the South Vietnamese government in the countryside. In April 1967, Lodge again resigned the ambassadorship.

In March 1968, Lodge was a member of the "Wise Men," who met with President Johnson to assess the course of the war following the Tet Offensive; he recommended an end to search-and-destroy operations in South Vietnam and suggested that U.S. troops be used as a shield to protect the South. In January 1969, President Nixon appointed Lodge chief negotiator to the Paris peace conference. Frustrated by North Vietnamese intransigence, he asked to be relieved in October 1969. In July 1970, Lodge became the president's special envoy to the Vatican, a post he held until 1977. He died on February 27, 1985.

Lon Nol (1913–1985)

Cambodian general; prime minister of Cambodia, 1966–67, 1970–72; president of Khmer Republic and supreme commander of armed forces 1972–75

Born in Prey Veng Province in Cambodia, he was educated in Saigon and then became a provincial civil servant in Cambodia. He was one of the founders of the Khmer Renovation Party in 1947,

which was allied with Prince Norodom Sihanouk from 1951 onward. Lon Nol became chief of the Cambodian National Police in 1950 and chief of staff of the Cambodian armed forces in August 1955. In 1966, he became prime minister, but Sihanouk became distrustful of him and removed him from control of the army. He resigned as prime minister in 1967, citing grounds of bad health. After going to France for medical treatment, he returned, becoming minister of defense in May 1968 and prime minister again in August 1969. In March 1970, while Sihanouk was away from Cambodia, Lon Nol and Deputy Prime Minister Prince Sisowath Sirik Matak took over the government in a bloodless coup. Lon Nol had a stroke in early 1971 and went to the United States for treatment. Upon his return, he resigned his positions as prime minister, defense minister, and army chief of staff, but took the new title of marshal. His poorly led forces suffered a string of defeats by the Khmer Rouge and the North Vietnamese Army, and popular discontent against his regime mounted. On March 10, 1973, he became president of a newly designated Khmer Republic. He proved to be an inept leader, and Cambodia fell into violence and social chaos. On April 1, 1975, he fled to Indonesia as the Khmer Rouge were about to overrun Phnom Penh.

Mansfield, Michael Joseph (1903–2001)

U.S. representative (D-Montana), 1943–53; U.S. senator (D-Montana), 1953–77

Mansfield was an early supporter of Ngo Dinh Diem and of the U.S. commitment to South Vietnam, but after several visits to Vietnam, he became disillusioned with the war effort, concluding that the South Vietnamese government enjoyed little popular support and that military action was doomed to failure. In 1965, he counseled President Johnson against sending ground troops to Vietnam and urged him to pursue peace negotiations rather than escalate the war, but his advice was disregarded. Mansfield became one of the most vocal critics of the war, supporting legislation to counter the precedent established by the Gulf of Tonkin

Resolution and to reassert Congress's war powers. After President Nixon assumed office, Mansfield was one of the leading Democratic critics of the administration's Vietnam policy. In 1969, he called for a cease-fire, and in 1970 Mansfield enthusiastically supported the Cooper-Church and McGovern-Hatfield amendments. The following year he introduced his own end-the-war amendment, which required the withdrawal of U.S. military forces within nine months after the bill's passage, subject to the release of all American prisoners of war. It passed the Senate but failed in the House. Mansfield decided to retire from the Senate following the 1976 election. In 1977, President Carter appointed him ambassador to Japan.

Martin, Graham Anderson (1912–1990)

Last U.S. ambassador to South Vietnam, 1973–75

A longtime diplomat and protégé of Averell Harriman, Martin was U.S. ambassador to Thailand (1963–67) and Italy (1969–73), before President Nixon appointed him the last U.S. ambassador to South Vietnam in 1973. Arriving in Saigon after the Paris Peace Accords, Martin tried to assure President Nguyen Van Thieu of continued U.S. support, while also lobbying Congress to provide that support. His encouragement of Thieu and his optimistic reports to Washington about the situation in Saigon delayed recognition that the war was lost. To avoid creating panic during North Vietnam's Spring Offensive of April 1975, Martin declined to implement contingency plans for an orderly departure from Saigon. When he belatedly began the last-minute evacuation of the embassy on April 29–30, 1975, it turned into a harrowing helicopter lift of people from rooftops and courtyards. The hasty departure also left behind many South Vietnamese who were closely associated with the Americans and who fell victim to the North Vietnamese. Martin himself was one of the last Americans to leave Saigon. He bitterly blamed the North Vietnamese victory on Congress' termination of military aid to South Vietnam. Martin served as special assistant to Secretary of State Henry Kissinger until his retirement in 1977.

McCain, John Sidney, Jr. (1911–1981)

Admiral, U.S. Navy; commander in chief, Pacific, 1968–72

A highly decorated submarine commander in World War II, Admiral McCain was the first admiral's son to become a full admiral himself. He held important navy staff posts, including that of top congressional lobbyist, and he commanded amphibious landings in the Dominican Republic in 1968–72. McCain succeeded Admiral Ulysses S. Grant Sharp as commander-in-chief Pacific on July 31, 1968. He long advocated mining Haiphong harbor, which President Nixon approved in May 1972. McCain also called for increased bombing of Hanoi even though his son, Lieutenant Commander John S. McCain III, a U.S. Navy aviator, was held prisoner there. Admiral Noel Gayler replaced McCain in September 1972.

McCarthy, Eugene (1916–2005)

U.S. senator (D-Minnesota), 1959–71; presidential candidate, 1968

McCarthy won election to the U.S. House of Representatives in 1948 and to the Senate in 1958. As a congressman, he criticized cold war anticommunist hysteria and helped to found the liberal Democratic Study Group. However, as a senator, he was not an early dissenter, having voted for the Tonkin Gulf Resolution in August 1964 and avoided any public criticism of President Johnson's war policy until January 1966. At that time, he joined 14 other senators in sending a letter to the president calling for a continuation of the suspension of air strikes against North Vietnam begun in December. In early 1967, McCarthy grew more vocal in his opposition and soon he became one of the foremost critics of Johnson's Vietnam policy, exerting a profound impact on the course of American foreign policy. As a member of the Senate Foreign Relations Committee, he skeptically interrogated administration spokesmen and ridiculed the idea that South Vietnam's survival was necessary to contain the People's Republic of China. He spoke often against the war, questioning the morality and constitutionality of the war. In 1967, after persistent urging by antiwar liberals, McCarthy announced that he was running for the Democratic presidential nomination to further the campaign for a negotiated settlement of the war. His candidacy attracted a legion of idealistic young volunteers. McCarthy made a strong showing in the New Hampshire Democratic primary, winning 42 percent of the vote to Johnson's 48 percent. McCarthy's moral victory and Senator Robert Kennedy's announcement that he would also contend for the Democratic nomination may have influenced President Johnson's decision not to seek reelection. McCarthy's campaign, however, was soon overshadowed by those of Kennedy and, after Kennedy's assassination, that of Vice President Hubert Humphrey. At the Democratic National Convention in Chicago in August 1968, McCarthy was defeated by Humphrey when the convention minority rejected McCarthy's proposal for a bombing halt and negotiations to establish a coalition government in South Vietnam. He refused to campaign for the Democratic ticket and offered only grudging endorsement in late October. McCarthy unexpectedly resigned from the Foreign Relations Committee in 1969 and retired from the Senate in 1970.

McGovern, George S. (1922–   )

U.S. representative (D-South Dakota) 1957–63; U.S. senator (D-South Dakota), 1963–81; presidential candidate, 1972

A decorated bomber pilot during World War II, McGovern was elected to the U.S. House of Representatives in 1956 and in 1962 he became South Dakota's first Democratic senator in 26 years. He was an early, outspoken critic of the Vietnam War. He first criticized U.S. involvement in September 1963, although he voted for the Tonkin Gulf Resolution the following August partly in hope of derailing Barry Goldwater's presidential

campaign. However, he soon began criticizing U.S. participation in what he believed to be a Vietnamese civil war. In January 1965, he proposed a negotiated solution, leading to a gradual withdrawal of U.S. troops and the neutralization of Vietnam protected by a UN presence. After the invasion of Cambodia by U.S. and South Vietnamese troops in April 1970, McGovern voted for the Cooper-Church amendment to cut off funds for U.S. operations in Cambodia. Later that year, he introduced with Senator Mark Hatfield an "end-the-war" amendment to a military appropriations bill that would have legislated the withdrawal of all U.S. combat troops from Southeast Asia by the end of 1971. The Senate rejected the amendment. In 1972, McGovern won the Democratic presidential nomination. His platform called for an immediate end to the Vietnam War. His more radical supporters alienated many working-class Democrats, and the Republicans effectively stigmatized him as the candidate of "acid, abortion, and amnesty." He was decisively defeated by President Nixon in the 1972 election. In 1974, he won reelection to the Senate, but his radical reputation led to his defeat in the conservative electoral sweep of 1980. In 1984, McGovern made an unsuccessful bid for the Democratic presidential nomination.

McNamara, Robert Strange (1916–   )

U.S. secretary of defense, 1961–68

Born on June 9, 1916, in San Francisco, McNamara graduated from the University of California at Berkeley in 1937 and from Harvard School of Business Administration in 1939. During World War II, he set up a statistical control system for the U.S. Army Air Corps and rose to the rank of lieutenant colonel before returning to civilian life in April 1946. Together with other Air Corps statistical control experts who came to be known as the "whiz kids," he joined the Ford Motor Company after the war and in 1960 was named its president.

In December 1960 he accepted the post of secretary of defense in the incoming Kennedy administration and served in that office until March 1968. In 1961, McNamara supported the recommendations of Maxwell Taylor and Walt Rostow, who advocated that the United States commit all the necessary resources to prevent the fall of South Vietnam to the Communists. He promoted this position throughout President Kennedy's administration, assuming greater day-by-day responsibility for conducting the war in Vietnam and overseeing the gradual escalation of the U.S. commitment.

In February 1965, following attacks on U.S. bases in Vietnam, McNamara approved retaliatory air strikes and sent the first contingent of 3,500 marines to defend the American base at Danang. After meeting with Westmoreland in July, McNamara approved the general's request that 185,000 troops be sent to Vietnam by the end of the year. McNamara also supported a call-up of the Reserves and a tax increase to pay for the war. Johnson rejected both measures as politically unpalatable.

By late 1965, McNamara, though publicly optimistic, had begun to have growing doubts about the situation in Vietnam and whether a military solution was possible. Communist victory had been prevented, but American casualties were high, and the secretary was pessimistic about chances of bringing an end to the conflict in the near future. Nor was McNamara pleased with the pace of reform within the government of South Vietnam. By 1967 he had become openly skeptical about the effectiveness of bombing the North to cut down the infiltration of men and materiel to the South.

While concerned about the military conduct of the war, McNamara became increasingly interested in finding a way to end the conflict through a negotiated settlement. In the summer of 1967 he helped draft the San Antonio Formula, a peace proposal asking the North Vietnamese only to begin productive discussion in exchange for an end to U.S. bombing. The proposal was rejected by North Vietnam in October. A month later McNamara submitted a memorandum to Johnson recommending that the United States lower its political goals, freeze its troop levels, cease bombing of the North, and turn over major responsibility for the ground war to the South Vietnamese. Johnson rejected these proposals outright and lost confidence in his secretary of defense, deciding to replace him. Increasingly at odds with the president, McNamara accepted Johnson's offer to resign and left the Pentagon in 1968 to become the head of the World Bank.

McNaughton, John T. (1921–1967)

Assistant secretary of defense for international security affairs, 1964–67

McNaughton strongly influenced Secretary of Defense Robert McNamara's Vietnam policy throughout McNamara's tenure. In 1964, after Congress passed the Gulf of Tonkin Resolution, McNaughton advocated increased U.S. military involvement and endorsed bombing of North Vietnam. In 1964 and 1965, he drafted many of the memoranda to McNamara and President Johnson that argued strongly in favor of committing substantial U.S. ground forces in South Vietnam. He was a major architect of the strategy of limited air war, which resulted in the 1965 Rolling Thunder bombing campaign. By late 1966, however, McNaughton was skeptical that the United States could prevail in South Vietnam, believing that the United States was fighting primarily to avoid defeat and humiliation. He revised his earlier position that a Communist Vietnam would threaten U.S. interests in Asia; the domino theory, he now believed, did not apply to the Vietnam situation, and the loss of Vietnam would therefore be of no grave consequence for the United States. Accordingly, McNaughton began advocating a U.S. withdrawal. McNaughton's change of view influenced McNamara who, in turn, resisted further troop requests and called for disengagement before President Johnson forced him out of the Defense Department. McNaughton, his wife, and one of his sons were killed in a plane crash in July 1967.

Medina, Ernest L. (1936–)

U.S. Army captain implicated in the My Lai massacre
Medina, an army captain, was commander of
Charlie Company, 1st Battalion, 20th Infantry of
the 11th Infantry Brigade, 23rd Infantry Division
(Americal), 1966–68. He was in command during the March 16, 1968, action that later became
known as the My Lai massacre. He was charged in
1970 with manslaughter, assault, and the murder
of 102 Vietnamese civilians at My Lai. On September 22, 1971, Medina, defended by attorney F. Lee
Bailey, was acquitted in a U.S. Army court-martial,
primarily as a result of flawed instructions by the
military judge. He resigned his commission on
October 15, 1971.

Mendenhall, Joseph (1920–)

U.S. Foreign Service officer, 1946–75
President Kennedy sent Mendenhall, who had been
counselor for public affairs at the U.S. embassy in
Saigon, and General Victor Krulak to Vietnam on
a four-day investigative trip in September 1963.
Mendenhall, the director of the State Department's
Far East Planning Office, reported that the Diem
government could not win the war, but Krulak
concluded that South Vietnam was winning the
war. These conflicting reports astonished Kennedy
and reflected the split over Vietnam policy among
the president's advisers.

Mendès-France, Pierre (1908–1982)

French prime minister, 1954–55
Elected premier June 17, 1954, following the French
defeat at Dien Bien Phu, Mendès-France promised
to end France's involvement in Indochina within
30 days or resign. He met his deadline by helping secure a settlement at the Geneva Conference.
Last-minute negotiations between Mendès-France,
Pham Van Dong, Zhou Enlai (Chou En-lai), and
Vyacheslav Molotov broke the conference deadlock; the latter two abandoned Communist unity
with the Viet Minh to pursue their respective geo-
political goals. Chou and Molotov pressured Pham
Van Dong to retreat from the strong positions won

by the Viet Minh on the battlefield and to accept
partition and late elections. Mendès-France extri-
cated France militarily from a lost war and won
much for France by negotiation, while denying the
Viet Minh the total victory they had won on the
battlefield.

Momyer, William Wallace (1916–)

*U.S. Air Force general; commander, Seventh Air
Force, 1966–68*
A highly decorated World War II pilot, General Momyer was assigned as commander of the
Seventh Air Force in Vietnam and concurrently
deputy commander of U.S. Military Assistance
Command Vietnam in July 1966. As such he was
responsible for Operation Rolling Thunder, the
prolonged bombing campaign against North Vietnam, and the massive air effort in South Vietnam.
A vocal advocate for air power, Momyer believed
that it could have done more if restraints had been
lifted. Returning from Vietnam in August 1968, he
commanded the Tactical Air Command until he
retired from active duty on October 1, 1973.

Moorer, Thomas Hinman (1912–2004)

*U.S. Navy admiral; chief of naval operations, 1967–
70; chairman, Joint Chiefs of Staff, 1970–74*
Moorer graduated from the U.S. Naval Academy in 1933 and served as a navy aviator during
World War II. On October 13, 1962, Moorer was
appointed commander in chief of the Seventh Fleet
in the Pacific. On June 26, 1964, he was named
commander in chief of the Pacific Fleet. Moorer
strongly advocated using naval and air power to
dissuade North Vietnam from its support of insurgents in South Vietnam and Laos. In August 1964
he helped persuade Washington to launch retaliatory air strikes against North Vietnam in the wake
of the Gulf of Tonkin incident, which precipitated
direct U.S. combat involvement in the Vietnam
War. Before he departed the theater in March 1965
to assume the position of commander in chief
of the Atlantic Command, he strongly endorsed
the use of U.S. warships to stop Communist sea-

borne infiltration, the deployment of U.S. Marines to Danang, and the start of systematic bombing operations in Laos and North Vietnam. In August 1967, he again assumed a leading role in the Vietnam War when President Johnson appointed him chief of naval operations and in July 1970 he was appointed chairman of the Joint Chiefs of Staff. As chairman, Admiral Moorer played a major role in withdrawing U.S. forces from Vietnam and in the "Vietnamization" of the war. He also coordinated U.S. military responses to the 1972 North Vietnamese Army Easter Offensive and convinced President Nixon to resume the bombing of North Vietnam as well as the mining of Haiphong Harbor. He directed the intensified bombing of Hanoi in late 1972, which led to the Paris Peace Accords in 1973. In July 1974, his tour as chairman complete, Admiral Moorer retired from active duty. Until his death in 2004, he remained critical of U.S. conduct of the war, maintaining that the United States should have invaded North Vietnam.

Morse, Wayne L. (1900–1974)

U.S. senator (D-Oregon), 1945–69

Morse, a former Republican, was an early, outspoken opponent of U.S. participation in the Vietnam War. He and Senator Ernest Gruening cast the only votes against the Gulf of Tonkin Resolution in 1964, arguing that it violated the Constitution. Morse unsuccessfully fought to repeal the resolution. Divisions among Oregon Democrats over the war and local issues led to Morse's defeat for reelection in 1968.

Navarre, Henri (1898–1983)

Commander in chief, French forces in Indochina, 1953–54

A career soldier, General Navarre shared the colonial military background of his post–World War II peers, with service in Syria and French Morocco in the 1920s and 1930s. He also distinguished himself as a Resistance leader from 1943 to 1945, earning a promotion to brigadier general. In 1953, Navarre was named to replace Raoul Salan as commander in chief of French forces in Vietnam.

Navarre was optimistic in public, forecasting victory. Ultimately, his forces were defeated in the Battle of Dien Bien Phu. He retired from the army in 1956 and the same years published *Agonie de la'Indochine*, a book in which he blamed the defeat on the French political system, intellectuals, politicians, and Communists.

Ngo Dinh Diem (1901–1963)

Prime minister and president of South Vietnam, 1954–63

Born in Hue to a family that had been converted to Catholicism as early as the 17th century, his grandparents had been poor peasants and fishermen in the province of Quang Binh. However, at the time of his birth, Diem's father, Ngo Dinh Kha, had become a high mandarin at court, thanks to the French colonial conquest that had helped Christian Vietnamese climb quickly up the ladder of success. Third in a family of eight children, Diem attended Le Lyceum Pellerin, a Catholic secondary school in Hue. After graduation, Diem enrolled in the French school of administration, Collège Hau Bo. Diem became minister of the interior under Emperor Bao Dai in 1933, but resigned to protest French colonial rule. Diem's anticommunist and anti-French attitude thereafter made him appear as a credible nationalist figure to many in Vietnam and in the West. In the eyes of others, however, his nationalist credentials had been tarnished by his willingness to work with the Japanese.

Diem's nationalist stature was reestablished when Diem refused an offer of a high position in Ho Chi Minh's government in late 1945, partly because he regarded the Viet Minh as ultimately responsible for the assassination of his brother Ngo Dinh Khoi, governor of Quang Ngai Province.

From 1950 to 1954, Diem lived in Europe and the United States. During a stay at a Catholic seminary in New Jersey, he met many American religious and political leaders, including Francis Cardinal Spellman and Senators John F. Kennedy and Mike Mansfield. After the May 1954 surrender of the French at Dien Bien Phu, the United

States pressured Emperor Bao Dai to appoint Diem prime minister. On July 7, Diem returned to Saigon to take over the government. In 1955 he made his family the core of the political struggle. Diem's brother, Ngo Dinh Can, ran the northern provinces around Hue. Bishop Ngo Dinh Thuc, Diem's older brother, ran the Catholic Church, which was composed largely of northern refugees who gave the regime its only appearance of mass support.

In a country that was more than 90 percent non-Catholic, the majority of high officials in the government were members of the church. Another brother, Ngo Dinh Nhu, was Diem's chief political adviser, and by 1956, the creator and chief of the Can Lao Party, which also served as a secret police. Membership in the party was a prerequisite for advancement to higher posts in the administration and military. Nhu and his wife exercised enormous influence over Diem and power over the government and the country.

In an effort to consolidate power and stabilize the regime, Diem mounted a repressive campaign against all potential opposition in the urban area and a merciless pacification program against the countryside. As part of pacification, Diem instituted a land reform program that in effect allowed landlords to reclaim lands the revolution had already parceled out to the peasants and to collect land rents for as many years back as the landlords could claim. With the help of U.S. and British experts, in 1959 Diem began a wholesale resettlement program that forced the resident population into so-called agrovilles—and later on, strategic hamlets—in an effort to weed out the Communists and control the population.

After the insurrection of January 1960 in Ben Tre, which resulted in the takeover of nearly the entire province by former Viet Minh cadres and caused a chain reaction throughout the Mekong Delta, North Vietnam approved the shift to armed struggle in the South. With North Vietnam's blessing, on December 20 some 20 organizations opposed to the United States and the Diem regime merged with former southern Viet Minh revolu-tionaries into the National Liberation Front, whose program included the overthrow of the Diem regime. From then on the NLF dealt the Diem regime repeated military and pacification setbacks, and the urban opposition created such turmoil and instability that the United States became convinced that Diem was no longer equal to his task.

When South Vietnamese troops killed nine Buddhist protesters in Hue on May 8, 1963, tensions between Diem and the United States reached a crisis. By mid-June the United States threatened to break with Diem over the issue of Buddhist repression. In October 1963, the U.S. ambassador, Henry Cabot Lodge, secretly informed a group of South Vietnamese military officers plotting a coup against Diem that the U.S. government would not oppose a change in leadership. On November 1–2, 1963, Diem and his brother were ousted and murdered, and Duong Van Minh became leader of South Vietnam.

Ngo Dinh Khoi (unknown–1945)
Governor of Annam, 1933–43

Khoi, elder brother of Ngo Dinh Diem, became governor of Annam, the central provinces of Vietnam, in 1933. During the early 1940s, Khoi reportedly had personal disagreements with Pham Quynh, a famous scholar and high mandarin, and retired from public office in 1943. In August 1945, the Communists assassinated Khoi as part of their campaign to eliminate all potential rivals. His death was a principal factor in Ngo Dinh Diem's rejection of Ho Chi Minh's offer of a cabinet post in the newly formed Democratic Republic of Vietnam

Ngo Dinh Nhu (1910–1963)
Brother and principal adviser to Ngo Dinh Diem

Younger brother of South Vietnamese president Ngo Dinh Diem, Nhu was Diem's chief political adviser and ran the Can Lao Party, the base of Diem's power. A master of intrigue and organization, he served as the minister of the interior, a position in which he wielded immense power, creating a network of intelligence, security, police, paramilitary, and undercover groups to report on opponents of the Diem regime. With such information Diem and Nhu were able to thwart all attempts to remove them from power. Many Americans blamed Nhu for the dictatorial nature of Diem's regime. Calls for Diem to get rid of Nhu intensified after Nhu sent his Special Forces into Buddhist pagodas on August 21, 1963. U.S. officials repeatedly told Diem that Nhu and his wife had to be removed, but Diem refused. Nhu's brutal suppression of Buddhist demonstrations against the government set in motion a sequence of events that climaxed in a military coup that took place on November 1; Diem and Nhu were murdered on November 2.

Ngo Dinh Nhu, Madame (1924–   )

Wife of Ngo Dinh Nhu

Born Tran Le Xuan in 1924 in Hanoi to a wealthy family that was active in the French colonial government, she married Ngo Dinh Nhu, brother of Ngo Dinh Diem, in 1943 and converted from Buddhism to Catholicism. When Diem became president, Madame Nhu acted as surrogate first lady and official hostess for her bachelor brother-in-law from 1955 to 1963. She organized and headed an anti-Communist paramilitary organization, the Vietnamese Women's Solidarity Movement, using it to lobby the government and promote legislation outlawing divorce, dancing, prostitution, and other activities she considered immoral. Particularly outspoken and vitriolic, her 1963 comment that Buddhist immolations were a "barbeque" helped turn American public opinion against President Diem. She was traveling abroad when President Diem and her husband were assassinated on November 2, 1963; she eventually went into exile in Rome.

Ngo Dinh Thuc (1897–1984)

Roman Catholic archbishop of Hue

Eldest brother of Ngo Dinh Diem, Thuc exercised considerable influence in his brother's regime. An ardent anti-Communist and nationalist priest, Thuc served as the liaison to South Vietnam's 1.2 million Catholics. Diem lobbied for Thuc's appointment

as archbishop of Saigon, but the Vatican refused because it would appear as a public endorsement by the Vatican of Diem's government. In 1961, Thuc became archbishop of Hue, where in 1963 he intervened to forbid display of the Buddhist flag during celebrations of Buddha's birthday, which subsequently resulted in demonstrations and a chain of events that culminated with the November 1, 1963, coup that overthrew Diem. Thuc was in Rome at the time of the coup; he lived in exile for the rest of his life. He was later excommunicated from the church twice for investing priests without the Vatican's permission, but was twice forgiven.

Ngo Quang Truong (1929–2007)

General, Army of the Republic of Vietnam (ARVN)

Born in Kien Hoa Province in the Mekong Delta, Truong received his commission in the South Vietnamese Army in 1954. He served with distinction, becoming commander of the ARVN 1st Division in June 1966. Widely regarded as one of the most competent commanders in the ARVN, he and his troops played a major role in the bitter fighting in Hue during the 1968 Tet Offensive. In August 1970, Truong was promoted and assumed command of IV Corps in the Delta, where he continued to perform admirably. In May 1972, after Quang Tri in the north fell to the invading North Vietnamese Army, he was sent to Hue to replace General Hoang Xuan Lam as commander of I Corps. Truong planned and led the counterattack that regained lost territory and saved the ARVN's reputation. After the cease-fire in 1973, he remained in command until the Communist victory of 1975. With the fall of South Vietnam, Truong and his family escaped to the United States; he died of cancer on January 22, 2007.

Nguyen Cao Ky (1930–   )

Prime minister of South Vietnam, 1965–67; Vice President, 1967–71

Nguyen Cao Ky was born in Son Tay Province, northwest of Hanoi. After graduation from junior high school, he joined the French air force as a corporal. A short tour of training in France and a

French wife helped him rise quickly through the ranks.

Although officially only the air vice-marshal during the November 1963 coup against Diem, the absence of the air force chief and the personal loyalty of the men toward Ky gave him effective control of the air force and considerable leverage over other military leaders. In January 1964, Ky joined General Nguyen Khanh in a coup against Duong Van Minh's government. In February, Ky was appointed head of the air force. After General Khanh purportedly sought secret negotiations with the NLF, in February 1965, General Maxwell Taylor and General William Westmoreland relied on Ky to urge the Armed Forces Council to remove Khanh from his position of commander in chief. On 24 February Khanh left South Vietnam as "roving ambassador."

In June 1965 Ky joined with General Nguyen Van Thieu and General Nguyen Chanh Thi to oust South Vietnamese premier Phan Huy Quat, and with U.S. backing Ky became the new prime minister. The U.S. mission judged that among the triumvirate Ky, a nominal Buddhist, would be the safest bet to be the new prime minister.

Ironically, Ky became the most effective oppressor of the Buddhists. On April 3, 1966, with the approval of both Ambassador Henry Cabot Lodge and General Westmoreland, Ky announced that the Buddhist movement had fallen into Communist hands and requested U.S. aid in shuttling loyal troops to Danang. In early May, Ky fed troops in and launched his attack. Aided by U.S. Marines, Ky brutally crushed the Buddhists and their supporters. In June, Ky turned against the city of Hue and once more succeeded in ending that opposition. Remnants of the movement in Saigon were similarly crushed.

In 1967, Ky effectively used his protégés, including General Nguyen Ngoc Loan, head of South Vietnam's police and intelligence services, and General Le Nguyen Khang, commander of the 3rd Army Division, to rig the presidential election and intimidate the National Assembly into ratifying the results that allowed Ky and

Thieu to become vice president and president, respectively.

Relations between Ky and Thieu deteriorated after the 1968 Tet Offensive. Ky retired from politics in 1971. He fled Vietnam for the United States just before the collapse of Saigon in April 1975.

Nguyen Chi Thanh (1914–1967)
General, People's Army of Vietnam

Also known as Truong Son, Thanh was born in Thua Thien Province, where he began his revolutionary activity at the age of 17. He became secretary of the Thua Thien Province Committee of the Indochinese Communist Party in 1938 and subsequently served time in French prisons. From 1945 to 1950, he held various positions in central Vietnam. From 1950 to 1961, he was head of the People's Army of Vietnam General Political Directorate, becoming a member of the Politburo in 1950 or 1951. In the early 1960s, Thanh was responsible for overseeing the struggle in the South. In 1964, he was sent south to take control of the Central Office of South Vietnam, which made him the commander of Communist military operations in the southern half of South Vietnam. He sought a quick victory using conventional tactics, and his forces sustained heavy losses when U.S. troops were deployed in 1965–66. General Giap opposed Thanh's use of conventional methods. The Tet Offensive of 1968 was originally Thanh's idea, but he died in July 1967 during the early stages of planning for the operation. There remain some disagreement on how he died; one version says that he died of a heart attack while attending strategy meetings in Hanoi, but another version insists that he was killed in the South by American bombs. Recent scholarship reveals that the first version is correct.

Nguyen Huu Tho (1910–1996)
Chairman, National Liberation Front

A French-trained lawyer, Tho was active in the anti-French movement, but is not known to have joined the Communist Party. He was imprisoned by the French from 1950 to 1952 for his role in leading a demonstration in Saigon against U.S. support of the French. It is generally believed that he was placed under arrest by the Diem government and escaped only in 1961, but some think he spent this time in North Vietnam, returning only in 1961. In 1962, he became chairman of the National Liberation Front (NLF). He was apparently chosen for his broad public appeal to anti-Diem elements, giving the impression that the NLF as a whole was not a Communist organization. It appears that he was actually a figurehead without significant power during the war. However, he became one of the two vice presidents of the Socialist Republic of Vietnam in 1976, and served briefly as acting president, 1980–81.

Nguyen Khanh (1927–   )

General, Army of the Republic of Vietnam; prime minister, South Vietnam, 1964–65; president, South Vietnam, 1965

At age 16, Khanh ran away from his wealthy, well-connected family, joined the Viet Minh, and fought the French for a year before he was dismissed for poor discipline. Khanh then switched sides, attended a French officers school, and led colonial troops against the Viet Minh.

As deputy chief of staff to General Duong Van Minh, Khanh joined the coup that killed President Diem in November 1963. Two months later, Khanh led the Young Turk faction of officers who overthrew Duong Van Minh. Khanh then named himself prime minister. He never won over his own people, and he alarmed U.S. advisers by jeopardizing the war effort with repeated attempts to establish a dictatorship. His purging of the ARVN officer corps turned Khanh's fellow generals against him, while stepping up draft calls angered the populace.

Amid rising protests against his rule, Khanh used the Tonkin Gulf incident to proclaim a state of emergency on August 7, 1964. He proclaimed himself president, but angry mobs in Saigon forced him to resign on August 25. Khanh returned to power on August 27 as a member

of the Provisional Leadership Committee, which reappointed him prime minister on September 3. He foiled a coup attempt by Catholic officers on September 13, and appointed a civilian council to draw up a new constitution. Tran Van Huong was named prime minister of the new government on November 4, but Khanh retained supreme command of the military. He led the Armed Forces Council in yet another coup on December 20.

Ambassador Maxwell Taylor then suspended U.S. military aid in hopes of forcing Khanh to resign, but a month later Khanh dismissed the rest of the Armed Forces Council and assumed dictatorial powers. Khanh's supporters, General Nguyen Van Thieu, General Nguyen Van Cao, and Air Vice-Marshal Nguyen Cao Ky, deposed him on February 21, 1965. Khanh left the next day to become South Vietnam's "roving ambassador." He spent the rest of the war in France. After the war he moved to the United States.

Nguyen Ngoc Loan (1932–1998)

General, Army of the Republic of Vietnam; chief of South Vietnamese national police

Born in Hue, Loan joined the Vietnamese National Army in 1951 and entered officer training school, where he was a classmate of Nguyen Cao Ky. He went to Morocco to be trained as a pilot. Upon his return to Vietnam, he served 10 years in the Vietnamese Air Force (VNAF). He flew as wingman to his old friend Ky, by that time commander of VNAF, on the Flaming Dart air strikes against North Vietnam in February 1965. When Ky became prime minister of the Republic of Vietnam in June 1965, he gave Loan control of military intelligence and security. In April 1966, Loan was made, in addition, director general of the National Police. In that role, he helped to crush the dissident Buddhist movement in Danang and Hue several months later. During the 1968 Tet Offensive, a Viet Cong officer in civilian clothes was captured by the police in Cholon, the Chinese section of Saigon. General Loan walked up to the prisoner, whose arms were bound, and shot him in the head. An Associated Press photographer caught the execution in a still photo, and an NBC-TV crew recorded it with a movie camera. The images caused an uproar worldwide. Loan initially explained that this particular Viet Cong had killed a lot of Vietnamese and Americans; a subsequent story was circulated that he had killed the family of a subordinate and personal friend of Loan. In 1975, Loan fled to the United States, where he operated a pizza restaurant in Virginia.

Nguyen Thi Binh (1927–   )

Minister of foreign affairs, People's Revolutionary Government (PRG)

Madame Binh was born near Saigon and became active in revolutionary activities as a student. She was imprisoned by the French from 1951 to 1954. In the early 1960s, she became a member of the Central Committee of the National Liberation Front and vice president of the South Vietnamese Women's Union for Liberation. From 1962 until 1969, she served in the front's diplomatic corps and toured the world as a diplomatic spokesman for the front. When the Paris peace talks opened in 1969, the Provisional Revolutionary Government appointed her as its foreign minister, sending her to Paris as its official representative at the talks. There she focused on exacting a settlement that diminished Nguyen Van Thieu's monopoly on political power in the South. Eventually, she signed the final accord on behalf of the PRG. After the war, Binh served in various government positions in Hanoi, and she was vice president of the Socialist Republic of Vietnam 1992–93.

Nguyen Van Thieu (1923–2001)

General, Army of the Republic of Vietnam; president, Republic of Vietnam 1967–75

Born near Phan Rang, Thieu served as a combat officer with French forces during the French-Viet Minh War. He received military command and staff training in the United States in the 1950s, converted from Buddhism to Catholicism, and joined the Can Lao Party to gain advancement in

the ARVN. As a colonel, he led an ARVN division against the presidential palace during the coup against Ngo Dinh Diem and gained promotion to general from the new government. Along with Air Vice-Marshal Nguyen Cao Ky, Thieu became a leader of a military faction known as the Young Turks, who gained control of the government in June 1965. With Thieu as head of state and Ky as premier, the two men shared power for awhile. They met with Lyndon Johnson in 1966 and pledged to strengthen the South's armed forces and to prepare a constitution. Rivalry developed between the two officer-politicians, and Thieu was able to secure the presidency of South Vietnam in a manipulated election in 1967 that made the younger and brasher Ky vice president. In 1971, Thieu gained reelection as president in another rigged process from which Ky ultimately withdrew, leaving the South basically with one-man rule.

As president, Thieu made some attempts at allowing elected village governments, initiating land reform and rent controls, and removing corrupt officials, but he also repressed dissent, eventually suspended local elections, and amassed a personal fortune. He consistently resisted a negotiated settlement with Hanoi, and on several occasions—most notably in November 1968 and November–December 1972 during U.S. elections—he refused to cooperate with major American diplomatic efforts. With secret promises of generous financial support from Richard Nixon, Thieu took the offensive in attacking North Vietnamese Army forces in the South in 1973. The NVA began effective counterattacks in 1974, and in the spring of 1975, the North launched its final, successful offensive against the South. Military, political, and economic conditions in the RVN were poor, and Thieu's government had little popular support. Nixon had resigned, and the American Congress was not willing to provide Thieu more aid. Thieu bitterly denounced the United States for abandoning his government and then fled to Taiwan before the fall of Saigon. He later settled in the United States.

Nixon, Richard Milhous (1913–1994)

U.S. vice president, 1953–61; president of the United States, 1969–74

Born on January 9, 1913, in Yorba Linda, California, Nixon graduated from Whittier College in 1934 and Duke University Law in 1937. He served as a U.S. Navy officer in the South Pacific in World War II. Elected to the House of Representatives in 1946 and the Senate in 1950, he was chosen to be Dwight D. Eisenhower's running mate in the 1952 presidential race and served as vice president from 1953 to 1961. Defeated in his attempt for the presidency in 1960, Nixon ran successfully in 1968, becoming the 37th president of the United States.

Nixon entered office after the war in effect had been lost, since by 1969 both the American people and Congress had turned against the war. Following large-scale antiwar demonstrations in several cities in October, some 250,000 people gathered in Washington, D.C., in November to protest the war. Facing the difficult problem of honoring U.S. security guarantees to South Vietnam and preserving U.S. prestige abroad while responding to the desire of the American people to disengage from the war, President Nixon implemented a five-part strategy: a military campaign to "Vietnamize" the war by building up the South Vietnamese armed forces so they could assume responsibility for the fighting; increased emphasis on pacification of the South Vietnamese countryside; withdrawal of U.S. combat forces as "Vietnamization" and pacification proceeded; and diplomatic strategies aimed at driving a wedge between North Vietnam and its Soviet and Chinese allies while conducting peace talks with the North Vietnamese.

To gain maneuvering room for U.S. military withdrawals, President Nixon ordered the secret bombing (Operation Menu) of North Vietnamese Army staging areas and supply bases in Cambodia on March 18, 1969, and on April 29, 1970, he ordered a 60-day "incursion" into Cambodia to destroy NVA base and assembly areas. Despite widespread public opposition and campus protests, some of which turned violent, Nixon persisted in this military campaign. When the NVA sought to take advantage of U.S. withdrawals with its Eastertide Offensive in March 1972, he not only ordered a massive U.S. air campaign against the attacking NVA divisions but also resumed the bombing of North Vietnam that his predecessor, President Johnson, had halted three and a half years before, making good on his pledge that "the bastards have never been bombed like they're going to be bombed this time."

Meanwhile, on the diplomatic front, Nixon had been working to undermine North Vietnamese alliances with the Soviet Union and China. In February 1972 he visited Beijing, breaking more than 20 years of Sino-U.S. hostility. This overture to China increased Soviet interest in a détente with the United States; even though Nixon ordered the bombing of Hanoi and the mining of Haiphong harbor on May 8, a U.S.-Soviet summit meeting was held as scheduled in Moscow on May 22.

The North Vietnamese began negotiating in earnest in August 1972, three months before the U.S. presidential elections. Hanoi's chief negotiator Le Duc Tho and National Security Advisor Henry Kissinger held frequent private talks in a Paris suburb, and by October it appeared that a peace settlement was imminent. The United States dropped its demand for the withdrawal of NVA forces from the South, and North Vietnam no longer insisted on the removal of South Vietnamese president Nguyen Van Thieu. However, after hearing the details, President Thieu denounced the settlement. Kissinger and Le Duc Tho resumed negotiations but they stalled in December over the future of South Vietnam. It was a contest of wills, and Hanoi evidently believed that U.S. antiwar sentiment would cause Nixon to capitulate.

Nixon, on December 17, 1972, ordered an intensive bombing of Hanoi, which critics dubbed the Christmas bombing, and after an 11-day air campaign (Operation Linebacker II) the North Vietnamese agreed to resume the talks. When negotiations reconvened on January 8, 1973, Hanoi soon agreed to terms. The January agreement was substantially the same as the one in October. Nixon repeatedly assured Thieu of continued U.S. support and advised him to approve the settlement and a formal agreement, the Paris Peace Accords, was signed on January 27.

Earlier, seeking to overcome South Vietnamese objections to a peace that allowed substantial numbers of NVA forces to remain in the South, Nixon had assured Thieu that the United States would take "swift and severe retaliatory action" if the North Vietnamese failed to abide by the terms of the agreement. However, when the North Vietnamese tested the U.S. response with a multi-division attack on Phuoc Long Province in December 1974, Nixon was no longer president. Undone by the Watergate scandal, he had left office four months before. Nixon suffered a stroke on April 18, 1994, and died four days later at the age of 81.

Nolting, Frederick E. (1911–1989)
U.S. ambassador to South Vietnam, 1961–63
Born in Richmond, Virginia, Nolting served in the navy during World War II, then joined the Foreign Service in 1946. He was chosen by President John F. Kennedy to become U.S. ambassador to South Vietnam early in 1961. As ambassador, Nolting believed that President Diem's anticommunism made him worthy of unqualified U.S. support despite his repressive rule. Diem promised democratic reforms in exchange for more U.S. advisers, whose numbers increased from 2,000 to 16,000 during Nolting's tenure. The reforms never materialized, but Nolting did not press Diem and continued to praise Diem, sending back positive reports on his government and military. The Buddhist crisis that erupted in May 1963 demonstrated that Nolting's praise and positive reports were unfounded. In August, Nolting, whom President Kennedy felt had become too identified with the favored Diem regime, was replaced by Henry Cabot Lodge. Shortly thereafter, Diem sent troops on raids against Buddhist temples only days after assuring Nolting he would respect Buddhist rights. Back in Washington, Nolting's devotion to Diem never wavered and he argued against U.S. support for a coup. In early 1964, he left government

service in disgust over the U.S.-approved coup that killed Diem in November 1963.

Norodom Sihanouk (1922–   )
Twice king of Cambodia, 1941–55 and 1933–2004; premier, Cambodia, 1955–70; Cambodian head of state, 1993
Born on October 31, 1922, into the royal family of Cambodia, Prince Sihanouk was educated in French schools in Indochina and Paris before being elected by the royal council to the Cambodian throne in 1941. When Japan occupied Indochina during World War II, Sihanouk was kept a virtual prisoner. After the post–World War II French reoccupation, Sihanouk proclaimed a limited monarchy, and elections in 1947 made him head of state. Two years later Cambodia became one of the three "associated states" of Indochina, and at the Geneva Conference in 1954 it won total independence. When war broke out in Vietnam in 1959, Sihanouk bent with the wind. In 1956, he announced Cambodia would follow a neutralist policy. When it appeared the North Vietnamese would be victorious, he allowed them to use the port of Sihanoukville (Kampong Som) to bring in war supplies and to rent Cambodian trucks to haul the supplies to their base areas along the Vietnamese border. By the late 1960s when North Vietnam appeared to be losing, he intimated that he would not object if these base areas were attacked. In March 1969, the secret bombing of Cambodia began. In reaction the North Vietnamese began supplying the poorly armed Cambodian Communist Party—the Khmer Rouge. While Sihanouk was traveling abroad, Cambodian general Lon Nol seized power on March 18, 1970. Sihanouk lived in exile in Beijing and allied himself with the Khmer Rouge guerrillas. After the 1975 Khmer Rouge takeover, he returned to Cambodia and was placed under house arrest. He was released when Vietnam invaded Cambodia in 1978. Sihanouk served briefly as the symbolic head of state in 1993 following UN-supervised elections.

O'Daniel, John W. (1894–1975)

U.S. Army general; chief of U.S. Military Assistance Advisory Group–Indochina (MAAG–I), 1954–56

Lieutenant General John "Iron Mike" O'Daniel, a veteran of three wars, had trained South Korea's army and was U.S. Army commander in the Pacific when he was sent to Vietnam by President Eisenhower to assess French military needs in 1953. A year later, O'Daniel returned to head the first U.S. MAAG in Indochina. He expressed confidence that the French and, later, President Diem, would win against the Communists. He trained South Vietnam's military to repel a Korea-style conventional invasion, but not to counter a guerrilla war. O'Daniel departed Vietnam in October 1955, retired, and was the first chairman of the American Friends of Vietnam (AFV), a private advocacy group dedicated to strengthening U.S. support for the Republic of Vietnam. He remained loyal to Diem, even after most of the other members of the organization had lost faith in Diem's ability to stop the Communists. He resigned from the AFV in September 1963.

Peers, William R. (1914–1984)

U.S. Army general

Peers, who commanded the army's 4th Infantry Division and the I Field Force in Vietnam, headed a special army board to investigate the American Division's cover-up of the My Lai massacre. The board's strongly worded 225-page report, known as the Peers Report, released in 1970, fixed responsibility at several levels and led to court-martial charges against 12 army participants. Peers served a final tour of duty as deputy commanding general of the Eighth Army in Korea before retiring in 1973. He died in 1984 at the age of 69 at the Presidio of San Francisco.

Pham Hung (1912–1988)

Chief, Central Office of South Vietnam (COSVN), 1967–75

Born Pham Van Thien, Pham Hung joined the newly formed Indochinese Communist Party in 1930. A protégé of Pham Van Dong's, in 1956 he became the highest-ranking party official from southern Vietnam elected to the Politburo. Nine years later, Hung secretly returned to take charge of the Viet Cong insurgency. As head of COSVN, he oversaw the Tet Offensive in 1968 and served as political commissar for General Van Tien Dung during the 1975 Spring Offensive that resulted in the fall of South Vietnam.

Pham Van Dong (1906–2000)

Premier of Democratic Republic of Vietnam, 1955–76, and of the Socialist Republic of Vietnam, 1975–86

Born on March 1, 1906, into a gentry family in central Vietnam's Quang Ngai Province, he attended school in Hue with Vo Nguyen Giap and Ngo Dinh Diem. In 1926, he joined Ho Chi Minh's Revolutionary Youth League, and from 1931 to 1937 he was in France's infamous Poulo Condore prison. With Ho and Giap he founded the Viet Minh. He was named finance minister of the DRV in 1946 and, as foreign minister, represented the DRV at the Geneva Conference of 1954. As prime minister, he strongly opposed a negotiated settlement with the United States, and upon Ho's death in 1969, he became the most visible international leader of the DRV. He played a key role in approving Hanoi's tactical concessions in the 1973 cease-fire agreement and then the subsequent decisions to continue the fighting. He approved the April 1975 final North Vietnamese offensive and supervised the Communist takeover of the South, where 400,000 people were sent to "reeducation" camps. After 1976, he received considerable blame for an economic collapse that followed in the postwar years. In 1981, he was forced to introduce capitalist incentives, especially in the South. The Politburo replaced him as prime minister in December 1986. He retained respect, however, as one of the heroes of the revolution and served as an adviser to the Party Central Committee from 1987 to 1997.

Phan Boi Chau (1867–1940)

Anticolonial nationalist leader

Phan Boi Chau began working against French colonialism in 1903, forming revolutionary organizations and writing patriotic tracts. While in exile in China, he formed the Vietnam Restoration Society and encouraged resistance in Vietnam between 1907 and 1918. In 1925, he was arrested by the French in Shanghai and imprisoned in Hanoi. Eventually paroled, he lived in retirement until his death in 1940 in Hue.

Phoumi Nosavan (1920–1985)
Rightist leader in Laos

Nosavan was born in Savannakhet. He served in the colonial administration, but became a leader in the Lao Issara (Free Laos) movement, cooperating with the Vietnamese. In 1950, he switched sides and joined the Lao National Army allied with the French. He became chief of the General Staff in 1955, and in 1958 he became a leader of the CIA-supported Committee for the Defense of National Interests, a group of mostly young, rightwing officers and government officials. Despite considerable U.S. aid in the late 1950s, Phoumi was unable to develop an effective national army. In August 1960, a coup organized by Kong Le brought the neutralists to power and Phoumi retreated to Savannakhet. However, before the end of the year, Phoumi and his forces, supported by the CIA and Thailand, drove the neutralists from power. Although he made Prince Boun Oum prime minister, Phoumi was the real head of government until 1962, when he became deputy prime minister and minister of finance in the Second Coalition Government, headed by a neutralist, Prince Souvanna Phouma. Phoumi fled to Thailand after a failed rightist coup in 1965. He remained there in exile until his death.

Pol Pot (1925–1998)
Leader of the Khmer Rouge, prime minister, Democratic Kampuchea, 1976–79

Born Saloth Sar in Kompong Thom Province, Cambodia. His parents were landowners and had royal connections. Sar was sent to Phnom Penh at the age of six to join his brother Loth Suong, who worked in the palace as an administrator. Sar's upbringing was strict, and he was isolated from Cambodia's vernacular culture. In 1948, he received a scholarship to study radio electricity in Paris, where he joined the Cambodian section of the French Communist Party. His scholarship ended after he failed his course three years in a row, and he arrived home in January 1953, just after King Sihanouk declared martial law to suppress Cambodia's independence movement, which was becoming radicalized in response to French colonial repression.

In 1953, Sar joined the Cambodian and Vietnamese Communists. Following independence in 1954, Sar rose within the Cambodian Communist movement, becoming party leader in 1962. He believed that under his rule Cambodia would recover its pro-Buddhist glory by rebuilding the powerful economy of the medieval Angkor kingdom and regaining ancient territory from Vietnam and Thailand. Pol Pot's group treasured the Cambodian "race," not individuals, and believed that impurities included the foreign-educated (himself and his colleagues excepted) and "hereditary enemies," especially the Vietnamese. He wanted to return Cambodia to its "pure" origins. Pol Pot saw the need for war and for secrecy as "the basis of the revolution." In 1966, he began planning an uprising against the Cambodian ruler, Prince Sihanouk.

In 1975, after defeating Lon Nol, the U.S.-backed general who overthrew Sihanouk in a 1970 coup, Pol Pot became prime minister.

Immediately after the fall of Phnom Penh, the Khmer Rouge began to implement reforms to return the nation to "Year Zero," ordering the evacuation of the capital city and other recently captured towns and cities. Pol Pot then instituted a draconian agrarian program that resulted in the murder and starvation of hundreds of thousands of Cambodians, including politicians, intellectuals, and those from many other walks of life.

A true nationalist chauvinist, Pol Pot could not see Cambodia among its neighbors in a community of nations. He shared the traditional Khmer elite's racism and grandiose designs on "lost territories." Raids on Laos, Thailand, and Vietnam began simultaneously in 1977.

He imposed policies that resulted in a holocaust against his own countrymen in which some 1.5 million Cambodians died. His identity as Saloth Sar was realized in late 1978, when his brother, Loth Suong, recognized him in a poster. Two months later the Pol Pot regime was overthrown by the invading army of the Socialist Republic of Vietnam. He led a guerrilla campaign against the Vietnam-supported government until 1985 when he resigned from the Khmer Rouge party, citing asthma as a contributing factor, but he continued as the dominant force in the anti-Vietnam movement. In 1989 when the Vietnamese withdrew from Cambodia, Pol Pot and the Khmer Rouge refused to cooperate with the peace process and continued to fight against the forces of the new government in Phnom Penh. In June 1997, Pol Pot ordered the execution of his life-long right-hand man, Son Sen. This caused a backlash among other Khmer Rouge leaders, who arrested him and subjected him to a slow trial for the death of his subordinate. He was placed under house arrest, during which he died, reportedly from heart failure.

Porter, William J. (1914–1988)

U.S. deputy ambassador to South Vietnam; delegate to the Paris Peace Talks

For 18 months in 1965, Porter was responsible for coordinating the pacification programs of U.S. government agencies in South Vietnam. He pulled together several overlapping agencies under the umbrella of his Office of Civilian Operations (OCO). Ultimately, however, the effort fell short and pacification was reassigned to military control. In September 1971, President Richard Nixon appointed Porter to replace David K. E. Burns as chief of the U.S. delegation at the Paris peace talks.

Radford, Arthur W. (1896–1973)

Admiral, U.S. Navy; chairman, Joint Chiefs of Staff (JCS), 1953–57

A veteran of three wars, Admiral Radford helped devise President Eisenhower's "New Look" defense

policy in the 1950s. In March 1954 when the French asked for U.S. help during the siege of Dien Bien Phu, Admiral Radford proposed massive U.S. air strikes, possibly including nuclear weapons, against the Viet Minh. President Eisenhower rejected the plan, code named Operation Vulture, after Congress and the European Allies refused their support. In later discussions about how to deal with the developing situation in Vietnam, Radford argued that the United States should contain the Democratic Republic of Vietnam with airpower while American ground forces played only a limited role. In his view, South Vietnamese ground forces would be responsible for stopping any invasion by the North Vietnamese Army. Radford retired from the navy in 1957.

Ridgway, Matthew Bunker (1895–1993)

U.S. Army general; U.S. Army chief of staff, 1953–55

General Ridgway, who commanded army combat divisions in World War II and was the senior U.S. commander in the latter years of the Korean War, was opposed to U.S. involvement in the French war in Indochina, 1953–55. He also argued against providing U.S. air support to the French during the Dien Bien Phu crisis in 1954, believing that ground operations would inevitably follow. In later years, he remained skeptical of U.S. Vietnam policy and, as one of President Johnson's senior advisers known as the "Wise Men," Ridgway urged him to de-escalate the Vietnam War in 1968.

Rogers, William P. (1913–2001)

Deputy attorney general, 1953–1957; secretary of state, 1969–73

Rogers, an attorney who served as a naval officer in World War II, was deputy attorney general of the United States from 1953 to 1957, and attorney general from 1957 to 1961. He then left government service for eight years, becoming a senior partner in a law firm. When Richard Nixon, a close friend, was elected president in 1968, he selected Rogers as his secretary of state. During Rogers's tenure at the State Department, Vietnam policy was formulated by President Nixon and National Security Advisor Henry Kissinger, with little input from Rogers. Rogers was a strong supporter of Nixon's Vietnamization program and U.S. troop withdrawal, but strongly disagreed with Nixon's covert bombing of Cambodia, which began in 1969, and the invasion of Cambodia in 1970. He resigned in September 1973; Kissinger replaced him as secretary of state. Rogers returned to the private practice of law; in 1986 he chaired the committee that investigated the explosion of the space shuttle *Challenger*.

Rostow, Walt Whitman (1916–2003)

Special assistant for national security affairs, 1961–66; National Security Advisor, 1966–69

An economics professor, Rostow served as part of the Kennedy administration "brain trust," as Deputy National Security Advisor under McGeorge Bundy. In the early 1960s, Rostow advocated a strong U.S. diplomatic and military role in Vietnam and Laos to combat Communist insurgencies. As the Viet Cong insurgency grew, Rostow suggested bombing the North to defeat the guerrillas in the South, because he believed that the Viet Cong were controlled from the Democratic Republic of Vietnam. President Kennedy rejected the idea, but President Johnson approved it in 1965. When bombing of North Vietnam began in earnest, Rostow succeeded Bundy as National Security Advisor to President Johnson and continued in that capacity until January 1969, when he left government service.

In his new position, Rostow repeatedly recommended systematic and continued bombing of critical targets in North Vietnam, including petroleum facilities. When public opinion turned against the war, President Johnson relied heavily on Rostow's optimism and perseverance. In 1967, Rostow moderated his commitment to bombing by seemingly supporting a proposal to limit bombing raids to the southern panhandle of North Vietnam, although he maintained that the bombing of the Hanoi-Haiphong area had to

be left as an option. When Secretary of Defense Robert McNamara proposed a bombing halt in November, however, Rostow opposed it. After the 1968 Tet Offensive, Rostow served on the "wise men," where he advocated intensifying the bombing, mobilizing the Reserves, and sending more troops to Vietnam. However, Johnson was swayed by the other members of the group, who almost unanimously recommended de-escalation, a decision that he announced on March 31, 1968, and that included a partial bombing halt as an inducement to negotiations.

Rusk, David Dean (1909–1994)

Assistant U.S. secretary of state for Far Eastern affairs, 1950–1952; secretary of state, 1961–69

Born on February 9, 1909, in Cherokee County, Georgia, Rusk graduated from Davidson College in 1931 and later studied at Oxford as a Rhodes Scholar. As a U.S. Army infantry officer, Rusk served in the China-Burma-India theater as operations officer to General Joseph Stilwell. In 1946, Rusk joined the State Department. He was appointed Assistant Secretary of State for Far Eastern Affairs at the beginning of the Korean War. In 1952, he left the State Department to head the Rockefeller Foundation.

In December 1960, president-elect Kennedy selected Rusk as his secretary of state. Rusk attempted to limit the role of the State Department in Vietnam, believing that American involvement there should be primarily military. But as the U.S. advisory role expanded and as the United States became increasingly concerned with South Vietnamese president Ngo Dinh Diem's ability to carry out internal reforms, Rusk played a more active role.

In August 1963, top U.S. foreign policy advisers began to reevaluate American support for Diem. Rusk, sensing Diem's isolation from the people of South Vietnam and his inability or unwillingness to stop the government's repression of Buddhists, advised that a change in government might be necessary. Prepared by State Department officials, the initial instructions sent to Ambassador Henry Cabot Lodge reflected Rusk's position. Lodge was told Diem must be given every chance to rid himself of elements hostile to reform, but that if he remained obdurate, the United States must "face the possibility that Diem himself cannot be preserved." Lodge was also instructed to inform military leaders, who had been planning to overthrow Diem, that the United States would not attempt to thwart a coup. Rusk's role in the complicated decision making that preceded a coup on November 1 is not clear, as he preferred to let his subordinates, including Lodge, Averell Harriman, and Roger Hilsman, expound the need for change in South Vietnam.

Rusk's influence on Vietnam policy increased markedly after Lyndon Johnson assumed the presidency. He helped Johnson make important decisions on escalation of the conflict. During 1964 and 1965, Rusk opposed attempts to negotiate a settlement, arguing that with the VC controlling more than half of South Vietnam, the United States could not bargain from a position of strength. Until military pressure on Hanoi tilted the balance of power in favor of the Saigon government, Rusk asserted, the North Vietnamese would have little incentive to negotiate. Rusk opposed the bombing halt of December 1965–January 1966 for similar reasons.

In addition to serving as a key adviser to the president, Rusk emerged as a chief public defender of administration policy. In February 1966, he appeared at televised hearings of the Senate Foreign Relations Committee, chaired by Senator J. William Fulbright, to explain administration policy on Vietnam. Rusk sought to refute Fulbright's charge that the conflict was a civil war in which the United States had no strategic interest by describing what he believed to be a long-term pattern of Communist Chinese aggression. In an October 1967 press conference, he justified the U.S. presence in Southeast Asia as necessary to protect the region from the future threat of "a billion Chinese ... armed with nuclear weapons."

When the military requested an additional 200,000 troops after the Tet Offensive of February 1968, Rusk recommended that the president approve the increase. However, after the "Wise Men," a bipartisan panel of statesmen, recommended disengagement from the war because of its detrimental effects on the American economy and society, Johnson announced a policy of de-escalation and his desire to enter into negotiations with the North Vietnamese. Hanoi accepted Johnson's offer with the provision that initial meetings deal only with the conditions required for a total bombing halt. Rusk appears to have felt that such talks were not in the best interests of the United States. When the talks began in Paris in May 1968, Rusk played little part in them.

Rusk saw the conflict in Southeast Asia as an attempt by a militant Chinese government to expand its influence throughout Asia by means of "wars of liberation." Consequently, he argued, the United States was not in Vietnam simply because of commitments but because of the need to show that such expansion was doomed to failure. Although Rusk asserted that victory in Vietnam was necessary for American security, he did not define the war primarily as a battle for a strategic area but rather emphasized that it was a "psychological struggle for the conquest of minds and souls." The loss of Vietnam, he said, would mean "a drastic loss of confidence in the will and capacity of the free world to oppose aggression." Rusk left office in January 1969.

Russell, Richard B. (1897–1971)
U.S. senator (D-Georgia), 1933–71

Born in Winder, Georgia, Russell was elected to the U.S. Senate in 1932 and served there from 1933 until his death. As chairman of the Armed Services Committee, 1951–1953 and 1955–1969, he greatly influenced military appropriations and policy. He advised President Eisenhower in 1954 not to intervene militarily to help the French at Dien Bien Phu, and initially opposed U.S. involvement in Vietnam because he did not consider North Vietnam a threat to U.S. interests. However, once U.S. troops were committed, Russell, a close friend of President Johnson, advocated that victory should be pursued vigorously. After the 1968 Tet Offensive, he rejected piecemeal escalation of the ground war and called for full-scale bombing of North Vietnam. In 1969, he stepped down from the chairmanship of the Armed Services Committee to become chairman of the Appropriations Committee. Russell was one of the few Democratic senators who supported the Cambodian Incursion of 1970.

Sainteny, Jean (1907–1978)

French diplomat

Sainteny represented the French government during negotiations with Ho Chi Minh following World War II. In March 1946, Sainteny and Ho agreed to accords in which France would recognize the Democratic Republic of Vietnam as a free state within the French Union. By December, however, the agreement broke down, resulting in the eight-year Indochina War. Sainteny represented France on three later diplomatic missions, including a 1966 peace effort. In 1969, he brokered correspondence between Nixon administration national security advisor Henry Kissinger and the North Vietnamese leadership. Sainteny also arranged the 1972 secret meetings between Kissinger and Le Duc Tho in Paris.

Salisbury, Harrison E. (1908–1993)

Journalist

Salisbury was a reporter for United Press from 1930 to 1948. He joined the *New York Times* in 1949 and won a Pulitzer Prize in 1955 for his reporting while serving as *Times* bureau chief in Moscow. He played a controversial role in the reporting of the Vietnam War. In December 1965, he was the first American newsman to travel to the Democratic Republic of Vietnam, where he reported that U.S. planes were bombing civilian targets, a claim that the Johnson administration denied. He was strongly criticized by President Johnson, Pentagon officials, and some of his fellow journalists, for providing aid and comfort to the enemy.

Schlesinger, James Rodney (1929–)

Director of the Central Intelligence Agency (CIA), 1973; U.S. secretary of defense, 1973–75

As secretary of defense, Schlesinger, like his predecessor, Elliot Richardson, and William Rogers at the State Department, was largely bypassed in Vietnam policy-making by Henry Kissinger. Schlesinger was considered a hard-liner and as secretary of defense made several speeches defending the bombing of Cambodia in 1969–70. He coordinated the May 1975 military response to Cambodian seizure of the *Mayaguez,* the U.S.-registered container ship. Schlesinger, who often disagreed with President Ford, was fired in November of 1975 and was replaced by Donald Rumsfeld.

Sharp, Ulysses S. Grant (1906–2001)

Admiral, U.S. Navy; commander in chief, Pacific, 1964–68

Sharp graduated from the U.S. Naval Academy in 1927 and commanded several combat vessels during World War II. Appointed commander-in-chief of the Pacific Fleet on September 30, 1963, he controlled the Seventh Fleet's air operations over North Vietnam and Laos and surface operations in the western Pacific. On June 30, 1964, he was promoted to commander-in-chief, Pacific. Six weeks later, after the Tonkin Gulf incident, he planned the retaliatory airstrikes, the first U.S. bombing of North Vietnam. He was one of the most hard-line proponents of the war, which he supported as necessary to "stop communist-supported aggression." He believed that the war could be won "by keeping the pressure on North Vietnam through air attacks," and he often argued against bombing halts and target restrictions. He was responsible for overseeing the U.S. buildup in Vietnam and for executing American strategy in the theater of war. On July 31, 1968, Admiral Sharp relinquished his command and retired from active duty. He later wrote his memoirs, in which he was strongly critical of the way the war was handled, saying that "The war was lost in Washington, not on the battlefield."

Sheehan, Neil (1936–   )
Journalist
Sent to Saigon in April 1962 as the Saigon bureau chief for United Press International, Sheehan at first was supportive of U.S. involvement in the war, but soon became very suspicious of what he decided was the false optimism of senior U.S. military officials such as General Paul Harkins. He initially incurred official ire with his eyewitness reporting of the stunning defeat suffered by South Vietnamese troops at the Battle of Ap Bac in January 1963. Harkins, wanting to put a positive spin on the situation, proclaimed the battle a great victory for the South Vietnamese. Washington accepted Harkins's account and assailed Sheehan and the other journalists who had reported otherwise. Sheehan continued to report from Vietnam until he departed in 1964 to join the staff of the *New York Times*. He returned in 1965 and was among the first to dispatch firsthand accounts of the bloody fighting in the Ia Drang Valley. He left Vietnam in 1966, but continued to report on the war from Washington. In 1968, he broke the story of Westmoreland's large troop request in the wake of the Tet Offensive. Daniel Ellsberg later leaked the Pentagon Papers to Sheehan, who published them in the *Times*.

Shoup, David M. (1904–1983)
General, U.S. Marine Corps; Commandant of the Marine Corps, 1960–1963
General Shoup, a highly decorated marine who commanded the spearhead battalion at the Tarawa landing in World War II, became the 22nd commandant of the Marine Corps. While commandant, Shoup counseled against U.S. involvement in Vietnam, but never openly questioned policy. However, after his retirement in 1963, he spoke out against the war. In a May 1966 speech, he said he believed that all of Southeast Asia was not "worth the life and limb of a single American." In an April 1969 edition of *Atlantic Monthly,* Shoup warned that anti-communism provided the perfect climate to nurture a "new American militarism" in the defense establishment.

Souphanouvong, Prince (1909–1995)
Leader of Pathet Lao movement; first president of the Lao People's Democratic Republic, 1975–86
The younger half-brother of the Lao prime minister, Prince Souvanna Phouma, was a leader in the post-World War II Lao Issara (Free Laos) independence movement. However, he became disenchanted with the group's political policies and sought assistance from the Viet Minh. He was closely associated with Ho Chi Minh from before World War II and he became a leader in the Viet Minh-supported Communist Pathet Lao. During the Vietnam War, Souphanouvong and other Pathet Lao leaders lived in a cave complex in northeastern Laos. Following the U.S. withdrawal from Vietnam, the prince returned to the Lao capital and in mid-1974 joined the new coalition government as president of the newly formed National Political Consultative Council, but this government eventually collapsed. In December 1975, the communists established the Lao People's Democratic Republic and Souphanouvong became its first president.

Souvanna Phouma, Prince (1901–1984)
Prime minister of Laos, 1951–54, 1956–58, 1960, 1962–75
An older half-brother of Prince Souphanouvong, Souvanna Phouma was head of the wartime Pathet Lao Communist movement. A proclaimed neutralist for most of his life, Souvanna was often called upon to head the politically fractured government of Laos. His willingness in the 1950s to allow participation in the central government by members of the Pathet Lao led to charges by right-wing Lao officials and the U.S. government that Laos would be taken over by Communist agents. After 1962, Souvanna, under pressure from the Lao right wing and the U.S. government, abandoned the Pathet Lao in a coalition government. From 1963 until the 1973 American withdrawal from South Vietnam, Souvanna's government publicly declared a neutral policy with regard to the Vietnam War. In reality the prime minister allowed the United

States to conduct bombing and reconnaissance campaigns against Communist supply routes in Laos and supported U.S. efforts to use Lao hill tribes in ground and air operations against Pathet Lao and North Vietnamese forces in Laos. Upon the December 1975 Communist takeover of Laos, Souvanna was named special adviser to the president of the Lao People's Democratic Republic.

Spock, Benjamin (1903–1998)
Author; pediatrician; antiwar activist

Dr. Spock's reputation as America's preeminent child care authority earned him a leading role in U.S. domestic opposition to the Vietnam War. He first became known as a peace activist when he joined the National Committee for Sane Nuclear Policy in 1962. He supported Lyndon Johnson during the 1964 election, believing his campaign promises for peace. As the United States became more involved in the Vietnam War, Spock began to speak against the war and urge draft resistance. An active participant in many protests, he tried to unite moderate and radical antiwar groups. In January 1968, he and four others were indicted for conspiring to aid and encourage violations of the Selective Service law and hinder administration of the draft. All but one of the "Boston Five" were found guilty, fined, and sentenced to two years' imprisonment. However, the U.S. First Circuit Court of Appeals overturned the conviction of Spock and one other defendant.

Stennis, John Cornelius (1901–1995)
U.S. senator (D-Mississippi), 1947–89

Born on August 3, 1901, in Kemper County, Mississippi, Stennis graduated from Mississippi State College in 1923 and received a law degree from the University of Virginia in 1928. He became a circuit judge in 1937 and 10 years later succeeded Theodore Bilbo in the U.S. Senate. A conservative Democrat, Stennis opposed social welfare programs and supported military appropriation requests. He was initially skeptical about the propriety of U.S. involvement in Southeast Asia, but believed

that once the United States had committed itself, it could not shrink from that commitment, and he supported the Johnson administration's war effort in Vietnam. An influential member of the Armed Services Committee who became its chairman in 1969, Stennis favored maximum use of air power against the North Vietnamese and the VC to achieve a prompt victory and he believed that direction of the war effort should be left to the military. Although he strongly backed President Nixon's Southeast Asia policy, Stennis worked to curb the president's war-making power, co-sponsoring the War Powers Act with Jacob Javits in 1971.

Stevenson, Adlai E. III (1900–1965)
U.S. ambassador to the United Nations, 1961–65

In 1964, Stevenson, a cold war liberal, discussed with UN Secretary-general U Thant the prospects for secret U.S.-North Vietnamese negotiations. Stevenson passed the information on to Secretary of State Dean Rusk, but the administration did not respond. Although he believed that military intervention was a bad idea and favored political and economic means of countering communism, Stevenson consistently defended U.S. policy in Vietnam.

Sullivan, William H. (1922–   )
U.S. ambassador to Laos

A career Foreign Service officer, Sullivan served as deputy U.S. representative to the 1962 Geneva Conference. In 1964, President Lyndon Johnson appointed Sullivan ambassador to Laos. In that position, he exerted more control over U.S. military operations in Laos than his counterpart in Saigon was able to do. He directed the secret U.S. bombing campaign in Laos. He left Laos in March 1969 to return to the State Department, where he helped draft the proposals that the United States put forth at the Paris peace talks. Sullivan then served as Henry Kissinger's chief deputy in Paris and played a major role in negotiating the agreement signed on January 27, 1973.

Taylor, Maxwell Davenport (1901–1987)

U.S. Army general; U.S. Army chief of staff, 1955–59; chairman, Joint Chiefs of Staff (JCS), 1962–64; ambassador to South Vietnam, 1964–65

Capping a brilliant military career in World War II and Korea, he was appointed army chief of staff in 1955. Opposed to the idea of total reliance on nuclear weapons for America's defenses that prevailed at the time, General Taylor advocated building up conventional (nonnuclear) forces as an alternative to nuclear war, though his attempts to persuade the budget-minded Eisenhower administration, which saw nuclear weapons as a "cheap" way to provide national security, met with only limited success. General Taylor retired from active duty on July 1, 1959.

His 1959 book, *The Uncertain Trumpet*, which detailed his proposals for a more flexible response, brought Taylor to the attention of Senator John F. Kennedy and some of Taylor's arguments were used in Kennedy's successful 1960 presidential campaign. On July 1, 1961, Taylor, who would become one of Kennedy's most influential advisers, was named Military Representative to the President, a post reportedly established because President Kennedy had lost faith in the military advice he was getting from the Joint Chiefs of Staff. Returning from a special mission to South Vietnam in November, Taylor recommended sending more military aid and advisers to Vietnam and pressing President Ngo Dinh Diem to carry out reforms. In a report kept secret at the time, Taylor also advised dispatching 8,000 combat troops to South Vietnam as a sign of U.S. commitment and as a reserve emergency force. Kennedy decided not to send combat troops, but approved the other recommendations.

In 1962, General Taylor was recalled to active duty and named chairman of the Joint Chiefs of Staff. After President Kennedy's assassination, President Johnson appointed Taylor ambassador to South Vietnam in July 1964. As ambassador, he pressed for the return of civilian rule after the military coup that overthrew Diem in 1963. In July 1965, General Taylor relinquished that post and served as a special consultant to President Johnson. He was a member of the "Wise Men" convened in March 1968 to advise President Johnson on the course of the war, but he opposed the policy of disengagement recommended by a majority of the group. In 1969, he returned to private life.

Thich Quang Duc (1907–1963)

Buddhist monk

Thich Quang Duc was the first Buddhist monk to immolate himself in public to protest the Ngo Dinh Diem regime's treatment of the Buddhists. The immolation took place in Saigon on June 11, 1963. It provoked widespread shock and led to months of confrontation between South Vietnamese police and Buddhist monks. This unrest helped convince the Kennedy administration that Diem would never win the support of his people and provided the catalyst for the coup by South Vietnamese generals that resulted in the murder of Diem and his brother Nhu.

Thompson, Robert G. K. (1916–1992)

British counterinsurgency expert

Sir Robert Thompson was a noted counterinsurgency authority who had helped the British suppress the insurgency in Malaya. As head of the British advisory mission to Vietnam from 1961 to 1965, he was very influential in his attempts to have the "lessons" of the British effort in Malaya applied to Vietnam. Based on his experience, he urged President Ngo Dinh Diem to adopt the Strategic Hamlet program, which proved to be fatally flawed. Later in the 1960s, Thompson served as a key unofficial adviser to President Nixon, endorsing the Vietnamization strategy.

Tran Do (1922–2002)

General, People's Army of Vietnam

General Tran Do moved south in 1963 to become head of the Political Department of the Central Office for South Vietnam (COSVN), which controlled and directed the political and military activities of the National Liberation Front against the Saigon government. During the war, he was one of five deputy commanders of the People's Liberation Armed Forces (PLAF). One of the key field commanders in the South, he increased the number of North Vietnamese commanders, political officers, and technical experts within the NLF to insure the North's oversight and control. One of the architects of the 1968 Tet Offensive, he later acknowledged that the offensive failed in its main goal of inciting uprisings across the South, although it had the unintended result of turning American public opinion against the war.

Tran Thien Khiem (1925–   )
General, Army of the Republic of Vietnam

General Tran Thien Khiem was chief of staff when he helped overthrow President Diem in November 1963. He then held many offices in South Vietnam's government: defense minister (1964) under General Nguyen Khanh, ambassador to the United States (1965–68) under President Nguyen Cao Ky, and prime minister (1969–75) under President Nguyen Van Thieu. As prime minister, Khiem was believed to be involved in the narcotics trade, using money from the sale of heroin to fund his political activities. When Communist forces captured Saigon in April 1975, Khiem escaped to Taiwan and from there to France.

Tran Van Don (1917–   )
General, Army of the Republic of Vietnam

Don, attending the University of Paris, was called to active duty as a cadet in the French army when World War II began in 1939; he won the Croix de Guerre at the Battle of the Loire, but was captured by the Nazis in the blitzkrieg that led to the fall of France in 1940. Released after France's surrender, he returned to Vietnam and in 1942 was promoted to second lieutenant in the French Army Reserves, in which he served until the Republic of Vietnam was established in 1954. In December 1962, he returned to Saigon as commander of the army. Although initially a Diem supporter, he joined three other generals who orchestrated the November 1963 coup against Ngo Dinh Diem and

controlled the government until they were subsequently overthrown by Nguyen Khanh's coup in January 1964. He retired from the army in 1965 and won election to the Senate, where he served until 1970, but then won election to the House of Representatives in 1971. He escaped to the United States just before Saigon fell in April 1975.

Tran Van Huong (1903–1982)
Prime minister of South Vietnam, 1964–65, 1968–69, 1975; vice president, 1971–75

Tran Van Huong, the mayor of Saigon, was named prime minister in October 1964. In December 1964, the Armed Forces Council led by Khanh seized control of the government in a bloodless coup; Huong was left in office but had no real power. He left office in January 1965. He was again prime minister under Nguyen Van Thieu from May 1968 to August 1969. In the election of 1971, he was Thieu's running mate and served as vice president from 1971 through 1975. When Thieu fled Saigon on April 25, 1975, ahead of advancing North Vietnamese forces, he appointed Huong president, but he quickly resigned in favor of General Duong Van Minh on April 28, two days before the final collapse of the Republic of Vietnam. He remained in Vietnam after the end of the war.

Tran Van Tra (1918–1996)
General, People's Army of Vietnam; military leader of National Liberation Front (NLF); chairman, Military Affairs Committee of the Central Office of South Vietnam (COSVN), 1964–76

Tran Van Tra fought with the Viet Minh against the French from 1946 to 1954. He went to the North in 1955, where he became a lieutenant general and one of the deputy chiefs of staff of the People's Army of Vietnam (PAVN). Tra returned to the South in 1963 to assume command of the B2 Front responsible for military operations in the southern half of South Vietnam. In 1968, he was one of the commanders in charge of the assault on the capital city in the Tet Offensive. While minister of defense for the Provisional Revolutionary Government (PRG) of South Vietnam, as the NLF was renamed after the Tet Offensive, he advocated a national military campaign in 1973–75 in order to prevent the Army of the Republic of Vietnam from deploying its forces region by region. His strategy for the final push—in which he served as deputy commander—was an attack on Route 14 across Phuoc Long Province and a quick assault on Saigon from five directions. In 1982 Tran Van Tra was purged from the Vietnamese Communist Party after publishing a book about the 1975 campaign that offended powerful members of the Central Committee.

Truman, Harry S. (1884–1972)

U.S. senator (D-Missouri), 1934–44; vice president, 1944–45; president of the United States, 1945–53

Truman reversed President Franklin D. Roosevelt's tentative policy of abandoning support for a continued French presence in Indochina. Truman viewed Ho Chi Minh as a Communist puppet in the global cold war and invoked the domino theory and the policy of containment in discussing his Indochina policy. In a 1950 speech announcing his decision to send U.S. troops to Korea, Truman called for aid to the French in Vietnam. Congress appropriated funds for the French war in Indochina, a policy continued by President Eisenhower until the French defeat at Dien Bien Phu in 1954.

Truman's financial commitment to fighting the communists in Vietnam was significant in establishing U.S. interests in the country, but his ideological constructs were even more fundamental. In viewing Ho Chi Minh's forces as Communist tools in the cold war and in his repeated references to containment, Truman established the ideological framework within which the conflict would be viewed for the next two decades. In the 1960s, President Lyndon Johnson made several attempts to persuade Truman to back his Vietnam policies, but Truman would not make any public statement about the war.

Truong Chinh (1907–1988)

General secretary, Indochinese Communist Party, 1941–56; president, National Assembly, Democratic Republic of Vietnam (DRV), 1960–76; co-president, DRV, 1981–87

Born Dang Xuan Khu, Chinh helped found the Indochinese Communist Party in 1930. For the next 26 years, Chinh ranked second only to Ho Chi Minh on the Politburo. In 1956, after the excesses of his radical land reform program, Chinh resigned as general secretary of the party, but remained a member of the Politburo and the party's top ideologist. Although long opposed to capitalist reforms, Chinh, serving as general secretary, relented and initiated the Doi Moi program, which permitted the reintroduction of private enterprise in 1986. However, by the end of that year, he had stepped down from his position and gave up his membership in the Politburo.

U Thant (1909–1974)

Burmese diplomat; secretary-general, United Nations, 1961–1971

Secretary General U Thant tried to organize peace talks between U.S. and Democratic Republic of Vietnam (DRV) officials in 1964. In 1966, he called for a halt to the bombing of North Vietnam, negotiations that would include the National Liberation Front (NLF), and a reduction in military activities on all sides. In the late 1960s, U Thant sought to ban the use of U.S. herbicides in Vietnam. His pressure helped bring about the Nixon administration's renunciation of herbicide use in 1969 and led to an April 1972 international treaty outlawing the production of biological weapons.

Van Tien Dung (1917–2002)

General, People's Army of Vietnam; chief of staff, People's Army of Vietnam (PAVN), 1954–1974; PAVN commander in chief, 1974–80; Socialist Republic of Vietnam defense minister, 1980–86

Van Tien Dung, born in Ha Deng Province in Tonkin on May 1, 1917, became an active Communist revolutionary in 1936. He fought in the Viet Minh guerrilla movement against the French and the Japanese during World War II, and commanded the North Vietnamese Army's 320th Division from 1951 to 1953. Dung was appointed chief of staff of the North Vietnamese Army in 1953 and throughout the 1960s, he was second in command to General Vo Nguyen Giap. In 1971, he directed the PAVN forces that fought against the South Vietnamese in Laos during their Operation Lam Son 719. In 1972, he directed the forces that attacked south across the Demilitarized Zone during the Easter Offensive. In March 1973, he oversaw the infiltration of PAVN troops into South Vietnam after the signing of the Paris Peace Accords. He was promoted to senior general in 1974. Named commander of the PAVN forces in the South, General Dung planned and led the North Vietnamese blitzkrieg that conquered South Vietnam in March and April 1975. Dung later led the 1979 invasion of Cambodia and also directed the 1979 Sino-Vietnamese clash. In February 1980, he replaced Giap as minister of national defense. In 1986, however, he was dismissed from that position and expelled from the Politburo, but remained a member of the Central Committee until 1991.

Vang Pao (1929–)

Hmong military leader

Vang Pao worked with the French against the Viet Minh and then commanded Hmong troops against the North Vietnamese and the Pathet Lao. The CIA recruited Vang Pao as leader of the Hmong in 1960. By mid-decade he led a Hmong army of 300,000 troops. Ruthless in his domination of Hmong villagers, Vang Pao used his CIA connections to make them dependent upon his support for rice supplies. He withheld shipment of U.S. aid from villages that tried to keep their sons from entering his army. When the Pathet Lao overran his army in 1975, Vang Pao escaped to the United States with several thousand Hmong followers, and became a leader of the expatriate Hmong community.

Vann, John Paul (1924–1972)

Lieutenant colonel, U.S. Army; senior Adviser, Military Region II, 1971–72

As a U.S. Army officer and senior adviser to the ARVN in 1962–63, John Paul Vann charged that many ARVN commanders were corrupt, incompetent, and cowardly, accusations that were unpopular with his superiors. Vann retired from the army in 1963 and in March 1965, he returned to Saigon as a civilian Foreign Service Officer, to run the programs of the U.S. Operations Mission, which was controlled by the U.S. Agency for International Development (AID). In June 1967, he became head of the newly created Civil Operations and Revolutionary Development Support (CORDS) program for the area around Saigon. As such, he was responsible for all pacification activities in III Corps. In February 1969, he was moved south to take control of the CORDS effort in the Mekong Delta. In 1971, General Creighton Abrams appointed Vann, a civilian, to command all U.S. forces in II Corps and serve as the senior adviser to the ARVN commander of II Corps. He personally directed the defense of Kontum and surrounding area during the North Vietnamese 1972 Easter Offensive. On June 9, 1972, he was killed in a helicopter crash near Kontum.

Vogt, John W., Jr. (1920–)

General, U.S. Air Force; commander, Seventh Air Force, 1972–73

Born on March 19, 1920, in Elizabeth, New Jersey, Vogt enlisted in the U.S. Army Air Corps in 1941 and served as a fighter pilot during two European combat tours. From 1965 to 1968, Vogt served as deputy for plans and operations, Pacific Air Force (PACAF), in Honolulu, participating in the planning and direction of the air campaign against North Vietnam. In 1972, he was appointed commander of the Seventh Air Force in Vietnam and concurrently deputy commander of MACV and in that position commanded the massive U.S. air response to the 1972 North Vietnamese Eastertide offensive, which proved critical in turning back that invasion. He also presided over the draw-down of U.S. forces in Vietnam and the final withdrawal in March 1973 after the signing of the Paris Peace Accords. Moving his headquarters to Nakhon Phnom Royal Thai Air Force Base, he departed in the fall of 1973, thereafter to become commander of PACAF. After a subsequent tour as commander in chief, U.S. Air Forces Europe, General Vogt retired from active duty on August 1, 1975.

Vo Nguyen Giap (1911–   )

General and commander, People's Army of Vietnam (PAVN), 1946–72; minister of defense and commander in chief, Democratic Republic of Vietnam, 1946–80

Born in Quang Binh Province in the French protectorate of Annam (which would become North Vietnam's southernmost province during the Vietnam War), Giap graduated from the French-run Lycée Albert Sarraut. He joined the Indochinese Communist Party in 1930 and was jailed from 1930 to 1932. He attended the University of Hanoi Law School, graduating in 1936. He then worked as a high school history teacher and journalist, while participating in various revolutionary movements. He married Nguyen Thi Quang in 1939. When France outlawed communism during the same year, Giap fled to China together with Pham Van Dong, where they joined up with Ho Chi Minh. While he was in China, his wife, sister, father, and sister-in-law were captured and executed.

Ho entrusted Giap with the organization and command of the fledgling Viet Minh guerrilla forces, which fought against the Japanese forces occupying Vietnam from 1940 to 1945. During the political vacuum following the end of World War II, Ho and the Communists seized power in northern Vietnam and Giap became a leading figure in the new government.

When France tried to reestablish control over Vietnam the First Indochina War broke out in December 1946. At first the Viet Minh had difficulty in coping with the better trained and equipped French forces, but Giap ordered his troops into the mountainous north and began to shape his army into a potent fighting force. When Mao Zedong defeated the nationalists in China, he offered weapons and equipment to Giap and his army. The war degenerated into a bloody stalemate, but by 1953 the Viet Minh controlled several remote areas of northern Vietnam while the French controlled the Red River Valley in the north and most of the south.

The war reached a climax in 1954 when Giap directed the Viet Minh siege that overwhelmed the French garrison at Dien Bien Phu and effectively won Vietnam its independence. Giap became North Vietnam's minister of defense, a member of the ruling Politburo, and commander in chief of the People's Army of Vietnam (PAVN).

In the late 1950s and 1960s, Giap remained a key military figure in the Democratic Republic of Vietnam. Giap was a proponent of protracted war, focused on guerrilla operations and the advancement of a Communist political base in the South. He disagreed with the aggressive way that Nguyen Chi Thanh prosecuted the war in the South; Giap's tactical concerns were largely validated after PAVN forces suffered extensive defeats in 1965–66.

The 1968 Tet Offensive was originally Nguyen Chi Thanh's idea, but after Thanh's death, Giap had the responsibility for planning and directing the campaign. The offensive resulted in a tactical disaster for the Communists when the expected popular uprising in support of their forces failed to develop.

In 1972, Giap convinced the Politburo that because the majority of U.S. ground combat forces had been withdrawn, the time was ripe to commit the entire NVA to combat in the South. Launching some 14 infantry divisions reinforced by Soviet-supplied tanks and artillery in what became known as the Eastertide Offensive of March 1972, Giap's forces were initially successful, capturing the provincial capital of Quang Tri in I Corps. However, his attacks in the Central Highlands and at An Loc in III Corps were stopped cold by a determined South Vietnamese defense supported by massive American fire power, including air strikes by U.S. B-52 bombers. Estimates are that the PAVN suffered more than 100,000 casualties and lost more than half of its tanks and heavy artillery.

Tarnished by these successive failures, General Giap was eased from power in favor of his protégé, the PAVN chief of staff, Senior General Van Tien Dung, who had commanded a division under Giap at Dien Bien Phu. It was Dung, not Giap, who planned and commanded the final offensive that conquered South Vietnam in 1975. In 1980, General Giap was formally replaced as minister of defense by General Dung and in 1982 he lost his seat on the Politburo. He now lives in virtual retirement in Hanoi.

Walt, Lewis Williams (1913–1989)

General, U.S. Marine Corps; Commander, III Marine Amphibious Force in Vietnam, 1965–67

After graduation from Colorado State University, Walt became a Marine Corps second lieutenant in July 1936 and proved an outstanding combat leader in World War II and the Korean War. Lieutenant General Walt commanded the III Marine Amphibious Force (MAF) in Vietnam from June 1965 until June 1967, with responsibility for the five northern provinces of South Vietnam. Responsible for operations in I Corps, the northernmost region south of the Demilitarized Zone, Walt launched a balanced strategy of small unit patrolling, large unit operations, and an innovative pacification program using civic action and the U.S. Marine Combined Action Platoons (CAP) operating with local Vietnamese militia. However, in the middle of 1966, the North Vietnamese sent more troops into the extreme northern section of I Corps and Walt was compelled to shift the focus of III MAF efforts to fighting the PAVN main force units. Walt replaced Lieutenant General Leonard A. Chapman as assistant Marine Corps commandant in January 1968, was promoted to full general in June 1969, and retired in February 1971.

Warnke, Paul C. (1920–2001)

General Counsel, Defense Department, 1966–67; Assistant Secretary of Defense for International Security Affairs, 1967–69

Warnke became one of the Pentagon's leading proponents of de-escalation. When General Westmoreland requested an additional 206,000 troops in 1968, Warnke prepared a critical assessment of Vietnam policy, arguing that more troop deployments would lead to increased casualties and that it was time to reduce U.S. involvement. Warnke's analysis helped sway Defense Secretary Clark Clifford, especially when the Joint Chiefs of Staff failed adequately to address Clifford's concerns about further troop requests and the uncertain future of the war.

Westmoreland, William Childs (1914–2005)

General, U.S. Army; Commander, U.S. Military Assistance Command, Vietnam, 1964–1968

Born in Spartanburg County, South Carolina, on March 26, 1914, he graduated from the U.S. Military Academy in 1936. During World War II, Westmoreland, then a lieutenant colonel, commanded a field artillery battalion during the North African and Sicily campaigns and later was chief of staff of the Ninth Infantry Division during the invasion of Europe. After serving as an instructor at both the Command and General Staff College and Army War College, Colonel Westmoreland fought in the Korean War as commander of the 187th Airborne Infantry Regimental Combat Team. After his return to the United States and promotion to general, he commanded the 101st Airborne Division and later served as superintendent of the U.S. Military Academy. When Secretary of Defense Robert S. McNamara selected him as commander of U.S. Military Assistance Command, Vietnam, General Westmoreland was in command of America's rapid reaction force, the XVIII Airborne Corps.

Serving briefly as deputy commander, General Westmoreland assumed command of MACV on June 20, 1964. His initial task was to provide military advice and assistance to the government of South

Vietnam. Less than 60 days later, however, with the Gulf of Tonkin incident, General Westmoreland assumed the added responsibility of commanding America's armed forces in combat in Vietnam.

In 1965, when North Vietnamese regulars threatened to cut the country in two, Westmoreland and the Joint Chiefs of Staff recommended an increase of U.S. combat forces in South Vietnam to more than 100,000. Westmoreland favored a conventional style of warfare, using large units and massive firepower to seek out and destroy the Communist forces. He was instrumental in increasing the level of U.S. forces in Vietnam and developed the strategy of attrition for the ground war.

In late 1967, he made several public statements stressing the progress being made in the war. These statements came back to haunt him in January 1968 when the Communists launched a massive new offensive. Westmoreland and his commanders were taken by surprise by the new attacks, but his forces reacted quickly and decisively defeated the attackers. He then asked for 206,000 more troops to take advantage of what he saw as an opportunity to exploit the failed offensive. Stunned by the offensive and in political trouble within his own party, President Johnson rejected Westmoreland's request. He then recalled Westmoreland and made him army chief of staff, replacing him in Vietnam with General Creighton Abrams. He served in the new position from July 1968 until his retirement from the army in June 1972. In 1982, he sued the CBS television network for libel over a documentary that charged that Communist strength figures in South Vietnam in 1967 had been deliberately falsified, but a settlement was reached before the jury began deliberations. Both Westmoreland and CBS claimed victory.

Weyand, Frederick Carlton (1916–)

General, U.S. Army; Commander, U.S. Military Assistance Command, Vietnam, 1970–72; U.S. Army Chief of Staff, 1974–76

Born on September 15, 1916, at Arbunkle, California, Weyand graduated from the University of California at Berkeley in 1939. Originally commissioned in the Coast Artillery Corps, he served as an intelligence officer in the China-Burma-India theater in World War II. Transferring to the infantry in 1948, he won the Silver Star for gallantry in action as a combat infantryman during the war in Korea.

In March 1966, Weyand took the 25th Infantry Division into combat in Vietnam. After 12 months of battlefield activity with his division in western III Corps, he was selected to command the corps-level II Field Force Vietnam. During the Tet Offensive in 1968, his forces were instrumental in turning back the VC attack on Saigon. Departing Vietnam in August 1968, he later served as the military adviser to the U.S. Peace Delegation in Paris from March 1969 to June 1970.

In September 1970, General Weyand returned to Vietnam to serve as the deputy commander of MACV and in June 1972 succeeded General Creighton Abrams as COMUSMACV. Faced with the difficult and dangerous task of winding down the U.S. military presence in Vietnam, he was fated to be the last MACV commander. When the Paris accords were signed in January 1973, General Weyand withdrew the last U.S. military forces. Soon thereafter, he was named army vice chief of staff. Upon the death of the army chief of staff, General Creighton Abrams, on September 4, 1974, General Weyand assumed that office. Sent to Vietnam in April 1975 by President Gerald Ford to assess the military situation there, Weyand recommended $722 million in additional military aid for South Vietnam, which Congress refused to grant. He retired from active duty in September 1976.

Wheeler, Earle Gilmore (1908–1975)

General, U.S. Army; chief of staff, 1962–64; chairman, Joint Chiefs of Staff, 1964–70

General Earle "Bus" Wheeler was a lifelong staff officer with no combat experience when President Kennedy appointed him U.S. Army chief of staff in 1962. He shared Kennedy's enthusiasm for counterinsurgency warfare and Secretary of

Defense Robert McNamara's penchant for statistics, having taught mathematics at West Point. Wheeler was appointed chairman of the JCS in July 1964 to replace General Maxwell Taylor, who was sent to South Vietnam as U.S. ambassador by President Johnson. Soon after being appointed JCS chairman, Wheeler began promising success in Vietnam through further escalation. He resented Johnson's refusal to mobilize the Reserves and his reluctance to use the full might of U.S. power against North Vietnam. Wheeler went to Vietnam in February 1968, where he and General Westmoreland worked out a request for 206,000 additional troops; Wheeler returned with the request and recommended that the president call up the Reserves. The request leaked to the press and further undermined public faith in the military's claim that the Tet Offensive had been a major American victory that had seriously weakened Communist forces in South Vietnam. The president refused to mobilize the Reserves and sent only modest reinforcements to Westmoreland. During the first part of the Nixon administration, he tried unsuccessfully to get the president not to draw down U.S. forces so quickly. After serving longer than any other JCS chairman, Wheeler retired in 1970. He died on December 18, 1975.

Williams, Samuel T. (1897–1984)

U.S. Army general; commander, U.S. Military Assistance Group, Vietnam, 1955–60

A strict disciplinarian known as "Hanging Sam," Williams succeeded General John W. O'Daniel as commander of U.S. Military Assistance Advisory Group Indochina (MAAG-I) on October 24, 1955. It was very soon thereafter redesignated U.S. Military Assistance Group, Vietnam. Williams dismissed the Viet Cong guerrilla threat as a diversion and continued the U.S. policy of training South Vietnamese troops to become a conventional force designed to repel an invasion from the north. He cultivated close relations with South Vietnamese president Ngo Dinh Diem while feuding constantly with U.S. ambassador Elbridge Durbrow.

Williams retired in 1960 after completing his service in Vietnam.

Xuan Thuy (1912–1985)

Foreign minister, Democratic Republic of Vietnam (DRV), 1963–65; chief delegate, Paris Peace Talks, 1968–70

Born in Ha Dong Province near Hanoi, Thuy began revolutionary activities in 1926 and was imprisoned by the French from 1939 to 1945. He became a member of the Lao Dong Party Central Committee in 1951. He served as North Vietnam's foreign minister from 1963 to 1965. Xuan Thuy headed the official North Vietnamese delegation to the Paris peace talks from May 1968 until the signing of the cease-fire agreement in January 1973. Thuy, acting as Le Duc Tho's chief deputy, negotiated periodically with Henry Kissinger. He died in Hanoi on June 18, 1985.

Zumwalt, Elmo Russell, Jr. (1920–2000)

Admiral, U.S. Navy; commander of U.S. naval forces Vietnam, 1969–70; chief of naval operations, 1970–74

Born on November 29, 1920, in San Francisco, Zumwalt graduated from the U.S. Naval Academy in 1942. During World War II, he served on destroyers in the Pacific. On September 30, 1968, Admiral Zumwalt was appointed commander of U.S. Naval Forces Vietnam (COMNAVFOR) and as such was responsible for naval operations, which included the Coastal Surveillance Force, the River Patrol Force, and the Riverine Assault Force, as well as the Naval Advisory Group to the South Vietnamese Navy, the SEABEEs of the Third Naval Construction Brigade, and other activities that included Coast Guard Activities, Vietnam. While with COMNAVFOR, Admiral Zumwalt launched Operation Sealords, a concerted U.S. and South Vietnamese navy effort to disrupt enemy supply lines in the Mekong Delta. Named chief of naval operations, Zumwalt departed Vietnam in May 1970 and assumed his new office on July 1, 1970. He launched a number of reforms designed to improve conditions for the navy's enlisted men, and to relax regulations in matters like grooming standards. He retired from active duty on July 1, 1974. His son, Elmo R. Zumwalt, III, who had served as a navy officer commanding a swift boat unit of the Coastal Surveillance Force of Vietnam, died of cancer, which is believed to have been caused by Agent Orange, authorized by his father as a defoliant to reduce enemy ambush positions along coastal waterways.

GLOSSARY OF ACRONYMS AND ABBREVIATIONS

AAA antiaircraft artillery
ABC American Broadcasting Company
AATTV Australian Army Training Team Vietnam
AAR After Action Report
ACAV armored cavalry assault vehicle
AFB Air Force Base
AID Agency for International Development
AIM Air Intercept Missile
ANZAC Australian New Zealand Army Corps
AO area of operation
AP Associated Press
APC armored personnel carrier
ARVN Army of the Republic of Vietnam
ASA Army Security Agency
ASPB Assault Support Patrol Boat
AWOL Absent Without Leave
BDA bomb damage assessment
BOQ bachelor officers quarters
BTR Soviet-manufactured armored personnel carrier
CAP Combined Action Program
CAS close air support
CBU cluster bomb unit
CCC Command and Control, Central (SOG)
CCN Command and Control, North (SOG)
CCP Combined Campaign Plan
CCS Command and Control, South (SOG)
CEFEO Corps Espéditionnaire Français en Extrême-orient
CG Commanding General

CGDK Coalition Government of Democratic Kampuchea (Cambodia)
CI counterintelligence
CIA Central Intelligence Agency
CICV Combined Intelligence Center Vietnam
CIDG Civilian Irregular Defense Group
CINCPAC Commander-in-Chief, Pacific
CIO Central Intelligence Organization
CJCS Chairman, Joint Chiefs of Staff
CMD Capital Military District
CMR Capital Military Region
CNO Chief of Naval Operations
COMUSMACV Commander, U.S. Military Assistance Command, Vietnam
CORDS Civil Operations and Revolutionary Development Support
COSVN Central Office for South Vietnam
CP command post
CTC Central Training Command
CTZ Corps Tactical Zone
DCG Deputy Commanding General
DAO Defense Attaché Office
DEROS Date Eligible for Return from Overseas *or* Date of Expected Return from Overseas
DIA Defense Intelligence Agency
DIOCC District Intelligence and Operations Coordination Committee
DK Democratic Kampuchea (Cambodia under Khmer Rouge)
DMAC Delta Military Assistance Command
DMZ Demilitarized Zone

DOD   Department of Defense

DRAC   Delta Regional Assistance Command

DRV   Democratic Republic of (North) Vietnam

ELINT   electronic intelligence

FAC   forward air controller

FANK   Forces Armies Nationales Khmères (Cambodian Army from 1970 to 1975)

FAR   Forces Armées Royales (Laotian Army)

FFV   Field Force, Vietnam

FFORCEV   Field Force, Vietnam

FO   forward observer

FSA   Forward Support Area

FSB   Fire Support Base

FSCC   Fire Support Coordination Center

FULRO   Front Unitie de Lutte des Races Opprimees (United Front for the Liberation of Oppressed Races)

FWMAF   Free World Military Assistance Forces

GPWD   General Political Warfare Department

GVN   Government of (South) Vietnam

H&I   Harassment and Interdiction (Fire)

HES   Hamlet Evaluation System

Huey   UH–1 Iroquois helicopter

HUMINT   human intelligence

HQ   headquarters

ICC   International Control Commission

ICCS   International Commission of Control and Supervision

ICP   Indochinese Communist Party

IFFV   I Field Force, Vietnam

IG   Inspector General

IIFFV   II Field Force, Vietnam

IPW   interrogation of prisoners of war

JCS   U.S. Joint Chiefs of Staff

JGS   South Vietnamese Joint General Staff

JMC   Joint Military Commission

JUSPAO   Joint U.S. Public Affairs Office

KSCB   Khe Sanh Combat Base

KIA   Killed in Action

KIA/BNR   Killed in Action/Body Not Recovered

KPRP   Khmer People's Revolutionary Party

LAW   light antitank weapon

LCU   landing craft, utility

LBJ   Long Binh Jail

LLDB   Luc Luong Dac Biet (RVN Special Forces)

LOC   line of communication

LOH   Light Observation Helicopter

LRRP   long-rang reconnaissance patrol

LZ   landing zone

MAAG   Military Assistance Advisory Group

MAAG-V   Military Assistance Advisory Group-Vietnam

MAC   Military Airlift Command

MACCORDS   Military Assistance Command Civil Operations and Revolutionary Development Support

MACSOG   Military Assistance Command, Studies and Observations Group

MACV   Military Assistance Command, Vietnam

MAF   Marine Amphibious Force

MAP   Military Assistance Program

MAT   Mobile Advisory Team

MATT   Mobile Advisory Training Team

MEDCAP   Medical Civic Action Program

MEDTC   Military Equipment Delivery Team, Cambodia

MEDVAC   Medical Evacuation, also known as "dust off"

MIA   Missing in Action

MOS   Military Occupation Specialty

MP   Military Police

MR   Military Region

MRC   Military Revolutionary Council

MRF   Mobile Riverine Force

MSTS   Military Sea Transportation Service

MTT   Mobile Training Team

NAVFORV   Naval Forces, Vietnam

NCO   non-commissioned officer

NIC   National Interrogation Center

NICC   National Intelligence Coordination Committee

NKP   Nakhon Phanom Air Base (Thailand)

NLC   National Leadership Committee

NLF   National Liberation Front

NP   National Police

NSA   National Security Agency

NSC   National Security Council

NVA   North Vietnamese Army (PAVN)

NVN   North Vietnam

NZTTV   New Zealand Training Team Vietnam

OB   order of battle

OCO   Office of Civilian Operations

OJT   on-the-job training

ONTOS   Marine self-propelled multiple 106 mm recoilless rifle

OPLAN   operations plan

OSS   Office of Strategic Services

PAVN   People's Army of (North) Vietnam

PBR   Patrol Boat, River

PCF   Patrol Craft, Fast (Swift Boat)

PEO   Program Evaluation Office

PF   Popular Forces

PFF   Police Field Forces

PGM   Motor Gunboat

PHILCAG   Philippines Civic Action Group

PIOCC   Province Intelligence and Operations Coordinating Committee

PLAF   People's Liberation Armed Forces

POL   petroleum, oils, and lubricants

POW   prisoner of war

PRC   People's Republic of China

PRD   Pacification and Rural Development

PRG   Provisional Revolutionary Government

PRK   People's Republic of Kampuchea

PROVN   Program for the Pacification and Long-Term Development of Vietnam

PRU   Provincial Reconnaissance Unit

PSA   Province Senior Adviser

PSDF   People's Self-Defense Force

PSYOPS   Psychological Operations

PSP   pierced steel plate

PT   Motor Torpedo Boat (Patrol Torpedo)

PTSD   Post-Traumatic Stress Disorder

PW   prisoner of war

PX   Post Exchange

QL   Quoc Lo (National Route)

RAAF   Royal Australian Air Force

RAC   Regional Assistance Command

RAG   River Assault Group

RAR   Royal Australian Regiment

RD   Revolutionary (or Rural) Development

RDF   radio direction finding

RF/PF   Regional Forces/Popular Forces

RLAF   Royal Lao Air Force

RLG   Royal Lao Government

ROC   Republic of China

ROE   rules of engagement

ROK   Republic of Korea

ROTC   Reserve Officers Training Corps

RPDC   Regional Pacification and Development Council

RPG   rocket-propelled grenade

RRU   Radio Research Unit (ASA)

R&R   rest and recreation

RVN   Republic of (South) Vietnam

RVNAF   Republic of Vietnam Armed Forces

SAC   Strategic Air Command

SAM   surface-to-air missile

SAR   search and rescue

SDS   Students for a Democratic Society

SEALs   Sea, Air, Land Teams (U.S. Navy Special Forces)

SEATO   Southeast Asia Treaty Organization

SF   Special Forces

SIGINT   signals intelligence

SITREP   situation report

SLAR   side-looking airborne radar

SOG   Special Operations Group, later Studies and Observations Group

SOI   signal operating instructions

SOP   standard operating procedures

SRAG   Second Regional Assistance Group

STD   Strategic Technical Directorate (RVN)

SVN   South Vietnam

TAC   Tactical Air Command

TAOR   Tactical Area of Responsibility

TDY   temporary duty

TERM   Temporary Equipment Recovery Mission

TF   Task Force

TOC   Tactical Operations Center

TO&E   Table of Organization and Equipment

TOW   tube-launched, optically-tracked, wire-guided missile

TRAC   Third Regional Assistance Command

TRIM   Training Relations and Instruction Mission

UN   United Nations

UPI   United Press International

U.S.   United States

USA   United States of America; U.S. Army

USAF   U.S. Air Force

USIA   U.S. Information Agency

USAID   U.S. Agency for International Development

USARV   U.S. Army, Vietnam

USIS   U.S. Information Service

USMACV   United States Military Assistance Command, Vietnam

USMC   U.S. Marine Corps

USN   U.S. Navy

USO   United Services Organization

USOM   U.S. Operations Mission

USSAG   U.S. Support Activity Group

USSR   Union of Soviet Socialist Republics

VC   Viet Cong

VCI   Viet Cong Infrastructure

VNA   Vietnamese National Army

VNAF   Republic of Vietnam Air Force

VNMC   Republic of Vietnam Marine Corps

VNN   Republic of Vietnam Navy

VNQDD   Vietnam Quoc Dan Dang (Vietnamese Nationalist Party)

VOA   Voice of America

VVAW   Vietnam Veterans Against the War

WIA   wounded in action

WSO   weapons systems officer

APPENDIX I

U.S. MILITARY COMMITMENT IN SOUTH VIETNAM BY YEAR

DATE	TROOPS	DATE	TROOPS
December 31, 1960	900	December 31, 1967	485,600
December 31, 1961	3,205	June 30, 1968	534,700
June 30, 1962	9,000	December 31, 1968	536,100
December 31, 1962	11,300	April 30, 1969	543,400
June 30, 1963	15,400	June 30, 1969	538,700
December 31, 1963	16,300	December 31, 1969	475,200
June 30, 1964	16,500	June 30, 1970	414,900
December 31, 1964	23,300	December 31, 1970	334,600
June 30, 1965	59,900	June 30, 1971	239,200
December 31, 1965	184,300	December 31, 1971	156,800
June 30, 1966	267,500	June 30, 1972	47,000
December 31, 1966	385,300	December 31, 1972	24,200
June 30, 1967	448,800	March 30, 1973	240

Source: U.S. Department of Defense, OASD (Comptroller), Directorate of Information Operations, March 19, 1974, cited in Marc Leepson, ed., *Webster's New World Dictionary of the Vietnam War* (New York: Simon & Schuster Macmillan, 1999), p. 484.

 # APPENDIX II

U.S. MILITARY PERSONNEL IN SOUTHEAST ASIA OUTSIDE VIETNAM

DATE	TROOPS
December 31, 1965	42,900
December 31, 1966	54,200
December 31, 1967	80,300
December 31, 1968	87,400
December 31, 1969	82,900
December 31, 1970	57,200
December 31, 1971	48,200
November 30, 1972	84,700

Source: U.S. Department of Defense, OASD (Comptroller), Directorate for Information, cited in David L. Anderson, *The Columbia Guide to the Vietnam War* (New York: Columbia University Press, 2002), p. 287.

APPENDIX III

ALLIED MILITARY FORCES IN SOUTH VIETNAM*

COUNTRY	END 1964	END 1965	END 1966	END 1967	END 1968	END 1969	END 1970	END 1971	END 1972
Australia	200	1,500	4,530	6,820	7,660	7,670	6,800	2, 000	130
Korea	200	20,620	35,570	47,830	50,000	48,870	48,540	45,700	36,790
New Zealand	30	120	160	530	520	550	440	100	50
Philippines	20	70	2,060	2,020	1,580	190	70	50	50
South Vietnam#	514,000	643,000	735,900	798,000	820,000	897,000	968,0 00	1,046,250	1,048,000
Thailand	—	20	240	2,200	6,000	11,570	11,570	6,000	40
United States	23,310	184,310	385,300	485,600	536,000	484,330	335,790	158,120	24,000

*Countries providing nonmilitary personnel are not listed. An average of 30 Republic of China and 10 Spanish advisers served throughout period as well.

#Includes the Army, Navy, Marines, Air Force, Regional, and Popular Forces, but does not include paramilitary formations such as National Police, CIDG, "Armed Combat Youth," etc.

Sources: Shelby L. Stanton, *Vietnam Order of Battle* (New York: Galahad Books, 1986), p. 333.

 # APPENDIX IV

ALLIED CASUALTIES

U.S./RVNAF Military Casualties				
YEAR	KIA U.S.	KIA RVNAF	WIA* U. S.	WIA* RVNAF
1960	—	2,223	—	2,788
1961	11	4,004	2	5,449
1962	31	4,457	41	7,195
1963	78	5,665	218	11,488
1964	147	7,457	522	17,017
1965	1,369	11,242	3,308	23,118
1966	5,008	11,953	16,526	20,975
1967	9,377	12,716	32,370	29,448
1968	14,589	27,915	46,797	70,696
1969	9,414	21,833	32,940	65,276
1970	4,221	23,346	15,211	71,582
1971	1,381	22,738	4,767	60,939
1972	300	39,587	587	109,960
1973	237	27,901	24	131,936
1974	207	32,219	—	155,735
Total	46,370	254,256	153,313	783,602

*Required hospitalization.

Source: Jeffrey J. Clarke, *Advice and Support: The Final Years, 1965–1973* (Washington, D.C.: U.S. Government Printing Office, 1988), p. 275; Spencer C. Tucker, ed., *Encyclopedia of the Vietnam War: A Political, Social, and Military History.* 3 vols. (Santa Barbara, Calif.: ABC-CLIO, 1998), Vol. III, p. 1,093.

Free World Military Forces Casualties	
Republic of Korea, Killed	4,407
Australia/New Zealand, Killed	469
Thailand, Killed	352

Source: George Donelson Moss, *Vietnam: An American Ordeal,* 3rd ed. (Upper Saddle River, N.J.: Prentice Hall, 1998), p. 447; Lester H. Brune and Richard Dean Burns, *America and the Indochina Wars, 1945–1990: A Bibliographic Guide* (Clairmont, Calif.: Regina Books, 1992), p. 146.

APPENDIX V

Major U.S. Combat Unit Casualties in Vietnam

UNIT	KILLED IN ACTION	WOUNDED IN ACTION
III Marine Amphibious Force	13,082	88,633
1st Marine Division		
1st Marine Aircraft Wing		
3rd Marine Division		
7th Fleet Amphibious Force		
1st Cavalry Division	5,444	26,592
25th Infantry Division	4,547	31,161
American (23rd) Division	4,040*	13,828*
11th Light Infantry Brigade		
198th Light Infantry Brigade		
101st Airborne Division	4,011	18,259
1st Infantry Division	3,146	18,019
9th Infantry Division	2,624	18,831
4th Infantry Division	2,531	15,229
173rd Airborne Brigade	1,148	8,747
7th Air Force/SAC (Guam)	1,739	3,457
1st Aviation Brigade	1,701	5,163
7th Fleet/Naval Forces Vietnam	1,626	10,406
196th Light Infantry Brigade	1,183	5,591
5th Special Forces Group	792	2,704
199th Light Infantry Brigade	754	4,679
11th Armored Cavalry Regiment	728	5,761
5th Mechanized Infantry Division	403	3,648
1st Brigade		
82nd Airborne Division	184	1,009
3rd Brigade		
Coast Guard Squadrons 1 and 3	5	59

*Includes total for 196th Light Infantry Brigade, which served as a component of the American Division for part of its time in Vietnam.

The units listed above account for 98 percent of the Americans killed by hostile action in Vietnam. Wounded in action include both hospitalized and nonhospitalized.

Source: Richard K. Kolb, ed. *Vietnam War Combat Chronology: A Special Publication of VFW Magazine,* October 2005, p. 16.

APPENDIX VI

U.S. MILITARY CAMPAIGNS IN VIETNAM

CAMPAIGN	INCLUSIVE DATES
Advisory	March 15, 1962–March 7, 1965
Defense	March 8, 1965–December 24, 1965
Counteroffensive	December 25, 1965–June 30, 1966
Counteroffensive, Phase II	July 1, 1966–May 31, 1967
Counteroffensive, Phase III	June 1, 1967–January 29, 1968
Tet Counteroffensive	January 30, 1968–April 1, 1968
Counteroffensive, Phase IV	April 2, 1968–June 30, 1968
Counteroffensive, Phase V	July 1, 1968–November 1, 1968
Counteroffensive, Phase VI	November 2, 1968–February 22, 1969
Tet 69/Counteroffensive	February 23, 1969–June 8, 1969
Summer-Fall 1969	June 9, 1969–October 31, 1969
Winter-Spring 1970	November 1, 1969–April 30, 1970
Sanctuary Counteroffensive	May 1, 1970–June 30, 1970
Counteroffensive, Phase VII	July 1, 1970–June 30, 1971
Consolidation I	July 1, 1971–November 30, 1971
Consolidation II	December 1, 1971–March 29, 1972
Cease-fire	March 30, 1972–January 28, 1973

Source: U.S. Army Center of Military History, Fort McNair, Washington, D.C.

APPENDIX VII

U.S. GOVERNMENT MILITARY EXPENDITURES IN SOUTHEAST ASIA

FISCAL YEAR	FULL COST (IN MILLIONS)
1965	103
1966	5,812
1967	20,133
1968	26,547
1969	28,805
1970	23,052
1971	14,719
1972	9,261

Full costs are for all forces and include personnel, aircraft, operations, munitions used, and equipment lost in the Southeast Asia conflict

Source: U.S. Senate Appropriations Committee, cited in David L. Anderson, *The Columbia Guide to the Vietnam War* (New York: Columbia University Press, 2002), p. 287.

APPENDIX VIII

U.S. Army Troop Withdrawals from Vietnam, 1969–1972

INCRE-MENT	TIME FRAME	MAJOR UNIT(S) INVOLVED	ARMY REDUCTION	TOTAL U.S. REDUCTION	ARMY STRENGTH AT COMPLETION OF INCREMENT	TOTAL U.S. FORCES REMAINING
I	July 1–Aug. 31, 1969	9th Inf Div (-)#	15,712	25,000	352,400	519,000
II	Sep. 18–Dec. 15, 1969	3rd Bde, 82nd Abn Div	14,092	40,500	338,300	484,000
III	Feb. 1–Apr. 15, 1970	1st Inf Div 3rd Bde, 4th Inf Div	29,396	50,000	308,900	434,000
IV	July 1–Oct. 15, 1970	3rd Bde, 9th Inf Div 196th Lt Inf Bde	15,932	50,000	292,900	384,000
V	Oct. 16–Dec. 31, 1970	4th Inf Div (-) 25th Inf Div (-)	38,054	40,000	254,800	344,000
VI	Jan. 1–Apr. 30, 1971	1st Cav Div (-) 11th Ar Cav Regt (-) 2nd Bde, 25th Inf Div	41,848	60,000	213,000	284,000
VII	May 1–June 30, 1971	One Air Cav Sqdn Three Inf Bns	15,030	29,300	198,000	254,000
VIII	July 1–Sep. 1, 1971	173rd Abn Bde	21,769	28,700	176,200	226,000
IX	Sep. 1–Nov. 30, 1971	AMERICAL Div (-) 11th Inf Bde 198th Inf Bde	35,000	42,000	141,200	184,000
X	Dec. 1–Jan. 31, 1972	101st Abn Div (-)	36,718	45,000	104,500	139,000
XI	Feb. 1–Apr. 30, 1972	Two Cav Sqdns Five Inf Bns Four Air Cav Sqdns	58,096	70,000	46,400	69,000

(continues)

U.S. Army Troop Withdrawals from Vietnam, 1969–1972, *continued*

INCRE-MENT	TIME FRAME	MAJOR UNIT(S) INVOLVED	ARMY REDUCTION	TOTAL U.S. REDUCTION	ARMY STRENGTH AT COMPLETION OF INCREMENT	TOTAL U.S. FORCES REMAINING
XII	May 1–June 30, 1972	3rd Bde, 1st Cav 196th Inf Bde Four Inf Bns	14,552	20,000	31,900	49,000
XIII	July 1–Aug. 31, 1972	Two Inf Bns	8,484	10,000	23,400	39,000
XIV	Sep. 1–Nov. 30, 1972	Miscellaneous Units	7,282	12,000	16,100	27,000

*Approximate figures.

(-) indicates only partial withdrawal of this unit.

Sources:

Larry A. Niksch. *Vietnamization: The Program and Its Problems* (Washington, D.C.: Library of Congress, Congressional Research Service, January 1972), p. A–1.

Nguyen Duy Hinh. *Indochina Monographs: Vietnamization and the Cease-Fire* (Washington, D.C.: U.S. Army Center of Military History, 1980), p. 27.

Shelby L. Stanton. *Vietnam Order of Battle* (New York: Galahad Books, 1986), p. 333.

APPENDIX IX

MEDAL OF HONOR RECIPIENTS—VIETNAM WAR

(* - Posthumous Receipt)

NAME	SERVICE	RANK (AT TIME OF ACTION)	PLACE OF ACTION	DATE OF ACTION
*Adams, William E.	USA	Maj.	Kontum Province	May 25, 1971
*Albanese, Lewis	USA	PFC	Republic of Vietnam	Dec. 1, 1966
*Anderson, James, Jr.	USMC	PFC	Republic of Vietnam	Feb. 28, 1967
*Anderson, Richard A.	USMC	LCpl.	Quang Tri Province	Aug. 24, 1969
Anderson, Webster	USA	SFC	Tam Ky	Oct. 15, 1967
*Ashley, Eugene, Jr.	USA	SFC	Near Lang Vei	Feb. 6–7, 1968
*Austin, Oscar P.	USMC	PFC	West of Da Nang	Feb. 23, 1969
Baca, John P.	USA	SP4	Phuoc Long Province	Feb. 10, 1970
Bacon, Nicky D.	USA	SSG	West of Tam Ky	Aug. 26, 1968
Baker, John F., Jr.	USA	PFC	Republic of Vietnam	Nov. 5, 1966
Ballard, Donald E.	USN	HC2c	Quang Tri Province	May 16, 1968
*Barker, Jedh C.	USMC	LCpl.	Near Con Thien	Sept. 21, 1967
*Barnes, John Andrew III	USA	PFC	Dak To	Nov. 12, 1967
Barnum, Harvey C., Jr.	USMC	1st Lt.	Ky Phu, Quang Tin Province	Dec. 18, 1965
Beikirch, Gary B.	USA	SGT	Kontum Province	Apr. 1, 1970
*Belcher, Ted	USA	SGT	Plei Djerang	Nov. 19, 1966
*Bellrichard, Leslie A.	USA	PFC	Kontum Province	May 20, 1967
Benavidez, Roy P.	USA	SSG	West of Loc Ninh	May 2, 1968
*Bennett, Steven L.	USAF	Capt.	Quang Tri	June 29, 1972
*Bennett, Thomas W.	USA	CPL	Chu Pa Region, Pleiku Province	Feb. 9–11, 1969
*Blanchfield, Michael R.	USA	SP4	Binh Dinh Province	July 3, 1969
*Bobo, John P.	USMC	2nd Lt.	Quang Tri Province	Mar. 30, 1967
Bondsteel, James L.	USA	SSG	An Loc	May 24, 1969

(continues)

MEDAL OF HONOR RECIPIENTS—VIETNAM WAR, *continued*

NAME	SERVICE	RANK (AT TIME OF ACTION)	PLACE OF ACTION	DATE OF ACTION
*Bowen, Hammett L., Jr.	USA	SSG	Binh Duong Province	June 27, 1969
Brady, Patrick H.	USA	MAJ	Near Chu Lai	Jan. 6, 1968
*Bruce, Daniel D.	USMC	PFC	FSB Tomahawk, Quang Nam Province	Mar. 1, 1969
*Bryant, William M.	USA	SFC	Long Khanh Province	Mar. 24, 1969
Bucha, Paul W.	USA	CPT	Near Phuoc Vinh, Binh Duong Province	Mar. 16–19, 1968
*Buker, Brian L.	USA	SGT	Chau Doc Province	Apr. 5, 1970
*Burke, Robert C.	USMC	PFC	Southern Quang Nam Province	May 17, 1968
*Capodanno, Vincent R.	USN	LT (Chaplain)	Quang Tin Province	Sept. 4, 1967
*Caron, Wayne M.	USN	HC3c	Quang Nam Province	July 28, 1968
*Carter, Bruce W.	USMC	PFC	Quang Tri Province	Aug. 7, 1969
Cavaiani, Jon R.	USA	SSG	Republic of Vietnam	June 4–5, 1971
Clausen, Raymond M., Jr.	USMC	PFC	Republic of Vietnam	Jan. 31, 1970
*Coker, Ronald L.	USMC	PFC	Quang Tri Province	Mar. 24, 1969
*Connor, Peter S.	USMC	SSgt.	Quang Nam Province	Feb. 25, 1966
*Cook, Donald G.	USMC	Capt.	Republic of Vietnam	Dec. 31, 1964– Dec. 8, 1967
Crandall, Bruce P.	USA	MAJ	Ia Drang Valley, Pleiku Province	Nov. 14, 1965
*Creek, Thomas E.	USMC	LCpl.	Near Cam Lo	Feb. 13, 1969
*Crescenz, Michael J.	USA	CPL	Hiep Duc Valley	Nov. 20, 1968
*Cutinha, Nicholas J.	USA	SP4	Near Gia Dinh	Mar. 2, 1968
*Dahl, Larry G.	USA	SP4	An Khe, Binh Dinh Province	Feb. 23, 1971
*Davis, Rodney M.	USMC	Sgt.	Quang Nam Province	Sept. 6, 1967
Davis, Sammy L.	USA	PFC	West of Cai Lay	Nov. 18, 1967
Day, George E.	USAF	Maj.	North Vietnam	Aug. 26, 1967
*De La Garza, Emilio A., Jr.	USMC	LCpl.	Near Da Nang	Apr. 11, 1970
Dethlefsen, Merlyn H.	USAF	Capt.	Over North Vietnam	Mar. 10, 1967
*Devore, Edward A., Jr.	USA	SP4	Near Saigon	Mar. 17, 1968
*Dias, Ralph E.	USMC	PFC	Que Son Mountains	Nov. 12, 1969
*Dickey, Douglas E.	USMC	PFC	Republic of Vietnam	Mar. 26, 1967
Dix, Drew D.	USA	SSG	Chau Doc Province	Jan. 31–Feb. 1, 1968
*Doane, Stephen H.	USA	1LT	Hau Nghia Province	Mar. 25, 1969
Dolby, David C.	USA	SP4	Republic of Vietnam	May 21, 1966

NAME	SERVICE	RANK (AT TIME OF ACTION)	PLACE OF ACTION	DATE OF ACTION
Donlon, Roger H. C.	USA	CPT	Near Nam Dong	July 6, 1964
Dunagan, Kern W.	USA	CPT	Quang Tin Province	May 13–14, 1969
*Durham, Harold B., Jr.	USA	2LT	Republic of Vietnam	Oct. 17, 1967
*English, Glenn H., Jr.	USA	SSG	Phu My District	Sept. 7, 1970
*Estocin, Michael J.	USN	LCDR	Haiphong, North Vietnam	Apr. 20 & 26, 1967
*Evans, Donald W.	USA	SP4	Tri Tam	Jan. 27, 1967
*Evans, Rodney J.	USA	SGT	Tay Ninh Province	July 18, 1969
Ferguson, Frederick E.	USA	CWO	Hue	Jan. 31, 1968
*Fernandez, Daniel	USA	SP4	Cu Chi, Hau Nghia Province	Feb. 18, 1966
Fisher, Bernard F.	USAF	Maj.	Bien Hoa and Pleiku	Mar. 10, 1966
Fitzmaurice, Michael J.	USA	SP4	Khe Sanh	Mar. 23, 1971
*Fleek, Charles C.	USA	SGT	Binh Duong Province	May 27, 1969
Fleming, James P.	USAF	1st Lt.	Near Duc Co	Nov. 26, 1968
Foley, Robert F.	USA	CPT	Near Quan Dau Tieng	Nov. 5, 1966
*Folland, Michael F.	USA	CPL	Long Khanh Province	July 3, 1969
*Foster, Paul H.	USMC	Sgt.	Near Con Thien	Oct. 14, 1967
*Fournet, Douglas B.	USA	1LT	A Shau Valley	May 4, 1968
*Fous, James W.	USA	PFC	Kien Hoa Province	May 14, 1968
Fox, Wesley L.	USMC	1st Lt.	Quang Tri Province	Feb. 22, 1969
*Fratellenico, Frank	USA	CPL	Quang Tri Province	Aug. 19, 1970
Freeman, Ed	USA	CPT	Ia Drang Valley	Nov. 14, 1965
Fritz, Harold A.	USA	1LT	Binh Long Province	Jan. 11, 1969
*Gardner, James A.	USA	1LT	My Canh	Feb. 7, 1966
*Gertsch, John G.	USA	SSG	A Shau Valley	July 15–19, 1969
*Gonzalez, Alfredo C.	USMC	Sgt.	Near Thua Thien	Feb. 4, 1968
*Graham, James A.	USMC	Capt.	Republic of Vietnam	June 2, 1967
*Grandstaff, Bruce A.	USA	PSGT	Pleiku Province	May 18, 1967
*Grant, Joseph X.	USA	1LT	Republic of Vietnam	Nov. 13, 1966
*Graves, Terrence C.	USMC	2nd Lt.	Quang Tri Province	Feb. 16, 1968
*Guenette, Peter M.	USA	SP4	Quan Tan Uyen Province	May 18, 1968
Hagemeister, Charles C.	USA	SP4	Binh Dinh Province	Mar. 20, 1967
*Hagen, Loren P.	USA	1LT	Republic of Vietnam	Aug. 7, 1971
*Hartsock, Robert W.	USA	SFC	Hau Nghia Province	Feb. 23, 1969
*Harvey, Carmel B., Jr.	USA	SP4	Binh Dinh Province	June 21, 1967
Herda, Frank A.	USA	PFC	Near Dak To, Quang Trang Province	June 29, 1968
*Hibbs, Robert J.	USA	2LT	Don Dien Lo Ke	Mar. 5, 1966
*Holcomb, John N.	USA	SGT	Near Quan Loi	Dec. 3, 1968
Hooper, Joe R.	USA	SGT	Near Hue	Feb. 21, 1968
*Hosking, Charles E., Jr.	USA	SFC	Phuoc Long Province	Mar. 21, 1967

(continues)

MEDAL OF HONOR RECIPIENTS—VIETNAM WAR, *continued*

NAME	SERVICE	RANK (AT TIME OF ACTION)	PLACE OF ACTION	DATE OF ACTION
Howard, Jimmie E.	USMC	SSgt.	Republic of Vietnam	June 16, 1966
Howard, Robert L.	USA	SFC	Republic of Vietnam	Dec. 30, 1968
*Howe, James D.	USMC	LCpl.	Republic of Vietnam	May 6, 1970
*Ingalls, George A.	USA	SP4	Near Duc Pho	Apr. 16, 1967
Ingram, Robert R.	USN	HC3c	Quang Ngai Province	Mar. 28, 1966
Jackson, Joe M.	USAF	Lt Col.	Kham Duc	May 12, 1968
Jacobs, Jack H.	USA	1LT	Kien Phong Province	Mar. 9, 1968
Jenkins, Don J.	USA	PFC	Kien Phong Province	Jan. 6, 1969
*Jenkins, Robert H., Jr.	USMC	PFC	FSB Argonne	Mar. 5, 1969
Jennings, Delbert O.	USA	SSG	Kim Song Valley	Dec. 27, 1966
*Jimenez, Jose F.	USMC	LCpl.	Quang Nam Province	Aug. 28, 1969
Joel, Lawrence	USA	SP5	Republic of Vietnam	Nov. 8, 1965
Johnson, Dwight H.	USA	SP5	Near Dak To, Kontum Province	Jan. 15, 1968
*Johnson, Ralph H.	USMC	PFC	Near Quan Duc Valley	Mar. 5, 1968
*Johnston, Donald R.	USA	SP4	Tay Ninh Province	Mar. 21, 1969
*Jones, William A. III	USAF	Col.	Near Dong Hoi, North Vietnam	Sept. 1, 1968
*Karopczyc, Stephen E.	USA	1LT	Kontum Province	Mar. 12, 1967
*Kawamura, Terry T.	USA	CPL	Camp Radcliff	Mar. 20, 1969
Kays, Kenneth M.	USA	PVT	Thua Thien Province	May 7, 1970
*Kedenburg, John J.	USA	SP5	Republic of Vietnam	June 13, 1968
*Keith, Miguel	USMC	LCpl.	Quang Ngai Province	May 8, 1970
Keller, Leonard B.	USA	SGT	Ap Bac Zone	May 2, 1967
Kelley, Thomas G.	USN	LT	Ong Muon Canal, Kien Hoa Province	June 15, 1969
Kellogg, Allan J., Jr.	USMC	SSgt.	Quang Nam Province	Mar. 11, 1970
Kerrey, Joseph R.	USNR	LT (jg)	Near Nha Trang Bay	Mar. 14, 1969
Kinsman, Thomas J.	USA	PFC	Near Vinh Long	Feb. 6, 1968
Lambers, Paul R.	USA	SGT	Tay Ninh Province	Aug. 20, 1968
Lang, George C.	USA	SP4	Kien Hoa Province	Feb. 22, 1969
*Langhorn, Garfield M.	USA	PFC	Pleiku Province	Jan. 15, 1969
*Lapointe, Joseph G., Jr.	USA	SP4	Quang Tin Province	June 2, 1969
Lassen, Clyde E.	USN	LT (jg)	Republic of Vietnam	June 19, 1968
*Lauffer, Billy L.	USA	PFC	Near Bong Son, Binh Dinh Province	Sept. 21, 1966
*Law, Robert D.	USA	SP4	Tinh Phuoc Thanh Province	Feb. 22, 1969
Lee, Howard V.	USMC	Capt.	Near Cam Lo	Aug. 8–9, 1966

NAME	SERVICE	RANK (AT TIME OF ACTION)	PLACE OF ACTION	DATE OF ACTION
*Lee, Milton A.	USA	PFC	Near Phu Bai, Thua Thien Province	Apr. 26, 1968
*Leisy, Robert R.	USA	2LT	Phuoc Long Province	Dec. 2, 1969
Lemon, Peter C.	USA	SP4	Tay Ninh Province	Apr. 1, 1970
*Leonard, Matthew	USA	PSG	Near Suoi Da	Feb. 28, 1967
Levitow, John L.	USAF	A1C	Long Binh Army Post	Feb. 24, 1969
Liteky, Angelo J.	USA	CPT (Chaplain)	Near Phuoc Lac, Bien Hoa Province	Dec. 6, 1967
Littrell, Gary L.	USA	SFC	Kontum Province	Apr. 4–8, 1970
Livingston, James E.	USMC	Capt.	Dai Do	May 2, 1968
*Long, Donald R.	USA	SGT	Republic of Vietnam	June 30, 1966
*Lozada, Carlos J.	USA	PFC	Dak To	Nov. 20, 1967
*Lucas, Andre C.	USA	LTC	FSB Ripcord	July 1–23, 1970
Lynch, Allan J.	USA	SP4	Near My An, Binh Dinh Province	Dec. 15, 1967
Marm, Walter J., Jr.	USA	2LT	Ia Drang Valley	Nov. 14, 1965
*Martini, Gary W.	USMC	PFC	Binh Son	Apr. 21, 1967
*Maxam, Larry L.	USMC	Cpl.	Cam Lo District, Quang Tri Province	Feb. 2, 1968
McCleery, Finnis D.	USA	PSGT	Quang Tin Province	May 14, 1968
*McDonald, Phill C.	USA	PFC	Near Kontum City	June 7, 1968
McGinty, John J., III	USMC	SSgt.	Republic of Vietnam	July 18, 1966
McGonagle, William L.	USN	CDR	USS *Liberty*, eastern Mediterranean	June 8–9, 1967
*McKibben, Ray	USA	SGT	Near Song Mao	Dec. 8, 1968
*McMahon, Thomas J.	USA	SP4	Quang Tin Province	Mar. 19, 1969
McNerney, David H.	USA	1SG	Polei Doc	Mar. 22, 1967
*McWethy, Edgar L., Jr.	USA	SP5	Binh Dinh Province	June 21, 1967
*Michael, Don L.	USA	SP4	Republic of Vietnam	Apr. 8, 1967
Miller, Franklin D.	USA	SSG	Kontum Province	Jan. 5, 1970
*Miller, Gary L.	USA	1LT	Binh Duong Province	Feb. 16, 1969
Modrzejewski, Robert J.	USMC	Capt.	Republic of Vietnam	July 15–18, 1966
*Molnar, Frankie Z.	USA	SSG	Kontum Province	May 20, 1967
*Monroe, James H.	USA	PFC	Bong Son, Hoai Nhon Province	Feb. 16, 1967
*Morgan, William D.	USMC	Cpl.	Quang Tri Province	Feb. 25, 1969
Morris, Charles B.	USA	SGT	Republic of Vietnam	June 29, 1966
*Murray, Robert C.	USA	SSG	Near Hiep Duc	June 7, 1970
*Nash, David P.	USA	PFC	Giao Duc District, Dinh Tuong Province	Dec. 29, 1968
*Newlin, Melvin E.	USMC	PFC	Quang Nam Province	July 4, 1967

(continues)

MEDAL OF HONOR RECIPIENTS—VIETNAM WAR, *continued*

NAME	SERVICE	RANK (AT TIME OF ACTION)	PLACE OF ACTION	DATE OF ACTION
*Noonan, Thomas P., Jr.	USMC	LCpl.	Near Vandegrift Combat Base, A Shau Valley	Feb. 5, 1969
Norris, Thomas R.	USN	LT	Quang Tri Province	Apr. 10–13, 1972
Novosel, Michael J.	USA	CWO	Kien Tuong Province	Oct. 2, 1969
*Olive, Milton L., III	USA	PFC	Phu Cuong	Oct. 22, 1965
*Olson, Kenneth L.	USA	SP4	Republic of Vietnam	May 13, 1968
O'Malley, Robert E.	USMC	Cpl.	Near An Cuong	Aug. 18, 1965
*Ouellet, David G.	USN	SN	Mekong River	Mar. 6, 1967
Patterson, Robert M.	USA	SP4	Near La Chu	May 6, 1968
*Paul, Joe C.	USMC	LCpl.	Near Chu Lai	Aug. 18, 1965
Penry, Richard A.	USA	SGT	Binh Tuy Province	Jan. 31, 1970
*Perkins, William T., Jr.	USMC	Cpl.	Quang Tri Province	Oct. 12, 1967
*Peters, Lawrence D.	USMC	Sgt.	Quang Tin Province	Sept. 4, 1967
*Petersen, Danny J.	USA	SP4	Tay Ninh Province	Jan. 9, 1970
*Phipps, Jimmy W.	USMC	PFC	Near An Hoa	May 27, 1969
*Pierce, Larry S.	USA	SGT	Near Ben Cat	Sept. 20, 1965
*Pitsenbarger, William H.	USAF	A1C	Near Cam My	Apr. 11, 1966
Pittman, Richard A.	USMC	LCpl.	Near the DMZ	July 24, 1966
*Pitts, Riley L.	USA	CPT	Ap Dong	Oct. 31, 1967
Pless, Stephen W.	USMC	Capt.	Near Quang Ngai	Aug. 19, 1967
*Port, William D.	USA	PFC	Que Son Valley, Heip Duc Province	Jan. 12, 1968
*Poxon, Robert L.	USA	1LT	Tay Ninh Province	June 2, 1969
*Prom, William R.	USMC	LCpl.	Near An Hoa	Feb. 9, 1969
*Pruden, Robert J.	USA	SSG	Quang Ngai Province	Nov. 29, 1969
*Rabel, Laszlo	USA	SSG	Binh Dinh Province	Nov. 13, 1968
Rascon, Alfred V.	USA	SP4	Republic of Vietnam	Mar. 16, 1966
*Ray, David R.	USN	HC2c	Quang Nam Province	Mar. 19, 1969
Ray, Ronald E.	USA	1LT	Ia Drang Valley	June 19, 1966
*Reasoner, Frank S.	USMC	1st Lt.	Near Da Nang	July 12, 1965
*Roark, Anund C.	USA	SGT	Kontum Province	May 16, 1968
Roberts, Gordon R.	USA	SP4	Thua Thien Province	July 11, 1969
*Robinson, James W., Jr.	USA	SGT	Republic of Vietnam	Apr. 11, 1966
Rocco, Louis R.	USA	SFC	Northeast of Katum	May 24, 1970
Rogers, Charles C.	USA	LTC	Near Cambodian Border	Nov. 1, 1968
*Rubio, Euripides	USA	CPT	Tay Ninh Province	Nov. 8, 1966
*Santiago-Colon, Hector	USA	SP4	Quang Tri Province	June 28, 1968
*Sargent, Ruppert L.	USA	1LT	Hau Nghia Province	Mar. 15, 1967
Sasser, Clarence E.	USA	PFC	Ding Tuong Province	Jan. 10, 1968

NAME	SERVICE	RANK (AT TIME OF ACTION)	PLACE OF ACTION	DATE OF ACTION
*Seay, William W.	USA	SGT	Near Ap Nhi	Aug. 25, 1968
*Shea, Daniel J.	USA	PFC	Quang Tri Province	May 14, 1969
*Shields, Marvin G.	USN	CB3c	Dong Xoai	June 10, 1965
*Sijan, Lance P.	USAF	Capt.	North Vietnam	Nov. 9, 1967
*Sims, Clifford C.	USA	SSG	Near Hue	Feb. 21, 1968
*Singleton, Walter K.	USMC	Sgt.	Gio Linh District, Quang Tri Province	Mar. 24, 1967
*Sisler, George K.	USA	1LT	Republic of Vietnam	Feb. 7, 1967
*Skidgel, Donald S.	USA	SGT	Near Song Be	Sept. 14, 1969
*Smedley, Larry E.	USMC	Cpl.	Quang Nam Province	Dec. 21, 1967
*Smith, Elmelindo R.	USA	SSG	Republic of Vietnam	Feb. 16, 1967
Sprayberry, James M.	USA	1LT	Republic of Vietnam	Apr. 25, 1968
*Steindam, Russell A.	USA	1LT	Tay Ninh Province	Feb. 1, 1970
*Stewart, Jimmy G.	USA	SSG	Republic of Vietnam	May 18, 1966
Stockdale, James B.	USN	Capt.	Hoa Loa Prison, Hanoi, North Vietnam	Sept. 4, 1969
*Stone, Lester R., Jr.	USA	SGT	West of Landing Zone Liz	Mar. 3, 1969
*Stout, Mitchell W.	USA	SGT	Khe Gio Bridge	Mar. 12, 1970
*Stryker, Robert F.	USA	SP4	Near Loc Ninh	Nov. 7, 1967
Stumpf, Kenneth E.	USA	SP4	Near Duc Pho	Apr. 25, 1967
*Swanson, Jon E.	USA	CPT	Cambodia	Feb. 26, 1971
Taylor, James A.	USA	1LT	West of Que Son	Nov. 9, 1967
*Taylor, Karl G., Sr.	USMC	SSgt.	Republic of Vietnam	Dec. 8, 1968
Thacker, Brian M.	USA	1LT	Kontum Province	Mar. 31, 1971
Thornton, Michael E.	USN	PO	Republic of Vietnam	Oct. 31, 1972
Thorsness, Leo K.	USAF	Maj.	Over North Vietnam	Apr. 19, 1967
Vargas, Jay R.	USMC	Capt.	Dai Do	Apr. 30–May 2, 1968
*Versace, Humbert R.	USA	CPT	Ca Mau	Oct. 29, 1963– Sept. 26, 1965
*Warren, John E., Jr.	USA	1LT	Tay Ninh Province	Jan. 14, 1969
*Watters, Charles J.	USA	MAJ	Dak To	Nov. 19, 1967
*Wayrynen, Dale E.	USA	SP4	Quang Ngai Province	May 18, 1967
*Weber, Lester W.	USMC	LCpl.	Quang Nam Province	Feb. 23, 1969
Wetzel, Gary G.	USA	PFC	Near Ap Dong An	Jan. 8, 1968
*Wheat, Roy M.	USMC	LCpl.	Republic of Vietnam	Aug. 11, 1967
*Wickam, Jerry W.	USA	CPL	Near Loc Ninh	Jan. 6, 1968
*Wilbanks, Hilliard A.	USAF	Capt.	Near Dalat	Feb. 24, 1967
*Willett, Louis E.	USA	PFC	Kontum Province	Feb. 15, 1967
Williams, Charles Q.	USA	2LT	Dong Xoai	June 9–10, 1965
*Williams, Dewayne T.	USMC	PFC	Quang Nam Province	Sept. 18, 1968
Williams, James E.	USN	PO1	Mekong River	Oct. 31, 1966

(continues)

MEDAL OF HONOR RECIPIENTS—VIETNAM WAR, *continued*

NAME	SERVICE	RANK (AT TIME OF ACTION)	PLACE OF ACTION	DATE OF ACTION
*Wilson, Alfred M.	USMC	PFC	Quang Tri Province	Mar. 3, 1969
*Winder, David F.	USA	PFC	Republic of Vietnam	May 13, 1970
*Worley, Kenneth L.	USMC	LCpl.	Bo Ban, Quang Nam Province	Aug. 12, 1968
Wright, Raymond R.	USA	SP4	Ap Bac Zone	May 2, 1967
*Yabes, Maximo	USA	1SG	Near Phu Hoa Dong	Feb. 26, 1967
*Yano, Rodney J. T.	USA	SFC	Near Bien Hoa	Jan. 1, 1969
*Yntema, Gordon D.	USA	SGT	Near Thong Binh	Jan. 16–18, 1968
Young, Gerald O.	USAF	Capt.	Khe Sanh	Nov. 9, 1967
*Young, Marvin R.	USA	SSG	Near Ben Cui	Aug. 21, 1968
Zabitosky, Fred W.	USA	SSG	Republic of Vietnam	Feb. 19, 1968

Abbreviations to List of Medal of Honor Recipients

A1C	Airman First Class	PSgt.	Platoon Sergeant
Capt.	Captain (USN, USMC, USAF)	Pvt.	Private
CB3c	Construction Mechanic Third Class	SFC	Sergeant First Class
Col.	Colonel	Sgt.	Sergeant (USMC)
Cpl.	Corporal	SGT	Sergeant (USA)
CPT	Captain (USA)	SN	Seaman
CWO	Chief Warrant Officer	SP4	Specialist Fourth Class
GSgt.	Gunnery Sergeant	SP5	Specialist Fifth Class
HC2c	Hospital Corpsman Second Class	SP6	Specialist Sixth Class
HC3c	Hospital Corpsman Third Class	SSG	Staff Sergeant (USA)
LCpl.	Lance Corporal	SSgt.	Staff Sergeant (USMC)
LT	Lieutenant	1LT	First Lieutenant (USA)
LTC	Lieutenant Colonel (USA)	1st Lt.	First Lieutenant (USMC, USAF)
LtCol.	Lieutenant Colonel (USMC, USAF)	1SG	First Sergeant
Lt Cdr.	Lieutenant Commander	2LT	Second Lieutenant (USA)
LT (jg)	Lieutenant (junior grade)	2nd Lt.	Second Lieutenant (USMC)
Maj.	Major (USMC, USAF)	USA	U.S. Army
MAJ	Major (USA)	USAF	U.S. Air Force
MSgt.	Master Sergeant	USMC	U.S. Marine Corps
PFC	Private First Class	USN	U.S. Navy
PO	Petty Officer	USNR	U.S. Naval Reserve
PO1c	Boatswain's Mate First Class		

Sources: Marc Leepson, ed. *Webster's New World Dictionary of the Vietnam War* (New York: Simon & Schuster Macmillan, 1999), pp. 579–587. U.S. Army Center of Military History. "Medal of Honor," available online. URL: www.history.army.mil/moh.html. Accessed October 19, 2008.

 # MAPS

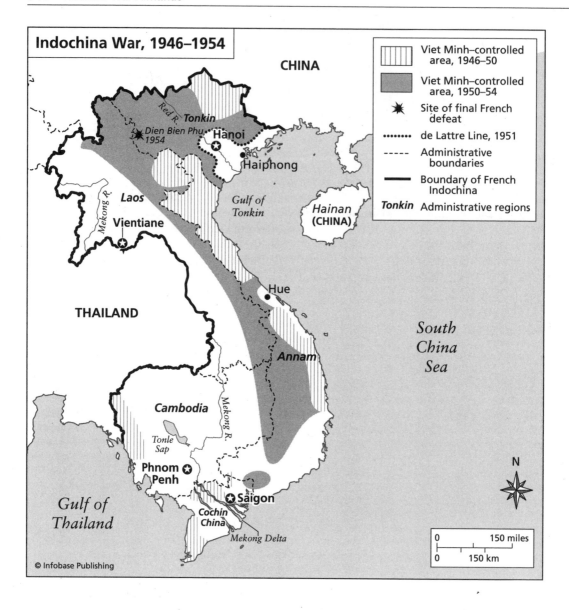

Indochina War, 1946–1954

CHINA

Red R.   *Tonkin*

Dien Bien Phu 1954   Hanoi

Haiphong

Laos

Gulf of Tonkin

Mekong R.

Vientiane

Hainan (CHINA)

THAILAND

Hue

Annam

South China Sea

Cambodia

Mekong R.

Tonle Sap

Phnom Penh

Saigon

Gulf of Thailand

Cochin China

Mekong Delta

N

Legend:

- Viet Minh–controlled area, 1946–50
- Viet Minh–controlled area, 1950–54
- ✳ Site of final French defeat
- ●●● de Lattre Line, 1951
- - - - Administrative boundaries
- ▬ Boundary of French Indochina
- *Tonkin* Administrative regions

0   150 miles
0   150 km

© Infobase Publishing

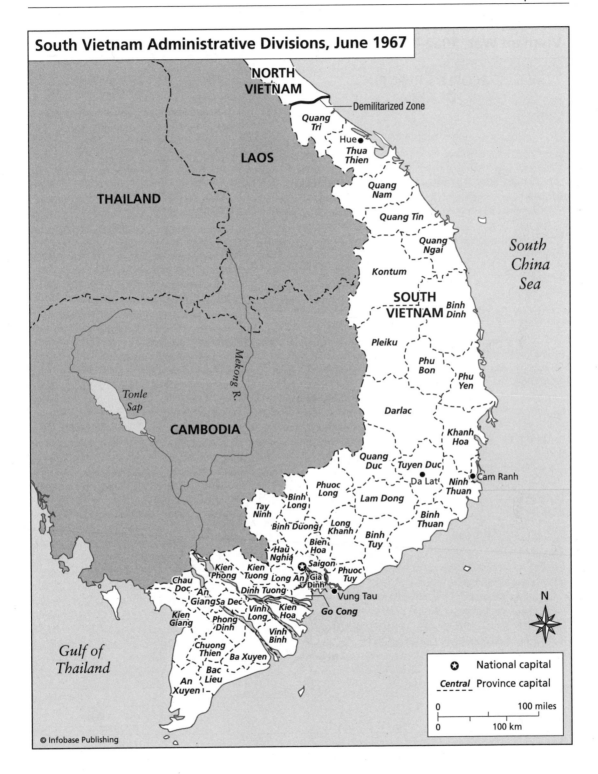

South Vietnam Administrative Divisions, June 1967

NORTH VIETNAM

— Demilitarized Zone

LAOS

THAILAND

Quang Tri

Hue ●
Thua Thien

Quang Nam

Quang Tin

Quang Ngai

Kontum

SOUTH VIETNAM

Binh Dinh

Pleiku

Phu Bon

Phu Yen

Darlac

Khanh Hoa

Quang Duc

Tuyen Duc

Da Lat ●

Ninh Thuan

● Cam Ranh

Phuoc Long

Lam Dong

Binh Long

Tay Ninh

Binh Duong

Long Khanh

Binh Thuan

Binh Tuy

Bien Hoa

Hau Nghia

Saigon ✪
Gia Dinh

Phuoc Tuy

Kien Phong

Kien Tuong

Long An

Chau Doc.

An Giang

Sa Dec

Dinh Tuong

● Vung Tau

Kien Giang

Phong Dinh

Vinh Long

Kien Hoa

Go Cong

Vinh Binh

Chuong Thien

Ba Xuyen

Bac Lieu

An Xuyen

South China Sea

Tonle Sap

CAMBODIA

Mekong R.

Gulf of Thailand

N

✪	National capital
Central - - - -	Province capital

0   100 miles

0   100 km

© Infobase Publishing

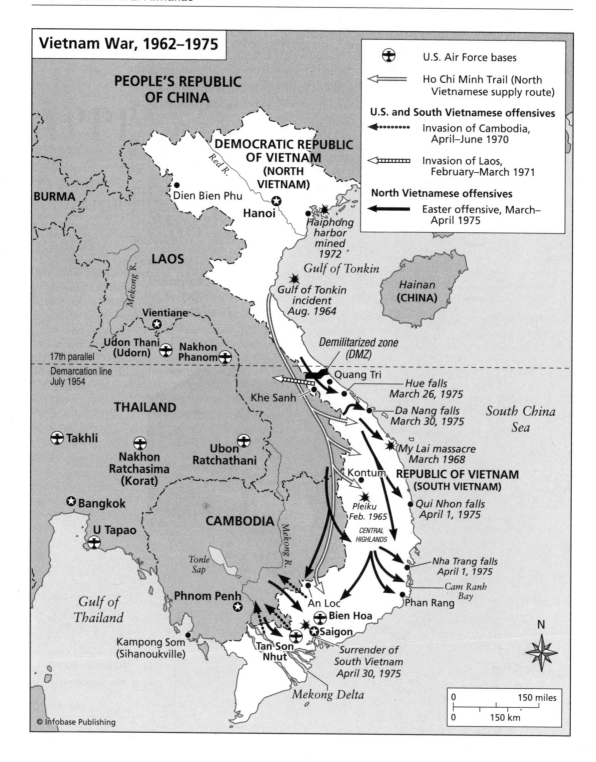

Vietnam War, 1962–1975

Legend:

- ☩ U.S. Air Force bases
- ⇐ Ho Chi Minh Trail (North Vietnamese supply route)

U.S. and South Vietnamese offensives
- ◄······· Invasion of Cambodia, April–June 1970
- ⇐▭▭▭ Invasion of Laos, February–March 1971

North Vietnamese offensives
- ◄━━ Easter offensive, March–April 1975

PEOPLE'S REPUBLIC OF CHINA

DEMOCRATIC REPUBLIC OF VIETNAM (NORTH VIETNAM)

Red R.

BURMA

Dien Bien Phu

Hanoi

Haiphong harbor mined 1972

Gulf of Tonkin

Gulf of Tonkin incident Aug. 1964

Hainan (CHINA)

LAOS

Mekong R.

Vientiane

Udon Thani (Udorn)

Nakhon Phanom

17th parallel

Demarcation line July 1954

Demilitarized zone (DMZ)

Quang Tri

Khe Sanh

Hue falls March 26, 1975

Da Nang falls March 30, 1975

South China Sea

THAILAND

Takhli

Nakhon Ratchasima (Korat)

Ubon Ratchathani

My Lai massacre March 1968

Kontum

REPUBLIC OF VIETNAM (SOUTH VIETNAM)

Bangkok

CAMBODIA

Mekong R.

Pleiku Feb. 1965

CENTRAL HIGHLANDS

Qui Nhon falls April 1, 1975

U Tapao

Tonle Sap

Nha Trang falls April 1, 1975

Cam Ranh Bay

Gulf of Thailand

Phnom Penh

An Loc

Phan Rang

Bien Hoa

Saigon

N

Kampong Som (Sihanoukville)

Tan Son Nhut

Surrender of South Vietnam April 30, 1975

Mekong Delta

© Infobase Publishing

| 0 | 150 miles |
| 0 | 150 km |

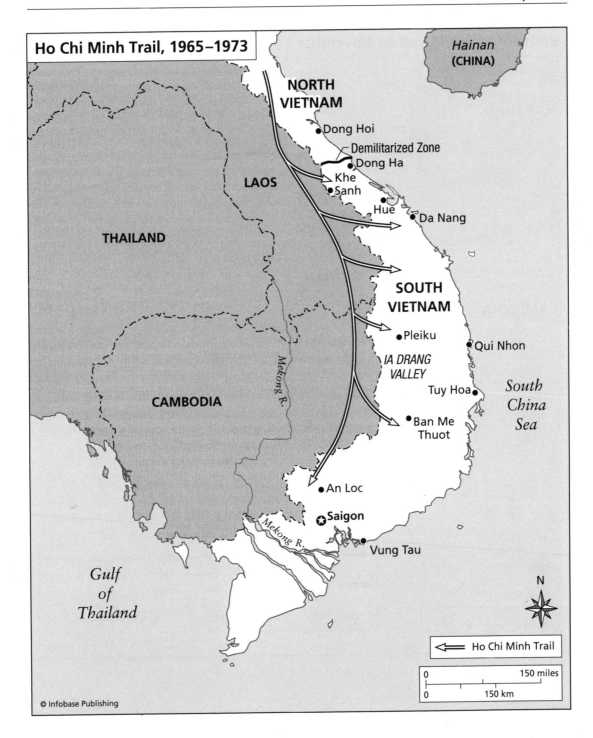

Ho Chi Minh Trail, 1965–1973

Hainan (CHINA)

NORTH VIETNAM

• Dong Hoi

Demilitarized Zone

• Dong Ha

LAOS

Khe • Sanh

Hue •

• Da Nang

THAILAND

SOUTH VIETNAM

• Pleiku

• Qui Nhon

IA DRANG VALLEY

Mekong R.

Tuy Hoa •

CAMBODIA

South China Sea

• Ban Me Thuot

• An Loc

☆ Saigon

Mekong R.

• Vung Tau

Gulf of Thailand

N

⇐ Ho Chi Minh Trail

| 0 | 150 miles |
| 0 | 150 km |

© Infobase Publishing

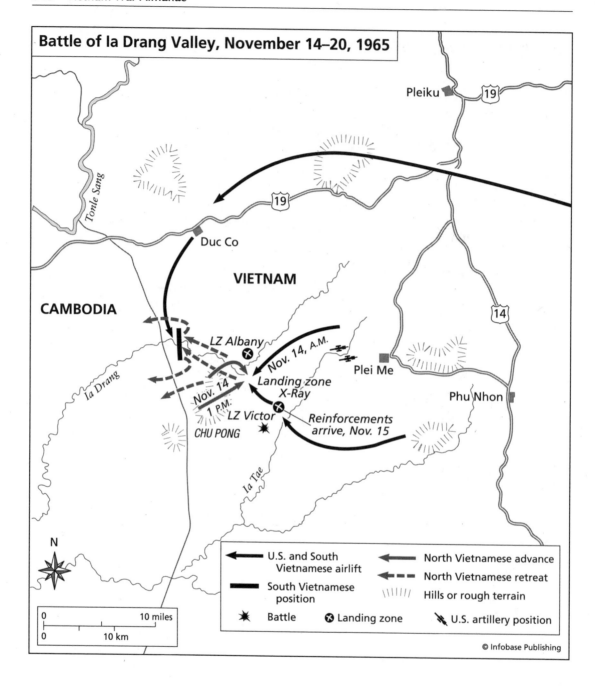

Battle of Ia Drang Valley, November 14–20, 1965

Pleiku

19

Tonle Sang

Duc Co

VIETNAM

CAMBODIA

19

14

LZ Albany

Nov. 14, A.M.

Plei Me

Landing zone
X-Ray

Phu Nhon

Ia Drang

Nov. 14
1 P.M.

LZ Victor

Reinforcements
arrive, Nov. 15

CHU PONG

Ia Tae

N

	U.S. and South Vietnamese airlift		North Vietnamese advance
	South Vietnamese position	|||||	North Vietnamese retreat
			Hills or rough terrain
✳	Battle	⊗ Landing zone	U.S. artillery position

| 0 | | 10 miles |
| 0 | 10 km | |

© Infobase Publishing

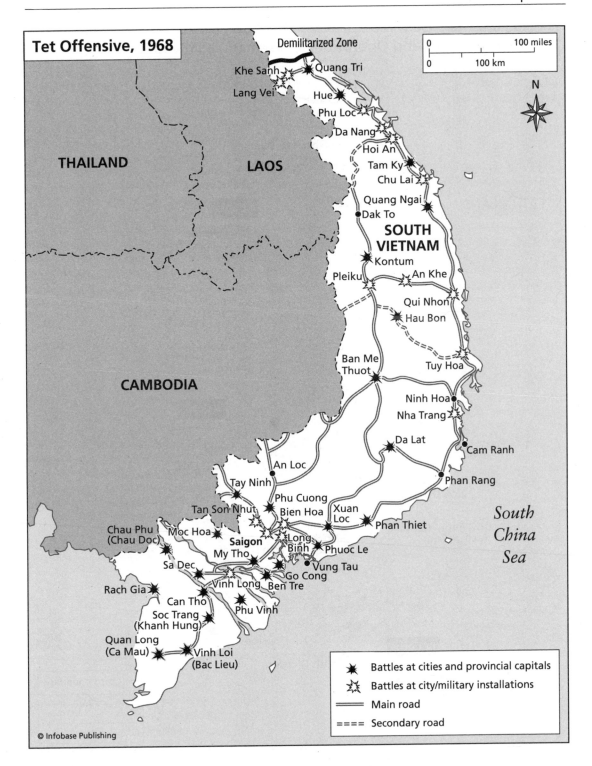

Tet Offensive, 1968

THAILAND

LAOS

CAMBODIA

SOUTH
VIETNAM

Demilitarized Zone

Khe Sanh
Lang Vei
Quang Tri
Hue
Phu Loc
Da Nang
Hoi An
Tam Ky
Chu Lai
Quang Ngai
Dak To
Kontum
Pleiku
An Khe
Qui Nhon
Hau Bon
Ban Me
Thuot
Tuy Hoa
Ninh Hoa
Nha Trang
Da Lat
Cam Ranh
Phan Rang
An Loc
Tay Ninh
Phu Cuong
Tan Son Nhut
Bien Hoa
Xuan
Loc
Phan Thiet
Chau Phu
(Chau Doc)
Moc Hoa
Saigon
Long
Binh
Phuoc Le
My Tho
Vung Tau
Sa Dec
Vinh Long
Go Cong
Ben Tre
Rach Gia
Can Tho
Phu Vinh
Soc Trang
(Khanh Hung)
Quan Long
(Ca Mau)
Vinh Loi
(Bac Lieu)

South
China
Sea

0 ____ 100 miles
0 ____ 100 km

N

★ Battles at cities and provincial capitals
✺ Battles at city/military installations
═══ Main road
==== Secondary road

© Infobase Publishing

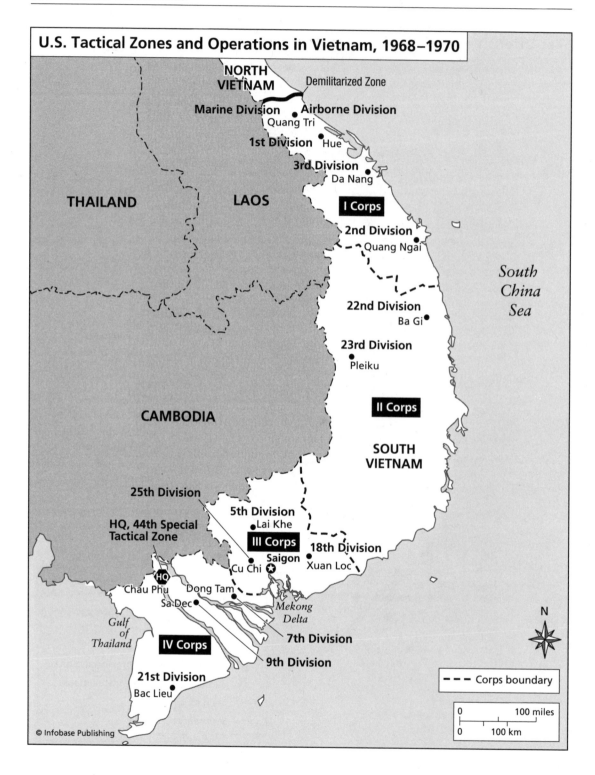

U.S. Tactical Zones and Operations in Vietnam, 1968–1970

NORTH VIETNAM

Demilitarized Zone

Marine Division **Airborne Division**
• Quang Tri

1st Division • Hue

3rd Division
• Da Nang

THAILAND

LAOS

I Corps

2nd Division
• Quang Ngai

22nd Division
Ba Gi •

23rd Division
• Pleiku

CAMBODIA

II Corps

SOUTH VIETNAM

25th Division

5th Division
• Lai Khe

HQ, 44th Special Tactical Zone

III Corps

18th Division

Saigon
Cu Chi • ✪ Xuan Loc •

HQ
Chau Phu • Dong Tam •
Sa Dec •

Mekong Delta

Gulf of Thailand

IV Corps

7th Division

9th Division

21st Division
• Bac Lieu

South China Sea

N

- - - Corps boundary

| 0 | 100 miles |
| 0 | 100 km |

© Infobase Publishing

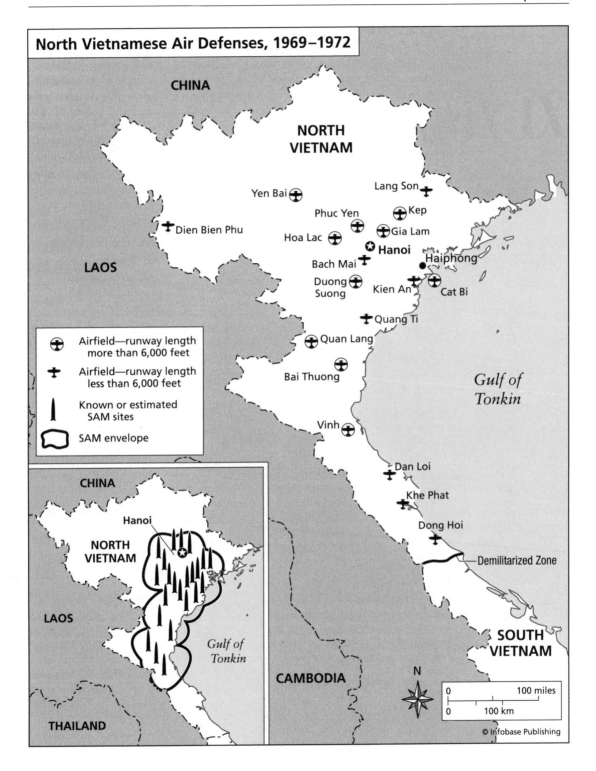

North Vietnamese Air Defenses, 1969–1972

CHINA

NORTH VIETNAM

Yen Bai

Lang Son

Phuc Yen

Kep

Dien Bien Phu

Hoa Lac

Gia Lam

LAOS

Bach Mai

Hanoi

Haiphong

Duong Suong

Kien An

Cat Bi

Quang Ti

Quan Lang

Gulf of Tonkin

Bai Thuong

Airfield—runway length more than 6,000 feet

Airfield—runway length less than 6,000 feet

Known or estimated SAM sites

SAM envelope

Vinh

Dan Loi

Khe Phat

CHINA

Dong Hoi

Hanoi

Demilitarized Zone

NORTH VIETNAM

LAOS

Gulf of Tonkin

CAMBODIA

SOUTH VIETNAM

THAILAND

N

0   100 miles

0   100 km

© Infobase Publishing

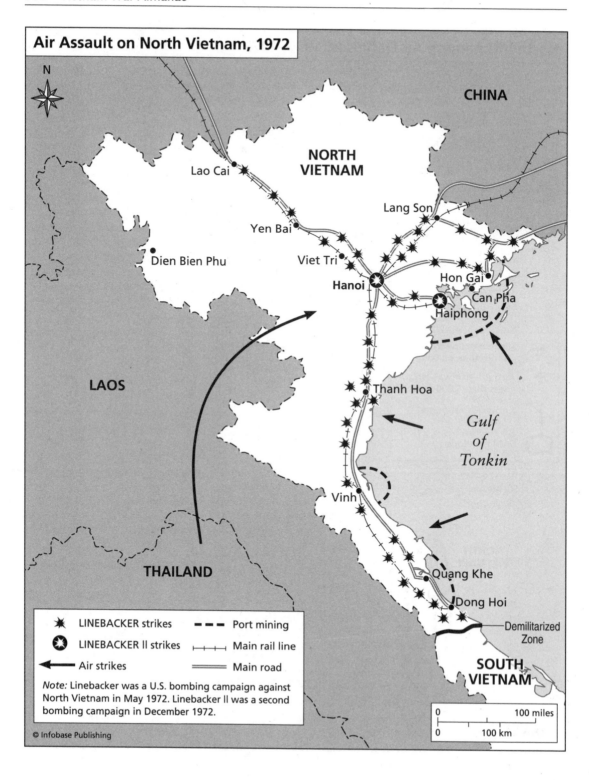

Air Assault on North Vietnam, 1972

N

CHINA

NORTH VIETNAM

Lao Cai

Lang Son

Yen Bai

Viet Tri

Dien Bien Phu

Hon Gai

Hanoi

Can Pha

Haiphong

LAOS

Thanh Hoa

Gulf of Tonkin

Vinh

THAILAND

Quang Khe

Dong Hoi

Demilitarized Zone

SOUTH VIETNAM

✳ LINEBACKER strikes	– – – Port mining
✸ LINEBACKER II strikes	⊢⊢⊢ Main rail line
← Air strikes	═══ Main road

Note: Linebacker was a U.S. bombing campaign against North Vietnam in May 1972. Linebacker II was a second bombing campaign in December 1972.

© Infobase Publishing

0		100 miles
0		100 km

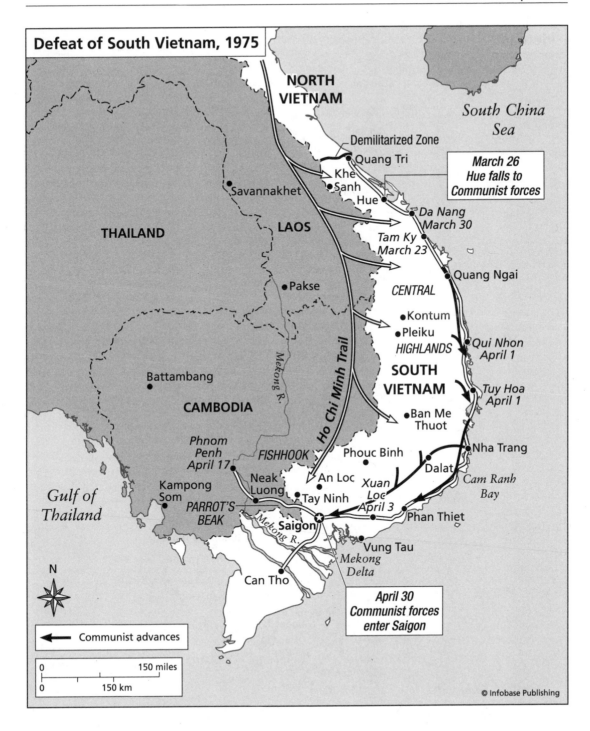

Defeat of South Vietnam, 1975

NORTH VIETNAM

South China Sea

Demilitarized Zone

Quang Tri

Khe Sanh

Savannakhet

Hue

**March 26
Hue falls to
Communist forces**

THAILAND

LAOS

Da Nang
March 30

Tam Ky
March 23

Pakse

Quang Ngai

CENTRAL

Kontum

Pleiku

HIGHLANDS

Qui Nhon
April 1

SOUTH
VIETNAM

Tuy Hoa
April 1

Battambang

CAMBODIA

Ban Me
Thuot

Nha Trang

Phnom
Penh
April 17

FISHHOOK

Phouc Binh

Dalat

Cam Ranh
Bay

Kampong
Som

Neak
Luong

An Loc

Xuan
Loc
April 3

Gulf of
Thailand

PARROT'S
BEAK

Tay Ninh

Saigon

Phan Thiet

N

Vung Tau

Mekong
Delta

Can Tho

**April 30
Communist forces
enter Saigon**

Ho Chi Minh Trail

Mekong R.

Mekong R.

← Communist advances

0   150 miles
0   150 km

© Infobase Publishing

Vietnam

CHINA

Cao Bang

Lao Cai

Lai Chau

Red R.

Thai
Nguyen

Viet Tri

Lang Son

Yen Bai

Bac Ninh

Dao Cai Bau

Hoa Binh

Ha Long

Hanoi

Cam Pha

Hai
Duong

Ha Long Bay

Ha Dong

Haiphong

Ninh Binh

LAOS

Thanh
Hoa

*Gulf of
Tonkin*

Dien Chau

Hainan

Vinh

Dong Hoi

*South China
Sea*

Quang Tri

Hue

THAILAND

Da Nang

Mekong R.

Quang Ngai

Pleiku

Qui Nhon

CAMBODIA

Buon Me Thuot

Dak
Nong

Nha Trang

Loc Ninh

Da Lat

Cam Ranh

Phan Rang

Ho Chi Minh City
(Saigon)

Bien Hoa

Cu Lao Thu

Tan An

N

*Dao Phu
Quoc*

Long
Xuyen

Mekong R.

Vung Tau

Ben Tre

Vinh Long

Can Tho

Gulf of Thailand

Soc Trang

Con Son

Ca Mau

0   150 miles

0   150 km

© Infobase Publishing

SELECTED BIBLIOGRAPHY

Adams, Sam. *War of Numbers: An Intelligence Memoir.* South Royalton, Vt.: Steerforth Press, 1994.

Addington, Larry H. *America's War in Vietnam: A Short Narrative History.* Bloomington: Indiana University Press, 2000.

Adler, Bill, ed. *Letters From Vietnam.* New York: Ballantine Books, 2003.

Albright, John, John A. Cash, and Allan W. Sandstrum. *Seven Firefights in Vietnam.* Vietnam War Studies. Washington, D.C.: Department of the Army, 1970.

Allen, George W. *None So Blind: A Personal Account of the Intelligence Failure in Vietnam.* Chicago: Ivan R. Dee, 2001.

Allison, William Thomas. *Military Justice in Vietnam: The Rule of Law in an American War.* Lawrence: University Press of Kansas, 2007.

Alvarez, Everett, Jr. *Chained Eagle: The Heroic Story of the First American Shot Down over North Vietnam.* Dulles, Va.: Potomac Books, 2005.

Ambrose, Stephen E. *Nixon, Volume Two—the Triumph of Politician, 1962–1972.* New York: Simon and Schuster, 1989.

———. *Nixon, Volume Three—Ruin and Recovery, 1973–1990.* New York: Simon and Schuster, 1991.

Anderson, David L. *The Columbia Guide to the Vietnam War.* New York: Columbia University Press, 2002.

Anderson, David L., ed. *Facing My Lai: Moving Beyond the Massacre.* Lawrence: University Press of Kansas, 1998.

———, ed. *Shadow on the White House: Presidents and the Vietnam War, 1945–1975.* Lawrence: University Press of Kansas, 1993.

Anderson, David L., and John Ernst, eds. *The War That Never Ends: New Perspectives on the Vietnam War.* Lexington: University of Kentucky Press, 2007.

Andrade, Dale. *America's Last Vietnam Battle: Halting Hanoi's 1972 Easter Offensive.* Lawrence: University Press of Kansas, 2001.

———. *Ashes to Ashes: The Phoenix Program and the Vietnamese War.* Lexington, Mass.: Lexington Books, 1990.

Appy, Christian G. *Patriots: The Vietnam War Remembered From All Sides.* New York: Viking, 2003.

———. *Working-Class War: American Combat Soldiers and Vietnam.* Chapel Hill: University of North Carolina Press, 1993.

Arlen, Michael J. *Living-Room War.* New York: Penguin Books, 1982.

Atkinson, Rick. *The Long Gray Line.* London: Harper, 1990.

Baker, Mark. *Nam: The Vietnam War in the Words of the Soldiers Who Fought There.* New York: William Morrow, 1981.

Baritz, Loren. *Backfire: A History of How American Culture Led Us into Vietnam and Made Us Fight the Way We Did.* New York: Morrow, 1985.

Barrett, David M. *Uncertain Warriors: Lyndon Johnson and His Vietnam Advisers.* Lawrence: University Press of Kansas, 1993.

Bartholomew-Feis, Dixee R. *The OSS and Ho Chi Minh: Unexpected Allies in the War Against Japan.* Lawrence: University Press of Kansas, 2006.

Basel, G. I. *Pak Six: A Story of the War in the Skies of North Vietnam.* New York: Jove (Berkley), 1987.

Belknap, Michael R. *The Vietnam War on Trial: The My Lai Massacre and Court-Martial of Lieutenant Calley.* Lawrence: University Press of Kansas, 2002.

Berger, Carl, ed. *The United States Air Force in Southeast Asia, 1961–1973: An Illustrated Account.* Washington, D.C.: Office of Air Force History, 1984.

Bergerud, Eric M. *The Dynamics of Defeat: The Vietnam War in Hau Nghia Province.* Boulder, Colo.: Westview Press, 1990.

———. *Red Thunder, Tropic Lightning: The World of a Combat Division in Vietnam.* Boulder, Colo.: Westview, 1993.

Berman, Larry. *Lyndon Johnson's War.* New York: Norton, 1989.

———. *No Peace, No Honor: Nixon, Kissinger, and Betrayal.* New York: Free Press, 2001.

———. *Perfect Spy: The Incredible Double Life of Pham Xuan An, Time Magazine Reporter and Vietnamese Communist Agent.* Washington, D.C.: Smithsonian Books, 2007.

———. *Planning a Tragedy: The Americanization of the War in Vietnam.* New York: Norton, 1992.

Beschloss, Michael R., ed. *Taking Charge: The Johnson White House Tapes, 1963–1964.* New York: Simon and Schuster, 1997.

Bey, Douglas. *Wizard 6: A Combat Psychiatrist in Vietnam.* College Station: Texas A&M Press, 2006.

Bilton, Michael, and Kevin Sim. *Four Hours in My Lai.* New York: Viking, 1992.

Blackburn, Robert M. *Mercenaries and Lyndon Johnson's "More Flags": The Hiring of Korean, Filipino, and Thai Soldiers in the Vietnam War.* Jefferson, N.C.: McFarland, 1994.

Blaufarb, Douglas S. *The Counterinsurgency Era: U.S. Doctrine and Performance 1950 to Present.* New York: Free Press, 1977.

Blood, Jake. *The Tet Effect: Intelligence and the Public Perception of War.* New York: Routledge, 2005.

Bowman, John S., ed. *The Vietnam War: An Almanac.* New York: Pharos Books, 1985.

———, ed. *The Vietnam War: Day by Day.* New York: Brompton Books, 1989.

Braestrup, Peter. *Big Story: How the American Press and Television Reported and Interpreted the Crisis of Tet 1968 in Vietnam and Washington.* 2 vols. Boulder, Colo.: Westview, 1977.

Brands, H. W. *The Wages of Globalism: Lyndon Johnson and the Limits of American Power.* New York: Oxford University Press, 1995.

Brigham, Robert K. *Guerrilla Diplomacy: The NLF's Foreign Relations and the Vietnam War.* Ithaca, N.Y.: Cornell University Press, 1998.

———. *ARVN: Life and Death in the South Vietnamese Army.* Lawrence: University Press of Kansas, 2006.

Broughton, Jack. *THUD Ridge.* New York: Lippincott, 1969.

Broyles, William, Jr. *Brothers in Arms: A Journey from War to Peace.* New York: Knopf, 1986.

Bui Diem, with David Chanoff. *In the Jaws of History.* Boston: Houghton Mifflin, 1987.

Bui Tin. *Following Ho Chi Minh.* Honolulu: University of Hawaii Press, 1995.

———. *From Enemy to Friend: A North Vietnamese Perspective on the War.* Annapolis, Md.: Naval Institute Press, 2002.

Burkett, B. G. *Stolen Valor: How the Vietnam Generation Was Robbed of Its Heroes and History.* Dallas: Verity Press, 1998.

Butler, David. *The Fall of Saigon.* New York: Simon and Schuster, 1985.

Buttinger, Joseph. *Vietnam: A Dragon Embattled.* 2 vols. New York: Praeger, 1967.

———. *Vietnam: A Political History.* New York: Praeger, 1969.

Buzzanco, Robert. *Masters of War: Military Dissent and Politics in the Vietnam Era.* New York: Cambridge University Press, 1996.

Caputo, Philip. *A Rumor of War.* New York: Holt, Rinehart, and Winston, 1977.

Carland, John M. *The United States Army in Vietnam. Combat Operations: Stemming the Tide, May 1965 to October 1966.* Washington, D.C.: Government Printing Office, 2000.

Cash, John A., John Albright, and Allan W. Sandstrum. *Seven Firefights in Vietnam.* New York: Bantam, 1985.

Castle, Timothy N. *At War in the Shadows of Vietnam: U.S. Military Aid to the Royal Lao Government, 1955–1975.* New York: Columbia University Press, 1999.

———. *One Day Too Long: Top Secret Site 85 and the Bombing of North Vietnam.* New York: Columbia University Press, 1999.

Catton, Philip E. *Diem's Final Failure: Prelude to America's War in Vietnam*. Lawrence: University Press of Kansas, 2002.

Chanoff, David, and Doan Van Toai. *Portrait of the Enemy*. New York: Random House, 1986.

Chinnery, Philip D. *Vietnam: The Helicopter War*. Annapolis: Naval Institute Press, 1991.

Cincinnatus (Cecil B. Currey). *Self-Destruction: The Disintegration and Decay of the United States Army During the Vietnam Era*. New York: Norton, 1981.

Clarke, Jeffrey J. *The United States Army in Vietnam: Advice and Support: The Final Years, 1965–1973*. Washington, D.C.: U.S. Government Printing Office, 1988.

Clifford, Clark, with Richard C. Holbrook. *Counsel to the President: A Memoir*. New York: Random House, 1991.

Clodfelter, Mark. *The Limits of Airpower: The American Bombing of North Vietnam*. New York: Free Press, 1989.

Coan, James P. *Con Thien: The Hill of Angels*. Tuscaloosa: University of Alabama Press, 2004.

Colby, William. *Lost Victory: A Firsthand Account of America's Sixteen-Year Involvement in Vietnam*. Chicago: Contemporary Books, 1989.

Coleman, J. D. *Incursion*. New York: St. Martin's Press, 1991.

———. *Pleiku: The Dawn of Helicopter Warfare*. New York: St. Martin's Press, 1988.

Collins, James L., Jr. *The Development and Training of the South Vietnamese Army, 1950–1972*. Washington, D.C.: U.S. Government Printing Office, 1975.

Conboy, Kenneth, and Dale Andrade. *Spies and Commandos: How America Lost the Secret War in North Vietnam*. Lawrence: University Press of Kansas, 2000.

Cooper, Chester L. *The Lost Crusade: America in Vietnam*. New York: Dodd, Mead, 1970.

Currey, Cecil B. *Edward Lansdale: The Unquiet American*. Boston: Houghton Mifflin, 1989.

———. *Victory at Any Cost: The Genius of Viet Nam's Gen. Vo Nguyen Giap*. Washington: Brassey's, 1997.

Cutler, Thomas J. *Brown Water, Black Berets: Coastal and Riverine Warfare in Vietnam*. Annapolis: Naval Institute Press, 1988.

Dallek, Robert. *Flawed Giant: Lyndon Johnson and His Times, 1961–1973*. New York: Oxford University Press, 1998.

———. *Nixon and Kissinger: Partners in Power*. New York: Harper Collins, 2007.

Dougherty, Leo. *The Vietnam War: Day by Day*. Miami: Lewis International, 2002.

Davidson, Phillip B. *Vietnam at War: The History, 1946–1975*. Novato, Calif.: Presidio Press, 1988.

Dawson, Alan. *55 Days: The Fall of South Vietnam*. Englewood Cliffs, N.J.: Prentice Hall, 1977.

Deac, Wilfred P. *Road to the Killing Fields: The Cambodian War of 1970–1975*. College Station: Texas A&M Press, 1997.

DeBenedetti, Charles, with Charles Chatfield. *An American Ordeal: The Antiwar Movement of the Vietnam Era*. Syracuse, N.Y.: Syracuse University Press, 1990.

Denton, Jeremiah A. *When Hell Was in Session*. New York: Reader's Digest Press, 1976.

Dillard, Walter Scott. *Sixty Days to Peace*. Washington, D.C.: U.S. Government Printing Office, 1982.

DiLeo, David. *George Ball, Vietnam, and the Rethinking of Containment*. Chapel Hill: University of North Carolina Press, 1991.

Donovan, David. *Once a Warrior King: Memories of an Officer in Vietnam*. New York: McGraw-Hill, 1985.

Dorland, Gil. *Legacy of Discord: Voices of the Vietnam War Era*. Washington, D.C.: Brassey's, 2001.

Downs, Frederick, Jr. *The Killing Zone*. New York: Norton, 1978.

Doyle, Jeff, Jeffrey Grey, and Peter Pierce. *Australia's Vietnam War*. College Station: Texas A&M University Press, 2002.

Drake, Hal. *Vietnam Front Pages*. New York: Macmillan Publishing, 1986.

Drew, Dennis M. *Rolling Thunder 1965: Anatomy of a Failure*. Maxwell AFB, Ala.: Air University Press, 1998.

Duiker, William J. *Historical Dictionary of Vietnam*. 2nd ed. Metuchen, N.J.: Scarecrow, 1989.

———. *Ho Chi Minh*. New York: Hyperion, 2000.

———. *Sacred War: Nationalism and Revolution in a Divided Vietnam*. New York: McGraw-Hill, 1995.

———. *The Communist Road to Power in Vietnam*. 2nd ed. Boulder, Colo.: Westview Press, 1996.

Dunnavent, R. Blake. *Brown Water Warfare: The U.S. Navy in Riverine Warfare and the Emergence of a Tactical Doctrine, 1775–1970*. Gainesville: University Press of Florida, 2003.

Ebert, James R. *A Life in a Year: The American Infantryman in Vietnam, 1965–1972*. Novato, Calif.: Presidio, 1993.

Edelman, Bernard, ed. *Dear America: Letters Home from Vietnam*. New York: W.W. Norton, 2002.

Emerson, Gloria. *Winners and Losers: Battles, Retreats, Gains, Losses and Ruins from the Vietnam War.* New York: Harcourt Brace Jovanovich, 1976.

Engelmann, Larry. *Tears before the Rain: An Oral History of the Fall of South Vietnam.* New York: Oxford University Press, 1990.

Fall, Bernard B. *Hell in a Very Small Place.* Philadelphia: Lippincott, 1967.

———. *Last Reflections on a War.* Garden City, N.Y.: Doubleday, 1967.

———. *Street without Joy.* Rev. ed. New York: Schocken, 1972.

———. *The Two Vietnams: A Political and Military Analysis.* New York: Praeger, 1967.

Fall, Dorothy. *Bernard Fall: Memories of a Soldier-Scholar.* Washington, D.C.: Potomac Books, 2006.

FitzGerald, Frances. *Fire in the Lake.* Boston: Little, Brown, 1972.

Ford, Ronnie E. *Tet 1968: Understanding the Surprise.* Portland, Oreg.: Frank Cass, 1995.

Franklin, H. Bruce. *M.I.A. or Mythmaking in America.* Brooklyn, N.Y.: Lawrence Hill Books, 1992.

Frankum, Ronald B., Jr. *Like Rolling Thunder: The Air War in Vietnam, 1964–1975.* New York: Rowman and Littlefield, 2005.

Fry, Joseph A. *Debating Vietnam: Fulbright, Stennis, and Their Senate Hearings.* New York: Rowman and Littlefield, 2006.

Fulbright, William. *The Arrogance of Power.* New York: Vintage Books, 1996.

Gaiduk, Ilya V. *The Soviet Union and the Vietnam War.* Chicago: Ivan R. Dee, 1996.

Galluci, Robert L. *Neither Peace nor Honor: The Politics of American Military Policy in Vietnam.* Baltimore: Johns Hopkins University Press, 1975.

Gardner, Lloyd C. *Approaching Vietnam: From World War II Through Dienbienphu.* New York: Norton, 1988.

———. *Pay Any Price: Lyndon Johnson and the Wars for Vietnam.* Chicago: Ivan R. Dee, 1995.

Gargus, John. *The Son Tay Raid.* College Station: Texas A&M Press, 2007.

Garland, Lt. Col. Albert N., ed. *A Distant Challenge: The U.S. Infantryman in Vietnam 1967–1972.* Nashville, Tenn.: Battery Press, 1983.

———. *Infantry in Vietnam: Small Unit Actions in the Early Days, 1965–1966.* Nashville, Tenn.: Battery Press, 1982.

Gelb, Leslie, and Richard K. Betts. *The Irony of Vietnam: The System Worked.* Washington, D.C.: Brookings Institution, 1979.

Gettleman, Marvin E., ed. *Vietnam: History, Documents, and Opinions on a Major World Crisis.* New York: Fawcett Premier, 1965.

Gilbert, Marc Jason, and William Head, eds. *The Tet Offensive.* Westport, Conn.: Praeger, 1996.

———, eds. *Why the North Won the Vietnam War.* New York: Palgrave, 2002.

Gitlin, Todd. *The Whole World Is Watching: Mass Media and Vietnam.* New York: Oxford University Press, 1986.

Glasser, Ronald J. *365 Days.* New York: B. Braziller, 1971.

Glenn, Russell W. *Reading Athena's Dance Card: Men Against Fire in Vietnam.* Annapolis: Naval Institute Press, 2000.

Goff, Stanley, and Robert Sanders, with Clark Smith. *Brothers: Black Soldiers in the Nam.* Novato, Calif.: Presidio, 1982.

Goldman, Peter, and Tony Fuller. *Charlie Company: What Vietnam Did to Us.* New York: Ballantine, 1983.

Goodman, Allan E. *The Lost Peace: America's Search for a Negotiated Settlement of the Vietnam War.* Stanford, Calif.: Hoover Institution Press, 1978.

Goulden, Joseph C. *Truth Is the First Casualty: The Gulf of Tonkin Affair—Illusion and Reality.* Chicago: Rand McNally, 1969.

Grant, Zalin. *Survivors: Vietnam POWs Tell Their Stories.* New York: Da Capo Press, 1989.

Grinter, Lawrence E., and Peter M. Dunn, eds. *The American War in Vietnam: Lessons, Legacies, and Implications for Future Conflicts.* Westport, Conn.: Greenwood Press, 1987.

Guilmartin, John F., Jr. *A Very Short War: The Mayaguez and the Battle of Koh Tang.* College Station: Texas A&M Press, 1995.

Guin, Larry. *Baptism: A Vietnam Memoir.* New York: Ivy Books, 1999.

Halberstam, David. *The Best and the Brightest.* New York: Random House, 1972.

———. *The Making of a Quagmire.* New York: Random House, 1964.

Haldeman, H. R. *The Haldeman Diaries.* New York: Putnam, 1994.

———. *The Ends of Power*. New York: Times Books, 1978.

Haley, P. Edward. *Congress and the Fall of South Vietnam and Cambodia*. East Brunswick, N.J.: Fairleigh Dickinson University Press, 1982.

Hallin, Daniel C. *The "Uncensored War": The Media and Vietnam*. New York: Oxford University Press, 1986.

Hammel, Eric. *Fire in the Streets: The Battle for Hue, Tet 1968*. Chicago: Contemporary Books, 1991.

———. *Khe Sanh, Siege in the Clouds: An Oral History*. New York: Crown, 1989.

Hammer, Ellen J. *A Death in November: America in Vietnam*. New York: E. P. Dutton, 1987.

Hamilton-Merritt, Jane. *Tragic Mountains: The Hmong, the Americans, and the Secret Wars for Laos, 1942–1992*. Bloomington: Indiana University Press, 1993.

Hammond, William M. *Reporting Vietnam: Media and Military at War*. Lawrence: University Press of Kansas, 1998.

Hargrove, Thomas R. *A Dragon Lives Forever: War and Rice in Vietnam's Mekong Delta*. College Station: Texas A & M Press, 2008.

Harrison, James P. *The Endless War: Vietnam's Struggle for Independence*. New York: Columbia University Press, 1989.

Harrison, Marshall. *A Lonely War*. Novato, Calif.: Presidio Press, 1989.

Hayslip, Le Ly, with Jay Wurts. *When Heaven and Earth Changed Places: A Vietnamese Woman's Journey from War to Peace*. New York: Doubleday, 1989.

Head, William, and Lawrence E. Grinter, eds. *Looking Back on the Vietnam War: A 1990s Perspective on the Decisions, Combat, and Legacies*. Westport, Conn.: Praeger, 1993.

Hemingway, Albert. *Our War Was Different: Marine Combined Action Platoons in Vietnam*. Annapolis: Naval Institute Press, 1994.

Hendrickson, Paul. *The Living and the Dead: Robert McNamara and Five Lives of a Lost War*. New York: Alfred A. Knopf, 1996.

Herring, George C. *America's Longest War: The United States and Vietnam, 1950–1975*. 4th ed. New York: McGraw-Hill, 2002.

———. *LBJ and Vietnam: A Different Kind of War*. Austin: University of Texas Press, 1994.

Herrington, Stuart A. *Peace with Honor? An American Reports on Vietnam, 1973–1975*. Novato, Calif.: Presidio Press, 1983.

———. *Stalking the Vietcong*. Novato, Calif.: Presidio, 1997.

Hersh, Seymour M. *The Price of Power: Kissinger in the Nixon White House*. New York: Summit Books, 1983.

———. *My Lai 4: A Report on the Massacre and Its Aftermath*. New York: Random House, 1970.

———. *Cover-Up: The Army's Secret Investigation of the Massacre at My Lai 4*. New York: Random House, 1972.

Hess, Gary R. *Vietnam and the United States: Origins and Legacy of War*. Rev. ed. Boston: Twayne Publishers, 1998.

———. *The United States' Emergence as a Southeast Asian Power, 1949–1950*. New York: Columbia University Press, 1987.

Hickey, Gerald C. *Village in Vietnam*. New Haven, Conn.: Yale University Press, 1964.

Hoopes, Townsend. *The Limits of Intervention*. New York: David McKay, 1969.

Hosmer, Stephen T., Konrad Kellen, and Brian M. Jenkins. *The Fall of South Vietnam: Statements by Vietnamese Military and Civilian Leaders*. New York: Crane, Russak, 1990.

Hunt, Michael H. *Lyndon Johnson's War: America's Cold War Crusade in Vietnam, 1945–1968*. New York: Hill and Wang, 1996.

Hunt, Richard A. *Pacification: The American Struggle for Vietnam's Hearts and Minds*. Boulder, Colo.: Westview Press, 1995.

Isaacs, Arnold R. *Vietnam Shadows: The War, Its Ghosts, and Its Legacy*. Baltimore: Johns Hopkins University Press, 1997.

———. *Without Honor: Defeat in Vietnam and Cambodia*. Baltimore: Johns Hopkins University Press, 1983.

Isaacson, Walter. *Kissinger: A Biography*. New York: Simon & Schuster, 1992.

Jamieson, Neil L. *Understanding Vietnam*. Berkeley: University of California Press, 1993.

Johnson, Lyndon Baines. *The Vantage Point: Perspectives on the Presidency, 1963–1969*. New York: Holt, Rinehart, and Winston, 1971.

Jones, Charles. *Boys of '67: From Vietnam to Iraq, the Extraordinary Story of a Few Good Men*. Mechanicsburg, Pa.: Stackpole Books, 2006.

Kahin, George McTurnan. *Intervention: How America Became Involved in Vietnam.* New York: Knopf, 1986.

Kahin, George McTurnan and John W. Lewis. *The United States in Vietnam.* Rev. ed. New York: Delta, 1969.

Kaiser, David. *American Tragedy: Kennedy, Johnson, and the Origins of the Vietnam War.* Cambridge, Mass.: Harvard University Press, 2000.

Karnow, Stanley. *Vietnam: A History.* Rev. ed. New York: Viking Press, 1992.

Kattenburg, Paul L. *The Vietnam Trauma in American Foreign Policy 1945–1975.* New Brunswick, N.J.: Transaction, 1980.

Kearns, Doris. *Lyndon Johnson and the American Dream.* New York: Harper and Row, 1976.

Kerrey, Bob. *When I Was a Young Man: A Memoir.* New York: Harcourt, 2002.

Kimball, Jeffrey. *Nixon's Vietnam War.* Lawrence: University Press of Kansas, 1998.

King, Peter, ed. *Australia's Vietnam.* Boston: George Allen and Unwin, 1983.

Kinnard, Douglas. *The War Managers.* Hanover, N.H.: University Press of New England, 1976.

Kissinger, Henry A. *White House Years.* Boston: Little, Brown, 1979.

Kittfield, James. *Prodigal Soldiers: How the Generation of Officers Born of Vietnam Revolutionized the American Style of War.* New York: Simon and Schuster, 1995.

Kolko, Gabriel. *Anatomy of a War: Vietnam, the United States, and the Modern Historical Experience.* New York: Pantheon Books, 1985.

Komer, Robert W. *Bureaucracy at War: U.S. Performance in the Vietnam Conflict.* Boulder, Colo.: Westview Press, 1986.

Kovic, Ron. *Born on the Fourth of July.* New York: McGraw-Hill, 1976.

Krepinevich, Andrew F., Jr. *The Army and Vietnam.* Baltimore: Johns Hopkins University Press, 1986.

Kutler, Stanley, ed. *Encyclopedia of the Vietnam War.* 3 vols. New York: Macmillan Library Reference USA, 1996.

LaFeber, Walter. *The Deadly Bet: LBJ, Vietnam, and the 1968 Election.* New York: Rowman and Littlefield, 2005.

Lam Quang Thi. *The Twenty-Five Year Century.* Denton: University of North Texas Press, 2001.

Lanning, Michael Lee. *The Only War We Had.* New York: Ivy Books, 1987.

———. Vietnam, *1969–1970: A Company Commander's Journal.* New York: Ivy Books, 1988.

Lanning, Michael Lee, and Dan Cragg. *Inside the NVA.: The Real Story of North Vietnam's Armed Forces.* New York: Fawcett Columbine, 1992.

Lansdale, Edward G. *In the Midst of Wars.* New York: Harper and Row, 1972.

Larsen, Stanley Robert, and James Lawton Collins, Jr. *Allied Participation in Vietnam.* Washington, D.C.: U.S. Government Printing Office, 1975.

Laurence, John. *The Cat from Hue: A Vietnam War Story.* New York: Public Affairs, 2002.

Lee, J. Edward, and Toby Haynsworth, eds. *White Christmas in April: The Collapse of South Vietnam, 1975.* New York: Peter Lang, 1999.

Leepson, Marc, ed. *Webster's New World Dictionary of the Vietnam War.* New York: Simon and Schuster Macmillan, 1999.

LeGro, William E. *Vietnam from Cease-Fire to Capitulation.* Washington, D.C.: Government Printing Office, 1981.

Lehrack, Otto J. *No Shining Armor: The Marines at War in Vietnam.* Lawrence: University Press of Kansas, 1992.

Lewy, Guenther. *America in Vietnam.* New York: Oxford University Press, 1978.

Lind, Michael. *Vietnam: The Necessary War.* New York: Free Press, 1999.

Logevall, Fredrick. *Choosing War: The Lost Chance for Peace and the Escalation of War in Vietnam.* Berkeley: University of California Press, 1999.

Lomperis, Timothy J. *From People's War to People's Rule: Insurgency, Intervention, and the Lessons of Vietnam.* Chapel Hill: University of North Carolina Press, 1996.

MacGarrigle, George L. *The United States Army in Vietnam: Combat Operations: Taking the Offensive, October 1966 to October 1967.* Washington, D.C.: U.S. Government Printing Office, 1998.

MacPherson, Myra. *Long Time Passing: Vietnam and the Haunted Generation.* Garden City, N.Y.: Doubleday, 1984.

Mangold, Tom, and John Penycate. *The Tunnels of Cu Chi.* New York: Random House, 1985.

Mann, Robert A. *A Grand Illusion: America's Descent into Vietnam.* New York: Basic Books, 2001.

Maraniss, David. *They Marched into Sunlight.* New York: Simon and Schuster, 2003.

Marolda, Edward J. *By Sea, Air, and Land: An Illustrated History of the U.S. Navy in the War in Southeast Asia.* Washington, D.C.: Navy Historical Center, 1994.

Marr, David G. *Vietnamese Anti-colonialism 1885–1925.* Berkeley: University of California Press, 1981.

———. *Vietnamese Tradition on Trial, 1920–1945.* Berkeley: University of California Press, 1981.

Marshall, S[amuel] L. A. *Ambush.* Nashville, Tenn.: Battery Press, 1969.

———. *Battles in the Monsoon.* New York: William Morrow, 1967.

———. *Bird.* Nashville, Tenn.: Battery Press, 1968.

———. *West to Cambodia.* Nashville, Tenn.: Battery Press, 1968.

———. *The Fields of Bamboo.* New York: Doubleday, 1971.

Maslowski, Peter, and Don Winslow. *Looking for a Hero: Staff Sergeant Joe Ronnie Hooper and the Vietnam War.* Lincoln: University of Nebraska Press, 2004.

Maurer, Harry. *Strange Ground: Americans in Vietnam: 1945–1975, An Oral History.* New York: Henry Holt, 1989.

McAulay, Lex. *The Battle of Long Tan.* New York: Arrow, 1987.

McGarvey, Patrick J. *Visions of Victory: Selected Vietnamese Communist Military Writings, 1965–1968.* Stanford, Calif.: Hoover Institute on War, Revolution, and Peace, 1989.

McMahon, Robert J. *The Limits of Empire: The United States and Southeast Asia since World War II.* New York: Columbia University Press, 1999.

McMaster, H. R. *Dereliction of Duty: Johnson, McNamara, the Joint Chiefs of Staff, and the Lies That Led to Vietnam.* New York: HarperCollins, 1997.

McNamara, Francis Terry, with Adrian Hill. *Escape with Honor: My Last Hours in Vietnam.* Washington, D.C.: Brassey's, 1997.

McNamara, Robert. *In Retrospect: The Tragedy and Lessons of Vietnam.* New York: Times Books, 1995.

McNamara, Robert, James G. Blight, and Robert K. Brigham. *Argument without End: In Search of Answers to the Vietnam Strategy.* New York: Public Affairs, 1999.

McNeill, Ian. *The Team: Australian Army Advisors in Vietnam 1962–1972.* Canberra: Australian War Memorial, 1984.

———. *To Long Tan: The Australian Army and the Vietnam War 1950–1966.* Sydney: Allen and Unwin, 2003.

Melanson, Richard A. *American Foreign Policy since the Vietnam War: The Search for Consensus from Nixon to Clinton.* 3rd ed. Armonk, N.Y.: M. E. Sharpe, 2000.

Melson, Charles D. *The War That Would Not End: U.S. Marines in Vietnam, 1971–1973.* Central Point, Oreg.: Hellgate Press, 1998.

Metzner, Edward P. *More Than a Soldier's War: Pacification in Vietnam.* College Station: Texas A&M University, 1995.

Michel, Marshall L. *The 11 Days of Christmas: America's Last Vietnam Battle.* San Francisco: Encounter Books, 2001.

Military History Institute of Vietnam. *Victory in Vietnam: The Official History of the People's Army of Vietnam, 1954–1975* (tr. Merle L. Pribbenow). Lawrence: University Press of Kansas, 2002.

Millett, Allan R., ed. *A Short History of the Vietnam War.* Bloomington: Indiana University Press, 1978.

Moïse, Edwin E. *Historical Dictionary of the Vietnam War.* Lanham, Md.: Scarecrow Press, 2001.

———. *Tonkin Gulf and the Escalation of the Vietnam War.* Chapel Hill: University of North Carolina Press, 1996.

Moore, Harold G., and Joseph L. Galloway. *We Were Soldiers Once . . . And Young: Ia Drang: The Battle That Changed the War in Vietnam.* New York: Random House, 1992.

Moore, John Norton, and Robert F. Turner. *The Real Lessons of the Vietnam War.* Durham, N.C.: Carolina Academic Press, 2002.

Morris, Roger. *Uncertain Greatness: Henry Kissinger and American Foreign Policy.* New York: Harper and Row, 1977.

Moss, George Donelson. *Vietnam: An American Ordeal.* 4th ed. New York: Prentice Hall, 2002.

Moyar, Mark. *Phoenix and the Birds of Prey.* Annapolis: Naval Institute Press, 1997.

———. *Triumph Forsaken: The Vietnam War, 1954–1965.* New York: Cambridge University Press, 2006.

Mrozek, Donald J. *Air Power and the Ground War in Vietnam: Ideas and Actions.* Washington, D.C.: U.S. Government Printing Office, 1989.

Murphy, Edward F. *Semper Fi Vietnam: From Da Nang to the DMZ: Marine Corps Campaigns, 1965–1975.* Novato, Calif.: Presidio Press, 1997.

Murphy, John. *Harvest of Fear: A History of Australia's Vietnam War.* Boulder, Colo.: Westview Press, 1994.

Neu, Charles E. *America's Lost War—Vietnam: 1945–1975.* Wheeling, Ill.: Harland Davidson, 2005.

Newman, John M. *JFK and Vietnam: Deception, Intrigue, and the Struggle for Power.* New York: Warner, 1992.

Nguyen Cao Ky, with Marvin Wolf. *Buddha's Child: My Fight to Save Vietnam.* New York: St. Martin's Press, 2002.

———. *Twenty Years and Twenty Days.* New York: Stein and Day, 1976.

Nguyen Tien Hung, and Jerrold J. Schechter. *The Palace File.* New York: Harper and Row, 1986.

Nixon, Richard M. *No More Vietnams.* New York: Arbor House, 1985.

———. *RN: The Memoirs of Richard Nixon.* New York: Grosset and Dunlap, 1978.

Nolan, Keith. *Battle for Hue: Tet 1968.* Novato, Calif.: Presidio, 1983.

———. *House to House: Playing the Enemy's Game in Saigon, May 1968.* St. Paul, Minn.: Zenith Press, 2006.

———. *Into Laos: The Story of Dewey Canyon II/Lam Son 719.* Novato, Calif.: Presidio, 1986.

———. *Ripcord, Screaming Eagles Under Siege, Vietnam 1970.* Novato, Calif.: Presidio, 2003 (Reissue edition).

———. *Sappers in the Wire: The Life and Death of Firebase Mary Ann.* College Station: Texas A&M University, 1995.

O'Balance, Edgar. *The Wars in Vietnam, 1954–1980.* New York: Hippocrene, 1981.

Oberdorfer, Don. *Tet! The Turning Point in the Vietnam War.* Garden City, N.Y.: Doubleday, 1971.

Olson, James S. *Dictionary of the Vietnam War.* Westport, Conn.: Greenwood Press, 1988.

Olson, James S., and Randy Roberts. *Where the Domino Fell: America and Vietnam, 1945 to 1995.* 3rd ed. St. James, N.Y.: Brandywine Press, 1999.

Page, Tim, et al. *Another War: Pictures of the War from the Other Side.* Washington, D.C.: National Geographic Society, 2002.

Palmer, Bruce, Jr. *The 25-Year War: America's Military Role in Vietnam.* Lexington: University Press of Kentucky, 1984.

Palmer, Dave Richard. *Summons of the Trumpet: U.S.-Vietnam in Perspective.* San Rafael, Calif.: Presidio Press, 1978.

Palmer, Laura. *Shrapnel in the Heart: Letters and Remembrances from the Vietnam Veterans Memorial.* New York: Random House, 1987.

Patti, Archimedes L. A. *Why Vietnam? Prelude to America's Albatross.* Berkeley, Calif.: University of California Press, 1980.

Peers, W. R. *The My Lai Inquiry.* New York: Morton, 1979.

Pentagon Papers: The Defense Department History of United States Decisionmaking on Vietnam. Senator Gravel edition, 5 vols. Boston: Beacon Press, 1971.

Peterson, Michael E. *The Combined Action Platoons: The U.S. Marines' Other War in Vietnam.* New York: Praeger, 1989.

Phillips, William R. *Night of the Silver Stars: The Battle of Lang Vei.* Annapolis: Naval Institute Press, 1997.

Pike, Douglas. *Viet Cong: The Organization and Techniques of the National Liberation Front of South Vietnam.* Cambridge, Mass.: MIT Press, 1966.

———. *A History of Vietnamese Communism, 1923–1978.* Stanford, Calif.: Hoover Institute Press, 1978.

———. *PAVN: People's Army of Vietnam.* Novato, Calif.: Presidio Press, 1986.

Pisor, Robert. *The End of the Line: The Siege of Khe Sanh.* New York: Norton, 1982.

Plaster, John. *SOG: The Secret Wars of America's Commandos in Vietnam.* New York: Penguin Onyx Books, 1998.

Podhoretz, Norman. *Why We Were in Vietnam.* New York: Simon and Schuster, 1982.

Porter, Gareth. *A Peace Denied: The United States, Vietnam and the Paris Agreement.* Bloomington: Indiana University Press, 1975.

Prados, John. *The Hidden History of the Vietnam War.* Chicago: Ivan Dee, 1995.

———. *The Blood Road: The Ho Chi Minh Trail and the Vietnam War.* New York: John Wiley and Sons, 1999.

Prados, John, and Ray W. Stubbe. *Valley of Decision: The Siege of Khe Sanh.* Boston: Houghton Mifflin, 1991.

Pratt, John Clark, ed. *Vietnam Voices: Perspectives on the War Years, 1941–1982.* New York: Viking Press, 1984.

Prochnau, William. *Once Upon a Distant War.* New York: Random House, 1995.

Qiang Zhai. *China and the Vietnam Wars, 1950–1975.* Chapel Hill: University of North Carolina Press, 2000.

Quang X. Pham. *A Sense of Duty.* New York: Ballantine Books, 2005.

Race, Jeffrey. *War Comes to Long An: Revolutionary Conflict in a Vietnamese Province.* Berkeley: University of California Press, 1972.

Randolph, Stephen P. *Powerful and Brutal Weapons: Nixon, Kissinger, and the Easter Offensive.* Cambridge: Harvard University Press, 2007.

Reardon, Carol. *Launch the Intruders: A Naval Attack Squadron in the Vietnam War, 1972.* Lawrence: University Press of Kansas, 2005.

Record, Jeffrey. *The Wrong War: Why We Lost in Vietnam.* Annapolis: Naval Institute Press, 1998.

Reporting Vietnam: American Journalism, 1954–1971. New York: Library of America, 2000.

Rusk, Dean, with Richard Rusk. *As I Saw It.* New York: Norton, 1990.

Safer, Morley. *Flashbacks: On Returning to Vietnam.* New York: Random House, 1990.

Santoli, Al. *Everything We Had: An Oral History of the Vietnam War.* New York: Random House, 1981.

———. *To Bear Any Burden: the Vietnam War and Its Aftermath in the Words of Americans and Southeast Asians.* New York: Dutton, 1985.

Schandler, Herbert Y. *The Unmaking of a President—Lyndon Johnson and Vietnam.* Princeton: Princeton University Press, 1977.

Schell, Jonathan. *The Real War.* New York: Pantheon, 1987.

———. *The Village of Ben Suc.* New York: Knopf, 1967.

Schemmer, Benjamin F. *The Raid: The Son Tay Prison Rescue Mission.* Reissue ed. New York: Ballantine Books, 2002.

Schmitz, David F. *The Tet Offensive: Politics, War, and Public Opinion.* New York: Rowman and Littlefield, 2005.

Schultz, Richard H., Jr. *The Secret War against Hanoi: Kennedy and Johnson's Use of Spies, Saboteurs, and Covert Warriors.* New York: HarperCollins, 1999.

Schulzinger, Robert D. *A Time for Peace: The Legacy of the Vietnam War.* New York: Oxford University Press, 2006.

———. *A Time for War: The United States and Vietnam, 1941–1975.* New York: Oxford University Press, 1997.

Shaplen, Robert. *The Lost Revolution: The U.S. in Vietnam, 1946–1966.* Rev. ed. New York: Harper Colophon, 1966.

———. *The Road from War: Vietnam, 1965–1970.* New York: Harper & Row, 1970.

Shapley, Deborah. *Promise and Power: The Life and Times of Robert McNamara.* Boston: Little, Brown, 1992.

Sharp, U.S. Grant. *Strategy for Defeat: Vietnam in Retrospect.* Novato, Calif.: Presidio Press, 1978.

Shaw, John M. *The Cambodian Campaign.* Lawrence: University Press of Kansas, 2005.

Shawcross, William. *Sideshow: Kissinger, Nixon, and the Destruction of Cambodia.* New York: Simon and Schuster, 1970.

Sheehan, Neil. *A Bright Shining Lie: John Paul Vann and America in Vietnam.* New York: Random House, 1988.

Shulimson, Jack. *U.S. Marines in Vietnam. The Defining Year, 1968.* Washington, D.C.: History and Museums Division, Headquarters, U.S. Marine Corps, 1977–1997.

Sigler, David Burns. *Vietnam Battle Chronology: U.S. Army and Marine Corps Combat Operations, 1965–1973.* Jefferson, N.C., and London: McFarland, 1992.

Small, Melvin. *Covering Dissent: The Media and the Anti-Vietnam War Movement.* New Brunswick, N.J.: Rutgers University Press, 1988.

———. *Johnson, Nixon, and the Doves.* New Brunswick, N.J.: Rutgers University Press, 1988.

Smith, George W. *The Siege at Hue.* Boulder, Colo.: Lynne Rienner, 1999.

Snepp, Frank. *Decent Interval: An Insider's Account of Saigon's Indecent End.* New York: Random House, 1977.

Solis, Gary D. *Son Thang: An American War Crime.* Annapolis: Naval Institute Press, 1997.

Sorley, Lewis. *A Better War: The Unexamined Victories and the Final Tragedy of America's Last Years in Vietnam.* New York: Harcourt Brace, 1999.

———. *Honorable Warrior: General Harold K. Johnson and the Ethics of Command.* Lawrence: University Press of Kansas, 1998.

———. *Thunderbolt: General Creighton Abrams and the Army of His Times.* New York: Simon and Schuster, 1992.

Sorley, Lewis, ed. *Vietnam Chronicles: The Abrams Tapes, 1968–1972.* Lubbock: Texas Tech University Press, 2004.

Spector, Ronald H. *After Tet: The Bloodiest Year in Vietnam.* New York: Free Press, 1992.

———. *The United States Army in Vietnam: Advice and Support: The Early Years, 1941–1960.* Washington, D.C.: U.S. Government Printing Office, 1983.

Stanton, Shelby L. *Anatomy of a Division: The 1st Cav in Vietnam.* Novato, Calif.: Presidio, 1987.

———. *Green Berets at War.* Novato, Calif.: Presidio Press, 1985.

———. *The Rise and Fall of an American Army: U.S. Ground Forces in Vietnam, 1965–1973.* San Rafael, Calif.: Presidio Press, 1985.

———. *Vietnam Order of Battle: A Complete Illustrated Reference to the U.S. Army Ground Forces in Vietnam, 1961–1973.* New York: Galahad Books, 1981.

Starry, Donn A. *Armored Combat in Vietnam.* Indianapolis: Bobbs-Merrill, 1980.

Steinman, Ron. *The Soldiers' Story: Vietnam in Their Own Words.* New York: TV Books, 1999.

Summers, Harry G., Jr. *Historical Atlas of the Vietnam War.* Boston: Houghton Mifflin, 1995.

———. *On Strategy: A Critical Analysis of the Vietnam War.* San Rafael, Calif.: Presidio Press, 1982.

———. *Vietnam War Almanac.* New York: Facts On File, 1985.

Swift, Earl. *Where They Lay: Searching for America's Lost Soldiers.* New York: Houghton Mifflin, 2003.

Taylor, Maxwell. *Swords and Plowshares.* New York: Norton, 1972.

Taylor, Richard. *Prodigals: A Vietnam Story.* Havertown, Pa.: Casemate, 2003.

Terry, Wallace. *Bloods: An Oral History of the Vietnam War by Black Americans.* New York: Random House, 1984.

Terzani, Tiziano. *Giai Phong! The Fall and Liberation of Saigon* (tr. John Shepley). New York: St. Martin's Press, 1976.

Thayer, Carlyle. *War by Other Means: National Liberation and Revolution in Viet-Nam, 1954–60.* Cambridge, Mass.: Unwin Hyman, 1989.

Thayer, Thomas C. *War without Fronts: The American Experience in Vietnam.* Boulder, Colo.: Westview Press, 1986.

Thies, Wallace J. *When Governments Collide: Coercion and Diplomacy in the Vietnam Conflict, 1964–1968.* Berkeley: University of California Press, 1980.

Thompson, James Clay. *Rolling Thunder: Understanding Policy and Program Failure.* Chapel Hill: University of North Carolina Press, 1980.

Thompson, W. Scott, and Donaldson D. Frizzell, eds. *The Lessons of Vietnam.* New York: Crane, Russak, 1977.

Thompson, Wayne. *To Hanoi and Back: The U.S. Air Force and North Vietnam, 1966–1973.* Washington, D.C.: Smithsonian Institution Press, 2000.

Tilford, Earl H., Jr. *Crosswinds: The Air Force's Setup in Vietnam.* College Station: Texas A&M University Press, 1993.

Timberg, Robert. *The Nightingale's Song.* New York: Simon and Schuster, 1995.

Toczek, David M. *The Battle of Ap Bac, Vietnam.* Annapolis: Naval Institute Press, 2001.

Todd, Olivier. *Cruel April: The Fall of Saigon* (tr. Stephen Becker). New York: Norton, 1987.

Tolson, John J. *Airmobility 1961–1971.* Washington, D.C.: Department of the Army, 1973.

Tourison, Sedgwick. *Secret Army, Secret War: Washington's Tragic Spy Operation in North Vietnam.* Annapolis: Naval Institute Press, 1995.

Tran Van Don. *Our Endless War: Inside South Vietnam.* San Rafael, Calif.: Presidio Press, 1978.

Tripp, Nathaniel. *Father, Soldier, Son: Memoir of a Platoon Leader in Vietnam.* South Royalton, Vt.: Steerforth Press, 1996.

Truong Nhu Tang, with David Chanoff and Doan Van Toai. *A Vietcong Memoir.* New York: Harcourt Brace Jovanovich, 1985.

Tucker, Spencer C. *Vietnam.* Lexington: University Press of Kentucky, 1999.

Tucker, Spencer C., ed. *Encyclopedia of the Vietnam War: A Political, Social, and Military History.* 3 vols. Santa Barbara, Calif.: ABC-CLIO, 1998.

Turley, G. H. *The Easter Offensive: Vietnam 1972.* Novato, Calif.: Presidio Press, 1985.

Turley, William S. *The Second Indochina War: A Short Political and Military History.* Boulder, Colo.: Westview Press, 1986.

Turner, Kathleen J. *Lyndon Johnson's Dual War: Vietnam and the Press.* Chicago: University of Chicago Press, 1985.

Valentine, Douglas. *The Phoenix Program.* New York: William Morrow, 1990.

VanDeMark, Brian. *Into the Quagmire: Lyndon Johnson and the Escalation of the Vietnam War.* New York: Oxford University Press, 1991.

Vandiver, Frank E. *Shadows of Vietnam: Lyndon Johnson's Wars.* College Station: Texas A&M University Press, 1997.

Van Dyke, Jon M. *North Vietnam's Strategy for Survival.* Palo Alto, Calif.: Pacific Books Publishers, 1972.

Van Tien Dung. *Our Great Spring Victory: An Account of the Liberation of South Vietnam.* New York: Monthly Review Press, 1977.

Vo Nguyen Giap. *The Military Art of People's War.* New York: Monthly Review Press, 1970.

Walker, Keith. *A Piece of My Heart: The Stories of Twenty-Six American Women Who Served in Vietnam.* Novato, Calif.: Presidio, 1985.

Walt, Lewis W. *Strange War, Strange Strategy.* New York: Funk and Wagnall, 1976.

Warner, Roger. *Back Fire: The CIA's Secret War in Laos and Its Link to the War in Vietnam.* New York: Simon and Schuster, 1995.

Warr, Nicholas. *Phase Line Green: The Battle for Hue, 1968.* Annapolis: Naval Institute Press, 1997.

Webb, James. *Fields of Fire.* Englewood Cliffs, N.J.: Prentice Hall, 1978.

Wells, Tom. *The War Within: America's Battle over Vietnam.* Berkeley: University of California Press, 1994.

Werner, Jayne S., and Luu Doan Huynh, eds. *The Vietnam War: Vietnamese and American Perspectives.* Armonk, N.Y.: M. E. Sharp, 1993.

West, Francis J. *The Village.* New York: Harper and Row, 1972.

Westmoreland, William C. *A Soldier Reports.* New York: Doubleday, 1976.

Wiest, Andrew, ed. *Rolling Thunder in a Gentle Land: The Vietnam War Revisited.* New York: Osprey, 2006.

———. *Vietnam's Forgotten Army: Heroism and Betrayal in the ARVN.* New York: New York University Press, 2007.

Willbanks, James H. *Abandoning Vietnam: How America Left and South Vietnam Lost Its War.* Lawrence: University Press of Kansas, 2004.

———. *The Battle of An Loc.* Bloomington: Indiana University Press, 2005.

———. *The Tet Offensive—A Concise History.* New York: Columbia University Press, 2006.

Williams, William Appleman, Thomas McCormick, Lloyd Gardner, and Walter LaFeber, eds. *America in Vietnam: A Documentary History.* New York: Norton, 1985.

Windrow, Martin. *The Last Valley: Dien Bien Phu and the French Defeat in Vietnam.* New York: Da Capo Press, 2004.

Wirtz, James J. *The Tet Offensive: Intelligence Failure in War.* Ithaca, N.Y.: Cornell University, 1992.

Woodruff, Mark W. *Unheralded Victory: The Defeat of the Viet Cong and the North Vietnamese Army, 1961–1973.* Arlington, Va.: Vandamere Press, 1999.

Wyatt, Clarence R. *Paper Soldiers: The American Press and the Vietnam War.* New York: Norton, 1993.

Young, Marilyn B. *The Vietnam Wars: 1945–1990.* New York: HarperCollins, 1991.

Zaffiri, Samuel. *Hamburger Hill, May 11–20, 1969.* Novato, Calif.: Presidio Press, 1988.

———. *Westmoreland: A Biography of General William C. Westmoreland.* New York: William Morrow, 1994.

Zaroulis, Nancy, and Gerald Sullivan. *Who Spoke Up? American Protest against the War in Vietnam, 1963–1975.* New York: Doubleday, 1984.

Zumwalt, Elmo R., Jr., Elmo R. Zumwalt, III, and John Pekkanen. *My Father, My Son.* New York: Macmillan, 1986.

WEB SITES

Battlefield Vietnam. URL: http://www.pbs.org/battlefieldvietnam/

The Vietnam Center and Archive. URL: http://www.vietnam.ttu.edu/

The Vietnam Database. URL: http://thevietnamdatabase.co.uk/Index.htm

The Wars for Viet Nam: 1945 to 1975. URL: http://vietnam.vassar.edu

Vietnam War.Com. URL: http://www.vietnamwar.com/veteranslinks.htm

Vietnam War Internet Project. URL: http://vwip.org/vwiphome.html

Vietnam: Yesterday and Today. URL: http://servercc.oakton.edu/~wittman/

INDEX

Italic page numbers indicate illustrations.